This book is dedicated to our immediate families, who through their sensitivity and understanding, encourage us to take the time to commit to preparing the words, structure, and elements.

Vania, Nicholas, Isabella, Art, Rose, Celio, Dulcina, Mark, and Brad

Pegi, Dan, Jill, Dana, Susan, David, Katie, Hunter, and Hailey

Preface

The major objective of *Global Management and Organizational Behavior: Text, Readings, Cases, and Exercises* is to provide a clear picture, analysis, and set of suggestions for managers and leaders to operate in international settings. Numerous management and organizational behavior textbooks address primarily local or domestic management issues. Books from the United States, Canada, Great Britain, and France offer a dominant view of managing human assets in a neutral or domestic setting. Each book includes elements concerning global issues, but the bulk of the content, examples, and settings are from the nations from which the authors work and reside.

Globalization has had a sobering impact on the thinking, research, and frameworks being proposed by theorists and organizational scientists. To sustain competitive advantage, more and more management teams around the world are reaching the conclusion that open-minded, flexible thinking and practice must be applied to managing workers in different cultures and in an array of heterogeneous groups and teams. As globalization continues, there will be an increased need for managers and leaders who can be effective, sensitive, and flexible in working with employees from diverse backgrounds, having an array of needs, expressing various workplace values, and possessing many different skill levels. The application of management and leadership practices in a universal way is likely to create a misfit between the employees and managers' performance expectations and needs. Assuming that managerial techniques and applications can be universally applied across the world is myopic, ethnocentric, and not supported by empirical research.

Preparing this book has presented an opportunity to explore many countries, managerial practices in terms of local and international settings, cross-border alliances, acquisitions, and adjustments, and the cultural impacts on global management and leadership. The book's creation and development also forced us to utilize our own global experiences, projects, relationships, successes, mistakes, and failures while challenging our own stereotypes and notions of managerial practices throughout the world. This open and reflective approach has helped in formulating conceptual and theoretical frameworks that can lead to specific, challenging, and meaningful applications.

ARCHITECTURE OF THE BOOK

The book consists of three major parts. Part 1 includes two chapters: Chapter 1 focuses on establishing the intent of the book and discusses globalization trends and developments. Chapter 2 addresses an extremely important factor—national culture.

Part 2 includes six key signature chapters. Chapter 3 addresses social responsibility, ethics, and ethical dilemmas faced by transnational organizations and managers. Chapter 4 focuses on communications, while Chapter 5 covers motivation and leadership. Chapter 6 looks at negotiations and what managers must be prepared for when dealing with alliance formation, government policies, labor issues, and a host of other negotiated agreements. Chapter 7 examines the management of diversity, which takes on a set of complex challenges in transnational firms. Chapter 8 discusses groups and teams and special challenges managers and leaders face with them.

Part 3 provides an overview of the issues affecting global human resource management (Chapter 9) and discusses many of the family and career considerations that play major roles in managers' and leaders' current and future success (Chapter 10).

Many other topics could have been added, but the decision was made to be concise, yet thorough, and to provide enough material to either supplement another set of course materials or to use this book as the main resource for the course. We believe this book is especially well-suited for the following classes: organizational behavior, international organizational behavior, and international or cross-cultural management. Also, it can be used as an international supplement to many principles of management and organizational behavior textbooks.

SUPPLEMENT RESOURCES

To support the content, examples, and models provided in the book's 10 chapters, each part includes readings, cases, and exercises. The 10 readings will elaborate further or provide additional insights into the chapter content and material.

The 8 cases provide a rich array of examples, dilemmas, and problems that managers and leaders in transnational organizations are faced with and must solve. The cases require student involvement and analysis.

Eight experiential exercises are provided to encourage students individually and in groups to participate so that they acquire a more accurate picture of how flexible and open-minded they are, and how knowledgeable they are about transnational management and leadership. The self-portrait will be tested and challenged in those exercises in which group formation is utilized. This is usually an enlightening learning experience.

Also, five Internet exercises are provided. These exercises require students to surf, aggregate, organize, and examine organizations, best practices, and issues facing transnational organization managers and leaders. Using the World Wide Web will be enlightening and will require making judgments about the quality of the material being aggregated.

TEACHING FEATURES AND ELEMENTS

To make the book and supplements more relevant, motivational, and practical, a number of teaching elements and features are embedded in the chapters. Each chapter contains exhibits and element boxes. We find that a limited number of well-designed exhibits and boxed elements generate in-class questions and critical thinking that support the learning process.

Chapter Objectives—These actions-oriented objectives set the tone for key points to be learned.

Opening Vignette—This short element explains a best-in-class example, situation, issue, or trend that can help students prepare for the chapter's content coverage.

Global Focus—This element provides a transnational company example that is linked to the content being discussed at a specific place in the chapter.

Review, Critical Thinking, and Discussion Questions—These 10 questions are designed to provoke the rereading, analysis, and discussion of the chapter and its elements.

Glossary—Key terms are defined.

Endnotes—This complete set of citations and references supports the content base of the book.

The book is a self-contained set of materials designed for instructors and students who realize that globalization requires a different course than the traditional treatment of management or organizational behavior. We envision that the use of this book will generate feedback on each chapter, the supplements, and its organization. This input will be used in future revisions to strengthen every aspect of the book. We want to provide students and instructors with an accurate, up-to-date, scholarly, and user-friendly set of materials.

ACKNOWLEDGMENTS

The creation and development of a textbook requires a team effort. First, we would like to thank the readings' authors, case writers, and exercise creators for providing what is compelling, interesting, and learning-enriched materials. These are the important contributors.

The intellectual offerings of our academic colleagues are listed with each of their contributions. People already recognize many of their contributions to the field of globalization. They have provided valuable learning material that we believe is student- and instructor-relevant, friendly, and congruent with the content base of this book.

John Biernat and John Weimeister of McGraw-Hill/Irwin are key team members who reviewed this book concept, encouraged us to prepare the book, and kept us on schedule. The entire McGraw-Hill/Irwin team of editors, production and marketing specialists, and development support staff is tremendous in every respect.

A key part of the team are Peggy Adams and Ginger Roberts. They take notes, scribbles, margin suggestions, and cards with words and somehow prepare manuscripts. These two colleagues do the heavy-lifting work with pleasantness, which is appreciated, respected, and honored.

Robert Konopaske

John M. Ivancevich

February 2003

Brief Contents

Table of Contents

Introduction to Globalization

Global Developments and Trends: Management Perspective

Learning Objectives

After completing Chapter 1, you should be able to:

- Discuss why an organization can benefit and grow by becoming a multinational corporation.
- Describe why managing diversity is such a crucial requirement in a global organization.
- Discuss why some individuals are antiglobalization and opposed to the creation of multinational organizations.
- Explain the environmental (external to the organization) forces that influence what global managers do in performing their roles.
- Describe how the use of SA8000 can become a part of the global manager's performance assessment of how he or she is doing.

Dependence in a Borderless World

A television commercial for UPS shows planes flying all around the world. Whether it's a Honda fuel pump, Baxter intravenous-infusion equipment, or Pierre Cardin apparel, the average modern product contains parts produced or assembled in Asia, South America, Europe, Central America, or the United States. The globalized network is spreading across the world.

On September 21, 1999, an earthquake measuring 7.6 on the Richter scale wreaked havoc in Taiwan and around the world. Within days, the stock prices of Dell Computer, Apple, and Hewlett-Packard fell like a rock because these companies depend on Taiwan-based factories. Although most of the island's suppliers and workers were back on the job within a week, the worldwide orders for electronics fell 7 percent. The world is so interconnected that an event such as an earthquake affected production in the global supply network.

Dell Computer has formed international strategic alliances with firms that have plants in Mexico, Malaysia, and Korea. These plants and their workers provide more than 4,500 parts used in Dell products. If the workforce in Korea produces below expected levels, Dell can be stopped cold in fulfilling orders. Dell is a large multinational firm that depends on global suppliers and workers for the timely shipment of high-quality components. The suppliers are dependent on Dell for orders, while Dell depends on global suppliers for its computer components.

The ability to sell in global markets and to manufacture in many countries has created two conditions: Firms must now compete with companies in different countries, and the management of operations must optimize the performance of workers so that costs are kept low while employee needs are met. Aided by advances in information management, communications, and management practices, organizations are taking an increased global perspective. The world of business is becoming borderless, allowing each company and each country to concentrate on what it does best. This work can be perfected and improved upon if capable, efficient, and knowledgeable managers and leaders are in place performing their jobs effectively.

Source: Barry Lynn, "Unmade in America," *Harpers*, June 2002, pp. 33–44.

Since the collapse of communism, the world has witnessed an accelerated pace of globalization, privatization, and improved standards of living. It is estimated that approximately $1.3 trillion moves around the world every day on the foreign exchange markets.[1] Workers in organizations around the world are fueling the growth and the reach of economic systems and institutions.

Managers in global organizations are expected to deal with workers in a way that sustains economic gains and captures increased market share. As the world becomes more interdependent, the flow of workers, the complexity of alliances, the negotiations of transactions, the coping with local rules, regulations, and cultures require a special type of understanding and set of management skills. Managing globally calls for international, complex, and challenging information. The skills needed are globally oriented and more comprehensive than what is required of domestic managers.[2]

This book will examine the process of managing organizational behavior in a global context. That is, the book will examine managers who are now faced with a diverse and electronically interconnected world dispersed across more than 200 countries with many historical, religious, and regional patterns that affect the work and flow that occurs within organizations. As the opening vignette illustrates, an earthquake in Taiwan can have an impact on business transactions in a number of countries. Taiwan felt the physical effects, while other countries experienced economic, supply, managerial, and worker effects.

THE GLOBAL ORGANIZATIONAL BEHAVIOR PERSPECTIVE

Since about the mid-1960s the study of organizational behavior has earned a respected position as a source of theory, research, and application among organizational scientists and practitioners. **Organizational behavior** (OB) is defined as:

> The study of human behavior, attitudes, and performance within organizational settings; drawing on theory, methods, and principles from such disciplines as psychology, sociology, and cultural anthropology to learn about individuals, groups, structures, and processes.[3]

This multidisciplinary-focused view illustrates that OB: (1) is studied at the individual, group, process, and organizational levels, (2) is an area that integrates theories, research, and applications from multiple disciplines, (3) is people and behaviorally anchored, (4) is concerned about how people perform their jobs, (5) accumulates knowledge and uses it as a learning source, and (6) has a generalization power in that what is learned in one setting may be useful for study and applications in other settings.

The definition of **global organizational behavior** used in this book is an extension of the traditional OB definition cited above. Adding the notion of studying "human behavior in organizations in any world setting" introduces a global orientation of organizational behavior. In this book we are interested in using discipline-based knowledge, methods, and principles to learn about individuals, groups, structures, and processes in global organizations.

A more globally oriented perspective of managing organizational behavior is well suited for today's world because of:

- The increasing pace and spread of globalization.
- The understanding that "one approach" or a favorite domestic approach may not work well in different countries, regions of the world, and cultural settings.
- Numerous joint ventures and alliances that require diverse and different managerial styles and methods to achieve success, which can be defined as sustaining competitive advantage, increasing profit and market share, or contributing to the economic development of a community, region, or country.
- The limited supply of well-educated, multilingual, articulate, and astute managers to lead diverse teams of employees.
- The need to be especially aware of variations in national cultures and the role played by culture on employee behavior and performance.

CAPTURING THE STUDY OF GLOBAL ORGANIZATIONAL BEHAVIOR

The management challenge in a global setting includes many issues, but none is more crucial than the integration of activities that occurs among a diverse workforce.[4] The complexity of the phenomenon becomes more pressing if a firm has operations in different countries. The manager facing these challenges must blend the skills, competencies, and talents of workers by being cognizant of their needs, perceptions, attitudes, and goals. The manager's job is made more difficult when he or she is operating in another setting. For example, one of Toyota's competitive advantages is the superior value-to-price ratio, which is made possible by using the Toyota lean manufacturing and management system.[5] This lean system depends on a superior supplier network and a loyal Japanese workforce. When Toyota exports autos from Japan, these advantages result in economic gains and market share. But when Toyota invests and produces automobiles in Georgetown, Kentucky, it does not have its supplier network and Japanese workforce. It must through astute global management practices re-create these resources, patterns, and approaches in a new location and national culture.

MULTINATIONAL ORGANIZATIONS

Following World War II, **multinational organizations** began to evolve. Defined as an organization that has operations in more than one country, sales revenue generated globally, and a diverse mix of managers, employees, and owners, multinationals' growth was spurred by reconstruction efforts in Europe and Japan. As the European and Japanese economies became stronger, many U.S. companies increased business operations overseas. By the late 1970s and early 1980s, U.S. firms had lost their dominance in international markets.[6] European and Japanese firms in such industries as oil, banking, autos, telecommunications, and electronics became major players. The emergence of Japanese-owned firms in Europe, Asia, and Latin America, and European firms in Latin America, the United States, Africa, and Asia illustrated how globalization resulted in complexities of operating multinational firms. The management of organizational behavior in multinational firms is portrayed in three brief profiles.

Sony Corporation (Japan)

Sony Corporation, based in Tokyo, is a major world manufacturer of televisions, videotape recorders, and other electronic equipment. Since the late 1940s, Sony has continued a steady growth in product lines and innovative sales strategies. Sony has manufacturing facilities in Europe, Latin America, South Korea, and Singapore. It manages a diverse workforce, hires and retains outstanding local engineering and technical talent to continue its growth pattern. The company also maintains and advocates productive strategic collaborative alliances with companies from other countries.[7]

Nestlé SA (Switzerland)

Nestlé is the world's leading food processor with a wide global reach. Based in Vevey, Switzerland, the company employs more than 140,000 people from and in many different countries. Drinks, dairy products, and sundry products produce the bulk of the company's sales revenue. Nestlé maintains plants and owns restaurants and hotels in Europe and the United States. Employees in Nestle's

Global Focus Globalization: A Formula Is Difficult to Find

If poor nations are denied a chance to produce products and sell their goods to developed nations, hatred and terrorism can be expected to follow. Many of Afghanistan's neighbors, as well as much of Africa and other economies that were once a part of the Soviet Union, are trapped in grinding poverty, limited education, malnutrition, few work and compensation opportunities, and poor health care. These countries are breeding grounds for civil disorder, terrorism, and even hunger. Economic development and transnational organizations can improve living standards.

Knowing exactly how and what to do in terms of globalizing is a difficult challenge. Simple prescriptions usually fail. Opening borders to trade, providing global firms with incentives and assurances, and encouraging entrepreneurialism are some of the methods that have promise for developing nations in Africa, Asia, Latin America, and Central America. These efforts can result in the building of multinational organizations having an interest in working within a country.

The United States, Europe, Japan, Singapore, and South Korea rarely use trade barriers against manufacturers, farmers, and merchants in developing countries. Government policies need to strengthen the business attachments between developed and developing countries. There will not be immediate results, but globalization offers one of the best hopes for integrating countries into the world economic community. To advance globalization, developed economies must creatively find ways to bring about more alliances, partnerships, and joint ventures. Working with local and national communities in developing nations should also be a top priority. Humanitarian assistance, business enterprise coaching, business transaction education, and developing joint-venture alliances are very productive and promising ways to accomplish globalization. One of the first steps is for developing country governments to show and express an interest in using foreign support, aid, and help.

In attempting to globalize developing nations, it is important to focus on more than economic gain. Showing concern about traditional values, mores, customs, and humanitarian basic needs is needed. For globalization to be a force for good, it must be careful not to destroy the valued aspects of a country's value system and culture.

Source: Adapted from Christopher Farrell, "Globalism, The Cure For War and Misery," *Business Week Online*, December 14, 2001, and Courtney Fingar, "Crossing Cultures," *Global Business Magazine*, July 2000, p. 81.

facilities are impressed with the firm's open culture, sensitivity to local worker issues, and concern about being responsive to worker's needs.[8]

Citicorp (United States)

Citicorp projects itself in advertisements as a global financial services company. The firm employs 90,000 people (about 40,000 outside the United States) who work in more than 3,000 offices around the world. The firm is organized into three divisions—individual, institutional, and investment banking. Citicorp global managers work hard at learning the local culture and business environment and then providing the services that fit the customer. Personalizing its approach to fit the customer emphasizes that differences across cultures and regions of the world must be properly managed.[9]

These examples provide a snapshot of how three successful multinationals have incorporated into their management approaches a distinct global approach. Instead of using a "single method" or universal approach in different global settings, each of these firms, Sony, Nestlé, and Citicorp, use what is considered a contingency approach for the particular employee group, customer-base, or national culture it engages. As indicated in the Global Focus there is "no" one best method or formula for globalizing.

THE TRANSNATIONAL ORGANIZATION

Toward the late 1980s as more research on multinational organizations began to raise questions about its robustness in explaining global operations, the "transnational organization" took center stage.

The theoretical work and research of Bartlett and Ghoshal highlight the evolution and shift toward transnational management. They emphasized that because of accelerating global competitiveness, firms would be required to be locally responsive and more globally integrated. That is, a firm such as Volvo or Barclay's would have to pay attention to local tastes, needs, expectations, politics, labor-management conditions, and environmental concerns, but at the same time improve its global practices, efficiencies, and ability to compete.

Ghoshal and Bartlett state:

> Managers in most worldwide companies recognize the need for simultaneously achieving global efficiency, national responsiveness, and the ability to develop and exploit knowledge on a worldwide basis. Some, however, regard the goal as inherently unattainable. Perceiving irreconcilable contradictions among the three objectives, they opt to focus on one of them at least temporarily. The transnational company is one that overcomes these contradictions.[10]

The **transnational firm** is not a specific structure or form. Instead, it is a philosophy or a management mentality calling attention to the flexibility needed to respond locally and globally. Not all firms will become transnational. However, it is the primary reference that will be used when this book focuses on flexibility, competitiveness, and a global mind-set. We will also use the term *global* to describe organizations doing business domestically and across borders. To some industries such as automobiles, computers, telecommunications, and pharmaceuticals, a transnational orientation is very important. In other less dynamic and changing industries, such as steel and paper, the move toward a transnational philosophy and practice is not as important.

THE VALUE ADDED BY GLOBAL ORGANIZATIONAL BEHAVIOR

Companies such as Sony, Nestlé, and Citicorp each believe that by being globally astute and knowledgeable they can gain and sustain distinct competitive advantages. The companies who understand the environmental system in which

EXHIBIT 1.1
Global Organization and Interacting Systems

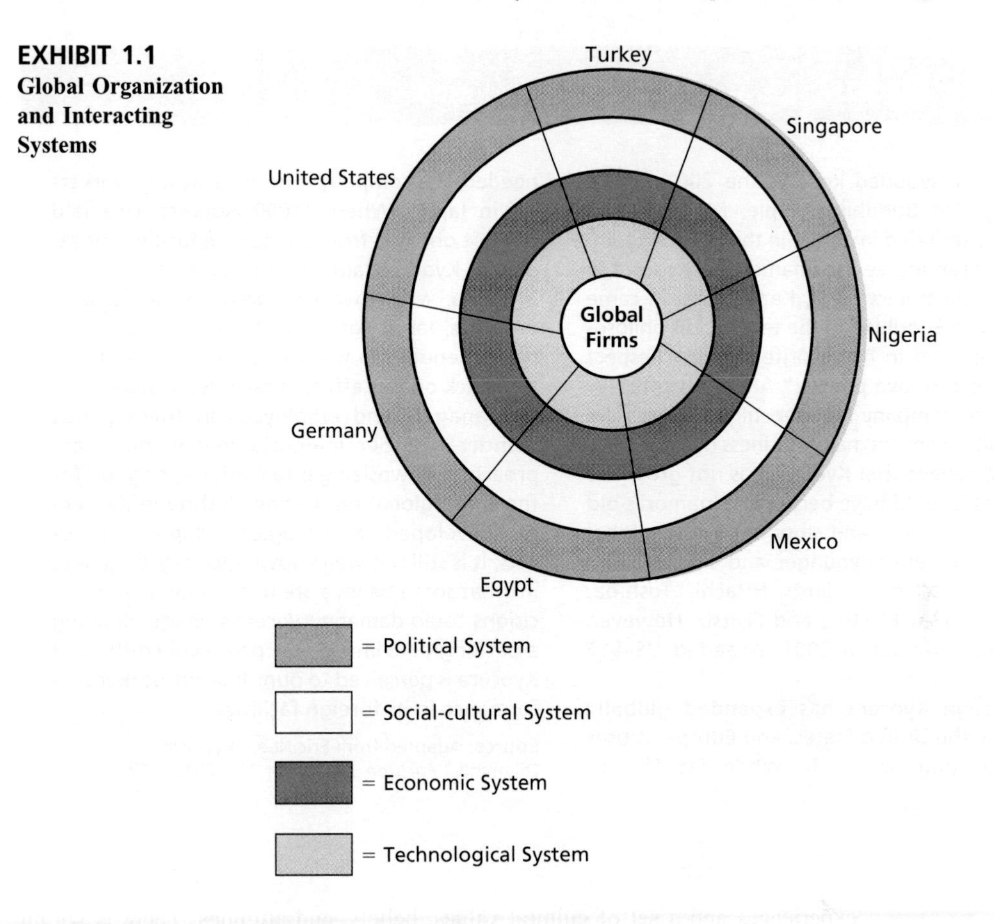

global firms operate are positioned to capture and leverage competitive advantages because of this knowledge. Exhibit 1.1 is a graphical portrayal of four interrelated global environmental systems—social-cultural, economic, political, and technological.

Social-Cultural

Suppose that the organization is a global Japanese firm (e.g., Honda, Toyota). The firm operates plants, belongs to joint ventures, and engages in business transactions in the United States. The United States has a political environment and national government that has jurisdiction over the nation's territory.[11] Through laws and regulations, the U.S. government establishes the "rules" of operating a business in the country. The existence of the Japanese firm depends on the willingness of the government to allow entry of foreign ownership, management, capital, technology, and products.

The global social-cultural system is a subsystem of the nation-state system. The United States, Turkey, Mexico, Egypt, and more than 200 other countries each contain a national culture—a group of citizens sharing common social

Global Focus Laying Off the Best Performers: What?

Nested in a wooded knoll is the 200-year-old Enfuku-ji Zen Buddhist temple. Monks spend their days secluded in prayer in this working temple. After retiring as chairman of the Kyocera, a Japanese electronics giant, Kazuo Inamori came to study Zen Buddhism in the temple. His philosophy is captured in his favorite saying, "Respect the divine and love people." Although officially retired, the company founder still influences the firm's culture and its major business decisions.

Some believe that Kyocera has not grown as rapidly as it could have because of Inamori's old ways of managing and slow entry into global markets. Kyocera is younger and smaller than Japanese electronic giants Hitachi, Toshiba, NEC, Mitsubishi Electric, and Fiyitsu. However, Kyocera's revenues in 2001 exceeded US $12 billion.

Although Kyocera has expanded globally into Asia, the United States, and Europe, it uses an interesting approach. When layoffs are needed, the company refuses to lay any workers off in Japan. When 10,000 workers were laid off, not one was from a Japanese facility. For example, Kyocera laid off employees at factories in China, where workers produce high-quality products, labor costs are cheap, and the company's reputation was growing, instead of cutting back on less efficient facilities in Japan.

Managers and employees in these plants wonder whether Inamori's management approach to downsizing is fair, ethical, or good for the firm's global reputation. Although Kyocera has developed technologically superior products, it is still not well known globally. Engaging in what some believe are unfair managerial decisions could damage Kyocera's image. Building a better global image may prove very difficult if Kyocera is perceived to punish good worker performance in its foreign facilities.

Source: Adapted from Eric Nee, "Kyocera's Dilemma," *Fortune,* December 10, 2001, p. 57.

experiences and a set of cultural values, beliefs, and attitudes. There is within each national culture subcultures and a variety of cross-cultural relations, communications, and beliefs. These variations result in cross-cultural gaps that must be understood and bridged by managers of the global firm.

One particular social-cultural set of attitudes and values is very important in conducting and managing global business: namely, nationalism, or the loyalty and identification with a given society, culture, and state. **Nationalism** can shift and change from time to time.[12] As a political concept, nationalism may run from love of a country (patriotism) to glorification of the state (chauvinism). Nationalism can inject emotions into managerial situations such as who should manage local employees—a host-country national, an expatriate manager, or a parent company national (PCN).

Negative attitudes toward foreign states and people are common components of nationalism. When a global firm enters a foreign country, the reception by the government and the public depends to some degree on the degree of nationalism that exists. Nationalism can distort organizational behavior approaches and needs to be considered when applying specific management techniques.

The Global Focus above provides an example of how nationalism can possibly play a role in management practices.

Values, which vary from culture to culture, are defined as the concepts people believe in and the standards they live by.[13] What an organization and its employees value is open to scrutiny, critical analysis, and skepticism. This is especially the case for global firms. For example, trust can influence behavior. Trust as a value is being questioned in U.S. firms such as Enron, WorldCom, Tyco, and Grand Crossing because of a breakdown in ethical practices and decision making.[14] Being involved in a business scandal can reduce employees' trust in their employers as well as society's trust in the organization. The loss of someone's trust in a firm's integrity is hard to recoup. Understanding how to respond to expectations and values that call for trust, integrity, and ethics is part of the global manager's job responsibility. If host-country citizens do not want to work for an unethical organization or an organization that has been convicted of fraud, conspiracy, or discrimination, the supply of human assets required for success will not be available.

Increasingly, motivation to perform well is based on values in global organizations, rather than primarily on financial reward. For decades, loyalty was bought. The employer provided gradual pay raises, promotional opportunities, and job security. In return, the employee offered loyalty, a hard day's work, and cooperation. Today, values impact loyalty and motivation.

ECONOMIC SYSTEM

Each nation in the world has an economy. The world's economies engage in transactions. Flows of human resources, merchandise, money, capital, technology, and information create an interconnectedness among the nation-states. Private business firms perform global transactions in North America, Europe, Africa, Asia, and Latin America.[15] The motivation behind these transactions is economic gain.

In the more centrally planned economies of China, North Korea, and Cuba, the speed, type, and flow of transactions with global companies is in the hands of state agencies. These agencies are motivated by economic gain, but also must function within the constraints of a national plan.

An organization becomes a global institution when its management seeks to achieve economic gain and market share by extending its reach and operations across national boundaries. The evolution of a global firm typically starts by exporting goods or services to foreign markets. As exports increase, the company may establish sales and service units in foreign countries. It may also license foreign firms to undertake the manufacture of its products for sale in local markets.

The next growth step of a global enterprise is the establishment of production units or offices (for service firms) abroad under its own managerial control and direction. This step requires a bigger stake in the foreign market in terms of hiring, retaining, developing, and motivating host-country employees.[16] The organization is shifting from a domestic to a global perspective, which requires unique managerial competencies and understanding. When management begins to plan, organize, control, and direct from a global perspective, the distinction between domestic and foreign becomes muted and eventually fades away. A global perspective takes control.

POLITICAL SYSTEM

Aggressive and proactive global firms compile, maintain, and analyze the political environment of the countries in which transactions occur or where operations are established or are being considered. Managers are involved in studying the political risks to which they and their companies are exposed in certain countries. A **political risk** is a government action or motivated event that could negatively affect the economic gains, market share, value, ownership, and opportunities of the firm.[17] Expropriation, which has been very rare in the past two decades, occurs when the host-country government seizes the foreign-owned assets of the global firm without providing any or fair compensation. The risk of expropriation is highest in countries that are unstable politically.

In parts of the world, terrorism poses a significant political risk to company employees and assets. **Terrorism** is the use or threat of use of violence for political purposes. Global firms must assess political risk to manage their assets and exposure to risk.[18] Exhibit 1.2 presents a checklist for determining political risk. A country scoring low would suggest a "high degree" of political risk. Scores over 70 would indicate a low political risk. Countries such as Switzerland, Norway, Singapore, Denmark, the United Kingdom, Brunei, and the Netherlands score as some of the best in terms of political risk.

TECHNOLOGY FACTORS

Innovative technology represents a significant competitive advantage to firms. The key issue is whether a global firm can benefit from its technology. A global firm can reap many technological benefits from worldwide operations. The technology can be diffused and transferred to operations around the world. Nation–states have various regulations for the use and transfer of technology. For example, in Italy a patent is good for 20 years and a trademark has a 20-year life span and is renewable. But in Mexico, patents have a 14-year duration and trademarks are usable on a 5-year, renewable schedule. Countries can control the flow, use, and creation of technology by developing and enforcing specific laws.[19] For example, the U.S. controls and has an embargo on the transfer of various nanotechnologies to China because the technology could be used in producing advanced military missile weapon systems.[20]

Some countries use their investment laws to acquire needed technology to create jobs, to train local citizens, and to improve productivity. This allows them to produce products that can be traded and result in economic gains. Strategy expert Michael Porter has shown clearly that a key to successful global growth is the ability to create, use, and innovate technology.[21] Nintendo is an example of a firm that continues to innovate. It uses technology to produce game units that can easily slide into a book bag and provide users with a high-resolution, clear screen that competitors have a difficult time matching.

EXHIBIT 1.2 Political Risk Assessment—Country X

Source: E. Dichtl and H.G. Koglmayr, "Country Risk Ratings," *Management International Review* 26, no. 4 (1986), p. 6.

Subindex	Criteria	Factor Ratings Score Range	
		Minimum	**Maximum**
I. Political and economic environment	1. Stability of the political system	3	14
	2. Imminent internal conflicts	0	14
	3. Threats to stability emanating from the outside world	0	12
	4. Degree of control of economic system	5	9
	5. Reliability of the country as a trading partner	4	12
	6. Constitutional guarantees	2	12
	7. Effectiveness of public administration	3	12
	8. Labor relations and social peace	3	15
		Σ 20	100
II. Domestic economic conditions	9. Size of population	4	8
	10. Per capita income	2	10
	11. Economic growth during previous 5 years	2	7
	12. Prospective growth during next 3 years	3	10
	13. Inflation during previous 2 years	2	10
	14. Accessibility of domestic capital market to foreigners	3	7
	15. Availability of energy resources	2	8
	16. Possibility of giving employment to foreign nationals	2	8
	17. Availability of medical resources	2	14
	18. Legal requirements concerning environmental protection	4	8
	19. Traffic system and communication channels	2	14
		Σ 28	100
III. External economic relations	20. Restrictions imposed on imports	2	10
	21. Restrictions imposed on exports	2	10
	22. Restrictions imposed on foreign investments in the country	3	9
	23. Freedom to set up or engage in partnerships	3	9
	24. Legal protection for brands and products	3	9
	25. Restrictions imposed on monetary transfers	2	9
	26. Revalorizations against the DM during previous 5 years	2	8
	27. Development of the balance of payments	2	7
	28. Drain on foreign funds through oil and other energy imports	3	14
	29. International financial standing	3	8
	30. Restrictions imposed on the exchange of local money into foreign currency	2	8
		Σ 27	100
Total Risk Evaluation—County X:		75	300

An important technological development is provided by telecommunication. Wireless telephones, beepers, and other personal digital assistant (PDA) devices allow people to use wireless technology. Telecommunication systems have enabled countries to become partners in the world's business transactions. Without adopting telecommunication devices, countries will likely fall behind economically.

Technology has affected the size of workforces around the world. Robots, automated teller machines (ATM), smart systems, and voice-recognition systems have resulted in job displacement. For certain technical jobs, such as software engineers, technicians, and computer support personnel, there is an increased market demand. On the other hand, the demand for low-skilled, blue-collar workers is decreasing. Job gain and job loss are global managerial realities when new or improved technologies are introduced.

The knowledgeable global manager in preparing plans, organizing work, controlling, and directing must pay attention to environmental forces—sociocultural, political, economic, and technological. Examining and being attuned to these forces will influence the manager's style and techniques. Scanning the environment for changes, trends, and events that may require an adjustment in style or technique must be part of the global manager's approach.

GLOBAL TRENDS THAT IMPACT MANAGEMENT

A number of powerful trends influence the management of global employees in transnational firms. These trends affect the management and leadership decisions that will be discussed throughout the book.

Ecosystem Factors

Managers need to be sensitive to ecosystem factors such as energy consumption, recycling, and waste management. Managerial concern about ecology is very important and a top priority in transnational organizations. There are now over 6 billion people in the world, and attention to ecosystems has become a major issue in the past two decades. High rates of consumption encourage markets to meet higher demand.

An increasing proportion of the world's inhabitants have high expectations as consumers as images portraying high levels of consumption are available through global media.

Greater consumption produces more waste. In developed economies, regulations are in place to ensure that waste disposal is carried out in an acceptable manner. In 1999, the European Union (EU) adopted a regulation that waste disposal must be effectively managed.[22] Global managers are not able to ignore or give just a passing reference to ecosystems balance in operating their organizations.

Work/Life Balance

An increasing number of workers around the world have shifted their attitudes, values, and priorities to achieve a greater sense of work/life balance. Thus, companies must become more creative in responding to work/life needs such as child care, elder care, flexible work schedules, and more vacation time. Ignoring this trend can result in recruitment problems, decreasing performance, greater turnover, low morale, and declining customer relationships. Companies are offering extended parental leave, job sharing, sabbaticals, school-term work schedules, and compassionate leave to fulfill caregiving responsibilities. For example, the United Kingdom supermarket chain Sainburg's offers special leave of up to one year for caregiving. The right to take parental leave and leave for family reasons became national law in 15 EU member states in 1999.[23]

An international workforce study of 13 countries found that workers in every country except Russia rate work/life balance higher than a good salary.[24] Workers want quality time to enjoy what they earn. One-third of those surveyed would leave their current jobs for one that provides more flexibility.

Diversity

Globalization has led to more companies operating in countries with limited resources, inadequate infrastructure, social problems, and low skill levels. Lack of investment in education has stifled the growth in many nations. Global firms are coming into contact with many different demographic profiles, religions, races, customs, and traditions. The workforce that exists comes from a more diverse pool, which makes recruitment, retention, and motivation more complex for managers.

Companies will continue to serve or sell into diverse markets, which will require an ability on the part of managers to optimize the performance of a heterogeneous group of employees. Management practices that are free from age, gender, or racial discrimination, that support equal pay for equal work, and that are concerned about workplace conditions are important to diverse workforces.[25] Thus, managers need to explore the issues that are the most significant to different races, religions, and nationalities. The transnational firm's workforce is likely to become much more diverse in the next few decades.

Health, Well-Being, and Happiness

In many nations, proper nutrition and treatment of life-threatening diseases are common concerns. A larger proportion of a global firm's workforce is likely to be located in nations with poor standards of health care. Inadequate health care can influence worker attendance, the availability and size of the pool of candidates to perform work, and the type of health care benefits preferred and needed by workers.

A global firm can use its communication system to promote health care information. The Toy Manufacturers Association of Brazil, for example, requested that its member companies carry messages on product packages for parents about how to prevent dehydration in children. In countries in Asia and Africa, company communication channels carry information on HIV prevention.[26]

Working Conditions

Organized labor and activist consumers increasingly pressure managers about working conditions. Topics such as paying a fair, living wage, avoiding child or bonded labor, allowing freedom of association, and preventing discrimination are important workforce issues.

Global Focus World Values Survey

Geneticists, biologists, psychologists, economists, organizational scientists, and physiologists have all studied happiness. The newer, more preferred term is *subjective well-being*. The World Values Survey, coordinated by Ronald Inglehart at the University of Michigan, studies subjective well-being. Since 1981, the World Values Survey has sampled people in 60 societies representing 75 percent of the world's population.

A surprising result emerges in reviewing the survey results: An increase in wealth per capita makes a big difference in the happiness level of the poorer nations but has little impact on those that are reasonably well off. This is good news for some former communist countries. Moldova holds the record for misery with only 32 percent of the population saying it is happy, and Russia and Belarus are not far ahead. India and Poland, on the other hand, are zooming up on the charts.

Iceland is one of the happiest nations of all, even though its citizens are not nearly as rich as the gloomier Japan, Germany, and the United States. The survey determined that increasing wealth does not result in permanent happiness. Other factors, such as values, customs, and a sense of belonging, friendships, and self-expression, also affect subjective well-being.

Source: Adapted from Alan Anderson, "The Greatest Gift That We Possess: The World in 2002," *The Economist*, June 2002, pp. 107–8.

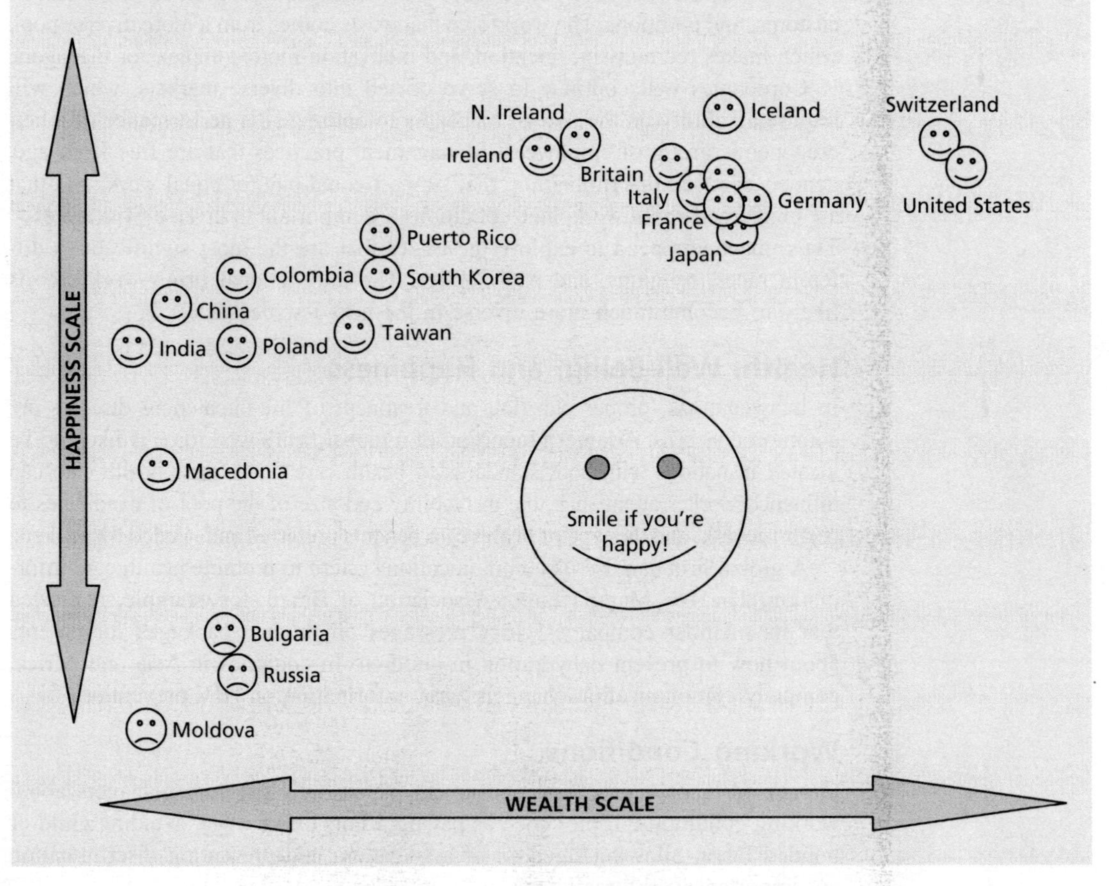

There have been reports of employees working under sweatshop conditions at Southeast Asian suppliers for Nike, Adidas, Gap, and Wal-Mart.[27] Nike and Adidas are tackling working condition issues by introducing codes of conduct, independent auditing and verification of workplace standards, and management training programs. Differences in working conditions and wages for comparable work in countries around the world have resulted in demonstrations, boycotts, and negative publicity.

In industrialized countries, the work relationship between managers and employees is also being examined. Laws relating to employee rights are presented in managerial training programs and coaching sessions. Microsoft, Lockheed Martin, and Nextel have all been named in lawsuits for violating employee rights. Companies in Turkey, Algeria, Saudi Arabia, Malaysia, Angola, and many others have been identified as places where denial of freedom, torture, forcible relocation, and harassment have been identified in management and worker relationships.

Quality

In the majority of the world today, quality is a vital factor in achieving global competitiveness and economic gains. The automobile industry has remained in the forefront in demanding high-quality production from workers. Careful recruitment, selection, and motivation can create and maintain a workforce dedicated to quality. Designing and producing quality at all price levels—low, medium, and high—is required of global managers. The following Global Focus describes how quality makes a difference.

Starbucks, the Seattle-based coffee company, is an example of a company with a wide global reach.[28] When the company broadened its reach into China, many skeptics pointed out that getting $4 for a high-quality cup of coffee would be impossible in this developing nation, where coffee wasn't even popular. But since Starbucks entered the market, trained a Chinese workforce, and charged a high price for high-quality coffee, consumption has skyrocketed. Starbucks has used a quality emphasis to expand internationally into more than 20 countries.

The quality service provided by the airlines of Singapore, Malaysia, and Thailand has attracted global attention and many job candidates wanting to join these exceptional organizations.[29] Asian hotel groups also receive high ratings for providing superior customer service. Being viewed as a quality service provider is a competitive advantage and also attracts large pools of job candidates. People want to be part of a global organization that is considered superior in the delivery of quality.

These six trends shape global businesses and multinational organizations. Concern for the environment, work/life balance, managing diversity, health care and well-being, working conditions, and quality transcend national boundaries. Managers in global firms certainly must carry out their roles and perform planning, organizing, controlling, and directing functions. These are crucial parts of the job. However, they must also weigh, observe, and analyze the trends that exist worldwide. Managerial performance is much more than meeting production schedules or completing a project within a budget's parameters. Managers

Global Focus Quality Makes a Difference Globally

Nagavara Ramarao Narayana Murthy, better known as NR, and six other cofounders of Bangalore-based Infosys Technologies had to borrow US $2,000 to start their software company in 1981. The idea of Infosys competing with world giants such as IBM in global markets was wishful thinking. Today, with 10,000 programmers Infosys is still small (about $545 million annual sales) compared to IBM ($9 billion annual sales), but it is a powerhouse in the world.

NR founded his firm on what are considered principles of globalization. He found capital where it was cheapest, produced where it was cost-effective, and sold products where it was most profitable.

In the past five years, repeat business, high-quality software developed in India at a fraction of the cost of European or American development, and investment in research and development have made Infosys a global success story. For example, Belgian mobile communication operator Belgacom Mobile wanted to develop a customer loyalty program that would handle data storage in different languages and provide flexibility for clients. Infosys delivered the program ahead of schedule, providing Belgacom with a high-quality, first-mover product.

Infosys has attracted business from Europe, Latin America, Canada, and the United States. NR gained the confidence of customers, some of whom were anxious about using foreign software outsourcing, by meeting quality standards and schedules, and Infosys now has a reputation of being one of the best in the world.

NR stresses quality in every phase of producing software. His quality initiative is a part of the Infosys company culture. He matches or benchmarks his quality against the world's most recognized multinational firms. Foreign and institutional investors who in the 1980s were wary of investing in India are no longer reluctant to invest in Infosys.

NR is proudest of Infosys' ability to compete with anyone in the world. He wanted to make a difference in India and throughout the world. Obviously, he has done so through a management system that requires employees to focus on quality production as the top priority.

Source: Adapted from Anthony Sibillin, "The Best of Both Worlds," *Eurobusiness*, April 2002, pp. 40–42.

must also address the type of questions, concerns, and problems associated with the environment, work/life balance, a diverse workforce, health care and well-being, working conditions, and quality. These are issues that involve people, their perceptions, values, attitudes, needs, and personalities. The people-related factors will be addressed in the book.

THE PEOPLE CHALLENGE

The primary duty of transnational managers operating in a globally connected world is to recruit, retain, and motivate the most talented, committed, and skilled workforce possible for their company. They will need to establish guidelines and policies on expectations of performance and conduct, which the company's employees understand, respect, and appreciate and which the managers also embrace. Exhibit 1.3 presents a partial list of what global managers must do. Some of these actions require time to become established. They may also

EXHIBIT 1.3 **The Global Manager's Actions: A Sample List**

Global Manager's Actions	Anticipated Results
• Create an attractive place to work, with open and flexible policies that permit workers to balance work and life. • Clearly communicate performance and conduct expectations. • Show how reward system is linked to performance and conduct. • Recruit from the local community the best talent and skill available. • Train and develop employees so that they can experience recognition and personal growth. • Provide process for workers to freely voice concerns, complaints, and work improvement suggestions. • Participate in local events, charities, and volunteer programs as a person and as a representative of the global business. • Serve as an ethical role model for employees. • Learn about local customs, language, religion, and traditions.	**Employees** • Feel respected • Motivated to learn • Motivated to perform • Interested in improving skills • Loyal and committed **Global Firm** • Increased number of job candidates • More stable workforce • Higher production • Respect • Lower training costs **Community** • Respect for firm • Appreciation • Positive image • Welcoming attitudes • Lower training costs

increase costs initially, but the improvements within the workforce and the community can be significant.

Global managers face the challenge of operating within the boundaries of acceptable and ethical company policies and programs, while taking local conditions into account. For example, the managers of a Dow Chemical plant in Australia made a commitment to create an environmental improvement plan to improve health and safety and reduce the environmental impact of the plant in the community. This commitment cost millions of dollars, but the positive image it created with the workers, government, and community was hailed as the most significant environmental management success in Australia in the past 10 years.[30]

The people challenges vary among industries—auto, financial services, information and communication technology, extraction and utilities, pharmaceutical, retail, transportation, and others. However, by paying close attention to the basic functions of management and the six trends outlined here, managers will be in a better position to recruit, retain, and motivate their workforces. More than domestic managers, global managers must develop people, operate the business, and build the global organization's reputation. The reputation concept is extremely important. Global managers can help to build the firm's reputation by gaining the trust of the employees, the community in which it operates, and the government that oversees operations.

For an organization to succeed globally, it needs qualified people and astute management. At the core is the need for managers to have cultural awareness and an understanding of the effects of culture on the day-to-day operations. Unfortunately, cross-cultural awareness appears to be in short supply among global managers. Cultural blunders are almost always avoidable. However, it takes training, knowledge, and experience to reach a level of acceptable and competent managerial behavior.

THE BOOK'S ARCHITECTURE AND FRAMEWORK

Whatever the size, location, or industry of a global firm, managers must be knowledgeable, skilled, and flexible to be effective. This book will show that specific knowledge, skills, and a flexible or contingency approach on the part of managers and leaders are needed to accomplish economic and market share goals. The book's architecture is centered around four parts, as shown in Exhibit 1.4. The

EXHIBIT 1.4 Global Organizational Behavior: Framework

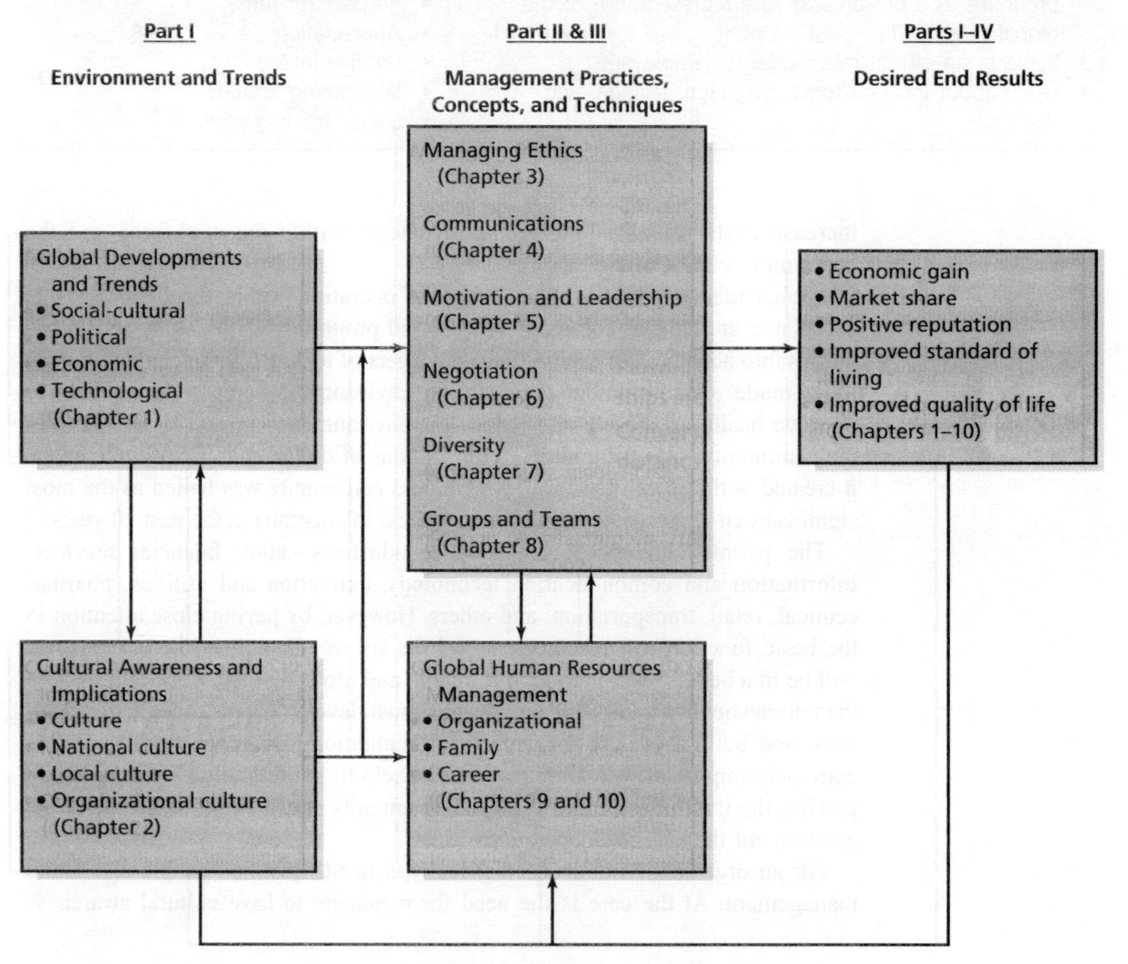

content and supplemental resources in Part 4 are designed to present the knowledge, skills areas, and rationale for a contingency approach.

In today's global environment, you could find yourself as a manager in a foreign subsidiary of a German firm, facing many of the issues presented in this book. Or you could end up at the home office of a Mexican firm coordinating with its 20 affiliates across the world. Or you could be a manager of a Japanese firm negotiating a major engineering project in Russia. Or you could be a frequent traveler from your firm in Ethiopia conducting business transactions in Canada and the United States. Many different kinds of managerial roles are available. An example of the types of managerial jobs is presented in Exhibit 1.5

EXHIBIT 1.5 Examples of Positions

European Sales Manager

Location: **London**

An ideal opportunity to join a small European hedge fund company within a new business development role. Strong track record across Europe required.

Ideal Experience:

- Strong track record in sales. Ideally within the institutional marketplace, with some high network individuals.
- Experience within the alternative investment sector would be advantageous. No less than five years of experience.
- Passionate about growing a business through European.
- Happy to work with a small team, although experienced in developing business independently.

HR Director

Location: **Tokyo, Japan**

A major Silicon Valley-based software firm has an exciting opening in Japan for an HR Director. As part of the management team, the HR Director is critical to the overall business achievement in Japan. The position will not only oversee the HR activities for Japan, but also work closely with management to drive change and growth within Japan. The HR Director will work closely with each of the regional directors, functional heads and managers to ensure that the HR programs support their business objectives and to ensure that the HR activities are effectively executed in accordance with regional goals and local laws and practices.

Requirements:

- Requires HR generalist experience in a rapidly changing environment in a senior position typically for an international company
- Requires 10+ years of experience, preferably in the IT industry
- Undergraduate degree in Human Resources, Organizational Psychology, or Business Administration is required
- A Masters degree or advanced diploma would be a plus

(*continued*)

(*concluded*)

Vice President Sales—France/Germany

Location: **Europe**

Europroprospectus.com requires two individuals to sell company products and services, train and maintain existing customers and develop new customers.

Scope of the position:
The company is looking to hire two individuals, one for France and one for Germany. They will sell the company's products and services, train and maintain existing customers, and develop new customers. The sales and business development team currently consists of 6 people, all of whom are based in London.

Location:
One person will work in France and the other one in Germany. The majority of their clients will be based in those countries. The company does not have offices in these countries at the moment and the person could work from home, at least initially.

Principal Responsibilities:
1. Looking after all aspects of the sales process
2. Solicit customer feedback on product and service to do things better or differently
3. Help develop and maintain a user group to generate important feedback
4. Negotiate subscriptions and documentation
5. Help promote company services at trade fairs
6. Organize and provide training for customers
7. Help develop new product ideas
8. Achieve targets based on client contact and sales revenue

Education Requirements: Educated to degree level

Work Experience Requirements:
Proven track record in sales for professional services, ideally in a legal/investment banking environment.

Skills/Personal Requirements:
- Fluent in English and either French or German
- Committed to the Internet as a way of doing business
- Good PC skills, including a working knowledge of MS Outlook, Word, and Excel
- Ability to be motivated and work on their own

CONTINGENCY APPROACH

Whatever managerial role a person plays, he or she will need to understand the environmental forces, the trends that exist, and the cultures in which the transactions occur and how these factors influence managerial style, techniques, and approach.

Global management practice is well suited for a **contingency or flexible approach.**[31] This approach suggests that the choice of "what to do," "how to do it," and "when to do it" depends on the people involved, the task at hand, and the forces impacting the decision. Working as a manager in a domestic setting is very difficult, but being an effective transnational manager with its unique mix of issues, situations, and environmental forces is even more challenging.

What a transnational manager can do in the job is established to some extent by each country. The educated and proficient global manager will study and learn about sociocultural customs, political agendas, technological status, laws and regulations, economic conditions, and competitors. This type of knowledge acquisition will result in more effective planning, organizing, controlling, directing, and decision making. These functional responsibilities are carried out by domestic managers; but in a global environment, managers need to be more flexible or contingency oriented. The contingency-oriented global manager will constantly need to use an "if → then" approach. If these are the conditions, tasks, environmental forces, and human assets, "then" I must act and do the following. Applying this method of addressing problems requires confidence, knowledge, the ability to work and motivate a diverse workforce, and some type of measure or measurement metric to determine accomplishments or areas that need improvement.

A Metric to Consider

Determining whether a transnational manager is effective is an important theme of this book. Organizations are constantly searching for ways to determine how they are performing. This determination is typically conducted by using a measurement system. Some firms measure employee satisfaction levels and monitor it so that morale issues can be immediately addressed. One global set of measures gaining widespread adoption is called Social Accountability 8000.[32] Based on conventions of the International Labor Organization, SA 8000 is being adopted across the world. Some of the adopters include Dole Food, Toys "Я" Us, and Otto Versand.

What Is SA 8000?

Social Accountability 8000 (SA 8000) is a code of conduct for companies seeking to make the workplace more humane. It can be used in any country and in any industry. Companies are adopting SA 8000 to enhance their reputations by improving workplace conditions and because they want to do the right thing. To certify compliance with SA 8000, qualified auditors visit facilities to assess performance on health and safety, working hours, compensation, child labor, management practices, and freedom of association. Managers need to document performance in all areas, and accredited auditors must verify compliance.

SA 8000 and ISO Standards

The SA 8000 system of measurement and audit is modeled after the **ISO 9000** and **ISO 14000** series of standards for quality control and environmental management systems.[33] Hundreds of thousands of global firms around the world use these ISO standards. The ISO standards were initially developed at the national level and then harmonized by the International Standard Organization in Geneva. The SA 8000 was developed from the beginning as a global standard.

The Proposed Benefits

SA 8000 compliance results in improving work conditions. Research indicates that among the benefits of adopting SA 8000 are greater employee retention, improved community reputation, additional customers, and enhanced product quality and productivity. Managers have made the following statements:

> SA 8000 has given us a formal method to publicly communicate to our employees, our customers, and to our suppliers the principles by which we manage our company. Our employees have expressed a positive response to the program.[34]
>
> Peter Venenma, chairman and CEO,
> L.E. Jones

> By continually conversing with the employees about the firm and raising its profile in the community, we have been able to develop pride and loyalty within the company and credibility in the eyes of outsiders, using SA 8000 as a management tool to achieve these ends.[35]
>
> P. Guerin, president, Celtiphram

De Nadai, a Brazilian catering company, credits SA 8000 with attracting new clients. SA 8000 provides companies with the ability to differentiate themselves in a crowded marketplace. With the advent of globalization, companies have more competitors attempting to be more socially accountable and SA 8000 offers proof, thus differentiating the business.[36]

Co-op Italia Case

Co-op Italia is the largest supermarket chain in Italy with more than 1,200 stores, controlling about 7 percent of the Italian market. The company has 36,000 employees.[37] SA 8000 is used by Co-op Italia to earn the trust of consumers. The SA 8000 standard is applied to 230 suppliers of Co-op's label food program. Co-op Italia audits a sample of its suppliers each year on SA 8000 performance criteria: child labor, safety and health, working hours, management, disciplinary actions, discrimination, and others. If the suppliers are not meeting acceptable standards (e.g., prohibition of child labor under the age of 15, forbidding mental or physical coercion and verbal abuse of workers), they can be and some are dropped from the business.

In terms of global management practices, SA 8000 is one of the fastest-growing standards. This type of standard sends a clear signal from transnational firms that they are concerned about workers, management practices, the community, and the firm's image and reputation. These are the type of concerns that this book, *Global Management and Organizational Behavior: Text, Readings, Cases, and Exercises,* will portray, analyze, and critique.

Action Now

Globalization and the rise in telecommunication have changed the way transactions occur and what is expected in terms of workplace standards. The emergence of a global assembly line has led some countries to lower standards to attract new production. The media and other groups have reported on workplace standards and management practices. Exposing a company with bad management practices and standards causes them harm and affects their economic and profit profile and market share negatively. Adopting SA 8000 is an indicator that the global organization is serious about workers, management, and conditions.

21ST CENTURY GLOBALIZATION

While globalization has occurred for centuries, today it is spread out further, faster, and deeper. Economists use the term *network effects* to refer to situations where a product becomes more valuable once many other people use it. The Internet is an example of further, faster, and deeper. As global organizations contemplate new markets, new customers, and new workforces, they will do so by examining environmental forces, trends, and the value they can bring to nation–states. Distance has become irrelevant in terms of economic gains and market share. What is not irrelevant is how managers can be effective in a global world. As this book will quickly show, local culture, local needs, local politics, and local human resources set significant boundaries on what, where, when, and how an organization can function.

Globalization is a two-edged sword. In some nations, activists protest foreign management, practices, and goals. Antiglobalization protesters oppose global organizations and networks on the grounds that they are undemocratic.[38] In other nations, there is a hope that globalization and the growth of transnational organizations can improve a nation's standard of living, infrastructure, and health and nutrition. As the future unfolds, an important part of the history of global organizations will be the role that managers play. Astute managers can help remove some of the antiglobalization criticisms and fulfill the hopes that global organizations will provide more benefits to a society than costs.

Key Terms

Contingency or flexible approach, *22*
Global organizational behavior, *5*
ISO 9000, *23*
ISO 14000, *23*
Multinational organizations, *6*
Nationalism, *10*
Organizational behavior, *5*
Political risk, *12*
Social Accountability 8000 (SA 8000), *23*
Terrorism, *12*
Transnational firm, *8*
Values, *11*

Review, Critical Thinking, and Discussion Questions

1. Why is global organizational behavior considered a multidiscipline concept?
2. Why would a firm's reputation globally be so carefully protected and worked on by managers?
3. What can transnational organizations contribute to globalization?
4. What are some of the criticisms of globalization that are meaningful and require managerial consideration?

5. Explain in your own words the contingency approach.
6. How can significant trends such as those presented in the chapter influence transnational management practices?
7. Is there one best or preferred way to manage a diverse workforce in a global organization? Why?
8. Why should nationalism be taken into consideration when transnational firms are considering a business transaction?
9. What particular managerial skills would be valuable in managing a diverse workforce in a transnational organization?
10. Would an increase in terrorism around the world have an effect on any of the trends discussed in this chapter? Explain.

Endnotes

1. Richard K. Lyons, *The Microstructure Approach to Exchange Rates* (Boston: MIT Press, 2000).
2. J. A. Galbraith, *Designing the Global Corporation* (San Francisco: Jossey-Bass, 2000).
3. James L. Gibson, John M. Ivancevich, James H. Donnelly, Jr., and Robert Konopaske, *Organizations: Behavior, Structure, Processes* (New York McGraw-Hill/Irwin, 2003), p. 6.
4. Michael S. Schell and Charlene Marmer Solomon, *Capitalizing on the Global Workforce* (Chicago: Irwin Professional, 1997).
5. Michael A. Cusumano, Kentaro Nobeoka, and Ketaro Nobeoka, *Thinking Beyond Lean* (New York: Simon & Schuster, 2002).
6. Susan C. Schneider and Jean-Louis Barsoux, *Managing Across Cultures* (Saddle River, NJ: Prentice Hall, 2002).
7. John Nathan, SONY, (Reading, MA: Houghton Mifflin, 2001).
8. Schneider and Barsoux, *Managing Across Cultures*.
9. Amey Stone and Mike Brewster, *King of Capital: Sandy Weill and the Making of Citicorp* (New York: John Wiley & Sons, 2002).
10. Christopher A. Bartlett and Sumantra Ghosal, *Managing Across Borders: The Transnational Solution* (Cambridge, MA: Harvard Business School Press, 1998), p. 65.
11. Joseph S. Nye, Jr., *The Paradox of American Power* (New York: Oxford, 2001).
12. Chris Cook, *World Political Almanac* (New York: Checkmark Books, 2001).
13. Carol Akright, *Funding Your Dreams Generation to Generation* (Chicago: Dearborn Trade, 2001).
14. David Rakoff, *Fraud* (New York: Broadway Books, 2002).
15. George S. Yip, *Total Business Strategy II* (Saddle River, NJ: Prentice Hall, 2003).
16. Michelle Maynard, *The Global Manufacturing Vanguard: New Rules from the Industry Elite* (New York: John Wiley & Sons, 1998).
17. Thomas A. Moran, *Managing International Political Risk* (London: Blackwell, 1998).
18. Joe Teeples, *Building Corporate Castles: Homeland Defense for Business* (New York: Dimensions, 2002).
19. Howard Smith and Peter Finger, *Business Process Management: The Tidal Wave* (Tampa, FL: Meghan-Kiffer, 2002).

20. *Ibid*.
21. Michael E. Porter, Jeffrey D. Sachs, and Cornelius McArthur Schwab, *The Global Competitiveness Report* (London: Oxford University Press, 2002).
22. G. Deburca and Joanne Scott, eds., *The EV & WTO: Legal and Constitutional Aspects* (New York: Hart Publishing, 2001).
23. *Ibid*.
24. Kathryn M. Denton, *Corporate Russian Roulette Behavior Management Through Understanding Human Nature* (Bloomington, IN: 1st Books, 2002).
25. Karen C. Knop, *Diversity and Self-Determination in International Law* (London: Cambridge University Press, 2002).
26. Zia Jaffrey, *The New Apartheid: AIDS in South Africa* (New York: Verso Books, 2002).
27. Theodore H. Moran, *Beyond Sweatshops* (Washington, DC: Brookings Institute, 2002).
28. Veronica Anne Starbuck, *August Magic* (New York: Windigo Harbor Media, 2001).
29. "Airlines and Airports in Singapore, Malaysia, and Brunei," *A Market Analysis,* 2001, PDF file.
30. Roger L. Miller, Daniel K. Benjamin, and D. C. North, *The Economics of Public Issues* (Reading, MA: Addison-Wesley, 2002).
31. Jose De La Torre, Yves Doz, and Timothy Devinney, *Managing the Global Corporation: Case Studies in Strategy and Management* (New York, McGraw-Hill/Irwin, 2000).
32. Deborah Leipziger, *SA 8000* (London: Pearson Education, 2001).
33. David Hoyle, *Quality Systems Handbook* (New York: Butterworth-Henemann, 2001), and David L. Goetsch and Stanley Davis, *Understanding and Implementing ISO9000 and Other ISO Standards* (Saddle River, NJ: Prentice Hall, 2001).
34. "SA8000: Another Measurement of Corporate Success," *Action Line,* June 2000, p. 1.
35. Brad Brown and Meredith McNabb, "Interview with Marie-Pierre Daniel and Patrick Guerin," *Celticpharm,* May 24, 2000, p. 1.
36. Fitz Hilaire, "Visionary Leadership Which Makes a Critical Difference," Presentation given at CEPAA Brussels conference, December 6, 1999.
37. Presentation by Alessandra Vaccari to Advisory Board of SAI, July 7, 1999.
38. Joseph E. Stigletz, *Globalization and Its Discontents* (New York: Norton, 2002).

Chapter Two

Cultural Awareness and Implications

Learning Objectives

After completing Chapter 2, you should be able to:

- **Distinguish between national, organizational, and subcultures.**
- **Identify major dimensions of culture that affect employee performance.**
- **Discuss the differences and characteristics of strong and weak organizational culture.**
- **Describe some of the research that has been done on culture.**
- **Describe how an employee's socialization occurs.**
- **Explain Schein's three levels of culture model.**

Notes on African Culture

Africa is a diverse continent in terms of cultures and subcultures. But there is a foundation of shared values, attitudes, and institutions that binds together the nations south of the Sahara, and in many respects those to the north as well. African culture is not easily classified. Africa appears to be a cluster of societies with weak controls over uncertainty. The control that is present is exercised through religion.

The African sees space and time as a single entity. The Nigerians say, "A watch did not invent man." Africans have always had their own time. The African, anchored in his ancestral culture, is so convinced that the past can only repeat itself that he worries only superficially about the future.

In Africa, a person must be born dominant, otherwise he has no right to power. Leaders or strong individuals are bestowed the power to make decisions.

If there is a single characteristic of the African national culture, it is the subordination of the individual by the community. African culture rejects the view that the individual (in society, in the workplace) is autonomous and responsible. The African working in an organization is linked first to the family. It is assumed that Africans can only grow and develop through family life and connectivity. The individual is suppressed at the time the person-family relationship is developed. Individual rights and responsibilities are not the key concepts in African culture.

The powerful cultural forces in Africa must be noted and considered by transnational organization managers in their decision-making roles. African culture is different from any other, and the range and type of differences is vital to managing workers, operations, and negotiations. The challenge of managers coping with national and subcultural differences will unfold as this chapter's content is considered.

Source: Adapted from Lawrence E. Harrison and Samuel P. Huntington, *Cultural Matters* (New York: Basic Books, 2000), and Mihnea C. Moldoveanu and Nitin Nohria, *Master Passions: Emotion, Narrative, and the Development of Culture* (Cambridge, MA: MIT Press, 2002).

In applying organizational behavior principles to a global workforce it is crucial to have an understanding of culture. Organizations as well as nations have cultures. Different organizations may have similar growth, market share, and performance goals, but their internal company cultures and their external nation-state culture will be different. Research has demonstrated that culture (internal and external) can dramatically influence an organization's performance and success. Consider the following story:

> Once upon a time there was a great flood; and involved in this flood were two creatures, a monkey and a fish. The monkey, being agile and experienced, was lucky enough to scramble up a tree and escape the raging waters. As he looked down from his safe perch, he saw the poor fish struggling against the swift current. With the very best of intentions, he reached down and lifted the fish from the water. The result was inevitable.[1]

The monkey meant well, but assumed the fish's environment and survival route were similar to his, which follows the thought processes of many global managers who assume that people think and work like they do. Simply applying or transferring managerial practices without consideration of the cultural setting and circumstances is not sound, effective, or efficient. Managerial ignorance of and resistance to the realities of cultural differences is not good for survival, growth, or morale.

Transnational company managers can avoid or reduce culture-based ignorance and resistance problems through a better understanding of organizational and national cultural phenomena such as those presented in the opening vignette on Africa. In this chapter, we introduce the concept of culture and how national cultures differ. Because global managers work with people from different cultures, much more than a simple application of a manager's most familiar cultural perception and knowledge is needed to achieve goals. The short culture quiz in the Global Focus provides a picture of your current cultural IQ. It is not a comprehensive quiz, but it offers a quick snapshot of where you are in terms of understanding China, a sleeping giant that is becoming a major participant in the global marketplace.

Global Focus What Would You Do When?

China is a giant emerging economy that is becoming more involved with global operations, markets, and communications than at any time in its history. Global managers and negotiators performing their work roles in China must be aware of the cultural forces that shape Chinese behavior, expectations, and interaction style. Try the brief quiz below to indicate your awareness of Chinese culture and style.

CULTURE QUIZ

1. You have been negotiating a business deal for weeks. There are only 36 hours left before your visit to China. In a sudden move with 10 hours left, the Chinese yield on a number of key points. The Chinese negotiators seem to be waiting for you to give in on some key issues.
2. You are introduced to Mr. Chou Chang at a meeting in a Chinese plant. You politely address him during the meeting as Mr. Chang. He appears to be upset when you refer to or call him Mr. Chang.
3. You visit a Chinese manager's office and admire a painting of the Great Wall of China. When you visit the following week, as you get up to leave the manager provides you with a wrapped gift. You go to your hotel room and open the gift. It is the picture you admired last week. What should you do?
4. You are invited to a formal business dinner in Hong Kong. Should you ask whether your spouse is invited?
5. You are in a meeting with Chinese managers who continue to ask questions about the software package you are attempting to sell them. The questioning continues for hours. You are very familiar with the software and answer so many questions you are exhausted. You are puzzled by all of the questions.
6. You indicate in a meeting that your Chinese colleague is excellent, knowledgeable, and wonderful to work with on the project. The colleague seems upset. You don't know why.

CULTURE AWARENESS ANSWERS

1. This is a usual Chinese negotiation approach. They wait until the last hours and then present some give and expect some give from the other side on key issues.
2. In China, the family name is used first. He is Mr. Chou and should be respectfully referred to this way.
3. You thank the manager. You also provide him with a gift that is about the same value if possible.
4. No. Spouses (wives or husbands) aren't invited to a business dinner.
5. Don't be. The Chinese don't think about time. They respect knowledge and you probably are doing very well.
6. He is upset because individualism is not highly prized in China. Singling him out among his Chinese colleagues is embarrassing. China is a collective society in which group is praised and singled out, not individuals.

How did you do on the quiz?

DEFINING CULTURE

Organizational culture is defined as the values, norms, customs, and assumptions held by people that serve as a guide to their behavior. Culture influences how people make decisions, treat others, and determine what is right and wrong.[2] A country's national culture is the set of beliefs, values, and style shared by the citizens within a nation.[3] **National culture,** like organizational culture, provides the basic assumptions used to guide behavior.

In addition to the national culture, there are ethnic and other cultural groups within a nation. Although these groups share national cultural values, they also have some unique cultural characteristics—food, language, dress, religion, and work ethic. The United States (e.g., Southerners, Midwesterners, Easterners), Canada (e.g., French, English), Belgium (Flemish and French), and Indonesia (Islamic Javanese, Hindu Balinese Malay, etc.) are nations that possess an array of **subcultures.** Countries such as Japan, South Korea, Sweden, and Denmark have few subcultures and are considered to have relatively homogeneous national cultures.

The increase in globalization elevates to a more prominent position not only organizational culture phenomena, but also the numerous national and subcultural considerations. More and more managers must now cope with the three levels of culture—national, subcultural, and organizational—to perform their jobs.

THE NATIONAL CULTURE: FRAMEWORKS

Global managers learn about a national culture in a variety of ways, but the most dominant is by visiting and living in the country. This is not always a perfect or complete way of learning about a national culture, but it is firsthand, realistic, and timely.

Dutch researcher Fons Trompenaars introduced a model that can help managers understand national culture.[4] He conducted field research studies of over 15,000 people in organizations in 47 countries. He concluded that cultures differ along the seven dimensions presented in Exhibit 2.1.

Dimensions 1 to 5 focus on how people interact with and relate to one another. The last two dimensions address the notion of perceptions of time and the environment. The first five dimensions suggest concepts and techniques to managers for addressing behavior. For example, in achievement-oriented and individually focused cultures such as the United States and Australia, relationships at work are ruled by clearly defined and objective phenomena that are not related to personal feelings. In collectivist, emotional, and diffuse national cultures such as Pakistan and Chile, work relationships are influenced dramatically by personal feelings.

Being aware of the dimensions developed by Trompenaars would help managers in a particular country deal with the impact of the national culture on workplace behavior and performance. Such awareness can provide hints, guidelines, and suggestions on managing organizational behavior.

Kluckhohn and Strodtbeck offer six dimensions of culture, represented in Exhibit 2.2.[5]

Characteristics regarding nature, history, human nature, ownership, activities, and relationships are spelled out by these two theorists. The Kluckhohn and Strodtbeck value-orientation model, like Trompenaars', provides an explanation of national culture characteristics that can empower managers with an understanding about why host-country nationals are behaving in a particular way. No

EXHIBIT 2.1 Trompenaars' Cultural Dimensions

Source: Adapted from Fons Trompenaars, *Riding the Waves of Culture* (London: Nicholas Brealey, 1994).

Dimensions and Countries	Description
• Universalism versus particularism *Universal cultures: United States, Switzerland, Germany, Sweden* *Particular cultures: France, Italy, Spain, the Middle East*	Universalist cultures develop rules that apply to all relationships and situations. Particularistic cultures focus on the uniqueness of each situation.
• Individualism versus collectivism *Individualist cultures: Canada, United States* *Collectivist cultures: Kuwait, South Korea, Singapore*	In individualism, value is placed primarily on the individual rather than on the community. Collectivist cultures place more value on the group than on the individual.
• Neutral versus emotional *Neutral cultures: Japan, United Kingdom, Indonesia* *Emotional cultures: Italy, France*	Interactions are based on objectivity and neutrality, or they are based on emotional bonds.
• Specific versus diffuse *Specific cultures: United States, Australia, Netherlands* *Diffuse cultures: France, Italy, Japan, Mexico*	Relationships are specific to situations or generalize to different situations.
• Achievement versus ascription *Achievement-based cultures: United States, Canada, Norway, Sweden, United Kingdom* *Ascription-based cultures: Middle East, Eastern Europe, France*	People's worth is judged by their recent performance and achievement, or by an ascribed status based on other factors such as birth or social class.
• Perception and use of time *Present based and linear: United States, Germany* *Past: Mexico*	Focus and value are placed on the present, the past, or the future.
• Perceptions of physical environment *Environment to be used: Brazil, Portugal, South Korea* *Environment to be respected: Japan, Egypt, Singapore, Sweden*	Either the individual or the environment is seen as dominant; the environment is either used or respected.

perfect portrayal can be provided, but a concise, useful explanation for behavior can be a helpful starting point in preparing a particular technique or approach to optimize workers' performance.

The most widely publicized classification of national culture was advanced by organizational researcher Geert Hofstede.[6] He conducted a field survey of over 116,000 IBM employees across 40 countries. Exhibit 2.3 presents Hofstede's five cultural dimensions.

Individualism/Collectivism

Individualism exists when people look at themselves primarily as individuals and secondarily as members of teams or groups. The self-concept, self-ego, and self-interest motivate behavior. **Collectivism** is the opposite of individualism.

EXHIBIT 2.2 Kluckhohn and Strodtbeck's Value Orientations

Source: Adapted from F. Kluckhohn and F.L. Strodtbeck, *Variations in Value Orientation* (Evanston, IL: Peterson, 1961), and H.W. Lane, J.J. DiStefano, and M.L. Maznevski, *International Management Behavior,* 3rd ed. (Malden, MA: Blackwell, 1997).

Cultural Dimensions	Description
Relation to nature: subjugation, harmony, or mastery	Views of nature and its relationship to people as either an object to be controlled or as a force with which to live in harmony
Time orientation: past, present, or future	Focus on past, present, or future
Basic human nature: evil, neutral, good	Views of human nature as positive or negative
Activity orientation: being, controlling, doing	Views on level or type of activity and being proactive or reactive to events
Relationship among people: individualistic, group, or hierarchy	Views relating to how people interact as individuals and groups and hierarchical relationships in society
Space orientation: private, mixed, or public	Views of ownership of private and public space

People view themselves as a working and connected member of a team, family, organization, or clan. The United States is more of an individualism culture, while China is more of a collectivism culture.

Masculinity/Femininity

Masculinity dominated cultures emphasize assertiveness, proaction, and acquisition of wealth as opposed to concern for people growth and development. **Femininity** dominated cultures emphasize emotional well-being, concern for people, and work/life balance.

EXHIBIT 2.3 Hofstede's Five Cultural Dimensions

Source: Adapted from G. Hofstede, "Cultural Constraints in Management Theories," *Academy of Management Executive 7,* no. 1 (1993), pp. 81–94, and G. Hofstede, *Culture's Consequence: International Differences in Work-Related Values* (Thousand Oaks, CA: Sage, 1980).

Dimension	Description
Power Distance	The extent to which people accept unequal distribution of power. In higher power distance cultures, there is a wider gap between the powerful and the powerless.
Uncertainty Avoidance	The extent to which the culture tolerates ambiguity and uncertainty. High uncertainty avoidance leads to low tolerance for uncertainty and to a search for absolute truths and predictability.
Individualism	Individualism leads to reliance on self and focus on individual achievement; the extent to which individuals or closely knit social structures such as the extended family (collectivism) are the basis for social systems.
Masculinity	The extent to which assertiveness and independence from others is valued. High masculinity leads to high sex-role differentiation, focus on independence, ambition, and material goods.
Long-Term Orientation	The extent to which people focus on past, present, or future. Present orientation leads to a focus on short-term performance achievements.

Power Distance

Power distance is a measure of the extent to which those who have less power in society accept that power is distributed unequally among members of the society. Some members of the society are assumed to have the "right" and privilege to have more power than others.

Uncertainty Avoidance

This measures the extent to which a culture programs its members to feel either comfortable or uncomfortable in unstructured situations. People in high uncertainty avoidance cultures feel threatened by risky or uncertain situations. Uncertainty avoidance cultures try to minimize risk and uncertainty by creating strict laws and rules, formal regulations, and intolerance of what are considered deviant behaviors.

Time Orientation

The extent to which people focus on the past, present, or future. A short-term perspective of time generates pressure to accomplish short-term performance results. A long-time perspective focuses on performance in the future, a year, two years, or five years ahead.

Hofstede's research finding for 10 countries is presented in Exhibit 2.4. The highest scores on the dimensions are the following: power distance (Russia), individualism (United States), masculinity (Japan), uncertainty avoidance (Japan), and long-term orientation (China).

Each of these three frameworks is only one set of information, assumptions, and insight for global managers to consider when executing their roles and respon-

EXHIBIT 2.4 Cultural Dimension Scores for 10 Countries

Source: Adapted with permission from A.M. Francesco and B.A. Gold, *International Organizational Behavior: Text, Reading, Cases, and Skills* (Upper Saddle River, NJ: Prentice Hall, 1998), p. 27.

	Power Distance	Individualism	Masculinity	Uncertainty Avoidance	Long-Term Orientation
United States	40L	91H	62H	46L	29L
Germany	35L	67H	66H	65M	31M
Japan	54M	46M	95H	92H	80H
France	68H	71H	43M	86H	30L*
Netherlands	38L	80H	14L	53M	44M
Hong Kong	68H	25L	57H	29L	96H
Indonesia	78H	14L	46M	48L	25L*
West Africa	77H	20L	46M	54M	16L
Russia	95H*	50M*	40L*	90H*	10L*
China	80H*	20L*	50M*	60M*	118H

Note: The numbers are the scores for each country on each dimension. The letter by each number indicates the comparative rankings for each country. H = top one-third, M = medium one-third, L = bottom one-third (among 53 countries for the first four dimensions; among 23 countries for the fifth dimension).
*Estimate.

Global Focus Guidelines for Parent Company Managers When Managing in Another Culture

When a manager is managing in another culture, a number of crucial cultural characteristics must be considered when performing various rules. A few pointers that apply to specific cultures could be invaluable.

CHINA

- Mandarin is spoken by over 70 percent of the population.
- Although the government encourages atheism, Buddhism, Islam, and Christianity are practiced in China. Confucianism, although not a religion, has a great influence on Chinese society.
- A collectivist society; individual rights and needs are subordinate to collective rights and needs.
- Harmony and family must be respected.
- Although women are purported to be equal to men, economic and work-related inequities exist.

INDIA

- Hinduism, Buddhism, and Islamic religions play a major role in the lives of most Indians.
- The caste system is followed closely.
- A moderately collective culture exists. Friendship is more important than work or technical expertise.
- Time is not a major important factor.
- Being passive is considered a virtue.
- Women have few privileges and male chauvinism is strong.

RUSSIA

- Literacy is almost 100 percent.
- Information is processed subjectively and outsider-initiated communication is viewed suspiciously.
- Specialists with technical expertise are respected.
- Sexual harassment is excessive in business organizations and in the government.
- Compromise is viewed as a sign of personal weakness.

MEXICO

- Citizens are impressed when noncitizens are familiar with the nation's history, customs, and art.
- Suspicious of foreigners.
- Time is not a crucial factor.
- Personal friendships and long-term relationships are very important.
- Conversations take place at close physical distance.

sibilities. Each of the frameworks introduces issues and also suggests that national culture needs to be carefully weighed before making work-related decisions.

THE MANAGER AND ORGANIZATIONAL CULTURE

As previously illustrated, countries and groups have their own distinct national cultures and subcultures. The same is true of organizations. The shared beliefs, customs, rituals, artifacts, and symbols of an organization guide the behavior of employees. The organization's culture provides a sense of identity, purpose, goals, and vision to its members. It informs its members about what is important, who is serving as leaders, and where the firm is going. By helping an organization define itself, organizational culture provides a road map and reference for not only its members but also for clients and other stakeholders.

Avis for many years has been attempting to overtake Hertz as the number-one car rental firm in the United States. The goal of moving from number two to number one is expressed in Avis' literature and advertisements. Avis has assembled a workforce that recognizes its goal to be number one. This steady message that "we are number two, but want to be number one" is now a part of the Avis culture and its purpose.[7]

Once managers can distinguish between the culture outside the organization (national) and the culture inside the organization, they are ready to focus on crucial daily work operations—planning, staffing, rewarding, training, and organizing. An organization's culture is embedded within the perceptions, memories, and understanding of employees. They use the culture to reinforce ideas, feelings, and information that are consistent with their beliefs.

The firm's culture can reflect the needs and aspirations of the employees. This makes embracing the culture satisfying and a potential motivational force. At its best, an organization's culture can serve as an inspiration that brings out the potential of employees.[8]

At 3M Corporation, the culture contains characteristics that admire, recognize, and reward innovative thinking and work.[9] Employees that value innovation, autonomy, and time to be creative thrive in the 3M culture. It is motivational, dynamic, and self-fulfilling.

Culture provides employees with a sense of community and identity that can be shared. Volvo and British Airways employees are proud to be working for organizations that are distinct, held in high esteem, and sought after by job applicants. The strong beliefs held by employees provide them with a sense of belonging to something—their work organizations—that is worthwhile.[10]

Cultures provide a set of values, beliefs, and processes that employees can share through experiences and communication. By sharing, communication networks and patterns are opened up and used. The increased communication and sharing provides a reason to come together to achieve and to grow.

Edgar Schein of MIT proposed that organizational cultures actually operate at three levels of more or less visibility.[11] His model is presented in Exhibit 2.5. Schein describes culture as:

> A pattern of basic assumptions invented, discovered, or developed by a given group as it learns to cope with its problems of external adaptation and internal integration that has worked well enough to be considered valid, and to be taught to new members as the correct way to perceive, think, and feel in relation to these problems.[12]

EXHIBIT 2.5
Schein's Three Levels of Culture

Source: Adapted from Edgar H. Schein, *Organizational Culture and Leadership* (San Francisco: Jossey-Bass, 1985), p. 9.

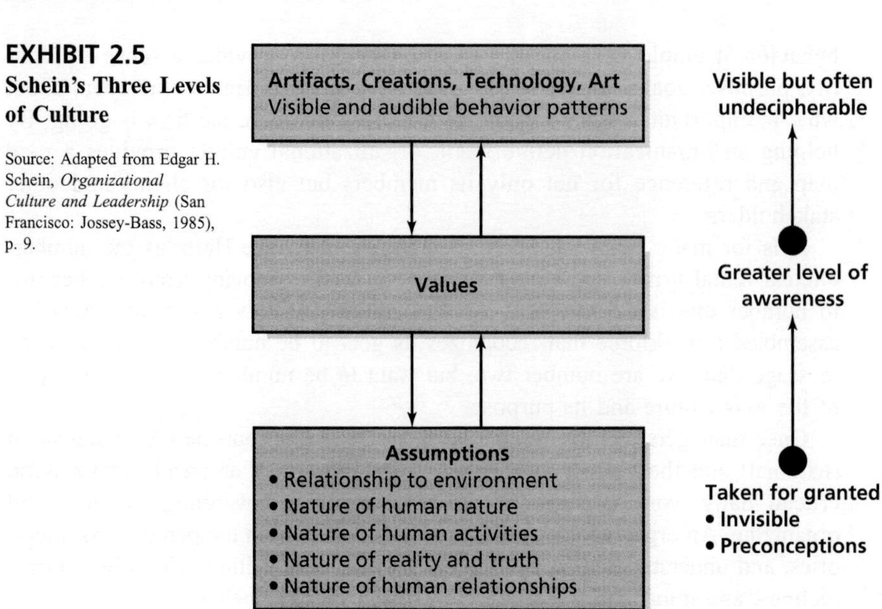

THE CHARACTERISTICS OF ORGANIZATIONAL CULTURE

Schein's presentation, theory, and assumption regarding three levels of culture emphasizes three major components: observable features of the culture, shared values, and basic assumptions.

Observable Components

The observable components are visible to people. They include such items as the company logo, dress code, language used, office layout, carpet color, and type of social events supported by the firm. There are also the stories, myths, and rituals. Stories are powerful reminders of where and how the firm began and developed. They tell current workers how the firm achieved its success and the role key people played. Stories about Walt Disney (Disney), Thomas Watson (IBM), Jorma Ollila (Nokia), John Browne (BP Amoco), and Cheong Choong Kong (Singapore Airlines) become repeated, embellished, and honored.

Rituals are the prescribed ceremonies that employees perform such as singing the company song, honoring a colleague's accomplishment, or saluting a colleague with a retirement party. The ritual can become a welcomed tradition and mark the link between the past and the present.

Shared Values

The second component is not easily observable. Values represent the core beliefs shared by employees about what is important. The shared values of a firm state, "What we are and what we stand for" and "What we want to provide to the community in which we operate." A company's statement of what and who it is

EXHIBIT 2.6 Hewlett-Packard's Statement of Principles

Source: Hewlett-Packard annual reports (www.hp.com).

We should strive to meet certain fundamental requirements:

FIRST, the most capable people available should be selected for each assignment within the organization. Moreover, these people should have the opportunity—through continuing programs of training and education—to upgrade their skills and capabilities. This is especially important in a technical business where the rate of progress is rapid. Techniques that are good today will be outdated in the future, and people throughout the organization should continually be looking for new and better ways to do their work.

SECOND, enthusiasm should exist at all levels. People in important management positions should not only be enthusiastic themselves, but they should be selected for their ability to engender enthusiasm among their associates. There can be no place, especially among the people charged with management responsibility, for half-hearted interest of half-hearted effort.

THIRD, even though an organization is made up of people fully meeting the first two requirements, all levels should work in unison toward common objectives and avoid working at cross purposes if the ultimate in efficiency and achievement is to be obtained.

It has been our policy at H-P not to have a tight military-type organization but, rather, to have overall objectives which are clearly stated and agreed to, and to give people the freedom to work toward those goals in ways they determine best for their own area of responsibility. Goals are:

1. *Profit*—To achieve profit to finance our company growth and to provide the resources we need to achieve our other objectives.
2. *Customers*—To provide products and services of the greatest possible value to our customers, thereby gaining and holding their respect and loyalty.
3. *Fields of Interest*—To enter new fields only when the ideas we have, together with our technical and marketing skills, assure we can make a needed and profitable contribution.
4. *Growth*—To let our growth be limited only by our profits and our ability to develop and produce technical products that satisfy real customer needs.
5. *Our People*—To help H-P people share in the company's success, which they make possible; to provide job security based on their performance; to recognize individual achievement; and to insure the personal satisfaction that comes from a sense of accomplishment in their work.
6. *Management*—To foster initiative and creativity by allowing the individual great freedom of action in attaining well-defined objectives.
7. *Citizenship*—To honor our obligations to society by being an economic, intellectual, and social asset to each nation and each community in which we operate.

can illustrate clear values. An example of a global organization's values is reflected in Exhibit 2.6 for Hewlett-Packard.

Basic Assumptions

The third component is difficult to observe. These basic assumptions serve as the foundation for the values and behaviors shared by organizational members. The way people are treated (e.g., customers, employees, vendors, job applicants) is affected by the organization's assumptions about people. The assumptions reflect the values of honesty, integrity, justice, sharing, beneficence, compassion, and humanity. Andy Grove of Intel developed his general assumptions about people from his struggle as a child in Hungary attempting to survive the German and Soviet occupations of his country. He is passionate about hard work, frugality, and achieving difficult goals, which he has made a part of Intel's culture around the world.

THE EVOLUTION OF ORGANIZATIONAL CULTURE

As soon as an organization is created, its cultural history begins. Over time the components of the culture become clearer. Once the cultural components become known and shared, they are difficult to change.

The Founders

Company founders such as Andy Grove at Intel, Henri Nestlé, Arman Peugeot, and Walt Disney put their own distinct philosophy and mark on their firms' culture. The founders came from specific backgrounds where their attitudes, values, beliefs, and philosophies of how to manage a globally diverse workforce took shape. The imprint of founders is powerful and initiates the theme, depth, and type of culture that survives and grows over the years.[13]

Socialization

As new employees enter the organization's culture, they are taught and they observe the three cultural levels. The process by which employees learn about the three cultural levels is called **organizational socialization.**

Exhibit 2.7 presents three specific stages of organizational socialization.[14]

EXHIBIT 2.7
The Stages of Organizational Socialization

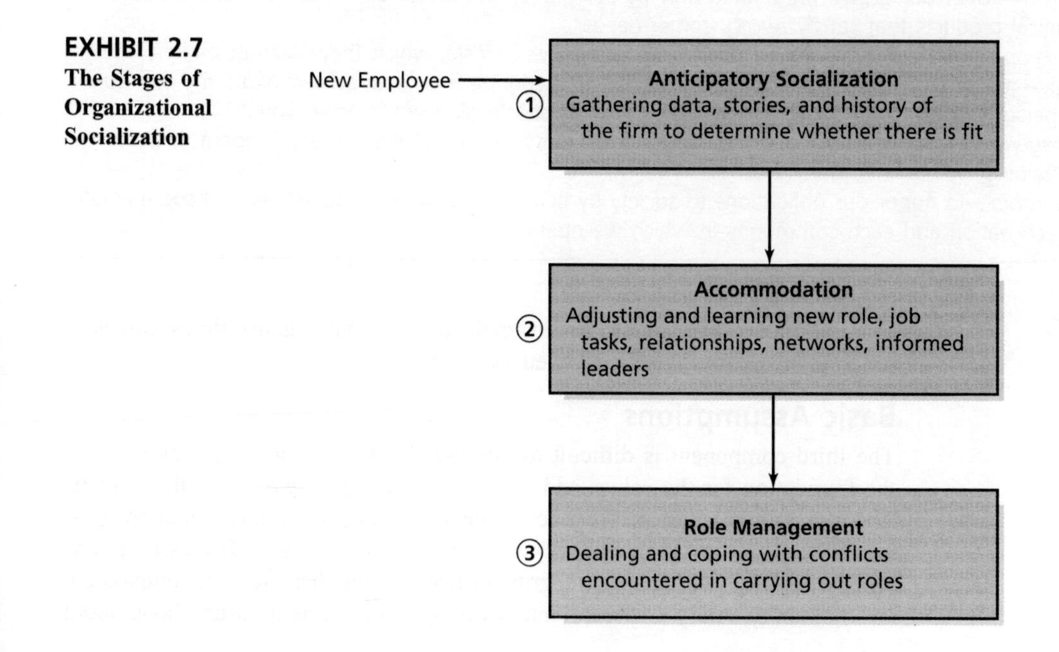

During stage one, the potential employee studies the organization and gathers as much information as possible. Reading, interacting with employees, and talking to customers provides technical and informal information about the company. This type of information gathering can help an individual determine if there is a fit between his or her philosophy, values, and beliefs and the organization's. Being on the outside attempting to acquire a valid picture of the inside culture is not easy and is not always accurate.

The second socialization stage, accommodation, begins when the new employee starts the job and attempts to fit, adjust, and cope with the organizational culture. Orientation programs, training, mentoring, and written materials are used in some firms to accommodate the new employee. During this stage, the issue of fit becomes very important. If there is a poor fit with the job and organizational culture, it will eventually result in poor performance, dissatisfaction, and perhaps even resignation or termination.

The third socialization stage is referred to as role management. The employee is on the job, being asked to perform multiple roles, and must meet requests of superiors, subordinates, peers, and in some cases outside parties such as customers, clients, or patients. These multiple requests and the expectations others have create role conflicts. What should I do first? Who should I respond to next? What does he or she expect me to do? These questions and the response each one triggers can cause conflict that must be resolved and managed. Successful employees handle the conflicts and become socialized, ultimately adding to the cultural fabric of the organization.

Hoechst Celanese considers the three stages to be crucial for sustaining its cultural norms and expectations.[15] To introduce and sustain more diversity among minority and women managers, a mentor/coach is assigned to each new employee. At Hoechst Celanese, the journey from anticipatory to accommodation to managing role conflicts is considered more productive and more impressive when top-level managers serve as one-on-one coaches and mentors of the most promising new minority and women managers.

Socialization is often given a low priority and sense of urgency, but when done effectively it can become a driver of higher and better performance. It is important not only for the job applicant to consider the person-culture fit, but also for the global organization to make fit a part of the recruitment and selection process. When the fit is optimal, the organization's culture is perpetuated and can even be strengthened.

CULTURAL STRENGTH

The strength and impact of an organization's culture depends on how strongly employees share its history, values, and assumptions. Philips, Ericsson, Toyota, Kao, and Procter & Gamble are global companies with reputations of possessing strong and influential organizational cultures. A firm considered to have a powerful culture is one that has employees who share its values and basic assumptions. Employees of IBM, another strong cultural organization, are task and goal oriented, concerned about providing excellent service, interested in the local community needs, and conservative dressers. In the past decade IBM has worked to instill within its strong, stable, and conservative culture a need to encourage innovation and competitiveness.

Organizations with strong cultures have more open communication, harmony, and understanding of where the organization is going. In weak cultural organizations, there is a lack of consistency, identity, and clarity about goals, expectations, and directions.

MANAGING AND CHANGING THE ORGANIZATION'S CULTURES

Can a weak culture be changed to a strong culture and can it be maintained? Some answer yes, some say no, and some are not sure. The shift in IBM's historically conservative culture to a more innovative culture suggests that change is possible.[16]

The following five-step approach can create cultural alterations.[17]

1. *Identify cultural violations*. Identification of cultural violations in behavior, tone, patterns, and techniques is a first step. Managers need to discover who, what unit, and what situation and context trigger violations or noncompliance behavior. Observation, interviews, surveys, and analysis of information and communication flow can pinpoint violations. Attempting to understand why the identified violations are occurring is a starting point.
2. *Probe violations*. Observing the violations or discussing them is important in eventually finding ways to change a culture. Interviewing by formal and informal leaders can reveal perceptions, behaviors, and attitudes. It is important to probe deeply among those formal and informal leaders who are identified by cultures. They can provide firsthand views of where cultural violations or mismatches are occurring. Step 1 involves preliminary and general observation, while Step 2 suggests that leaders are key individuals within the organization and involved in changing the culture.
3. *Review historical records and data*. Culture evolves over time and therefore offers a historical picture. Successes, failures, growth, downsizing, lawsuits, community relationships, and other historical events need to be analyzed and interpreted. After Steps 1 and 2, examining how culture evolves and is changing in terms of values, rituals, and behaviors can help spur the necessary changes.
4. *Develop a cultural learning system*. Based on Steps 1 through 3, an organizational learning system—people, repositories, records, databases—must be established, improved, and maintained. Leaders must serve as a "knowledge source," someone who can influence and cultivate other employees. They also can serve as a change initiator. Formal and informal leaders who respect and understand the organization's culture can be invaluable in bringing about

Global Focus Cross-Cultural Considerations in Russian Organizations

Some call the shift in Russia to a more free-enterprise system "one of the greatest natural experiments of our time." Privatization, stabilization of the ruble, upgrading manufacturing facilities, falling inflation, and changes in management practices are some of the dramatic changes occurring in Russia. A set of perplexing problems facing foreign businesses attempting to become involved in the growth of a new Russia centers on the cultural differences, value differences, and attitudes about how to manage employees in the workplace.

Researchers have found that one-person leadership had been the guiding principle until perestroika changed the entire political structure. For decades Russian organizations were operated with a "heavy hand" by a centralized power broker, the general director. Only the general director made decisions, allocated resources, and demanded collective actions by employees. Russians who attempted to excel beyond the group's expectation were often chastised and pulled back to the group's level of performance.

The most recent research indicates that there are still leftover, from an earlier period, influences of the communist system. The national culture in Russia is still characterized by high power distance and a strong collective mentality. Russian employees expect managers to be autocratic and not participative. Building consensus among diverse groups is part of the manager's responsibilities in Russia.

The application of an individualistic approach in rewarding performance is not likely to work well in Russia where there is a high uncertainty avoidance tendency. A sense of belonging and security are important motivational forces in Russian organizations.

Research suggests that applying a U.S., Canadian, or British managerial style and approach that emphasizes individualism, low power distance, and low uncertainty avoidance will currently result in failure, resistance, or substantial barriers. Russian employees are more comfortable with larger power distance and uncertainty avoidance and expect to be managed in a way that supports their expectations.

Source: Adapted and based on Detelin S. Elenkov, "Can American Management Concepts Work In Russia? A Cross-Cultural Comparative Study," *California Management Review,* Summer 1998, pp. 133–56, and Sylvie Roussillon, Frank Gournois, and C. Brooklyn Derr, eds., *Cross-Cultural Approaches to Leadership Development* (Westport CT: Quorum, 2002).

cultural changes because of their power and influence. Leading by example or role modeling can be a powerful way to show others how to behave, perform, and work in an organization.

5. *Anticipate slow change.* Because an organization's culture evolves over time, it becomes embedded and fixed. Thus, changes to strengthen culture or to make it more observable will require time. Even if leaders serving as role models are very influential and effectively disseminate change messages and examples, bringing about cultural change is likely to be slow. Artifacts, creations, values, and assumptions become fixed in strong, powerful cultures. Creating new artifacts, building new preferred behaviors, altering values, and changing assumptions will require altering attitudes, perceptions, emotions, and feelings. These changes require unlearning, relearning, and reinforcement. The socialization of new employees requires time. Introducing

new philosophies and values, and instituting new rituals and ceremonies, will take time, years in some cases. The changes introduced by leaders can range from hiring different kinds of employees, done relatively quickly, to changing the culture from a nonrisk-taking to a more risk-taking and innovative one. Often, as was the case with IBM, this change may be difficult and take years. The same slow, deliberate, and painstaking changes in organizations are true for national culture changes, as shown in the accompanying Global Focus. Both organizational and national culture changes should be thought of as difficult, slow, incremental processes that will take interventions, time, and patience.

Leaders can use many approaches to bring about culture change. But, as discussed, quick changes in culture are unlikely, and any type of culture change will typically encounter barriers (people, resource limitations, technology) and implementation problems. Many firms involved in mergers and acquisitions, such as Daimler-Chrysler, Compaq-Hewlett-Packard, Nestlé-Saint Springs (in Russia), and Ford-Jaguar, find that merging divergent cultures into a new culture is extremely difficult and in these cases continues to be an ongoing effort.

MANAGING ACROSS CULTURES

The discussion about managing organizational culture needs to incorporate the concept of managing across cultures. National and organizational culture discussions should consider and focus on global managers moving closer to the host-country workforce, vendors, and customers. For years Renault manufactured automobiles primarily in France. To extend its market reach across borders, Renault bought controlling interests in Nissan Motor of Japan, Samsung of South Korea, and Dacia of Romania. Renault also built plants in South America and in Russia.

Currently, Renault operates on four continents and recruits and hires employees (managers and nonmanagers) from dozens of countries. By 2010, Renault intends to have 10 common manufacturing platforms or underbodies of automobiles that will enable it to build Renaults and Nissans around the world, while maintaining the look, feel, and identity of their separate brands.[18] In addition, Renault is working to improve its dealings, negotiations, and managerial effectiveness with employees, unions, and governments.

The Renault case illustrates some of the problems faced by managers of globally based firms. Managers prefer to direct, reward, appraise, team-build, and perform activities in global settings similar to the way they carry out these roles at home. Using a familiar approach is easier, faster, and more comfortable than attempting to understand the global setting, rituals, customs, attitudes, values, and expectations.

A major barrier facing most global managers is referred to as **ethnocentrism.** This is the belief that one's native country, culture, language, customs, mores, and way of conducting an operation are superior to any other nation's. Ethnocentrism is described as follows:

> Ethnocentrism is often not attributable to prejudice as much as to inexperience or lack of knowledge about foreign persons and situations. This is not too surprising since most executives know far more about employees in their home environments. As one executive put it, "At last I understand why our managers make mistakes. With foreigners, I never know. The foreign managers may be better. But if I can't trust a person, should I hire him or her just to prove we're multinational."[19]

Being aware of one's ethnocentrism tendencies is a good starting point in cross-cultural management applications. However, it is not enough. Managers need a much broader approach for managing across cultures. One useful framework for moving cross-cultural understanding is offered by the Windham International Cultural Model (WICM).[20] The model is concise, understandable, thorough, and usable. It is a template and knowledge-based framework that can teach managers first to understand themselves and then to understand the people they're working and living with. The model was developed by Michael Schell, Marian Stolz-Locke, and others in the Windham International Organization.

The WICM uses the theories and research of Geert Hofstede, Fons Trompenaars, and Edward T. Hall.[21] It serves as a training framework and as a model for counseling programs at Windham International. The model proposes that once managers understand the cross-cultural impact on behavior, they can adapt their behaviors more readily to fit the local circumstances. The WICM is depicted as a cultural prism that provides insight about nine cultural dimensions, presented in Exhibit 2.8. There is overlap between each of these nine dimensions, defined

EXHIBIT 2.8 Windham International Cultural Prism

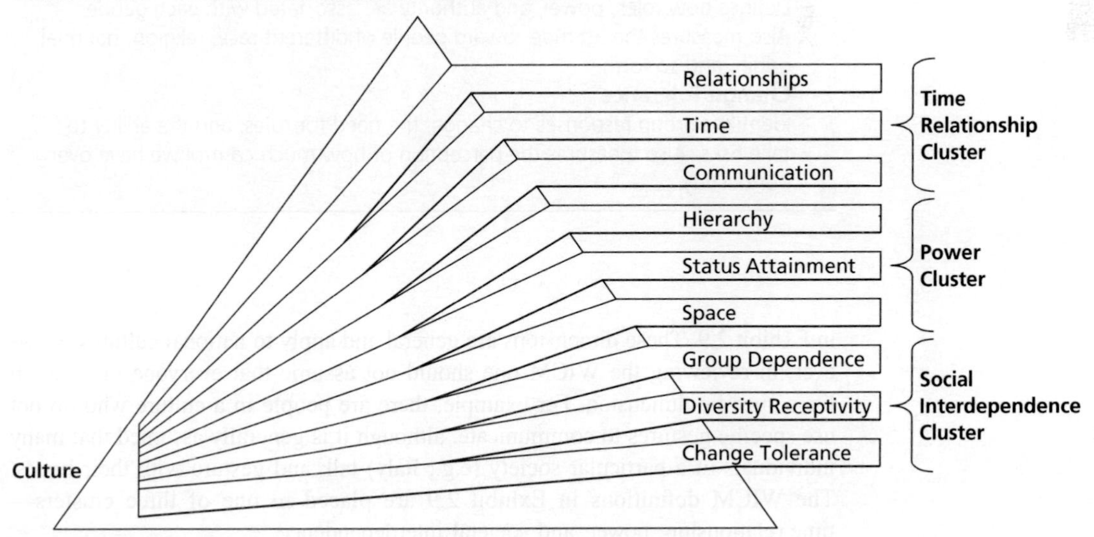

EXHIBIT 2.9
The Cultural Dimensions

Source: Adapted from Michael S. Schell and Charlene Marmer Solomon, *Capitalizing on the Global Workforce* (New York: Times-Mirror, 1997), p. 28.

Time/Relationship Cluster

- **Relationships**
  Focuses on whether an organization places primary importance on completing a job or devoting time to building relationships among business associates.
- **Time**
  Measures the degree to which a society believes an individual can focus on one or more tasks and evaluates the importance of personal relationships compared with adherence to schedules.
- **Communication**
  Addresses the way societies communicate, including the use of nonverbal gestures.

Power Cluster

- **Hierarchy**
  Measures the way individuals interact with one another within an organizational hierarchy.
- **Status Attainment**
  Measures the importance of personal achievement and accomplishment to an overall sense of well-being.
- **Space**
  Views how individuals in societies use space to define themselves, including spatial distances used when speaking, and the amount of space needed for comfort in business and living environments.

Societal Interdependence Cluster

- **Group Dependence**
  Measures the importance of the individual versus the group in diverse social and business situations.
- **Diversity Receptivity**
  Defines how roles, power, and authority are associated with each gender. Also measures the attitude toward people of different race, religion, national origin, and so forth.
- **Change Tolerance**
  Identifies group responses to change, the need for rules, and the ability to take risks. Also measures the perception of how much control we have over our destiny.

in Exhibit 2.9. These dimensions are general and apply to national cultures. However, in reviewing the WICM one should not assume that everyone in a nation fits a specific dimension. For example, there are people in a culture who do not use specific gestures to communicate, although it is generally assumed that many individuals in a particular society (e.g., Italy) talk and gesture with their hands. The WICM definitions in Exhibit 2.9 are placed in one of three clusters—time/relationship, power, and societal interdependence.

Time/Relationship Cluster

Managers operating globally will notice that different cultures place varying emphasis on time, relationships, and how people communicate. High-time cultures, such as those found in Northern Europe and North America, view time as a finite commodity that must be controlled. These high-time cultures emphasize scheduling, meeting deadlines, and being prompt.

In contrast, people living in low-time cultures, such as Southern Europe, Latin America, and the Middle East, consider time to be uncontrollable. Scheduling and promptness are not sacred and everything is subject to change.

These opposite views of time can result in misunderstandings, frustration, and conflicts. The high-versus-low-time issue is not an either/or example. What is more crucial is recognizing that time is viewed, evaluated, and used differently in different cultures. The culture is not likely to change or adapt. It is the manager who needs to adapt. Living by the clock is simply not valued in low-time cultures. Building stronger, more personal relationships may be more important than time concerns.

The relationship dimension explains the importance individuals place on others—people versus things, people versus time, people versus promptness. In low-relationship cultures such as Sweden and the United States, relationships are expected to evolve rapidly, but they may exist for only short periods. There is a more superficial undertone to relationships in low-relationship cultures.

In high-relationship cultures, people spend time getting to know each other—eating together, talking, traveling, and sightseeing. In France, Italy, Mexico, and Japan, relationships are expected to be deep and to grow slowly through interactions. A relationship is considered long-term, to last for years. In high-relationship cultures, one is expected to hold off on talking about and doing business until people first become comfortable with and trust each other.

Managers are much more job, work, or task oriented in low-relationship cultures. Completing the job on time and within budget constraints is valued more than building a long-term friendship. Often, individuals from low-relationship cultures prefer to immediately transact discussions and business. They are abrupt, direct, and interested in completing the discussions quickly or as fast as possible.

Hall refers to cultures as being high or low in context in communicating.[22] In low-context cultures, individuals expect to receive only what they need to do the job. When too much information is provided, there is confusion, frustration, and annoyance. By contrast, people in high-context cultures want a full accounting, a total picture, and a complete set of communication.

A British manager (low-context upbringing) who wants a quick resolution to an equipment purchase dilemma would become frustrated with an Italian (high-context) colleague who wants every possible detail before making a decision on how to proceed. The British manager would prefer quick meetings, while the Italian manager would want fewer meetings and a more comprehensive view of the situation delivered at one time.

Cultures also evaluate nonverbal aspects of communication differently. Nonverbal communication can either improve or detract from the verbal exchanges between managers. Not making eye contact is considered rude in some cultures, while other cultures believe that eye contact is not at all necessary to communicate and can be perceived as intimidating or disrespectful.

The directness and assertiveness of communication can lead to problems. Some cultures believe that openness and being blunt, "telling it like it is," is valuable. Individuals from these cultures are direct, no-nonsense, and specific communicators. On the other hand, people in some cultures (Asia) believe that bluntness, being specific, and directly addressing someone is unfriendly, impolite, and insensitive. People from these cultures will try to avoid saying "no" so that the other people can save face.

More Than 3,000 Different Languages Are Spoken Around the World

One view, called *relativist,* is that language influences perception and behavior. A second view, called *universalist,* states that all languages share common elements and therefore result in common thought processes and perceptions. Those attempting to communicate across cultures can (1) use their own language, (2) rely on translators, or (3) learn the local language. There is no substitute for learning the local language. However, many individuals have difficulty learning another or a second language. Whatever option is taken, communication does not mean that understanding occurs. Communication is irreversible, and communication occurs in a specific context. Perhaps it is better to listen carefully, use a local context to interpret the communication, and take your time before communicating. Each of these behaviors is easy to say or think about, but may be difficult to apply in a cross-cultural situation.

Power Cluster

Three cultural dimensions—hierarchy, status attainment, and space—are referred to as the power cluster. They define how authority and position are used in different nations. How a society perceives power, who holds it, and how it is acquired can range from birthrights to earned stature. Cultures such as the United States, Canada, Australia, and New Zealand pride themselves on rags-to-riches stories. However, in India and China a person's rank, stature, and position are fixed at birth and will not change. These national cultures are referred to as high hierarchical and fixed. Respect and deference are directed to those at the top of the hierarchical system. In low-hierarchical national cultures, less deference is shown toward people in higher-level positions.

The hierarchical structure of a culture can be reflected in the size of one's office, dress, titles, formality of communication, and expectations. In high-hierarchical cultures, managers are expected to know what to do, how to do a job, and how to behave. Subordinates do not expect to participate in decision making, negotiation, and problem solving. The manager is assumed to know what is needed or is best. The chain of command is a dominant feature. Asking subordinates to participate and discuss an important decision in a high-hierarchical culture is likely to produce stares, silence, and perhaps confusion.

In contrast in a low-hierarchical culture, participation, worker empowerment, sharing, and collaborating are considered important. Rejection of an opportunity to participate in an important job-related decision would be considered immature and would suggest a lack of competence and ability.

Status attainment is the cultural dimension that explains how people connect what they do at work to how they feel about themselves (e.g., self-esteem). It refers to the importance of personal achievement compared to family or birth-entitled position. Attitudes about status attainment affect what is referred to as work/life balance and the amount of time devoted to the job.

In nations with a high-achievement orientation, people believe that one can accomplish goals by hard work. If an individual doesn't achieve or receive a promotion, a desired work assignment, or a pay raise, it is because of his or her efforts and talents. Hard work, recognition, and rewards are thought to lead to a strong sense of self-esteem.

In low-status achievement cultures, value is placed on having the best connections. Family connections and inherited position are crucial. Individuals from Canada and the United States discuss their job context in detail before introducing family issues. In contrast, individuals from Africa, the Middle East, and Latin America—low-status achievement national cultures—discuss family connections before the job situation is considered. The job, status, or position is not important enough to interfere with the family connection.

In high-status cultures, doing whatever it takes to complete the project is acceptable. This means working late and on weekends. However, in low-status cultures such as Portugal and Spain, working extra or long hours or giving up a vacation would be considered insensitive and inappropriate.

Space refers to how a culture uses space and what is comfortable in terms of spatial distances when talking or interacting with others. When two Arab friends are talking to each other, often little distance separates them. They are talking almost nose-to-nose. In Belgium, men stand three or four feet from each other to communicate. The comfort of personal space differs in different countries. Exhibit 2.10 shows a personal space difference from one foot to about three feet. Arabs are in what is classified as an intimate distance zone, while Northern Europeans use a personal distance zone. Hall uses the term *proxemics* to describe the study of cultural expectations about interpersonal space.

The issue of interpersonal space spills over into how homes are designed, offices are arranged, and privacy is regarded. Knowing how a nation views space—close, restricted, tight versus open, extensive—is important for designing work settings. In a low-space culture such as Japan, land and space are scarce. The benefit of having one's own office is not as highly valued as would be the case in a high-space culture (Canada and England).

Societal Interdependence Cluster

This cluster includes a society's attitudes about individual versus group behavior, interactions with strangers, and adaptability to new situations. Cultures low on group dependence focus on individual achievements, have laws protecting

EXHIBIT 2.10
Distance Zones for Communication between Individuals: Cultural Norms

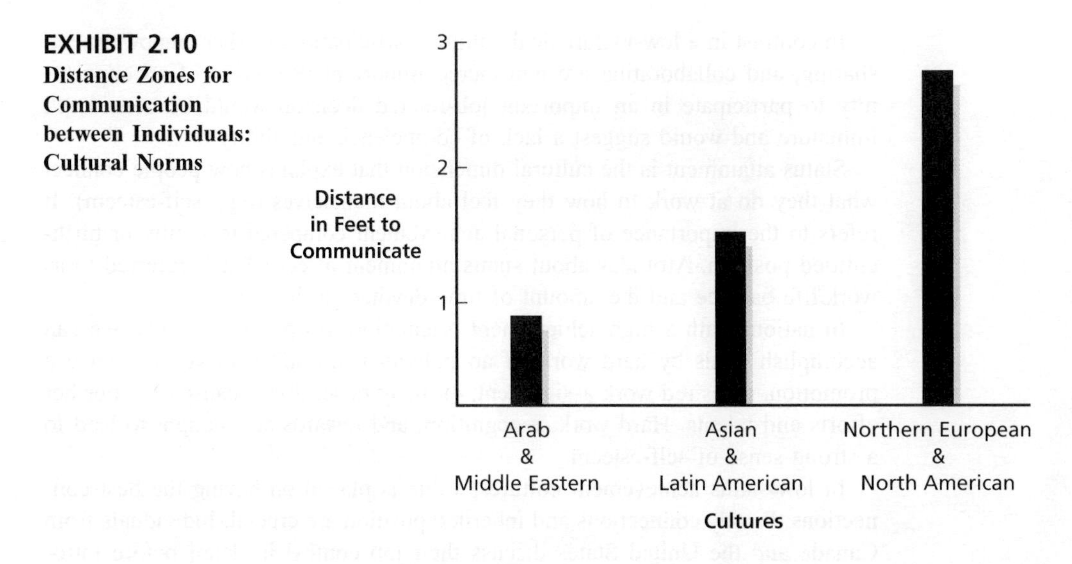

individual rights, and encourage individuals to excel. Cultures high in group dependence emphasize, reward, and encourage group achievement and avoid calling attention to individual behavior or achievement.

Individualistic national cultures use heroes as references, role models, and examples of achievement. The United States is individualistic-oriented, and this is reflected in the reading materials that schoolchildren use. Mexico and Japan are more group oriented. Loyalty, commitment, and association to the group is very important. People in group-dependent nations believe that the group is always more significant and contributes more than the sum of the individuals who are in the group.

Group dependence influences how people work together and how they can be motivated and rewarded. This dimension affects how a manager recognizes and evaluates performance, determines how people are assigned to groups, and influences whether individual or group assignments should be made.

In low-group-dependence nations, using group reward systems would be resisted. Individuals take responsibility and want to be individually rewarded and recognized. People are hired, promoted, and terminated because of the value placed on individual skills and competencies. The group versus individual dimension is very powerful and needs to be addressed by managers very carefully. If a manager comes from an individually oriented culture (e.g., United States) and is working in a group-oriented culture (e.g., Australia), there will have to be adjustments. Introducing an individual approach in a group-dependent setting would be difficult, if not impossible. This concept is best captured by the Japanese saying: "The nail that stands out gets hammered back in."

The attitude a society has about gender role expectation is a powerful factor.[23] Hofstede's masculine versus feminine dichotomy points this out. In masculine cultures, people are encouraged to be assertive, passionate, and high energy. Feminine cultures encourage people to be sensitive and collaborative.

Beyond the gender diversity issue are race, background, and social class factors. High-diversity cultures believe that these factors are not major issues in terms of someone's ability to succeed. These differences are considered important in being able to produce and market products to an increasingly diverse world market. Differences are considered an asset.

Change tolerance refers to the nation's attitudes about change, innovation, and newness. Cultures that are low in this dimension attempt to maintain a routine, status quo approach to work. Managers are expected to be in favor of maintaining the tradition, rituals, and approaches that have been used for years. History, tradition, and folklore are very important. Change, modification, and newness is frowned on in nations with low tolerance for change.

In contrast, nations that encourage, reward, and desire change are constantly interested in innovation, creativity, and economic advancement. There is an expectation that change will improve the quality of life and well-being in the society.

France, Japan, and Italy embrace changes in technology and work practices, but also cherish long-standing traditions, history, and the status quo in terms of art, foods, language, and music. These nations have a high tolerance for technological changes and a low tolerance for noneconomic, family tradition changes. This tug-of-war is something transnational managers need to explore because these issues will affect managerial practices.

A FINAL NOTE ON CULTURE

As the 21st century moves forward, organizations will become more aware of the importance of managerial understanding of organizational, national, and subcultural dimensions. Workers and managers will increasingly be selected and assigned from a worldwide talent pool. Cultural issues will become embedded in the roles managers play with a diverse, globally oriented workforce. These issues spell out how people will relate and work with each other.

Managers (domestic and global) must meld a common vision and establish and nurture a workplace culture in which optimal performance can be achieved. The glue that keeps employees working productively together will be the managerial behavior, tone, and competence applied to an organization's culture, which is affected by host-country cultures and subcultures. This is a challenging responsibility for managers. The uninformed, rigidly ethnocentric, and unknowledgeable manager is likely to fail. Failure is a harsh sentence, but it is realistic to state that traditional management practices will not be sufficient in a globally oriented world. The traditional technical skills of being competent in planning, organizing, and controlling will still be important. However, in the globally oriented world managers must also be culturally aware of and fluent in the language of the host country; possess international experience; be comfortable working with a diverse global talent pool; possess exceptional people skills; be able to work with ambiguity; and know how to build, motivate, and retain a productive global team.

Key Terms

Collectivism, *33*
Ethnocentrism, *44*
Femininity, *34*
Individualism, *33*
Masculinity, *34*
National culture, *32*
Organizational culture, *31*
Organizational socialization, *40*
Power distance, *35*
Subculture, *32*

Review, Critical Thinking, and Discussion Questions

1. If someone claimed that cultural values are the same worldwide, how would you respond?
2. Why should parent company managers learn as much as possible about a nation's culture in which they live and work?
3. Can ethnocentrism be reduced? How?
4. What are the dimensions that were found by Geert Hofstede? What value is provided to a manager by being aware of these dimensions?
5. What is meant by the view that "cross-cultural communication must be cautiously conducted"?
6. Why is the understanding and awareness of an organization's culture an insufficient knowledge base when performing managerial roles in a country other than your own?
7. What did Schein mean when he referred to "observable components of an organization's culture"? What are examples of "unobservable" components of an organization's culture?
8. Explain each of the three stages of socialization?
9. Why would it be difficult to manage effectively in a situation where the manager lacks respect, knowledge, and understanding of subcultures that exist within a national culture?
10. A so-called expert states that "changing an organization's culture can be accomplished relatively quickly if a strong, charismatic leader takes charge of the change process." Comment.

Endnotes

1. Don Adams, "The Monkey and the Fish: Cultural Pitfalls of An Educational Advisor," *International Development Review,* 2 (1969), p. 22.
2. Stanley D. Truskie, *Leadership in High-Performance Organizational Cultures* (Westport, CT: Quorum, 2002).
3. Martin J. Gannon, *Working Across Cultures* (Thousand Oaks, CA: Sage, 2001).
4. F. Trompenaars, *Riding the Waves of Culture: Understanding Culture and Diversity In Business* (London: Nicholos Brealey, 1994).
5. F. Kluckhohn and F. L. Strodtbeck, *Variations in Value Orientations* (Evanston, IL: Peterson, 1961).
6. Geert Hofstede, *Cultures and Organizations* (Cambridge, UK: University Press, 1991).
7. J. R. Biasi, M. Conte, and L. Kruse, Employee Ownership National Center for Employee Ownership Resort, Washington, DC 1999.
8. Martin J. Gannon, ed., *Cultural Metaphors: Readings, Research Translations, and Commentary* (Thousand Oaks, CA: Sage, 2001).

9. Julian Birkenshaw and Neil Hood, “Unleash Innovation in Foreign Subsidiaries,” *Harvard Business Review*, March 2001.
10. Harry Korine and Pierre-Yves Gomez, *The Leap to Globalization: Creating New Value of Business Without Borders* (Upper Saddle River, NJ: Prentice Hall, 2002).
11. Edgar H. Schein, *Organizational Culture and Leadership* (San Francisco: Jossey-Bass, 1985).
12. *Ibid.*
13. Michael J. Marquardt and Nancy O. Berger, *Global Leaders to the 21st Century* (Albany, NY: State University of New York Press, 2000).
14. John M. Ivancevich and Michael T. Matteson, *Organizational Behavior and Management* (New York: McGraw-Hill/Irwin, 2002), pp. 74–77.
15. Greg Steinmeitz and Matt Marshall, “How a Chemical Giant Goes About Becoming a Lot Less German,” *Wall Street Journal,* February 21, 1997, p. A18.
16. M. Dalton, *Success for the New Global Managers: How to Work Across Distances, Countries, and Cultures* (San Francisco: Jossey-Bass, 2002).
17. M. S. Schell and C. M. Solomon, “Global Culture: Who Is the Gatekeeper?” *Workforce,* 76 (1997), pp. 35–39.
18. Michael M. Hodgetts and Fred Luthans, *International Management* (New York: McGraw-Hill/Irwin, 2003).
19. A. Inkeles and M. Saski, eds., *Company Nations and Cultures: Readings in a Cross-Disciplinary Perspective* (Upper Saddle River, NJ: Prentice-Hall, 1996).
20. Michael S. Schell and Charlene Marmer Solomon, *Capitalizing on the Global Workforce* (Chicago: Irwin Professional, 1997).
21. *Ibid.*
22. Edward T. Hall, *Understanding Cultural Differences* (Yarmouth, ME: Intercultural Press, Inc., 1990).
23. Hofstede, *Cultures and Organizations.*

Part 1/Reading 1

Difference and Danger: *Cultural Profiles of Nations and Limits to Tolerance*

Geert Hofstede

In spite of internal differences, most nation-states display a common mental programming of a majority of their inhabitants. This programming consists of shared symbols, heroes, and rituals that provide a national identity, and shared values that serve to stabilize the national society. Dominant values in nation-states around the world have been classified according to four dimensions. One of these is *Uncertainty Avoidance,* which among other things stands for the degree of tolerance for whatever or whoever is different, for the strength of the feeling that *what is different, is dangerous.* The counselling process is affected by the mental programming of counsellor and client. Effective counselling of persons not sharing the same cultural profile demands special efforts, especially if the level of *Uncertainty Avoidance* for either or both parties is high.

THE CONCEPT OF MENTAL PROGRAMMING

Mental programming is an informatician's metaphor for the pattern of thinking, feeling, and acting that every person has acquired in childhood and carries along throughout life. Without such mental programmes, the behaviour of people would be unpredictable, and social life, impossible.

A person's mental programming is partly unique, partly shared with others. One can distinguish three levels of uniqueness in mental programmes:

1. The one furthest from being unique and the most basic is the *universal level* of mental programming which is shared by all, or almost by all, mankind. This level is the biological *operating system* of the human body, which includes a range of expressive behaviours such as laughing and weeping, and kinds of associative and aggressive behaviours which are also found in the higher animals. This level of programming has been popularized by ethologists (biologists specialized in animal behaviour such as Eibl-Eibesfeldt, who has called one of his books *Der vorprogrammierte Mensch* [Man the Pre-Programmed] Munich: Deutscher Taschenbuch Verlag, 1976).
2. The *collective level* of mental programming is shared with some but not with all other people. It is common to people belonging to a certain group or category, but different among people belonging to other groups or categories. The whole area of subjective human culture (as opposed to objective culture that consists of human artifacts; see Triandis, 1972, p. 4) belongs to this level. It includes the language in which people express themselves, the deference they show to their elders, the physical distance from other people they maintain in order to feel comfortable, the way they carry out basic human activities like eating, making love, or toilet behaviour, and the ceremonials surrounding them.
3. The *individual level* of human programming is the truly unique part. No two people are programmed exactly alike, not even identical twins reared together. This level is that of individual personality, the one providing for a wide range of alternative behaviours within the same collective culture.

The borderlines between the three levels are a matter of debate within the social sciences. To what

Source: "Difference and Danger: Cultural Profiles of Nations and Limits to Tolerance," *Higher Education in Europe* 21, no. 1 (1996) Taylor & Francis, Ltd, P.O. Box 25, Abingdon Oxford, OX14 3UE.

extent are individual personalities the product of a collective culture? Which behaviours are human universals, and which are culture-dependent?

Mental programmes can be inherited, that is, transferred in our genes, or they can be learned after birth. Of the three levels, the universal level must be entirely inherited. It is part of the genetic information common to the human species. Programming at the individual level should be at least partly inherited, that is, genetically determined. It is otherwise difficult to explain the differences in capabilities and temperament between successive children of the same parents raised in very similar environments. At the middle, collective level, however, all mental programmes are learned. They are shared with people who went through the same learning process, but who do not have the same genes. As an example, one should think of the existence of the people of the United States of America. A mixture of all the world's genetic roots, present-day Americans display a collective mental programming very recognizable to the outsider. They illustrate the force of collective learning.

Mental programming manifests itself in several ways. From the many terms used to describe mental programmes, the following four together cover the total concept rather neatly: *symbols, heroes, rituals,* and *values*. Of these, *symbols* are the most superficial, and *values,* the most profound, with *heroes* and *rituals* in between.

Symbols are words, gestures, pictures, or objects which carry a particular meaning only recognized as such by those who share the mental programme. The words in a language or a jargon belong to this category, as do dress, hairdos, Coca-Cola, flags, and status symbols. Heroes are persons, alive or dead, real or imaginary, who possess characteristics that are highly prized by those sharing the mental programme, and thus serve as models for behaviour. Rituals are collective activities, technically superfluous to reach desired ends, but considered socially essential. They are therefore carried out for their own sake. Ways of greeting and paying respect to others, and social and religious ceremonies are examples of rituals. Symbols, heroes, and rituals together constitute the visible part of mental programmes; elsewhere, they have been subsumed under the term, *practices* (Hofstede, 1991, p. 7).

Values are the invisible part of mental programming. Values can be defined as "broad tendencies to prefer certain states of affairs over others" (Hofstede, 1980, p. 19). They are feelings having a plus and a minus side.

The transfer of collective mental programmes through learning goes on throughout life. The most fundamental elements, the values, are learned first, when the mind is still relatively unprogrammed. A baby learns to distinguish between dirty and clean (hygienic values) and between evil and good, unnatural and natural, abnormal and normal (ethical and moral values). Somewhat later, the child learns to distinguish between ugly and beautiful (aesthetic values), and between paradoxical and logical, irrational and rational (intellectual values). By the age of 10, most children have their basic value system firmly in place, and after that age, changes are difficult to make.

Because they were acquired so early, values as a part of mental programming often remain unconscious to those who hold them. They therefore cannot normally be discussed, nor can they be directly observed by outsiders. They can only be inferred from the way people act under various circumstances.

The transfer of collective mental programmes is a social phenomenon which, according to Durkheim (1937 [1895], p. 107), should be explained socially. Societies, organizations, and groups have ways of conserving and passing on mental programmes from generation to generation with an obstinacy which many people tend to underestimate. The elders programme the minds of the young according to the way they were once programmed themselves. What else can they do, or who else will teach the young? Theories of race, very popular among past generations, were an erroneous genetic explanation for the continuity of mental programmes across generations.

Collective mental programming takes place within the collectivities of which people are a part.

Everybody belongs to different categories at the same time; therefore, everybody carries different levels of mental programming.

The most obvious ones are the following:

- A family level, determined by the family or family substitute in which a person grew up.
- A sex-determined level, according to whether a person was born as a girl or as a boy.
- A generational level, according to the decade in which a person was born.
- A social class level, associated with educational opportunities and with a person's occupation or profession.
- A linguistic level, according to the language or languages in which a person was programmed.
- A religious level, according to the religious tradition in which that person was programmed.
- For those who are employed, an organizational or corporate culture level according to the way a person was socialized by his or her work environment.
- An occupational level, representing the shared mental programming, across national borders, of persons within the same type of occupation (like counsellors).
- A nation-state level according to one's country (or countries for people who migrated during their lifetimes).
- Within nation-states, possibly a regional and/ or ethnic level.

This article will focus on the level associated with the nation-state. It corresponds partly with what was once called *national character*, and later, *national culture*. National characters are intuitively evident, and have been so for hundreds and even thousands of years. However, because of the value elements in national mental programmes, statements about national characters were almost without exception extremely biased. They often contained more information about the person making the statement than about the nation that was the object of the statement.

In order to avoid this bias, only comparative information about differences in nation-state-linked mental programmes that treat the data of every nation-state as equivalent will be used.

NATIONAL CULTURAL DIFFERENCES

Human societies as historically and organically developed forms of social organization have existed for at least 10,000 years. Nation-states as political units into which the entire world is divided and to one of which any human being is supposed to belong are a much more recent phenomenon in human history. The concept of a common mental programming applies, strictly speaking, more to societies than to nation-states. Nevertheless, many nation-states do form historically developed wholes even if they are composed of different regions and ethnicities, and even if less integrated minorities live within their borders.

Nation-states contain institutions that standardize mental programmes: a dominant language (sometimes more than one), common mass media, a national education system, a national army, a national political system, national representation in sports events with a strong symbolic and emotional appeal, and a national market for certain skills, products, and services. Today's nation-states do not attain the degree of internal homogeneity of the isolated, usually nonliterate, societies traditionally studied by field anthropologists, but most nation-states are the source of a considerable amount of common mental programming of their citizens.

A popular term at the present time is *national identity*. National identity is part of the mental programming of a national population, but at the conscious level of practices, symbols, heroes, and rituals. There is an increasing tendency for ethnic, linguistic, and religious groups to fight for recognition of their own identity, if not for national independence. Ulster, the republics of the former Yugoslavia, and parts of the former Soviet Union are evident examples. But the groups struggling are not necessarily very different in terms of their deepest level of mental programmes: values. They may struggle on the basis of rather similar values, as has been found to be the case for the Flemish and Walloons in Belgium, and for the Croats and Serbs in former Yugoslavia.

In the first half of the 20th century, social anthropology developed the conviction that all societies, traditional or modern, faced and still face the same basic problems; only the answers differ. Attempts at identifying these common basic problems used conceptual reasoning, interpretation of field experiences, and statistical analysis of data about societies. In 1954, two Americans, the sociologist Alex Inkeles and the psychologist Daniel Levinson, published a broad survey of the literature in English on what was then still called *national character*. They suggested that the following issues qualify as common basic problems worldwide, with consequences for the functioning of societies, of groups within these societies, and of individuals within these groups:

1. Relation to authority.
2. Conception of self, in particular:
   - The relationship between individual and society.
   - The individual's concept of masculinity and femininity.
3. Ways of dealing with conflicts, including the control of aggression and the expression of feelings (Inkeles and Levinson, 1969 [1954], p. 447).

Twenty years later, the author had the opportunity to study a large body of survey data about the values of people in over 50 countries around the world. These people were working in the local subsidiaries of one large multinational corporation: IBM. At first sight it might seem strange that employees of a multinational corporation—a very special kind of people—could be used to identify differences in *national* value systems. However, a crucial problem in cross-national research is always to sample respondents who are functionally equivalent. The IBM employees represented almost perfectly matched samples. They were similar in all respects except nationality, which made the effects of nationality differences in their answers stand out unusually clearly.

A statistical analysis of the answers to questions about the values of similar IBM employees in different countries revealed common problems, but solutions differing from country to country, in the following areas:

1. Social inequality, including the relationship to authority.
2. The relationship between the individual and the group.
3. Concepts of masculinity and femininity: the social implications of having been born as a boy or as a girl.
4. Ways of dealing with uncertainty, relating to the control of aggression and the expression of emotions.

These four problem areas could be expressed in four dimensions of national cultures, labelled *Power Distance* (large versus small), *Individualism versus Collectivism, Masculinity versus Femininity,* and *Uncertainty Avoidance* (strong versus weak). Every country studied could be located somewhere between the extremes (poles) of each dimension.

These empirical results covered amazingly well the areas predicted by Inkeles and Levinson 20 years earlier. The author only discovered the prediction made by Inkeles and Levinson *after* he had identified the four dimensions in the IBM data. It provided strong support for the theoretical importance of the empirical findings. Problems basic to all human societies should turn up in different studies regardless of the approaches followed.

A dimension associates a number of phenomena in a society that were empirically found to occur in combination; even if at first sight there does not always seem to be a logical necessity for their going together. The logic of societies, however, is not the same as the logic of individuals looking at them.

The IBM research results have been replicated by others on other samples of respondents: on students (Hofstede and Bond, 1984) and on national elites (Hoppe, 1990). These research results correlate significantly with the results of other cross-national studies of values, like the European

Value Systems Study (Ester *et al.*, 1993), and the worldwide values surveys by Schwartz (1994).

More recently, a fifth dimension of differences among national cultures was identified, opposing a *Long Term Orientation* in life to a *Short Term Orientation*. East Asian nations tend to score *Long Term;* European countries more *Short Term*. Data allowing for the computation of scores on this dimension have so far only been collected for 23 nations.

POWER DISTANCE AND UNCERTAINTY AVOIDANCE

Power Distance has been defined as "the extent to which the less powerful members of institutions within a country expect and accept that power is distributed unequally." It represents the degree of social inequality in the mental programming of people. All societies are unequal, but some are more unequal than others, and this inequality is reflected in the mental programmes of people.

Uncertainty Avoidance has been defined as "the extent to which the members of a culture feel threatened by uncertain or unknown situations." It stands for the need for structure, social conformity, and absolute truths. People in a strongly uncertainty avoiding society have been preprogrammed to be active, anxious, precise, and to dislike the unpredictable. People in weakly uncertainty avoiding societies have been preprogrammed to be passive, relaxed, imprecise, and to dislike the predictable. Obviously, individual personalities within these societies vary in regard to these counts.

Exhibit 1 illustrates the relative positions of the answers by the respondent samples from 54 countries and regions on *Power Distance* and *Uncertainty Avoidance*.

The IBM survey data, collected around 1970, did not cover Eastern Europe, except for what was then still Yugoslavia. In 1993, the author went back to the old Yugoslavia data, which could be split into data from Croatia, Serbia, and Slovenia. More recent replications on samples more-or-less matched with the IBM employee data samples were collected in Hungary (Varga, 1986) and Russia (Bollinger, 1988). Attempts have been made to collect data with the same questionnaire in other Eastern European countries, but the survey populations were poorly matched with the IBM employee population, so that the results are not useful.

The top left quadrant of Exhibit 1 contains six Northern and Western European countries: Denmark, Sweden, Norway, the Netherlands, Ireland, The United Kingdom, and overseas countries initially populated by British migrants. These combine small *Power Distance* with weak *Uncertainty Avoidance*. In the mental programmes of these people, there is little social inequality and little need for structure.

The bottom left quadrant contains the German-speaking countries of Austria, Switzerland, and Germany, plus Finland, Hungary, and Israel. These combine small *Power Distance* with stronger *Uncertainty Avoidance*. The mental programmes still display little social inequality, but more need for structure.

The two quadrants to the left thus host all Germanic countries, plus Finland and Hungary. In all of these countries, survey respondents scored low on *Power Distance*. The closeness of Austria and Hungary is remarkable: the Austro-Hungarian empire survives in the mind-sets of people.

The top right quadrant (large *Power Distance* but weak *Uncertainty Avoidance*) contains countries in Africa, Asia, and the Caribbean, not populated by Europeans.

The bottom right quadrant contains all Latin European countries studied (including Belgium), all Latin American countries (Costa Rica being an exception), the South and East European countries of Slovenia, Croatia, Serbia, Turkey, Russia, and Greece, plus Japan and Korea, and some other Asian and Muslim countries (Taiwan, Thailand, Iran, Pakistan, and the Arab-speaking countries). In all of these countries, respondents scored high on both *Power Distance* and *Uncertainty Avoidance*.

Power and structure are the key elements in the organizations people build. Other research (described in Hofstede, 1991, p. 140) has suggested

EXHIBIT 1 **The Relative Position of 54 Countries or Regions on the *Power Distance* × *Uncertainty Avoidance* Dimensions (for country name abbreviations, see Exhibit 2 on page 60)**

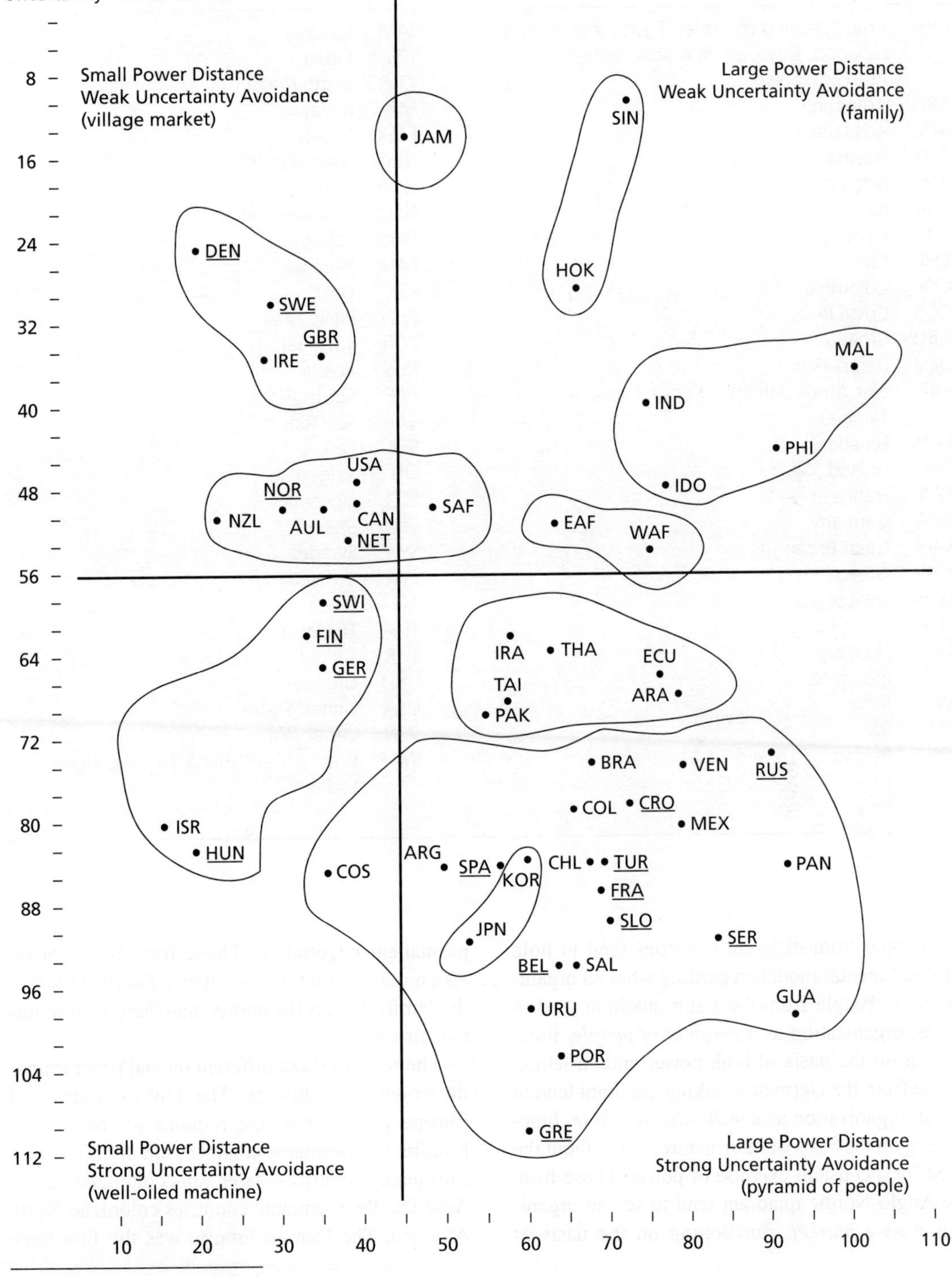

Note: European countries are underlined.

EXHIBIT 2 Abbreviations for Country Names

ARA	Arab-speaking countries (Egypt, Iraq, Kuwait, Lebanon, Libya, Saudi Arabia, United Arab Emirates)	JAM	Jamaica
ARG	Argentina	JPN	Japan
AUL	Australia	KOR	South Korea
AUT	Austria	MAL	Malaysia
BEL	Belgium	MEX	Mexico
BRA	Brazil	NET	Netherlands
CAN	Canada	NOR	Norway
CHL	Chile	NZL	New Zealand
COL	Colombia	PAK	Pakistan
COS	Costa Rica	PAN	Panama
CRO	Croatia	PER	Peru
DEN	Denmark	PHI	Philippines
EAF	East Africa (Ethiopia, Kenya, Tanzania, Zambia)	POR	Portugal
ECU	Ecuador	RUS	Russia
FIN	Finland	SAF	South Africa
FRA	France	SAL	Salvador
GER	Germany	SER	Serbia
GBR	Great Britain	SIN	Singapore
GRE	Greece	SLO	Slovenia
GUA	Guatemala	SPA	Spain
HOK	Hong Kong	SWE	Sweden
HUN	Hungary	SWI	Switzerland
IDO	Indonesia	TAI	Taiwan
IND	India	THA	Thailand
IRA	Iran	TUR	Turkey
IRE	Ireland	URU	Uruguay
ISR	Israel	USA	United States
ITA	Italy	VEN	Venezuela
		WAF	West Africa (Ghana, Nigeria, Sierra Leone)

that people from different countries tend to hold different mental models regarding what an organization is. People from the Latin quadrant tend to see an organization as a *pyramid of people,* functioning on the basis of both power and structure. Those from the German-speaking quadrant tend to see an organization as a *well-oiled machine,* functioning on the basis of its structure, but without the need for a constant exercise of power. Those from the Anglo-Nordic quadrant tend to see an organization as a *market,* functioning on the basis of permanent negotiation. Those from the African-Asian quadrant tend to see it as a *family,* in which the family head is the master, and there is little formal structure.

The roots of these different mental programmes lie evidently in history. The Latin countries of Europe grew out of the remains of the Roman Empire; the Germanic countries did not. The Latin European countries later on colonized Latin America, the Germanic countries colonized North America. The Roman Empire was the first large and effective state to be established in its part of the world. In the same way as early childhood experiences have a major impact on personality, these early societal experiences must have had a lasting impact on polity, affecting not only all institutions that have followed but also the corresponding mental programmes. One still speaks of the *Latin mentality*.

The Roman Empire combined two principles new to Europe: *i)* authority centralized in Rome, and *ii)* a system of codified laws, applicable to every Roman citizen. The centralized authority principle supports a large *Power Distance;* the codified law principle supports strong *Uncertainty Avoidance*. Of the two principles, the first dominated the second. The supreme power, the emperor, stood over the law. When the Roman Empire disintegrated, the absolute authority of the ruler was maintained by the Germanic invaders of France, who mixed with the country's Romanized Celtic population (Pirenne, 1939, p. 32), but not by the Germanic Anglo-Saxon invaders of Britain who chased the Romanized Celts without mixing with them.

In the Germanic tradition, the power of the king was subordinate to the assembly of freemen. Therefore, an absolutist rule could never take hold in Britain. When the Norman kings attempted to establish it, they were forced to recognize the rights of the people in the Magna Charta of 1215 (Pirenne, 1939, p. 257). In Germany up until the 19th century, a central authority could never last, and the country was composed of small principalities. Federal Germany is still much more decentralized than the countries of Latin Europe.

Russia, Greece, and Serbia inherited the Byzantine culture, which in turn was an offspring of Roman culture. We find their scores on the extreme fringe of the Latin quadrant in Exhibit 1, with extreme *Power Distances* in Russia and Serbia and extreme *Uncertainty Avoidance* in Greece. The Byzantine empire seems to have developed and transferred a hypertrophy of Latin mental programming traits.

The Germanic countries in Exhibit 1 are relatively close on *Power Distance* but display a wider spread on *Uncertainty Avoidance*. The countries turned towards the sea avoided uncertainty less than the countries turned towards the land. How, why, and when exactly this split took place is a question best left to historians.

UNCERTAINTY AVOIDANCE AND TOLERANCE

The term *Uncertainty Avoidance* has been borrowed from American organization sociology, in particular from the work of James G. March (e.g., Cyert and March, 1963, p. 118ff). March and his colleagues recognized it in American organizations. Ways of handling uncertainty, however, are part and parcel of any human institution in any country. All human beings have to face the fact that we do not know what will happen tomorrow. The future is uncertain, but one must live with it anyway.

Extreme uncertainty creates intolerable anxiety. Every human society has developed ways to alleviate this anxiety. These ways belong to the domains of technology, law, and religion. Technology, from the most primitive to the most advanced, helps to avoid uncertainties caused by nature. Laws and rules try to prevent uncertainties in the behaviour of other people. Religion is a way of relating to the transcendental forces that are assumed to control the personal future of humankind. Religion helps one to accept the uncertainties against which one cannot defend oneself. Some religions offer the ultimate certainty of a life after death or of victory over one's opponents.

Anthropologists studying traditional societies have devoted a good deal of their attention to technology, law, and religion. They have illustrated the enormous variety of ways in which human societies deal with uncertainty. Modern societies do not vary essentially from traditional societies in this respect. In spite of the availability of the same information virtually anywhere around the globe, technologies, laws, and religions continue to vary. Moreover, there are no signs of spontaneous convergence.

The essence of uncertainty is that it is a subjective experience, a feeling. A lion tamer may feel reasonably comfortable when surrounded by his animals, a situation which would make most people die of fear. Some people may feel reasonably comfortable when driving on a crowded motorway at 70 miles per hour or more, a situation that is statistically about as risky as that of the lion tamer.

Feelings of uncertainty are not only just personal, but may also be partly shared with other members of one's society. Feelings of uncertainty are acquired and learned. Such feelings and ways of coping with them belong to the cultural heritage of societies and are transferred and reinforced through basic institutions like the family, the school, and the state. They are reflected in the collectively held values of the members of a particular society. Their roots are nonrational. They lead to collective patterns of behavior in one society which may seem aberrant and incomprehensible to members of other societies.

Among the first things a child learns are the distinctions between *clean* and *dirty,* and between *safe* and *dangerous*. What is considered clean and safe, or dirty and dangerous, varies widely from one society to the next and even among families within a society. The British-American anthropologist Mary Douglas has written a book, *Purity and Danger*. Dirt—that which pollutes—is, Douglas argues, a relative concept, which depends entirely on cultural interpretation. Dirt is basically matter that is out-of-place. Dangerous and polluting things are those that do not fit one's usual framework of thinking and normal classifications, from a given point of view. What a child has to learn is to distinguish clean things from dirty things and safe things from dangerous things. And in strongly uncertainty avoiding cultures, classifications with regard to what is dirty and dangerous are tight and absolute.

Dirt and danger are not limited to matter. They also refer to people. Racism is bred in families. Children learn that persons from a particular category are dirty and dangerous. Ideas too can be considered dirty and dangerous. Children in families learn that some ideas are good and others, taboo. In some cultures, the distinction between good and evil ideas is very sharp. There is a concern about Truth with a capital T. Ideas which vary from this Truth are dangerous and polluting. Little room is left for doubt or relativism. Taboos are supposed to be a characteristic of traditional, primitive societies, but modern societies too are full of taboos. The family is the place in which these taboos are transmitted from generation to generation.

Weak *Uncertainty Avoidance* cultures also have their classifications as to dirt and danger, but these are wider and more prepared to give the benefit of the doubt to unknown situations, people, and ideas. Norms are expressed in basic terms, like being honest and being polite, but allowing a range of personal interpretation as to what both concepts mean in given cases. Deviant behaviour is not so easily felt as threatening. Norms as to dress, hair style, and speech are looser, and children are expected to treat other people equally regardless of their appearance.

The strong *Uncertainty Avoidance* sentiment can be expressed by the credo of xenophobia: *What is different is dangerous*. The weak *Uncertainty Avoidance* sentiment on the contrary is: *What is different is curious*. Somewhere in between is the prevailing sentiment in the author's country, the Netherlands (UAI = 53): *What is different is ridiculous*.

Fundamentalisms are more frequent in strongly than in weakly uncertainty avoiding societies. Tolerance, mysticism, and meditation are more characteristic of weakly than of strongly uncertainty avoiding societies. But the relationship between *Uncertainty Avoidance* and religion is even broader. The grouping of countries according to *Uncertainty Avoidance* scores reflects their dominant religion. Orthodox and Roman Catholic Christian countries score high (except the Philippines and Ireland). Judaic and Muslim countries tend to score in the middle. Protestant Christian countries score low. Eastern religions score medium to very low, with Japan as an exception.

The dominant religious affiliation in a country may have been a *result* of previously existing mental programmes as much as a *cause* of such programmes. All of the great religions of the world at some time in their history underwent profound schisms: between Roman Catholics, Eastern Orthodox, and various Protestant groups in Christianity; between Sunni and Shia in Islam; between liberals and various fundamentalist groups in Judaism; and between Hinayana and Mahayana in Buddhism. Differences in mental programming between groups of believers have probably played a major role in these schisms. Religious conversion does not mean a total change in cultural values.

The value complexes described by the dimensions of *Power Distance, Uncertainty Avoidance, Individualism or Collectivism,* and *Masculinity and Femininity* seem to have survived religious conversions. These value complexes are likely to have influenced to what extent a population has been receptive to certain religions, and how the accepted religion has evolved in that country. Indonesian (Javanese) mysticism, for example, implying weak *Uncertainty Avoidance,* has survived Hindu, Buddhist, Muslim, and Christian conversions.

The split between Germanic and Latin countries as portrayed in Exhibit 1 could also be explained as a split by religion: Protestant versus Roman Catholic. According to the Belgian historian, Henri Pirenne (1939, p. 397), the Roman Catholic Church is in many respects a continuation of the Roman Empire; therefore, the influences of old Rome and new Rome are difficult to separate. However, Ireland, predominantly Roman Catholic, but never part of the Empire, scored like the United Kingdom and not like, for example, Italy, a fact that suggests that the crucial factor is the Empire and not the Church. The Reformation in the Christian churches separated almost exactly those European countries once under the Roman Empire from the rest. All the ex-Roman countries (the ones now speaking Romance languages, with the exception of Romania) refuted the Reformation and remained Roman Catholic; most others became Protestant or mixed. Poland and Ireland were never part of the Roman Empire, but in their case, Roman Catholicism provided them with an identity against non-Roman Catholic oppressors.

In establishing a relationship between *Uncertainty Avoidance* and religious belief, it makes sense to distinguish between western and eastern religions. The western religions, Judaism, Christianity, but also Islam, are based on divine revelation, and all three originated from what is now called the Middle East. What distinguishes the western from the eastern religions is their concern with Truth with a capital T. The western revealed religions share the assumption that there is an absolute Truth that humans can possess which excludes all other truths. The difference between strong and weak *Uncertainty Avoidance* societies adhering to these religions lies in the amount of certainty one needs about having this Truth. In strong uncertainty avoiding cultures, the frequently held belief is that *There is only one Truth and we have it. All others do not have it.* Possessing this Truth is the only road to salvation and the main purpose in a person's life. The consequence of the error of others may be an effort to convert them, to avoid them, or to kill them.

Weak *Uncertainty Avoidance* cultures from the west still believe in Truth, but they have less of a need to believe that they alone possess it. *There is only one Truth and we are looking for it. Others are looking for it as well, and we accept as a fact of life that they look in different directions.* Part of this Truth, anyway, is that God wants nobody to be prosecuted for their beliefs.

Eastern religions are less concerned about Truth. The assumption that there is one Truth which man can possess is absent in their thinking. Buddhism instead stresses the acquisition of insight by meditation. Thus in the east, people will easily absorb elements of different religions. Most Japanese perform both Buddhist and Shinto rituals; however, by standards of western logic, the two religious traditions are mutually exclusive.

What applies to religions applies also to political ideologies which are often difficult to separate from religious inspiration. Marxism in many places took on the form of a secular religion. When East Germany was still solidly communist, the façade of the University of Leipzig was decorated with an enormous banner reading "*Der Marxismus ist allmächtig, weil er wahr ist!*" (Marxism is all-powerful because it is True!). In strong *Uncertainty Avoidance* cultures, we find intolerant political ideologies; in weak *Uncertainty Avoidance* cultures, tolerant ones.

The respect of what is commonly called *human rights* assumes a tolerance for people with different political ideas. One reason for violations of human rights in some countries is a strong *Uncertainty Avoidance* in their culture; however, the same strong *Uncertainty Avoidance* may stimulate a careful application of laws that protect human rights.

INDIVIDUALISM/ COLLECTIVISM AND MASCULINITY/FEMININITY

Exhibit 3 displays the relative positions of the respondent samples from 56 countries and regions, in regard to the two dimensions of *Individualism-Collectivism* and *Masculinity-Femininity* (for these two dimensions no data are available for Hungary).

Individualism stands for a society in which the ties between individuals are loose. Everyone is expected to look only after him- or herself and his or her immediate family. Collectivism stands for a society in which people from birth onwards are integrated into strong, cohesive, in-groups, which throughout their lifetimes continue to protect them in exchange for unquestioning loyalty.

Collectivism is the normal state of mind of agricultural societies. Hunting and gathering societies are more individualist. Modern individualism developed in England, Scotland, and the Netherlands and was taken to North America by the Pilgrim Fathers. Individualism in countries increases with national wealth (increased individualism is an *effect,* not a *cause* of economic growth). Asian nations that have recently become wealthy have also become more individualistic but not as much as Western European countries at the same level of wealth.

The scores regarding individualism in Exhibit 3 closely follow the *Per Capita Gross National Product* of the countries. All wealthy western countries are found in the lower part of the diagram. Japan that combines an Asian tradition of collectivism with western-style modernity scores half-way.

Individualist mental programmes are a precondition for political democracy and for a free market economy. One-person-one-vote presupposes that those persons have been programmed to hold personal opinions. The invisible hand of the market economy presupposes that persons will attempt to maximize their individual economic advantage. Both do not apply in nations with collectivist mental programmes and institutions.

Collectivism plays an important role in the ethnic conflicts that regularly erupt in different parts of the world: like those in Bosnia, Somalia, and Burundi. Children in collectivist societies have learned to differentiate between *us* and *them,* to oppose their own in-group to various out-groups. If, in addition, *Uncertainty Avoidance* in these societies has increased under political or ecological threat, the growing feeling that *what is different is dangerous* is projected on the nearest out-groups. The call, *let's hit them first before they hit us,* becomes credible in such situations.

The second dimension in Exhibit 3, *Masculinity,* stands for a society in which social sexual roles are clearly distinct: Men are supposed to be assertive, tough, and focused on material success; women are supposed to be more modest, tender, and concerned with the quality of life. *Femininity* stands for a society in which social-sexual roles overlap. Both men and women are supposed to be modest, tender, and concerned with the quality of life.

On the bottom left, the individualistic and feminine side of the diagram, we find a cluster of Nordic countries: Sweden, Norway, Denmark, and Finland, plus the Netherlands. Slightly feminine scores were obtained for France, Spain, and Israel. On the bottom right, individualistic, and masculine side of the diagram, we find the German-speaking countries: Germany, Switzerland, and Austria (moderately individualistic but strongly masculine);

EXHIBIT 3 The Relative Position of 54 Countries or Regions on the *Individualism* × *Masculinity* Dimensions (for country name abbreviations, see Exhibit 2)

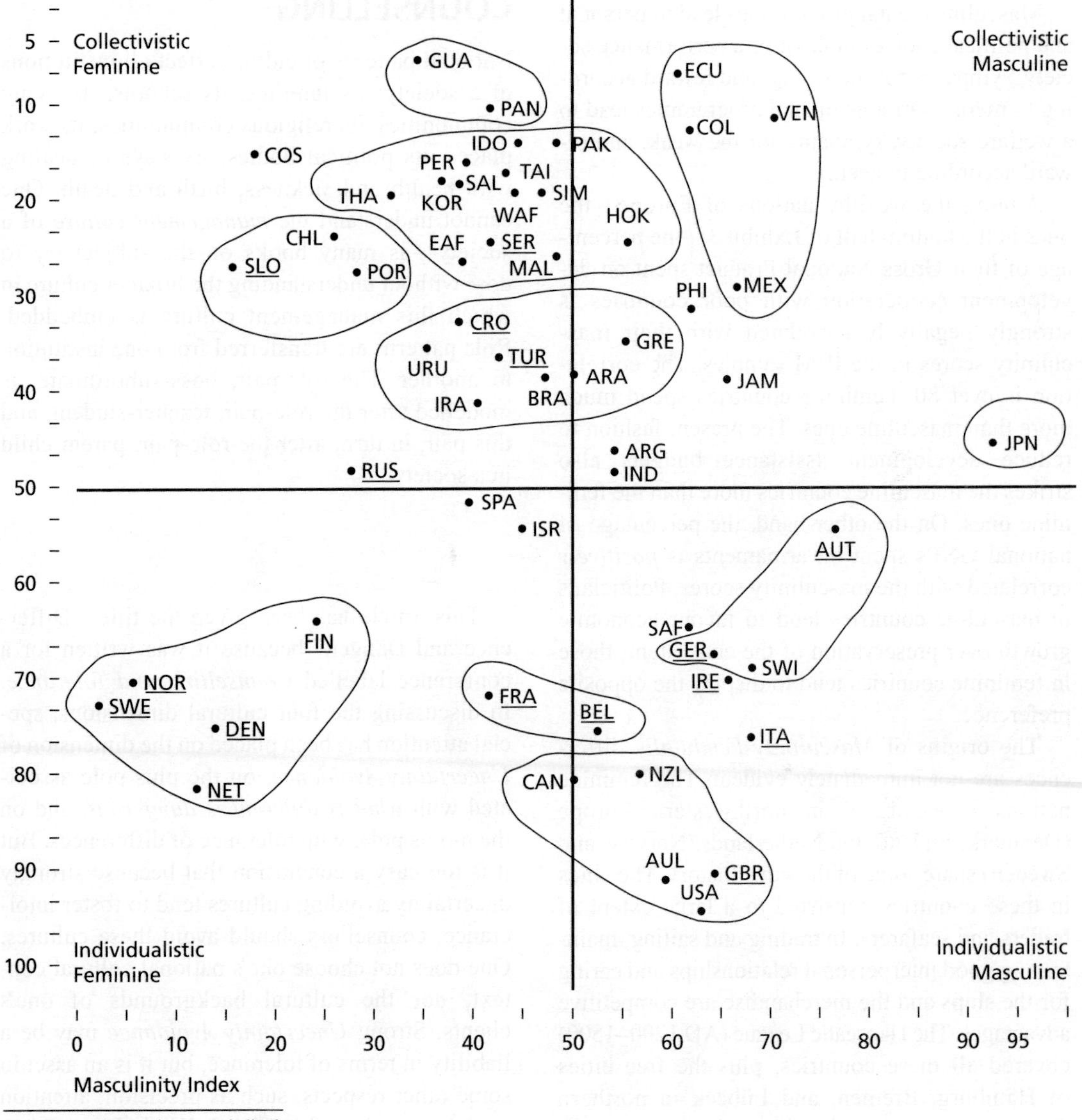

Note: European countries are underlined.

the United Kingdom and other Anglo-Saxon countries (very individualistic and fairly masculine), plus some other countries: Italy, Ireland, Belgium, and South Africa (where scores were only based on the white population).

The poorer countries (top half of Exhibit 3) vary in *Masculinity,* from Costa Rica, Slovenia, Russia, Chile, Portugal, and Thailand (quite feminine); to Jamaica, Colombia, Ecuador, Venezuela, and Mexico (quite masculine). (South) Korea distinguishes itself from Japan by a feminine score opposing Japan's extremely high score on *Masculinity*.

Masculine mental programmes lead to personal and political choices in favor of a performance society, sympathy for the strong, and reward according to merit. Feminine mental programmes lead to a welfare society, sympathy for the weak, and reward according to need.

Among the wealthy nations of Europe—the ones in the bottom half of Exhibit 3—the percentage of their Gross National Product spent on development cooperation with poor countries is strongly negatively correlated with their masculinity scores in the IBM samples. The correlation is over 80. Feminine countries spend much more than masculine ones. The present fashion to reduce development assistance budgets also strikes the masculine countries more than the feminine ones. On the other hand, the percentage of national GNPs spent on armaments is *positively* correlated with the masculinity scores. Politicians in masculine countries tend to favour economic growth over preservation of the ecosystem; those in feminine countries tend to display the opposite preference.

The origins of *Masculinity-Femininity* differences are not immediately evident. The feminine nations concentrated in northwestern Europe (Denmark, Finland, the Netherlands, Norway, and Sweden) share some of the same history. The elites in these countries consisted to a large extent of traders and seafarers. In trading and sailing, maintaining good interpersonal relationships and caring for the ships and the merchandise are competitive advantages. The Hanseatic League (AD 1200–1500) covered all these countries, plus the free cities of Hamburg, Bremen, and Lübeck in northern Germany and the Baltic states. The Hansa was a free association of trading towns and, for the maintenance of such a system, values associated with *Femininity* were functional. Women played an active role in the Hansa trading families. While the Hansa does not explain the origin of North-European *Femininity,* it at least benefited from it and reinforced it.

NATIONAL CULTURE DIFFERENCES AND COUNSELLING

National patterns of culture affect all institutions of a society: its families, its schools, its living communities, its religious communities, its work places, its political bodies, its ways of dealing with health and sickness, birth and death. One cannot understand the *management culture* of a society—as many books on the subject try to do—without understanding the broader culture in which this management culture is embedded. Role patterns are transferred from one institution to another. The role-pair, boss-subordinate, is modelled after the role-pair, teacher-student, and this pair, in turn, after the role-pair, parent-child in a society.

. . .

This article has been given the title, "Difference and Danger," because it was written for a conference labelled *Counselling and Tolerance*. In discussing the four cultural dimensions, special attention has been placed on the dimension of *Uncertainty Avoidance,* on the plus pole associated with *what is different is dangerous,* and on the minus pole, with tolerance of differences. But it is too easy a conclusion that because strongly uncertainty avoiding cultures tend to foster intolerance, counsellors should avoid these cultures. One does not choose one's national cultural context, nor the cultural backgrounds of one's clients. Strong *Uncertainty Avoidance* may be a liability in terms of tolerance, but it is an asset in some other respects, such as precision, attention to detail, and working hard. Weak *Uncertainty Avoidance* cultures may be more tolerant, but their tolerance might also take the form of ignoring the other party's problems; of simply not caring. With a dubious term, such tolerance could be labelled, *repressive*.

. . .

monochronic or polychronic the cultures of your employing organization and department are.[2]

Many of these fundamental variations are so subtle that they often go unrecognized because they exist beneath the level of conscious awareness. Differences in patterns related to time horizon, pace, and punctuality can be found as well as tendencies to use time monochronically or polychronically. However, individuals are sometimes unaware of the particular aspects of their "time personalities," although they can readily report actual time use preferences and behaviors. Furthermore, polychronicity is important, not only because it is a fundamental distinction in and of itself, but because pioneering research indicates that it is related to many of our other important behaviors and attitudes.

Anthropologist Edward Hall has observed that differences in space utilization and the priorities given to human relationships over task accomplishment vary with monochronic and polychronic cultural orientations.[3] His observations indicate that people with a monochronic orientation are task-oriented, emphasize promptness and a concern for others' privacy, stick to their plans, seldom borrow or lend private property, and are accustomed to short-term relationships with other people. Conversely, people with a polychronic orientation tend to change plans, borrow and lend things frequently, emphasize relationships rather than tasks and privacy, and build long-term relationships with family members, friends, and business partners. Because of these relationships and polychronicity's stature as a core defining characteristic of temporal attitudes and behaviors, an understanding of monochronic and polychronic orientations is vital to understanding our own behaviors, the ability to manage in the international arena, and the ability to manage in an increasingly culturally diverse workplace.

HOW POLYCHRONIC ARE YOU?

Researchers Carol Kaufman, Paul Lane, and Jay Lindquist conducted an extensive survey of polychronic time use in which they examined individuals' tendencies to use time either polychronically or monochronically. They developed a scale, the Polychronic Attitude Index (PAI), which attempted to capture the respondent's general attitude toward performing more than one activity at a time.[4] Respondents were also requested to report the likelihood of their participation in some specific types of activity combinations. As anticipated, several activity combinations were found to be significantly correlated with the PAI. Thus, one's score on the PAI provides a preliminary indication of whether an individual has the potential and desire to combine activities in the same block of time. In contrast, prior research on polychronicity has been primarily qualitative and observational.

Kaufman, Lane, and Lindquist's work produced the four-item scale presented in Exhibit 2. We suggest that you complete the four-item scale right now and then score yourself. By completing this scale you will gain a better understanding of the monochronic/polychronic continuum and learn about an element of your own personality most people do not know about themselves.

Kaufman et al.'s survey was completed by 310 employed adults in southern New Jersey. Their sample is fairly representative of the general U.S. population and provides the only existing baseline against which your response may be compared. The mean score in their sample was 3.128, which you can use as a point of comparison for your own score. Kaufman et al. found that polychronic time use was negatively correlated with role overload (the more polychronic the individual, the less role overload the individual tended to experience), and positively correlated with education (the higher the education level, the more polychronic the respondent tended to be), working more than 40 hours per week (the more polychronic tended to work more than 40 hours per week), and social group and club membership (the more polychronic were more likely to belong to social groups and clubs). Polychronic time use was not, however, correlated with gender (contrary to Hall's suggestion), age, income, or marital status.

EXHIBIT 2 Polychronic Attitude Index

Please consider how you feel about the following statements. Circle your choice on the scale provided: strongly agree, agree, neutral, disagree, or strongly disagree.

	Strongly Disagree	Disagree	Neutral	Agree	Strongly Agree
I do not like to juggle several activities at the same time.	5 pts	4 pts	3 pts	2 pts	1 pt
People should not try to do many things at once.	5 pts	4 pts	3 pts	2 pts	1 pt
When I sit down at my desk, I work on one project at a time.	5 pts	4 pts	3 pts	2 pts	1 pt
I am comfortable doing several things at the same time.	1 pt	2 pts	3 pts	4 pts	5 pts

Add up your points, and divide the total by 4. Then plot your score on the scale below.

1.0	1.5	2.0	2.5	3.0	3.5	4.0	4.5	5.0
Monochronic								Polychronic

The lower the score (below 3.0) the more monochronic your orientation; and the higher the score, (above 3.0) the more polychronic.

HOW POLYCHRONIC ARE YOUR DEPARTMENT AND ORGANIZATION?

After Kaufman et al. had completed the first phases of their work, Bluedorn built upon it to develop a five-item scale for measuring the monochronic/polychronic continuum as a component of organizational culture.[5] Unlike Kaufman et al.'s original scale, his scale asks respondents to report on the general time use orientations they perceive in their departments and organizations rather than about their own individual orientations. This scale, tested in a sample of 205 employees drawn from a medium-size bank in Missouri, is presented in Exhibit 3. We suggest that you complete the scale in Exhibit 3 for both your department and your entire organization at this time. Then follow the instructions to score your department and organization.

The results in Exhibit 3 reveal your perceptions of your department's and organization's location on the monochronic/polychronic continuum (they will not necessarily be at the same place on the continuum). To determine the "real" locations of your department and organization on the continuum, a survey drawn from a large sample of your department and organization would be necessary. However, your perception by itself is still useful because you can now use it to compare to your own orientation, as measured by the scale in Exhibit 2, your perceptions of your department and organization in Exhibit 3. We suggest that you now plot your results from Exhibit 2 and Exhibit 3 on the scales in Exhibit 4, which will allow you to compare your personal time use orientation with that which you perceive in your department and organization.[6]

The more polychronic the department, the more externally focused it tended to be. The more polychronic departments also tended to have longer time horizons. These results, which should be considered preliminary findings, may indicate that more polychronic individuals would also have better matches with departments that have longer time horizons and more of an external orientation.

EXHIBIT 3 Monochronic/Polychronic Orientation Scale

Please use the following scale to indicate the extent to which you agree or disagree that each statement is true about 1) your organization and 2) your department.

Statement		Strongly Disagree	Somewhat Disagree	Slightly Disagree	Neutral	Slightly Agree	Somewhat Agree	Strongly Agree
We like to juggle several activities at the same time.	Organization	1 pt	2 pts	3 pts	4 pts	5 pts	6 pts	7 pts
	Department	1 pt	2 pts	3 pts	4 pts	5 pts	6 pts	7 pts
We would rather complete an entire project everyday than complete parts of several projects.	Organization	7 pts	6 pts	5 pts	4 pts	3 pts	2 pts	1 pt
	Department	7 pts	6 pts	5 pts	4 pts	3 pts	2 pts	1 pt
We believe people should try to do many things at once.	Organization	1 pt	2 pts	3 pts	4 pts	5 pts	6 pts	7 pts
	Department	1 pt	2 pts	3 pts	4 pts	5 pts	6 pts	7 pts
When we work by ourselves, we usually work on one project at a time.	Organization	7 pts	6 pts	5 pts	4 pts	3 pts	2 pts	1 pt
	Department	7 pts	6 pts	5 pts	4 pts	3 pts	2 pts	1 pt
We prefer to do one thing at a time.	Organization	7 pts	6 pts	5 pts	4 pts	3 pts	2 pts	1 pt
	Department	7 pts	6 pts	5 pts	4 pts	3 pts	2 pts	1 pt

Add up your points, for your organization, and your department. Divide each total by 5. Then plot both scores on the scale below.

1.0 1.5 2.0 2.5 3.0 3.5 4.0 4.5 5.0 5.5 6.0 6.5 7.0

Monochronic — Polychronic

The lower the score (below 4.0) the more monochronic your organization or department; and the higher the score, (above 4.0) the more polychronic.

EXHIBIT 4 Orientation Comparison

To compare your individual Monochronic/Polychronic orientation with your department and organization, copy your scores from the three scales onto this chart.

Individual

1.0	1.5	2.0	2.5	3.0	3.5	4.0	4.5	5.0
Monochronic								Polychronic

Department

1.0	1.5	2.0	2.5	3.0	3.5	4.0	4.5	5.0	5.5	6.0	6.5	7.0
Monochronic												Polychronic

Organization

1.0	1.5	2.0	2.5	3.0	3.5	4.0	4.5	5.0	5.5	6.0	6.5	7.0
Monochronic												Polychronic

To interpret the scores, rather than using exact numerical values, use general comparisons such as "middle of the scale" or "clearly above" or "clearly below" the midpoint.

MANAGERIAL IMPLICATIONS

Although the monochronic-polychronic distinction creates as many potential implications for behavior and action as there are people, three behavioral domains are particularly prominent: individual time management, supervision/coordination, and cultural diversity.

Individual Time Management

Much of traditional prescriptive time management emphasizes a monochronic orientation. To wit: In an orderly fashion carefully plan your day by organizing a schedule based on your priorities with a specific allotment of time allocated for each activity. Kaufman et al. have suggested that more polychronically oriented consumers may be more successfully marketed to by learning which types of activities they would like to have combined with others. For example, many people may like to drive and conduct business at the same time (cars and cellular phones) or watch the news and a ball game at the same time (picture-in-picture televisions). Their idea of identifying activities whose combination is attractive to customers can readily be extended to the personal time management enterprise through a series of questions.

- Which activities require your undivided attention?
- Which activities do you prefer to do in combination with other tasks?
- Which activities do you prefer to have grouped together?
- Which activities would you prefer not to be grouped together?

Candid answers to these questions and their corollaries can lead to a more sophisticated approach to time management by moving beyond the

The closer your individual preference score is to that of your organization or department, the closer your "fit" or "match" in terms of the monochronic/polychronic orientation, but the closeness of the match may indicate more than just a fit or misfit with the monochronic/polychronic continuum alone. Bluedorn's bank study revealed some very large correlations between a department's polychronicity and the extent to which it emphasizes an external focus (on customers, suppliers, changing technologies, etc.) rather than an internal focus (interpersonal relations and development, rules, procedures, etc.).

general use of priorities to establish schedules. Using this approach in addition to priorities establishes multiple criteria for deciding what things you plan to do when. By identifying which types of things seem to go together and which do not, a self-managed process of job enrichment can accompany the more traditional time management task.

Your own orientation—relatively monochronic or relatively polychronic—will naturally make some of the preceding questions and issues easier to deal with than others, and it will also lead you to different ways to deal with them.[7]

Earlier in this article we discussed behaviors associated with monochronic and polychronic orientations, one of which was the individual's degree of flexibility in regard to plans and schedules. The time management fundamental of the daily To-Do list that identifies your activities and assigns priorities to them is a plan and a schedule. Given the association of polychronic orientations with greater flexibility toward plans and schedules, polychronic individuals may be more flexible in their approach to the To-Do list.

If you are relatively polychronic, you may find it more difficult giving an activity your undivided attention than will your monochronic counterpart. Conversely; if you are relatively monochronic, you may have more difficulty than your polychronic colleague grouping certain tasks together to be performed during the same time period; and the more diverse the activities, the more difficulty you are likely to have grouping them together.

First, they are likely to be less precise in scheduling completion times for tasks, if they even use them at all. Second, they should be more likely to modify the items on their lists (add, postpone, delete) as well as alter item priorities as the day proceeds; but this flexibility is neither a universal advantage nor a disadvantage. Flexibility in one situation may lead to the exploitation of an unanticipated opportunity, but in other situations it may lead to unproductive dithering. Third, the practice of using priorities to say no to lower priority requests, especially when the requested activities involve interaction with other people, should be more difficult for more polychronic people too.

Supervision and Coordination

Regardless of whether you are a first-line supervisor managing a single work group or a CEO managing multiple divisions or departments, the polychronicity issues described for individual time management have direct analogues at these higher levels. Which tasks and assignments do your people seem to be able to handle simultaneously (e.g., selling computers and teaching customers how to use them), and which do they have trouble handling if assigned together (e.g., selling computers and repairing them)? Which tasks do they like to handle simultaneously and which ones are better if given one at a time (e.g., taking inventory)? And which tasks might the organization be able to *learn* to handle simultaneously (e.g., designing new computers and repairing current models), giving it competitive advantages in any environment where time-based competition exists?

All of these issues imply the universal management activity of *delegation,* an act that can be influenced by your own monochronic/polychronic orientation as well as that of your subordinate.

Or consider the very monochronic boss. He is so insistent on a tightly planned schedule—everything

Although similarity between delegator's and subordinate's degree of polychronicity would seem to be the obvious route to harmony and successful delegation outcomes, the issue may be more complex than it appears at first glance. For example, an extremely polychronic boss may so enjoy the stimulation of multiple activities carried out simultaneously or in a short period that she fails to delegate enough tasks to subordinates. Not only would polychronic subordinates be potentially experiencing a too-monochronic environment for their own work satisfaction; but they would not be developing skills in a variety of activities which is a major benefit and purpose of delegation

has its time and only one thing at a time is scheduled—that he delegates almost everything to ensure his ability to be working on only one task at a time. The resulting avalanche of delegated tasks may overwhelm the constantly inundated subordinate, especially if the subordinate has a relatively monochronic orientation too. The subordinate in this case will gain very little in terms of skill enhancement from the delegated tasks and will probably feel continuously overwhelmed and miserable.

Overall, you need to recognize your own orientation and that of your subordinate because you must take *both* into account to successfully delegate over the long term. If you and your subordinates differ in orientation, do not consider such differences impediments. Such differences may actually be complementary and provide opportunities to improve the results of delegation in your department.

Cultural Diversity

". . . When people or groups with different [temporal] perspectives interact, conflicts often arise. Misunderstandings occur when intention and action are judged, by different participants, on different temporal scales. Values are attached to these scales. *The differences in temporal perspective often go unrecognized by the participants.* [Emphasis added] But the differing temporal scales have values associated with them nonetheless, and the temporally divergent actions lead to value inferences by the participants about each other."[8] Thus has James Jones succinctly described the *raison d'etre* for understanding temporal concepts such as monochronic/polychronic orientation when working with culturally diverse groups. To illustrate the problems that may occur if you do not understand these temporal differences, put yourself into the following situation.

> You are a sales representative for a U.S.-based company that is attempting to expand into overseas markets. As part of the expansion effort, you are travelling around the world to call on several potential customers. Your itinerary includes appointments in New York, Paris, Berlin, Tunis, and Seoul. You want to make a good impression on your firm's prospective clients in each location, but you are far from an expert on France and Germany, let alone Tunisia and South Korea. Thus, you are quite anxious about how people in these different cultures will react to your behavior, and you are equally concerned about your own abilities to attribute the correct meanings to the treatment you will receive from the French, Germans, Tunisians, and Koreans.
>
> That there will be language differences is obvious, but you were recently briefed that some of the greatest non-language difficulties in cross-cultural interactions are those arising from differences in beliefs, values, and behaviors concerning time. For example, what does it mean when a French manager keeps you waiting for 30 minutes after your scheduled appointment time? Does it mean the same thing that it means when an American or a Korean manager keeps you waiting? Similarly, should you end your appointment at the scheduled time if you have not covered everything you want to discuss, or should you attempt to continue your meeting even if you would be going beyond your scheduled time allotment? And should you try to keep going in Tunis, but not in Berlin?

Although you may not know the exact answers to the questions raised in the scenario, you have a competitive advantage over anyone who does not even know that there are questions, that there may be a difference in these matters between cultures, and that these differences are often crucial differences.

It is hackneyed now to expound on the increasingly diverse nature of the American workforce, let alone the greater diversity of the global economy. But if, as analysts such as Hall and Jones assert, the temporal components of culture are the most fundamental, recognizing and understanding those components, and hence the differences among cultures concerning them, becomes essential for productive cross-cultural management and interaction.

For example, when a relatively monochronic North American interacts with a more polychronic Latin American, misinterpretations and misattributions of behavior, if not friction and conflict, are likely to occur unless some attention has been paid to identifying and learning such differences in temporal behavior and norms. The situation may be even more complex in interactions with the Japanese who tend to be monochronic in their use of technology and in dealing with non-Japanese, but who are very polychronic in respect to most other matters. Similarly, misunderstandings may occur among major subcultures within the United States.[9] And monochronic/polychronic time use, however important is but one of many ways cultures may differ temporally. If people coming from different cultures and traditions understand these differences, or even that there may be differences, conflicts related to polychronicity and other temporal differences can be managed more effectively.

CONCLUSION

The more polychronically oriented among you have not only finished this article, but have also finished lunch or are about to change the subject of your conversation; the more monochronically oriented are about to begin lunch or will now make that phone call. Either way, you have learned about one of the subtler yet more profound ways individuals can differ from one another.

As we have seen, an understanding of the monochronic/polychronic continuum can lead to better self-management as well as better management of our organizations and our relationships with people from different cultures and traditions. Given the increasingly international nature of business and management, the strategic competitive advantages will be held by the individuals, companies, and nations who learn how to successfully manage cultural diversity. And temporal differences such as monochronic/polychronic orientations are among the most basic cultural differences to manage.

ENDNOTES

1. Edward T. Hall developed the concepts of monochronic and polychronic time and presented them most extensively in his book, *The Dance of Life: The Other Dimension of Time,* which was published in 1983 by Anchor Press. Additional material is provided in *Understanding Cultural Differences* by Edward T. Hall and Mildred Reed Hall, published in 1990 by Intercultural Press.
2. Some time writers (not all) such as James W. Gentry, Gary Ko, and Jeffrey J. Stoltman in "Measures of Personal Time Orientation," in *Time and Consumer Behavior,* eds. Jean-Charles Chebat and Van Venkatesan (Val Motin, Quebec, Canada: Universite du Quebec a Montreal, 1990) reserve the use of the word "orientation" to refer to an individual's relative emphasis on the past, present, or future. Throughout this article we have used "orientation" in its more traditional, more generic sense of establishing a location or position with respect to some phenomenon.
3. See Hall and Hall, *Understanding Cultural Differences*.
4. Kaufman, Lane, and Lindquist's research is reported in their article, "Exploring More Than 24 Hours a Day: A Preliminary Investigation of Polychronic Time Use," *Journal of Consumer Research,* 18 (1991), pp. 392–401. The

scale presented in Exhibit 2 produced an alpha reliability coefficient of 0.67 in their study.

5. Allen Bluedorn's study is reported in the working paper, "Time and the Competing Values Model of Culture: Adding the Fourth Dimension," which is available from him at the University of Missouri-Columbia. The scale in Exhibit 3 produced an alpha reliability coefficient of 0.74 in the bank sample, and he is currently involved in research on a large insurance company to see if his results will replicate.
6. Carol Kaufman, Paul Lane, and Jay Lindquist provide a much more extensive discussion of matching individual and organizational time styles and orientations in their article, "Time Congruity in the Organization: A Proposed/Quality of Life Framework," which is forthcoming in *The Journal of Business and Psychology*.
7. We would like to thank the following individuals who suggested some of the implications of MP orientation for individual time management: Kevin Adam, Barbara Braungardt, Greg Boivin, Steven Briggs, James Dawes, Matthew Harper, Mary Hass, Mike Ondracek, and Julie Witte.
8. The quotation is from page 27 of James M. Jones' article, "Cultural Differences in Temporal Perspectives," in J. E. McGrath, ed., *The Social Psychology of Time* (Newbury Park, CA: Sage Publications, 1988).
9. The relative orientations of North and Latin Americans are taken from Hall, *The Dance of Life*. The description of the Japanese is from Edward T. Hall and Mildred Reed Hall, *Hidden Differences: Doing Business With the Japanese,* which was published in 1987 by Anchor Press/Doubleday.

Part 1/Reading 3

European Competencies—Some Guidelines for Companies

Bruno LeBlanc

In 1991, a small group of European executives, all of whom were directors of human resources at an international, European or group level in their companies, joined up, with the present author, into a task force to identify the specific competencies required for companies to develop in Europe in the context of the Single Market. The task force was an off-shoot of a European club of companies. A major objective of the club was to help the member companies increase their understanding of the implications of the emerging Single Market on the development and management of their human resources.[1]

The task force met in Paris for eight one-day sessions and produced a number of conclusions and recommendations. The present text is a further development of those issues.

Source: *Journal of Management Development* 13, no. 2 (1994).

ORIGINS AND OBJECTIVES OF THE TASK FORCE

The task force was set up to help clarify what specific competencies companies and their managers need in order to respond successfully to the demands of the emerging Single European Market (SEM).

A number of member companies of the club felt that people talk a great deal about these competencies, but that they have never been clearly defined. Also, that they are not easily distinguishable from the more general set of skills and capabilities considered necessary for international development outside Europe. This was partly explained by the fact that many companies do not find it necessary to separate out their specific goals and objectives in Europe from their broader international ambitions.

We also wanted to distinguish between the individual skills needed by, say, expatriate managers, and the more collective corporate competencies required to develop and implement international strategies and policies. The ability of an international manager to operate effectively within a given foreign culture seemed to us distinct from his or her ability to manage pluri-national/pluri-cultural teams. And both of these abilities are different from a company's corporate ability to introduce and develop policies of staff recruitment on a European level, to integrate staff from different European countries, including into its domestic operations, or to develop new transnational modes of corporate organization (e.g. allocating Europewide product line management or other Europewide responsibility along with traditional country/national subsidiary responsibilities).

Task force members quickly realized that their companies had reached quite different stages of international and European development, and therefore had very different midterm priorities in this area. So we decided to develop a general framework to help characterize the different stages of European and international development. The framework would include tasks a company has to accomplish at each stage and the competencies needed to do this successfully. We saw this framework as a tool that could help companies identify where they were in the internationalization process and, subsequently, the specific range of competencies that were likely to be of greatest relevance to them.

STAGES IN THE ORGANIZATION PROCESS

Taking the companies represented in the task force as a working sample, we first identified three broad stages in the internationalization process. We found that each one also corresponds to a strategic choice of how to develop in Europe.

1. *"First landing" stage:* A national company with a strong national base expands its interests into Europe for the first time through a series of acquisitions in different European countries. The main focus of concern is to be successful in preparing, implementing and managing the "foreign" acquisitions.
2. *"Go native" stage:* A company which has become well-established in Europe through a network of branches and subsidiaries, in which each national subsidiary has gradually been granted autonomy for the day-to-day management of its operations and marketing activities. Human resource policies reinforce the percentage of national managers in each subsidiary: the expatriate general manager of the subsidiary is responsible for the medium and long-term career development of the high calibre members of his/her local staff.
3. *Integration stage:* A company which is truly European because it has manufacturing facilities and a commercial presence throughout Europe. It now considers that national boundaries must give way to the European perspective and seeks to organize and pursue its development on a continental rather than national basis. It gradually develops a pan-European strategy, within a global strategy, generates awareness of that policy within the company and finds practical ways of implementing it.[2]

DIFFERENTIATION AND INTEGRATION SKILLS

We identified two types of business and management skills as essential in these stages, although they vary in importance depending on the stage of European development a company is at. We called the first set, most relevant to the "landing stage" and "going native" stages, "differentiation skills," and the second set, essential to the "integration stage," "integration skills."

Foreign subsidiaries in the "first landing" and "go native" stages, for example, are very often involved only with the production and/or sale of goods and services locally, not with any export or re-export activities. These foreign subsidiaries are then viewed as so many local units of a "multi-domestic" company, rather than as fully integrated members of an international ensemble, in which *each* geographic territory can have international roles and responsibilities. They need to be sure their expatriate managers have the differentiation skills needed to adjust to a foreign environment.

Differentiation Skills

These skills are essential to successful "local" management, and include:

- Recognizing the diversity of Europe.
- Accepting differences between countries as a fact.
- Adjusting to these differences effectively.

They imply the following abilities to:

- Obtain and interpret information about foreign national contexts (local institutions, legislations, practices, market specificities, etc.).
- Inform, and communicate effectively with a foreign environment about the home company's policies.
- Negotiate contracts, partnerships, etc. in a foreign environment.
- Be accepted as a foreign representative of one's company abroad.
- Manage local operations and personnel abroad effectively.
- Tolerate and adjust to local conditions personally (tolerance of expatriation/foreign posting).
- Cope in the long term with a large variety of foreign contexts.

We considered that essential to this group of competencies is the corporate ability, and indeed the willingness, to *import* foreign practices and choices into the home environment of the company when this is a condition for success abroad. For example the ability to:

- Identify and accept adjustments to basic product specifications in order to meet the needs of the foreign market, and ability to persuade the company at home to make the necessary changes.
- Recruit foreign managers into both the foreign operations and the home environment, integrate them and manage their career development.

The "integration stage" involves setting up and promoting novel, complex, multilateral relationships among the different geographic units of the same company. These relationships can even include allocating strategic or developmental responsibilities to different—domestic or foreign—subsidiaries of the company. Indeed, the very notions of "domestic" and "foreign" units and systems tend to become irrelevant and counterproductive to achieving cohesive international development.

The ability to implement this type of development, which has been called "getting rid of the headquarters mentality" and "decomposing the centre" into equally important and legitimate co-operating territorial units,[3] obviously requires extensive changes of attitudes in the parent company as well as in its subsidiaries. It will be an important factor in the successful emergence of truly pan-European companies.

Integration Skills

These skills provide a company with the ability to build a European perspective and European policies from the diversity of national considerations and viewpoints. They include the ability to:

- View Europe as a single region, within which traditional (national) or new (subregional) differentiations must be accepted or developed (e.g. new market segmentations).
- Develop elements of a common framework for company strategies, policies and operations at a European level (e.g., ability to develop a common company culture).
- Build commonalities, at both company and functional levels (common procedures, product specifications, standards, policies, etc.) with a

view to achieving economies of scale or minimizing the cost of company development at a European level.

- Organize cooperation at a European level (e.g., ability to manage international/pluri-cultural teams and develop international projects).

Thus, a corporate skill that is essential in the process of European development and integration is for the parent company to accept that the best, or most realistic solutions at a European level, are not necessarily those which it has traditionally adopted in its national environment. This implies an ability to acknowledge that in a European perspective, each country's "home" practices are only a special case among other special cases, *and that this includes the head office.*

The task force members agreed that the skills most relevant to meeting the challenges of the emerging Single Market are integration skills, and that there is probably need for more work in this area. However, we believe that differentiation skills are very important to many companies, especially those in the first two stages of internationalization.

THE COMPETENCIES—STAGE BY STAGE

After having identified the different stages of European development and the types of skills needed, the task force looked more closely at the managerial and organizational competencies for each stage.

"First Landing"

For the first landing stage the task force was especially interested in the behavioural and general managerial qualities which managers would need to operate effectively in a foreign environment. We looked at behaviours (personal, interpersonal, managerial), which we believe can serve as a general check-list for the recruitment, guidance and evaluation of expatriate managers (see Exhibit 1).

All members of the task force agreed that the amount of cultural information and knowledge specific to a particular country, which a manager needs in order to adopt locally effective behaviours, should never be underestimated. Our recommendation is that companies organize exposure to the country or special preparation for their managers before the foreign assignments.

Our discussions revealed that, failing this, serious mistakes are likely despite the best of intentions. Task force members spoke of managers having difficulties interpreting local situations, events, and behaviours, as well as in responding to local expectations. Local ideas about proper behaviour and acceptable business and management practice could simply not be guessed at! The result was often failure to meet company objectives and, more generally, an inability to make the most of local business opportunities. Nor did these unprepared managers obtain the confidence of local employees or business partners.

Our group agreed that in order to learn to accept cultural differences between countries, a

EXHIBIT 1 Major Tasks of Company Managers during the Three Stages of European Development

Responsibility	First Landing	Go Native	Integration
Commercial	Open up new national market abroad	Increase market share Optimize results in national context	Develop Euro-brands Pricing policy in Single Market
Industrial	Build or acquire production facilities	Improve productivity and quality performance	Rationalize capacity across boundaries
Human resources	Recruit and train new teams Design compensation	Industrial relations Management development	Euro social legislation Pan-Euro IR Multi-cultural team building

manager has to consider him/herself as initially "blind and deaf" to local realities and insist on getting properly briefed. We also agreed that it takes time to develop this ability, and that it is possibly one of the most valuable characteristics of an experienced international manager. A manager who has performed well in his/her own home environment will not necessarily find it easy to cope with the intellectual and psychological adjustments necessary in a foreign context.

All this also meant that companies and, more specifically, human resource managers, with international, or European, ambitions, have the difficult responsibility of identifying, preparing and then supporting their expatriate managers. We decided it was also their role to promote attitudes of open-mindedness towards and knowledgeability about the cultures of the company's business partners abroad. This task was likely to become even more important as increasingly large proportions of people in companies became, directly or indirectly, involved in cross-border activities, if only for short periods of time.

Go Native Stage

In this stage, the general managers of foreign subsidiaries have larger areas of responsibility and their activities take on a more international dimension. Additional skills become necessary, for which they have not necessarily received specific training. For example:

- Management skills concerning career management of the better qualified, locally employed staff. This involves knowing how to identify those high caliber staff members capable for an international career, and building an international team of managers among the local staff.
- Analysis and reporting skills on such local factors as new opportunities for take-overs and mergers and the activities of their competitors.
- Product development skills: extending the product or service range locally to respond to, or anticipate, new local competition, by introducing innovations possibly developed by the company in its other territories of operation.

On the corporate level, this requires an increased ability to organize the systematic dissemination of information about international competitive trends and about its own new products and services to all its local managers, at home and abroad. This promotes fruitful cross-fertilization of different subsidiaries Europe-wide (or worldwide), even if the final objective is still a "multi-domestic" model and not a full international, or European, integration of its activities.

The Stage of Integration

Companies which pursue the integration strategy have to reconcile several objectives and sources of competitive advantage simultaneously, which are always partly contradictory. They are seeking to:

- Achieve the maximum benefits from economies of scale, and generate a unique capacity for innovation thanks to rationalizing and consolidating a number of their activities (e.g., R & D, product development, manufacturing, sourcing of materials, components, finance, etc.), on the one hand.
- Respond rapidly to local markets and situations in a way that matches more decentralized "local companies" on the other.
- Organize and foster the effective transfer of learning from any geographic point of the company to any other, so as to maximize the overall rate of innovation of the company in all its markets and operations.

There can be many reasons for engaging the integration process, for example to:

- Satisfy the needs of an emerging "European customer." For instance as automobile companies become increasingly international, it is virtually impossible to have different pricing policies on a national basis. In addition, the development of trans-European fleet operations within the Single Market will gradually lead to integration in the replacement market.

- Take full advantage of Single Market opportunities.
- Revitalize European operations, which may be old and entrenched in national traditions and need to be modernized and streamlined in order to face fierce worldwide competition.
- Organize or rationalize their European activities.
- Remain a player in Europe, the major "playing field" for most of their international business opportunities.

The members of our task force felt that the problems are more cultural and motivational than technical. The issues revolve around how to achieve the best result for Europe as a whole (the team) as opposed to what might appear best for a national manager (the individual player). The balancing act involves how to:

- Centralize some decision making without taking responsibility away from the national managers.
- Get the national managers in partnership with each other while still developing their competitive national spirit.
- Push a "European solution" while remaining sensitive to national culture, tradition, pride in performance, and local social legislation.

We agreed that a simple or rigid organizational answer will only defeat the business objectives of the company. These issues of centralization (Europeanization) versus decentralization ("localization") of decision making must be accepted as permanently live and uneasy ones, needing on-going flexibility and adaptation.

Most importantly, we stressed that the European identity can never be the private domain of the central team, but must be equally shared and developed by everyone in Europe. All general managers of the company have to learn how to learn from each other and develop a measure of "dual membership and loyalty." They have to be equally committed members of their national team and of a European/International group. This is a new and unusual mind-set requirement for many managers, and has sometimes been referred to as an ability to "hold the matrix (of the organization) in one's mind." It means constantly introducing European perspectives into their respective areas of responsibility (see Exhibit 1). This ability, central to success in the future development of European companies, does not easily cohabit with the more traditional notions of a single command structure.

This means that when it comes to real integration, European competencies of individual managers are not enough. The company needs to integrate European competencies at its different levels, and in its different areas of activity.

CONCLUSIONS—IMPLICATIONS FOR TRAINING AND DEVELOPMENT

Top management's responsibility in advocating and pushing through European goals and objectives and the role of the human resources function in developing the corresponding competencies are critical. The tasks include:

Recruitment

- Develop a European recruitment policy.
- Favour mobile, multilingual candidates.
- Develop selection procedures which identify European integration skills and behaviours.

Career Management

- Systematically build expatriate experience into career development programmes.
- Centralize career planning information.
- Give national personnel functions European responsibilities in this area.

Communication

- Communicate the European integration message.
- Explain the importance of mobility for the company to achieve its integration goal.

It is disconcerting that a number of surveys, carried out in different European countries in the last few years by professional organizations or consulting firms, show that in many companies, including large international ones, the personnel and human resources functions lag behind other management functions (such as sales, production, or finance), in developing a European perspective and agenda. The members felt that by implementing the following recommendations, human resources would better contribute to successful Europeanization:

1. The skills and capabilities requirements of companies differ according to the stage of European development. They also differ according to the mode of European development—ownership of foreign subsidiaries or alliances, partnerships, joint ventures, etc.
2. The task force found that there is a real need to develop training programmes focused around the following topics:
   - Discovering the diversity of a company's national environments (economic, social, cultural, etc.) and developing the ability to tolerate and take into account that diversity in fulfilling individual company responsibilities.
   - Understanding the meaning and implications of developing and managing from a (pan)-European perspective rather than on a nation-by-nation basis.
   - Organizing for transnational/Europe-wide work and cooperation: managing pluricultural teams, developing Euro-strategies and organizations.

   Training groups should include participants of different nationalities and teaching staff from different countries. This also holds for one-on-one or on-the-job programmes developed internally.
3. There is a clear need to redefine the organization of the human resources function within companies at a European level. Discussions between companies with similar development objectives would be useful in moving this process forward.

NOTES AND REFERENCES

1. Regular members of the task force included: Alan Duke (Michelin), Mike Donogan (Dalgety PLC), Michel Durier (Ciments Français), Carmelo Florez Cosio (Banco Bilbao & Vizcaya), JeanPierre de Hochepied (Banque Nationale de Paris). The present author, who chaired the discussions and wrote the final report, was also at that time European Director of a management school (EAP), with institutions in France, Germany, Spain and the UK.

   Several members of the task force contributed very valuable position papers, which provided the initial basis of the discussions. None of them, however, bears any responsibility for the present text, given that they have not had an opportunity to comment on it in any way. Nor can the viewpoints expressed here be taken to represent the policies of their companies in any way.
2. Notwithstanding the relevance of the model to our large organizations, we also recognize its limitations. Our companies have created or acquired their own operations abroad. As a result, our model does not consider the problems which can arise from attempts to develop and manage other types of close association with partners abroad (e.g. joint ventures, strategic alliances, etc.). Nor did we really consider the problems of companies developing their presence abroad through independent local distributors. This is an important limitation, since many medium- and small-size companies can only hope to expand quickly into other European markets on the basis of such co-operative arrangements.

   The ability to enter into and manage such arrangements effectively is crucial to their future European development. It is, of course, also important for larger companies forming joint ventures; the problems of properly managing such joint ventures and maintaining satisfactory relationships with one's foreign partner(s) can be formidable and a source of considerable frustration for many companies. Indeed, specialists working in this area have documented the fact that the rate of failure of cross-border joint ventures founded by European companies in Europe tends to be very high (over 60 percent after three years of life together). A better understanding of the specific skills and competencies of joint venture management will therefore be increasingly important as the European economies become more integrated.

3. Ohmae, K. *The Borderless World,* 1990.

Part 1/Case 1

The Road to Hell

John Baker, Chief Engineer of the Caribbean Bauxite Company of Barracania in the West Indies, was making his final preparations to leave the island. His promotion to production manager of Keso Mining Corporation near Winnipeg—one of Continental Ore's fast-expanding Canadian enterprises—had been announced a month before and now everything had been tidied up except the last vital interview with his successor, the able young Barracanian Matthew Rennalls. It was vital that this interview be a success and that Baker should leave his office uplifted and encouraged to face the challenge of his new job. A touch on the bell would have brought Rennalls walking into the room but Baker delayed the moment and gazed thoughtfully through the window considering just exactly what he was going to say and, more particularly, how he was going to say it.

John Baker, an English expatriate, was 45 years old and had served his 23 years with Continental Ore in many different places: in the Far East; several countries of Africa; Europe; and, for the last two years, in the West Indies. He hadn't cared much for his previous assignment in Hamburg and was delighted when the West Indian appointment came through. Climate was not the only attraction. Baker had always preferred working overseas (in what were termed the developing countries) because he felt he had an innate knack—better than most other expatriates working for Continental Ore—of knowing just how to get on with regional staff. Twenty-four hours in Barracania, however, soon made him realize that he would need all of this "innate knack" if he was to deal effectively with the problems in this field that now awaited him.

At his first interview with Hutchins, the production manager, the whole problem of Rennalls and his future was discussed. There and then it was made quite clear to Baker that one of his most important tasks would be the "grooming" of Rennalls as his successor. Hutchins had pointed out that, not only was Rennalls one of the brightest Barracanian prospects on the staff of Caribbean Bauxite—at London University he had taken first-class honors in the B.Sc. Engineering Degree—but, being the son of the Minister of Finance and Economic Planning, he also had no small political pull.

The company had been particularly pleased when Rennalls decided to work for them rather than for the government in which his father had such a prominent post. They ascribed his action to the effect of their vigorous and liberal regionalization program which, since the Second World War, had produced 18 Barracanians at mid-management level and given Caribbean Bauxite a good lead in this respect over all other international concerns operating in Barracania. The success of this timely regionalization policy has led to excellent relations with the government—a relationship that had been

Source: Prepared by Gareth Evans for Shell-BP Development Co. of Nigeria Ltd., Intercollegiate Case Clearinghouse, Soldiers Field, Boston, 01263.

given an added importance when Barracania, three years later, became independent, an occasion which encouraged a critical and challenging attitude toward the role foreign interests would have to play in the new Barracania. Hutchins had therefore little difficulty in convincing Baker that the successful career development of Rennalls was of the first importance.

The interview with Hutchins was now two years old and Baker, leaning back in his office chair, reviewed just how successful he had been in the "grooming" of Rennalls. What aspects of the latter's character had helped and what had hindered? What about his own personality? How had that helped or hindered? The first item to go on the credit side would, without question, be the ability of Rennalls to master the technical aspects of his job. From the start he had shown keenness and enthusiasm and had often impressed Baker with his ability in tackling new assignments and the constructive comments he invariably made in departmental discussions. He was popular with all ranks of Barracanian staff and had an ease of manner which stood him in good stead when dealing with his expatriate seniors. These were all assets, but what about the debit side?

First and foremost, there was his racial consciousness. His four years at London University had accentuated this feeling and made him sensitive to any sign of condescension on the part of expatriates. It may have been to give expression to this sentiment that, as soon as he returned home from London, he threw himself into politics on behalf of the United Action Party who were later to win the preindependence elections and provide the country with its first Prime Minister.

The ambitions of Rennalls—and he certainly was ambitious—did not, however, lie in politics for, staunch nationalist as he was, he saw that he could serve himself and his country best (for was not bauxite responsible for nearly half the value of Barracania's export trade?) by putting his engineering talent to the best use possible. On this account, Hutchins found that he had an unexpectedly easy task in persuading Rennalls to give up his political work before entering the production department as an assistant engineer.

It was, Baker knew, Rennalls's well-repressed sense of race consciousness which had prevented their relationship from being as close as it should have been. On the surface, nothing could have seemed more agreeable. Formality between the two men was at a minimum: Baker was delighted to find that his assistant shared his own peculiar "shaggy dog" sense of humor so that jokes were continually being exchanged; they entertained each other at their houses and often played tennis together—and yet the barrier remained invisible, indefinable, but ever present. The existence of this "screen" between them was a constant source of frustration to Baker since it indicated a weakness which he was loath to accept. If successful with all other nationalities, why not with Rennalls?

But at least he had managed to "break through" to Rennalls more successfully than any other expatriate. In fact, it was the young Barracanian's attitude—sometimes overbearing, sometimes cynical—toward other company expatriates that had been one of the subjects Baker had raised last year when he discussed Rennalls's staff report with him. He knew, too, that he would have to raise the same subject again in the forthcoming interview because Jackson, the senior draftsman, had complained only yesterday about the rudeness of Rennalls. With this thought in mind, Baker leaned forward and spoke into the intercom. "Would you come in Matt, please? I'd like a word with you," and later, "Do sit down," proffering the box, "have a cigarette." He paused while he held out his lighter and then went on.

"As you know, Matt, I'll be off to Canada in a few days' time, and before I go, I thought it would be useful if we could have a final chat together. It is indeed with some deference that I suggest I can be of help. You will shortly be sitting in this chair doing the job I am now doing, but I, on the other hand, am 10 years older, so perhaps you can accept the idea that I may be able to give you the benefit of my longer experience."

Baker saw Rennalls stiffen slightly in his chair as he made this point so added in explanation,

"You and I have attended enough company courses to remember those repeated requests by the personnel manager to tell people how they are getting on as often as the convenient moment arises and not just the automatic 'once a year' when, by regulation, staff reports have to be discussed."

Rennalls nodded his agreement, so Baker went on. "I shall always remember the last job performance discussion I had with my previous boss back in Germany. He used what he called the 'plus and minus' technique. His firm belief was that when a senior, by discussion, seeks to improve the work performance of his staff, his prime objective should be to make sure that the latter leaves the interview encouraged and inspired to improve. Any criticism must, therefore, be constructive and helpful. He said that one very good way to encourage a person—and I fully agree with him—is to tell him about his good points—the plus factors—as well as his weak ones—the minus factors—so I thought, Matt, it would be a good idea to run our discussion along these lines."

Rennalls offered no comment, so Baker continued: "Let me say, therefore, right away, that, as far as your own work performance is concerned, the plus far outweighs the minus. I have, for instance, been most impressed with the way you have adapted your considerable theoretical knowledge to master the practical techniques of your job—that ingenious method you used to get air down to the fifth-shaft level is a sufficient case in point—and at departmental meetings I have invariably found your comments well taken and helpful. In fact, you will be interested to know that only last week I reported to Mr. Hutchins that, from the technical point of view, he could not wish for a more able man to succeed to the position of chief engineer."

"That's very good indeed of you, John," cut in Rennalls with a smile of thanks. "My only worry now is how to live up to such a high recommendation."

"Of that I am quite sure," returned Baker, "especially if you can overcome the minus factor which I would like now to discuss with you. It is one which I have talked about before so I'll come straight to the point. I have noticed that you are more friendly and get on better with your fellow Barracanians than you do with Europeans. In point of fact, I had a complaint only yesterday from Mr. Jackson, who said you had been rude to him—and not for the first time either.

"There is, Matt, I am sure, no need for me to tell you how necessary it will be for you to get on well with expatriates because until the company has trained up sufficient people of your caliber, Europeans are bound to occupy senior positions here in Barracania. All this is vital to your future interests, so can I help you in any way?"

While Baker was speaking on this theme, Rennalls had sat tensed in his chair and it was some seconds before he replied. "It is quite extraordinary, isn't it, how one can convey an impression to others so at variance with what one intends? I can only assure you once again that my disputes with Jackson—and you may remember also Godson—have had nothing at all to do with the color of their skins. I promise you that if a Barracanian had behaved in an equally peremptory manner I would have reacted in precisely the same way. And again, if I may say it within these four walls, I am sure I am not the only one who has found Jackson and Godson difficult. I could mention the names of several expatriates who have felt the same. However, I am really sorry to have created this impression of not being able to get on with Europeans—it is an entirely false one—and I quite realize that I must do all I can to correct it as quickly as possible. On your last point, regarding Europeans holding senior positions in the Company for some time to come, I quite accept the situation. I know that Caribbean Bauxite—as they have been doing for many years now—will promote Barracanians as soon as their experience warrants it. And, finally, I would like to assure you, John—and my father thinks the same too—that I am very happy in my work here and hope to stay with the company for many years to come."

Rennalls had spoken earnestly and, although not convinced by what he had heard, Baker did not think he could pursue the matter further except to say, "All right, Matt, my impression *may* be wrong, but I would like to remind you about the truth of that old saying, 'What is important is not what is true but what is believed.' Let it rest at that."

But suddenly Baker knew that he didn't want to "let it rest at that." He was disappointed once again at not being able to "break through" to Rennalls and having yet again to listen to his bland denial that there was any racial prejudice in his makeup. Baker, who had intended ending the interview at this point, decided to try another tack.

"To return for a moment to the 'plus and minus technique' I was telling you about just now, there is another plus factor I forgot to mention. I would like to congratulate you not only on the caliber of your work but also on the ability you have shown in overcoming a challenge which I, as a European, have never had to meet.

"Continental Ore is, as you know, a typical commercial enterprise—admittedly a big one—which is a product of the economic and social environment of the United States and Western Europe. My ancestors have all been brought up in this environment for the past two or three hundred years and I have, therefore, been able to live in a world in which commerce (as we know it today) has been part and parcel of my being. It has not been something revolutionary and new which has suddenly entered my life. In your case," went on Baker, "the situation is different because you and your forebears have only had some 50 or 60 years' experience of this commercial environment. You have had to face the challenge of bridging the gap between 50 and two or three hundred years. Again, Matt, let me congratulate you—and people like you—once again on having so successfully overcome this particular hurdle. It is for this very reason that I think the outlook for Barracania—and particularly Caribbean Bauxite—is so bright."

Rennalls had listened intently and when Baker finished, replied, "Well, once again, John, I have to thank you for what you have said, and, for my part, I can only say that it is gratifying to know that my own personal effort has been so much appreciated. I hope that more people will soon come to think as you do."

There was a pause and, for a moment, Baker thought hopefully that he was about to achieve his long-awaited "breakthrough," but Rennalls merely smiled back. The barrier remained unbreached. There remained some five minutes' cheerful conversation about the contrast between the Caribbean and Canadian climate and whether the West Indies had any hope of beating England in the Fifth Test before Baker drew the interview to a close. Although he was as far as ever from knowing the real Rennalls, he was nevertheless glad that the interview had run along in this friendly manner and, particularly, that it had ended on such a cheerful note.

This feeling, however, lasted only until the following morning. Baker had some farewells to make, so he arrived at the office considerably later than usual. He had no sooner sat down at his desk than his secretary walked into the room with a worried frown on her face. Her words came fast. "When I arrived this morning I found Mr. Rennalls already waiting at my door. He seemed very angry and told me in quite a peremptory manner that he had a vital letter to dictate which must be sent off without any delay. He was so worked up that he couldn't keep still and kept pacing about the room, which is most unlike him. He wouldn't even wait to read what he had dictated. Just signed the page where he thought the letter would end. It has been distributed and your copy is in your 'in tray.' "

Puzzled and feeling vaguely uneasy, Baker opened the "Confidential" envelope and read the following letter:

> *From:* Assistant Engineer
> *To:* The Chief Engineer, Caribbean Bauxite Limited
>
> 14th August
>
> ASSESSMENT OF INTERVIEW BETWEEN MESSRS. BAKER AND RENNALLS
>
> It has always been my practice to respect the advice given me by seniors, so after our interview, I decided to give careful thought once again to its main points and so make sure that I had

understood all that had been said. As I promised you at the time, I had every intention of putting your advice to the best effect.

It was not, therefore, until I had sat down quietly in my home yesterday evening to consider the interview objectively that its main purport became clear. Only then did the full enormity of what you said dawn on me. The more I thought about it, the more convinced I was that I had hit upon the real truth—and the more furious I became. With a facility in the English language which I—a poor Barracanian—cannot hope to match, you had the audacity to insult me (and through me every Barracanian worth his salt) by claiming that our knowledge of modern living is only a paltry fifty years old whilst yours goes back 200–300 years. As if your materialistic commercial environment could possibly be compared with the spiritual values of our culture. I'll have you know that if much of what I saw in London is representative of your most boasted culture, I hope fervently that it will never come to Barracania. By what right do you have the effrontery to condescend to us? At heart, all you Europeans think us barbarians, or, as you say amongst yourselves, we are "just down from the trees."

Far into the night I discussed this matter with my father, and he is as disgusted as I. He agrees with me that any company whose senior staff think as you do is no place for any Barracanian proud of his culture and race—so much for all the company "clap-trap" and specious propaganda about regionalization and Barracania for the Barracanians.

I feel ashamed and betrayed. Please accept this letter as my resignation which I wish to become effective immediately.

c.c. Production Manager
Managing Director

Part 1/Case 2

Pacific-Western Oil: The Sembilan Plant

In February 2000, Jack Stevens, President of Pacific-Western Oil Inc.'s (Pac-West) Gas Division, had to decide whether or not he would recommend reducing production at the P.T. Sembilan (Sembilan) liquefied natural gas (LNG) plant. Pac-West Oil was one of the world's largest integrated oil and gas companies. The firm, headquartered in Denver, had been involved in international operations almost since its founding more than 90 years earlier. Pac-West was involved in exploration activities in every continent and had a strong presence in gas exploration and processing in Indonesia.

 This case was prepared by Professor Andrew Inkpen for the purpose of classroom discussion only, and not to indicate either effective or ineffective management. Various company and individual names, including Pacific-Western Oil, event, and other information are disguised.

The Sembilan LNG plant was located in the Indonesian province of Aceh and was jointly owned by Pac-West; Indonesia's state owned oil monopoly, Pertamina; and Samco, a Tokyo-based consortium. For more than a decade, the Indonesian military had been involved in an effort to suppress dissent in Aceh. Many Acehnese had been killed and, allegedly, tortured. In October 1999, a coalition of 17 Indonesian human rights groups issued a statement claiming that Pac-West and Sembilan were responsible for human rights abuses during the military operation in Aceh. In late 1999, secessionist guerrillas in Aceh made threats against foreign investors, hinting that a prime target would be the Sembilan liquefaction plant. Moreover, various human rights groups were pressuring Pac-West and other Aceh investors to take a stance against the Indonesian government in an effort to resolve the conflict. In December, Pac-West suspended its gas exploration activities in the troubled province.

According to Stevens:

> Sembilan is very important for the three partners and for the Aceh area. The three shareholders' ultimate decision on the future of the plant must be governed by economic and commercial considerations. Although we are certainly aware of the secessionist actions in Aceh, we cannot allow human rights groups to dictate the relationship Pac-West has with governments. As well, we cannot allow our business to be held hostage by terrorists. Our actions in Aceh are beyond reproach and we will continue to operate in a manner that is consistent with the goals of Pac-West shareholders.

INDONESIA'S NATURAL GAS AND OIL INDUSTRIES

Indonesia was one of the world's largest producers of natural gas, ranking sixth in total gas produced and 13th in proven reserves. The country's gas reserves were concentrated in several areas: the Arun field in Aceh, the Badak field in East Kalimantan, in smaller offshore fields of Java, the Kangean Block offshore East Java, a number of blocks in Irian Jaya, and the Natuna D-Alpha field, the largest in Southeast Asia. Despite its significant gas reserves and its position as the world's largest exporter of LNG, Indonesia still relied heavily on oil to supply about 60 percent of its energy needs. As Indonesia's oil production flattened in the mid-to-late 1990s, the country tried to shift towards using its natural gas resources for power generation. However, the domestic gas market was considered immature, and the country lacked a domestic network and pipeline infrastructure to provide widespread gas distribution.

Indonesia was also a major oil producer and the only Asian member of OPEC. Indonesia had proven oil reserves of about 5 billion barrels. Much of Indonesia's proven reserve base was located onshore. Central Sumatra was the country's largest oil-producing province. Other significant oil field development and production was located in accessible areas such as offshore northwestern Java, East Kalimantan, and the Natuna Sea. To meet its goal of increasing production and to deal with declining output, Indonesia was stepping up efforts to sign new oil exploration contracts.

Indonesia's oil and gas industries were controlled by P.N. Pertamina (Pertamina), a state-owned organization. Pertamina was formed in 1968 when the government combined two state-owned companies to form a single organization that controlled all oil and gas exploration, production, processing, marketing, and distribution activities in Indonesia. In Indonesia, 90 percent of oil and gas production operations were operated by foreign companies under production-sharing contracts that allowed the foreign company a profit after tax and cost recovery of about 15–35 percent on oil and 30–40 percent on gas. Under production-sharing contracts with Pertamina, Indonesia's largest gas producers included Arco, Mobil, Total, Unocal, and Vicol, as well as Pac-West. In 2000, Pertamina had about 30,000 employees.

Over the years, Pertamina had become a bloated and inefficient bureaucracy and, according to one report:

> . . . operated almost as a sovereignty unto itself, ignoring transparent business practices, often acting independently of any ministry, and increasingly taking on the role of a cash cow for then-President Suharto and his cronies. During the 32-year tenure of President Suharto, Pertamina awarded 159 contracts to companies linked to his family and cronies. These contracts were awarded without formal bidding or negotiation processes. . . . (Indonesian petroleum law dictated that every aspect of operation in the country was subject to approval by Pertamina's foreign contractor management body, Bppka. Dealing with the incomprehensible Bppka bureaucracy on simple matters, such as acquiring work permits for expatriate personnel, can take hours of filling in applications and months of waiting.[1]

[1] "Indonesia Considers Legislation That Would End Pertamina's 30-Year Petroleum Monopoly, *Oil & Gas Journal,* July 26, 1999, pp. 27–32.

percent. Samco was a Tokyo-based consortium of six Japanese companies: Nissho Iwai Corp., Chubu Electric Power Co., Kansai Electric Co., Nippon Steel Corp., Osaka Gas Co., and Kyushu Electric Power Co. Samco was a major customer of Sembilan and had long-term agreements for the purchase of Indonesian LNG.

Pac-West had been doing business in Indonesia for decades. The initial contract between Pac-West and the Indonesian government that would lead to the Sembilan plant was in 1965. This contract gave Pac-West exploration access to the rich oil and gas fields in the Lhokseumawe area, in north Aceh. The discovery of natural gas in 1971 resulted in the development of one of the world's richest onshore reserves of gas, estimated at 40 billion cubic meters. This gas field, named Arun, quickly became Indonesia's largest producing gas field (subsequently surpassed by the Natuna field) and the most important source of revenue for the Indonesian government. By the late 1980s, Aceh oil and gas reserves provided an estimated 11 percent of Indonesia's total exports. The Sembilan plant processed the gas for export. The plant, based in the village of Blang Lancang in North Aceh, was one of the largest LNG processing facilities in the world, P.T. Sembilan was one of two LNG plants operated by Pertamina.

Through various production-sharing contracts, Pac-West was a major producer of gas from the Arun field. Pac-West's investment in Sembilan was made through its wholly owned subsidiary in Indonesia, Pac-West Oil Indonesia. The joint venture agreement for Sembilan specified that Pertamina would be responsible for operational management of the plant. Pac-West's official role was mainly in a technical advisory capacity. The general manager of Sembilan, Umar, was a native of Java and was appointed by Pertamina. Five Pac-West expatriates were working in Sembilan and living in Aceh. Their primary responsibility was working closely with Pac-West Oil Indonesia and ensuring that Pac-West's investment was properly managed. Pac-West Oil Indonesia and Pac-West's global operations were a source for much of the technology in the plant. As well, Pac-West Oil Indonesia provided various advisory services in the finance, accounting, and human resource areas. In addition to the Pac-West expatriates working in Sembilan, Pac-West had a team of expatriates running Pac-West's gas exploration and production in the Arun field. About 70 percent of the Sembilan employees were Acehnese.

Production at the Sembilan plant had been declining for the past six years. Maximum production of 224 cargoes of LNG was reached in 1994 (a cargo has a capacity of 125,000 cubic meters of LNG). In 2000, Sembilan planned to produce 194 cargoes of LNG. This production represented 40 percent of Indonesia's LNG output. About 70 percent of the production would be shipped to Japan and 30 percent to South Korea. The plant generated about $350 million in annual revenue for Pac-West in 1999. In about 15 years it was expected that gas production would be depleted and production at Sembilan would stop.

UPGRADES IN THE ARUN GAS FIELD

The Arun field had been producing since 1977 and, within the oil and gas industry, was viewed as Pac-West's aging cash cow. The Arun field had been acquired relatively cheaply by Pac-West and was vastly profitable, accounting in recent years for at least 25 percent of Pac-West's net income according to industry estimates. With Arun maturing, it was critical for Pac-West to achieve both higher well deliverability in the gas field and greater efficiency in the LNG plant. Through 1998 and 1999, Pac-West had achieved a major technological breakthrough in obtaining higher well deliverability. Production had been maximized with the successful application of new drilling technology that allowed the gas to flow more freely.

HUMAN RIGHTS ISSUES IN ACEH

After the fall of Indonesian President Suharto in May 1998, after 32 years of rule, many allegations of corruption and human rights abuses by the former government surfaced. There was little agreement as to the number of people involved. The Indonesian Human Rights Commission (Komnas HAM) claimed it had evidence of 782 people killed by the military in Aceh, 368 cases of torture, and 168 disappearances. Other human rights groups in Aceh, however, contended that at least 3,000 people were killed, and they accused the national commission of being controlled by the military. The New York-based Human Rights Watch estimated that as many as 1,000 people were killed from 1989 to 1992 by the military and Free Aceh guerrillas. Other estimates were that 3,000 women were widowed because their husbands were killed or disappeared and that the number of children orphaned as a direct result of military activity was in the thousands.

A stream of witnesses came forward with tales of torture and other atrocities. A prison camp survivor's ordeal is described:[5]

> For six months he languished in a military prison camp in Aceh. One day Bintara, then the headman of a nearby village, was put inside a room whose walls were splattered with human blood and hair. During an interrogation that left him blind in one eye, Bintara claims that an Indonesian army officer whipped his scalp with a frayed cable, burned him with a match, and held live electric wires to his body.

Sembilan and Pac-West

According to various human rights and environmental groups, Pac-West had been a heavy burden on Acehnese communities that depended on agriculture and fish farming. The list of alleged abuses included land seizures with minimum compensation; explosions that destroyed farmland and villagers' homes; numerous oil and industrial spills into the rivers, sea, and bay; erosion of villagers' riverside gardens; and extreme noise pollution. In 1991, it was reported that around 60 percent of fisherfolks in traditional villages in the Lhokseumawe area were living below the poverty line, and were even close to starvation as a result of critically low catches over the previous few years. In 1992, villagers whose fields were flooded by liquid waste from a Pac-West operation filed a lawsuit against the company. The villagers lost. In December 1997, some 1,600 people had to leave their homes after eruptions from three natural gas wells spewed out tons of mud over their villages. Nine houses collapsed and almost 200 were damaged as a result.

In addition to alleged environmental abuses, Indonesian human rights organizations and government officials identified 12 mass graves in Aceh. One grave was located on Pertamina-owned land less than three miles from a Pac-West gas drilling site. Other suspected graves were in close proximity to Pac-West sites. Indonesian human rights groups alleged that Pac-West provided logistical support to the Indonesian army, including the lending of earth-moving equipment used to dig mass graves. Indonesian human rights groups were demanding that Pac-West and Sembilan apologize, pay compensation, and rehabilitate the victims of human rights abuses carried out by the military with the support of Pac-West and Pertamina. They also urged Amnesty International and Human Rights Watch to investigate Pac-West's finances, especially funding for military operations.

Both Pac-West and Pertamina executives denied allegations that they knew of any human rights abuses in the Aceh area. In November 1998, Pac-West's president met with the U.S. Ambassador to Indonesia in Jakarta and denied knowledge of any misuse of Pac-West equipment or facilities. In December, Joseph Watson, vice president for production and exploration of Pac-West Oil Indonesia, publicly disclaimed any knowledge of human rights abuses happening on or near Pac-West facilities. A Pertamina public relations executive echoed that response, saying, "Incidents connected to human rights violations were beyond Pertamina's and Pac-West's authority and knowledge." Pac-West acknowledged that it loaned the army excavators and supplied troops with food and fuel on occasion for three decades.

[5] M. Shari, P. Engardio, and S. Prasso, "What Did Mobil Know?" *Business Week*, December 28, 1998, pp. 68–75.

But the company insisted that Pac-West managers had no record that the army was using this help for anything but peaceful purposes. A Pac-West spokesman said:

> We were told the equipment was used for roads and other community projects. If facilities and equipment were used for any other purposes, we cannot be held responsible. We are aware that we were operating in the middle of a conflict but no reports on alleged mass graves and military abuses were ever brought forward to Pac-West's management in Indonesia.

As well, Pac-West said that all equipment and land was owned by Pertamina or leased from outside contractors. The Indonesian army, which was helping to excavate the graves, said that it regretted any suffering but denied that the deaths were caused by the army. Complicating matters was a December 1999 report in which one of the rebel leaders claimed that Sembilan had been willingly giving contributions to the movement. Sembilan did not respond to this report, which meant that if contributions were being made, it was not clear if they were a tax for protection or because Sembilan supported the rebel movement.

Various individuals argued that Pertamina and Pac-West had to know what was going on. A former Sembilan manager maintained that everybody in Aceh knew that massacres were taking place. A former Sembilan employee said that rumors of massacres and other atrocities near the Sembilan plant were frequently discussed in the workplace. A contractor said he told local Pac-West managers that he had found human body parts close to Pac-West sites, which he claimed was reported to a Pac-West heavy-equipment supervisor. The discovery was made on land owned by Pertamina and acquired for Pac-West to develop, subsequently named Skull Hill by local villagers. According to villagers, the stench of rotting flesh from Skull Hill could be smelled half a mile away.

The public spotlight on Pac-West emboldened some local communities to take action against Pac-West. One Aceh attorney, who intended to sue Pac-West on behalf of victims, said, "The crimes occurred over a long period of time. Pac-West cannot utter the words, 'We didn't know.'"

In December 1999 in North Aceh, four inhabitants took Pac-West Indonesia to court for 10 billion rupiah (about U.S. $1.33 million) for forcibly taking their land and a cemetery to use as an airfield. Pac-West's response was that the lawsuit had no implications for the U.S. parent company and that Pac-West could not have taken anything from anyone in Indonesia, because the company did not own anything in Indonesia, including land and vehicles.

Finally, according to Human Rights Watch, the international community (including business and government) should be pressing Indonesia to address three of the key underlying causes of the conflict: failure to prosecute past abuses; failure to reduce a hated military presence and diversion of locally produced revenues to Jakarta.

RECENT ACTIVITIES

By December 1999, local military and police commanders reported that GAM began stepping up its campaign of terror, which included a wave of arson incidents that destroyed government and school buildings, and the murder and kidnapping of many security personnel. The police reported that rebels had destroyed many government offices, police and military posts, and court facilities. As a consequence, the local economy was in dire straits, with massive bank withdrawals and prices spiraling upwards due to stockpiling and business closures. The city of Lhokseumawe was almost closed down, government services had virtually stopped, most businesses had ceased functioning, and dozens of schools, shops, and government offices had been burned down. A senior Indonesian military commander conceded that the army and government authorities had lost control of the territory and that the rebels had taken control.[6]

Indonesian President Abdurrahman Wahid's government indicated that it was looking for a

[6] T. Dodd, "Rebels Have Taken Control in Aceh: Military Leader," *Australian Financial Review*, December 2, 1999.

peaceful solution to the Aceh situation and was trying to win support by investigating past army atrocities in the province and prosecuting those responsible. The Government announced a five-member team of judges to try 20 military and civilian personnel accused of murdering 56 people at an Islamic boarding school in July 1999. The military was less conciliatory, with some officers renewing calls for the government to declare martial law. President Wahid had previously said he opposes martial law for Aceh.

Pac-West Suspends Gas Exploration Activities

In December Pac-West suspended exploration activities in the Arun gas field and evacuated 41 dependents of its expatriate staff and 150 dependents of its local staff to the North Sumatran capital of Medan. Umar, the general manager of Sembilan, was one of the few general managers who had remained in north Aceh. Production at existing fields in Aceh was expected to continue through 2018 as planned. As well, the Sembilan plant maintained its production despite the threat of possible attacks from the rebels.

To reassure foreign investors and Western governments, Aceh rebels had, so far, refrained from attacking Pac-West facilities. Pac-West, in a written statement, maintained once again that it had strict neutrality and had had no contact with the rebels. However, rebel leader Syafie indicated that the rebels might not hold off attacks much longer. According to Syafie, "Foreigners have taken a lot of wealth out of Aceh. If we have to fight our own struggle by ourselves, we cannot guarantee that their investments won't be damaged."[7] Rebel leaders were also threatening to attack ships passing through the Malacca Strait. Syafie maintained that if Jakarta refused to give in to rebel demands, then Indonesia must expect all-out war. According to a report in *Business Week,* the rebels faced huge odds. They would be up against at least 36,000 well-equipped, uniformed Police Mobile Brigade and army troops who had recently been moved into the province. Some Indonesian generals told diplomats that an offensive in Aceh could be more brutal than the recent East Timor bloodshed.[8]

A final issue that complicated matters for Pac-West was that apart from the very uncertain security situation, the economic prospects for the Arun gas field had been damaged by a slowdown in growth of electricity demand in Japan. Japanese electricity companies were the primary customers for the Sembilan LNG.

[7] M. Shari, "The Next East Timor? Aceh Wants Independence from Indonesia and Control of its Vast Gas Fields. That May Cause a Brutal War," *Business Week International Editions: Asian Business,* December 6, 1999.

[8] Ibid.

Part 1/ Exercise 1: The Culture Quiz

Objectives

- To stimulate awareness of cultural differences.
- To promote consideration of the impact of cultural differences in a global economy.
- To stimulate dialogue between domestic and international students.
- To explore issues raised by culturally diverse workforces.

Background

Few, if any, traditions and values are universally held. Many business dealings have succeeded or failed because of a manager's awareness or lack of understanding of the traditions and values of his/her foreign counterparts. With the world business community so closely intertwined and interdependent, it is critical that managers today become increasingly aware of the differences that exist.

How culturally aware are you? Try the questions below.

Instructions

Working alone or with a small group, answer the questions (without peeking at the answers). When you do look at the answers, be sure to read the explanations. If you are taking the quiz with students from other countries than your own, explore what the answer might be in your country and theirs.

1. In Japan, loudly slurping your soup is considered to be
   a. rude and obnoxious.
   b. a sign that you like the soup.
   c. okay at home but not in public.
   d. something only foreigners do.
2. In Korea, business leaders tend to
   a. encourage strong commitment to teamwork and cooperation.
   b. encourage competition among subordinates.
   c. discourage subordinates from reporting directly, preferring information to come through well-defined channels.
   d. encourage close relationships with their subordinates.
3. In Japan, virtually every kind of drink is sold in public vending machines except for
   a. beer.
   b. diet drinks with saccharin.
   c. already sweetened coffee.
   d. soft drinks from U.S. companies.
4. In Latin America, managers
   a. are most likely to hire members of their own families.
   b. consider hiring members of their own families to be inappropriate.
   c. stress the importance of hiring members of minority groups.
   d. usually hire more people than are actually needed to do a job.
5. In Ethiopia, when a woman opens the front door of her home, it means
   a. she is ready to receive guests for a meal.
   b. only family members may enter.
   c. religious spirits may move freely in and out of the home.
   d. she has agreed to have sex with any man who enters.

6. In Latin America, businesspeople
   a. consider it impolite to make eye contact while talking to one another.
   b. always wait until the other person is finished speaking before starting to speak.
   c. touch each other more than North Americans do under similar circumstances.
   d. avoid touching one another as it is considered an invasion of privacy.
7. The principal religion in Malaysia is
   a. Buddhism.
   b. Judaism.
   c. Christianity.
   d. Islam.
8. In Thailand
   a. it is common to see men walking along holding hands.
   b. it is common to see a man and a woman holding hands in public.
   c. it is rude for men and women to walk together.
   d. men and women traditionally kiss each other on meeting in the street.
9. When eating in India, it is appropriate to
   a. take food with your right hand and eat with your left.
   b. take food with your left hand and eat with your right.
   c. take food and eat it with your left hand.
   d. take food and eat it with your right hand.
10. Pointing your toes at someone in Thailand is
    a. a symbol of respect, much like the Japanese bow.
    b. considered rude even if it is done by accident.
    c. an invitation to dance.
    d. the standard public greeting.
11. American managers tend to base the performance appraisals of their subordinates on performance, while in Iran, managers are more likely to base their performance appraisals on
    a. religion.
    b. seniority.
    c. friendship.
    d. ability.
12. In China, the status of every business negotiation is
    a. reported daily in the press.
    b. private, and details are not discussed publicly.

c. subjected to scrutiny by a public tribunal on a regular basis.
d. directed by the elders of every commune.

13. When rewarding a Hispanic worker for a job well done, it is best not to
    a. praise him or her publicly.
    b. say "thank you."
    c. offer a raise.
    d. offer a promotion.
14. In some South American countries, it is considered normal and acceptable to show up for a social appointment
    a. 10 to 15 minutes early.
    b. 10 to 15 minutes late.
    c. 15 minutes to an hour late.
    d. one to two hours late.
15. In France, when friends talk to one another
    a. they generally stand about three feet apart.
    b. it is typical to shout.
    c. they stand closer to one another than Americans do.
    d. it is always with a third party present.
16. When giving flowers as gifts in Western Europe, be careful not to give
    a. tulips and jonquils.
    b. daisies and lilacs.
    c. chrysanthemums and calla lilies.
    d. lilacs and apple blossoms.
17. The appropriate gift-giving protocol for a male executive doing business in Saudi Arabia is to
    a. give a man a gift from you to his wife.
    b. present gifts to the wife or wives in person.
    c. give gifts only to the eldest wife.
    d. not give a gift to the wife at all.
18. If you want to give a necktie or a scarf to a Latin American. It is best to avoid the color
    a. red.
    b. purple.
    c. green.
    d. black.
19. The doors in German offices and homes are generally kept
    a. wide open to symbolize an acceptance and welcome of friends and strangers.

b. slightly ajar to suggest that people should knock before entering.
c. half-opened suggesting that some people are welcome and others are not.
d. tightly shut to preserve privacy and personal space.

20. In the area that was formerly West Germany, leaders who display charisma are
    a. not among the most desired.
    b. the ones most respected and sought after.
    c. invited frequently to serve on boards of cultural organizations.
    d. pushed to get involved in political activities.
21. American managers running business in Mexico have found that by increasing the salaries of Mexican workers, they
    a. increased the numbers of hours the workers were willing to work.
    b. enticed more workers to work night shifts.
    c. decreased the number of hours workers would agree to work.
    d. decreased production rates.
22. Chinese culture teaches people
    a. to seek psychiatric help for personal problems.
    b. to avoid conflict and internalize personal problems.
    c. to deal with conflict with immediate confrontation.
    d. to seek help from authorities whenever conflict arises.
23. One wedding gift that should not be given to a Chinese couple would be
    a. a jade bowl.
    b. a clock.
    c. a basket of oranges.
    d. shifts embroidered with dragon patterns.
24. In Venezuela, New Year's Eve is generally spent
    a. in quiet family gatherings.
    b. at wild neighborhood street parties.
    c. in restaurants with horns, hats, and live music and dancing.
    d. at pig roasts on the beach.
25. If you order "bubble and squeak" in a London pub, you will get
    a. two goldfish fried in olive oil.
    b. a very cold beer in a chilled glass, rather than the usual warm beer.
    c. Alka Seltzer and a glass of water.
    d. chopped cabbage and mashed potatoes fried together.
26. When a stranger in India wants to know what you do for a living and how much you earn, he will
    a. ask your guide.
    b. invite you to his home and, after getting to know you, will ask.

c. come over and ask you directly, without introduction.

d. respect your privacy above all.

27. When you feel you are being taken advantage of in a business exchange in Vietnam, it is important to

a. let the anger show in your face but not in your words.

b. say that you are angry, but keep your facial expression neutral.

c. not show any anger in any way.

d. end the business dealings immediately, and walk away.

28. When a taxi driver in India shakes his head from side to side, it probably means

a. he thinks your price is too high.

b. he isn't going in your direction.

c. he will take you where you want to go.

d. he doesn't understand what you're asking.

29. In England, holding your index and middle fingers up in a vee with the back of your hand facing another person is seen as

a. a gesture of peace.

b. a gesture of victory.

c. a signal that you want two of something.

d. a vulgar gesture.

Answers to the Culture Quiz

1. b. Slurping your soup or noodles in Japan is good manners in both public and private. It indicates enjoyment and appreciation of the quality. (Source: Eiji Kanno and Constance O'Keefe, *New Japan Solo.* Tokyo: Japan National Tourist Organization, 1990, p. 20.)

2. b. Korean managers use a "divide-and-rule" method of leadership that encourages competition among subordinates. They do this to ensure that they can exercise maximum control. In addition, they stay informed by having individuals report directly to them. This way, they can know more than anyone else. (Source: Richard M. Castaldi and Tjipyanto Soerjanto, "Contrasts in East Asian Management Practices." *The Journal of Management in Practice,* 2:1, 1990, pp. 25–27.)

3. b. Saccharine-sweetened drinks may not be sold in Japan by law. On the other hand, beer, a wide variety of Japanese and international soft drinks, and so forth, are widely available from vending machines along the streets and in buildings. You're supposed to be at least 18 to buy the alcoholic ones, however. (Source: Eiji Kanno and Constance O'Keefe, *New Japan Solo.* Tokyo: Japan National Tourist Organization, 1990, p. 20.)

4. a. Family is considered to be very important in Latin America, so managers are likely to hire their relatives more quickly than hiring strangers.

(Source: Nancy J. Adler, *International Dimensions of Organizational Behavior,* 2nd ed. Boston: PWS-Ken, 1991.)

5. d. The act, by a woman, of opening the front door, signifies that she has agreed to have sex with any man who enters. (Source: Adam Pertman, "Wandering No More," *Boston Globe Magazine,* June 30, 1991, p. 10 ff.)
6. c. Touching one another during business negotiations is common practice. (Source: Nancy J. Adler, *International Dimensions of Organizational Behavior,* 2nd ed. Boston: PWS-Kent, 1991.)
7. d. Approximately 45 percent of the people in Malaysia follow Islam, the country's "official" religion. (Source: Hans Johannes Hoefer, ed., *Malaysia.* Englewood Cliffs, NJ: Prentice Hall, 1984.)
8. a. Men holding hands is considered a sign of friendship. Public displays of affection between men and women, however, are unacceptable. (Source: William Warren, Star Black, and M.R. Priya Rangsit, eds., *Thailand.* Englewood Cliffs, NJ: Prentice Hall, 1985.)
9. d. In India, as in many Asian countries, toilet paper is not used. Instead, water and the left hand are used, after which the left hand is thoroughly cleaned. Still, the left hand is considered to be polluted and therefore inappropriate for use during eating or touching another person. (Source: Gitanjali Kolanad, *Culture Shock! India* Portland. OR: Graphic Arts Center Publishing Company, 1996, p. 117.)
10. b. This is especially an insult if it is done deliberately, since the feet are the lowest part of the body. (Source: William Warren, Star Black, and M.R. Priya Rangsit, eds., *Thailand.* Englewood Cliffs, NJ: Prentice Hall, 1985.)
11. c. Adler suggests that friendship is valued over task competence in Iran. (Source: Nancy J. Adler, *International Dimensions of Organizational Behavior.* 2nd ed. Boston: PWS-Kent, 1991.)
12. b. Public discussion of business dealings is considered inappropriate. Kaplan et al. report that, "The Chinese may even have used a premature announcement to extract better terms from executives," who were too embarrassed to admit that there was never really a contract. (Source: Frederic Kaplan, Julian Sobin, Arne de Keijzer. *The China Guidebook.* Boston: Houghton Mifflin, 1987.)
13. a. Public praise for Hispanics and Asians is generally embarrassing because modesty is an important cultural value. (Source: Jim Braham, "No, You Don't Manage Everyone the Same," *Industry Week,* February 6, 1989.) In Japan, being singled out for praise is also an embarrassment. A common saying in that country is, "The nail that sticks up gets hammered down."
14. d. Though being late is frowned upon in the United States, being late is not only accepted but expected in some South American countries. (Source: Lloyd S. Baird, James E. Post and John F. Mahon, *Management: Functions and Responsibilities.* New York: Harper & Row, 1990.)

15. c. Personal space in most European countries is much smaller than in the United States. Americans generally like at least two feet of space around themselves, while it is not unusual for Europeans to be virtually touching. (Source: Lloyd S. Baird, James E. Post, and John F. Mahon, *Management: Functions and Responsibilities.* New York: Harper & Row, 1990.)
16. c. Chrysanthemums and calla lilies are both associated with funerals. (Source: Theodore Fischer, *Pinnacle: International Issue,* March–April 1991, p. 4.)
17. d. In Arab cultures, it is considered inappropriate for wives to accept gifts or even attention from other men. (Source: Theodore Fischer, *Pinnacle: International Issue,* March–April 1991, p. 4.)
18. b. In Argentina and other Latin American countries, purple is associated with the serious fasting period of Lent. (Source: Theodore Fischer, *Pinnacle: International Issue,* March–April 1991, p. 4.)
19. d. Private space is considered so important in Germany that partitions are erected to separate people from one another. Privacy screens and walled gardens are the norm. (Source: Julius Fast, *Subtext: Making Body Language Work.* New York: Viking Penguin Books, 1991, p. 207.)
20. a. Though political leaders in the United States are increasingly selected on their ability to inspire, charisma is a suspect trait in what was West Germany, where Hitler's charisma is still associated with evil intent and harmful outcomes. (Source: Nancy J. Adler, *International Dimensions of Organizational Behavior.* 2nd ed., Boston: PWS-Kent, 1991, p. 149.)
21. c. Paying Mexican workers more means, in the eyes of the workers, that they can make the same amount of money in fewer hours and thus have more time for enjoying life. (Source: Nancy J. Adler, *International Dimensions of Organizational Behavior.* 2nd ed. Boston: PWS-Kent, 1991, pp. 30 and 159.)
22. b. Psychological therapy is not an accepted concept in China. In addition, communism has kept most Chinese from expressing opinions openly. (Source: James McGregor, "Burma Road Heroin Breeds Addicts, AIDS Along China's Border," *Wall Street Journal,* September 29, 1992, p. 1.)
23. b. The Chinese regard a clock as a bad omen because the word for clock, pronounced *chong,* is phonetically similar to another Chinese word that means the end. Jade is highly valued as symbolizing superior virtues, and oranges and dragon patterns are also auspicious symbols. (Source: Dr. Evelyn Lip, "Culture and Customs." *Silver Kris,* February 1994, p. 84.)
24. a. Venezuelans do the reverse of what most people in other countries do on Christmas and New Year's. On Christmas, they socialize. While fireworks are shot off on both nights, most restaurants are closed, and the streets are quiet. (Source: Tony Perrottet. ed., *Venezuela.* Boston: Houghton Mifflin. 1994, p. 97.)
25. d. Other popular pub food includes Bangers and Mash (sausages and mashed potatoes). Ploughman's lunch (bread, cheese, and pickled onions),

and Cottage pie (baked minced meat with onions and topped with mashed potatoes). (Source: Ravi Desai, ed., *Let's Go: The Budget Guide to Britain and Ireland.* London: Pan Books, 1990, p. 83.)

26. c. Indians are generally uninhibited about staring at strangers and asking them about personal details in their lives. Social distance and personal privacy are not common social conventions in India. (Source: Frank Kusy, *India.* The Globe Pequo Press: Chester, Conn., 1989, p. 27.)
27. c. Vernon Weitzel of the Australian National University advises never to show anger when dealing with Vietnamese officials or businesspeople. Showing anger causes you to lose face and is considered rude. Weitzel also recommends always smiling, not complaining or criticizing anyone, and not being inquisitive about personal matters. (Source: Daniel Robinson and Joe Cummings, *Vietnam, Laos & Cambodia.* Lonely Planet Publications: Australia, 1991, p. 96.)
28. c. What looks to Westerners like a refusal is really an Indian way of saying "yes." It can also express general agreement with what you're saying or suggest that an individual is interested in what you have to say. (Source: Gitanjali Kolanad, *Culture Shock! India.* Graphic Arts Center Publishing Company: Portland, Oregon, 1996, p. 114.)
29. d. In England, this simple hand gesture is considered vulgar and obscene. In a report to *The Boston Globe,* an American who had been working in London wrote, "I wish someone had told me before I emphatically explained to one of the draftsmen at work why I needed two complete sets of drawings." (Source: "Finger Gestures Can Spell Trouble," *The Berkshire Eagle:* January 26, 1997, p. E5.)

Part 1/ Exercise 2: The Owl: Cross-Cultural Sensitivity

Purpose

To experience and understand how cultural values influence behavior and relationships.

Group Size

Any number of groups of five to seven members.

Time Required

50 minutes or more.

Preparation Required

Roles to be assigned are: three X-ians and two Americans/Westerners per group. Larger classes may have one or two observers per group. X-ians must meet for about an hour prior to class to prepare for the role-playing. Americans/Westerners meet for no more than 15 minutes before the role-play begins.

Room Arrangement Requirements

Circles of five chairs set up in various places around the room.

Exercise Schedule

1. **Preparation (pre-class)**
   X-ians, Americans/Westerners, and observers' roles are assigned. Each group reads only its role sheet. Observers read both role sheets.

	Unit Time	*Total Time*
2. **Role-play, Part 1**	**15 min**	**15 min**
X-ians take their places in groups of chairs and wait for the American/Western couple to arrive. Then the conversation begins.		
3. **Time out**	**5 min**	**20 min**
The instructor signals time up and the American/Western couple leaves the room while X-ians remain.		
4. **Role-play, Part 2**	**25 min**	**25 min**
The Americans/Westerners return and make their request. X-ians give a "yes" or "no" reply.		
5. **Class discussion**	**25+ min**	**50 min**
The instructor will lead a discussion on the exercise covering the following areas:		

a. Which groups got a "yes"? Which ones got a "no"?
b. What were the reasons for the "success" or "failure"?
c. What did the Americans/Westerners understand about Culture X?
d. How does this exercise relate to stereotyping?

Role for "The Owl"

Briefing 1: To be read ONLY by the Americans/Westerners

You are two Americans/Westerners, male and female, both of you well-known journalists.

Both of you have master's degrees in journalism from recognized schools, and have spent several years in international travel and reporting on political, cultural, and artistic subjects in a number of countries.

Never at a loss to detect a possible "story," you are pleased to encounter three people in a restaurant in Athens whom you have met once before briefly. You do not remember their names, but do remember that they are from Country X, a rather exotic and unusual place not often visited by foreigners. Country X is one of those places in the world about which there are more legends than facts. It is known, however, to be a society with highly developed arts, literature, and gardens (which are apparently some kind of art form), with an atmosphere of being inaccessible and not too interested in getting into the world tourism business. One of the intriguing things about which speculation sometimes appears in the Sunday Supplements is the X-ian Queen's Garden Festival, which takes place apparently once a year, and which no one has ever visited or photographed. To do so, especially to be the first, would be a true journalistic "coup."

In this exercise, you will approach the X-ians at their restaurant table and ask to join them. Talk with them for about 15 minutes. Then, find a pretext and leave the table for two or three minutes and decide together what would be the best way to approach your real subject: Can you get permission to observe the next Queen's Garden Festival and do a story with pictures?

Try not to let your conversation run on too long. After you return from your two or three minutes of conferring, make your request to the X-ians. You will get a "yes" or "no" answer. At that point, the exercise is over, and you then excuse yourselves again and leave.

Role for "The Owl"

Briefing 2: To be read ONLY by X-ians

You are a member of Country X, an ancient land of high culture which has, in the course of the centuries, tended to develop along somewhat isolationist lines. X-ians have a deep and complete acceptance of a way of life that no outside influence has altered in any appreciable way for many years due to the sense of perfection and harmony of life that each X-ian derives from her/his culture.

In Country X, women are the natural leaders, administrators, heads of households, principal artistic creators, owners of wealth through whom inheritance functions, and rulers of the state. Men rarely work outside the home—where they keep house, cook, mind children, etc.—and then only in menial positions where heavy labor is required. Among X-ian women, education is important, with a high percentage going on to the university level. Among men, there is little interest and no encouragement to go beyond basic literacy. In all respects, women know themselves to be superior to men, and are acknowledged to be superior by the men, both in individual attitudes and as expressed institutionally. There is a well-known expression, for example, which goes, "Don't send a man on a woman's errand."

Knowing much of the outside world—and rendered somewhat uncomfortable by what they know of male-female relationships in many other countries—X-ians have tended to withdraw into themselves. In Country X, marriage is between two women, forming what is known as the Bond. The two women (the Bond) then may wish to receive jointly a man into their household, for purposes of creating children, for tending the home, etc. Two women in the Bond are equal in all respects, jointly agree in all decisions, and mutually have responsibility for a man, should he be affiliated with them. Relating to a Bond, a man is legally regarded as an entity, having protection from the Bond. The man is considered "cherished" by the Bond. The women are "married"; his relationship is to the Bond, whereby he is "cherished." A state of being "cherished" is considered very desirable among men.

The artistic powers of X-ian women are famous, particularly in having developed the design and care of gardens into a unique art form. In Country X, the

Queen's Garden is open once a year on her birthday to the women of the country (no men allowed) in celebration of the natural processes of growth and rebirth. No foreigners have been able, so far, to observe this Queen's Garden Festival, though there is no law to the contrary that would prevent it from happening.

X-ians share with some cultures of the world a marked discomfort with prolonged eye contact. They, of course, look at another person with brief, polite glances when they are in conversation, but do not hold another person's eyes with their own. In Country X, one is very careful not to "stare," since it is very impolite, and considered to be the worst kind of aggressiveness.

You are an X-ian Bond, Ms. Alef and Ms. Beh, with your Cherished Man Peh. Ms. Alef holds an important position in the Ministry of Foreign Affairs as Directress of Cultural Affairs. Ms. Beh holds a position, also in the Ministry of Foreign Affairs, as Special Assistant to the Minister. Both women are distantly related to the Queen. Cherished Man Peh has been taken along by the two women of the Bond on one of their official trips outside Country X. The three of you are now in a restaurant in Athens, and have been spotted by an American/Western couple whom you have met once before but do not know very well.

When speaking with the Americans/Westerners, you must limit your vocabulary to words of only one or two syllables. The purposes for this are: (1) your native language is that of Country X, and thus it is quite natural for you to be limited in your command of English, and (2) by making you conscious of your language, it is an easy way to prevent a use of vocabulary and concepts that people rarely use except as sociologists and anthropologists.

This American/Western couple will attempt to gain your help in getting permission to observe the next Queen's Garden Festival. They will talk with you for about 15 minutes. At that time, on some pretext, the American/Western couple will excuse themselves for a few minutes, then return to the three of you. At that time they will ask you for your help.

You must decide whether to say "yes" or "no." Basically, you should decide "yes" if, in your judgment, the Americans/Westerners have shown cultural sensitivity to what X-ians like. This means looking for and considering three main things:

1. The American/Western woman must be the one asking for permission, and she must ask the X-ian Bond (not Peh). The men in the role play (both the American/Western man and Peh) must not be involved in the request.
2. You must decide how thoughtful the Americans/Westerners have been about your limitations in use of English. They should not just rattle on when it is obvious by your speech that you may not understand them very well. If they show sensitivity in this, it will be one factor toward saying "yes."
3. The Americans/Westerners must also show sensitivity to your customs in eye contact. If they continue to "stare" at you during the conversation (and the request), then your answer would be "no."

Part 1/ Exercise 3: The East-West Game (Emperor's Pot)

Purpose

To explore dynamics of cross-cultural interactions when one group wants something from the other.

Group Size

An even number of groups with 10 to 19 people in each group.

Time Required

One class period of 90 minutes, or two class periods of 50 minutes each.

Exercise Schedule

	Unit Time	Total Time
1. **Groups form**	**5 min**	**5 min**

Students are assigned a group, either "West" or "East." If the class is large enough to have more than one East/West group, each East group is paired with a West group. Within each group, role assignments are made. Participants within each group decide who will play which role.

	Unit Time	Total Time
2. **Groups prepare**	**30+ min**	**35 min**

Groups discuss what their culture and behaviors will be like and they practice various interactions. This part may be done the class before, or assigned as a group project for outside class.

	Unit Time	Total Time
3. **Role play**	**20 min**	**55 min**

A delegation from the East visits the West group, while simultaneously a delegation from the West visits the East group.

	Unit Time	Total Time
4. **Debrief**	**20+ min**	**75 min**

Instructor leads a discussion on what occurred. What was it like to play a part in your culture? How different was it from your own culture? How well did the West group do in asking the favor of the East group? Were members sensitive to cultural differences? How can cultural insensitivity get in the way of business negotiations?

East Group

Instructions: Situational note: The West will be sending delegates to your culture to find a way to persuade you to relinquish the national treasure. You will observe their style and make notes on your assumptions, based on the way they behave and talk in your culture during the Phase II negotiations. At the same time (Phase II), a delegation of your people will visit the West (to their embassy, let's assume), where their officials will try to persuade some of your people on their home ground.

Only to Be Read By the East Group

Your group represents an ancient Eastern culture. You are poor but proud.

Source: Donald Batchelder, "The Emperor's Pot," from *Experiential Activities for Intercultural Learning,* Volume 1, edited by H. Ned Seelye.

A highly treasured artifact is in your possession. It dates back to A.D. 400. It is a national treasure, in fact THE national treasure. Culturally, you cannot give it up under any circumstances. The other side (West) wants it. Their delegation is under strong pressure from the West to return with the artifact. (You may wish to identify one key behavior that, if demonstrated by the West, will win the treasure.)

However, it is in the nature of your culture to be very agreeable, to be very polite, to try always to answer affirmatively, whether you mean it or not. You never come out directly with a flat negative in the negotiations. You never tell their delegates that they will never get the artifact. You dissemble if necessary; you seem to agree and go along, because culturally you never wish to offend.

Culturally, it is important for you to avoid strong, direct eye contact with the delegates or visitors from the West. You look them in the eye, but never a fixed, hard, direct look of any duration.

Typically, even your negotiating team (your delegates to the West) will practice the ancient art of dealing through a third party. Example: One of you has the role of Chief Spokesman (a senior scholar and official), who may act as one of your delegates to the West, or may negotiate at home with the delegates from the West. And while he will do some of the talking in either situation, he will defer often to one of the other members of your group, allowing that other person to carry on some, if not most, of the conversation with the other side. The West will not understand what dynamic is operating here, but that is its problem.

Your list of cultural values follows. A staff person in your room will help with questions during the Phase I planned period. During that time, you will sort out your various roles, decide who and how many should go to the West, and who should remain in the East to negotiate with the West delegates. You should decide on your approach in Phase II.

Roles:

Chief Spokesman
Minister of Education and Culture
Security officer
Political officer
Protocol officer
Information officer
Recorder: to list all the assumptions and values of other side
Astrologer/timekeeper: to keep each phase exactly on schedule
GOD (Group Organizational Director): organizer of the East
Most Honored Grandmother
Spokesman #2 (most honored)
Advisers: all others

East Cultural Traits (These are the items governing your behavior)

WE Performance is conditioned by role in society, as opposed to individualism.

OVERLAPPING EGO Expectations/morality of community more important than those of the individual. Individual always in social role. Cannot do anything to conflict with group.

FORM Outward form is of major importance. Manners extremely important. Must participate in activities considered important by group, even if one disagrees.

PASSIVISM Confucian idea of endurance is prevalent. Acceptance of fate, life, etc.

PRAGMATISM Confucian or community morality is applied to social issues and problems.

PROGRESS Change is both negative and positive. Technical change is necessary; social change is bad.

NATURE Nature is considered beautiful/good. Conformity to rule of nature considered good.

EFFICIENCY Considered less important than higher values such as form, face, conformity to custom.

TIME Not precisely measured, except in business/science. Time not a primary consideration. The present, not the future, is given utmost consideration.

HISTORY History is seen as a cyclical phenomenon rather than a linear progression.

HUMILITY Humility is related to social status. One never takes advantage of one's rank. One must always defer to another of higher social rank, must always try to appear humble. Persons of higher rank must even make attempts to defer to and honor special inferiors.

DISCIPLINE Pre-school: much freedom, little discipline. School age: discipline begins at home and from teachers in school. Considered a function of the school system at this age rather than a function of the parents. Adulthood: many responsibilities to family and community. Old age: great freedom, shown much respect, considered to have great wisdom.

MOBILITY Important because of duties to family and community.

WORK A means to an end rather than an end in itself. Has no value in itself.

MONEY Saving for the sake of saving is seldom considered a virtue. Some attitudes toward money involve concepts of "face"—i.e., spending an entire year's income for elaborate ceremonies, wedding, etc., to increase or maintain family prestige. Price is regarded as an index of quality.

AGE Great reverence for age, which means wisdom, authority, great perspective on life. Age brings certain privileges (a girl is not a woman until married and a mother). One always uses honorific terms when addressing an elder.

EDUCATION A discipline and a reflection on family prestige. Means of raising whole family's status. Confucian idea of education to create the true gentleman.

AUTHORITY Confucian values stress the cautions. Obedience to authority. Individual rights bear little consideration. Vertically organized hierarchy regarded as most orderly and harmonious.

MORAL SUPERIORITY A moral smugness stemming from a conviction that East's people are a special people with a set of values and conditions that have made them unique.

West Group

Instructions: Situational note: When told, you will send your delegation to the East. While they are negotiating, this team will also be recording observations about the ways in which the Easterners operate and making assumptions about them. At the same time, a delegation from the East will come to the West. During the visit you will try to persuade their delegates about the merits of your case for the artifact and to simultaneously find out from them what the price might be, etc.

Only to Be Read By the West Group

Your group represents an authentic Western culture. You are rich and powerful.

A highly treasured artifact is in the possession of the East. It is a most valuable part of their ancient cultural heritage, and although they are a poor country, they will be reluctant to give it up. You have been assigned the task, however, by your national museum, with strong urging from the government itself, to obtain this national treasure for your country's own collection. Money is no problem.

Thus your task is to assemble a delegation and send it to the East. You decide who goes, how many, what approach they should use . . . as long as the approach appears to you to be compatible with the cultural values listed on the next page. In plainest terms, your group has been sent to the East to bring back the artifact at whatever cost, although you cannot come right out and say this during negotiations with the East. They are known as shrewd traders, even though they are relatively poor, but you have been instructed to operate on the supposition that "every man has his price."

Culturally, it is important for you and your negotiators to figure out which approaches are acceptable on the other side, in order to smooth out the path to your objective of gaining the artifact. At the same time, you should try to stay within the value system defined for you in the next pages.

Typically, you tend to be success-oriented, hardworking and efficient; you plan ahead and try to use time productively.

Your list of cultural values follows. There will be a staff person in your room to help with questions during the Phase I planning period. During that time, you will sort out, consult the value list, decide who and how many should go to the East to negotiate, and who and how many should remain in the West to negotiate with their delegation.

Roles:

Curator of National Museum (expert on Oriental Art)
Diplomatic officer
Public Relations person
CIA agent posing as an Area Studies specialist
Journalist

Chief of your task group (forceful administrator)
Recorder: to list all assumptions, values, etc., of other side
Timekeeper: to keep each phase of exercise exactly on schedule
GOD (Group Organizational Director): organizer of the West
Advisers: all others

West Cultural Traits (These are the items governing your role behavior)

"I" Ego-centrism

INDIVIDUALISM Self-reliance. Initiative expected from each. Status achieved by own efforts. Economic, social, political equal opportunity regarded as right of individual. Achievement is good and requires competitiveness. Competition expected.

SOCIAL CONFORMITY Outward conformity to opinions of others and to dress has certain value in society.

ACTIVISM Being active, especially in face of uncertainty, is a virtue. Achievement and goal-oriented activities are strongly stressed.

PRAGMATISM Practical ingenuity applied to social as well as materialistic problems.

PROGRESS Change in itself is good. Improvement, especially personal, is a duty. Man is supposed to work in order to control nature.

EFFICIENCY Applies not only to machines but to social organizations and personalities.

TIME Precisely measured and must be used productively and efficiently.

HISTORY Seen as a linear progression.

AGGRESSIVENESS Ambition, competition, self-assertiveness to achieve success are emphasized. High status, once attained, does not confer right to treat lower class as "inferior." Personal excelling is good, but empty boasts and boasting about success are bad.

DISCIPLINE Pre-school: discipline from parents. School age: increased freedom and responsibility. Adulthood: time of greatest freedom. Old age: considered less productive, less active, an epoch of incapability, less freedom.

MOBILITY Great physical and social mobility seen as good.

WORK Valued as an end in itself. Personal effort and energy output are good. Laziness is bad.

MONEY An economic tool, plus a yardstick for social status, influence, and power satisfaction.

YOUTH Highly valued. Old people wish they were young again. Elders feel outmoded by rapid change.

EDUCATION Means to an end. Reflections on family prestige. Means to attain skill, money, status.

AUTHORITY Rules/law generally obeyed, but don't like to be ordered to obey. Authorities must not infringe upon individual rights. Mild suspicion of authority.

MORAL SUPERIORITY A moral smugness stemming from convictions that West's people are a special people with a set of values and conditions that have made them unique.

Part 1/ Exercise 4: Pros and Cons of Free Trade

Purpose
To examine the arguments for and against free trade.

Group Size
Initially conduct an individual analysis of the pro and con free trade arguments. Form into class groups of five to eight people to share ideas, concerns, and opinions.

Time Required
A few hours individually and 50-minute in class group discussion.

Exercise
The events of the past 100 years demonstrate how global trade can provide benefits and some costs to countries. Trade can be a stimulus for economic growth and improving the quality of life of citizens. However, some critics of free, unbalanced trade present various counterarguments.

Prepare a two-page, pro and con free trade paper that will be used in group discussions. In the paper present some of the benefits for a nation when markets are open. Also present some of the disadvantages that a nation can face by having a free and open trade policy. What special interest groups stand out in opposing free trade? Why?

Source: Robert Konopaske and John M. Ivancevich ©.

Part 1/Internet Exercise 1: World-Class Brands

Purpose
To learn about world-class brands that have developed over the years.

Group Size
To be performed individually.

Time Required
Approximately two hours.

Other
Internet connection and search engine needed.

Exercise
As more globalization occurs there is often little information in one country about brands that are important in other countries. That is, citizens of other nations have little idea what kind of automobiles are popular in Russia or India. This Internet assignment is intended to explore the world's different preferences

for products. Listed below are a number of countries and products. Determine by using **Internet resources** the most popular brands for these products in the countries indicated. Also, where is the parent company headquarters for each of these products located?

Country	Product	Most Popular Brand	Origin of Parent Company
Russia	Automobile		
China	Computers (PCs)		
United Kingdom	DVD player		
Poland	Hiking boots		
India	Disposable diapers		
France	Children's toys		
Malaysia	Bicycle		
Canada	Toothpaste		
Kenya	Aspirin		
Mexico	Televisions		
Spain	Golf clubs		
Japan	Baseball bats		

Source: Robert Konopaske and John M. Ivancevich ©.

Part Two

Management and Organizational Behavior in a Global Environment

Chapter Three

Global Social Responsibility and Ethical Decision Making

Learning Objectives

After completing Chapter 3, you should be able to:

- Describe the difference between proactive and reactionary social responsibility.
- Define ethics and explain the crucial role it plays in conducting global business transactions.
- Evaluate how a nation's culture and customs influence the ethical decision making a manager performs each day.
- Describe a global manager's responsibility to address host-country issues involving human rights.
- Describe the "moral commonsense" rules that can guide a manager's ethical decision making.
- Explain what is meant by the notion that good ethics equals good business.

What the Public Expects!

The interest and motivation for socially responsible behavior and ethical behavior has become a front-page issue again and again. Questions about greed, fraud, conflicts of interest, excessive profit, pollution, greenhouse effect, and many others have raised the awareness of organizations that are moving across borders to transact operations.

In the United Kingdom, Anita Roddick's Body Shop, a soaps and cosmetics firm, promoted the image that all of the products sold were made from natural products. The company became a champion and role model for environmentalists. Unfortunately, the firm was accused of misleading the public and not following an environmental friendly program. Anita Roddick let down the public, and her image, the firm's market, and its stock value have tumbled because of a number of ethical impropriety allegations. A segment of the public was attracted to The Body Shop's natural products and its leader and then became disappointed.

The public expects responsible and ethical behavior from managers and leaders, but it is not able to accurately assess these qualities. An allegation such as the one made against The Body Shop was enough to bring about a consumer backlash even though it has not been proven. Unethical behavior accusations can cost a firm for many years.

China has been accused of human rights violations that carry over into the workplace. As China grows and its economy becomes more global, more attention must be paid to what partners, consumers, and potential alliance participants think about how workers are treated. Responsible firms willing to treat workers fairly and with respect are considered more reliable and better than firms that are not paying attention to human rights. A poor image domestically can be projected across oceans and borders and chill any business transaction or negotiations. Not complying with acceptable human rights treatment can stall or derail some of China's plans to become a dominant global player.

The stakeholders outside the organization receive impressions or become a judge and jury regarding ethical or unethical behavior. Companies around the world have to pay attention to the stakeholder's perception. In the case of the Body Shop and Chinese organizations, the public is observing and listening. The economic impact of an irate or skeptical public can result in less consumer traffic, as well as other negative reactions.

Source: Brian Cruver, *Anatomy of Greed: The Unshredded Truth from an Enron Insider* (New York: Avalon Publishing Group, 2002), and Anita Roddick, *Business As Unusual,* (New York: Thorsons, 2002).

As part of their global responsibilities, managers must deal with the issues of social responsibility and ethics as illustrated in the opening vignette. Anita Roddick found that allegations of unethical public relations could damage her image and business. The Chinese economic machine can be slowed significantly if human rights is not given a higher priority. The relationship between companies and their host countries requires paying careful attention to social responsibilities and ethical behavior. Ethics is concerned with decisions and behavior at the individual level, while social responsibility decisions are much more encompassing and reflect the companies' stance on a number of environmental and host-country issues. This chapter will examine the social responsibility and ethical behavior of companies and managers who are operating across different borders.

SOCIAL RESPONSIBILITY

The notion of global social responsibility suggests that global firms must concern themselves with the social, economic, and human asset effects of their decision making. Pressing issues regarding social responsibility have for the last decade focused on poverty, the lack of opportunity in developing countries, human rights, consumer welfare, the environment, and employee safety and health.[1] One view is that it is in a transnational firm's interest to use coachable talents, expertise, capital, and power to actively solve host-country problems such as protecting human rights or protecting the health of employees and the communities in which it is doing business.

Another viewpoint is that transnational firms by entering a host country, hiring and compensating employees, and investing capital are already addressing local social, human asset, and economics problems. A harsher viewpoint is that the only responsibility of a transnational firm is to earn a profit within the confines of the host-country's laws. The firm is responsible to its owners and to operate globally it should operate within the structure of the law.[2]

Exhibit 3.1 presents a corporate model addressing level of involvement, social issues, and responsibility categories. Three specific responsibilities are portrayed—ethical, legal, and economic. The responsiveness to these responsibilities ranges from being proactive to reactionary. Only a few social issues are presented in Exhibit 3.1 because this is only a representative sample.

Transnational companies have a responsibility to employees, customers, and owners, all of which are considered **internal beneficiaries** of responsible management. The responsive categories shown in Exhibit 3.1 indicate that a company can be proactive, accommodating, or reactionary.

The external beneficiaries of socially responsible behavior are of two types—general and specific.

Specific External Beneficiaries

Modern societies around the world consist of a number of diverse special-interest groups working to further the well-being of their members. These groups often represent well-defined populations seeking to redress historical grievances: racial and ethnic minorities, women, the handicapped, and the aged. They pursue their interests by bringing political and popular opinion to bear on actions. Some groups succeed in having laws implemented that motivate companies to support their efforts.[3] For example, equal employment opportunity and affirmative action legislation obligates corporations to recruit, hire, and develop women and members of minority groups. The fundamental contention of these groups is that they have been discriminated against in the past and that corporations have played major roles in this discrimination. Thus, transnational firms must take some responsibility to erase the vestiges of prior discrimination and to create programs of equal access to employment opportunities and economic advancement.

Actions involving specific **external beneficiaries** can be obligatory, reactive, or responsive. The transnational firm can be judged irresponsible, both socially and

EXHIBIT 3.1 A Three-Dimensional Model of Corporate Social Responsibility

Source: Adapted from original three-dimensional model, A.B. Carroll, "A Three-Dimensional Conceptual Model of Corporate Performance," *Academy of Management Review* 4 (1979), pp. 497–505.

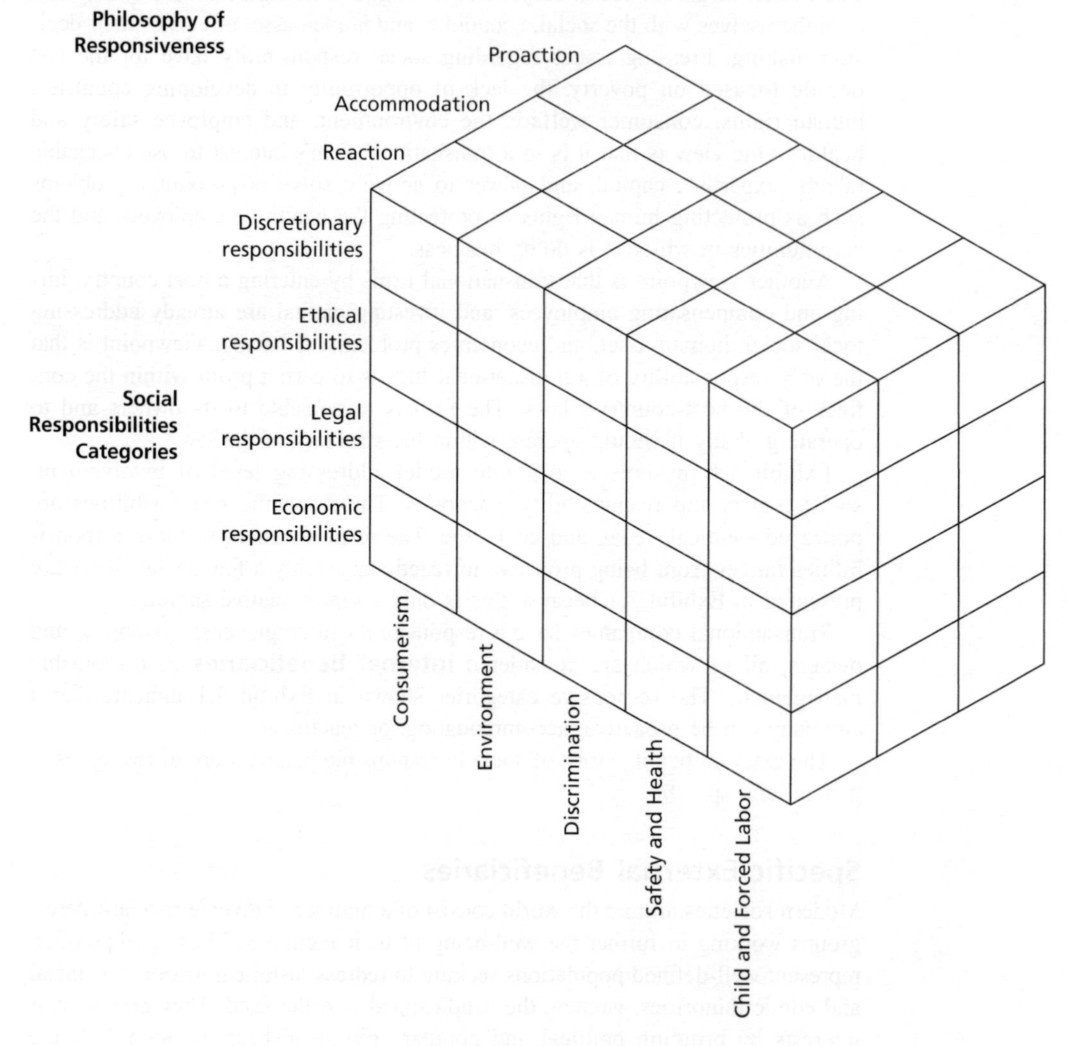

legally, if it violates host-country laws. But beyond minimal compliance, a corporation has considerable latitude in its implementation of socially beneficial activities. How rapidly it fills its managerial ranks with a group that represents the diversity of a host country's population is largely a matter of discretion as long as good faith can be demonstrated. A company can be deemed socially reactive if it goes beyond the letter of the law in implementing such actions. Socially responsive behavior not only seeks solutions to immediate problems but also attempts to go to the very heart of the causes. Such behavior could include creating programs to train the chronically unemployed and initiating career development programs for a diverse mix of host-country citizens. When such efforts are not prompted by any specific law or pressure, they are clearly socially responsive.

The most important characteristic of these actions—whether they are obligatory, reactive, or responsive—is that the economic, social, and political well-being of a specific group—and, hence, of all society—is enhanced through the corporation's efforts.

General External Beneficiaries

Programs involving general external beneficiaries often are considered to be socially responsible because they elicit company efforts to solve or prevent general social problems in a society. Companies have launched efforts to solve or prevent environmental or ecological problems such as water, air, and noise pollution, and waste and radiation disposal. **Stakeholder management devices (SMDs)** are mechanisms through which organizations respond to stakeholder concerns.[4] Research suggests that a firm's SMDs affect the perceived moral climates in the firm and affect managers' expectations about the consequences of good corporate social performance, but they do not affect organization members' attitudes about corporate social responsibility.[5]

The notion that a firm must balance the competing claims of multiple stakeholders in order to sustain their necessary cooperation goes back to the 1930s. The stakeholder concept is the subject of considerable scholarly research and theorizing. Stakeholder management devices provide a means for a firm to meet its responsibilities to various stakeholders. Some examples of SMDs are ethics committees on the board of directors, public affairs offices, written **codes of ethics,** corporate sponsorship of community functions, and employee newsletters. Given that socially responsive organizations establish such formal structures, processes, and procedures to address the concerns of external stakeholders, most SMDs have an external focus. However, the initial impact of SMDs in an organization must be internal, if they are to constrain the behavior of organization members and, thereby, shape the way the firm conducts its business. Because stakeholders define the individuals and groups to whom the firm must be responsible and responsive, stakeholders are central to the very concept of corporate social performance, which has been defined as a business organization's configuration of principles of social responsibility, process of social responsiveness, and policies, programs, and observable outcomes as they relate to the firm's societal relationships.

Novo Nordisk's approach to stakeholder responsibility is presented in the accompanying Global Focus.

Even though the focus of SMDs is primarily external, they impose internal constraints on organization members in their dealings with external stakeholders. Organizational effectiveness and survival require dependable behavior on the part of organization members. In pursuit of dependable behavior, the organization establishes (1) formal controls and structures, (2) rewards or instrumental satisfactions, and/or (3) internalized values. SMDs may serve in each of these ways as motivation for organization members to strive for and/or comply with the level of corporate social performance desired by top management.

Global Focus Novo Nordisk's Stakeholder Approach

Novo Nordisk, a health care transnational company in Denmark, is the world's leading producer of insulin. The manufacturer's other health care products include human growth hormones and drugs to treat hemophilia and menopause.

Novo Nordisk is dedicated to what it refers to as the Triple Bottom Line (TBL) approach to sustainability. This involves balancing social and environmental responsibility with economic success.

TBL and sustainability are driven by Novo Nordisk's Stakeholder Relations unit. The company reports annually on its performance and new targets for the TBL. The process of gathering data, tracking performance against targets, and setting new targets is the responsibility of Stakeholder Relations. A number of environmental, socio-economic and economic reports on the company's sustainability metrics are made public.

Novo Nordisk is determined to be profitable and also to be humanitarian. For example, the Stakeholder Relations group has been working on developing a sustainable business model that will work in six different developing countries. Making insulin available in poor countries at a reasonable price is the challenge. This is a long-term project, but is a model for other institutions that are humanitarian and also profitable.

Novo Nordisk believes that diabetes will double over the next decade and it will do so primarily in the less developed, poorer countries that need the most help and creative ways of treating the disease. Access to diabetes care is a life or death issue that Novo Nordisk believes is worth all of its concern and effort.

TBL has become so embedded in the company's culture that new recruits and employees are proud to be working for such a socially and morally responsible firm. Top managers are committed to the TBL approach because they consider responsibility, humanitarian support, and the future success of Novo Nordisk as part of management and employee duties.

Source: Adapted from "Novo Nordisk: Integrating CSR into Business Operations," Business For Social Responsibility, November 20, 2002, www.bar.org/print/printthispage.cfm.

Transnationals have considerable freedom in the area of social responsibility. They can choose which specific problems to become involved with, or they can choose not to become involved at all. But business leaders recognize the growing importance of issues such as the condition of the environment.

When companies engage in behavior that cannot be related, except remotely, to their primary economic and legal responsibilities, they do so in an atmosphere of controversy.

TRANSNATIONAL RESPONSIBILITY REGARDING HUMAN RIGHTS

Human rights are basic standards of treatment for all people, regardless of nationality, gender, race, economic status, or religion.[6] These standards include the avoidance of child labor in global operations, nonparticipation in a country's action that results in depriving citizens of civil liberties, and avoidance of using forced labor to produce products or services. Many countries have adopted the universal Declaration of Human Rights, the most widely recognized human rights benchmark.

Companies can avoid legal challenges to their global operations by following human rights principles, as contained in international law. Environmental factors have elevated the importance of human rights responsibilities for those conducting global business. Privatization, technological advances, increased information technology, globalization, and the rise of stakeholder groups have combined to create concern for human rights.

Global human rights groups such as Amnesty International have focused attention on the responsibility of companies to incorporate operating standards that do not violate human rights.[7] Because of the increased attention, human and labor abuses are publicized, and company violators are pointed out. Religious, shareholder, consumer, environmental, and student groups request strict standards and policies from global organizations. Some of these groups even submit reports of audited behavior regarding such human rights issues as labor conditions, environmental contamination, substandard wages, sweatshop working conditions, and mistreatment of employees.

Forced labor is considered a violation of human rights because a person is performing work involuntarily or under threat of a penalty. This type of human rights violation occurs at varying rates in different parts of the world. Forced labor has been alleged in China, Burma, and Saipan.[8] For example, in Saipan migrant workers have been forced to sign labor contracts prohibiting them from resigning their jobs for a specified length of time. In the United States, the use of prison labor to produce goods is considered a human rights violation.

Chinese political dissidents filed a $1.2 billion lawsuit accusing Adidas-Selomon AG of using slave labor in China to make World Cup soccer balls.[9] The complaint on behalf of former and current prisoners of a work camp in Shanghai charged that individuals were coerced into making Adidas soccer balls under inhuman working conditions. Adidas management conceded that unauthorized subcontracting of the production may have taken place. The company temporarily suspended soccer ball orders from China, established a full-time human rights department, and announced plans to centralize all Chinese production in one location under the guidance and oversight of a human rights management team.

Thai workers in an overseas El Monte garment factory were awarded $1.2 million to settle a lawsuit. The lawsuit accused the company of holding workers in indentured servitude, which is a human rights and legal violation.[10]

A number of organizational efforts and programs have been initiated to illustrate that companies accept the social responsibility to avoid human rights violations.[11]

- Reebok and Nike have established centralized stitching centers in Pakistan to ensure that this work is not outsourced where violations can't be determined.
- Rugmark, a private, voluntary certification program, uses monitoring that includes surprise inspections of employees, working conditions, and human rights policies. Until this program was implemented, bonded child labor was extensively used to produce carpets in India, Pakistan, and Nepal.
- California and Massachusetts legislators have banned imports that used forced labor, convict labor, or child labor.

Understanding the negative image, legal, and moral consequences of human rights abuse is the first step for transnational company managers in taking on responsibility to treat everyone fairly, honestly, and correctly. Establishing company human rights policies is another proactive and socially responsible step. The communication of the company's policy and position on human rights to employees, partners, customers, and other stakeholders also illustrates how the firm views and treats human assets. Training managers and monitoring compliance are proactive steps transnational companies should seriously consider.

There is no one way or best way for any transnational firm to address social responsibility or human rights. However, a growing number of firms have recognized the importance and benefits of being socially responsible. The experiences of leading firms such as Co-operative Bank in the United Kingdom, Natura cosmetics in Brazil, and Xerox combined with empirical research demonstrate that social responsibility has a positive impact on goodwill, brand and name image, and performance.[12]

BUSINESS ETHICS

The meaning of business ethics is difficult to pin down. Responses received from managers and nonmanagers asked for a one-sentence definition of business ethics include the following:

- "Ethics means complying with law."
- "Ethics is a guide to my feelings for making a distinction between right and wrong."
- "Ethics reflects my religious beliefs and faith."

Being ethical is not following the law. Laws can deviate from what is considered ethical. Feelings frequently deviate from what is ethical. Ethics should not be confined to religion since being ethical then would apply only to religious persons.

The diversity of these definitions, expert opinions, and logic suggests that business ethics is two things. First, it refers to standards of right and wrong. Second, ethics refers to the development of one's own ethical standards. Establishing a standard of conduct, belief, values, and sensitivity is what ethics means to people, communities, and institutions.

The proper role of the transnational corporation has reemerged as a topic of political debate. The contract between business and global societies had evolved from the traditional view that economic growth is the source of all progress to one holding forth an organizational imperative to work for social as well as economic improvement. This latter, expanded meaning of corporate social responsibility includes an implicit, informal social contract between the corporation and its employees. But this informal social contract is now breaking apart under the stress of economic transformations.

Many writers are talking about a new social contract between businesses and employees. This new contract will not guarantee lifetime employment for a job well done. However, it will offer employees new responsibilities, new benefits, and new power. Many of today's most effective organizations involve employees in every facet of the business. Managers are consulting employees on everything from strategic insights to feedback on the managers' performance. Such practices would have been unheard of even 20 years ago.

For their part, employees are benefiting from new compensation schemes such as stock options and gain sharing. These types of compensation systems draw employees into the heart of the business and tie their rewards to its success. A growing number of companies have used stock option plans as a reward. At high-tech companies, the value of options has often dwarfed earnings and even revenue. As Silicon Valley lost some of its luster after 2001, firms reacted to the down market by granting more stock options at lower prices.[13] Some critics claim, and research suggests, that a large percentage of stock options actually go to the top executives. At Oracle and Siebel Systems, two giant high-tech firms, more than 30 percent of the options are held by the highest-paid executives. Is this practice fair, ethical, and responsible?[14] Should boards of directors be allowing the few to own so much? These questions are and should be asked so that the cost and impact of options is presented in the light of day.

MANAGERIAL ETHICS

The word **ethics** commonly refers to principles of behavior that distinguish between what is good, bad, right, and wrong. Ethics are used by global managers as guidelines in making decisions that affect employees, the organization, consumers, and other parties.[15] The importance of ethics increases in proportion to the consequences of the outcome of a decision or behavior. As a manager's actions become more consequential for others, the more important are the ethics of that manager. The role and state of ethics in businesses continue to be a concern among managers and the public. Modern ethical issues are becoming more complex. They involve global transactions and cash flows, as well as individuals from vastly different cultural backgrounds.

A 100-year relationship between Ford Motor Company and Firestone/Bridgestone Tires highlights the complexity of ethics, the law, and global transactions. The U.S. Congress in 2000 became involved in a controversy after more than 100 deaths were linked to faulty auto tires. In 1997 Ford received reports of tread separations on its SUV Explorers in Saudi Arabia. Also, in 1998 State Farm Insurance notified the federal government about tread failures. At Ford's direction, Firestone/Bridgestone developed a tire in 1999 for countries with hot climates and rough roads.[16]

Who is responsible for the deaths (now estimated to be over 200) attributed to the tires? Ford CEO Jacques Nasser (now the ex-CEO) stated it was a tire problem. Firestone, however, pointed an accusatory finger at Ford and called the problem a vehicle design issue. Complaints, lawsuits, and congressional probes in the United States placed this issue in the headlines. There were calls for criminal charges against managers in both companies.

Evidence is unfolding that Ford and Firestone managers knew about the tire tread problems for nearly a decade. Lawmakers are examining the possibility of filing second-degree murder charges against managers who withheld information on defective products (tires or vehicles) that caused deaths. The long-term damage to careers, company image, and business is certain to be significant. As the Ford-Firestone charges and countercharges continue, the concept of ethical behavior will be raised again and again.

Business ethics continues to be a topic of concern because businesses are realizing that ethical misconduct by management can be extremely costly for the company and society as a whole. For example, sweatshop labor, once a low-profile issue, took center stage because of allegations that some clothing endorsed by TV personality Kathie Lee Gifford and sold by Wal-Mart stores had been manufactured under grueling conditions. Sensing an opportunity, human rights groups and labor unions stepped up their marketing efforts to reverse the situation. The Union of Needle Trades Industrial & Textile Employees, for example, ran ads that encouraged consumers who believe in human rights, fair wages, and ending child labor to "wear what they believe."[17]

Despite the seeming appropriateness of national policies on sweatshop labor, it's a controversial proposition. For example, some critics suggest that while a national government task force's code of business conduct may be appropriate for rich nations such as the United States, it's misapplied in Indonesia, Pakistan, Vietnam, and other countries that are the targets of the code. The poor in these countries send children to work because families desperately need their meager earnings. It's a hard life for children, but appalling poverty forces the whole family to struggle with malnutrition, poor health care, and dismal economic prospects.

Determining what is ethical is often difficult. In some situations, the task is easy. For example, accepting bribes from a supplier is clearly unethical as is falsifying records or dishonest advertising in promoting a product. However, business situations are often more complex. Every day, managers face ethical questions that have no easy answers. What, for example, is a "fair" profit? What is a "just" price for a product? How "honest" should a company be with the press?

Because of the complex ethics of a business situation, managers sometimes differ in their views of what actions are ethical. Currently, several ethical issues are being debated in the business environment. For example, managers are grappling with the ethics of employee surveillance (monitoring computer work and telephones to measure employee productivity) and with the ethical questions of conducting polygraph tests of job applicants.

Because the ethics of managerial decision making are often complex and managers often disagree on what comprises an ethical decision, two subjects are particularly relevant: (1) the basis that the individual manager can use in determining which alternative to choose in a decision-making situation; and (2) what organizations can do to ensure that managers follow ethical standards in their decision making.

Exhibit 3.2 presents a concise ethics test that can be completed to simply illustrate how difficult it is to determine the "right" ethical choices.

EXHIBIT 3.2 Ethics Quiz

Source: Adapted from Lowell G. Rein, "Is Your (Ethical) Slippage Showing?" *Personnel Journal,* September 1980.

Indicate the degree to which you agree or disagree with each statement.

Strongly Disagree –0– –1– –2– –3– Strongly Agree

Statement	–0–	–1–	–2–	–3–
1. Employees should not expect to inform on their peers for wrongdoings.	☐	☐	☐	☐
2. There are times when a manager must overlook contract and safety violations in order to get on with the job.	☐	☐	☐	☐
3. It is not always possible to keep accurate expense account records; therefore, it is sometimes necessary to give approximate figures.	☐	☐	☐	☐
4. There are times when it is necessary to withhold embarrassing information from one's superior.	☐	☐	☐	☐
5. We should do what our managers suggest, though we may have doubts about it being the right thing to do.	☐	☐	☐	☐
6. It is sometimes necessary to conduct personal business on company time.	☐	☐	☐	☐
7. Sometimes it is good psychology to set goals somewhat above normal if it will help to obtain a greater effort from the sales force.	☐	☐	☐	☐
8. I would quote a "hopeful" shipping date in order to get an order.	☐	☐	☐	☐
9. It is proper to use the company 800 line for personal calls as long as it's not in company use.	☐	☐	☐	☐
10. Management must be goal oriented; therefore, the end justifies the means.	☐	☐	☐	☐
11. If it takes heavy entertainment and twisting a bit of company policy to win a large contract, I would authorize it.	☐	☐	☐	☐
12. Exceptions to company policy and procedures are a way of life.	☐	☐	☐	☐
13. Inventory controls should be designed to report "underages" rather than "overages" in goods received.	☐	☐	☐	☐
14. Occasional use of the company's copier for personal or community activities is acceptable.	☐	☐	☐	☐
15. Taking home company property (pens, tape, paper, etc.) for personal use is an accepted fringe benefit.	☐	☐	☐	☐

If your score is:

0 Prepare for canonization ceremony
1–5 Bishop material
6–10 High ethical values
11–15 Good ethical values
16–25 Average ethical values
26–35 Need moral development
36–44 Slipping fast
45 Leave valuables with warden

GLOBALIZATION AND ETHICS

Questions about the ethical justification of human activity have occupied philosophers for centuries.[18] Whether Laotse, Confucius, Augustine, or Thomas of Aquinas, *they all have comparable concepts of what is good and bad human behavior and what constitutes sensible human existence.* Those wishing to discover suitable working principles can refer to Immanuel Kant, Max Weber, or Hans Jonas. *No one today can claim that there are no interesting impulses for appropriate ethical reflection.* However, anyone who examines the current social and environmental situation in the world is likely to be disappointed about the influence that the accumulated moral-philosophical wisdom is having in practice.

Over the past 30 years, the ethical perspective has been moving more and more to the forefront of managerial debate and concern. Every significant profession and every institution that thinks anything of itself has its "something ethics" to proclaim—environmental ethics, media ethics, research ethics, and even corporate ethics. The latter has recently, along with environmental ethics, gained the public's attention. Many national and international books, seminars, symposia, professorships, ethics networks, and journals are exclusively devoted to business ethics.

Why is there such an enthusiasm and interest in ethics? Has there been a fundamental shift in social value systems and has the "worth" of ethical argument increased as a result? When traditional ways of life and institutions are no longer taken for granted, philosophical ethics, guided by the idea of sensible human life, seeks generally valid arguments about good and just behavior in a methodical way. If social change were to move in the direction of higher morals, then all social groups and institutions—including business enterprises—would be faced with new legitimization demands. Economic performance alone is no longer enough to give businesses legitimacy. Noneconomic demands (e.g., the sustainable fulfillment of social and environmental responsibility in industrialized and developing countries) have been increasing their significance over the past two decades.

Or does the new interest in ethical debate stem from a publicly perceived violation of old "unspoken grounds for legitimization"? Is ethical thought so in demand because existing morals are in such dire straits? There is at least the suspicion that those who talk a lot about ethics may be on a rather shaky moral footing themselves and are using ethical alibis to appease a critical public. Looking over what has passed for "market economy" in many Eastern European countries following the demise of communism, one almost finds oneself agreeing with this argument.[19]

Philosophical reflection is without doubt a fulfilling and intellectually challenging matter. But if one wishes to do more than just impart traditional moral philosophical knowledge to people or preach romantic idealism, then ethics, including corporate ethics, must come down from its lofty realm of "ideas" or "values" and establish itself in day-to-day reality. Acting responsibly would then not mean swearing allegiance to higher notions of approved behavior, but would emerge from a very worldly setting in which a corporation's or individual's activity has to be justified in the light of different values in pluralistic societies. Such a debate would have to be based on real people with all their strengths and weakness, not on ideal people that we would all like to know but seldom meet.

Unethical conduct is behavior that focuses on supposed short-term advantages without considering mid- and long-term consequences. The impotence of ethics is shown in the fact that most people choose to maximize their own benefits when economic and political decisions have to be made, and are only prevented from acting against the common interest by governments branching out into many walks of life. A reflection on corporate ethics must always bear this in mind and, precisely because of it, must always aim higher and dig deeper than merely avoiding unintelligent behavior. Intelligent action is acting in one's enlightened self-interest and thus compatible with the selfish tendencies in our societies. To assume that altruism and a holistic worldview are predominant human characteristics would be unrealistic.

ETHICS PERCEPTIONS

In the past 10 years, society's image of private industry, and particularly of large corporations, has become shaped by distrust. The Enron scandal in the United States triggered a worldwide groundswell for addressing ethical dilemmas. Apparently, many managers believe that a corporation cannot simultaneously have high principles and high profits. In fact, an increasingly common view is that many corporations are ethically irresponsible, unscrupulously pursuing profits at the cost of the environment and the safety and health of consumers. The perception of the commitment of transnational companies in developing countries seems especially critical.

The November 2002 CNN/USA Today/Gallup poll asked the public to rate the honesty and ethics of 21 professions. The ratings of business professions has been low, but the 2002 ratings are lower than in the past. The very high and high ratings for ethics and honesty for eight of the professions are shown in Exhibit 3.3. Only a few professions such as labor union leaders, car sales personnel, and telemarketers rated below business executives in terms of ethics and honesty.[20]

Another survey focusing on business students brings little improvement in the public's image of business. In answer to the question "How ruthless are you prepared to be to get to the top of your chosen career?" 2 percent answered "extremely ruthless," 14 percent "very ruthless," and 39 percent "moderately ruthless." The same MBA students had a more than skeptical opinion of the moral state of the modern business world: 5 percent thought it had no morals at all, and 35 percent thought it had "very few" morals.[21]

Various studies of executives' moral perceptions of themselves confirm the existence of conflicts. Executives often feel they often have to decide between

EXHIBIT 3.3
Rankings of Perceived Ethics by Occupation

Source: Adapted from "Honesty and Ethics Rating" USA Today Gallup poll, November 2002.

	Very High	High
Nurses	27%	57%
Military officers	18	47
High school teachers	15	49
Medical doctors	11	52
Bankers	3	33
Building contractors	3	17
Business executives	2	15
Labor union leaders	2	12

economic performance within the time limits of the profit-and-loss account and the demands of their conscience. A study by the Düsseldorf Institute for Applied Marketing Science revealed an interesting distinction: Lower-level executives or middle management often seem to feel more pressure and to experience greater moral difficulties than upper-level executives, who showed great interest in ethical questions.[22]

CORPORATE ETHICS AND LEADERSHIP

How can a business enterprise respond successfully to the day-to-day challenge of corporate ethics? There are a number of ways to address the ethics test: (1) common sense or "moral reason," (2) "corporate codes of conduct," and (3) comprehensive policies and ongoing, rewarding management development.

Moral Common Sense

The following rules, which Goodpaster referred to as "moral common sense," are relevant in discussing ethics:

1. Avoid harming others.
2. Respect the rights of others.
3. Do not lie or cheat.
4. Keep promises and contracts.
5. Obey the law.
6. Prevent harm to others.
7. Help those in need.
8. Be fair.
9. Reinforce these imperatives in others.[23]

At first glance, these "commandments" are so convincing that further comment seems superfluous. When examined more closely, however, the picture is not so simple. Moral commonsense rules can be discussed using examples of the global chemical/pharmaceutical industry.

Avoid Harming Others

Drugs are not commodities in the sense of other consumer or investment goods. They are used because people are sick or in pain, or because they have physical or mental disorders, or because they are dying. "Consumer sovereignty"—the freedom to choose or refuse a product—is limited in this industry's market. The resulting ethical challenge for the pharmaceutical industry, therefore, is pronounced.

Similarly, the pharmaceutical industry's assessments of drug safety and risk/benefit evaluations have particularly fateful properties: If the company's specialists or managers err, they err not just for themselves and their company, but also for the sick people who are at their mercy. Particularly offensive are double standards in safety product information (indications, warnings on side effects), product quality, and everything else, which is significant for the health or even the maintenance of human life.

Respect the Rights of Others

Much of the responsibility for the global environmental equilibrium rests with a small, rich minority of about 15 percent of the world's people. Their alarming ability to consume resources and create waste is responsible for about 80 percent of the global environmental problems, including the depletion of the ozone layer and the potential greenhouse effect. Per capita emissions of carbon dioxide and other greenhouse gases of Americans, Germans, or Singaporeans is about 10 to 20 times higher than those of Indians and Chinese, and about 100 times higher than those of the people in Bangladesh.[24] The same picture arises if we look at the per capita consumption of nonrenewable resources. Clearly, those in the 10 to 15 percent "rich" minority live unsustainable lifestyles in regard to energy consumption, consumption of nonrenewable resources, water consumption, or pollution. Major ecological systems would probably already have collapsed if all human beings lived that same lifestyle.

The lifestyle repercussions of developed nations may include reduced options for future generations. This introduces the problem of intergenerational justice and a moral issue since, in contrast to former generations, we know the consequences of our actions and we have the political, technical, and economic means for a change of course.

Do Not Lie or Cheat

The "three dogs theory" illustrates how one can easily fall into one's own trap: A man knocks at your door and complains that your dog has bitten him. Your first answer, according to the theory, is: "I do not have a dog!" That is the moment when your dog comes running around the house, barking loudly. You now refer to the "second dog theory" and say: "I do have a dog, but it does not bite." That is unfortunately the moment where your dog bites the man again. You then have to refer to your third and last dog theory: "I do have a dog, it does bite once in a while, but it does not hurt!" Your credibility fades away with every theoretical reorientation, as you are clearly admitting only what has already been proven. Furthermore, a "supposition gap" arises: Even after you have said everything you know, everyone still keeps waiting for the "fourth dog theory."

An accident that went into legal history as the "Carnival Monday Case" shows the practical relevance of the "three dogs theory": After an incident, the company concerned announced the "yellow rain" that had fallen over residential areas of a town on a morning in February was "not particularly toxic."[25] After complaints from neighborhood residents, the chemical quantities were adjusted upward and after investigations by Greenpeace, the company finally admitted that there were 10 tons of chemicals and at least 11 different substances in the rain, among them o-Nitroanisole, which can cause cancer.

A similar series of events is conceivable in connection with information about unexpected side effects of a drug. "Do not lie or cheat" in practice means "tell the truth, the whole truth, and nothing but the truth," plus admit a lack of knowledge and promise clarification.

Keep Promises and Contracts

This commandment can be viewed from the perspective of the employee, and also from the perspective of the corporation. An example could be the employees' working ethos. To paraphrase a quote from the late John F. Kennedy, one might suggest, "Don't ask what your company can do for you, but what you can do for your company." Solidarity means the morally qualified, essential, and active dependence of the individual on the community and vice versa.

Obey the Law

Imagine you are traveling in a poor country in sub-Saharan Africa, Southeast Asia, or Latin America and you become seriously ill. You find a well-trained physician who diagnoses your illness and prescribes a medication. It is highly probable that you do not know anything about the substance prescribed, but you recognize the name or the logo of the manufacturer, and if you can tie the name or the logo to a well-known, reputed pharmaceutical manufacturer, almost certainly you will feel relieved.[26] You will expect that the worst will soon be over and you will be on your way to recovery.

You probably wouldn't fear that such a pharmaceutical company might have high ethical standards to govern its actions at home but would conceal dangerous or lethal side effects of its products in a poor country. Your gut feeling would tell you to trust the decency and the moral common sense of a widely respected, honorable company.

You wouldn't expect that such a drug firm would communicate openly and honestly with government authorities, the health profession, and patients in its home country—for example, New Zealand, Germany, or Switzerland—but allow serious inconsistencies or omissions to mark its communication in a developing country. With widespread poverty, illiteracy, sickness, hunger, and the scarcity of physicians, nurses, and pharmacists all influencing drug safety in many parts of the Third World, you might assume that a reputed company would try even harder to maintain the safest possible use of its products. Unfortunately, again and again publications demonstrate there is reason for worry.

For many companies doing business in developing countries, the commandment "obey the law" is not sufficient to prevent harm to people and society. Many Third World countries do not yet have state-of-the-art legislation (e.g., in product safety or environmental protection), or they may for various reasons be forced to tolerate social injustices that would not be allowed in industrialized nations (e.g., child labor, dismissal of pregnant women, etc.). Developing countries may be what Nobel laureate Gunnar Myrdal called "soft states," where the letter of the law has little to do with legal reality, because laws that have been passed are not enforced consistently.[27]

Perceived responsibility on the basis of better insight or knowledge must lead to appropriate action even where country-specific legislation does not require it. In areas such as product, industrial, and environmental safety; social welfare obligations; and correctness and completeness of information, standards that satisfy the stringent requirements of total responsibility must hold sway. Double standards would have doubly fatal consequences, not only for the corporation but also perhaps for the health and quality of life now or in generations to come.

Prevent Harm to Others

Pesticide safety is a matter of widespread concern. Particularly in countries where illiteracy and other social conditions of poverty are pronounced, there is considerable worry about pesticides' public health impact. And yet, safely and effectively used, chemicals can reduce losses due to insects, diseases, and weeds, thus increasing income for the farmer and food output for the nation.

How far does the ethical responsibility of a specific agrochemical corporation reach? An individual corporation cannot run literacy and training courses for hundreds of thousands of people working in the rural areas of the developing world. But a company's ethical responsibility certainly extends beyond selling its products to the next wholesale agent. How much more ought to be done? The answer to that question depends on the specific social, economic, and political framework of a specific country—and on the economic feasibility for the company concerned. Cooperation with the state extension services and the manufacturer's associations is almost always part of an appropriate answer.

Ethical reflection is needed on top of technical and economical considerations. Novartis Foundation for Sustainable Development is tackling the topic by running KAP (knowledge, attitude, practice) studies on the safe and effective use of plant protection products in India, Zimbabwe, and Mexico in order to develop tailor-made education and training programs.[28] The objective is to produce a pilot project from which others can learn and others can repeat elsewhere. Another approach might be to withdraw certain products from a country's market, if a company's endeavors do not lead to a measurable improvement of the public health impact of its products.

Help Those in Need

A number of managers suggest that it is not a primary function of business enterprises to become involved in charitable activities. However, other managers believe that operating in a country involves helping those in need. A sense of satisfaction is acquired when a manager, through the Novartis Foundation for Sustainable Development, helps host-nation citizens learn how to read, attends to their safety and health, and completes numerous projects for people living in poverty.

Be Fair

The Golden Rule opens a variety of reflections with regard to one's attitude toward colleagues on the same hierarchical level and toward those who have lower ranks in the company. Consider the following ethical dilemma.

Suppose you have just heard that one of the most important members of your staff is prepared to leave your department for an overseas position in another department within your company. The new job would be a challenge and provide excellent career opportunities. You have no doubt that your employee would fit in very well and would be able to meet the requirements of the new position. But you would lose your best team member, and your department's performance would suffer seriously, along with your bonus. The person would be very difficult to replace.

That person's potential new boss has asked for your opinion and has made it clear that your input will be crucial in deciding whether to offer the job to your team member. Will you give your honest opinion and provide a strong recommendation? Or will you want to keep your staff member and hence mislead the inquiring overseas manager?

Reinforce These Imperatives in Others

How can a corporation reinforce its moral imperatives in others? Should it have the courage to assume leadership responsibilities in ethically relevant questions, or should it seek conformity with convention as often happens in practice? Ethical guidelines of business associations are often the lowest common denominator and mostly fall short of what an individual corporation should be prepared to do with regard to higher ethical business standards.

The dilemma that arises when individual corporations impair the image of the entire industry must also be considered. Should one stay quiet and thus become a silent accomplice, or should one bring up the issue and run the risk of being accused of airing one's dirty laundry in public?

The accompanying Global Focus illustrates the perceptions that how managers conduct themselves with regard to corporate business ethics differs across countries.

Global Focus Managerial Stereotypes: Myth, Fun, or Accurate

Globally, people form images, impressions, and stereotypes of people who live and work in different countries. This practice is oversimplified and often full of exaggerations based on actual knowledge, stories, gossip, and opinions voiced by others. Asking a group of transnational employees about their stereotypes often results in caricature-based descriptions such as the following.

Japanese managers are clever and cunning. They are reserved, express no emotion, communicate indirectly (saying yes when they mean no), and consider themselves to be culturally superior to uncivilized foreigners. Rank and status are important, but the top man has the main responsibility to bring harmony and is not always the key decision maker.

Swedish managers are practical and technically competent, but are not very creative. Abstract thinking sometimes confuses them. They possess no sense of humor and usually focus on what is wrong with a product or service and not what is exceptional or good. They put off decisions and delegate responsibilities to the lowest level of an organization. They are neurotic about being prompt and meeting schedules.

American managers are arrogant, confident, and loud. They believe that everyone who is not American wishes he or she was. Everything they present or do is pushed as the best, newest, and most profitable. They use lawyers and accountants too much and prepare complex, convoluted, and time-consuming business deals. They organize their transnational companies in a many-layered maze of bureaucracy.

French managers are not always the most thorough, but are often the most negative. They love to talk, but not always about what is on the agenda. They love to show and exercise their power. Informal relations with foreigners are difficult to create and sustain. Information flows from the top down because top managers know what is the best.

German managers are focused on details and proceeding by the book. They usually have years of technical training. The top person is in complete control. Meetings are formal and attention is paid to every detail. Occasionally a loud voice or table pounding are tactics used to get concessions for managers or businesses from other countries.

British managers are well-educated, articulate, insular, and aloof. They have a broad, but not always relevant knowledge of their companies' products or services. Participative management, empowerment, and bottoms-up communication are not appreciated, respected, or used. They are polite and use stories with managers of other nationalities. Unfortunately, the stories are often not understood or funny.

CORPORATE CODES OF CONDUCT FOR SENSITIVE MATTERS AND LEADERSHIP

Not everything that is legal is legitimate. An active transnational corporation, which has to conduct operations in different legal and social frameworks and which strives for uniform ethical standards, is well advised to develop codes of conduct for its sensitive activities. There is no a priori harmony between corporate or individual profit and what is to be preferred from a social point of view. Indeed, a corporation needs to think about how to minimize a whole set of potential conflicts.

Corporate codes of conduct are defined here as standards of behavior that a corporation adopts without being compelled to by law, but which then become binding on all employees, to minimize potential conflicts arising from normal business activities' undesirable effects on society and the environment. Such corporate codes of conduct make it clear that the management of the corporation is not indifferent to how business goals are achieved. Corporate codes of conduct rule out what the corporation believes to be clearly unacceptable behavior.

Of importance here is the question of whether one should imperialistically enforce one's own standards in cases of doubt, or whether one should opt more for an "ethical relativism" that argues for doing what the Romans do when in Rome. Even though one can concede that many traditional ways of thinking and behaving are based on sound assumptions, there are a number of situations where a corporation should have the courage to apply its own standards and philosophy and not that of the different social and cultural framework of the host country.

For instance, sensitive areas might be marketing, information policy, environmental protection, animal experiments, and research policy. Ethically acceptable maneuverability must be clarified, and its effects on people, environment, and society analyzed. The desirable and undesirable must be defined and formulated.

Unfortunately, behavior forbidden by corporate codes of conduct occurs again and again in corporations. Pitt and Groskaufmanis have proposed criteria that can increase the practical effectiveness of internal codes of conduct.[29]

Criteria for the formulation of corporate codes of conduct are as follows:

- The principles of the code must be tailored to the specific corporate culture, merely taking over general codes is not enough.
- The code of conduct addresses those corporation activities that are particularly sensitive or that concern the greatest vulnerability (legal, sociopolitical, and other).
- Corporate codes of conduct have to be pragmatic; that is, they must reflect the circumstances of the corporation and should set only standards that can reasonably be expected to be followed.

Criteria for the implementation of corporate codes of conduct are as follows:

- A communication program must ensure that all people affected by the code of conduct actually know and understand it. It is not enough merely to distribute it; the content should be explained and someone made available to answer questions.
- There should be at least one person who may be approached in confidence (ombudsperson).
- Employees should certify in writing that they have read, understood, and complied with the code of conduct in their work.

Criteria for the enforcement of corporate codes of conduct are as follows:

- Codes of conduct make sense if the managers concerned are accountable for the objectives.
- Audit committees, ombudspersons, a hot line, or other means should ensure that employees can have their concerns heard by the appropriate office.
- Violations of the code of conduct must be investigated and resolved. The message should be clear and leave employees in no doubt: Violation of the code leads to penalties, including dismissal, irrespective of whether the violation had positive or detrimental consequences for the corporation.

Most global institutions have a tendency to be self-referential (i.e., to live in a rather closed value and interest system). It is important that codes of conduct are based on a broad social consensus. Therefore, they should not only reflect the philosophy of management, but also should, before their adoption, be challenged by external, independent review and as far as possible result from a consensus based on dialogue.

To firmly represent a point of view, relevant facts have to be collected, illuminated, and evaluated from different angles. This requires broad discussions to consider all the pluralistic opinions and interests. Ideological lines of demarcation or fundamentalist rejections do not improve the quality of solutions. On the contrary, prejudice acts like a wall, preventing awareness.

If conflicting opinions are considered untenable in a company, then that company lacks more than just an opposition culture and ability to cope with conflict. Openness to pluralistic opinions is essential for a comprehensive perception of reality. Especially for the social acceptance of an organization's practices, the search for consensus through dialogue is vital for survival.

Many expert and sociopolitical positions that were represented only by fringe minorities 10 or 15 years ago now are associated with "sound common sense." If one reads the publications of some companies on environmental protection and compares them with the earlier manifestos of "green" groups, one can identify similarities.

Corporate decision making becomes more difficult when including host-country concerns and interests based on other value systems. Because dialogues

Global Focus Codes of Conduct

Codes of conduct are being used in different countries and organizations. The following is a sample of a few codes of conduct used to establish responsibility, ethics, practice, and philosophy of organizations.

- **Codes of Conduct** (http://www.codesofconduct.org/): a website providing a useful resource for those interested in the full text of various codes of conduct, and their provisions, sponsors, and effects on business practices.
- **IEPCE (European Initiative for Ethical Production and Consumption)** a European forum between the main social and economic players who wish to encourage ethical production and consumption (employers, trade unions, nongovernment organizations, public institutions).
- **Social Accountability 8000 (SA8000)** (http://www.cepaa.org/sa8000.htm): a voluntary standard for corporate social responsibility launched in 1997 by the Council on Economic Priorities Accreditation Agency (CEPAA), recently renamed Social Accountability International (SAI). Focuses mainly on labor practices (e.g. child labor, freedom of association, hours of work, and wages). This global corporate responsibility code is modeled after ISO 9000 and includes accreditation of auditors and independent monitoring.
- **Caux Round Table Principles for Business** (http://www.cauxsroundtable.org/): a code of conduct focusing on global corporate responsibility adopted by a trilateral business organization.
- **Global Sullivan Principles** (http://www.globalsullivanprinciples.org/): a set of principles drafted by the Rev. Leon H. Sullivan to guide corporate social, economic, political, and environmental policies.
- **ICFTU Basic Code of Labor Practice** (http://www.icftu.org/displaydocument.asp?Index = 991209513&Language=EN): the International Confederation of Free Trade Unions; model code regarding worker rights (1997).
- **Investors in People** (http://www.iipuk.co.uk/): a U.K. quality standard, which sets a level of good practice for improving an organization's performance through its people.
- **Ethical Trading Initiative (ETI)** (http://www.eti.org.uk/): a U.K. code developed through partnership between retail and consumer goods companies, nongovernment organization, trade unions, and the U.K. government.
- **Amnesty International's Human Rights Principles for Companies** http://www.amnesty.org/ailib/aipub/1998/ACT/A7000198.htm): an international code requiring companies to protect human rights and abide by several labor standards in countries in which they have facilities.
- **Clean Clothes Campaign Code of Labor Practices for the Apparel Industry** (http://www.cleanclothes.org/codes/ccccode.htm): a model code for labor standards and a monitoring system for companies in the apparel industry.

are open processes, how they will develop cannot be planned, and the effects and consequences are visible only to a limited extent. Dialogues do not automatically lead to agreement. They run the risk of overflowing endlessly and getting involved in controversies that are less and less relevant instead of working out an acceptable, practical compromise for both sides. Dialogues are particularly vulnerable if one or the other side sets itself up as morally superior or crosses into other worlds without sufficient expert knowledge.

Nevertheless, controversies must be argued out. Although the final decision on corporate policy lies within the corporation itself, the harmonization of controversial views is more sustainable through discussion than through power. Those involved must refrain from claiming superiority, think over their own positions, and if necessary revise them. Openness and pluralism are required, though not arbitrariness or cheap tolerance to avoid arguments. True dialogue, in this case, differs from manipulative persuasion and modern advertising by dealing critically both with the necessity of acting in an economically reasonable manner and with wider public interests.

Corporate codes of conduct are not standardized instructions on ethical dealing that can always clearly determine what is ethically acceptable. Guidelines such as those outlined here can give company employees a basis for setting priorities when commercial decisions have to be made under time and financial constraints.

Codes of conduct web links and information can be found in the accompanying Global Focus.

GOOD ETHICS IS GOOD BUSINESS

Why should a transnational company consider ethics—on top of law, self-interest, and convention—in directing its managerial behavior? The worst conceivable result of high moral standards would be competitive or other tangible detriment because the special efforts and costs a company attaches to ethical consideration result in net disadvantages. There are a number of indications that losing short-term profit from being unethical does not exactly burst into the limelight.

But there are a number of empirical examples in which unethical corporate behavior caused a great social outcry and intervention from the authorities, and presented no acceptable options even in the short-term. In these cases it is easy to show that unethical conduct can be a burden on a corporation and that high ethical standards can be seen as an asset.

A second conceivable possibility is that financial disadvantages due to investments over and above those required by law (for instance in environmental, social, or safety areas) or withdrawing from sale for ethical reasons could be compensated and balanced out by nonfinancial advantages (e.g., the company's reputation). The problem here is that investments and falling sales are easier to measure than increased opportunities from an enhanced reputation.

For enlightened corporations, commercial success now means more than just how big the year's profit is. Profits to companies are like food to people: an absolute necessity, without which they die. But only a few—sick—people would consider eating to be the central or only purpose of life. The reputation of a company is one of its most valuable assets, even if it does not appear directly in the balance sheet (Swanda therefore suggests that "goodwill" should become a balance-sheet item).[30] The verdict of the public depends significantly on the company's perceived contribution to socially valued ends. Acting in a socially and environmentally responsible way and using energy and nonrenewable resources wisely are important blocks in the mosaic of commercial success.

EMPLOYEES' MOTIVATION

Morale and job satisfaction suffer in a transnational firm that is the focus of public criticism or that rewards employees who promote their careers in unethical ways. This can lead to good employees, a corporation's most valuable "capital," leaving the corporation. This alone is reason enough to avoid unethical conduct.

Various empirical studies reveal a positive correlation between ethical conduct in a corporation and job satisfaction.[31] Where top management is seen as giving strong support for ethical conduct, job satisfaction increases together with the degree of employee identification with the corporation. Everything points to the conclusion that a positive reciprocal relationship exists between job satisfaction and ethical conduct. Applied business ethics becomes a component of corporate identity, the totality of value systems, thought and decision patterns, modes of behavior, and structures within a corporation that transmits a positive "us-feeling" to employees and thus boosts motivation to work.

Corporations whose ethical conduct is considered above reproach are seen as more attractive employers than those that have been publicly criticized due to failure to recognize their responsibilities or even due to willful damage to the welfare of the community or the environment. A poll of business studies students carried out by Prognos AG revealed that 88 percent regard "work satisfaction," 67 percent a "good working atmosphere," and 66 percent a "job that makes sense" as an important criterion in choosing an employer.[32]

Corporations are now no longer measured on what they produce, but on what they present. The strength of such trends can change again, especially when the labor market develops unfavorably for those seeking employment. But an increasing number of citizens, whether as employees or consumers, are taking ethical viewpoints seriously—more seriously than 10 years ago.

CORRUPTION AND BRIBERY

The globalization of business has created a new perspective toward corruption, bribery, and fraud. Once viewed by many global managers as a necessary requirement for conducting business around the world, corruption, bribery, and fraud are increasingly seen as unacceptable behaviors. **Bribery,** a subset of corruption and fraud, is the paying of money or providing a benefit to someone in business or government to obtain an inappropriate market, workplace, or individual economic advantage. Corruption, bribery, and fraud are not defensible in economic, ethical, or national cultural terms. Exhibit 3.4 lists a number of bribe motivations.

Companies and individuals must now comply with an increasingly pervasive set of international and national laws governing corruption, bribery, and fraud.

EXHIBIT 3.4
Factors Responsible for Bribes

Home Country Factors	Host-Country Factors
Competitors are giving bribes to obtain business.	Permits and licenses from government officials are required to conduct normal business functions.
Top management and shareholders pressure for higher levels of performance.	Government officials are poorly paid, use bribes to supplement salary.
This is an accepted practice in the host country; cannot expect to get any business without conforming.	Bureaucratic delays can be costly for business (e.g., clear products through customs on time to meet delivery schedules).
Tax laws of the country encourage bribery. Bribes can be written off as a business expense in Germany (not in the United States).	Politicians pressure for contributions to political parties or favorite political organizations or causes.

Committing such acts can and has resulted in large fines, criminal punishment including imprisonment, complex litigation, and distraction from needed management practices. In the United States, prosecutions under the **Foreign Corrupt Practices Act** (FCPA), a 1977 antibribery law, have resulted in fines of up to $25 million and being banned from government contracts.[33]

Transnational firms have an interest in fighting corruption, bribery, and fraud because they can lead to a secret advantage to competitors on projects, proposals, and bids, reduce innovation and creativity advantages, and take business away from a merit-based system. Corruption, bribery, and fraud also stymie the economic development resulting from free market competition. Research shows that corruption, bribery, and fraud hamper the creation of acceptable legal systems, encourage red tape and bureaucracy, erode public confidence and trust, and block the development of the type of infrastructure on which organizations depend.

A number of best-in-class examples illustrate how some transnationals are proactively addressing corruption, bribery, and fraud.[34]

- Hong Kong's second-largest bank, Hang Seng, conducts corruption and bribery seminars on a regular basis. Managers are then expected to impart to employees through training, videos, discussions, and personal meetings the bank's position on eliminating corruption and bribery.
- Motorola, a large American global electronics firm, has a clear code of conduct and lessons for managers in dealing with bribes. The lessons are delivered in ongoing training programs. Case studies, practice feedback sessions, videos, speakers, and international experts are used in the programs. Motorola also funds ethics training programs to combat corruption, bribery, and fraud in countries in which it operates.
- Rohm and Haas publishes and disseminates a code of conduct to all directors, officers, and employees of the global firm. Exhibit 3.5 presents a concise version of this specific code, which is circulated in English, French, German, Italian, Portuguese, Spanish, and Japanese.

EXHIBIT 3.5 Rohm and Haas Company: Political Payments, and Gifts and Entertainment

Source: Rohm and Haas, *Code of Business Conduct*, November 2002, pp. 1 & 3. Reprinted by permission.

The Company

Rohm and Haas Company is an ethical company which complies with applicable laws. This Code of Business Conduct applies to all directors, officers, and employees of the Company, its subsidiaries and controlled affiliates.

Political Payments

(a) We encourage participation in the political process, and we recognize that participation is primarily a matter for individual involvement.

(b) Any payment of corporate funds to any political party, candidate, or campaign may be made only if permitted under applicable law and approved in advance by the General Counsel. U.S. laws generally prohibit payments of corporate funds to any U.S. political party, candidate, or campaign.

Gifts and Entertainment

(a) Gifts of cash or property may not be offered or made to any officer or employees of a customer or supplier or any government official or employee unless the gift is (1) nominal in value, (2) approved in advance by the appropriate Regional Director, Business Group Executive, or Corporate Staff Division Manager, and (3) legal. In most countries it is illegal for corporations to make gifts to government officials or employees; any gift to a government official or employee must be approved in advance by the General Counsel as well as the appropriate Regional Director, Business Group Executive, or Corporate Staff Division Manager.

(b) Employees of the Company should decline or turn over to the Company gifts of more than nominal value or cash from persons or companies that do (or may expect to do) business with Rohm and Haas.

(c) Business entertainment (whether we do the entertaining or are entertained) must have a legitimate business purpose, may not be excessive, and must be legal. Business entertainment of government officials or employees is illegal or regulated in most countries; therefore, the propriety of such entertaining should be reviewed in advance with the General Counsel or his delegates.

Translation

Translations of the Code will be prepared in French, German, Italian, Portuguese, Spanish, and Japanese. Other translations will be prepared if necessary to ensure that recipients of the Code are able to understand it fully. The General or Resident Manager in each country will be responsible for translations.

Dissemination

(a) A copy of the Code in the appropriate language will be given to all employees of the Company (including employees of domestic and foreign subsidiaries and controlled affiliates). New employees will be given a copy of the Code at the time of their employment.

(b) The Regional or Staff Division Personnel Directors are responsible for dissemination of the Code.

(*continued*)

(concluded)

Compliance

(a) All salaried employees of the Company (its subsidiaries and controlled affiliates) will be asked to certify annually in writing their compliance with the Code substantially as follows (with such exceptions as may be noted therein):

"I have reviewed and understand the Code of Business Conduct. I hereby confirm that (1) I have complied with the Code during the preceding year, and (2) each recipient of the Code who reports to me has certified in writing his or her compliance with the Code."

(b) The Regional and Business Directors will be responsible for obtaining certifications not later than February 1 with respect to the preceding year.

TRANSNATIONAL COMPANY ACTIONS TO PROMOTE ETHICS

Similar to most management practices, no one approach is always successful or effective in providing answers and guidance on ethical matters. Research and best practices, however, suggest that ethics can become part of a firm's culture, history, and folklore when:

1. Top executives are committed and involved in the ethics training and initiatives.
2. A clearly communicated company code of ethics and code of conduct is prepared, continuously upgraded, and used. The Rohm and Hass example in Exhibit 3.5 illustrates how clarity can be achieved.
3. A center, person, ombudsman, committee, or unit is established as the company's formal point of reference for training, advisory services, and resources. Transnational companies can establish this type of center to fit the type of dilemmas and situations faced in their particular countries.
4. Once codes of conduct and support services are in place, violations must be strictly enforced. No exceptions should be tolerated, and the code must be applied fairly from the board level to the lowest-level operating employee.
5. Monitoring the program and enforcement should be formally conducted. Data and information of ethical incidents, lawsuits, settlements, and situations should be carefully prepared, reviewed, and established as a part of this company database and history. This type of evaluation can help a transnational company determine weaknesses and repeat violators.

There is no universally applicable set of laws, ethical codes, or codes of conduct that can cover every situation, country, and context. Global managers faced with ethical dilemmas and decisions will apply their values, standards, and perspective. They will be tested again and again in transnational settings when making decisions regarding discrimination, child or forced labor, safety and health, intellectual property, and a host of dilemmas. For example, some societies give preferences to certain racial, geographic, and religious groups. There is active and legal discrimination in terms of hiring, rewarding, and promoting. Such societially sanctioned discrimination can pose problems for global managers from countries in which discrimination is illegal.

One area in which ethical problems occur involves the use of intellectual property (e.g., computer software, compact discs).[35] When a company's intellectual property is pirated, a major element of its competitive position is no longer its exclusively. Governments are generally sincere in their efforts to champion their transnationals' causes, yet laws, trade agreements, contracts, personal relationships, and other factors often reduce the home-country government's efforts.

As discussed in this chapter, the theft of intellectual property is only one area that cuts across cultures and countries. Corruption, bribery, fraud, the environment, and determining what constitutes ethical and socially responsible decisions also have cross-cultural consequences.

Social responsibility and ethics are limited by the host-country precedents, laws, infrastructure, and culture. How social responsibility and ethics are managed differs across cultures. Reviewing and considering the host-country setting is a necessity in making the right decisions. Global managers face social responsibility and ethics issues that require creativity, patience, and knowledge to resolve.

Key Terms

Bribery, *138*
Corporate codes of Conduct, *134*
Code of ethics, *119*
Corruption, *138*
External beneficiaries, *117*
Ethics, *123*
Foreign Corrupt Practices Act, *139*
Fraud, *138*
Human rights, *120*
Internal beneficiaries, *117*
Stakeholder Management Devices (SMDs), *119*
Unethical conduct, *127*

Review, Critical Thinking, and Discussion Questions

1. Ethics are not the same as law. Comment on the meaning of this statement.
2. Why are small bribes to transact business in the global marketplace so widespread around the world?
3. What is the social responsibility of a transnational company toward the environment (e.g., pollution, greenhouse gases)?
4. What are some of the human rights responsibilities of transnational organizations?
5. What ethical issues are faced by Ford Motor Co. and Firestone/Bridgestone regarding SUV tire problems?
6. The United States has the Foreign Corrupt Practices Act, a law governing transnational company global business transactions. Does the law create a disadvantage or an advantage for U.S. firms against competitors from other countries?
7. What are some major ethical and social responsibility arguments leveled against transnational companies regarding their business style, programs, and activities in less developed countries?
8. Can global managers be trained to use better decision-making processes when faced with ethical dilemmas? How?

9. What managerial implications are there for a global manager to understand, respond to, and monitor local customs, norms, and expectations regarding employee recruitment, selection, reward, and evaluation programs?
10. Some claim that a love-hate relationship exists between transnational companies and host countries. Explain.

Endnotes

1. Jeffrey E. Garten, *The Politics of Fortune* (Cambridge, MA: Harvard Business School Publishing, 2002).
2. Chris Cook and James Allan, *Profit from the Core: Growth Strategy in an Era of Turbulence* (Cambridge, MA: Harvard Business School Publishing, 2001).
3. Thomas N. Duening and John M. Ivancevich, *Managing Organizations: Principles & Guidelines* (Cincinnati: Atomic Dog Publishing, 2003).
4. Sara A. Morris, "Internal Effects of Stakeholder Devises," *Journal of Business Ethics,* March 1997, pp. 413–24.
5. Evan M. Dudik, *Strategic Renaissance* (New York: AMACOM, 2000).
6. Thomas Hartman, *Unequal Protections: The Rise of Corporate Dominance and the Theft of Human Rights* (New York: Rodale, 2002).
7. Jonathan Power, *Like Water on Stone: The Story of Amnesty International* (Boston: Northeastern University, 2001).
8. Business for Social Responsibility, *Forced Labor,* 2002; see www.bsr.org/print/printthispage/cfm.
9. Ibid.
10. Ibid.
11. Ibid and Business for Social Responsibility, *Human Rights,* 2002; see www.bsr.org/print/printhispage/cfm.
12. Ibid.
13. Ibid.
14. Ibid.
15. David Drickhamer, "Under Fire," *Industry Week,* June 2002, pp 30–36.
16. Jayne O'Donnell, "Rep. Tauzin Turns Business Scandals into Must-See TV," *USA Today,* July 28, 2002, p. A-1, A-2
17. "Kathie Lee Treated Worse than Michael Jordan," www.newsmax.com/articles/?a=2000/7/30/163520.
18. The next three sections are based on the structure, outline, and writings of Klaus M. Leisinger, *Corporate Ethics and International Business: Some Basic Issues,* (Basle, Switzerland, Novartis Foundation for Sustainable Development, 1994). Although this material is almost a decade old, it is still one of the best treatments of this subject. The issues the author raises are relevant and apply to current transnational and global issues.
19. Barbara Wejnert, *Transition to Democracy in Eastern Europe and Russia* (New York: Greenwood Publishing, 2002).
20. Jeffrey M. Jones, "Effects of Year's Scandals Evident in Honesty and Ethics Rankings," *Gallup Organization Poll,* December 4, 2002, www.gallup.com/poll/releases/pr02/204.asp.
21. Leisinger, *Corporate Ethics.*

22. D. Hochstetler, Lorbeer and Mammon, In Wirtshaftswoche, 1990.
23. K. E. Goodpaster, *Ethics in Management* (Cambridge, MA: Harvard Business School Press, 1984).
24. G. Eidan, *Emission Standard* (Cologne: Verlag, 1993), and *World Resources Institute, A Guide to the Global Environment* (Washington, DC: Oxford University Press, 1994).
25. Ibid.
26. M. Silverman and M. Lydecker, *Bad Medicine: The Prescription Drug Industry in the Third World* (Palo Alto, CA: Stanford University, 1992).
27. Leisinger, *Corporate Ethics.*
28. Ibid.
29. H. L. Pitt and K. A. Groskaufmanis, "Why a Corporate Code May Not Protect You," *Across The Board,* 1990.
30. V. R. Swanda, Jr., "Goodwill, Going Concern, Stocks, and Flows: A Prescription for Moral Analysis, *Journal of Business Ethics* 9 (1990), pp. 751–59.
31. S. J. Vitell and D. L. Davis, "The Relationship Between Ethics and Job Satisfaction: An Empirical Investigation," *Journal of Business Ethics* 9 (1990), pp. 489–94.
32. Leisinger, *Corporate Ethics.*
33. Arthur Aronof, Antibribery Provisions of the Foreign Corrupt Practices Act, National Trade Data Bank, June 16, 1992.
34. "Corruption and Bribery," Business and Social Responsibility white paper, November 2002, pp. 1–27.
35. George T. Haley, Intellectual Property Rights and Foreign Direct Investment in Emerging Markets, 2000; see www.asia-pacific.com/rights.pdf.

Communicating in Global Settings

Learning Objectives

After completing Chapter 4, you should be able to:

- Describe the six elements of the cross-cultural communication process model.
- Understand how language can either inhibit or enhance cross-cultural understanding.
- Discuss how nonverbal cues influence cross-cultural communication effectiveness.
- Identify the major barriers to effective cross-cultural communication and means to overcome these barriers.
- Learn the difference between high-context and low-context communication cultures.

So, What Are You Saying?

"Let me give you a more detailed explanation," the German manager exclaimed to her French colleague at their global headquarters in Frankfurt. Unfortunately, the French manager had heard enough about the new plans to expand into China and walked out of the German's office in a hurried manner. The German manager was also frustrated and could not understand why her French colleague made so much small talk, tried to speak in such a sophisticated manner, and rarely provided all of the details necessary to understand the complete situation. "Why can't he communicate more clearly," she said to herself, "direct and factual while adding several examples to illustrate his points."

This scenario is not uncommon when two global managers from different cultures attempt to communicate with one another. The Germans and French have very different communication styles. German managers favor a more direct and fact-based communication approach that is filled with illustrative examples to reinforce key points. The term *zum Beispiel* ("for example") is a commonly used phrase. Also, these individuals tend to like a great deal of information, facts, figures, and future forecasts and projections. Communication should be orderly and logical with thorough summaries provided at the end of discussions and presentations.

In contrast, French managers are much more likely to consider auxiliary information as well as written and spoken words when evaluating the overall context of a communication exchange. Also, the French tend to enjoy eloquence and the art of conversation more than their German counterparts. Similar to the Japanese, French managers will leave some information out of the conversation, thus leaving room for listeners to interpret the complete meaning of the communication. But unlike the Japanese, French managers will not hesitate to engage in spirited conversations and arguments.

These differences in communication style are an example of what 21st century global managers need to know to be successful in today's global marketplace.

Source: Edward T. Hall and Mildred R. Hall, *Understanding Cultural Differences: Germans, French, and Americans* (Yarmouth, ME: Intercultural Press, 1989).

Communication pervades all aspects of organizational activity; it's the process by which things are accomplished in global organizations. Employees and managers are continually involved in and affected by the communication process. For global managers, effective communication is a critical skill because the manager's planning, organizing, controlling, and facilitating functions become operationalized only through communication. Because of communication's importance to organizations throughout the world, this chapter provides an understanding of the cross-cultural communication process and of how to become a better communicator in different cultural environments.

IMPORTANCE OF CROSS-CULTURAL COMMUNICATION

Cross-cultural communication occurs when two managers from different cultures exchange meanings with one another. Meanings can be exchanged in both verbal and nonverbal ways. On the surface, the communicator (Culture A) attempts to convey meaning to the receiver (Culture B). The relationship between the German and French colleagues in the opening vignette has become strained as a result of ineffective communication between two individuals from different cultures. Their attempt at cross-cultural communication was not as successful as both had hoped it would be. This scenario is common. Whether in a small-group setting around a conference table in Bogotá or in front of 100 employees announcing the month's manufacturing quality numbers in an international joint venture in Singapore, breakdowns in communication are pervasive but should be avoided whenever possible. *Every global manager is a communicator.* Everything a global manager does and says communicates something in some way to somebody or some group.

The Cross-Cultural Communication Process Model

Based on the early work of Shannon and Weaver, and Schramm,[1] the **communication process model** can be applied to cross-cultural settings. The model consists of several elements as illustrated in Exhibit 4.1.

1. Communicator: In a global organizational framework, the communicator is a global manager from Culture A with ideas, intentions, and other information to relay to an individual from Culture B.
2. Encoding/sending: The manager from Culture A packages these ideas and information in a form (verbal, nonverbal, etc.) that the manager from Culture B should understand.
3. Message: The manager from Culture A can send a message that is verbal or nonverbal, intentional or unintentional. The manager has many reasons to communicate: to have others understand ideas, to understand the ideas of others, to gain acceptance, and to produce action.
4. Medium: The medium is the channel for the message—the means by which the message is sent. The manager from Culture A can utilize a variety of media to exchange information, including face-to-face interactions, e-mail, voice mail, video teleconferencing, and company intranet postings.
5. Decoding/receiving: Using his or her own culturally based frame of reference and previous experience, the manager from Culture B interprets the message that was sent by the manager from Culture A. The receiver can provide feedback to the communicator, which is often used to determine if the message was understood and had the intended effect on the receiver.

EXHIBIT 4.1 **A Cross-Cultural Communication Process Model**

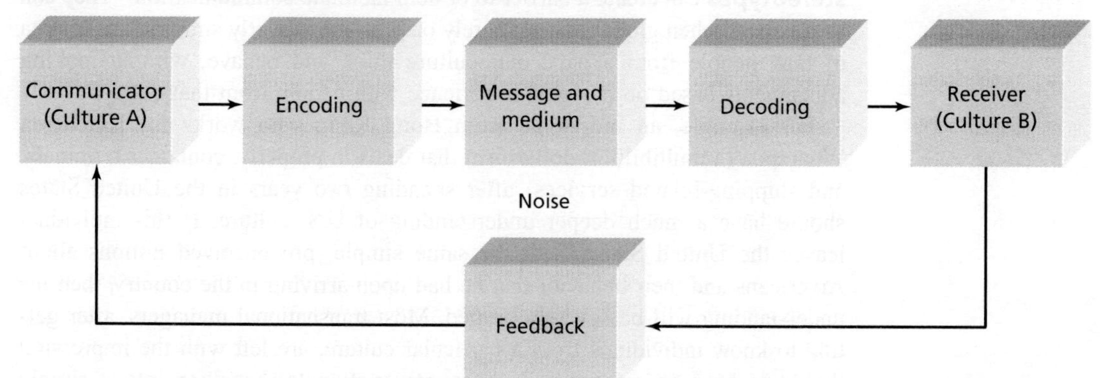

6. Noise: These are factors that can distort the communication process at any stage in the model. For example, a severe time constraint may force the manager from Culture A to send the manager from Culture B a hastily written e-mail that comes off as being rude and insensitive. Or, the manager from Culture B may nod his or her head up and down (which means "yes" or "affirmative" in some cultures) while the manager from Culture A is speaking. In reality, all the manager from Culture B meant was "I'm listening to you," not "Yes, I agree with you." These are examples of noise in the cross-cultural communication process.

As mentioned earlier, cross-cultural communication occurs when two managers from different cultures exchange meanings with one another. On the surface, the communicator (Culture A) attempts to convey meaning to the receiver (Culture B). Though verbal communication in the form of words and language are the primary ways to encode a message, the communicator can also convey a great deal of additional information through facial expressions, tone of voice, gestures, posture, eye contact, punctuality, and use of personal space.[2]

A challenging area for global managers is the encoding and decoding of messages so that their original meaning is interpreted in the intended way. When a global manager from Mexico wants to communicate his concern about a manufacturing defect to his Argentinean counterpart, the Mexican must create a message that will accurately reflect this concern and not create ill will with the Argentinean. Simultaneously, the Argentinean manager must apply knowledge of his Mexican counterpart's culture, communication style, and training when decoding and interpreting the meaning of the message. Proactive steps by both the communicator and receiver will help improve the overall cross-cultural communication process. In addition, feedback can be sought by the communicator to assess whether the original message was received as intended. If not, follow-up messages can be sent.

In this situation, stereotyping might be used constructively to help the Mexican manager craft an effective communication approach for his Argentinean counterpart. Referred to as a type of categorization that organizes previous experiences and guides future behavior regarding various groups and nationalities, **stereotypes** can create a barrier to or help facilitate communication.[3] They can be a barrier when global managers rely only on these overly simplistic schemata of how people from a particular culture think and behave, without making adjustments based on personal experience with people from that culture.

For example, an individual from Hong Kong who works for Hutchison Whampoa (a multibillion-dollar firm that deals in property, container terminals, and shipping-related services) after spending two years in the United States should have a much deeper understanding of U.S. culture. If this individual leaves the United States with the same simple, preconceived notions about Americans and their behavior that he had upon arriving in the country, then his understanding will be severely limited. Most transnational managers, after getting to know individuals from a particular culture, are left with the impression that it is hard to categorize host-country nationals' behavior into a simple framework. Experienced transnational managers observe that members of the same culture can have vastly different values, communication styles, habits, interests, education, and so on.

In contrast to being a barrier to effective cross-cultural communication, stereotypes can be helpful when they are used appropriately by global managers. Here are three suggestions on how to use stereotypes in a meaningful manner:[4]

1. *The first best guess* about a culture or group before receiving information about the specific individual with whom you are interacting.
2. *Descriptive rather than evaluative* so that the behavior of a culture or group can be described in objective terms rather than judged as good or bad.
3. *Modified,* based on further observation and experience with the actual people and situations within the culture.

Effective global managers need to have some idea of the stereotypes other nationalities hold about them. By knowing how one is stereotyped, that individual can try to dispel those notions early in the working relationship. Exhibit 4.2 illustrates the wide range of characteristics most and least frequently associated with American businesspeople.[5]

To communicate effectively with employees, customers, vendors, government officials, and other key stakeholders in host countries, knowledge about culture, communication style, and preferences is critical. Unfortunately, many global organizations do not provide adequate cross-cultural and language training to their soon-to-be global assignees (or their spouses and families). Such training programs (discussed in Chapter 9) could help global managers to understand their own culturally determined stereotypes and communication preferences in an attempt to make them more understanding and accepting of the communication preferences of managers from different cultures. Without this type of training, global managers are more prone to misinterpret and misevaluate the messages of key stakeholders in different parts of the world. Such misinterpretation tends to occur when the global manager is receiving and decoding the

EXHIBIT 4.2
How Other Nationalities Perceive Americans

Source: Adapted from *Newsweek,* July 11, 1983, as presented in Nancy J. Adler, *International Dimensions of Organizational Behavior,* 4th ed (Cincinnati: South-Western, 2002).

Characteristics *Most* Commonly Associated with Americans			
France	**Japan**	**Brazil**	**Mexico**
Industrious	Nationalistic	Intelligent	Industrious
Energetic	Friendly	Inventive	Intelligent
Inventive	Decisive	Energetic	Inventive
Decisive	Rude	Industrious	Decisive
Characteristics *Least* Commonly Associated with Americans			
Lazy	Industrious	Lazy	Lazy
Rude	Lazy	Self-indulgent	Honest
Honest	Honest	Sexy	Rude
Sophisticated	Sexy	Sophisticated	Sexy

Global Focus Communicating in Global Virtual Teams: Know Thyself

Global virtual teams are cross-functional teams that operate across time, space, organizational boundaries, and cultures whose members communicate mainly through electronic technologies (e.g., e-mail, teleconferencing, voice mail, etc.). With infrequent face-to-face contact, these teams are faced with the challenge of building and maintaining trust as they work toward accomplishing the team's objectives and goals. Miscommunication between team members from diverse cultures and backgrounds can block the development of trust and, ultimately, effective team functioning. Internationally savvy companies can manage this potential problem by providing each virtual team member with cross-cultural training.

The first part of the cross-cultural training should focus on helping each team member understand his or her own cultural beliefs, verbal and nonverbal communication style, and attitudes toward time, space, work ethic, and so on. The rationale behind this inward-looking portion of the training is based on the research of Edward T. and Mildred R. Hall, anthropologists and pioneers in the field of culture and communication who wrote: "Like people all over the world, Americans take their culture for granted. Indeed, it's only in juxtaposition with other cultures that Americans begin to understand the influence of their own culture on their behavior." The second part of the cross-cultural training for virtual team members will focus on learning how to work effectively with teammates from diverse cultures. Team members will learn how to interpret the verbal and nonverbal communication styles and cultural backgrounds of teammates and how to respond effectively to these cues.

For example, assume an American is placed on a global virtual team with individuals from Mexico. First, she would learn about her own cultural biases and communication style. Like many Americans, she prefers the following approaches to business: likes to tackle projects in monochronic fashion (i.e., one thing at a time); has a strong work ethic; favors direct, get-to-the-point communication; and likes to keep work and home life separate. In contrast, her Mexican counterparts tend to be more polychronic (i.e., juggle many activities at once), work hard but spend more time with family and friends, prefer a less direct approach to communication (to allow ample time to build trust), and do not refrain from discussing family issues at work.

Without some cross-cultural training, these global virtual team members are going to have a difficult time communicating and building trust. Without such trust, the likelihood of the team performing at an optimal level will be greatly diminished.

Sources: Edward T. Hall and Mildred R. Hall, *Understanding Cultural Differences: Germans, French, and Americans* (Yarmouth, ME: Intercultural Press, 1987); Douglas N. Ross, "Electronic Communications: Do Cultural Dimensions Matter?" *American Business Review,* June 2001, pp. 75–81; Sirkka L. Jarvenpaa and Dorothy E. Leidner, "Communication and Trust in Global Virtual Teams," *Organization Science,* November–December 1999, pp. 791–815; Maurice Cleasby, "Managing Global Contact," *The British Journal of Administrative Management,* March–April 2000, pp. 4–12; Lee Gardenswartz and Anita Rowe, "Cross-Cultural Awareness," *HRMagazine,* March 2001, pp. 139–42; and Steven L. McShane and Mary Ann Von Glinow, *Organizational Behavior* (New York: Irwin McGraw-Hill, 2000).

message sent by a communicator from a different culture. The more culturally distant or different the receiver's culture is from that of the communicator's, the more likely misinterpretation will occur. As the Global Focus above demonstrates, these problems are especially important when virtual team members are from diverse cultures and spread out geographically.

POTENTIAL BARRIERS TO EFFECTIVE CROSS-CULTURAL COMMUNICATION

When two or more managers from different cultural backgrounds and perspectives communicate, several factors may inhibit an effective exchange of meaning. Cross-cultural miscommunication can occur for a variety of reasons. Cultural anthropologists Edward T. Hall and Mildred R. Hall theorized that culture is communication and communication can be divided into several culturally determined parts.[6] Drawing on aspects of their research, some of the main barriers to effective cross-cultural communication include differences in spoken language, the extent to which information is exchanged, consideration of time, and the use of nonverbal behavior.

Language

Approximately 6,000 languages are spoken in the world today. As a result, there will be many occasions when one or both global managers will need to communicate in a second or third language that both individuals will understand. Regardless of one's fluency in that second or third language and understanding of the receiver's host culture, cross-cultural misunderstandings and miscommunications are still likely to occur. For example, Americans are fond of stating agreement with an idea or statement by saying "yeah." In Japan, this term is not recommended because it sounds a lot like the Japanese word for "no," the exact opposite meaning than in the United States. Interestingly, saying "no" should create no problems because it means the same in both English and Japanese.[7]

To help prevent problems from occurring, successful global managers in the 21st century need to be able to communicate in the language of their customer, no matter where that customer is located. Which language or languages are most influential and thus should be part of any global managers' skill set? This question can be considered from a variety of perspectives. If considering the number of primary and secondary speakers, then the top three most commonly spoken languages in the world are Mandarin Chinese (1.2 billion), English (480 million), and Spanish (320 million). If assessing the importance of language in terms of the number of countries where each is spoken, then English (115 countries), French (35 countries), and Arabic (24 countries) would be considered the most influential. Another approach rates languages on six separate criteria—number of primary speakers, number of secondary speakers, number and population of countries where used, number of major fields using language internationally, economic power of countries using languages, and socio-literary prestige.[8] Based on these criteria, the most influential languages turned out to be:

1. English (37 points)
2. French (23 points)
3. Spanish (20 points)
4. Russian (16 points)
5. Arabic (14 points)
6. Chinese Mandarin (13 points)
7. German (12 points)
8. Japanese (10 points)
9. Portuguese (10 points)
10. Hindi/Urdu (9 points)

Before one can conclude that English is sufficient to engage in most global business activities, global managers need to consider the number and languages of the countries they will be working with and the degree of interaction with host-country nationals. An Australian IT manager who will be setting up a new network in a subsidiary in England for a month would have no need to study English (it's her native tongue, the assignment is short, and there will be modest interaction with the host-country nationals). However, if a Chinese manufacturing engineer is being assigned to Brazil for two years to learn the latest innovations in Brazilian manufacturing technology of small jet aircraft (e.g., Embrair series), then intensive language training in Portuguese should be pursued by the Chinese engineer before departure and during the early part of the assignment.

Information Exchange

Cultures differ in the amount of contextual information that is necessary when people interact with one another. Individuals from **high-context communication cultures** do not require a detailed exchange of information, but rather rely on the knowledge they already have about the individual before the interaction. In addition to facts and figures, individuals from these cultures consider such things as one's education, socioeconomic status, family situation, and rank within the organization when interacting and assessing the content of a given message. Japanese and Latin American cultures tend to fall into this category. In contrast, **low-context communication cultures** like in Germany and the United States prefer explicit, detailed exchange of information (e.g., contracts, expansion proposals, budget reports) when two or more individuals are conducting business.[9] Facts, figures, and future projections are all commonly used in business situations.

Problems can occur when an individual from a high-context culture must conduct business with a counterpart from a low-context culture. When a Japanese manager signals to his German counterpart that he is not interested in a particular real estate deal, he will most likely indicate his disinterest by saying, "This deal will be very difficult," or "I'll have to think about it." The German, interpreting this message as a negotiating tactic to lower the price of the deal, counters with a onetime-only offer to lower the asking price by 5 percent. The Japanese, disturbed that his message of "no deal" was not heard, is confused by the German's behavior.[10]

Time

Individuals in Asia, the Middle East, and Africa tend to view time differently from most individuals in the United States, England, and Germany. Managers from **polychronic time cultures** are more prone to multitasking and doing many things at once, are subject to interruptions, are committed to human relationships, change plans often, and base punctuality on the relationship with the person being visited. However, managers from **monochronic time cultures** tend to be linear and do one thing at a time, treat time commitments consistently, adhere to long-term plans, follow rules of privacy and show respect for private property, and emphasize promptness.[11]

The common example of misunderstandings occurs with regard to appointment time. One of the authors (who lived and worked in Mexico City) often found that upon arriving at a Mexican colleague's office for an appointment 10 minutes early, he would be informed that the colleague was running late and would not be at the office for another hour or so. The administrative assistant would indicate that the Mexican manager would be arriving *ahorita* (diminutive for the Spanish word meaning *now*), which could mean in a few minutes or a few hours. As it would often turn out, the Mexican businessperson had bumped into an old friend on the way to the office and could not just rush by him without saying hello. After several such episodes and angry reactions, the author learned to take work along to do in the lobby area while waiting for his Mexican counterpart to arrive.

Nonverbal Behavior

As an effective global manager, one needs to develop the ability to interpret another person's nonverbal behavior. This is done subconsciously with members of one's own culture. When arriving for a two-day business visit or living as a long-term global assignee in another culture, a deliberate effort is often required to make sense of the plethora of differences in nonverbal behavior: body movements, facial expressions, gestures, eye contact, head movements, and other cues that carry with them important communication. The interpretation involves subjectively evaluating the nonverbal behavior of another individual without the use of self-correcting feedback. The task becomes more difficult for American managers who work in global environments, where meanings of nonverbal cues often differ strikingly from those in the United States. Many people around the world know much more about American gestures and nonverbal communication (due to the international popularity of U.S. television and movies) than Americans know about others.

Consider, for example, a nod of the head, which means *yes* in the United States but *no* in Bulgaria and *I'm listening* in England. The OK sign with thumb and forefinger means *money* in France, *worthless* in Japan, and something very obscene in Brazil. Waving to another person, a greeting or farewell in the United States, is a grave insult in Greece and Nigeria.[12]

Facial expressions, an important element in a global manager's daily interpersonal dealings with individuals from other cultures, were studied to determine whether differences existed between how American and Japanese individuals recognized facial expressions.[13] The subjects were 41 American and 44 Japanese college undergraduates. Each group was shown 48 photographs of six universal emotions (eight each of anger, disgust, fear, happiness, sadness, and surprise) to evaluate. For each emotion, two males and two females of both Japanese and American descent were depicted in the photograph.

The study's findings revealed that several differences exist between the two cultures. First, Americans were more accurate than the Japanese at recognizing four of the six emotions (anger, disgust, fear, and sadness), regardless of culture or gender of the poser in the photographs. Second, neither the culture nor gender of the poser affected Americans' judgments of the photos, whereas female emotions were more easily identified than male emotions by the Japanese. Last, both Americans and Japanese agreed that happiness was the easiest emotion to identify and that fear was the most difficult.

Proxemics

An important but often overlooked element of nonverbal communication is **proxemics,** defined as a global manager's use of space when interpersonally communicating with others. According to Edward T. Hall, a prominent researcher of this phenomenon, people have four zones of informal space, spatial distances they maintain when interacting with others: (1) *the intimate zone*—from physical contact to 18 inches apart; (2) *the personal zone*—from 18 inches to 4 feet; (3) *the social zone*—from 4 feet to 12 feet; and (4) *the public zone*—more than 12 feet.[14] For Americans, manager-subordinate relationships begin in the social zone and progress to the personal zone after mutual trust has developed.[15] A manager's personal and intimate zones make up a "bubble" of space that is considered private territory, not to be entered by others unless invited to do so.

Proxemics can create a significant communication barrier when the proxemics of the communicator and receiver differ.[16] Individuals from many Latin American cultures, for example, tend to stand more closely in social situations compared with North Americans. For example, assume that a U.S. transnational manager is invited to a cocktail party reception to celebrate the opening of a new sales and distribution center in Venezuela. Two Venezuelan managers gather around the American to discuss recent competitive information. The Venezuelans, who naturally prefer a personal-zone distance for conversation, are annoyed to see that the American appears nervous and backs away from them (albeit subtly) as the conversation progresses. This behavior signals to the Venezuelans that the American does not trust them or that he does not want to be at the reception. The American, who prefers a little more distance (social zone) around him, feels uncomfortable and is attempting to reestablish his privacy bubble. Conflicting proxemics behavior can affect each individual's perceptions of the other—the North American may view his South American counterparts as pushy and aggressive; they may see him as cold and impolite. Neither perception is healthy for building trust.

IMPROVING CROSS-CULTURAL COMMUNICATION

Global managers striving to become better cross-cultural communicators must accomplish two separate tasks. First, they must improve their messages—the information they wish to transmit. Second, they must seek to improve their own understanding of what people from other cultures are trying to communicate to them. In other words, they must become more sophisticated encoders and decoders. Cross-culturally savvy managers must strive not only to be understood, but also to understand.[17] Further reinforcement for this idea comes from cultural anthropologists Edward T. Hall and Mildred R. Hall who captured the important role the sender plays in the cross-cultural process when they wrote:[18] "Remember it is more important to release the right responses in others than it is to send what you think are the right messages."

Global managers can take many steps to become more effective cross-cultural communicators. First, they need to have an objective understanding of their own culture, communication norms, and mores.[19] Once this is achieved, global managers need to learn about the culture and communication practices of the cultures with which they will be interacting. Depending on the role of the global manager and the degree of interaction with host-country nationals, they will need to develop at least some proficiency, if not fluency, in the host-country language. As in all domestic and international business communications, best practices, such as expressing empathy, using repetition, and following up, are always recommended.[20]

Start With Your Own Culture

For many individuals, it takes an international living, working, and/or studying experience to gain insight into understanding the subtle aspects of their own culture. If one thinks of culture as an iceberg, only the most obvious artifacts and characteristics of the culture are visible from above the surface. In contrast, nonverbal communication practices such as facial expressions, proxemics, and eye contact are rarely taught directly to young children in school as they become socialized to the culture.[21] To be effective, global managers need to step outside of their culture and see it from the perspective of a non-home-country national. Whether this learning occurs through personal reflection, reading books on cross-cultural business practices, searching the Internet, asking for opinions from individuals from other countries, or international experience, global managers need to understand their own culture (those aspects above and below the "waterline") before they can effectively interact, communicate, and build empathy with individuals from other cultures.

Learn About the Host Culture

Assume a global manager with British Petroleum Oil Company is about to be transferred to Saudi Arabia for a year. What should he know about the culture? At the very least, he should understand the basics about Saudi geography, history, government structure and regulations, economy, population, religion, and geopolitical issues. All of this can be found in resources on the Internet such as the *CIA World Factbook,* which profiles over 200 countries.[22] Specifically, individuals can use this information when developing business plans, staffing approaches, and company policies. In addition, savvy managers can engender

Global Focus Toyota in France: Culture Clash?

Hiroaki Watanabe, the Japanese general manager of the first major Toyota plant in Valenciennes, France (and in continental Europe), has a lot at stake. He is in charge of a modern and efficient $570 million Toyota Motor factory designed to manufacture the Yaris, a subcompact car. The plant was designed to employ 2,000 workers. Currently, there are about 200 Japanese managers and 150 Japanese trainers on staff. The remaining employees are mostly French. Culturally, there were many potential areas of conflict between the Japanese and French customs. For example, the plant holds calisthenics at 8:00 A.M. every day to avoid starting off the day cold and more prone to injuries. This is a common Japanese practice that is not frequently done in France. Also, the plant does not serve wine at lunch, a common practice in other French organizations. As is common in other Japanese firms, blue and gray windbreaker jackets are made available with the word Toyota on the back and the employee's name on the front.

To help bridge these and other potential cultural gaps, the leadership of the venture needs to understand the potential cultural clashes that these issues can cause. How did Mr. Watanabe prepare himself for this high-profile assignment? Although fluent in English, he decided that he would learn French and as much about French culture as possible. After all, the vast majority of workers at the plant would be from northern France. To prepare himself, he traveled to France as a tourist and visited the Toyota plant in Canada. He conducted interviews in French, with the assistance of an interpreter, to improve his language skills.

Will his efforts succeed? Toyota has high hopes for this first major undertaking in continental Europe. Its goal is to increase its market share, which is currently at 3.7 percent, less than half its share in the United States. The French employees also have a lot at stake. The Valenciennes area, a former coal and steel region, suffers from high unemployment with the shuttering of many companies in heavy industry over the past 20 years. To underscore the importance of Toyota to this region, more than 30,000 people applied for the 2,000 jobs at the factory.

Source: John Tagliabue, "At a French Factory, Culture Is a Two-Way Street," *New York Times*, February 25, 2001, sec. 3, p. 4.

some goodwill with their host-country counterparts by demonstrating knowledge of the host country and its culture. This signals that the visiting global manager respects the host culture enough to take time out of a busy schedule to become culturally proficient. The accompanying Global Focus describes what one global manager for Toyota Motor did to be effective in France.

Know the Host-Country Language

One of the more challenging activities for many global managers is to become fluent in one or more host-country national languages. Although many individuals (especially native English speakers) believe that English is the language of world business and is sufficient for most common business transactions,[23] others would argue that a global assignee should always speak the language of the

EXHIBIT 4.3
Examples of Survival Language Phrases

Sources: Adapted from *German at a Glance,* 3rd ed. (Hauppauge, N.Y.: Barron's Educational Series, 2000), and *Italian at a Glance,* 3rd ed. (Hauppauge, N.Y.: Barron's Educational Series, 2000).

In English: **"Good morning. Do you speak English?"**
In Spanish: *"Buenos días. ¿Habla usted español?"*
In German: *"Guten Morgen. Sprechen Sie Englisch?"*
In Italian: *"Buon giorno. Parla inglese?"*
In Portuguese: *"Bom dia. Você fala português?"*

In English: **"My name is ________."**
In Spanish: *"Me llamo ________."*
In German: *"Ich heiße ________."*
In Italian: *"Mi chiamo ________."*
In Portuguese: *"Meu nome é ________."*

In English: **"I don't understand. What does that mean?"**
In Spanish: *"No entiendo ¿Que significa?"*
In German: *"Ich verstehe nicht. Was bedeutet das?"*
In Italian: *"Non ho capito. Che cosa significa?"*
In Portuguese: *"Naõ entendo. O que significa?"*

In English: **"Good luck!"**
In Spanish: *"¡Buena suerte!"*
In German: *"Viel Gluck!"*
In Italian: *"Buona fortuna!"*
In Portuguese: *"Boa sorte!"*

customer, no matter what. Every attempt should be made by global assignees to learn the host-country language. This is especially important for managers who will be living and working in a host country for extended periods. For those other individuals who visit multiple countries each year and spend only a few weeks in each, then learning several key phrases such as "Good morning, my name is so and so," and "It's nice to meet you," and "Hello, thank you, and goodbye" will help the global assignee function and gain the respect of the host-country nationals. By showing some humility and trying hard to speak another's language, one shows respect for the people who speak that language. Exhibit 4.3 lists examples of some "survival language" phrases.

Use "Best Practices" Communication Skills

There are several best practices that can help global managers enhance their cross-cultural communication effectiveness, including developing mutual trust and using empathy, repetition, and effective listening.[24]

Mutual Trust

Time pressures and hectic travel schedules often mean that global managers cannot follow up their messages and encourage feedback every time they communicate with stakeholders from different cultures. Under such circumstances, an atmosphere of mutual confidence and trust between managers from diverse cultures can help facilitate communication. In cultures that require a longer amount of time to get to know one another and more disclosure about one's personal life, the trust building often requires several initial face-to-face visits before mutual trust can be established. For example, in his business travels from the United States to Chile, a global manager found that it took three or four visits and several long dinners to develop solid working relationships with key Chilean host-country nationals, including customers, vendors, and employees. The manager resisted the temptation to get down to business during the early visits and instead focused on building rapport and getting to know the host-country nationals. He waited until they initiated business discussions and as a result was perceived as *simpático* (meaning *nice, friendly*) and able to be trusted.

Empathy

Empathy is the ability to put oneself in the other person's role and to assume that individual's viewpoints and emotions. This involves being receiver-oriented rather than communicator-oriented. The form of communication should depend largely on what is known about the receiver. This underscores the importance of having a good understanding of the receiver's culture and communication style. Global managers must understand and appreciate the process of decoding. Often a simple phrase from the communicator can express empathy to the receiver. For example, a software salesperson from India might say to a potential Chinese customer in Beijing that she understands it will take time before the Chinese company can decide whether to purchase her software products. Knowing China to be a collectivist culture where team decision making is often the rule, the Indian salesperson demonstrated empathy in her communication. Global managers who can relate and express their understanding of another's situation tend to be more successful. The greater the gap between the experiences and background of the communicator and the receiver, the greater should be the effort to find a common ground of understanding where functional areas, business training, education, and/or experience overlap.

Repetition

Tell them what you're going to tell them, tell them, and tell them what you told them. Repetition is an accepted principle of learning. Introducing repetition or redundancy into communication (especially if the communicator and receiver are not fluent in a mutual language) ensures that if one part of the message is not understood, other parts carry the same message. When repeating key concepts to one or more host-country nationals who are not fluent in the global assignee's language, a good communicator will seek feedback from the receivers to check if the message is being interpreted as originally intended. When a distributor from a company in Morocco is finalizing the deal with her counterpart in Spain, she would be well-advised to confirm the final sales price for the farming equipment by repeating it at different times during the meeting and then, after the meeting, sending a follow-up written summary of the highlights of the meeting (with the sales price included) to the Spanish buyer.

Effective Listening

One of the best ways to encourage someone to express true feelings, desires, and emotions is to listen. But just listening is not enough; one must listen with *understanding.* One writer cites numerous ways to become a more effective listener in organizational settings: stop talking to put the listener at ease, show the listener you want to listen by removing distractions, empathize with the speaker, be patient, hold your temper, refrain from criticism, ask questions, and stop talking.[25] Notice "stop talking" is the first and last suggestion. This underscores how important listening is when dealing with individuals from diverse cultures.

Such guidelines can be useful to global managers. More important, however, is the decision to listen. Guidelines are useless unless the manager makes the conscious decision to listen. Only after the realization that effective communication involves understanding as well as being understood can guidelines for effective listening become useful.

In conclusion, all aspects of a global manager's job involve communication. If everyone with whom the global manager has contact had a common point of view, communicating would be easy. Unfortunately, such is not the case in the international business arena—customers and colleagues from diverse cultures come to the table with a unique personality, language, background, experience, and frame of reference. All of these factors can influence the ability of individuals to communicate effectively across cultures.

This chapter has described basic elements in the process of cross-cultural communication and what it takes to communicate effectively with individuals from diverse cultural heritages. These elements are necessary whether the communication is delivered by face-to-face talking, telephone, e-mail, intranet or teleconference. Several common cross-cultural communication barriers and several means to improve communication were discussed. Often, time does not permit global managers to utilize many of the techniques for improving communication, and skills such as empathy and effective listening are not easy to develop. However, for global managers to be effective when crossing cultures, they must understand as well as be understood.

Key Terms

Communication process model, *147*
Decoding, *147*
Empathy, *158*
Encoding, *147*
High-context communication cultures, *152*
Low-context communication cultures, *152*
Monochronic time cultures, *152*
Polychronic time cultures, *152*
Proxemics, *154*
Stereotypes, *148*

Review, Critical Thinking, and Discussion Questions

1. Why is being a good communicator in multicultural contexts so important to today's global managers?
2. Why is the process of decoding and receiving a message so important to the cross-cultural communication process?
3. Do you think global managers should just rely on English whenever possible or take the time to learn one or more host-country languages? Explain.
4. Do you think low- or high-context communication cultures are more likely to emphasize the importance of written contracts in their business practices? Why?
5. Assume you are about to visit a culture where one is expected to hug members of the same sex and kiss on the cheek those of the opposite sex. If you are not comfortable with this, how would you deal with the situation without insulting the host-country nationals?
6. In general, how skilled are transnational managers at picking up the subtleties of nonverbal communication of people from another country? How can they improve?
7. Why is it important to start with and learn about your own national culture before trying to learn about another national culture?
8. Thinking about your own national culture, try to identify and describe the five most important values that most individuals in that culture share.
9. Think about a foreign language that you are interested in learning. What would be the fastest way that you could learn basic "survival phrases"? Follow up on this idea and learn five key phrases that will help you get around in the country.
10. Most everyone relies on stereotypes until they are proven inaccurate. Think about three national cultures. What stereotypes do you think of when describing the people from these three cultures? How can you learn more about these cultures so you don't have to rely just on stereotypes?

Endnotes

1. Claude Shannon and Warren Weaver, *The Mathematical Theory of Communication* (Urbana, IL: University of Illinois Press, 1948), and Wilbur Schramm, "How Communication Works," in *The Process and Effects of Mass Communication,* ed. Wilbur Schramm (Urbana, IL: University of Illinois Press, 1953), pp. 3–26. These works are considered classics in the field of communication.
2. Nancy J. Adler, *International Dimensions of Organizational Behavior,* 4th ed. (Cincinnati: South-Western, 2002), p. 74.
3. Anne Marie Francesco and Barry Allen Gold, *International Organizational Behavior: Text, Readings, Cases, and Skills* (Upper Saddle River, NJ: Prentice Hall, 1998), p. 64.
4. Adler, *International Dimensions of Organizational Behavior.*
5. Adapted from an article in *Newsweek,* July 11, 1983, as presented in Adler, *International Dimensions of Organizational Behavior,* p. 86.
6. Edward T. Hall and Mildred R. Hall, *Understanding Cultural Differences: Germans, French, and Americans* (Yarmouth, ME: Intercultural Press, 1989), p. 3.
7. David A. Ricks, *Blunders in International Business* (Oxford: Blackwell Business, 1993).
8. George Weber, "The World's 10 Most Influential Languages," *Language Today,* Vol. 2, 1997, pp. 4–10.
9. Hall and Hall, *Understanding Cultural Differences.*

10. Adler, *International Dimensions of Organizational Behavior.*
11. Hall and Hall, *Understanding Cultural Differences.*
12. C. Barnum and N. Wolniansky, "Taking Cues from Body Language: International Business Transactions," *Management Review,* June 1989, pp. 59–60.
13. D. Matsumoto, "American-Japanese Cultural Differences in the Recognition of Universal Facial Expressions," *Journal of Cross-Cultural Psychology,* March 1992, pp. 72–84.
14. Edward T. Hall, *The Hidden Dimension* (Garden City, NY: Doubleday, 1966).
15. Phillip L. Hunsaker, "Communicating Better: There's No Proxy for Proxemics," *Business Week,* March–April 1980, pp. 41–48.
16. Hall, *Hidden Dimension.*
17. Ernest G. Bormann, "Symbolic Convergence Theory: A Communication Formulation," *Journal of Communication,* Fall 1985, pp. 128–38.
18. Hall and Hall, *Understanding Cultural Differences.*
19. Edward T. Hall, *Beyond Culture* (Garden City, NY: Anchor Press/Doubleday, 1976).
20. James L. Gibson, James H. Donnelly, Jr., John M. Ivancevich, *Organizations: Behavior, Structure, Processes,* 11th ed. (New York: McGraw-Hill/Irwin, 2003).
21. Edward T. Hall, *The Silent Language* (Garden City, NY: Doubleday, 1959).
22. *CIA World Factbook* on the Web at http://www.cia.gov/cia/publications/factbook/.
23. John Tagliabue, "In Europe, Going Global Means, Alas, English," *New York Times,* May 19, 2002.
24. Gibson et al., *Organizations,* pp. 432–33.
25. Keith Davis, *Human Behavior at Work* (New York: McGraw-Hill, 1980), p. 394.

Chapter Five

Motivation

Learning Objectives

After completing Chapter 5, you should be able to:

- Explain how and why motivation should be treated as being culture-bound.
- Discuss why a managerial global mind-set is better suited for an expatriate manager than using a universal prescriptive approach to motivation.
- Explain the role that family and work-unit play in motivating employees in some cultures.
- Describe the meaning of work and its role in creating motivational opportunities.
- Explain why it is correct to state that motivation is an internal process that is not directly observable.
- Examine why various reward systems must be modified to fit host-country employees in transnational organizational settings.

Does What Works in New York Work in Tokyo?

Pay is considered a motivator of performance and job satisfaction. The role of pay, however, in these relationships is questioned. For American and Canadian sales forces, perhaps the most widely accepted viewpoint of performance/satisfaction determinants is as follows: Internal variables, such as aptitude and motivation, influence performance, which influences rewards received from others, rewards from the job itself, which then results in satisfaction. This explanation is largely tested in Western developed nations.

Japan, the second-largest U.S. trading partner, provides a useful comparison for studying sales force motivation, performance, and satisfaction. Approaches to motivating Japanese and American sales forces are quite different. Most U.S. firms use some combination of salary and commission to motivate their sales forces. The ratio between the two compensation components often varies from year to year as policy and business changes. Straight salary is much more frequently used in Japanese firms. Both Japanese and U.S. firms also include bonuses as part of the compensation packages. The Japanese base bonuses on company performance, while U.S. bonuses are usually tied to individual performance.

Japanese companies that are subsidiaries of U.S. firms, however, provide compensation packages with commission or individual bonus components. For example, National Cash Register pioneered commission selling in Japan.

Assuming that what typically works for an American sales force will motivate a Japanese sales force is not accurate. A better way of motivating Japanese sales representatives is by encouraging their commitment to the firm. Thinking in terms of motivational differences across countries appears to be valid when managers are considering how to improve opportunities for their employees to become and stay motivated.

Source: Adapted from Paul Verdin and Nick Van Heck, *From Local Champions to Global Masters* (New York: Global Publishing, 2002), and C. Brooklyn Derr, Sylvie Roussillon, and Frank Bournois, *Cross Cultural Approaches to Leadership Development* (Westport, CT: Greenwood Publishing Group, 2002).

Once managers establish a firm's operations through planning, organize jobs and the structure, set up control systems, and find and hire the talent needed to accomplish the mission, they become involved with motivation and leadership. Human assets must perform effectively for the company to survive.

This chapter will examine motivation in a global context. Are some motivational principles universal, or should there be no expectation that what works in one country's culture may work in another country? This question should be asked for any management application being considered.

THE MOTIVATIONAL PUZZLE

The concept of **motivation** refers to an individual's selection of behaviors and what lies behind making these choices.[1] Motivation is an internal process that can't be directly observed. Each individual internally can turn on his or her personal motivation. Managers can play a role by creating a work environment or opportunities that are attractive to individuals, which results in the initiation and sustaining of a high degree of internal motivation. To better understand what happens internally, there must be a discussion of needs, goals, value systems, expectations, and preferences.

Theories and studies of cross-cultural comparisons of motivation have largely centered on what are referred to as the content theories of motivation. The most recognized content theories were originally presented in the United States by Maslow, Herzberg, and McClelland.[2] Their theories focused on individual needs that are based on value systems. No matter what their nationality, cultural background, or physical location, people are motivated by the desire and aspiration to fulfill needs, which results in goals being accomplished. Of course, individual needs differ and they change.

Maslow's Theory

Most behavioral scientists agree that human beings are motivated by the desire to satisfy many needs. But there is a wide difference of opinion as to what those needs and their relative importance are. Abraham Maslow, a clinical psychologist, developed a widely publicized theory of motivation called the **hierarchy of needs.**

Maslow's hierarchy of needs is still widely accepted today in management theory and practice because it seems to make sense and is easy to understand.[3] This theory of motivation is based on two important assumptions:

1. Each person's needs depend on what he already has. Only needs not yet satisfied can influence behavior. A satisfied need cannot influence behavior.
2. Needs are arranged in a hierarchy of importance. Once one need is satisfied, another emerges and demands satisfaction.

Maslow believed five levels of needs exist. These levels are (1) physiological, (2) safety, (3) social, (4) esteem, and (5) self-actualization. He placed them in a framework he called the *hierarchy of needs,* presented in Exhibit 5.1.

EXHIBIT 5.1 **Maslow's Hierarchy of Needs**

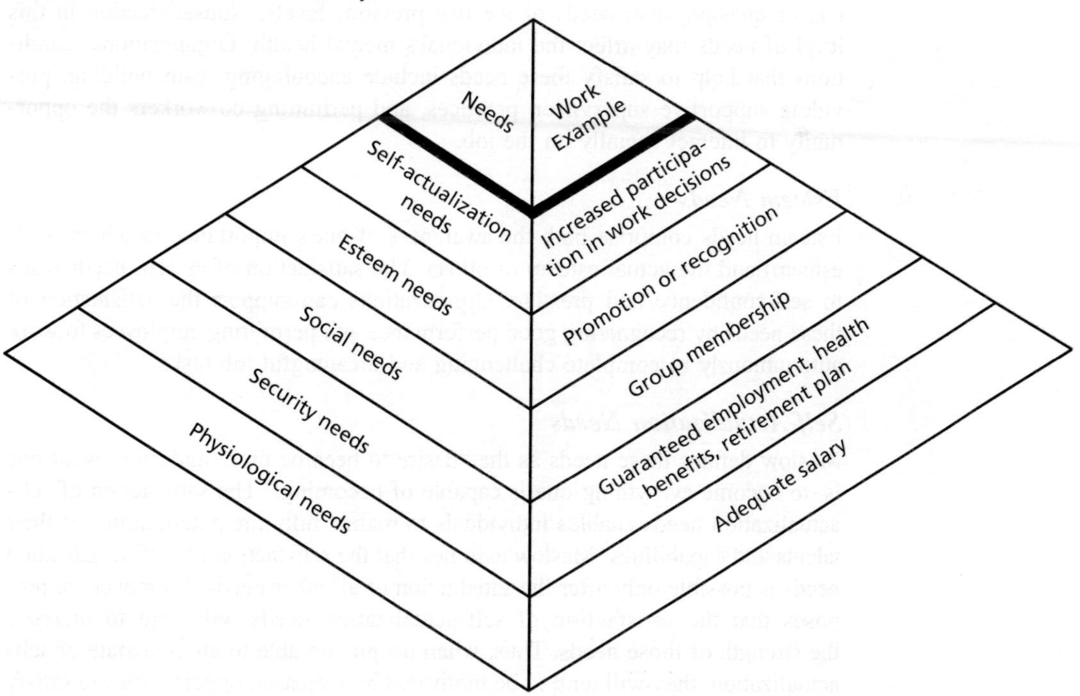

Maslow stated that if all of a person's needs are unsatisfied at a particular time, the most basic needs will be more pressing than the others. Needs at a lower level must be satisfied before higher-level needs come into play, and only when they are sufficiently satisfied do the next needs in line become significant.

Physiological Needs

This category consists of the basic needs of the human body, such as food, water, and sex. Physiological needs will dominate when all needs are unsatisfied. In such a case, no other needs will serve as a basis for motivation. As Maslow states, "A person who is lacking food, safety, love, and esteem would probably hunger for food more strongly than for anything else." Organizational factors that might satisfy physiological needs include enough pay to permit an employee to survive and working conditions that permit a healthy environment.

Safety Needs

Safety needs include protection from physical harm, ill health, economic disaster, and the unexpected. From a managerial standpoint, safety needs manifest themselves in attempts to ensure job security and to move toward greater financial support.

Social Needs

Social needs are related to the social nature of people and to their need for companionship. This level in the hierarchy is the point of departure from the physical or quasiphysical needs of the two previous levels. Nonsatisfaction in this level of needs may affect the individual's mental health. Organizational conditions that help to satisfy these needs include encouraging team building, providing supportive supervision practices, and permitting co-workers the opportunity to interact socially on the job.

Esteem Needs

Esteem needs comprise both the awareness of one's importance to others (self-esteem) and the actual esteem of others. The satisfaction of esteem needs leads to self-confidence and prestige. Organizations can support the satisfaction of these needs by recognizing good performance and permitting employees to work autonomously to complete challenging and meaningful job tasks.

Self-Actualization Needs

Maslow defines these needs as the "desire to become more and more what one is, to become everything one is capable of becoming." The satisfaction of self-actualization needs enables individuals to realize fully the potentialities of their talents and capabilities. Maslow assumes that the satisfaction of self-actualization needs is possible only after the satisfaction of all other needs. Moreover, he proposes that the satisfaction of self-actualization needs will tend to *increase* the strength of those needs. Thus, when people are able to attain a state of self-actualization, they will tend to be motivated by increased opportunities to satisfy that level of needs. Organizations can help employees satisfy self-actualization needs by encouraging creativity, allowing risk-taking decision making, and supporting workers in their efforts to develop their skills.

Maslow's ideas are easy to recall and continue to play an influential role among practicing managers and human resource professionals. However, there are significant problems with this perspective. First, Maslow recognized that the hierarchy is not a stair-step approach. Human needs are multiple and they often occur simultaneously. Second, we have to consider the relative level of the need that is present at a given time. Being thirsty is a relative concept. If you're in a desert and have no water, the need will probably influence 100 percent of your behavior. On the other hand, if you're mildly thirsty all morning but you're writing the weekly report, your behavior may be more determined by a deadline than your thirst. Third, Maslow's theory describes needs as internal; it says nothing about the environment's effect on behavior. How are needs determined? For example, the need for new clothes may be determined by comparing our clothes with those worn by friends, models, or prestigious people. Functionally our clothes may be fine, but by comparison to our friends' clothing, they might look old or out of style. So what might be considered a lower-order need for clothing becomes translated into a higher-order need for self-esteem.

Global Application of Maslow's Theory

Do the Maslow-type needs described and established as a hierarchy fit everywhere in the world or are they country-bound? Research suggests that needs are universal. However, the Maslow hierarchy is different across countries.[4] A dated, yet comprehensive study of more than 3,600 managers in 14 countries showed that the Maslow-type needs were important across countries. In Latin Europe, United States/England, and Nordic country clusters, the autonomy and self-actualization needs were most significant. This study focused on managers and not operating employees, but it showed overall congruence with the Maslow explanation of need preferences and satisfaction.

A study of Indian managers suggested more emphasis on lower-order needs such as security, salary, and benefits.[5] This result may illustrate the importance of culture and family traditions in a country such as India. As India develops economically, it will be interesting to monitor need preferences to determine if they begin to align with other more developed countries.

In the Middle East, self-actualization needs have been found to be important. Badawy reported that cultural conditions that place the male in an influence and power position may be the reason higher-order need satisfaction is preferred.[6]

The exact arrangement of needs in a hierarchy should be questioned in any consideration or application of Maslow's theory. The original hierarchy is a presentation of a Western culture explanation. Other national cultures may focus on belonging, safety, and security needs more strongly because of their traditions, conditions, religion, or other reasons. As will be the case in explaining each motivational approach in this chapter, do not assume universal, perfect transferability as a managerial or organizational approach to motivation.

Herzberg's Theory

Frederick Herzberg advanced a theory of motivation based on a study of need satisfactions and on the reported motivational effects of those satisfactions on 200 engineers and accountants. His approach is termed the **two-factor theory of motivation.**[7]

Herzberg asked the participants in his study to think of times when they felt especially good and especially bad about their jobs. Each person was then asked to describe the conditions that caused those feelings. Significantly, the individuals identified different work conditions for each of the feelings. For example, if managerial recognition for doing an excellent job led to good feelings about the job, the lack of managerial recognition was seldom indicated as a cause of bad feelings.

Based on this research, Herzberg reached the following two conclusions:

1. Although employees are dissatisfied by the absence of some job conditions, the presence of those conditions does not cause strong motivation. Herzberg called such conditions *maintenance or hygiene factors,* since they are necessary to maintain a minimum level of need satisfaction. He also noted that these have often been perceived by managers as factors that can motivate subordinates, but that they are, in fact, more potent as dissatisfiers when they are absent. He concluded that there were 10 maintenance factors, namely:

- Company policy and administration.
- Technical supervision.
- Interpersonal relations with supervisor.
- Interpersonal relations with peers.
- Interpersonal relations with subordinates.
- Salary.
- Job security.
- Personal life.
- Work conditions.
- Status.

2. Some job factors, which Herzberg calls *motivators,* cause high levels of motivation and job satisfaction when present. However, the absence of these factors does not prove highly dissatisfying. Herzberg described six of these motivational factors:

- Achievement.
- Recognition.
- Advancement.
- The work itself.
- The possibility of personal growth.
- Responsibility.

EXHIBIT 5.2
Contrasting Views of Satisfaction-Dissatisfaction

Traditional View

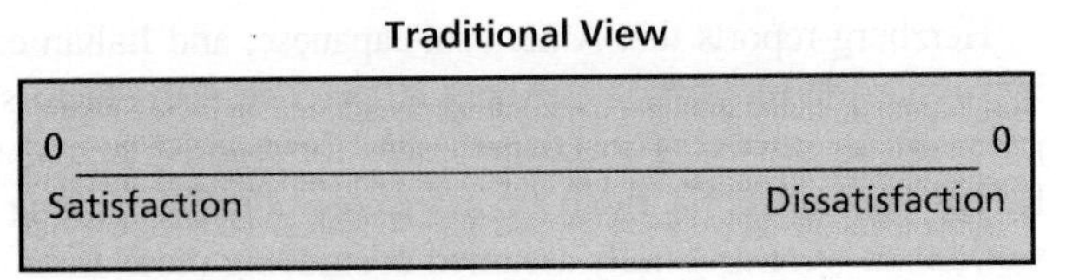

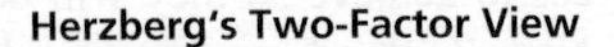

Motivators

0 ——— 0

No Satisfaction — Satisfaction

Maintenance factors

0 ——— 0

Dissatisfaction — No Satisfaction

Before Herzberg's research, managers viewed job satisfaction and dissatisfaction as opposite ends of the same continuum, as shown in Exhibit 5.2. Herzberg's research findings introduced the notion of two continuums. If employees are not satisfied, they indicate no satisfaction, and not dissatisfaction.

The motivational factors are job centered. They relate directly to the job itself; that is, the individual's job performance, the job responsibilities, and the growth and recognition obtained from the job. The maintenance factors are peripheral to the job and are more related to the external environment of work. The distinction between motivational and maintenance factors is similar to the distinction between intrinsic and extrinsic rewards. Intrinsic rewards are part of the job and occur when the employee performs the work; the work itself is rewarding. Extrinsic rewards are external rewards (e.g., receiving a paycheck) that have meaning or value after the work has been performed or away from the workplace. They provide little, if any, satisfaction when the work is being performed.

Global Application of Herzberg's Theory

Since conducting the original study, Herzberg has cited numerous replications supporting his position. These studies were conducted with professional women, hospital maintenance personnel, agricultural administrators, nurses, food handlers, manufacturing supervisors, engineers, scientists, military officers, managers ready for retirement, teachers, technicians, and assemblers.[8] Some of the studies were conducted in cultural settings beyond the United States, in Finland, Hungary, the Soviet Union, and Yugoslavia.

Herzberg reports that American, Japanese, and Italian employees are motivated by similar job motivations.[9] About 80 percent of the factors that are intrinsic to the job result in satisfying job experiences for workers across these different cultures. He has concluded that there are more commonalties among workers throughout the world than were originally assumed in studying motivation. Employees in Italy, like those in the United States, are motivated by their own inherent need to succeed at a challenging task. The manager in Rome or Chicago needs to provide opportunities for employees to achieve so they will become motivated.

A study of New Zealand managers and salaried employees used a rating of 12 job factors and overall job satisfaction to examine whether Herzberg's explanation of two-factors theory was accurate for the sample studied. Only the hygiene factors were reported to be sources of dissatisfaction.[10]

A study in Zambia examined Herzberg on six factors: work nature, growth and advancement, material and physical provisions, relations with others, fairness/unfairness in organizational practices, and personal problems.[11] The findings suggested that in an economically developing country such as Zambia, the two-factor explanation was valid.

McClelland's Theory

Psychologist David McClelland studied the conditions under which people develop a motive to achieve and its impact on behavior. The term *achievement* is used to mean both a need and a motive. McClelland and his colleagues devised a way to measure the strength of a need and then looked for relationships between strength of needs in different societies, conditions that had fostered the needs, and the results of needs in work organizations.[12]

Participants were shown pictures and asked to make up stories about them; that is, to describe what was happening in the picture and what the probable outcome would be. McClelland assumed that what a person perceived and reported in the pictures (called the **Thematic Apperception Test (TAT)** reflected the person's values, interests, and motives. McClelland stated, "If you want to find out what's on a person's mind, don't ask him, because he can't always tell you. Study his fantasies and dreams. If you do this over a period of time, you will discover the themes to which his mind returns again and again. These themes can be used to explain his actions."

From individuals' responses to a series of pictures, McClelland calculated scores for three human needs—need for achievement, need for affiliation, and need for power. The need for achievement was designated as n Ach. For example, one picture was of a boy holding a violin. Exhibit 5.3 provides hypothetical stories prepared by a person who scored high on need for achievement and one who scored low on need for achievement.

Self-motivated need achievers like to set their own goals. Goals that they set are moderately difficult but are not impossible to achieve. Also, those with high needs for achievement like to receive feedback on their performance. Successful salespeople usually have a high achievement motivation, for example. These people set moderately difficult, but achievable goals for themselves.

EXHIBIT 5.3
Examples of n Ach Stories

High n Ach Story	Low n Ach Story
The boy just completed a long, daily violin lesson. He is happy with his improvement and thinks that his daily practice is well worth the hard work. He knows that to become a top concert violinist by the time he turns 19 he will have to practice when his friends are partying, playing baseball, dating, and attending musical concerts. He wants to be the best and is willing to pay the price.	Jim is simply holding his dad's violin. He likes the music it makes, but feels that his dad spends too many hours playing the instrument. If only he could play without having to practice like his dad. It seemed that practicing was boring and would take away valuable time from his friends and his girlfriend. Maybe there are other instruments that are easier to learn to play. Then again, maybe he should be a good listener of music performed by others.

Global Application of McClelland's Theory

A number of research studies have examined McClelland's achievement-oriented theory. McClelland and his colleagues developed and implemented a training program to increase need for achievement in Mexico (schoolchildren), India (business employees), and the United States (executives). With the exception of one group of high school students in Mexico, those who received the training were more successful two years later than those who took another course or no course.[13]

Subsequent research with business executives in India indicates that achievement improvement through training could not be sustained. One explanation for this may be that India's national culture did not support the concept of individual achievement satisfaction and behavior. India's group culture values could work against individualism reflected in seeking personal achievements.

Studies of Russian entrepreneurs indicated a strong need for achievement. However, there has been a problem in Russia with this need.

> Achievement, ambition, and initiative have been denigrated in Russia. People with a high need for achievement have been condemned for being individualists, antisocial, and enemies of the people. Personal ambition has aroused feeling of envy, vindictiveness, and decision.[14]

Again culture, history, and economic stage of development need to be considered when discussing achievement motivation.

A study of Confucianism and need preference in China reported comparisons of Chinese versus American MBA students on achievement, affiliation, change, and other factors. The Chinese MBAs scored lower than their American counterparts on each of these factors.[15]

The growth of economic development of China more recently may help generate additional research on achievement needs. Reports suggest that within China the sense that achievement is a worthy pursuit is increasing among the educated and younger Chinese.

Research in Poland indicated that Polish managers had high achievement motivation. The average Polish versus American manager scores were 6.58 (Polish) versus 6.74 (American). However, when Czech managers were studied, they reported much lower achievement scores of 3.32.[16] These studies of central Europeans were conducted before glasnost and the end of the Eastern bloc. Today, the findings in the Czech Republic and Poland may be different because of the post-communist changes that have occurred in the economic systems, culture, society, and values.

Research on motivation typically illustrates that local culture, history, mores, and society play such a major role in motivation that they must all be carefully evaluated and considered before attempts are made to (1) understand the motivation triggers of host-nation employees, (2) intervene with specific motivation enhancement programs, and (3) train host-nation employees to help them understand and generate their own motivational strategies.

PROCESS MOTIVATION EXPLANATIONS

A number of process theories also help explain how behavior is initiated, sustained, and changed. They add some value and insight to the global managers' motivation, knowledge, considerations, and approaches.

Expectancy Theory of Motivation

One process theory of motivation was developed by Victor H. Vroom, and it expands on the work of Maslow and Herzberg.[17] Vroom's **expectancy theory of motivation** views motivation as a process governing choices. Thus, an individual who has a particular goal must practice a certain behavior to achieve it. He or she weighs the likelihood that various behaviors will achieve the desired goal, and if a certain behavior seems to be more successful than others, that behavior likely will be the one the goal-seeker selects.

In the expectancy motivation model, motivation, or the force to perform, is defined as expectancy times instrumentality times valence, or $M = E \times I \times V$. The theory proposes three determinants of motivation:

1. *The expectancy that individual effort will result in performance.* Employees generally are motivated to exert effort if they believe their effort will result in high performance.
2. *The belief that performance will result in reward.* Employees are motivated if they believe performance will lead to desired rewards. The employee considers whether performance is instrumental in achieving rewards.
3. *The valence of rewards.* Valence refers to an employee's preference for rewards he believes will result from performing well. A manager who provides rewards that have low valence (are not highly preferred) is not likely to see that rewards bring much improvement in performance.

Expectancies are probabilities calculated by a person's thought processes. If a person decides that if she works hard, she will be a high performer, expectancy is likely to be close to 1.00, or certainty. On the other hand, if a person decides that no matter how hard she works, there is little likelihood that she will be a high performer, expectancy will be close to 0.

Whether or not high performance is associated with desired outcomes is determined by examining what is called **instrumentality** in the expectancy theory. Instrumentalities are correlations or indicators of association, which range from -1.00 to $+1.00$. If a person sees no association between high performance and an outcome such as a merit pay increase, the instrumentality is 0. On the other hand, if a person believes high performance is always associated with a merit pay increase, the instrumentality is $+1.00$.

Valences are the values an individual attaches to work outcomes, such as a merit pay increase, a promotion, a transfer to a new group, more job responsibility, or having a longer workday. If one desires an outcome, it has a positive valence; if one does not prefer an outcome, it has a negative valence; if one is indifferent to a particular outcome, it is considered to have a zero valence.

Expectancy theory predicts that motivation to work will be high in the following instances:

1. *Expectancy is high*—The employee feels that high performance can be attained.
2. *Instrumentality is high*—The employee associates high performance with a desired (positive valence) outcome such as a merit pay increase.
3. *Valence is high*—The employee has a high preference for a merit pay increase.

Since $M = E \times I \times V$, all three components in the equation must be high to achieve optimal motivation. A zero for expectancy, instrumentality, or valence means there is no motivation. Exhibit 5.4 illustrates a general and a work-related example of the expectancy theory.

An important contribution of the expectancy theory is that it explains how the *goals* of individuals influence their *effort,* and that the behavior individuals select depends on their assessment of whether it will successfully lead to the goal. For example, members of an organization may not place the same value on efforts to increase employee involvement. Research has shown that employees who volunteer for such programs evaluate their outcomes more favorably than those who don't volunteer. In fact, individual commitment to employee involvement programs is directly related to appraisal of potential program outcomes.[18]

Vroom believes that what is important is the perception and value that the individual places on certain goals. Suppose one individual places a high value on a bonus and perceives high performance as instrumental in reaching that goal. Accordingly, this individual will strive toward superior performance to achieve the bonus. However, another individual may value relationships with co-workers. The individual, therefore, is not likely to emphasize superior performance to achieve the goal. Think of expectancy theory in terms of two workers,

EXHIBIT 5.4
Expectancy Theory from a Manager's Perspective

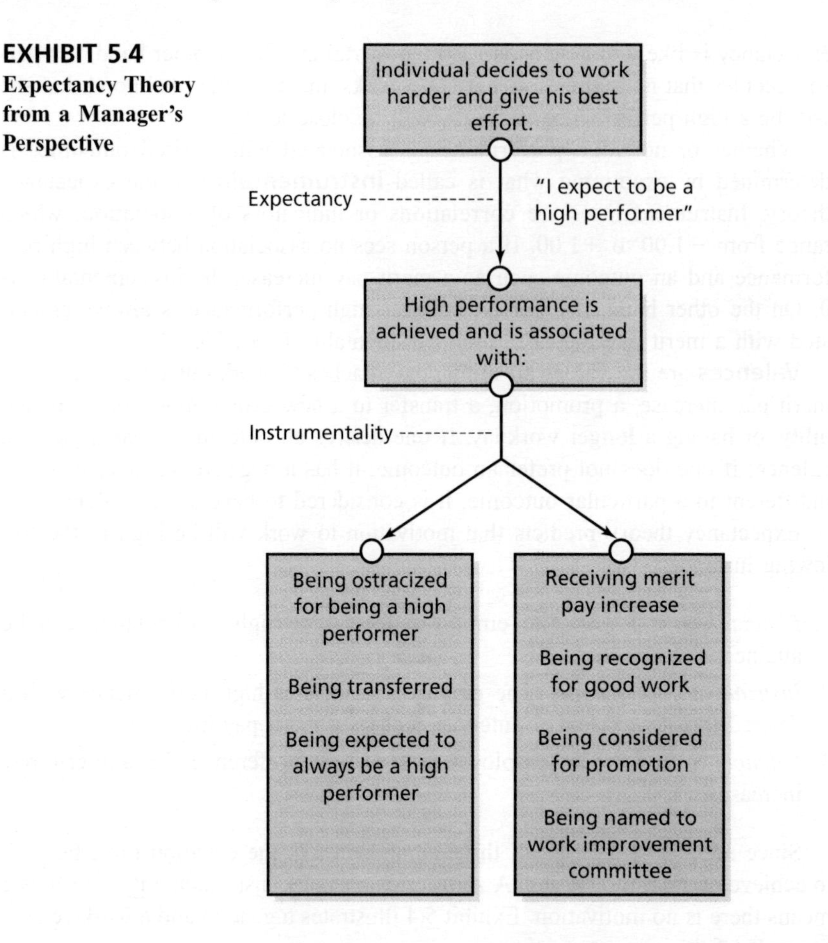

where one worker has the goal of selling e-learning software worth $28,000 and the other is attempting to provide some pro bono help to senior citizens for completing their income tax. How might their respective efforts and behaviors vary?

Research studies of expectancy theory usually involve asking employees to estimate the expectancy they have of being an outstanding, good, or average performer. In addition, the employees are asked to estimate the association (instrumentality) of performance and outcomes (pay, promotion). They also are asked to rate or rank the valence of outcomes. Their responses then are combined to determine the degree of effort (motivation) expended.

For the most part, empirical studies provide some support for the expectancy theory. However, many factors besides expectancy, instrumentality, and valence may influence the amount of effort expended on the job, and accurately measuring any of the factors in the expectancy theory is difficult. Is it really possible to have people report on their expectancies, instrumentalities, and valences? How can their answers be measured? Researchers who have tested various portions of the expectancy model have not yet resolved these different measurement questions.

The expectancy theory does have several important practical implications managers should consider, such as:

1. *Determine what outcomes employees prefer.* Communicating with employees to determine their preferences is important for developing reward packages that can stimulate motivation.
2. *Define, communicate, and clarify the level of performance that is desired.* An employee needs realistic and meaningful performance goals before he can exert proper effort.
3. *Establish with the individual attainable performance goals.* Setting impossible goals will create frustration and confusion and lower motivation.
4. *Link desired outcomes to performance goal achievement.* A manager should spell out how and when performance will be rewarded. Every effort should be made to link performance and rewards.

Global Application of Expectancy Theory

There has been a limited amount of research on expectancy theory's application in global settings. Eden studied expectancy theory in an Israeli kibbutz and found that the processes spelled out in the theory were supported.[19] A study of Japanese employees also supported the expectancy explanation of how behavior is initiated and sustained.[20]

Luthans and Hodgetts point out that expectancy theory is anchored in the premise that employees can control the environment, expression of preferences is tolerated, and changes in behavior are expected. That is, there is freedom, tolerance, and change in the workers' lives. However, they suggest that in some national cultures (e.g., Cuba, North Korea, Iraq, Iran) the locus of control has an external orientation. That is, change, freedom, and control are considered beyond the means of the individual. Luthans and Hodgetts offer words of caution, "The theory seems culture bound and international managers must be aware of this."[21]

Goal-Setting Theory

Ryan proposed that behavior is affected by conscious purposes, plans, intentions, and tasks. From this premise **goal-setting theory** evolved. A goal is the object of an action. Locke and Latham, two prominent goal-setting theorists and researchers, became involved in presenting a goal-setting explanation of behavior and motivation.[22] Their work has stimulated numerous studies of applied goal setting.

Goals are believed to affect the performance of individuals by (1) serving as a directive function, (2) energizing action, (3) fostering persistence, and (4) encouraging the use of task-relevant knowledge and strategy.

The goal–performance relationship is strongest when individuals are committed to their goals. Commitment is most important when relative, important, and moderately difficult goals are the target.[23] Researchers have determined that self-efficacy (feeling confident that you can do the task successfully) enhances goal commitment. People with high self-efficacy appear to be more likely than those with low self-efficacy to initiate and develop effective task accomplishment (goals) strategies.

Research has also found that specific goals lead to better performance than "do your best" goals. Being specific provides more direction and involves a commitment to a stated target, the goal.[24]

Managers should consider why individuals would establish and be motivated by moderately difficult goals. Why wouldn't people want easier work performance goals? The issues of pride, ego, future benefits, satisfaction, and fulfillment may be valid explanations for establishing moderately difficult goals.

Global Application of Goal-Setting Theory

The majority of goal-setting research has been conducted in countries with an individualistic orientation, and the results are similar, but not identical, across different country settings. A study in Norway, a collectivist country, examined worker participation and involvement in goal setting.[25] The sample resisted participative goal setting. The researchers concluded that the reason for the resistance stemmed from an inconsistency between union policies on participation and management's use of participative goal setting. The union expectation that participation amounts were governed by it appears to dampen the influence of the goal-setting program.

Before a conclusion can be reached about the value of goal setting in global settings, more research must be conducted. The limited number of available cross-cultural studies in goal setting is surprising considering the popularity of employing such a motivational approach on an individual or team basis in any nation or organizational setting. Until more research is available, however, it is recommended that goal setting not be implemented without considering cultural and work-related impediments and reluctance.

The Meaning of Work (MOW)

An ongoing research project that examines work motivation across countries is referred to as the **meaning of work (MOW) international research team.**[26] A group of global researchers created, designed, and conducted a series of studies. The MOW survey collects data on such factors as work centrality, work life, relationships to work, and employer responsibilities.

Exhibit 5.5 presents the results of work centrality findings for eight countries. The Japanese (7.78) report that work is the most important part of their lives, while British (6.36) participants report that work is not as important. This study also determined that 86.1 percent of all respondents indicated they would continue to work even if their financial needs were already met.[27]

A second area studied by the MOW researchers is societal norms and expectations about working. An entitlement norm that represents the underlying work rights of individuals and the work-related responsibilities of organizations and society toward individuals was examined.

EXHIBIT 5.5
Work Centrality Scores

Source: Adapted from MOW International Research Team, *The Meaning of Work: An International Perspective* (London: Academic Press, 1987), p. 83.

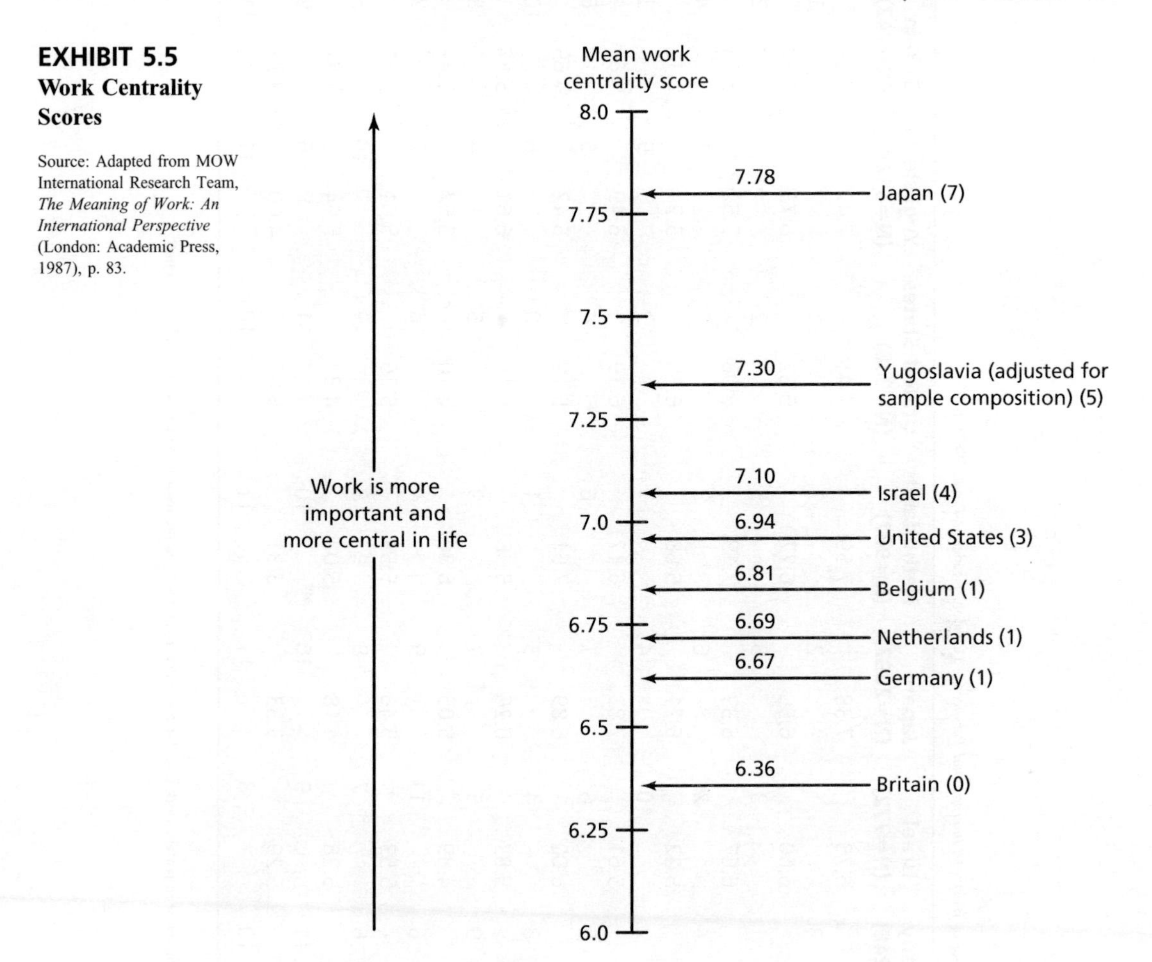

Also, an obligation norm representing duties of individuals to society with regard to working was determined. The Netherlands participants reported the highest entitlement scores and the lowest obligation scores. U.S. participants reported the lowest entitlement scores and the highest obligation scores.[28]

Exhibit 5.6 reports on the role of different work goals in the eight countries. "Interesting work" is the highest-rated work goal, while good pay also rates high. The least important goals were "good physical working conditions" and "good opportunity for upgrading for promotion."[29]

In a study of Asian managers in six countries—India, Mongolia, Singapore, Malaysia, Thailand, and Brunei—11 work goals were examined. The Malaysian and Singapore managers rated salary at the highest level when compared to managers in the other countries.[30] The most important goal to the total sample was "interesting work" and the least important was "promotion opportunities."

EXHIBIT 5.6 Importance of Work Goals

Source: Adapted from MOW International Research Team, *The Meaning of Work: An International Perspective* (London: Academic Press, 1987), p. 122.

Work Goals	Belgium (N=446)		Germany (N=1248)		Israel (N=772)		Japan (N=2897)		Netherlands (N=967)		United States (N=988)		Yugoslavia (N=512)*		Britain (N=742)	
Interesting work	8.25	1	7.26	3	6.75	1	7.38	2	7.59	2	7.41	1	7.47	2	8.02	1
Good pay	7.13	2	7.73	1	6.60	3	6.56	5	6.27	5	6.82	2	6.73	3	7.80	2
Good interpersonal relations	6.34	5	6.43	4	6.67	2	6.39	6	7.19	3	6.08	7	7.52	1	6.33	4
Good job security	6.80	3	7.57	2	5.22	10	6.71	4	5.68	7	6.30	3	5.21	9	7.12	3
A good match between you and your job	5.77	8	6.09	5	5.61	6	7.83	1	6.17	6	6.19	4	6.49	5	5.63	6
A lot of autonomy	6.56	4	5.66	8	6.00	4	6.89	3	7.61	1	5.79	8	5.42	8	4.69	10
Opportunity to learn	5.80	7	4.97	9	5.83	5	6.26	7	5.38	9	6.16	5	6.61	4	5.55	8
A lot of variety	5.96	6	5.71	6	4.89	11	5.05	9	6.86	4	6.10	6	5.62	7	5.62	7
Convenient work hours	4.71	9	5.71	6	5.53	7	5.46	8	5.59	8	5.25	9	5.01	10	6.11	5
Good physical working conditions	4.19	11	4.39	11	5.28	9	4.18	10	5.03	10	4.84	11	5.94	6	4.87	9
Good opportunity for upgrade or promotion	4.49	10	4.48	10	5.29	8	3.33	11	3.31	11	5.08	10	4.00	11	4.27	11

Left: Mean ranks.
Right: The rank of each work goal within a given country. Rank 1 is the ***most*** important work goal for a country and rank 11 is the ***least*** important work goal for a country.
*Combined target group data were used for Yugoslavia.

The MOW research and interpretation provide an opportunity to examine country-by-country differences. Managers could use this type of survey information to formulate, experiment with, and implement different motivational strategies. Of course, the MOW findings are not perfect, nor are they complete. However, like the research on the motivational theories, the MOW work points out that there is no best universal prescription, model, or theory available. Knowing what workers prefer and value provides managers with some knowledge to address the motivational puzzle that exists for all workers and in all countries.

MOTIVATIONAL INCIDENTS: MANAGERIAL RESPONSES

Motivation is a difficult concept to apply and to alter because of cultural differences and the internal aspect of its origins. Motivation is a powerful internal process that influences behavior, effort, and performance. Elashmawi and Harris provide a number of examples that illustrate the difficulty managers face in different countries when motivation is the goal. A few of Elashmawi and Harris's examples and a few other examples are provided for analysis, consideration, and review of the motivation process.[31]

- Fred was recently hired as an operations manager for a French company in Saudi Arabia. He wanted to immediately ship an order to Madrid customers for the firm's electronic template board, which his five Saudi employees were working on. It was 5 o'clock, which is the regular quitting time. Fred wanted the workers to finish the job and ship the order before leaving. However, at 5 o'clock exactly, the whistle blew and all five workers left. Fred was not happy and wondered what he could have done to keep the workers until the job was finished and the order was shipped to the Spanish customers.
- Yun Ming, a Chinese worker, was employed by a Canadian subsidiary in Shanghai, China. His boss, Brett, was a Canadian assigned to the plant for the last three years. At Yun's first performance appraisal, Brett asked him whether he would like to work as a team leader, which meant more pay and more responsibility. The day after the performance review, which Brett considered as excellent for Yun, Brett was called to his manager's office. Yun had quit and stated he didn't wish to work for the firm ever again. Brett was surprised by the events—a very positive performance review filled with compliments and then a sudden resignation. What went wrong?
- Mayidin Bin Omar, a Malaysian worker in a Japanese plant in Kuala Lumpur, had been working on an electrical lathe machine and came up with an idea. He believed that the productivity of the machine could be improved with some alteration. Omar met with his Japanese supervisor Sinjo Tanaka to discuss his idea. Omar briefly explained his idea while Sinjo sat, listened, and made no comments. Omar got up, thanked Sinjo, and left. Omar was

wondering why his idea triggered no observable response. He vowed to never again meet with Sinjo to discuss any ideas that could improve productivity.

- Barbara was an American worker for a South Korean auto company in Georgetown, Kentucky. She had a sick mother and needed to take a month long leave of absence. She met with her boss, Ling Dui, who asked her about her leave request. He said he would think about the request. About five weeks went by with no response, so Barbara met again with Ling. He suggested she quit the job and take care of her mother. Ling stated that the family must come before the job so quitting is the honorable and expected course to take immediately. Barbara was upset that Ling asked her to quit.

These four incidents point out the role that cultural differences play in motivation, needs, and expectations from a managerial perspective. There is no way to provide the "best" course of action for each of the managers. However, global managers must adopt a mind-set that allows them to frame the type of motivational dilemmas they will face when managing in another country.

The concept of mind-set can be traced to the work of cognitive psychologists who studied the question of how people make sense of the world with which they interact.[32] This work illustrates that individuals are limited in their ability to absorb and process information. The transnational manager must observe, experiment, and work in host-country work settings with host-country employees. This requires some ability to absorb signals and cues and to be knowledgeable about local customs, culture, and rituals.

A manager's mind-set has two attributes—differentiation (the number of elements in the person's knowledge base) and integration (the person's ability to synthesize the elements). Knowledge, differentiation, and integration can be coordinated better by a manager who is open-minded; willing to learn; observant; respectful of customs, mores, and rituals of other cultures; and patient. These skills are important to transnational managers who often face new opportunities to differentiate and integrate the knowledge that bombards them on the job.

Fred, Brett, Sinjo, and Ling could help provide better responses in each of their situations by being more globally aware, knowledgeable, and sensitive. They are each serving as managers working with host-country nationals. In each case, the managerial responses displayed in the incidents indicate the managers did not differentiate or integrate the knowledge necessary to handle the circumstances and people they are managing.

A CEO of an American household accessory firm provides an excellent example of how the global mind-set could operate. The CEO, an immigrant from China, states that the company's strategy is one that combines Chinese costs with Japanese quality, European design, and American marketing. The statement suggests the CEO is open and willing to use and practice differentiation and integration to help produce a very competitive product line for the global marketplace.

The accompanying Global Focus offers a set of questions to determine if an individual possesses a global mind-set.

Global Focus Testing for a Global Mind-set

1. When working with others, does national origin have an impact on the quality and depth of the encounter?
2. Are you as aware of and open to ideas from other countries and cultures as you are to ideas from your own country?
3. Are you anxious or stressed by being in a national cultural setting other than your own country?
4. Are you aware of family and work traditions in the country you are working in presently?
5. Do you respect and know about the history and religion of the country you are working in presently?
6. Do you have any close friends from the host nation (where you now work) in whom you confide and spend time with outside of work?
7. Do you make an effort to eat the foods, visit the museums, and listen to the music of the host country? Do you enjoy these?
8. Are you fair in evaluating the work performance of host-country employees?
9. Do you strive to understand everything you can about host-country nationals who report to you?

Answering "no" to two or more of these suggests that you may lack the open-mindedness needed to work in host countries with a diverse employee group.

MANAGEMENT APPLICATION

Since motivation is an internal process that is not directly observable, transnational managers must help develop and then implement activities, projects, and programs to create motivational opportunities. A wide range of motivational opportunities can be used. A few of these will be presented for consideration and possible use with transnational companies.

Meaningful Work Opportunities

The MOW centrality concept suggests the importance of work in a person's life must be weighed against other central areas of interest such as family, religion, nationhood, and leisure. The Japanese report the highest levels of work centrality. Moderate levels of work centrality exist for Americans, Germans, and the Dutch.

Because work is highly or moderately important for many employees in the world, it is necessary to determine what constitutes meaningful work. Meaningfulness is a personal attitude, a thought process held by the worker. Transnational managers are advised to determine how their employees view meaningfulness.

Meaningfulness can mean working with others or collaborating on projects, helping others achieve their goals, making decisions about how to complete the job, or a number of different job-related behaviors. The manager of host-nation workers has the responsibility to determine what meaningfulness actually means and whether the opportunities provided are sufficient to positively motivate workers.

Job satisfaction is an individual's positive or negative attitudes toward a job. In general, a majority of workers in different countries report high to moderate levels of job satisfaction.[33] However, some dramatic differences appear when countries are partitioned on the basis of being economically advanced or developing.

Exhibit 5.7 illustrates that workers in Denmark, India, and Norway are significantly more satisfied with their jobs than workers in Hungary, China, and the Ukraine. Countries undergoing a transition from a closed-economic system to an open-economic system (Hungary) show the highest level of job dissatisfaction. Lost jobs, withdrawal of government protection, and uncertainty about the future may be contributing to the lower levels of job satisfaction in some countries.

Work plays a role in every society. In some it is more significant, more central to a person's self-image, family roles, and responsibilities, and contribution

EXHIBIT 5.7 Are Workers Satisfied? It Depends on Where They Live

Percentage of workers reporting very satisfied with their jobs.

Source: Adapted from M. Boyle "Nothing Is Rotten In Denmark" *Fortune,* February 19, 2001.

Happiest Workers (Top 5)

Country	Percentage
Denmark	61%
India	55%
Norway	54%
United States	50%
Ireland	49%

Unhappiest Workers (Bottom 5)

Country	Percentage
Estonia	11%
China	11%
Czech Republic	10%
Ukraine	10%
Hungary	9%

to others. There are differences that must be determined before attempting to address performance difficulties, low or decreasing job satisfaction, or less commitment to the organization. The exact mix of various approaches attempted by the transnational manager involves learning about what works best and then applying a global mind-set to the motivation issues being faced.

Reward Systems

In basic economic terms, labor is a commodity no different from a personal computer or a tangerine. The employer (domestic or transnational) buys the labor services, skills, and talents needed at a going market price. The market wage times the amount of labor is the wage bill to be paid. The wage rate depends on the going market rate. The wage per hour of an autoworker in Germany is about US$27 per hour; that of similar work of autoworkers in Dothan, Alabama, is about US$15 per hour, and the rate for a similar autoworker in Mexico is about US$5 per hour. The work is similar, the skills required are about the same, and the experience is about equal, but there is a different rate per hour. Different rates, different markets, and different country payments influence the employer's decision about where to produce automobiles. The decision is based on economics.

Agency theory, the principal-agent model, and the economic theory of incentives are three names for the same thing. The basis assumption is that there is a connection between time and effort exerted by the worker, but this can't always be individually controlled. Work environment, leadership, available resources, and other factors may be outside the control of the worker. Thus, providing the effort and the time may be blocked by forces outside the control of the individual the manager is attempting to motivate without success.

These few comments about economics are presented because reward systems do not always work as planned and typically work differently in one country versus another country. Exhibit 5.8 presents a number of differences across countries in regard to performance appraisal systems and how they can provide rewards.

At a general level, a reward system includes everything an employee values and desires that an employer is able and willing to offer in exchange for employee time, effort, and contributions. Reward systems include financial and nonfinancial rewards such as those displayed in Exhibit 5.9.

Rewards are used to link worker expectations and the employer's goals. Effective reward systems provide employees with (1) sufficient rewards to fulfill basic, preferred needs, (2) assurance that it is fair in terms of market notes, (3) assurance that it is fair inside the organization, and (4) assurance that it is fair as perceived by the individual or group.

In New Zealand, Britain, Canada, and other developed countries, reward amounts and allocations vary on the basis of position in the company, type of occupation, skill level, and job experience. In Japan, however, a major determinant of the compensation reward is based on seniority. Also, too much emphasis on individual rewards is not positively received in countries that believe that

EXHIBIT 5.8 Characteristics of Performance Appraisal Systems in the United States, Saudia Arabia, and Korea

Source: Adapted from W.F. Cascio and E. Bailey, "International HRM: The State of Research and Practice" in *Global Perspectives of Human Resource Management,* ed. O. Shenkar (Englewood Cliffs, NJ: Prentice Hall, 1995), p. 29, and P.R. Harris and R.T. Moran, *Managing Cultural Differences,* (3rd ed. Houston: Gulf Publishing, 1990).

Issue	United States	Saudi Arabia	Korea
Objective	Administrative decisions, employee development	Placement	Develop relationship between supervisor and employee
Done by?	Supervisor	Manager several layers up who knows employee well	Mentor and supervisor
Authority of appraiser	Presumed in supervisor role	Reputation (prestige determined by nationality, age, sex, family, tribe, title, education)	Long tenure of supervisor with organization
Motivators	Money, upward mobility, career development	Loyalty to supervisor	Money, promotion, loyalty to supervisor
How praised	Individually	Individually	Given to entire group
Style	Supervisor takes the lead, with employee input	Authority of appraiser is important: never say "I don't know"	Supervisor takes the lead, with informal employee input
Frequency	Usually once per year	Once per year	Developmental appraisal once per month for first year, annually thereafter
Feedback	Criticisms are direct; may be in writing	Criticisms are more subtle; not likely to be given in writing	Criticisms subtle and indirect; may be given verbally
Employee acknowledgment and possible rebuttal	Employee acknowledges receipt; may rebut in writing	Employee acknowledges receipt; may rebut verbally	Employee does not see or sign formal appraisal; would rarely rebut

such rewards spur competition. Competition is considered to be a problem for advancing and supporting the group or work unit.

China is undergoing significant changes, but the core foundation of the nation still impacts how reward systems operate. Even today, the majority of Chinese citizens believe that they must provide service to the state and exert energy and time to perpetuate the state. China is largely a collective society that emphasizes the importance of the family and belonging to a work unit. In China, one's work unit defines the person's status. It establishes compensation, pension amounts, and health care support. The importance of the group or work unit must be considered by managers of Chinese employees in China when reward programs are being selected or evaluated for implementation. The group and the worker's accountability to the group are considered a powerful motivational

EXHIBIT 5.9 Transnational Reward Systems: Financial and Nonfinancial Dimensions

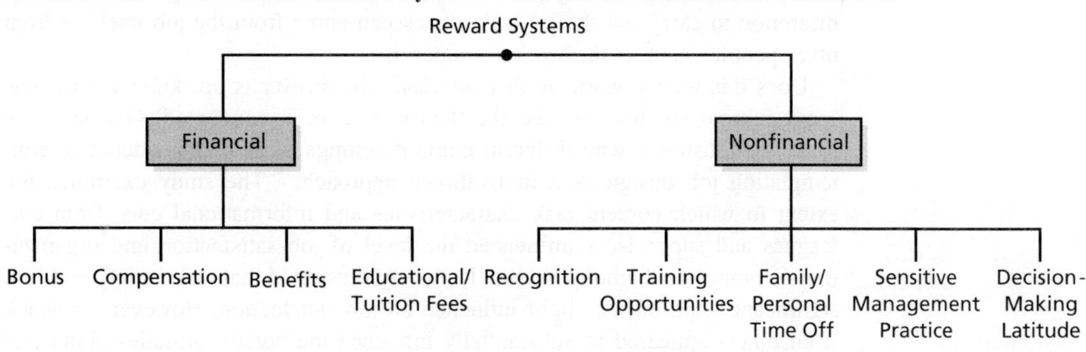

force. The motivation to perform is internalized by the Chinese through the concept of "moral encouragement." In seeking to make contributions to the state, the Chinese worker will usually make sacrifices for the good of the work unit. Any incentives such as a bonus payment would be allocated on the basis of the work unit's contribution.

In other high collectivist countries such as Peru, Guatemala, Ethiopia, Guam, Sierra Leone, and Thailand, the work group would also need to be considered when attempting to use a reward program to improve effort and time on a project. Using individually oriented merit, bonus, and nonfinancial factors in the most collectivist countries will likely be ineffective or even disruptive.

Job Design

Job performance is accomplished by the assignment of people to specific jobs. Consequently, matching people and jobs is a management responsibility. One strategy for bringing about a match is to select from the labor market and pool those individuals who seem to have the skills and abilities to perform the work effectively. A second strategy is to train and develop current employees so they can become effective performers.

The two strategies assume that people must be either recruited and attracted or changed to fit the job. Another approach is to redefine or reengineer the job to fit the abilities and needs of available people.

One theory of job design programs proposes that a worker will experience internal motivation from a job when the job generates three psychological states. First, the employee must feel personal responsibility for accomplishing the job. Second, the worker must feel that the work being performed is meaningful. Third, the person must receive knowledge or feedback so that his or her effectiveness can be judged. This theory suggests that jobs should be defined with responsibility, meaningfulness, and feedback dimensions.[34]

Meaningfulness can be built into jobs through adding skill variety (variety of different activities), task identity (completing a "whole" part of the work), and task significance (job has impact on the lives of other people). Responsibility can be enhanced through increasing autonomy (providing freedom and discretion to carry out the job). Feedback can come from the job itself or from other people, such as the worker's supervisor.

Does this theory work in all countries? The answer is not known since few cross-cultural studies that test the theory have been conducted. One study in Malaysia illustrates why different cultural settings must be considered in contemplating job design as a motivational approach.[35] The study examined the extent to which content task characteristics and informational cues from colleagues and supervisors influenced the level of job satisfaction and organizational commitment among nurses. The study illustrated that task variety and task significance had only a slight influence on job satisfaction. However, feedback from others appeared to substantially influence the nurses' attitudes about and satisfaction with their jobs. Most of the dimensions, except for feedback, favorably contributed to stronger organizational commitment. In addition, the data suggest that the Malaysian societal values and attitudes affected the nurses' impressions of their job. Local cultural conditions were more important than anything else in how the nurses reacted to the job design dimensions. Once again, simply adopting and applying the job design theory presented or available would have failed to create motivational opportunities.

A CONCLUDING NOTE

The chapter points out the importance of work motivation. Numerous theories and applications are available for analysis and use. After completing the chapter, it should be obvious that universal applicability across cultures of any motivational approach is dangerous. Effective transnational managers must look beyond the theory, research, personal background, biases, values, and belief systems while introducing the work and cultural environment as employees perceive and interpret it. This means that developing motivational opportunities in host countries is a culture-contingent approach. A close examination of the culture, norms, and rituals in a society should be the first step taken by a transnational manager who wants to practice management with a global mind-set.

Key Terms

Esteem needs, *166*
Expectancies, *172*
Expectancy theory of motivation, *172*
Goal-setting theory, *175*
Hierarchy of needs, *165*
Instrumentality, *173*
McClelland's Theory, *170*
Meaning of work (MOW) international research team, *176*
Motivation, *164*
Physiological needs, *166*
Safety needs, *166*
Self-actualization, *166*
Social needs, *166*
Thematic Apperception Test (TAT), *170*
Two-factor theory of motivation, *168*
Valence, *173*

Review, Critical Thinking, and Discussion Questions

1. In managing operations in countries with a large power distance (collectivist) such as Mexico, Portugal, Peru, and Salvador, what modifications in Maslow's need hierarchy should be considered?
2. A French manufacturing plant will begin operations in China and wants to develop reward systems that are motivational. What factors should French managers include in their analysis of what will be the most effective reward system?
3. What are some limitations of individual goal setting applied in developing countries?
4. What does a Japanese company establishing operations in Tennessee and Kentucky need to consider in terms of employee motivation?
5. What role does culture play in clarifying how the internal process of motivation operates?
6. Why isn't achievement motivation always the most significant aspect of motivating employees?
7. Since motivation is not directly observable, how can a transnational manager determine the state of motivation in employees?
8. How can transnational managers increase their ability to apply a global mind-set in terms of differentiating and integrating?
9. Herzberg's two-factor theory and explanation of motivation is the best in terms of having a positive influence on host-nation employees. True or false? Why?
10. In establishing operations in African countries, what should transnational managers consider when deciding the mix of motivational opportunities for employees?

Endnotes

1. Judy Cameron and W. David Pierce, *Rewards and Intrinsic Motivation* (Westport, CT: Ouorum, 2002).
2. Annette Moser Wellman, *The Five Faces of Genius* (New York: Penguin, 2002).
3. A. H. Maslow and A. R. Kaplan, *Maslow on Management* (New York: John Wiley, 1998).
4. Mason Haire, Edwin E. Guiselli, and Lyman W. Porter, *Managerial Thinking: An International Study* (New York: John Wiley, 1966).
5. B. Jaggi, "An Analysis of Perceived Need Importance of Indian Managers," *Management International Review,* 19 (1979), p. 108.
6. M. K. Badawy, "Managerial Attitudes and Need Orientations of Mid-Eastern Executives: An Empirical Cross-Cultural Analysis," *Academy of Management Proceeding,* August 1979, pp. 293–97.
7. Frederick Herzberg, *Work and The Nature of Man* (Cleveland: World Publishing, 1966).
8. Frederick Herzberg, "Worker Needs the Same Around the World," *Industry Week,* September 17, 1986, pp. 29–32.
9. Ibid.
10. George H. Hine, "Cross-Cultural Differences in Two-Factor Motivation Theory," *Journal of Applied Psychology* 58 (1973), p. 376.
11. Peter D. Machungwa and Neil Schmitt, "Work Motivation in a Developing Country," *Journal of Applied Psychology* 55 (1983), pp. 31–42.
12. David C. McClelland, *Motivational Trends in Society* (Morristown, NJ: General Learning Press, 1971).

13. Ibid.
14. S. Puffer, "A Riddle Wrapped in an Enigma: Demystifying Russian Managerial Motivation," *European Management Journal* 11 (1993), p. 479.
15. B. J. Burnet, "Preliminary Considerations of Confucianism and Needs in the PRC," *Journal of Asia-Pacific Business* 1 (1995), pp. 25–42.
16. Data presented in David C. McClelland, *The Achieving Society* (Princeton, NJ: Van Nostrand, 1961).
17. Wendelien Van Eerde and Hank Thierry, "Vroom's Expectancy Models and Work-Related Criteria: A Meta-Analysis," *Journal of Applied Psychology* 81 (1996), pp. 575–86.
18. Robert E. Allen, Margaret A. Lucero, and Kathleen L. Van Norman, "An Examination of the Individual's Decision to Participate in an Employee Involvement Program," *Group & Organization Management,* (March 1997), pp. 117–43.
19. Dov Eden, "Intrinsic and Extrinsic Rewards and Motives: Replication and Extension with Kibbutz Workers," *Journal of Applied Social Psychology* 5 (1975), pp. 348–61.
20. T. Matsui, T. Kakuyama, and M. C. Onglatzo, "The Effects of Goals and Feedback on Performance in Groups," *Journal of Applied Psychology* 72 (1987), pp. 407–15.
21. Richard M. Hodgetts and Fred Luthans, *International Management* (New York: McGraw-Hill/Irwin, 2003), p. 395.
22. Edwin A. Locke and Gary P. Latham, "Building a Practically Useful Theory of Goal Setting and Task Motivation," *American Psychologist* 57 (2002), pp. 705–17.
23. H. Klein, M. Wesson, J. Hollenbeck, and B. Alge, "Goal Commitment and the Goal Setting Process: Conceptual Clarification and Empirical Synthesis, *Journal of Applied Psychology* 84 (1999), pp. 885–96.
24. Edwin A. Locke and Gary P. Latham, *A Theory of Goal Setting and Task performance,* (Englewood Cliffs, NJ: Prentice Hall, 1990).
25. J. P. French, J. Israel, and D. As, "An Experiment in a Norwegian Factory," *Human Relations* 13 (1960), pp. 3–19.
26. MOW International Research Team, *The Meaning of Work: An International Perspective* (London: Academic Press, 1987).
27. Ibid, p. 83.
28. Ibid, p. 96
29. Ibid, p. 122
30. Mishra, S. and R. N. Kanungo, "Bases of Work Motivation in Developing Societies: A Framework for Performance Management," R. N. Kanungo, and M. Mendonca, eds., Work Motivation: Models for Developing Countries (New Delhi: Sage, 1994), pp. 60–72.
31. Farid Elashmawi and Philip R. Harris, *Multicultural Management 2000* (Houston, Gulf Publishing, 1999), pp. 48–51.
32. Vijay Govindarajan and Anil K. Gupta, *The Quest for Global Dominance* (San Francisco: Jossey-Bass, 2001), pp. 105–36.
33. M. Boyle, *Fortune,* "Nothing Is Rotten in Denmark," (February 19, 2001), p. 242.
34. J. R. Hackman and G. R. Oldham, *Work Redesign* (Reading, MA: Addison-Wesley, 1980).
35. S. Parker and T. Wall, Job and Work Design: Organizing Work to Promote Well-Being and Effectiveness. (Thousand Oaks, CA: Sage, 1998).

Negotiating Cross-Culturally

Learning Objectives

After completing Chapter 6, you should be able to:

- Describe the different types of negotiation and how they can impact the outcomes of negotiations.
- Identify the six steps in the cross-cultural negotiation process.
- Explain several ways in which culture influences the negotiation process.
- Learn about general, verbal, nonverbal, and unethical negotiation tactics.
- Understand several best practices that can enhance performance in cross-cultural negotiations.

Intercultural Negotiations: Avoid the Pitfalls!

Negotiating with individuals from different cultures requires a great deal of preparation, flexibility, and knowledge of the other party's cultural background and negotiation style. But in this fast-moving global business arena, many managers do not take the time to adequately understand the values of negotiators from other cultures. For example, one U.S. company lost a major contract opportunity in Greece because its managers tried to impose American customs on the Greece negotiators. In addition to being too direct and outspoken in the eyes of the Greeks, the Americans tried to set time limits for the meetings. The Greek negotiators considered time limits to be an insult and to limit their ability to fully explore the issues that were up for negotiation. The American negotiators also wanted the Greeks to agree to an initial set of principles to help guide the negotiation process. This would be followed by having their direct reports work out and finalize the details. The Greek negotiators perceived this as an attempt to be deceptive and indicated a strong preference to handle all arrangements regardless of the time required to do so.

In another example, a large U.S. global computer firm asked its U.S. software engineers (based in California) to work with the firm's French software engineers (based in Grenoble, France) to develop a joint project. While attempting to negotiate how best to proceed with the complicated project, the Americans and French experienced a variety of cross-cultural miscommunications that brought the project to a painfully slow crawl. To improve the teamwork among the two trans-Atlantic teams, a cross-cultural training firm was hired to help both sides understand the other.

Many global companies take a proactive approach to improving their chances of successful outcomes in cross-cultural negotiations. For example, Intel Corporation trained its employees in interpreting cultural nuances to improve their cross-cultural negotiation skills. A consulting company organized 55 classes for Intel employees to learn about cross-cultural negotiation. Helping businesses to avoid committing intercultural errors has become a $100 billion industry in the United States.

Sources: Lalita Khosla, "You Say Tomato," *Forbes,* May 21, 2001, pp. 36–37, and David A. Ricks, *Blunders in International Business* (Malden, MA.: Blackwell Publishers, 1993).

As the opening vignette demonstrates, strong growth in global trade and investment in the first part of the 21st century has made the development of cross-cultural negotiation skills a top priority for an increasing number of transnational managers.[1] As a result of globalization, cross-cultural interactions have been proliferating in recent years as witnessed by increases in cross-border interfirm agreements (e.g., joint ventures, strategic alliances, etc.), development and expansion of regional trade agreements (e.g., North American Free Trade Agreement, Asia-Pacific Economic Cooperation, and the European Union), and China's entry into the World Trade Organization. The global deals, markets, and relationships with customers, vendors, and host-country government officials require careful attention and a great deal of cross-cultural savvy. Such global managers need to possess worldwide vision, boundary-crossing skills, and resources to develop international networks that extend far beyond their home base.[2]

Research in the area of international negotiations has focused primarily on making cross-cultural comparisons of negotiations in different national cultural contexts and on the influence that cultures exert on negotiation practices.[3] Cultural values possess a strong link to negotiation. Defined as desirable goals that serve as guiding principles that are shared by members of a culture, cultural values encourage individuals from a particular culture to employ those negotiation strategies that will achieve results that are compatible with the cultural environment.[4] For example, Chinese negotiators tend to favor negotiation strategies that preserve social harmony and face.[5] Brazilian negotiators rely heavily on developing excellent interpersonal rapport with the other party through lengthy discussions and socializing.[6] Thus, global managers need to incorporate these factors when developing effective cross-cultural negotiation strategies.

In this chapter, we will define the different types of negotiation approaches, present the basic aspects of the cross-cultural negotiation process, discuss negotiation tactics, demonstrate how cultural differences can impact the negotiation process, and provide several concrete steps and suggestions to improve cross-cultural negotiation effectiveness. Ultimately, however, the success of any cross-cultural negotiation depends on the global manager or team involved in the transaction. Excellent preparation and a thorough understanding of the issues presented in this chapter will increase the likelihood of global managers achieving positive outcomes in their negotiations.

CROSS-CULTURAL NEGOTIATION: THE BASICS

Negotiation has been defined as the process by which two or more parties decide what each will give and take in a given exchange.[7] It is a process in which two or more parties attempt to reach acceptable agreement in a situation characterized by some level of disagreement. In a cross-cultural organizational context, negotiation may take place: (1) between two people (as when an international sales representative from Italian tire manufacturer Pirelli visits a purchasing manager at General Motors Corporation in the United States); (2) within a group (an international start-up team for U.S.-based Wal-Mart cannot decide on critical project dates); (3) between groups (a Brazilian labor union disputing job cuts with a team of managers from the Argentinean parent company); or (4) over the Internet. The Internet now serves as a place to negotiate international jobs, global consulting projects, cross-cultural training program prices, and overseas supplier product prices. One major difference in negotiating over the Internet is that it is done with written communication only. Many of the skills discussed in this section apply to both face-to-face negotiations and Internet-based transactions.

Regardless of the setting, medium, or parties involved, domestic and international negotiations usually possess at least four elements.[8] First, some disagreement or *conflict* exists. This may be perceived, felt, or manifested. Second, there is some degree of *interdependence* between the parties involved. Third, the situation must be conducive to *opportunistic interaction*. This means that each party has both the means and inclination to attempt to influence one another. Finally, some *possibility of agreement* exists. In the absence of this latter element, of course, negotiations cannot bring about a positive resolution. When negotiations are successful, each party feels that it has significantly benefited from the resolution. When they fail, however, the conflict often escalates. As the accompanying Global Focus illustrates, Jack Welch (once referred to as Neutron Jack), former CEO of General Electric, experienced considerable frustration while negotiating with European Union regulators over the proposed General Electric-Honeywell merger. Unfortunately for Welch and GE, the proposed merger failed to win approval and talks were subsequently abandoned.

Global Focus Cross-Atlantic Negotiations: *Super Mario* vs. *Neutron Jack*

On one side of the Atlantic, a legendary American CEO of a powerful U.S. corporation wanted to purchase and merge with another large U.S. multinational corporation for a price tag of US$45 billion. On the other side, a strong-willed European Union (EU) politician rejected the proposed merger on grounds that it would limit competition throughout member nations. Ending in the summer of 2001, Jack Welch ("Neutron Jack"), then chairman of General Electric, and Mario Monti ("Super Mario"), EU commissioner for competition, found themselves in heated global negotiations over the fate of the proposed General Electric-Honeywell International merger.

The two negotiators had very different agendas. For Welch, this deal would signify a crowning achievement in a long and successful career. Although he was turning 65 years old at the time, he decided to postpone retirement for a year to oversee the successful purchase of Honeywell International. He wanted to buy Honeywell International, a manufacturer of advanced electronics for the aviation industry, because its business would be a great fit with GE's airplane engine manufacturing business. From Monti's perspective, he believed that such a merger would create unfair competition in the EU's aviation sector, shutting out competitors. In the EU, GE alone has approximately 85,000 employees and collected $25 billion in sales revenue in 2000.

Welch, now retired from GE, recently admitted that he seriously underestimated Monti during the regulatory process for GE's proposed merger. Welch did not anticipate that the world's toughest "trustbuster" now works in Brussels, not Washington, D.C. In just a few years as EU commissioner for competition, Monti has blocked other high-profile would-be mergers, including MCI WorldCom and Sprint. As globalization continues to create new and powerful parties, global leaders must constantly prepare and refine their cross-cultural negotiation skills to achieve the kind of spectacular results that Jack Welch achieved during the majority of his 40-year career.

Sources: Michael Elliott, "How Jack Fell Down," *Time*, July 16, 2001, pp. 40–44; Tony Emerson and Daniel McGinn, "Super Mario Trips Up Neutron Jack," *Newsweek*, June 25, 2001, pp. 36–37; and "Business: The Next Battleground: Microsoft and the EU," *The Economist*, November 10, 2001, pp. 58–59.

Types of Negotiation

The classical view of the negotiation process suggests that negotiations are frequently a zero-sum game. That is, to whatever extent one party wins something, the other party loses. A zero-sum situation holds an assumption of limited resources, and the negotiation process is to determine who will receive these resources. This is also known as **distributive negotiation.** The term refers to the process of dividing, or distributing, scarce resources. Such a win-lose or fixed-pie approach characterizes numerous negotiating situations. Buying an automobile is a classic example. As the buyer, the less you pay the less profit the seller makes; your "wins" (in the form of less money paid) are the seller's "losses" (in terms of less profit made). Note that in win-lose negotiating, one party does not necessarily "lose" in an absolute sense. Presumably the party selling can still make a profit, but to the extent the selling price is lowered to make the sale, the profit is lower.

In global organizations, win-lose negotiating can be common. It characterizes some of the bargaining involving contracts, strategic alliances, joint ventures, franchises, distributorship arrangements, and the purchase or supply of manufacturing goods and services. The more variable examples of distributive negotiations in organizations are those that occur between labor and management. Issues involving wages, benefits, working conditions, and related matters are often seen as a conflict over limited resources.

In contrast, an alternative approach to cross-cultural negotiation is known as a win-win, or **integrative negotiation.** Unlike zero-sum orientation in distributive negotiating, the win-win approach leads to positive-sum results. Positive-sum situations are those where each party gains without a corresponding loss from the other party. This does not necessarily mean that everyone gets everything they wanted, for seldom does that occur. It simply means that an agreement has been achieved that leaves all parties better off than they were before the agreement.

Not every global management negotiating situation is appropriate for an integrative approach. In some situations, resources are indeed limited and an integrative payoff is not feasible. For example, assume a key supplier of chemical resins from Nigeria experienced a plant explosion, curtailing all production of a resin that is used in the production of self-adhesive paper products by a South African company. Knowing that resin production will begin again in a week, the South African company attempts to negotiate with the Nigerian supplier to be the first customer to receive the output of the next production run. Unfortunately, there is not enough resin to meet the needs of all of the company's large Nigerian customers, so the South African company gets only a fraction of what it needs. An integrative outcome is not possible due to the production constraints. This is essentially a distributive or win-lose situation.

Even if the nature of what is being negotiated lends itself to a win-win approach, the organizations to which the negotiators belong may not. Win-win or integrative negotiating can work only when the issues lend themselves to a positive outcome and all parties are committed to an integrative process. In Canada, union and management bargaining includes issues that are both distributive and integrative in nature. For example, the rising burden of health care costs can be negotiated in such a way that both parties feel that they are paying their "fair share," but unfortunately both parties want the other to absorb and pay for the majority of these cost increases. Since negotiators for both parties often see the total process as distributive in nature, even those issues that truly may be integrative become victims of a win-lose attitude, to the detriment of both parties.

Bargaining Zone Model of Negotiations

The **bargaining zone model** explains how win-win negotiations occur. Each party in a negotiation has a starting point, a target point, and a resistance point. The *starting point* is when each party in a negotiation makes an opening offer. For example, a potential buyer from a large department store chain in Europe may give a Hong Kong-based clothing manufacturer a very low price for 5,000 men's suits. The European does not expect his or her offer to be accepted, but rather uses it to set the stage for subsequent bargaining. On the other extreme, the Hong Kong business owner provides an exorbitant price for the suits, knowing that the EU buyer will not take the bait. The *target point* is the realistic goal or expectations for a final price that both parties believe they can achieve. The **resistance point** is the final stopping point at which time each party will not make any additional concessions or, in this case, adjustments in price. The potential area for agreement falls between each party's target point and resistance point.[9]

Impact of Personalities on the Negotiation Process

The process of negotiating is a very people-oriented experience. In addition to understanding the goals, needs, and wants of the other side, the successful negotiator tries to understand the relevant personality traits of the other individuals negotiating.[10] Negotiators come to the bargaining session from varied cultural backgrounds; their experiences, like their perspectives, can differ markedly. Their propensities to take risks vary, and their personalities and attitudes are diverse. All this affects their behaviors and actions.[11] Global managers must look beyond the roles the other party to the negotiation is playing and ask what really motivates the other individual.[12] Knowing these traits allows the global manager to "read" and understand the opposing side, a valuable tool in negotiations.

Four of the most common types of personalities a manager will face at the negotiation table are:[13]

1. The power seeker, who is task- and results-oriented, seeking challenges and opportunities, and potentially confrontational; a good decision maker.
2. The persuader, who tends to be outgoing, socially oriented, ambitious, and tough under a cloak of affability; a dangerous opponent at the negotiation table.
3. The reliable performer, who is solid, dependable, comfortable in supportive surroundings, and resistant to sudden change; dependent on past precedents for confidence in decision making.
4. The limited performer, who tends to lack in self-confidence, is in need of a sheltered environment, appears nondecisive, and is introverted.

The degree of a global manager's ability to successfully understand and handle people will ultimately determine his or her success at cross-cultural negotiation.

COMPONENTS OF THE CROSS-CULTURAL NEGOTIATION PROCESS

The components of the cross-cultural negotiation process include prenegotiation planning, steps in the negotiation process, negotiation style, and negotiation tactics.

Prenegotiation Planning

Many factors can make a cross-cultural negotiation more productive and more predictable. Such factors can be thought out well in advance of the actual negotiation. In their review of the research literature dealing with the components of prenegotiation, Peterson and Lucas[14] reported that prenegotiation behaviors have been categorized into four unique areas: (1) information gathering, (2) formulation, (3) strategy and tactics, and (4) preparation.

Information Gathering

Some of the best cross-cultural negotiators spend considerable time learning as much as possible about their counterpart's organization, culture, personality, needs, goals, and prior decision making on similar deals. In addition, a conscientious negotiator will study and understand market conditions, competitive threats, and other macroeconomic issues that might affect the outcome of the negotiation.[15] At one Web-based intelligence firm (www.informationbuilders.com) thousands of customers and partners all over the world, including most of the Fortune 100, all major government agencies, and many educational institutions, use Information Builders software and services to turn data into business intelligence that helps their customers, citizens, employees, managers, and business partners make better decisions in critical operations.

Formulation

This entails developing general goals, objectives, and desired outcomes, and setting the parameters for each issue to be negotiated.[16] During this stage of prenegotiation, a prepared global manager will have taken the time to consult with others within his or her own company before making decisions during the negotiation.[17] In addition, each party will learn more about the other's strategy and tactics, and when each will be willing to cease negotiations and walk away from the table.[18]

Strategy and Tactics

A well-prepared global manager will enter negotiations with a strategy and set of tactics for what concessions can be made at what times during the process.[19] Strategies refer to the overall approach and may include which priorities a global manager chooses to emphasize. Tactics are sometimes referred to as playing games, being manipulative, or having a hidden agenda; these may include when to make the first offer, how much to offer, when to make concessions, and so on.[20]

Preparation

One study of interpersonal negotiation found that rehearsing for an important negotiation can help global managers in a variety of ways: (1) enhanced overall performance in the session; (2) increased control of emotions and improved ability to remain rational (thus, reducing anxiety and improving confidence); and (3) improved articulation through better word choice and organization.[21] As an extension of rehearsing, role-playing has also been shown to improve negotiators' performance.[22]

Steps in Negotiation Process

As can be seen in Exhibit 6.1, negotiators typically take six major steps when negotiating in a cross-cultural situation. The steps are preparing (which was discussed in the previous section), building relationships, exchanging information, creating win-win options, choosing the best alternative/solution, and agreeing to outcomes.[23]

Each of these steps requires a considerable amount of attention, sensitivity, and knowledge of the other negotiator's culture. For example, if one party attempts to skip over relationship building to quickly "get down to business," then the other party may feel rushed or rudely treated. In Japan, for example, negotiators want to spend time finding out about their counterpart's school background, relative status within the company, and family background; all of which contribute to the Japanese need for harmony and cooperation.[24] Rushing can often occur when a businessperson from a highly individualistic culture such as the United States, England, or Australia negotiates with a member of a collectivist culture such as China, Peru, or Saudi Arabia. Global managers should not

EXHIBIT 6.1
Steps in the Cross-Cultural Negotiation Process

Source: Adapted from Nancy J. Adler, *International Dimensions of Organizational Behavior*, 4th ed. (Cincinnati: South-Western, 2002), p. 222.

Step 1: Preparing
- Learn as much as possible about your counterpart and his or her interests, needs, organization, language, and communication style.
- Cross-cultural and language training is critical.

Step 2: Building relationships
- Build trust and rapport with your counterpart (subjects of conversation may include family, travel, etc.).
- Emphasize the problem, not the people discussing the problem.
- Make adjustments for counterpart's style, pace, and verbal and nonverbal communication patterns.

Step 3: Exchanging information
- Exchange task-, participant-, and organizational-related information.
- Clarify and frame parties' interests and customary approaches to the negotiation.

Step 4: Creating "win-win" options appropriate to both cultures
- Be creative and think outside the box.
- Try to achieve solutions that build on each party's unique cultural perspective.

Step 5: Choosing best alternative/solution
- Be patient and thorough when deciding on solution.
- Consider criteria from both cultures.

Step 6: Agreeing to outcomes
- Translate and back-translate final agreement.
- Refine and renegotiate when necessary.

abandon their way of conducting negotiations, but rather they should modify their approach to fit more closely with their counterpart's preferences to achieve win-win outcomes acceptable to both parties.

Negotiation Style

It would be easy to assume that individuals from the same cultural background will approach a cross-cultural negotiation in a very similar manner. Applying a label to a culture's negotiation style is too general and constraining; however, general characteristics and behavioral tendencies have been observed and noted. The former ambassador from Singapore to the United States noted that American negotiators generally: (1) are prepared, (2) are plain speaking, (3) are pragmatic, (4) understand that concessions may be required, and (5) are very specific and candid. Others have described U.S. negotiators as blunt, arrogant, and rushed.[25] The weaknesses of U.S. negotiators appear to center on impatience, legalism, and poor listening skills. The strengths of U.S. negotiators focus on friendliness, fairness, and flexibility.

Exhibit 6.2 provides a description of over 300 negotiators from 12 countries.[26] The Japanese emphasized a win-win or integrative approach more than any other country's negotiators. The results also indicate the direct communication styles used by Argentinean, American, and German negotiators.

The differences in negotiating styles are extensive. Political systems, legal policies, ideology, traditions, and culture certainly influence style. The international experience of the negotiations also has an impact on the style utilized. Becoming familiar with the communication style, time orientation, group versus individual orientation, religious orientation, and customs of the culture of the counterpart negotiator is important in preparing for negotiations.[27] Knowing something about another person's culture is a sign of respect that is appreciated at the negotiating table.

Negotiation Tactics

Transnational managers can think of cross-cultural negotiation tactics as falling into four categories: general, verbal, nonverbal, and unethical. By becoming familiar with each of these behaviors, managers will be much better prepared to achieve successful win-win outcomes as a result of negotiating with their international counterparts.

General Negotiation Tactics

Different situations call for different tactics. A global manager should be aware of the tactical options available and strive to understand the rationale behind the tactics. These tactical options are known as good guy/bad guy team, the nibble, joint problem solving, splitting the difference, and lowballing.

1. **Good guy/bad guy team:** This occurs when the "bad guy" member of the negotiating team advocates positions so much out of line that whatever the good guy says sounds reasonable.

EXHIBIT 6.2 Cultural Effects on Negotiating Style

Source: Adapted from J.W. Salacuse, "Ten Ways That Culture Affects Negotiation Style: Some Survey Results," *Negotiation Journal,* July 1998, pp. 221–40.

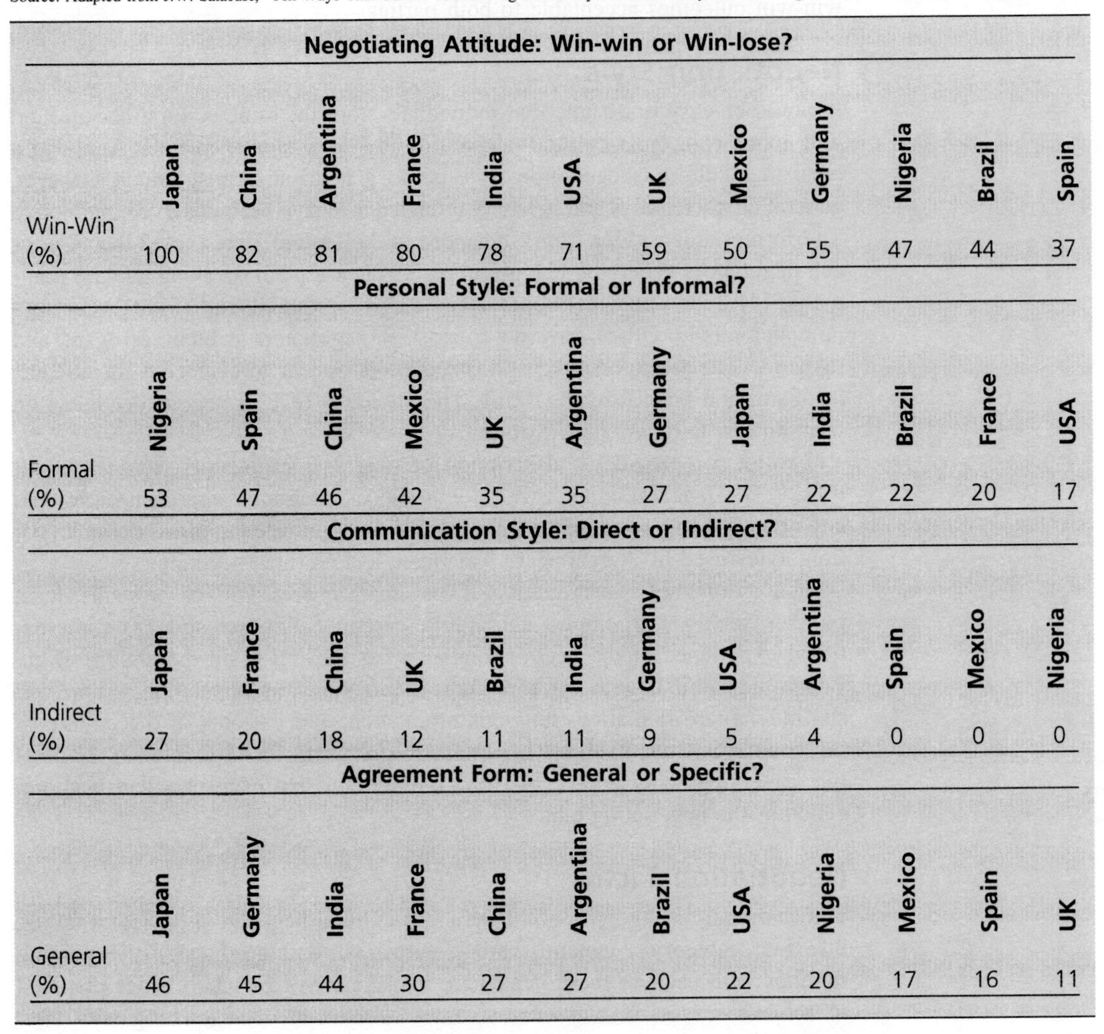

Negotiating Attitude: Win-win or Win-lose?

	Japan	China	Argentina	France	India	USA	UK	Mexico	Germany	Nigeria	Brazil	Spain
Win-Win (%)	100	82	81	80	78	71	59	50	55	47	44	37

Personal Style: Formal or Informal?

	Nigeria	Spain	China	Mexico	UK	Argentina	Germany	Japan	India	Brazil	France	USA
Formal (%)	53	47	46	42	35	35	27	27	22	22	20	17

Communication Style: Direct or Indirect?

	Japan	France	China	UK	Brazil	India	Germany	USA	Argentina	Spain	Mexico	Nigeria
Indirect (%)	27	20	18	12	11	11	9	5	4	0	0	0

Agreement Form: General or Specific?

	Japan	Germany	India	France	China	Argentina	Brazil	USA	Nigeria	Mexico	Spain	UK
General (%)	46	45	44	30	27	27	20	22	20	17	16	11

2. **The nibble:** This tactic involves getting an additional concession or perk after an agreement has been reached. An example would be the request for an additional staff position by a marketing manager after an agreement was reached between her group and another marketing group regarding division of market research duties.
3. **Joint problem solving:** A manager should never assume that the more one side wins, the more the other loses. Feasible alternatives not yet considered may exist. For instance, can manufacturing provide earlier completion dates

on products if the sales department increases the order size and reduces the order frequency?

4. **Splitting the difference:** This can be a useful technique when two groups come to an impasse. Managers should be careful, however, when the other group offers to split the difference too early. It may mean the other group has already received more than it thinks it deserves.
5. **Lowballing:** Ridiculously low offers and/or concessions are often used to lower the other group's expectations. A manager shouldn't let this type of offer lower her expectations or goals; nor should the manager walk out assuming the other group's position is inflexible. Communication should continue.

In addition to the general negotiation tactics, a variety of verbal behaviors occur in cross-cultural negotiation settings.

Verbal Tactics and Behaviors

One researcher studied the verbal and nonverbal behaviors of Japanese, American, and Brazilian businesspeople and reported some interesting differences and similarities in their approaches to negotiation.[28] As Exhibit 6.3 shows, American negotiators made slightly more promises than the Japanese and several more promises than their Brazilian counterparts. In terms of making recommendations, the Japanese made more than the Americans and Brazilians. When it came to making self-disclosing statements, asking questions, and making commands, the Brazilians engaged in this behavior more than their American and Japanese counterparts.

EXHIBIT 6.3
Frequency of Verbal Bargaining Behaviors by Nationality

Source: Adapted from John L. Graham, "The Influence of Culture on the Process of Business Negotiations: An Exploratory Study," *Journal of International Business Studies* 16, no. 1 (1985), pp. 81–96.

	Frequency of Use During 30-Minute Negotiation Session		
Verbal Bargaining Behavior	**Japanese**	**American**	**Brazilian**
Promise. A statement in which the source indicated his or her intention to provide the target with a pleasant, positive, or rewarding consequence.	7	8	3
Recommendation. Same as promise, except that the consequences are thought to be noxious, unpleasant, or punishing.	7	4	5
Self-disclosure. A statement in which the source reveals information about himself or herself.	34	36	39
Question. A statement in which the source asks the target to reveal information about himself or herself.	20	20	22
Command. A statement in which the source suggests that the target perform a certain behavior.	8	6	14

Nonverbal Tactics and Behaviors

In addition to cross-cultural differences in verbal tactics, there were several differences in the ways in which nonverbal tactics and behaviors were employed by Japanese, American, and Brazilian negotiators. Differences in silent periods, conversational overlaps, facial gazing, and touching were reported. Silent periods, or gaps in the conversation between the negotiators of 10 seconds or more, were used more by the Japanese (5.5 times per half hour) than by the Americans (3.5 times per half hour) or the Brazilians (0 times per half hour). **Conversational overlaps,** or periods when both negotiators are talking simultaneously, occurred more than twice as often with the Brazilian negotiators (28.6 times per half hour) than their Japanese (12.6 times per half hour) or American (10.3 times per half hour) counterparts. Brazilian negotiators gazed at other negotiators' faces for longer periods of time (5.2 minutes per half hour) than either the American (3.3 minutes per half hour) or Japanese (1.3 minutes per half hour) negotiators. Touching, or incidences of bargainers touching one another per half hour (excluding the beginning and ending handshakes), was not done at all by the Japanese or Americans, but was done approximately five times (over a half hour period) by the Brazilians.[29]

Unethical Negotiation Tactics

Beyond the general, verbal, and nonverbal negotiation tactics that exist, a global manager must also be savvy enough to recognize when he or she is being misled or deceived. It has been argued that the primary purpose of lying during a negotiation process is to increase the liar's power vis-à-vis the opponent by providing false or misleading information.[30] Two researchers, Lewicki and Robinson, summed up the issue this way: "Lies function to misinform the opponent, to eliminate or obscure the opponent's choice alternatives, or to manipulate the perceived costs and benefits of particular options that the opponent may wish to pursue."[31]

These researchers classify unethical negotiation behaviors as belonging to one of the following five categories:

1. Misrepresentation of position to an opponent: By distorting his or her preferred settlement point, an individual attempts to achieve highly favorable settlements. An example would be if the purchasing manager from the Swedish telecommunications company Ericsson offers to purchase electronic components from a Japanese vendor at an extremely low price. The Swedish manager is hoping that the final price, though not as low as the opening offer, is lower than his preferred settlement price.
2. Bluffing: Defined as either a false promise or false threat, bluffing is an attempt to get concessions from the other negotiator. Often, the person who bluffs does not intend to follow through on the stated consequences.
3. Falsification: This is the introduction of erroneous, false, or incorrect information as if it were true. The goal of this behavior is to influence the other negotiator's position by using distorted facts. For example, many U.S.

corporations have been accused of misleading investors by providing false information about their earnings, profitability, and cost structures.

4. Deception: This is an attempt to manipulate or influence the other negotiator's beliefs so as to lead him or her to incorrect conclusions.
5. Selective disclosure or misrepresentation to constituencies: When communicating with third parties (who are not present during the negotiation process), negotiators may misrepresent to their constituencies the events that occur at the negotiating table.

One research study tested some of these classification schemes by analyzing the negotiation attitudes and intentions of U.S. and Brazilian negotiators.[32] The most commonly used negotiation tactic was to exaggerate the opening demand. In other words, both U.S. and Brazilian negotiators would ask for much more than they believed they could reasonably receive from the process. This research also found that when one's opponent had a reputation of being an unethical negotiator, then both U.S. and Brazilian negotiators would increase the use of traditional competitive bargaining tactics, collecting information about the other party, misrepresenting certain information, bluffing, and attempting to influence the other's professional network. These behaviors were more likely to be used when the individual was up against skilled negotiators in a foreign city, the outcome of the negotiation was very important, and there was a time deadline. Offsetting the tendency to use unethical tactics was the prospect of future business relationships with the opponent and the possibility that the other party would learn details/secrets of the negotiation.

CULTURE'S IMPACT ON NEGOTIATIONS

Several issues can influence how a global manager from India might approach a major set of negotiations with her counterpart in the Philippines. Previous research studies have shown that negotiation differences exist between people of different cultures.[33]

Individualism versus Collectivism

One of the cultural dimensions identified by Geert Hofstede,[34] individualism versus collectivism refers to the tendency of a culture's norms and values to emphasize the satisfaction of individual needs or group needs. Individualism emphasizes the pursuit of individual goals, needs, and success. It is assumed that if each person takes care of her or his personal needs, then the entire society will benefit. In contrast, the collectivist perspective emphasizes group welfare and satisfaction. The individual is willing in a collectivist culture to make personal sacrifices to better the stature, performance, and well-being of the group.

Negotiators from individualistic cultures such as the United States, England, Australia, Canada, and the Netherlands will tend to have greater discretion to make decisions, argue points of view, and make concessions than will those negotiators from collectivist cultures such as Taiwan, Singapore, Peru, and Pakistan. The collectivist negotiators prefer to discuss key proposals and to make decisions with a great deal of input and feedback for group members. Individualistic negotiators often become impatient with the apparent lack of response and decision making of their collectivist counterparts. In actuality, the collectivist negotiators want to achieve a consensus among their constituents before committing to a course of action.[35] The accompanying Global Focus highlights several characteristics prevalent when negotiating in China, a collectivist culture.

Low Context versus High Context

Cultures differ in the amount of contextual information that is necessary when people interact and negotiate with one another. Individuals from **high-context communication cultures** do not require a detailed exchange of information, but rather rely on the knowledge they have about the other individual before the negotiation. Japanese and Latin American cultures tend to fall into this category. In contrast, low-context cultures like in Germany and the United States require an explicit, detailed exchange of information when two more individuals are negotiating with one another.

Problems can occur when an individual from a high-context culture negotiates with a counterpart in a low-context culture. When a Japanese businessman signals to his German counterpart that he is not interested in a particular real estate deal, he will most likely indicate his disinterest by saying, "This deal will be very difficult" or "I'll have to think about it." The German, interpreting this message as a negotiating tactic to lower the price of the deal, counters with a onetime-only offer to lower the asking price by 5 percent. The Japanese, disturbed that his message of "no deal" was not heard, is confused by the behavior of the German.

Proxemics

Every person has an invisible boundary of space that surrounds his or her person. In some cultures (e.g., Northern Europe), the boundaries are large; whereas in other cultures (e.g., Middle Eastern countries), this space can be quite small. The amount of personal space maintained by an individual can shift temporarily depending on his physical surroundings (e.g., a crowded elevator) or the degree of intimacy with the person he or she is interacting with (e.g., spouse). Misunderstandings can occur when a businessperson from a culture where men touch and embrace one another as part of normal life initiates physical contact with his counterpart from a culture where touching between men is rare and occurs only with family members.[36] The latter individual will feel uncomfortable and may misinterpret the intent of the physical contact. In one study of American, Japanese, and Brazilian negotiators, it was reported that the Brazilians touched their American and Japanese counterparts an average of five times during a 30-minute negotiation session. This stood in stark contrast to the touching behavior of the Americans and Japanese, who did not do any touching in the same 30-minute period. It is possible that the Americans and Japanese negotiators were uncomfortable with the Brazilian touching behavior.[37]

Global Focus Chinese-Style Negotiation: What Global Managers Need to Know

China is one of the most popular emerging markets with which to do business. There are many reasons for China's increased popularity as a place to invest and do business: Its economy is growing at a rate of 7 percent a year, it has joined the World Trade Organization, it has a population of approximately 1.3 billion people, Hong Kong is an important source of international capital, and its government is encouraging foreign direct investment. With this interest in China comes an increased opportunity for negotiation between global managers and Chinese nationals. The differences in negotiation style and tactics can be considerable. To negotiate effectively, global managers need to understand which cultural traits and characteristics tend to influence how Chinese nationals negotiate. Here are some traits global managers need to be aware of: status, face, trust, friendship, *Guanxi* networks, ambiguity, patience, and Chinese protocols.

1. Status: The Chinese prefer to negotiate with someone of equal or higher status. Status is inferred by a person's role and position within the company. Before the actual negotiation, a list of all members of the negotiation team should be submitted to the Chinese negotiators. Leaders of the respective negotiation teams should sit opposite from one another.
2. Face: Defined as having high status and prestige vis-à-vis one's peers, the Chinese believe it's of the utmost importance to preserve the face of other negotiators in order to maintain dignity and harmony. Criticizing others can cause one to lose face, while being polite, courteous, and sincere can help give or restore face.
3. Trust: Referred to as the basis of successful negotiation, the Chinese place a high value on a person's reputation for trustworthiness on both the professional and personal levels. Global managers can build trust with Chinese negotiators by referring to people whom both parties know and respect, and by avoiding asking too many questions that could imply distrust of the Chinese negotiators.
4. Friendship: The Chinese will attempt to establish a firm sense of friendship before engaging in serious negotiations. Friendship is important because it leads to trust, and trust helps to smooth out the inevitable conflicts that result in many negotiation processes. Global managers should draw on any possible connections and common interests with their Chinese counterparts.
5. *Guanxi* networks: Established through the exchange or reciprocity of favors, *Guanxi* is a type of network or set of connections. Chinese negotiators will often be part of a complex web of individuals; as such, global managers must understand that their Chinese counterpart may need to assist or provide favors for members of the *Guanxi* network. Savvy global managers will be aware of these networks so as to better understand the nature of the deal.
6. Communication ambiguity: Chinese negotiators have several ways of saying "yes," many of which actually mean "no" or "uncertain." In trying not to embarrass or offend foreign negotiators, Chinese will answer "yes" in an attempt to ensure that the negotiator does not lose face. This is more likely to occur if the request was made in front of other people. A rejection may be convened in the following ways: If a request cannot be met, the Chinese may indicate that "it is inconvenient" or "under consideration" or "yes, but it will be difficult/take some time."

Sources: Hone Seng Woo and Celine Prud'homme, "Cultural Characteristics Prevalent in the Chinese Negotiation Process," *European Business Review* 99, no. 5 (1999), pp. 313–22, and Huang Quanyu, Richard Andrulis, and Chen Tong, *Guide to Successful Business Relations with the Chinese* (New York: International Business Press, 1994).

Monochronic versus Polychronic Time Orientation

Individuals in Asia, the Middle East, and Latin America tend to view time differently from most individuals from the United States, Britain, and Germany. Managers from cultures with a **polychronic time orientation** do many things at once, are subject to interruptions, are committed to human relationships, change plans often, and base promptness on the relationship. However, managers from monochronic cultures do one thing at a time, take time commitments seriously, adhere to plans, follow rules of privacy and show respect for private property, and emphasize promptness.[38] Applied to cross-cultural negotiations, misunderstandings can occur when members from monochronic and polychronic time cultures are on opposite sides of the negotiation table. U.S., British, and German negotiators will want to take a more orderly, linear, step-by-step approach to the negotiation process. In contrast, a Chinese, Saudi, or Costa Rican will resist this overly structured approach and prefer a more dynamic, spontaneous approach characterized by interruptions and occasional changes in plans based on new information.

BEST PRACTICES—NEGOTIATING STRATEGIES

Global managers can follow a set of best practices that tend to work well in most cross-cultural settings.[39] The practices include the following:

1. Plan the negotiation carefully.
2. Adopt a win-win approach so both sides can feel they benefited.
3. Maintain high aspirations during the process.
4. Use language that is simple and easy to understand without talking down to others.
5. Ask an appropriate number of questions and listen carefully to the responses.
6. Establish solid interpersonal relationships and friendships.
7. Maintain personal integrity, even when faced with the temptation to digress.
8. Conserve concessions until later in the negotiation process.
9. Be very patient and seek to understand the other party's position.
10. Be cross-culturally literate and adapt negotiating strategies to the host-country environment.

By understanding these best practices and many of the other concepts presented in this chapter, global managers will be better prepared to enter into cross-cultural negotiations with the skills, preparation, and attitude necessary to be successful. As the world continues to become more globalized, the frequency and importance of cross-cultural negotiation will increase dramatically. Part of the success of joint ventures, export arrangements, international trade talks, sales and vendor agreements, and foreign direct investment will hinge on the initial and ongoing negotiations between organizational representatives and leaders who engage in productive and relationship-based negotiations that take culture into account and produce win-win outcomes for the parties involved in the process.

Key Terms

Bargaining zone model, *193*
Conversational overlap, *200*
Distributive negotiation, *192*
High context communication cultures, *202*
Integrative negotiation, *193*
Lowballing, *199*
The nibble, *198*
Polychronic time orientation, *204*
Proxemics, *202*
Resistance point, *194*

Review, Critical Thinking, and Discussion Questions

1. Assume you are about to negotiate with an individual from China. Identify five culturally related areas in which you and your Chinese counterpart will most likely differ? How will you go about overcoming these differences?
2. Provide an example of when distributive (or zero-sum) negotiation would be most appropriate. Also, give another example of when you think the integrative (or win-win) negotiation approach is superior.
3. Thinking about the bargaining zone model of negotiation, what would you do if your counterpart, who is from a culture where initial starting points are often exaggerated, makes an outrageous initial offer? How would you react? How would you get that person to agree to your target point?
4. In a negotiation, which personality type would you prefer to "go up against": a power seeker or a persuader? Why?
5. Assume you are from a country other than the United States. What do you know about typical U.S. negotiators? What are their strengths? Weaknesses?
6. How would you react if the other party in a negotiation provided you with false information and tried to deceive you? Would you confront the person directly? Ignore the behavior? Why or why not?
7. What can you expect when you deal with an individual or team of negotiators from a collectivist culture? In terms of decision making? In terms of saying "no"?
8. What in your opinion is the best way for a negotiator to prepare for a complex negotiation with a team of negotiators from another country?
9. Assume that your counterpart in a negotiation is from another country and begins the negotiation by offering to purchase your consulting services for an extremely low price. How should you react to this lowballing technique? How can you prepare yourself for these types of tactics?
10. Silent periods are sometimes used during cross-cultural negotiations as a way to unnerve the other party. Thinking about your national culture, how do members of the culture feel about periods of silence during conversations? Are they avoided, endured, or relished? Explain.

Endnotes

1. Roger J. Volkema and Maria T. Leme Fleury, "Alternative Negotiating Conditions and the Choice of Negotiation Tactics: A Cross-Cultural Comparison," *Journal of Business Ethics,* 2002, pp. 381–98.

2. R. M. Kanter, *World Class: Thriving Locally in a Global Economy* (New York: Simon and Schuster, 1995).
3. Jensen Zhao, "The Chinese Approach to International Business Negotiation," *The Journal of Business Communication,* July 2000, pp. 209–37; Jeanne Brett and Tetsushi Okumura, "Inter- and Intracultural Negotiation: U.S. and Japanese Negotiators," *The Academy of Management Journal,* 1998, pp. 495–510; and Catherine Tinsley and Madan Pillutla, "Negotiating in the United States and Hong Kong," *Journal of International Business Studies,* Fourth Quarter 1998, pp. 711–27.
4. Nancy J. Adler, *International Dimensions of Organizational Behavior,* 4th ed. (Cincinnati: South-Western, 2002); Tinsley and Pillutla, "Negotiating in the United States and Hong Kong"; and F. R. Kluckhohn and F. L. Stodtbeck, *Variations in Value Orientations* (New York: Row, Peterson, 1961).
5. Shi Xinping, "Antecedent Factors on International Business Negotiations in the China Context," *Management International Review,* Second Quarter 2001, pp. 163–79.
6. Jacqueline Oliveira, *Brazil: A Guide for Business People* (Yarmouth, ME: Intercultural Press, 2001).
7. Jeffrey Z. Rubin and Bert R. Brown, *The Social Psychology of Bargaining and Negotiation* (New York: Academic Press, 1975).
8. Roy J. Lewicki, David M. Saunders, and John W. Minton, *Negotiations* (Burr Ridge, IL: McGraw-Hill/Irwin, 1999).
9. Steven L. McShane and Mary Ann Von Glinow, *Organizational Behavior* (New York: McGraw-Hill/Irwin, 2000).
10. C. W. Barlow and G. P. Eisen, *Purchasing Negotiations* (Boston: CBI Publishing, 1983), chap. 5.
11. J. A. Wall Jr. and M. W. Blum, "Negotiations," *Journal of Management,* 1991, pp. 273–303.
12. G. Dangot-Simpkin, "Eight Attitudes to Develop to Hone Your Negotiating Skills," *Supervisory Management,* February 1992, p. 10.
13. Barlow and Eisen, *Purchasing Negotiations*.
14. Robert M. Peterson and George H. Lucas, "Expanding the Antecedent Component of the Traditional Business Negotiation Model: Pre-negotiation Literature Review and Planning-Preparation Propositions," *Journal of Marketing Theory,* Fall 2001, pp. 37–49.
15. G. Richard Shell, *Bargaining for Advantage* (New York: Penguin Books, 1999), and Roy J. Lewicki, David M. Saunders, and John W. Minton, *Essentials of Negotiation* (Chicago: Irwin, 1997).
16. Peterson and Lucas, "Expanding the Antecedent Component of the Traditional Business Negotiation Model."
17. Lewicki, Saunders, and Minton, *Essentials of Negotiation*.
18. Roy J. Lewicki and J. A. Litterer, *Negotiation* (Homewood, IL: Irwin, 1985).
19. Peterson and Lucas, "Expanding the Antecedent Component of the Traditional Business Negotiation Model," and Lewicki, Saunders, and Minton, *Essentials of Negotiation*.
20. Frank L. Acuff, *How to Negotiate Anything with Anyone Anywhere around the World* (New York: American Management Association, 1993), p. 30.

21. R.K. Stutman and S.E. Newell, "Rehearsing for Confrontation: Why and How Some Actors Rehearse," paper presented at Temple University Conference on Discourse, Philadelphia, 1988.
22. Sandra Younger, "Sales Savvy for the Nineties," *Training & Development,* December 1992, pp. 13–17.
23. Adler, *International Dimensions of Organizational Behavior*.
24. Don R. McCreary, *Japanese-U.S. Business Negotiations: A Cross-cultural Study* (New York: Praeger, 1986), p. 26.
25. Tommy T.B. Koh, "American Strengths and Weaknesses," *International Negotiation: A Journal of Theory and Practice,* 1996, pp. 44–50.
26. J.W. Salacuse, "Ten Ways That Culture Affects Negotiation Style: Some Survey Results," *Negotiation Journal,* July 1998, pp. 221–40.
27. Michele J. Gelfand and Anu Realo, "Individualism-Collectivism and Accountability in Intergroup Negotiations," *Journal of Applied Psychology,* October 1999, pp. 721–36.
28. John L. Graham, "The Influence of Culture on the Process of Business Negotiations: An Exploratory Study," *Journal of International Business Studies,* Spring 1985, pp. 81–97.
29. Ibid.
30. Roy J. Lewicki, "Lying and Deception: A Behavioral Model," in *Negotiating in Organizations,* ed. M.H. Bazerman and R.J. Lewicki (Beverly Hills, CA: Sage Publications, 1983).
31. Roy J. Lewicki and Robert J. Robinson, "Ethical and Unethical Bargaining Tactics: An Empirical Study," *Journal of Business Ethics,* April 1998, pp. 665–82.
32. Volkema and Fleury, "Alternative Negotiating Conditions and the Choice of Negotiation Tactics."
33. Peterson and Lucas, "Expanding the Antecedent Component of the Traditional Business Negotiation Model;" John L. Graham, Alma T. Mintu, and Raymond Rodgers, "Explorations of Negotiation Behaviors in Ten Foreign Cultures Using a Model Developed in the United States," *Management Science,* 1994, pp. 72–95.
34. Geert Hofstede, *Culture's Consequences: International Differences in Work-Related Values* (Newbury Park, CA: Sage, 1980).
35. Peterson and Lucas, "Expanding the Antecedent Component of the Traditional Business Negotiation Model."
36. Edward T. Hall, *The Hidden Dimension* (Garden City, NY: Doubleday, 1966).
37. Graham, "The Influence of Culture on the Process of Business Negotiations."
38. Edward T. Hall and Mildred R. Hall, *Understanding Cultural Differences: Germans, French, and Americans* (Yarmouth, ME: Intercultural Press, 1989).
39. Acuff, *How to Negotiate Anything with Anyone Anywhere around the World*.

Chapter Seven

Diversity Management

Learning Objectives

After completing Chapter 7, you should be able to:

- Describe some of the forces that are contributing to the increase in diversity of labor forces in many countries.
- Define diversity and understand how it can influence workplace productivity.
- Explain how diversity issues are affecting Japan, the European Union, and the United States.
- Identify the advantages that organizations receive from having successful diversity management programs.
- Understand the main characteristics of a multicultural organization.

Global Diversity: Knowledge Is Power

Brigitta Hochstrasser, vice president of marketing and sales for a large Swiss food products company, is responsible for staffing the new sales and distribution center in Los Angeles, California. After placing various job advertisements in the local newspapers, radio, and Internet, she flew to Los Angeles to begin the interviewing. To her surprise, most of the candidates for the open positions were very diverse in nature, including male and female Russians, Japanese, Koreans, Vietnamese, Armenians, Mexicans, Guatemalans, Salvadorans, and African-Americans.

Hochstrasser is no stranger to interviewing and hiring candidates from diverse backgrounds. In her native country of Switzerland, the population is a rich mixture of cultural and ethnic backgrounds: 65 percent German, 18 percent French, 10 percent Italian, and 7 percent Romansch and other. The Swiss found that it was important to learn more about the candidates' backgrounds and perspectives to assist them in making better hiring decisions. By doing some research, she was able to learn more about her diverse candidates and also decided this would be good information for students, global managers, and others to know.

What race are Hispanics (or Latinos)? The correct answer is they can be Caucasian, black, native, or some combination. Hispanic refers not only to a race but also to an origin or an ethnicity. There are many Hispanic segments in Los Angeles—Mexicans, Guatemalans, Salvadorans, and others who are different in their indigenous ancestry, origins, accents, and many other characteristics.

What is Confucianism? **Confucianism** is the major religious influence on Chinese, Japanese, Korean, and Vietnamese cultures. It emphasizes response to authority, especially to parents and teachers; hard work; discipline and the ability to delay gratification; harmony in relationships; and the importance of the group over individual needs.

Does the term African-American apply to all blacks? No. Black Americans came from cultures others than just those in Africa, including the Caribbean, Central America, and South America. Just as in the general population, there is great variety in lifestyle, career choice, educational level attained, and value systems across segments of the over 36 million black American (including African and other cultural backgrounds) population.

After she completes the Los Angeles hiring, Hochstrasser will fill similar assignments in France and India. She thinks to herself how important it's becoming to develop a style and pattern of behavior that appeals to and reaches all segments of the diverse recruits that she encounters. By relating better to these job candidates, Hochstrasser hopes this relationship building will generate enthusiasm for the company. She believes that a diverse set of employees will go a long way to dealing with the mix of diverse customers, suppliers, food inspectors, and the other important stakeholders that share in the success of his enterprise.

Sources: *CIA World Factbook* (http://www.cia.gov/cia/publications/factbook/); Lynette Clemetson, "Hispanics Now Largest Minority, Census Shows," *New York Times*, January 22, 2003; and John Naisbitt, *Global Paradox* (New York: Morrow, 1994), pp. 227–35.

As the opening vignette illustrates, labor forces in Los Angeles and in many other cities and countries in the world are becoming much more diverse than was the case several decades ago. There are a variety of reasons for this increase in labor force diversity, including globalization, sociopolitical events, immigration, and population trends. Here are some examples to illustrate the impact these forces are exerting on diversity.

- *From now until 2010, women, Asians, and Hispanics are projected to enter the U.S. labor force at a higher rate than white non-Hispanics.*[1] Added to this is the fact that with the aging of the baby-boom generation (born between 1946 and 1964), the percentage of employees age 55 and older is expected to increase from 13 to 20 percent by 2020.[2]

- *France and Germany have between 400,000 and 1.5 million illegal immigrants.* In 2001, France received 47,000 asylum applications (mostly from Chinese and Turks). In that same year, Germany received 90,000 asylum petitions.
- *In the Philippines, a traditional and conservative society, women are entering the workforce at a higher rate than ever before not only as employees, but also as entrepreneurs.* Economic necessity and opportunity are driving many women to enter the workforce and/or create businesses.[3]
- *Changing geopolitical landscapes, economic downturns, and regional conflicts are creating large-scale immigration movements between countries.* Turmoil in the Middle East, the demise of the Soviet Union, unification of the German Democratic Republic (East) and German Federal Republic (West), Chinese government crackdown on protesters in Tiananmen Square, fighting in Croatia and Serbia, and economic crises in countries like Argentina and Russia all lead to immigration. In the United States, Hispanics are now the largest minority group with a population of 37 million as of 2001.[4] This is nearly equal to the combined populations of Venezuela (24 million) and Chile (15.4 million); and it represents over one-third the population of Mexico (103 million).[5]

These trends show that workforce diversity is an important topic for global managers to understand. Not only will managers need to know how to organize, motivate, and lead "domestically diverse employees" of different gender, race, ethnic, religious, age, and racial backgrounds, but managers will also need to know how to relate effectively to key customers, joint-venture managers and employees, vendors, and government officials located around the globe. For these reasons, global managers should develop an effective approach to diversity management.

DIVERSITY: AN INTRODUCTION

Diversity refers to a vast array of physical and cultural variation that constitutes the spectrum of human differences. The six primary dimensions of diversity include age, ethnicity, gender, physical attributes, race, and sexual/affectional orientation. These core elements of diversity have a lifelong impact on behavior and attitudes. Secondary forms of diversity—the differences that people acquire, discard, or modify throughout their lives—can be changed. Secondary dimensions of diversity include educational background, marital status, religious belief, health disabilities, and work experience.[6]

Valuing diversity from an organizational and leadership perspective means understanding and accepting differences in core and secondary diversity dimensions in others. An increasingly important goal in a changing society is to understand that all individuals are different and to appreciate these differences.[7] From an international business perspective, the more global managers know and understand their diverse stakeholders, the more effective and productive they will be. Exhibit 7.1 illustrates the extent to which countries are diverse in terms of ethnicity, religions, and languages.

EXHIBIT 7.1 Diversity around the World

Sources: *CIA World Factbook*; J.L. Price and W.G. Barron, *Profiles of General Demographic Characteristics: 2000 Census of Population and Housing—United States* (Washington, DC: U.S. Department of Commerce, May 2001).

Country	Ethnic Groups	Religions	Languages
Germany	German 91.5%, Turkish 2.4%, Other 6.1% (comprised mostly of Serbo-Croatian, Italian, Russian, Greek, Polish, and Spanish)	Protestant 34%, Roman Catholic 34%, Muslim 3.7%, Other 28.3%	German
India	Indo-Aryan 72%, Dravidian 25%, and Other 3%	Hindu 81.3%, Muslim 12%, Christian 2.3%, Sikh 1.9%, Other 2.5% (includes Buddhist, Jain, and Parsi)	English for national, political, and commercial communication; Hindi is the national language and primary tongue of 30 percent of the people; 14 other official languages are spoken (Bengali, Telugu, Marathi, Tamil, Urdu, etc.)
Brazil	White (includes Portuguese, German, Italian, Spanish, Polish) 55%, mixed white and black 38%, black 6%, and Other (includes Japanese, Arab, and Amerindian) 1%	Roman Catholic (nominal) 80%	Portuguese (official), Spanish, English, and French
China	Han Chinese 91.9%, Other (Zhuang, Uygur, Hui, Yi, Tibetan, Miao, Manchu, Mongol, Buyi, Korean) 8.1%	Taoist, Buddhist, Muslim 1–2%, Christian 3–4% (note: officially atheist)	Mandarin (Putonghua, based on Beijing dialect), Yue (Cantonese), Wu (Shanghaiese), Minbei (Fuzhou), Minnan (Hokkien-Taiwanese), Xiang, Gan, Hakka dialects, and others
South Africa	Black 75.2%, white 13.6%, colored 8.6%, and Indian 2.6%	Christian 68%, Muslim 2%, Hindu 1.5%, and indigenous beliefs and animist 28.5%	11 official languages, including Afrikaans, English, Ndebele, Pedi, Sotho, Swazi, Tsonga, Tswana, Venda, Xhosa, and Zulu
Canada	British Isles origin 28%, French origin 23%, other European 15%, Amerindian 2%, Other (mostly Asian, African, Arab) 6%, and mixed background 26%	Roman Catholic 46%, Protestant 36%, Other 18%	English 59.3% (official), French 23.2% (official), and Other 17.5%

GLOBAL PERSPECTIVES ON DIVERSITY

Japan, the European Union, and the United States have very different views of diversity.

Japan

As one of the most homogenous societies in the world, being considered Japanese requires an individual to be born to Japanese parents, to look Japanese, to speak the Japanese language, and to behave like Japanese.[8] These considerations have led to a population that is 99 percent Japanese, with the remaining 1 percent being Korean, Chinese, Brazilian, or Filipino. Due to several years of low birthrates and an aging workforce, the Japanese exclusionary stance toward *gaijin* (foreigners) is beginning to be challenged. For example, Japan has liberalized its immigration laws allowing Brazilians of Japanese descent (and their spouses) to migrate to Japan on temporary work visas. Reflecting the cultural diversity of the 254,000 Brazilians in Japan, there are now 41 Brazilian schools, two Brazilian television stations, and four Brazilian weekly newspapers.[9] This more encouraging stance toward guest workers is expected to continue as Japan grapples with its labor shortage.

Another diversity-related issue, women in managerial and leadership positions, is gaining attention. Japanese women who enter the workforce often take positions of "office lady," meaning that they will be labeled as clerical workers with little to no promotability. These individuals often wear uniforms and perform jobs that include photocopying, serving tea, and creating a "pleasant atmosphere" in the office. These women can be high school or college educated, and it is expected that after being married for a few years, they will drop out of the workforce to raise children and provide a suitable home environment for their working spouses.[10]

Better career opportunities are slowly beginning to become available for women in Japan. For example, the percentage of women in management positions has grown in the past 10 years, from 6.0 to 8.9 percent of all managers. This is still disproportionate to the percentage of women in the workforce (40.6 percent).[11]

In 1986, an equal employment law was passed to encourage fair and equitable treatment for women in terms of recruitment, hiring decisions, and promotions. In addition, the law prohibited illegal discrimination against women in new employee training, retirement, and dismissal, and lifted the ban on overtime for women working in "professional positions" such as doctors, engineers, and so on. This law has paved the way for a two-tiered career track system, one for women with traditional aspirations and one for women who want equivalent career opportunities as their male counterparts.[12]

These diversity issues in Japan hold implications for global managers. For example, foreign managers operating out of companies in Japan might be able to attract talented Japanese female managers and employees if they offer more opportunities for equal treatment and career advancement. Also, Japanese expatriate managers will need to make adjustments in their policies and management style when working in subsidiaries located in host countries with diverse cultures. If not, they may place their companies at risk of lawsuits and damage public relations with future employees and customers in the host country. One example of this is the discrimination lawsuits filed against Mitsubishi Motor Manufacturing of America in the United States. In 1998, the automobile manufacturer agreed to a record $34 million deal to settle claims that 350 women were sexually harassed on the factory floor at one of the plants. Also in that same year, the company agreed to pay $3 million to settle the complaints of 87 people who alleged they were not hired because of their disabilities.[13] To combat some of these problems, Mitsubishi asked former U.S. Secretary of Labor Lynn Martin to conduct a third-party review of all the company's workplace policies and procedures, including those related to sexual harassment, discrimination, and diversity.[14]

Thus, the development and implementation of diversity management programs that are appropriate for a given host country can improve relations with the public in general, and employees, customers, and vendors in particular. The goodwill that is created can help a global organization gain and sustain competitive advantage in the markets in which it operates.

European Union

Historically, the European Union nations have provided generous protection and benefits to pregnant women and parents of infants, but have been less proactive in developing broad-based antidiscrimination legislation. To create a unified effort against workplace discrimination, the European Union is attempting to establish minimum standards. The Directorate-General for Employment and Social Affairs has issued a three-part strategy that forms the basis for future legislative action:[15]

1. Directive implementing equal treatment irrespective of racial and ethnic origin.
2. Directive establishing a framework for equal treatment in employment and occupation (covers discrimination on grounds of religion and belief, disability, age, and sexual orientation).
3. Community Action Program controlling the spending required to support development of new legislation in the member states and acceding countries.

The member states of the European Union will have to modify their existing legislation to make these into national law. In addition to this pan-European legislation, the EU is also taking steps and establishing programs to enhance women's participation in European business.[16] For example, WOMENCRAFT involves 25 women-managed or -owned small and medium-size businesses from all over Europe whose goal is to encourage technological research among member firms. The project is being run by Beta Technology, a center of excellence for innovation, which specializes in technology transfer, technology funding, and consulting. Another project, ProWomEn has been launched by the European Commission to promote women entrepreneurs. This project's main goal is to create a strong network of high-potential individuals from the member countries to discuss and exchange regional policies and actions to promote the creation of start-ups by women. Specific objectives of the ProWomEm project include:

- Build awareness among regional decision makers as to the importance of promoting women entrepreneurs.
- Collect and distribute supporting tools for women entrepreneurs, including case studies and best practice models.
- Set up regional networks for women entrepreneurs that include discussion and initiation of pilot projects.
- Develop ways to change education and training systems to create a culture of entrepreneurship for women, specifically focusing on the development of valuable life skills for women.

United States

By 2010, most of the new entrants into the civilian labor force in the United States will be individuals age 55 and older, Asians, Hispanics, blacks, and women.[17] In an attempt to ensure that all individuals have an equal chance for employment without concern for race, color, religion, sex, age, disability, or national origin, the U.S. government passed a series of **equal employment opportunity laws** over the past 40 years. A sample of major U.S. EEO laws and regulations can be found in Exhibit 7.2.

Although some progress has been made, sex discrimination in employment in the United States continues to be a problem. Though accounting for approximately 50 percent of the U.S. workforce, women occupy about 30 percent of all salaried managerial positions, 20 percent of middle-manager positions, and 5 percent of executive jobs. Contributing to this problem is occupational segregation,

EXHIBIT 7.2
Sample of Equal Employment Opportunity Laws in the United States

Source: Adapted from John M. Ivancevich, *Human Resource Management, 8th ed.* (New York: McGraw-Hill/Irwin, 2001), pp. 73–90.

Name of the Act	Stipulations
Equal Pay Act (1963)	Requires that men and women performing substantially equal work receive equal pay.
Title VII of Civil Rights Act (1964)	Prohibits illegal discrimination based on race, color, religion, sex, or national origin.
Executive Order 11246 (1965)	Requires federal contractors and subcontractors with contracts greater than $10,000 to implement affirmative action in hiring women and minorities.
Age Discrimination in Employment Act (1967)	Prohibits discrimination in employment against individuals 40 years of age and older.
Americans with Disabilities (1990)	Prohibits discrimination against individuals with Act disabilities who can perform the essential functions of a job.

in which at least 75 percent of workers in an occupation are male or female. Seven of the 10 most common jobs for women are sex-segregated and are characterized by low pay, low status, and short career ladders: secretaries, cashiers, registered nurses, nursing aides/orderlies/assistants, elementary school teachers, and servers.[18] Laws such as the Civil Rights Act of 1964 and the Equal Pay Act of 1963 were developed to help deal with some of these issues.

To combat the overt and subtle barriers to advancement faced by women in the U.S. workplace, a combination of individual and organizational strategies should be developed. Individual strategies that women can follow to break the **glass ceiling** include:[19]

- Exceed performance expectations on a consistent basis.
- Develop a style with which male managers are comfortable.
- Find difficult or challenging assignments.
- Identify influential mentors.

As a complement to these individual strategies, companies can be proactive in helping employees receive fair and equal treatment. The accompanying Global Focus discusses what some companies are doing to help employees break through the glass ceiling.

Signed by Lyndon B. Johnson in 1965, **Executive Order 11246** created affirmative action as a way to deal with some of the barriers to advancement for minorities. **Affirmative action** is a proactive, intervention-based approach that organizations follow to increase the participation of historically underrepresented groups in the workforce. Though its intent is to achieve fair employment for everyone in the United States, affirmative action has suffered from negative perceptions and poor implementation. Negative perceptions surrounding affirmative action are illustrated by the following statements:[20]

- Affirmative action has created a "spoils system" in which people who have not experienced discrimination are reaping benefits at the direct expense of white males.[21]
- Lower hiring and performance standards have been applied to minorities.[22]
- Minorities have achieved their professional goals and no longer need affirmative action. To illustrate this is not the case, women make about 77 percent of men's earnings, and African-Americans and Hispanics held 11.3 percent and 10.9 percent, respectively, of all managerial and professional jobs in 2001.

Add to these the perception that affirmative action hires are selected on the basis of irrelevant workplace characteristics,[23] and one can conclude that the future of affirmative action is in question. In contrast, the successor of affirmative action, diversity management, has been portrayed as a critical component to the survival of global organizations. Some have argued that a more inclusive approach to embracing diversity is needed to enhance overall U.S. competitiveness vis-à-vis other economic powers.[24]

Global Focus What Can Companies Do to Break the Glass Ceiling?

Global organizations can take a variety of steps to help their female employees advance within the company. First, place more women on boards of directors; this will signal to lower-level female employees that capable women are recognized and rewarded with the firm. Second, hold senior management accountable for identifying and promoting women into line and general management positions. Third, institute a support program to assist working women; this can include flexible work arrangements and child care vouchers. Fourth, facilitate networking and mentoring relationships with senior successful individuals within the company. Last, understand and appreciate that men and women may take varied approaches to management issues.

Several companies have made strides in creating a friendly work environment for their female and minority employees. Deloitte & Touche is attempting to facilitate advancement of all its employees by using task forces, focus groups, and questionnaires to gather data on problems causing the glass ceiling; creating awareness of how gender attitudes affect the work environment; encouraging accountability through reviews of promotion rates and assignment decisions; and promoting development opportunities for all employees. In 1993, the company established "The Initiative for the Retention and Advancement of Women" to identify and develop female leaders. The programs in the initiative focused on the following concepts:

- Men and women as colleagues.
- Enhanced career opportunities for women.
- Balance between work and personal life.
- Diversity goals built into business planning and HR processes.
- Communication of these changes to all employees.

How successful has this program been? Overall, the initiative has produced some strong results. Currently, about 13 percent of the partners and directors are women (growing at about 30 percent per year), and more than 90 women have key leadership positions. Turnover has decreased 25 percent and the company has been ranked in Fortune's Best 100 Places to Work list for three years. Additionally, it has been ranked on the *Working Mother's* list and has received Workforce's Optimas award.

Other notable efforts have been made by Corning, American Airlines, and DuPont. At Corning, the CEO and top executives attend a gender training program that is followed up by a three-year program that directs managers to incorporate what they learned into daily working life. The company also sponsors quality improvement teams that focus on issues confronted by blacks and women, and organizes mandatory seminars to reinforce its policies against racial bias and gender discrimination. American Airlines has issued a directive that mandates that all corporate officers submit detailed, cross-functional development plans for all high-potential women in middle-management jobs and above. DuPont uses a rotation process that moves men and women through at least two or three functions before reaching top management positions.

Sources: Douglas M. McCracken, "Winning the Talent War for Women: Sometimes It Takes a Revolution," *Harvard Business Review,* November–December 2000, pp. 159–67; Charlene M. Solomon, "Cracks in the Glass Ceiling," *Workforce* 79, (September 2000), pp. 86–94; and Alison Eyring and Bette Ann Stead, "Shattering the Glass Ceiling: Some Successful Corporate Practices," *Journal of Business Ethics* 17 (February 1998), pp. 245–51.

DIVERSITY MANAGEMENT

Global legislative efforts to deal with discrimination in the workplace are an important step to creating a more inclusive workplace. In addition, organizations have considerable incentive to not only follow the laws that prohibit discrimination, but also to voluntarily design and implement **diversity management** programs that lead to greater inclusion of all types of individuals into informal social networks and formal company programs.[25] Making all types of employees feel included and an important part of the organization can contribute to several positive organizational outcomes. For example, Cox and Blake argue that an organization's ability to attract, retain, and motivate individuals from diverse backgrounds (age, gender, ethnicity, etc.) helps it achieve and sustain competitive advantage in a variety of key areas:[26]

1. Cost savings: In many companies, turnover and absenteeism rates are higher while job satisfaction levels are lower among women and minorities. Diversity management initiatives such as flexible work scheduling, mentoring, and equal access to training and development opportunities will help an organization retain these valuable human resources, especially in times of labor shortages.
2. Resource acquisition: Competitive advantage in human resources can come from hiring and retaining top talent from different demographic groups. Companies are increasingly turning to creative ads that focus on diversity:[27]

   - Pitney Bowes—"We're interested in Genius . . . not Genes . . . Genius is diverse."
   - Prudential—"At Prudential, diversity has its rewards."
   - Morgan Stanley—"Diversity. It's not an obligation—It's an opportunity."
   - Bristol-Myers Squibb—". . . we believe that diversity is the cornerstone of a high performance organization . . ."

   Diversity recruitment efforts are boosted when a company earns a spot on a public listing such as Fortune's 50 Best Companies for Minorities.[28] In 2002, the large mortgage company Fannie Mae earned the top spot for the first time thanks largely to its many powerful minority executives. Rounding out the top five are Sempra Energy, fast-food company Advantica (Denny's parent and 2001's No. 1 winner), Baby Bell SBC Communications, and McDonald's.
3. Marketing: Having a workforce that is representative of an organization's customers and other stakeholders can add value in a variety of ways. First, global managers who are from the country or region in which operations are located are able to communicate with and understand the needs and preferences of the host-country customers. Possessing the appropriate intercultural communication skills is important for managing culturally diverse relationships with customers.[29] The same holds true for marketing to customers and consumers that are part of a subculture within the same country. Early in the 21st century, African-Americans, Asians, and Hispanics are expected to account for 25 percent of the U.S. consumer base and are projected to have annual

spending power of approximately $650 billion.[30] Some organizations are proactively marketing to these subcultures. For example, Avon Corporation made major improvements in its profitability in inner-city markets in the United States by giving its black and Hispanic managers much more authority over these markets. Another example is *People* magazine, which markets its Spanish-language version, *People en español,* to over 400,000 subscribers in the United States. Advertising revenues for the magazine in 2002 were estimated at $24.3 million, or about 25 percent of the $98 million Hispanic magazine advertising market.[31]

4. Creativity and problem solving: Research supports the idea that diverse teams tend to generate ideas and solutions to problems that are more creative and innovative compared to those produced by homogenous teams.[32] Although too much diversity can lead to a decrease in team cohesiveness, companies that foster diversity and openness internally may do better in attracting talented, creative people who can collaborate and produce innovative ideas and solutions.[33] In addition, the global nature of business today increasingly requires people to collaborate in teams that cross cultural and geographic boundaries. These teams are in a unique position to create competitive advantage by forging different ideas, pools of knowledge, and approaches to work.[34]
5. System flexibility: A successfully managed diversity program enhances organizational flexibility, or the ability to react to changes in the environment faster and at less cost. Women tend to have a higher tolerance for ambiguity than men, which has been linked to their ability to excel in performing complex and ambiguous tasks.[35] In addition, research on bilingual versus monolingual subcultures from several countries indicates that bilingual individuals have higher levels of divergent thinking and cognitive flexibility.[36] In countries such as Canada, the hiring and inclusion of bilingual (French and English) employees in organizations will provide openness and adaptability, both important characteristics for global organizations that are fighting for success and competitive advantage.

Monolithic, Plural, and Multicultural Organizations

Cox classified organizations based on the extent of their diversity initiative implementation.[37] **Monolithic organizations** are in the early stages of developing a diversity management orientation. Women and ethnic minority men tend to be segregated into low-status jobs, reflecting a low degree of integration and inclusiveness into the organizational structure. Ethnocentrism leads to little to no adoption of minority-culture norms by majority group members. An example of this would be Honda Motors in Japan in which most of the manager and higher-status positions are occupied by members of the majority, Japanese men. The women and Brazilian employees (of Japanese heritage) are not treated with the same respect as the Japanese male employees.

Some of the potential problems associated with this unequal treatment is that monolithic organizations lose out on reaping the benefits of high-performing minority employees who are blocked from higher-level positions within the organization. Because of blocked career paths, many of these companies will end up with higher costs due to employee turnover, and subsequent replacement and training expenditures. Research has shown that Japanese companies that utilize only Japanese expatriates in high-level positions in overseas subsidiaries tend to experience more international human resource management problems than do U.S. and European firms.[38]

Compared with the monolithic organization, the **plural organization** has a more heterogeneous membership and will take steps to be more inclusive of persons who are different from the majority group. Such steps can include giving preference to minority-culture groups in hiring and promotion decisions, as well as training all managers and supervisors on equal employment opportunity issues. These initiatives create organizations characterized by the integration of minorities into informal networks and reductions in discrimination and prejudicial attitudes. However, similar to the monolithic organization, plural organizations expect minority members to assimilate and adjust to the majority culture and behavioral norms. Thus, some of the same problems (albeit less severe) that can impact monolithic organizations can be found in plural organizations.

Multicultural organizations not only contain different cultural groups but also value the diversity that these groups bring to the table. Full integration is achieved in terms of including minorities in informal networks. Discrimination is minimized in employment decisions, and the diversity is used to gain competitive advantage in the marketplace. Steps that organizations can take to become more inclusive and accepting of diverse groups while simultaneously creating a motivated workforce include:[39]

- Training and orientation programs. Organizations can build employee awareness of diversity issues and provide the necessary skills to work effectively with diverse stakeholders. McDonnell Douglas has a program titled "Woman-wise and Business Savvy" that focuses on gender differences in work-related behaviors.
- Language training. For companies that hire individuals whose native tongue is different from that of the headquarters' language, language training is critical to ensure good communications. Motorola provides English as a second language classes at company expense on company time.
- Mentoring and access to senior management. Global organizations are encouraging diverse employees to seek out mentors who can help guide them regarding the organization's politics and unspoken rules. Also, some firms are establishing minority advisory groups that have direct access to high-level executives. At Equitable Life Assurance, groups of blacks, women, and Hispanics meet with the CEO to make suggestions on how to improve the organizational climate.

Diversity in Multicultural and Virtual Teams

In contrast to homogenous teams in which members are very similar in terms of cultural background, heterogeneous teams are those in which members hail from

Global Focus Advantages and Disadvantages of Multicultural Teams

MAJOR ADVANTAGES

1. *More creativity.* Cultural diversity among team members can lead to increased creativity due to a wider range of ideas and perspectives, and less influence of groupthink.
2. *Increased quality of output.* Diverse ideas and perspectives can lead to better problem identification, more alternatives, and better decision making.
3. *Enhanced exploration of problems.* As multicultural team members discuss their unique points of view, others are forced to concentrate more on the issues at hand in order to defend their positions. This enhanced concentration can lead to more thorough problem solving.

MAJOR DISADVANTAGES

1. *Lack of trust between team members.* This can be caused by lower interpersonal attractiveness, inaccurate stereotyping, and less cross-cultural conversation.
2. *Miscommunication.* Less accurate and slower speech, coupled with translation difficulties, can lead to misunderstandings among diverse team members.
3. *Lack of cohesion.* Problems with trust and miscommunication can lead to a lack of cohesion among team members. When teams suffer from low cohesion, this can lead to the inability to validate ideas, agree when necessary, and take action when appropriate.

Source: Adapted from Nancy J. Adler, *International Dimensions of Organizational Behavior,* 4th ed. (Cincinnati: South-Western, 2002), p. 143.

different cultures.[40] An example of a homogenous team would be when a group of five Chinese managers moves from Shanghai to Tokyo to launch a new joint venture with their Japanese partner. In contrast, members of the MERCOSUR free trade area make up a heterogeneous team in that they represent such diverse cultural backgrounds as Argentina, Brazil, Paraguay, and Uruguay.[41] In today's Internet-based environment, many teams operate in a virtual manner, whereby members are dispersed across different geographical and cultural boundaries. The advantages and disadvantages of multicultural teams are discussed in the accompanying Global Focus.

Special care needs to be taken when managing virtual teams whose members are from countries with distinct cultures and languages. Such team members can find communication and building trust more challenging.[42] Cultural nuances that might be detected in face-to-face meetings may go unnoticed during a teleconference or Webcast. As a result, virtual team members may experience misunderstandings and miscommunications while working on important projects. To decrease the risk of such problems, team members should be brought together for face-to-face meetings and cross-cultural training sessions in the early stages of the team process.

As companies such as GE, AT&T, Pfizer, Motorola, Shell Oil, and Sun Microsystems continue to experiment with and use virtual teams across their global businesses, such practices will become more common in organizations of all types and sizes.[43]

When working with culturally diverse teams, some steps can be taken to improve their effectiveness. One researcher has made the following suggestions:[44]

1. Use task-related selection. The primary selection criteria for team selection should be their task-related abilities and track record.
2. Recognize differences. Teams and team leaders should not ignore or minimize differences, but rather should accept team members' unique insights and contributions to the group.
3. Establish a vision or subordinate goal. To help team members overcome individual differences, direct their energies and attention to achieving important goals that benefit the entire group.
4. Create mutual respect. This can be done by selecting team members of similar ability, making prior accomplishments and task-related skills known to all team members, and minimizing the use of stereotypes and ethnocentrism.
5. Give feedback. Since heterogeneous teams can take longer in reaching agreements, managers should provide the team with feedback regarding the team's process and productivity. Also, suggestions for improvement and team-building training should be offered to enhance team functioning.

Creating a Successful Climate for Diversity

A global organization can control several factors to bring about positive outcomes from diversity initiatives. These factors include CEO leadership and support as well as modification of accountability, development, and recruitment practices.[45]

CEO Leadership and Ongoing Support

CEOs have the power to instill in the organizational culture that valuing differences makes sense both from a perspective of justice and improving the bottom line. At Xerox, CEOs have consistently viewed diversity management in terms of social responsibility and sound business practice. The company was one of the first to use caucus groups (discussion and advocacy groups representing ethnicity, sexual orientation, gender, and race) to advance the interests of minority employees through direct dialogue with top management.[46]

Accountability, Development, and Recruitment Practices

Ann Morrison conducted a large-scale study of diversity practices used by 16 organizations that had successful diversity management programs.[47] The results indicated three sets of practices contribute to successful diversity management: accountability, development, and recruitment practices.

- *Accountability practices* refer to managers' responsibility to treat diverse employees in a fair manner. Morrison's research found the most important practices to be top management's personal intervention, internal advocacy groups, emphasis on equal employment opportunity statistics, inclusion of diversity in performance evaluation goals and ratings, and inclusion of diversity in promotion decisions.

- *Development practices* focus on preparing diverse employees for greater responsibility and advancement. Key practices include diversity training programs, networks and support groups, development programs for all high-potential managers, informal networking activities, and job rotation.
- *Recruitment activities* attempt to attract job applicants from all levels and groups who are willing to work hard and seek challenging assignments. The study reported these best practices: targeted recruitment of nonmanagers; key outside hires; extensive public exposure on diversity (affirmative action); corporate image as liberal, progressive, or benevolent; and partnerships with educational institutions.

Implications for Global and Transnational Organizations

As globalization continues, organizations will continue to expand into new international markets. This expansion will bring the organizations into more direct contact with diverse sets of host-country employees and alliance partners, customers, suppliers, government officials, and union representatives. These individuals will be characterized by a variety of ages, religions, ethnicities, languages, and skin colors. To establish and maintain productive relationships with these stakeholders, global and transnational managers will need to have empathy and develop a thorough understanding of how to relate to these individuals.

In addition, many organizations are shifting to a team-based work environment. Driven by the need to enhance quality and promote innovation, organizations are helping diverse teams understand and accept one another in the name of higher productivity and group cohesion. For example, the employees at Corning Glass are organized into approximately 3,000 teams; the goal is to achieve higher quality through cooperation and team member involvement and commitment.[48]

Globalization and the movement toward team-based work are occurring in the midst of changing labor markets.[49] As discussed earlier, Japan, the European Union, and the United States as well as other countries and regions of the world are experiencing increases in the amount of gender, ethnic, and age diversity in their workforces. Combine this with the projected labor shortages that are occurring in many countries, and we can expect that organizations that successfully integrate valuing diversity into their organizational cultures will be an employer of choice for many new entrants into the workforce for years to come. Because the majority of the new entrants in the United States, for example, will be women, Hispanics, and blacks, then the organizations that value diversity will be in the best position to attract and retain these valuable employees.

Key Terms

Affirmative action, *216*
Confucianism, *210*
Diversity, *211*
Diversity management, *218*
EEO laws, *215*
Executive Order 11246, *216*
Glass ceiling, *216*
Monolithic organization, *219*
Multicultural organization, *220*
Plural organization, *220*

Review, Critical Thinking, and Discussion Questions

1. Assume you are working on a virtual team and teammates are from countries with very diverse cultural heritages. What are some diversity-related issues your team will need to confront to function effectively? What language will the team communicate in? To what extent will written e-mails and communications be used?
2. What are some of the influences affecting the labor force in Japan? How is it changing? Be sure to include in your answer information about women and ethnic minorities.
3. In your opinion, which of the equal employment opportunity laws in the United States has had the most impact on creating a more diverse workforce? Explain.
4. Should labor shortages in countries such as the United States, Germany, and Japan influence immigration policy? Explain.
5. What is the glass ceiling and how can it be broken by individuals and organizations?
6. This chapter has argued that successful diversity management is a source of competitive advantage for global and transnational organizations. Provide two examples of how a company such as Nestlé or Fiat can use diversity to their advantage.
7. Provide two advantages and two disadvantages of using multicultural teams. How can the disadvantages be mitigated or decreased?
8. Why do you think there are still barriers to advancement for many women, minorities, and the disabled? Explain.
9. Beyond the cost savings that can be realized due to lower absenteeism and turnover rates, identify and describe three additional benefits associated with making all types of individuals feel included and valued in a global organization.
10. Think about the organizations (companies, federal and state agencies, schools, etc.) with which you have had contact. Identify the one that appeared to be the most diverse in terms of gender, race, ethnicity, and so on. Then, identify the organization that seemed to be the least diverse. Can you think of any reasons to explain the differences?

Endnotes

1. Howard N. Fullerton, Jr., and Mitra Toossi, "Labor Force Projections to 2010: Steady Growth and Changing Composition," *Bureau of Labor Statistics Monthly Labor Review,* (November 2001), pp. 1–4.
2. Mitra Toossi, "A Century of Change: The U.S. Labor Force, 1950–2050," *Bureau of Labor Statistics Monthly Labor Review,* (May 2002), pp. 15–28.
3. Rene Mallari, "Toughing It Out," *Asian Business* 38 (March 2002), pp. 30–31.
4. Lynette Clemetson, "Hispanics Now Largest Minority, Census Shows," *New York Times,* (January 22, 2003), p. A1.
5. CIA World Factbook found on the Web at www.ciafactbook.com.
6. James L. Gibson, James H. Donnelly, Jr., John M. Ivancevich, and Robert Konopaske, *Organizations: Behavior, Structure, Processes,* 11th ed. (New York: McGraw-Hill/Irwin, 2003), p. 47.
7. Mark A. Williams, Mark W. Williams, and Donald O. Clifton, *The 10 Lenses: Your Guide to Living and Working in a Multicultural World* (New York: Capital Books, 2001).
8. John C. Condon, *With Respect to the Japanese: A Guide for Americans* (Yarmouth, ME: Intercultural Press, 1984).
9. James Brooke, "Sons and Daughters of Japan, Back from Brazil," *New York Times,* (November 27, 2001), p. A4.

10. John P. Fernandez and Mary Barr, *The Diversity Advantage: How American Business Can Out-Perform Japanese and European Companies in the Global Marketplace* (New York: Lexington, 1993).
11. Jean R. Renshaw, "Kimono in the Boardroom: The Invisible Evolution of Japanese Women Managers," (New York and Oxford: Oxford University Press, 1999).
12. Fernandez and Barr, *Diversity Advantage.*
13. Christopher Thorne, "Black Workers Sue Mitsubishi," *ABC News Corporation* (www.abcnews.com), (February 20, 2003); Jean P. Kamp, Steven J. Levine, and Reginald Welch, "EEOC Scores Major Victory in Mitsubishi Lawsuit," *The U.S. Equal Employment Opportunity Commission* (www.eeoc.gov/press/1-21-98.html), (January 21, 1998).
14. Jennifer J. Laabs, "Lynn Martin to Review Mitsubishi's Policies in Wake of Sexual-Harassment Charges," *Personnel Journal* 75, (July 1996), pp. 12–15.
15. Board Europe, "Embracing Diversity," (www.conference-board.org/publications/boardeurope/diversity.cfm), November–December 2002.
16. Sarah Clothier, "Cracking the Glass Ceiling in Europe," *The British Journal of Administrative Management* 24, (March/April 2001), pp. 21–32.
17. Fullerton and Toossi, "Labor Force Projections."
18. Myrtle P. Bell, Mary E. McLaughlin, and Jennifer M. Sequeira, "Discrimination, Harassment, and the Glass Ceiling: Women Executives as Change Agents," *Journal of Business Ethics* 37 (2002), pp. 65–76; C.E. Bose and R.B. Whaley, "Sex Segregation in the U.S. Labor Force," in *Gender Mosaics: Social Perspectives* ed. D. Vannoy (Los Angeles: Roxbury Publishing, 2001), pp. 228–48; B. Reskin, "Sex Segregation in the Workforce," in *Workplace/Women's Place,* ed. D. Dunn (Los Angeles: Roxbury Publishing, 1997), pp. 69–73; and E.A. Fagenson and J.J. Jackson, "The Status of Women Managers in the United States," *International Studies of Management and Organizations* 23 (1993), pp. 93–112.
19. B.R. Ragins, B. Townsend, and M. Mattis, "Gender Gap in the Executive Suite: CEOs and Female Executives Report on Breaking the Glass Ceiling," *The Academy of Management Executive,* (1998), pp. 28–42.
20. Jacqueline A. Gilbert, Bette Ann Stead, and John M. Ivancevich, "Diversity Management: A New Organizational Paradigm," *Journal of Business Ethics* 21 (1999), pp. 61–76.
21. R.K. Robinson, "Affirmative Action Plans in the 1990s: A Double-Edged Sword?" *Public Personnel Management* 21 (1992), pp. 261–72.
22. L.W. Wynter, "Diversity Is All Talk, No Affirmative Action," *The Wall Street Journal*, (December 21, 1994), p. B1.
23. M.E. Heilman, M.C. Simon, and D.P. Repper, "Intentionally Favored, Unintentionally Harmed? The Impact of Sex Based Preferential Selection on Self-Perceptions and Self-Evaluations," *Journal of Applied Psychology* 72 (1987), pp. 62–68.
24. Fernandez and Barr, *Diversity Advantage*.
25. Gilbert et al., "Diversity Management."
26. Taylor H. Cox and Stacy Blake, "Managing Cultural Diversity: Implications for Organizational Competitiveness," *The Academy of Management Executive* 5 (August 1991), pp. 45–57.
27. Ruth E. Thaler-Carter, "Diversify Your Recruitment Advertising," *HRMagazine* 46 (June 2001), pp. 92–100.
28. Fortune Magazine's 50 Best Companies for Minorities (www.fortune.com), July 8, 2002.

29. Victoria D. Bush, Gregory M. Rose, Faye Gilbert, and Thomas N. Ingram, "Managing Culturally Diverse Buyer-Seller Relationships: The Role of Intercultural Disposition and Adaptive Selling in Developing Intercultural Communication Competence," *Academy of Marketing Science Journal* 29, (Fall 2001), pp. 391–404.
30. Gilbert et al., "Diversity Management."
31. Christina Hoag, "People Leads Stack in Market for Hispanic Magazine Ads," Wilmington, North Carolina, *Star-News,* (February 23, 2003), p. E1.
32. William B. Johnston, "Global Work Force 2000: The New World Labor Market," In *Differences That Work: Organizational Excellence Through Diversity,* ed. Mary C. Gentile, (Cambridge, MA: Harvard Business Review, 1994).
33. Richard Florida, Robert Cushing, and Gary Gates, "When Social Capital Stifles Innovation," *Harvard Business Review* 80 (August 2002), pp. 20–26.
34. Martha L. Maznevski and Joseph J. DiStefano, "Global Leaders Are Team Players: Developing Global Leaders through Membership on Global Teams," *Human Resource Management* 39 (Summer/Fall 2000), pp. 195–208.
35. Naomi G. Rotter and Agnes N. O'Connell, "The Relationships Among Sex-Role Orientation, Cognitive Complexity, and Tolerance for Ambiguity," *Sex Roles* 8 (1982), pp. 1209–20.
36. Wallace Lambert, "The Effects of Bilingualism on the Individual: Cognitive and Sociocultural Consequences," in *Bilingualism: Psychological, Social, and Educational Implications,* ed. Peter A. Hurnbey, (New York: Academic Press, 1977), pp. 15–27.
37. Taylor Cox, Jr., "The Multicultural Organization," *The Academy of Management Executive* 5 (May 1991), pp. 34–48.
38. Kopp Rochelle, "International Human Resource Policies and Practices in Japanese, European, and United States Multinationals," *Human Resource Management* 33 (1994), pp. 581–99.
39. Cox, "Multicultural Organization."
40. R.C. Ziller, "Homogeneity and Heterogeneity of Group Membership," in *Experimental Social Psychology,* ed. C.G. McClintock (New York: Holt, Rinehart and Winston, 1972), pp. 385–411.
41. Charles W.L. Hill, *International Business: Competing in the Global Marketplace,* 4th ed. (New York: McGraw-Hill/Irwin, 2003) p. 259.
42. Richard Benson-Armer and Tsun-yan Hsieh, "Teamwork Across Time and Space," *The McKinsey Quarterly,* (November 4, 1997), pp. 18–27, Julekha Dash, "Think of People When Planning Virtual Teams," *Computerworld,* (February 2001), pp. 34–36.
43. Dash, "Think of People When Planning Virtual Teams."
44. Nancy J. Adler, *International Dimensions of Organizational Behavior,* 4th ed. (Cincinnati: South-Western, 2002), p. 74.
45. Ann M. Morrison, *The New Leaders: Guidelines on Leadership Diversity in America* (San Francisco: Jossey-Bass, 1992).
46. Gilbert et al., "Diversity Management."
47. Morrison, *New Leaders*.
48. B. Duhaime, "Who Needs a Boss?" *Fortune,* May 7, 1990, pp. 52–60.
49. Susan E. Jackson and Associates, *Diversity in the Workplace: Human Resource Initiatives* (New York: Guilford Press, 1992), p. 19.

Work Groups and Teams

Learning Objectives

After completing Chapter 8, you should be able to:

- Define *group* and *team* and identify the differences between the two concepts.
- Describe why social loafing would be more prevalent in individualistic-oriented national cultures.
- Explain how self-managed teams operate.
- Discuss the five stages of development groups and teams.
- Describe how a virtual team would function to achieve outstanding performance.

Manager Impact on Group and Team Success

Erran Carmel conducted extensive studies on how 17 major companies manage global software teams. Carmel found that the greatest impact on cross-national teams is how each culture reveres hierarchy. People in Russia, China, and Indonesia have a high regard and respect for hierarchy. Other cultures, such as German and American, revere equality. These kind of differences result in more or less personal initiative.

Another key cultural issue revolves around how communication is processed. In the United States, Northern European countries, and Australia, language must be precise. However, in Japan, China, Latin American countries, and India, communication preciseness is not as important. Building relationships is the top priority.

These differences play a role in the life of project managers who are dealing with different cultures, time zones, and languages. In attempting to build an effective global project team, the differences and how to cope with them are extremely important. An experienced manager shouldn't force an American approach to communications or hierarchy on a team member in India or China. If the manager attempts to force the approach, failure will probably result.

Managers working with people outside the immediate unit need to understand that cultural and communication differences are very powerful. The ability to cope with these differences can mean the success or failure of global projects, alliances, and teams.

Source: Adapted from Anthony R. Wheeler and M. Ronald Buckley, "Examining the Motivation Process of Temporary Employees: A Holistic Model and Research Framework," *Journal of Management Psychology* 16, no. 5 (2001), pp. 339–54, and Rochell Garner, "Round-the-World Teamwork," *Computerworld*, May 1999, p. 15.

This chapter focuses on managing work groups, group processes, and teams in transnational organizations. Managers and researchers have paid special attention to the group processes that affect individuals and organizations. Thus, any presentation of transnational management would be incomplete if it did not include a framework for understanding the nature and characteristics of work groups. A **work group** is defined as a collection of interacting employees (managerial or nonmanagerial) who share certain norms and are striving toward member need satisfaction through the attainment of group goals. The work group is the smallest formal organization of people within a firm. As such, a work group represents the most basic level of collective work activity.

The term **team** is often used interchangeably with the concept of group. Some experts propose a distinction between the two terms as follows:

> A working group's performance is a function of what its members do as individuals. A team's performance includes both individual results and what we call "collective work products." A collective work product is what two or more members work on together . . . [it] reflects the joint, real contribution of team members.[1]

The authors of this distinction also point out specific team versus group differences such as:

1. A work group has a strong leader; a team has shared leadership roles.
2. A work group focuses on individual accountability; a team has individual and mutual accountability.
3. A work group measures effectiveness indirectly while a team measures performance directly by assessing collective work products.
4. A work group's purpose is the same as the organization's; a team has a specific purpose.

Thus, teams have characteristics similar to work groups but they go beyond by having a collective effect. This chapter will discuss cross-functional, virtual, and self-managed teams; however, the discussion will use groups as the central unit for analysis.

This chapter will provide (1) a classification of the different types of groups and teams, (2) some knowledge about the reasons for the formation and development of groups and teams, (3) an understanding of some characteristics of groups, (4) some insights into the outcomes of group and teams members, and (5) some of the dysfunctional consequences associated with groups and teams.

A MANAGERIAL MODEL OF GROUP FACTORS

Exhibit 8.1 depicts a general model of group factors a manager can use to gain some understanding of group dynamics and outcomes.[2] The model indicates that two types of groups, formal and informal, exist in transnational organizations. These groups either are formed by management or naturally evolve.

EXHIBIT 8.1
Groups: Reasons for Types of Development, Characteristics, and Outcomes

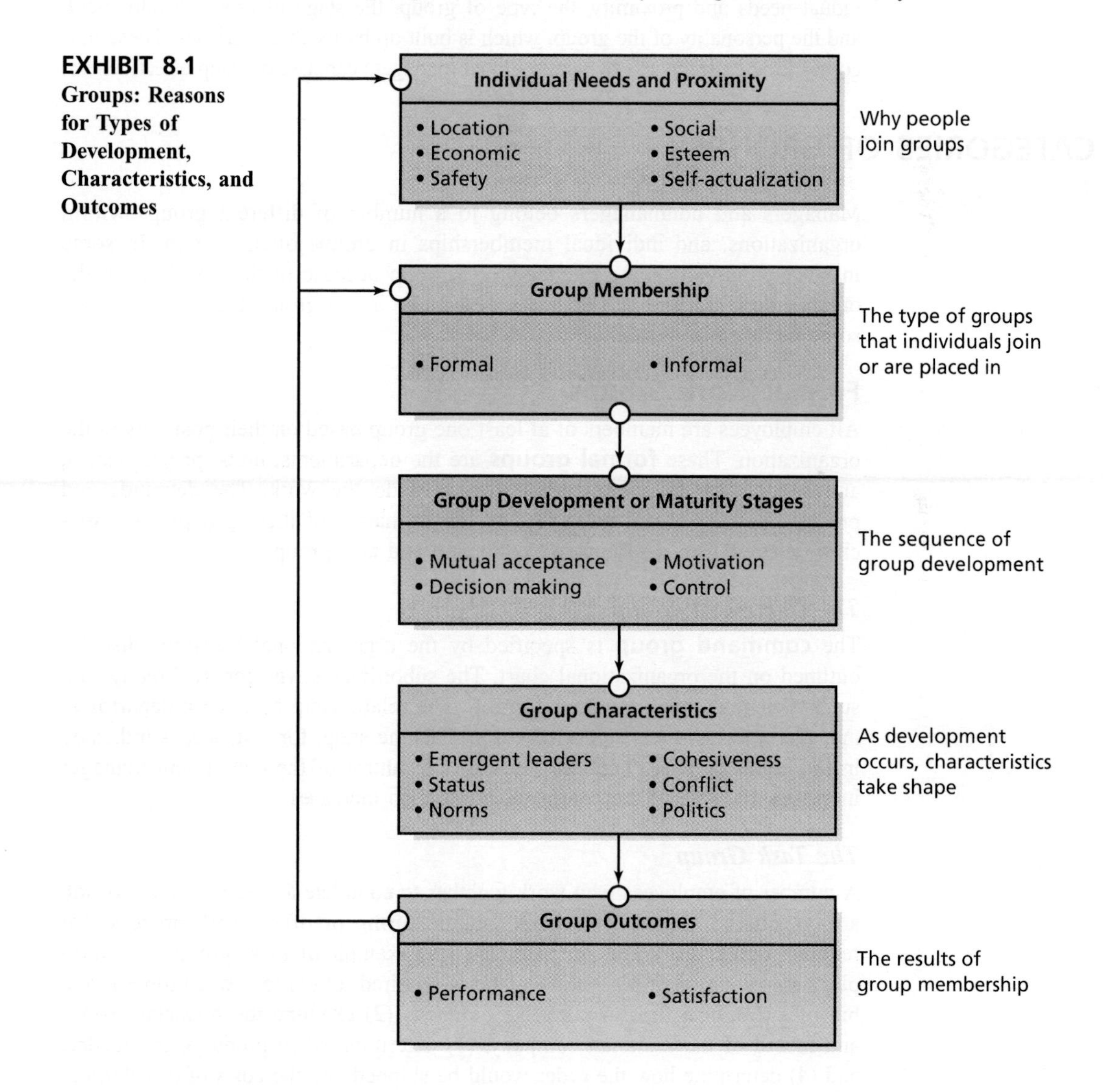

A group, once it evolves or is formed, begins a specific pattern of development or what is referred to as maturing. Like individuals, groups become more efficient and more productive over time. As a group develops, it begins to exhibit various typical characteristics such as norms, cohesiveness, and political maneuvering. The characteristics and their intensity, clarity, and frequency all culminate in a unique group personality.

A group's existence also has tangible consequences, called outcomes. They include performance, the number of units produced or services provided, and, for individual members, satisfaction arising from group affiliation.

According to the model in Exhibit 8.1, group outcomes are influenced by individual needs and proximity, the type of group, the stage of group development, and the personality of the group, which is built up by its characteristics. These outcomes provide standards by which global managers can assess group effectiveness.

CATEGORIES OF GROUPS

Managers and nonmanagers belong to a number of different groups within organizations, and individual memberships in groups often overlap. In some instances, individuals are members of a group because of their position in the organization. But through contacts they make in the group, they may also see some members informally.

Formal Work Groups

All employees are members of at least one group based on their positions in the organization. These **formal groups** are the departments, units, project teams, and so on, that the organization forms to do the work. The demands and processes of the organization lead to the formation of these groups. Two specific types of formal groups are command and task groups.

The Command Group

The **command group** is specified by the organizational hierarchy, usually outlined on the organizational chart. The subordinates who report directly to a supervisor make up a command group. The relationship between a department manager and his three supervisors in a machine shop, for instance, is indicated in the organizational chart. As the span of control of the department manager increases, the size of the command group also increases.

The Task Group

A number of employees who work together to complete a specific project or job are considered a **task group.** A manufacturing or office work process that requires a great deal of interdependence is an example of a task group. For example, suppose an organization in Poland is required to: (1) review a proposal and bid of a Zambian firm to purchase products, (2) examine the financial history and record of the Zambian company, (3) determine when products are needed, and (4) determine how the order would be shipped and the costs of distribution.

The activation group activities must be conducted before accepting or rejecting the Zambian proposal and bid. The process creates a situation in which group members must communicate and coordinate with each other if the proposal and bid is to be handled properly. Their interactions facilitate the formation of a task group.

Committees are common in organizations. Committees actually are task groups established for such purposes as:

- Exchanging views and information.
- Recommending actions.
- Generating ideas.
- Making decisions.

Committees can achieve all of these purposes. However, a group may have difficulty reaching a decision. Managers typically attempt to keep a committee's size relatively small, since size affects the quality of a group's decisions. Increasing a committee's size tends to limit the extent to which its members want to or can communicate, and members tend to feel threatened and less willing to actively participate. The perceived threat can lead to increased stress and conflict. Stress and conflict do not facilitate the generation of good committee decisions.

The committee chairperson is expected to provide proper direction. Ordinarily, successful committees have chairpersons who understand group processes. Such chairpersons see that the committee's objectives and purposes remain clear. They encourage committee members to participate and know how to move the committee toward its objectives.

The following guidelines apply to committee chairpersons:

1. Be a careful listener, and keep an open mind.
2. Allow each member to voice opinions; do not place your opinion above those of others.
3. Get everyone involved in the committee's activities.
4. Display an active interest in the purpose of the committee and in the ideas of its members.
5. Help the committee focus on the task at hand and on the progress being made.

Committee members also must be responsible for creating an atmosphere of cooperation within the group. Research indicates that in cooperative groups, as distinguished from competitive groups, one finds:

1. Stronger motivation to accomplish the task.
2. More effective communication.
3. More ideas generated.
4. More membership satisfaction.
5. More group performance.

Thus, when cooperation prevails, the results are generally positive. Communication, satisfaction, and productivity all tend to be more positive in a cooperative committee. Both the committee's chairperson and its members are important determinants of cooperative committee efforts.

Informal Work Groups

Whenever employees associate on a fairly regular basis, groups tend to form, and their activities may differ from those required by the organization. The **informal groups** are natural groupings of people in the workplace. They do not arise as a result of deliberate design but evolve naturally. The evolution of informal groups follows a path in response to the common interests, needs, or attraction of members. Informal groups often develop within formal groups because of certain values or needs that members share. The informal group is not sanctioned by management, and its membership usually cuts across a number of formal groups. Two types of informal work groups are interest and friendship groups.

The Interest Group

Groups often form because their members share a common interest in some particular job-related event or possible outcome. This type of group can be viewed as an **interest group,** since the members have joined together to achieve some objective, such as an equitable pension payment. The members of the group may or may not be members of the same command or task group.

The Friendship Group

In the transnational organization, people are drawn together by common characteristics such as age, ethnic background, political sentiment, or family structure. This attraction or drawing together results in the formation of **friendship groups.** These groups frequently extend their interaction and communication to off-the-job activities. For example, the members become friends in the workplace, then enjoy a meal together, or have their families spend time together.

The formation of informal groups in an organization does not signal anything especially good or bad about global management practices. The informal groups evolve naturally in response to the needs, interests, or characteristics of the members. Few, if any, organizations have no informal groups. Therefore, the formal groupings in an organization chart provide only a partial view of the important group memberships of employees.

Exhibit 8.2 classifies groups on the basis of formality, informality, and type. Many individuals are members of several or all of these groups at the same time. Not all groups can be neatly placed on a formal-informal continuum, however.

TEAMS IN TRANSNATIONAL ORGANIZATIONS

Teams are not a new concept. For example, Joseph Juran, a quality management expert, talked in the 1950s about the team approach to quality improvement. His concepts, along with those of other quality experts such as W. Edwards Deming, were adopted enthusiastically in Japan. In the 1970s, Volvo (Sweden), Toyota (Japan), and General Foods (United States) received significant attention when

EXHIBIT 8.2 **Contrasting Views of Satisfaction-Dissatisfaction**

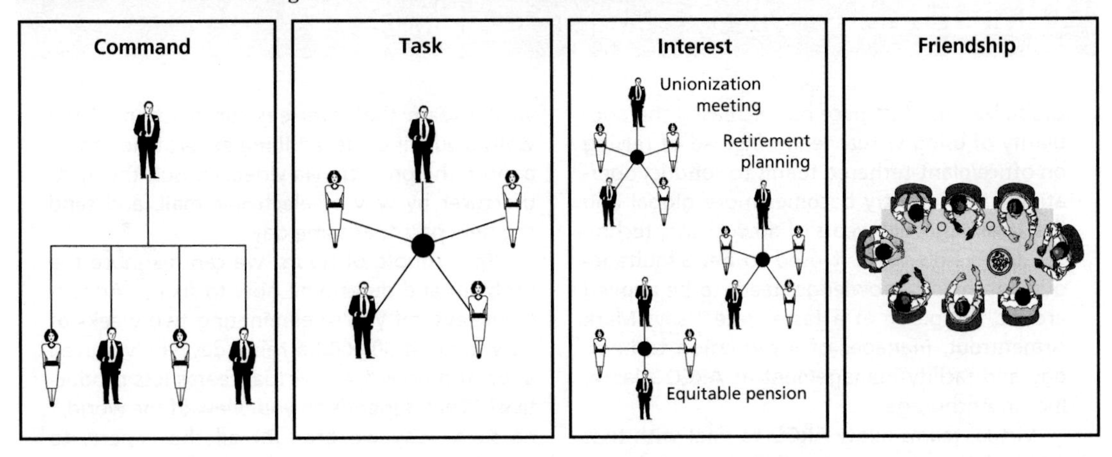

they introduced teams into their production processes.[3] Types of teams that have received increased interest include cross-functional, virtual, and self-managed teams.

Cross-Functional Teams

Organizations have used horizontal, boundary-spanning cross-functional teams to manage and coordinate projects. **Cross-functional teams** consist of individuals from about the same hierarchical level, but from different areas of expertise, who join to accomplish a task. In health care around the world, hospitals, clinics, and doctors use physicians from various specialties to treat and heal patients. This treatment is a form of cross-functional team application to health care. Each specialist brings complementary expertise to collectively help the patient.

In nonmedical organizations, pooling the expertise and skills of individuals from different functional departments (e.g., research and development, engineering, human resource management) is used to improve performance. Motorola's Iridium project is a good example of assembling a cross-functional team.[4] This team worked on the development of an information network that contained 66 satellites. In addition to Motorola team members, individuals with expertise were also included from other companies such as Lockheed Martin, General Electric, Russia's Khrunichev Enterprise, and Raytheon.

The Journey Zone, a multimedia exhibition inside Britain's Millennium Dome, the world's largest domed building, was designed by a 350-person, cross-functional team. The team consisted of graphic designers, engineers, software programmers, historians, architects, technicians, artists, and painters working for Imagination, Ltd. The company's director of marketing stated, "Our approach involves relationships, camaraderie, and working things through." Working in teams, he admits, can be more challenging than hiring a group of outside experts. "But when it clicks," he adds, "the result is a seamless experience."[5]

Global Focus ARCO's Virtual Team Approach

Globalization's fast pace has increased the popularity of using virtual teams instead of relying on office/plant-tethered teams to conduct operations. "As industry becomes more global and [has] gone through years of downsizing, technical depth isn't what it used to be. Simultaneously, technical knowledge needs to be applied around the globe at a faster rate," says Mark Armentrout, manager of information technology and facility management at ARCO Alaska, Inc., in Anchorage.

Virtual teams allow ARCO to deal with that reality. "We have expertise that distinguishes us in industry," Armentrout says. "Part of the application of that technology can be through virtual teams."

ARCO has set up what might be described as virtual centers of excellence: pools of experts in areas such as seismic technologies, reservoir management, and drilling. As projects come up worldwide, virtual team members are chosen from the specialty areas "to exploit [the] transfer of technology where it needs to be," he says.

For example, when an Algerian oil field partner faces a mechanical problem, the ARCO virtual team that oversees construction of the wells would include a drilling expert who can diagnose the problem via video, consult the manufacturer by way of electronic mail, and send the new part that same day.

"In a couple of hours, we can diagnose the problem and determine how to fix it," Armentrout says. "If you're eliminating two weeks of downtime at 50,000 barrels a day, you've saved a lot of money." Are virtual teams less productive? "That depends on your view of the world," he says. "Say we brought all the experts to Algeria and worked full time on it. Would that be more effective for Algeria? Yes."

"But I'm trying to multithread a number of projects where you only need these experts at certain points in the life of the project. I take a macro view of all ARCO opportunities and assets and find they're much more productive employed where they are," Armentrout says.

Source: Adapted from Vijay Govindaragan and Anil K. Gupta, "Building an Effective Global Business Team," *Sloan Management Review,* Summer 2001, pp. 63–71, and Kathleen Melymuka, "Virtual Realities," *Computerworld*, April 28, 1997, pp. 70–72.

Virtual Teams

Virtual teams are composed of individuals who operate across space and time and who communicate mainly through electronic technologies. E-mail, videoconferencing, electronic chat rooms, intranets, and networked computers let members in virtual teams work together in a coordinated manner. Decisions can be made from a distance and communicated to virtual team members.[6] The accompanying Global Focus about ARCO's virtual team approach, illustrates the value of virtual teams.

Technology, information, and knowledge databases make it possible to operate across space, time, and boundaries. Virtual team members can review, use, and implement resources that everyone can share. The issue of distance between team members is insignificant because of the reliance on electronic technologies. Team members from any geographical location can be in contact with all or some of the virtual team with the click of a mouse.[7]

Organizations have been able to assemble cross-functional virtual teams to solve problems, service customers, form alliances, and negotiate business transactions. Companies such as IBM, Shell International, Mazda, Honda, and Hewlett-Packard have partially or completely eliminated traditional offices for field sales and customer service. The old-fashioned office has been replaced with individuals and teams with portable computers, cellular phones, videoconferencing facilities, and fax machines that permit remote or mobile work flexibility.

The freedom and autonomy of being on a virtual team is appealing to some individuals. Executives like the concept, especially when it results in significant reductions in real estate cost. The virtual arrangements also make it possible for increased interaction between sales personnel and customers.

Self-Managed Teams

In a **self-managed team,** members have the autonomy to lead and manage themselves and determine how the team will perform its tasks. Self-managed teams exist at all levels in an organization.

The classic example of a self-managed team was reported by Volvo. The firm decided to not use the typical auto assembly line process and instead used self-managed teams. Each team was empowered and given total responsibility for a large or a specific section of the assembly of a car. The team planned, organized, controlled, and directed what was to be done, who on the team would be responsible, and when the work was to be accomplished. The reported results included improvements in the quality of the assembled cars and high levels of employee satisfaction.[8]

A number of conditions must exist to receive the greatest benefits from self-managed teams.

1. The team must be completely self-managed in setting its own goals, staff, schedule, quality standards, and work flow patterns. Managers are not allowed to intervene in establishing these thresholds or standards.
2. When the task is sufficiently complex, the self-managed team approach is more successful. Easy, routine tasks do not provide enough challenge for self-managed teams.
3. The team must have the power to implement its decisions. Management approval is not sought or needed. Managers can be asked for advice or coaching, but they do not have control or oversight on decisions.
4. Members of self-managed teams must be carefully selected by the members to implement the skills and expertise required to be successful.
5. Members of self-managed teams must have the ability to work with others on the team and with other teams. This requirement has to be examined when recruiting and selecting members for the self-managed team.

The lack of organizational commitment is the most common reason for the failure of self-managed teams. The impatience of managers waiting to intervene and take control of self-managed team decisions is an example of not being truly committed to empowering the team. Some managers do not support the self-managed approach and refuse to grant these kind of teams the authority to make decisions.[9]

THE FORMATION OF WORK GROUPS

By going to work for a transnational organization, an individual is actually joining a group. Once individuals become members of the organization, they are placed in, or volunteer for, various group memberships. They also join or create informal groups, because of common interests and characteristics. Location, economic background, and attitudes strongly influence people to join formal groups and join or establish informal groups.

Location

When people are in proximity, they tend to interact and communicate. Some degree of interaction and communication is necessary for group formation, particularly informal groups.

Organizations typically position workers with similar occupations together. For example, in the construction of a home, the bricklayers perform their jobs side by side. The same situation exists in offices, where clerks or information technology are located next to one another.

Economic Background

In some cases, work groups form because individuals believe they can gain economic benefits on their jobs if they band together. For example, individuals working at different stations on an assembly line in Slovakia may be paid on a group-incentive basis. Whatever the particular group produces determines the wages of each member. Because the workers all want to increase their wages, they will interact and communicate with one another. By working as a group instead of as individuals, they may actually obtain higher economic benefits.

Another example of how the economic motive affects the formation of informal work groups is a nonunion organization formed by workers to bring pressure on management for more economic benefits. The group members have a common interest—increased economic benefits—which leads to group affiliation.[10]

Attitude

Workers in organizations also are motivated to form work groups to satisfy more than economic needs. Workers who join together informally to improve productivity, quality, and customer satisfaction are acting only indirectly in their economic interests. They may have little or no clear understanding of the impact of their efforts on their economic benefits. Transnational firm managers must learn to appeal to the attitudinal needs and/or emotional needs of employees to reap additional productivity gains.[11]

THE DEVELOPMENT OF WORK GROUPS

While informal groups develop in a nonstructured way, formal groups usually go through various stages of group and team development. Research has identified five distinct stages that most groups and teams go through as they develop—forming, storming, norming, performing, and adjourning. Exhibit 8.3 presents these five stages.

Group development describes the progression from a collection of people brought together for a common purpose to a well-functioning unit whose individual members cooperate to pursue a common goal.

Stage 1: Forming

Forming is the beginning stage of group development where individuals are brought together for a specific purpose. In this stage, the group members come together as a functioning unit. They agree to rules of conduct and the goals of the team. Group hierarchy and roles begin to develop, and a formal group leader is typically appointed to facilitate further group development. Research suggests that after groups have become operational they return briefly to the "forming" stage at the beginning of each meeting.[12]

Stage 2: Storming

The most turbulent stage of group development, *storming* refers to the fact that, after initial niceties, the group confronts conflicts and discovers ways to keep the group focused. During this stage, group members learn to accept individual differences, and the beginnings of a collective "group personality" emerge. This personality is a result of shared values and purposes. An informal vying for power within the group also occurs in this stage. Group members negotiate roles that are needed for effective group functioning, and members tend to adopt and maintain those roles for the duration of the group.

EXHIBIT 8.3
Five Stages of Group Development

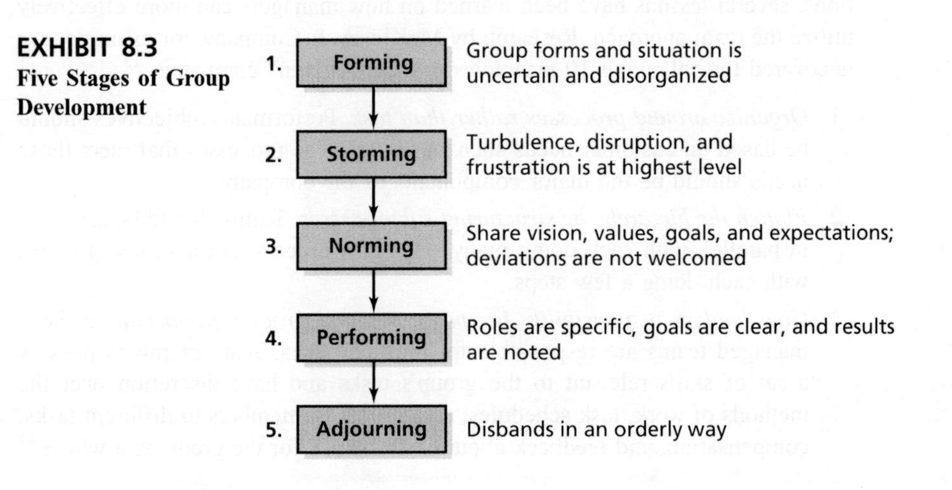

Stage 3: Norming

During the *norming* stage, the group establishes its long-term vision and how it will function over time. The agreement among members on a long-term vision is referred to as shared values. The group's norms are the unwritten rules of correct behavior and decorum. For example, most groups develop stable seating patterns for a meal or break. This informal seating pattern is a group norm. Although group norms are rarely formalized, deviation from them may subject a group member to punishment, humiliation, or ostracism.

Stage 4: Performing

The fourth stage of group development is reached when a group is able to begin *performing* the task it was designed to address. During this stage, a group begins to fine-tune its work patterns. Group members may carefully redefine roles as needed. The group will help develop the skills of individual members, as they are needed. The group may also recruit new members as it determines gaps in skill sets among existing members.

Stage 5: Adjourning

A functioning group or team is able to disband once the work tasks are completed. The adjourning stage is important in situations that use project teams, task teams, committees, or temporary teams to start and finish a set of tasks. Once the tasks are completed the members may return to their more permanent home base. The smoothness of disbanding and returning home is a measure of the success and maturity of the group or team.

UTILIZING TEAMS

Organizing, managing, and evaluating workplace teams is difficult. In the several decades since teams have become a more vital component of many organizations, several lessons have been learned on how managers can more effectively utilize the team approach. Research by McKinsey & Company, for example, has uncovered the following 10 principles of "team-driven" companies.[13]

1. *Organize around processes rather than task.* Performance objectives should be based on customer needs such as service. The processes that meet those needs should be the major components of the company.
2. *Flatten the hierarchy by structuring subprocesses.* Teams should be arranged in parallel, with each doing many steps in a process, not a series of teams with each doing a few steps.
3. *Give leaders responsibility for processes and process performance.* Self-managed teams are responsible for multiple tasks. Team members possess a set of skills relevant to the group's tasks and have discretion over the methods of work, task schedules, assignment of members to different tasks, compensation, and feedback about performance for the group as a whole.[14]

4. *Link performance objectives and evaluation of all activities to customer satisfaction.* Everything should be driven by the customer; successful performance also means customers have been satisfied.
5. *Assign performance objectives to teams, not individuals.* This makes teams the focus of organizational performance and design. Individuals cannot continuously improve quality and work flows.
6. *Assign managerial tasks to teams as much as possible.* Workers' teams should be responsible for activities such as hiring, evaluating, and scheduling.
7. *Emphasize the need for workers to develop several competencies.* In a team-driven company, only a few specialists are needed. Productivity can be increased by asking the team to take on more difficult tasks and asking team members to serve as consultants to other teams.[15]
8. *Train team members on a just-in-time, need-to-perform basis.* Information should go directly to those who can use it in their jobs. Trained and empowered workers know how to use information.
9. *Put team members in touch with customers.* Field trips and membership in problem-solving teams can bring team members closer to customers. Knowledge of customer needs is then reflected in teamwork.
10. *Reward skill development and team performance.* Performance evaluation should focus on team achievements rather than individual achievements. It is counterproductive to talk about teamwork while evaluating and rewarding individuals.

These are 10 obvious, yet not always implemented practices. The failure to consider these types of practices can result in the team not fully maturing and becoming an efficient unit.

CHARACTERISTICS OF WORK GROUPS

The creation and implementation of an organization's formal structure can result in such characteristics as specified relationships among subordinates, superiors, and peers; leaders assigned to positions; standards of performance; a status rank order according to the positions that individuals are filling; and group politics. Work groups also have characteristics similar to those of the formal organization, including leaders, standards of conduct, reward and sanction mechanisms, and political maneuvering. An effective group is one that fully utilizes the skills and abilities of each of its members. Groups continue to be effective as long as they are able to engage the enthusiasm, skills, and intelligence of members.

A good way of thinking about the relationship between a member and the group is as a type of exchange. The group member gives time, energy, knowledge, and emotion while the group provides the member with need satisfaction. Group membership has the potential to satisfy several common human needs, including the need for achievement, the need for power, and the need for affiliation.[16] Many group members derive satisfaction from knowing that their contributions to a

EXHIBIT 8.4
Characteristics of Effective Groups

Source: Adapted from Renis Likert, *New Patterns of Management* (New York: McGraw-Hill, 1961), pp. 162–71.

1. All group members understand group roles and expectations.
2. Group members have developed a good working relationship.
3. Group members are attracted to the group and are loyal to the leader.
4. Group members have a high degree of trust and confidence in one another.
5. Group activities such as decision making and problem solving occur in a supportive atmosphere.
6. The group leader creates a supportive atmosphere in which group work occurs. The leader (*a*) seeks information from group members about decisions that will affect them and (*b*) provides information that they need to do their jobs better.
7. The group attempts to develop each member's full potential.
8. An atmosphere that encourages members to influence each other is maintained. Influence ensures that new ideas enter the group and that dominant personalities work to the group's betterment.
9. The process for selecting a group leader is based on the qualities that the individual brings to the group that encourage a supportive and open atmosphere.
10. Communication among members and the leader is encouraged. If problems exist, free and open communication will bring problems to the surface.

group were essential in helping it reach its goals. Group membership is also a primary mode of social interaction for many people in organizations. Organizational citizenship behaviors play a big role in work group effectiveness. Research has indicated that helping behavior and sportsmanship had significant effects on performance quality among work groups.[17]

Exhibit 8.4 lists some important characteristics of effective groups.

ROLE MAKING IN GROUPS

All work groups are defined by roles that members in the group perform and by the hierarchy or status of these roles.[18] A **role** is a set of shared expectations regarding a member's attitude and task behavior within the group. At the most basic level, a group will have two roles: leader and member.

The greater the group's task complexity, the more roles will emerge. Group member agreement about the role to be performed is referred to as the sent role. The sent role is in essence the formal requirements of the role within the group. The **received role** is the role recipient's understanding of what the sent role means. In other words, the sent role may be received differently by different people. The enacted role is how the received role is expressed or redefined by the individual assuming the role.[19] This is how formal group expectations are transmitted, filtered, and processed by the role occupant. Everyone has different backgrounds, values, education, and beliefs about how the job should be done. All these factors are brought to the forefront during role creation and enactment.

PROBLEMS IN ROLE MAKING

Role creation with groups is not without problems. Common problems include role conflict, role ambiguity, and role overload.[20]

Role conflict represents the incompatibility between the role's requirements and the individual's own beliefs or expectations. Remember, employees assume multiple roles in many different aspects of their lives. For example, a worker in an Algerian plant could simultaneously hold the roles of father, brother, cousin, devoted religious practitioner, manager, and engineer. Many of these different roles have required behaviors that may conflict with one another.

Such internal conflict can come from a variety of sources. Interrole conflict occurs when two different types of roles collide. A manager may have to fire an employee who is also a friend. Because of friendship he doesn't want to fire the employee, but his job requires him to do so. Intrarole conflict occurs when two similar roles come in conflict—for example, when a boss informs subordinates to increase productivity and they are pushing for better working conditions. Intersender conflict occurs when contradictory messages come from the same source. A boss preaches that quality is the most important aspect of the work. However, he insists on hiring low-skilled workers who can't fully utilize the robotics that are a major determinant of quality in the company.

Person-role conflict occurs when an individual's beliefs are in direct conflict with the requirements of his or her role. For example, suppose a worker in Kenya knows that a product batch is defective and shipping the products could possibly cause consumer injury and cause harm to the image of the firm. The worker has also received a memo from the boss insisting that his job is to help build sales volume by expediting the shipment of as many products as possible. The worker knows that shipping the product is wrong but feels compelled to make the volume quota. Such role conflicts have a direct effect on organizational citizenship behaviors.[21]

In **role ambiguity,** role requirements are not clear. In general, role ambiguity results when the role occupant is not sure how to fulfill role requirements. Simple routine roles rarely generate ambiguity. In a routine role, such as an assembly-line job, role requirements are specific or decision criteria are simple. Professional roles present a greater chance of role ambiguity. Managers often face a technical situation that they are not trained to fully understand, and they must decide to rely on a subordinate's judgment. The ambiguity for the manager is whether to consult a staff specialist (which might waste time) or go with the subordinate's judgment. The manager knows he'll be held responsible regardless of a positive or a negative outcome. Managers should understand that role ambiguity is a stressor in the workplace. It can be mitigated to some extent by a worker's commitment to the firm.[22]

Role overload occurs when a task's demands overwhelm the role occupant's ability to perform the task. Too much, too little, or conflicting information may surpass the role occupant's ability to perform the task at a satisfactory level. With the emphasis on lean organizations and the corresponding reduction of white-collar employees, role overload is common contributory symptom of role stress reported by those who remain.

Role conflict, role ambiguity, and role overload are all potential problems that can decrease a group's effectiveness. Managers must recognize these potential problems that can undermine a group's overall performance.

THE GROUP LEADER

One of the most important group roles is that of the group leader. The leader emerges from within an informal group and is accepted by the group members. In the formal group, however, the leader is appointed.

Leaders in many formal groups are followed and obeyed because employees perceive them as possessing the power and influence to reward them or punish them if they do not comply with requests. However, this is not always an accurate perception. As organizations have continued to move toward self-managed teams, group leaders are often not in hire-fire or reward-punish positions.

The informal leader emerges from within the group and serves a number of functions. First, any group of individuals without a plan or some degree of coordination becomes an ineffective unit. Its members are not directed toward the accomplishment of goals, and this can lead to a breakdown in group effectiveness. The leader initiates action and provides direction. If there are differences of opinion on a group-related matter, the leader attempts to settle the differences and to move the group toward accomplishing its goals.

Second, some individual must communicate the group's beliefs about policies, the job, the organization, the supervision, and other related matters to nonmembers.[23] The nonmembers could include members of other groups, supervisory personnel, and the union. In effect, the group leader communicates the values of the group.

The characteristics of informal group leaders can be summarized as follows:

1. The leadership role is filled by the individual who possesses the attributes that members perceive as being critical for satisfying their needs.
2. The leader embodies the values of the group and is able to perceive those values, organize them into an intelligible philosophy, and verbalize them to nonmembers.
3. The leader is able to receive and interpret communication relevant to the group and to effectively communicate important information to group members.

In most groups, leaders perform two specific roles. A leader who performs the *task role* typically concentrates on accomplishing the desired goals, such as providing a number of units within quality and cost standards or delivering a product to a customer. The task role requires the leader to accomplish something specific of importance to the membership.

Leaders of groups also perform a *supportive,* or *maintenance, role,* which involves personally helping members, listening to their problems, and encouraging group cohesiveness. While the task role is job-oriented, the supportive role is people-oriented. Both orientations are important for accomplishing group performance and satisfaction.[24] In some groups, one person performs both roles. In other groups, two individuals perform the roles.

GROUP STATUS

Status is the rank, respect, or social position that an individual has in a group. Managers have relative status that depends on their positions in the hierarchy; that is, the top managers of the firm have more status than middle managers, and the middle managers have more status than lower-level managers. The top-level positions have more authority, responsibility, power, and influence—and thus are accorded more status.

A similar status system develops in groups. Members are accorded status by their groups for many different reasons. Individuals in leadership roles possess status because of their roles. Consequently, they are ranked highly in the status hierarchy. Many groups consider the seniority of a member to be important. A worker having more seniority is often thought of as being "organizationally intelligent," which means she knows how to adapt to the demands of supervisors, subordinates, or peers. This ability to adjust is an important status factor with group members.

The individual's skill in performing a job is another factor related to status. An individual with expertise in the technical aspects of the job is given a high status ranking in some groups. This type of status does not mean the individual actually utilizes the skill to perform more effectively, but simply that the group members admire this skill.

GROUP NORMS AND COMPLIANCE

A group norm is an implicit or explicit agreement among the group members as to how they should behave. The more a person complies with norms, the more the person accepts the group's standards of behavior.

Work groups can utilize norms to bring about acceptable job performance. Three specific social processes bring about compliance with group norms: group pressure, group review and enforcement, and personalization of the norms.

Group Pressure

The pressure to adhere to a specific group norm can bring conformity to the behavior of the group's membership. Conformity occurs when a person complies with a group's wishes because of the pressure the group applies or fear of future group pressure. Complying with group pressure does not mean the person agrees with the group's wishes.

Group Review and Enforcement

If group members, either veterans or newcomers, are not complying with generally accepted norms, a number of different approaches may be employed. One soft approach is a discussion between respected leaders and the nonconformists. If discussion does not prove effective, more rigorous corrective action is used, such as private and public scolding by the members. The ultimate enforcement is to ostracize the deviating members.

Personalization of Norms

Behavioral patterns are influenced significantly by values. Values, in turn, are influenced by the events occurring around individuals; values are learned and become personalized. For example, the norm of a work group may be to treat individuals from different social class backgrounds equally. This norm may be accepted by a group member as morally and ethically correct. Before group affiliation, the member may have displayed little interest in whether an individual is of a particular social class. However, based on a feeling of fairness, the member personalizes this group-learned norm, and it becomes a standard of her behavior.

Group norms can either be positive or negative as far as a manager is concerned. However, both types of norms typically are encountered when compliance is the issue of concern. Exhibit 8.5 lists some examples of work conditions for which groups often establish norms. Positive and negative norms are presented to portray what managers often must face.

EXHIBIT 8.5 Positive and Negative Group Norms

Condition Performance	Positive Group Norm +	Negative Group Norm −
Output	Members work hard to produce at optimal skill levels.	Members work just hard enough to get by.
Quality	Members take pride in producing quality products.	Members pay enough attention to quality to keep management minimally happy.
Absenteeism	Members pride themselves on being present.	Members are not interested in good attendance.
Supervisor relations	Members respect supervisors and are honest in their interactions.	Members distrust management and hold back vital information.
Honesty	Members are against stealing and slowdowns.	Members encourage some pilferage and slow down work performance when everyone seems tired.
Wages/salaries	Members expect a fair day's pay for a good day's work.	Members expect to be taken care of despite a lack of effort—the "organization owes me" attitude.

GROUP COHESIVENESS

Cohesiveness refers to the extent that group members are attracted to each other and to the group values and accept group goals. It is the pressure on the individual member to remain active in the group and to resist leaving it.[25] The concept of group cohesiveness is the esprit de corps of being part of a closer knit unit.

All characteristics of groups are influenced in some degree by group cohesiveness. For example, the greater the attraction within the group, the more likely its members will adhere closely to a group norm such as a production level.[26] Group cohesiveness influences a variety of outcomes, including organizational commitment, job satisfaction, motivation, and role conflict.[27]

Some of the conditions that can enhance or reduce cohesiveness are presented in Exhibit 8.6.

The Size of the Work Group

It is important that group members interact and communicate. If a group is so large that members do not know one another, it is unlikely that the group will be cohesive. Managers have learned that an inverse relationship exists between group size and group cohesiveness.[28] As the size of a group increases, its cohesiveness decreases.

The Dependence of the Members on the Work Group

The greater the individual's dependency on the group, the stronger will be his or her attraction for it. Individuals join groups because the groups can help them

EXHIBIT 8.6
Factors Affecting Group Cohesiveness

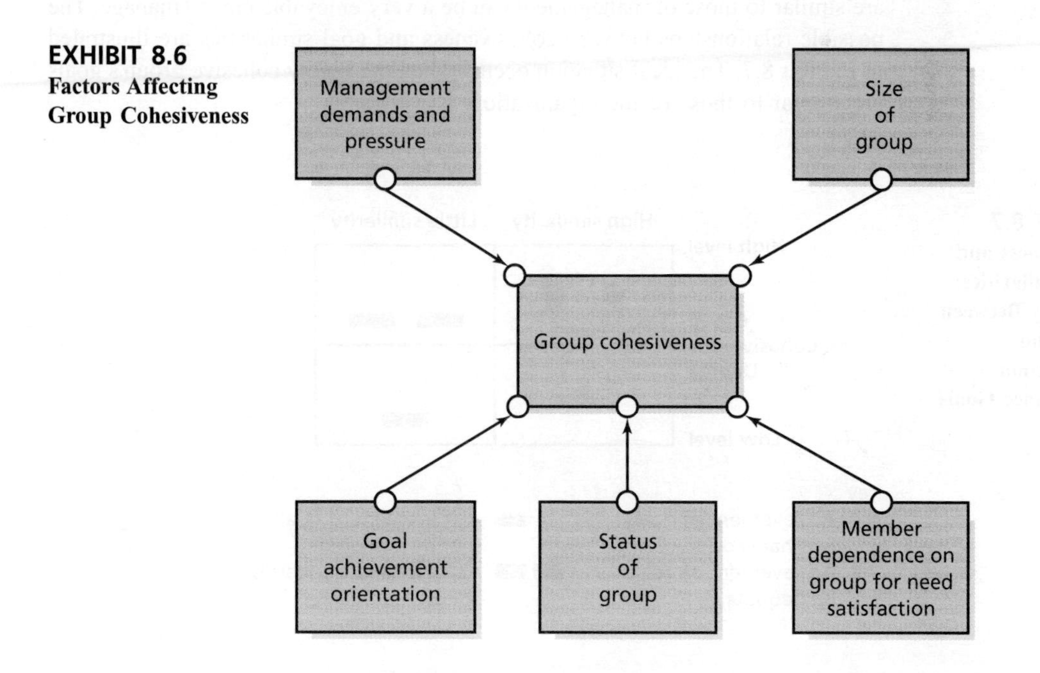

satisfy economic and sociopsychological needs. A group that is able to satisfy a significant portion of an individual's needs will be attractive to that individual. Group processes such as interaction with co-workers and overall friendship may make the group a key factor in the individual's life. Thus, what the group stands for, its norms, and its membership are bonds that tie the individual to the group.

The Achievement of Goals

The attainment of some set of group-established goals (e.g., better production than another group) influences the group's members. For example, if a work group attains a highly desired rating for completing a task, then a value of belonging to that group is enhanced. Its members feel pride in being part of a group that has achieved a superior performance.

Work groups that have successfully attained goals are likely to be highly cohesive units. The members tend to be more attracted toward one another because they have worked together in the past and their efforts have resulted in achieving goals. Thus, success and cohesiveness are interrelated: Success in goal achievement encourages cohesiveness, and cohesive work groups are more likely to attain goals. Managers know, however, that although group cohesiveness can lead to the achievement of goals, cohesiveness can prove detrimental when group and organizational goals are incompatible.

Transnational organization managers must recognize that they will have a difficult job if a group is highly cohesive but has performance goals that differ from those of the organization. On the other hand, a cohesive group whose goals are similar to those of management can be a very enjoyable unit to manage. The possible relationships between cohesiveness and goal similarities are illustrated in Exhibit 8.7. The ideal situation occurs when the highly cohesive group's goals are similar to those of the organization.

EXHIBIT 8.7
Cohesiveness and Goal Similarities: Similarity Between Group and Organization Performance Goals

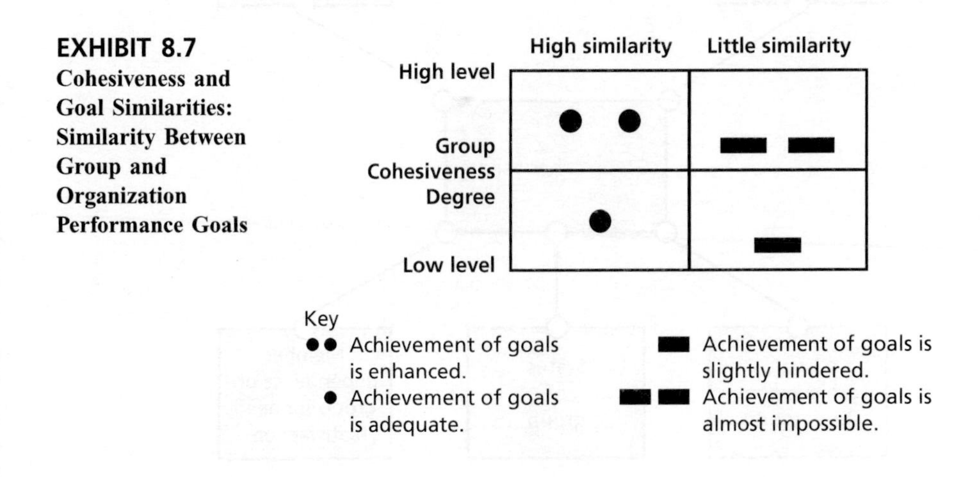

The Status of the Group

In an organizational setting, groups typically are ranked in a status hierarchy. A status hierarchy may develop among groups for many different reasons, including the following:

1. The group is rated higher than another group in overall performance; this rating measures success in an organization.
2. To become a member of the group, individuals must display a high level of skill.
3. The work being done by the group is dangerous, or financially more rewarding, or more challenging, than other work.
4. The group is less closely supervised than other groups.
5. In the past, members of the group have been considered for promotion more often than members of other groups.

These are only some of the criteria that affect the status hierarchy of groups. Generally, the higher a group ranks in the intergroup status hierarchy, the greater its cohesiveness. However, the higher-status groups appear attractive only to some nonmembers. Individuals outside the group may not want to become members of a high-status group because membership entails close adherence to group norms.

Management Demands and Pressure

Another agent for group cohesiveness is management demands and pressure. In many organizations, management has a significant impact on group cohesiveness. The members of groups tend to stick together when superiors pressure them to conform to some organizational norm.

The group cohesiveness attributed to managerial demands may be either a short-run or long-run phenomenon. In some cases, a loosely knit group (low in cohesiveness) may interpret a company policy statement as a threat to the job security of its members. Consequently the group may become a more cohesive and unified whole to withstand the perceived management threat. After the danger is past (i.e., the policy statement is rescinded), the group may drift back toward low cohesiveness. In other cases, the cohesiveness may be a longer-lasting phenomenon.

PROBLEMS IN GROUPS AND TEAMS

There are a number of potential problems when working with or managing groups or teams. The majority of research interest and debate has centered on such problems as groupthink, politics, intergroup conflict, and social loafing.

Groupthink

When groups are characterized by high conformity and cohesiveness, a phenomenon called **groupthink** might occur.[29] Groupthink exists when a group

EXHIBIT 8.8
Groupthink Symptoms

- **Having illusions of group invulnerability.** Members believe the group is basically beyond criticism or attack.
- **Rationalizing unpleasant and disconfirming data.** Members of the group refuse to accept contradictory data or to consider alternatives thoroughly.
- **Believing in inherent group morality.** Members believe the group is "right" and above any reproach by outsiders.
- **Stereotyping competitors as weak, evil, and stupid.** Members of the group refuse to look realistically at other groups.
- **Applying direct pressure to deviants to conform to group wishes.** Members of the group refuse to tolerate a member who suggests the group may be wrong.
- **Using self-censorship by members.** Members of the group refuse to communicate personal concerns to the group as a whole.
- **Having illusions of unanimity.** Members of the group accept consensus prematurely without testing its completeness.
- **Guarding minds.** Members of the group protect the group from hearing disturbing ideas or viewpoints from outsiders.

believes that it is invincible, rationalizes away criticisms, believes that everyone should comply with a group norm, and is characterized by unanimity among its members. Exhibit 8.8 identifies a number of symptoms of groupthink, which must be overcome if group effectiveness is to be restored.

Several managerial actions can minimize the groupthink phenomenon including the following:

- Assigning the role of critical evaluator to all members of the group. Critical thinking should be encouraged, supported, and rewarded.
- Encouraging members to be impartial and to engage in open interaction instead of sticking with predetermined preferences.
- Establishing subgroups to work on problem issues and to then share with the total group the proposed solutions.
- Including outside experts in group discussions and permitting them to challenge the views expressed by members.
- Having at least one group member play the devil's advocate and challenge the majority position.
- Developing an analysis of how the group's decision will affect other groups. Discuss the consequences of the group's proposal so that changes can be made before action is taken.
- Holding a "second chance" meeting at which every group member expresses any doubts about the decision.

These preventive actions do have disadvantages.[30] For instance, the open dialogue, debate, and exchange of ideas is likely to lead to prolonged delays in decision making. Can a transnational firm manager afford the time in a crisis situation? A crisis may require quick communications, quick discussions, and group meetings with time deadlines. Bringing in outside experts also can create problems. Although experts have much to offer, their use increases the risk of security leakage.

Politics

Political maneuvering to obtain limited resources is a common group and team characteristic. Because organizations typically work with scarce resources, politics is a problem that managers become involved with on a regular basis.

Group politics exists when the behavior of the group or team is specifically self-serving. When a group acts to enhance its own position, regardless of the costs of the action, it acts politically. Often, self-serving group or team behavior creates such strained relationships that both organizational and group performance suffer. When a situation becomes an "us" versus "them" or a "my group" versus "your group" controversy, there are self-serving overtones. Through their actions and their dealings with groups, managers set the tone for the political maneuvering that emerges.[31]

Two types of managerial behaviors can create the atmosphere for group politics—offensive and defensive. Offensive political behavior by a group manager includes power building, exploiting or calling attention to the weaknesses of others, and sabotaging the work of others.

Defensive political behavior by a group manager can mean maneuvering in response to others. Placing the blame on another group, covering up mistakes, or even working hard to direct attention away from weaknesses are examples of defensive political behavior.

By example, managers often can create the environment for the degree and kind of politics in organizations. Subordinates look to managers for direction. When managers use political maneuvers, subordinates tend to imitate this action. Managers can modify such behavior by examining their political tendencies:

- Is this action only self-serving?
- Will this action hurt another group or person?
- Will organizational performance be improved by this action?

Confronting these questions can help managers become more aware of the political impact of their behavior. When the behavior initiated by a manager involves working together with other groups, organizational performance can be enhanced.

Social Loafing

In some groups and teams, an individual's contribution or impact to the overall performance is not easily identified by other members or an outsider such as a manager. When this condition exists, social loafing may occur. **Social loafing** is the tendency of some individuals to exert less effort and attention when performing tasks when they work as a part of a group or a team.

Social loafing is also referred to as the Ringleman effect. Max Ringleman, a German psychologist, set up an experiment in which he asked people to pull as hard as possible on a rope.[32] He next asked them to join a group and pull as hard as possible on the rope. He found that the average productivity (pull power) dropped as more people joined the rope-pulling group. He suggested two explanations of why individuals may not work as hard as a member of a group or team as they would individually: (1) their individual contribution is less noticeable in the group setting, and (2) they permit or prefer others to carry the workload.

In individualistic cultures such as Northern Europe and the United States, people value individual contributions. However, in collectivist cultures such as China, people place a higher value on sharing the responsibility for work. In the collectivist culture social loafing would be unacceptable. An experiment conducted in the United States, China, and Israel tested the social loafing premise. Tasks were worked on alone and as a part of 10-person groups.[33] In the individual phase, the person was asked to write his or her name on each item completed and turned in. In the group condition, participants were informed that their group's overall performance would be evaluated.

The experiment data showed that social loafing occurred with U.S. participants. The individual performance was better than the group performance. However, the opposite was found for the Israeli and Chinese participants. In both these samples, individuals performed at higher levels when working in groups than when working alone. The identification with the group was much stronger than found with the U.S. participants.

This experiment suggests that national culture has an impact on social loafing. Research suggests the following techniques to reduce social loafing.[34]

1. Use public posting or identifying each performer's contribution in a group. When these postings are viewed by everyone (e.g., on a chart, on the bulletin board, posted on a website) individuals are less likely to socially loaf.
2. Make work assignments more interesting. This requires creativity and learning what subordinates consider to be interesting. Listening, observing, and discussing work goals, aspirations, and opinions with subordinates is time consuming, but it can be invaluable in providing ideas of how to enrich the work. When jobs are interesting, less social loafing is likely.
3. Reward individuals for contributing to the goals that are accomplished. Group or team incentives and bonuses can be used to encourage performance. Employees will focus more on the group or team goals if rewards are linked and this linkage can easily be determined by individual members.

These are three managerial-initiated approaches that may work effectively in reducing social loafing. Each of them requires managers who (1) understand how and why social loafing occurs and (2) attempt through their actions to create opportunities that use individual skills and talents to make noticeable and rewarded contributions to groups. Social loafing can become a major problem because it can lower group performance. Some group members, after observing social loafers, will decide not to carry an extra load and so reduce their own work.[35]

INTERGROUP CONFLICT

Conflict occurs when one party perceives that another party has frustrated, or is about to frustrate, the accomplishment of a goal. Conflict is not limited to interacting groups; it also occurs within groups, between individuals, and between organizations. This section focuses on **intergroup conflict** within organizations.

One way to view conflict is to consider it as a sequence of episodes. The sequence is as follows:[36]

- *Latent conflict*—conditions for conflict exist: two groups competing for scarce resources, for example.
- *Perceived conflict*—group members realize that there is conflict between groups.
- *Felt conflict*—the members involved feel tense or anxious.
- *Manifest conflict*—behaviors clearly demonstrate that one group is attempting to frustrate another group.
- *Conflict aftermath*—the situation after the conflict is minimized or eliminated.

Because conflict can progress to the manifest stage, it can have dysfunctional consequences for organizations and individuals. Conflict can arouse emotions and anxiety, lower satisfaction, and decrease performance. Research has shown that the greater the perceived threat, the greater the decrement in problem-solving effectiveness.[37] Managers must solve the conflict and get groups working cooperatively again toward the accomplishment of organizational and individual goals. Yet cooperation is not always the most desirable result of group interaction. For example, two groups may cooperate because they both oppose the introduction of new equipment being installed to improve cost control. In this instance, the cooperation of the groups can make the trial period of testing the new equipment a bad experience for management.

There are many reasons for conflict among groups. Some of the more important ones relate to limited resources, communication problems, differences in interests and goals, different perceptions and attitudes, and lack of clarity about responsibilities.

The management of intergroup conflict involves determining strategies to minimize each cause. Management reaction to disruptive intergroup conflict can take many different forms.[38] But management usually will first try to minimize the conflict indirectly, and if this fails, become directly involved.

The *indirect approach* refers to techniques managers might use that don't require their direct intervention. The *direct approach* refers to transnational managers becoming personally involved in resolving intergroup conflicts.

The Indirect Approach

Initially, managers often avoid direct approaches to solving conflict among groups. Unfortunately, avoidance does not always minimize the problem. Matters get worse because nothing is being done, and the groups become more antagonistic and hostile.

Another indirect strategy is to encourage the groups to meet and discuss their differences and to work out a solution without management involvement. This strategy can take the form of bargaining, persuasion, or working on a problem together.

Bargaining involves having the groups agree about what each will get and give to the other. For example, one group may agree to give another group quick turnaround time on the repairs of needed equipment if the second group agrees to bring complaints about the quality of repairs to it before going to management. Bargaining between two groups is successful if both groups are better off (or at least no worse off) after an agreement has been reached.

Persuasion involves having the groups find areas of common interest. The groups attempt to find points of agreement and to show how these are important to each of the groups in attaining organizational goals. Persuasion is possible if clashes between group leaders do not exist.

A problem can be an obstacle to a goal. For groups to minimize their conflicts through problem solving, they must agree at least generally on the goal. If there is agreement, then the groups can propose alternative solutions that satisfy all parties involved. For example, one group may want the company to relocate the plant to a specific rural area and the other group may want better working conditions. If both parties agree that a common goal is to maintain their jobs, then building a new facility in an area that does not have infrastructure problems may be a good solution.

The Direct Approach

To improve intergroup relations, greater integration or collaboration among groups must occur. Various strategies can be used effectively to increase integration. Management can use domination to minimize conflict by exercising its authority and requiring that a problem be solved by a specific date. If management uses authority, the groups may join together to resist domination. Management becomes a common enemy, and the groups forget their differences to deal with their opponent.

Another direct approach is to remove the key figures in the conflict. If a conflict arises because of personality differences between two individuals, removing them is a possible solution. This approach has three problems. First, the key figures who are to be removed may be leaders of the groups. Removing them could make the groups more antagonistic and lead to greater conflict. Second, it is difficult to pinpoint accurately whether the individuals in conflict are at odds because of personal animosities or because they represent their groups. Third, removal may create martyrs. The causes of the removed leaders may be remembered and fought for, even though the leaders themselves are gone.

Management also can establish a task force with representatives from the conflicting groups. The task force will develop ideas and procedures for improving group interaction.[39]

A final direct strategy to minimize conflict is to find superordinate goals. These are goals desired by two or more groups that can be accomplished only through the cooperation of the groups. When conflicting groups have to cooperate to accomplish a goal, conflict can be minimized. For example, a companywide profit-sharing plan may encourage groups to work together. If company profits are distributed among employees at the end of the year, conflict among groups can reduce the amount of profits that each employee receives. Thus, the superordinate goal, generating profit, may take precedence over group conflict.

Limited Resources

Groups that possess an abundance of materials, money, and time usually are effective. However, when a number of groups are competing for limited resources, conflict often results. The competition for equipment dollars or merit increase money or new positions can become fierce.

Communication Problems

Groups often become very involved with their own areas of responsibility. They tend to develop their own vocabulary. Paying attention to an area of responsibility is a worthy endeavor, but it can result in communication problems. The receiver of information should be considered when a group communicates an idea, a proposal, or a decision. Misinformed receivers often become irritated and then hostile.

Different Interests and Goals

A group of young workers may want management to do something about an inadequate promotion system. However, older workers may accuse management of ignoring improvements in the company pension plan. Management recognizes the two different goals but believes the pension issue is the more pressing and addresses it first. The groups want management to solve both problems, but this may not be currently possible. Thus, one group, that of the young workers, may become hostile because it feels it has been ignored.

Different Perceptions and Attitudes

Individuals perceive things differently. The groups to which they belong also can have different perceptions. Groups tend to evaluate in terms of their backgrounds, norms, and experiences. Since each of these can differ, there is likely to be conflict among groups. Most groups tend to overvalue their own worth and position and to undervalue the worth and position of other groups.

Lack of Clarity

Job clarity involves knowing what others expect in terms of task accomplishment. Yet, in many cases, it is difficult to specify who is responsible for a certain task. Who is responsible for the loss of a talented management trainee—the personnel department or the training department? Who is responsible for the increased sales revenue—marketing or research and development? The inability to pinpoint positive and negative contributions causes groups to compete for control over the activities that are more easily associated with specific effort.

CULTURAL DIVERSITY

Members in most organizational groups today will differ from each other in important ways, such as age, gender, ethnic background, disability, religious affiliation, and lifestyle. Research has shown that cultural diversity in the workplace is good for business. However, research has also shown that firms that pursue diversity for its own sake do not gain the advantages of firms that pursue diversity for performance reasons.

Cultural diversity has many implications for group performance. Different rules and traditions from the diverse backgrounds of individual group members complicate interpersonal interactions. Research has generally shown that groups with a substantial degree of cultural diversity are not able to solve complex problems as effectively as homogeneous groups. Managers often overlook the relationship between high performance and the ability of group members to work effectively with diverse individuals. To interact productively in a diverse group requires respecting other cultures and creating new ways of integrating diverse viewpoints, expanding the range of acceptable means for achieving organizational goals. Managing diverse groups can be a critical challenge in transnational organizations.

The characteristics of groups described in this section provide an overview of how transnational organization managers can think about and understand group behavior and performance. Despite being able to understand groups and their characteristics, managers won't be able to eliminate intergroup conflict. Conflict is a natural part of any system that has scarce resources. Managers must understand conflict as a natural occurrence.

MANAGING INTERGROUP CONFLICT

Certain cultures contain values, morals, and characteristics that lead to resistance to groups and teams. A study of executives from Mexico examined the use of self-managed teams in organizations.[40] The Mexican business culture supports collective, shared responsibility, respecting managers, and having managers make decisions, controlling operations, and disciplining employees. Some of these values are not compatible with self-managed teams, especially the role of managers. In self-managed teams, managers delegate, provide information, and refrain from direct control of operations. The Mexican executives believed that a lack of training, education, and maturity among employees would result in poorer self-managed team performance.

The accompanying Global Focus presents how a Chinese manufacturer imported and blended its corporate style to one of its oversees plants in Camden, South Carolina. Thus far, the success of this type of importing illustrates that it can be done.

A research study of what is designated to be a hybrid team involved a large multinational clothing producer with more than 17,000 employees.[41] The employees worked in plants and as subcontractors in Asia, Central and Eastern

Global Focus A Chinese Beachhead in the United States

Zhang Rumin, chairman and CEO of Chinese appliance maker Haier, plans to capture 10 percent of the U.S. market for full-size refrigerators in three years. Haier has the first Chinese major manufacturing plant in the United States. Typically, the traffic is in the other direction, since labor costs are so much lower in China. Haier has concluded that it wants the manufacturing and design to be close to its markets.

In 2003, Haier is the world's No. 2 refrigerator maker, after Whirlpool, and has expanded into washing machines, air conditioners, small appliances, televisions, computers, and cell phones. In China, it has 29 percent of the market share.

Haier is slowly but clearly importing its corporate philosophy and culture to its Camden, South Carolina, plant. The majority of the employees at the plant are Americans. The factory president, Zhang Zinmin, a support staff, and six engineers are from China. The upper management and the technical group is Chinese and the operating employees are American.

The Haier Chinese group is using the 6-S concept, which is an adaptation of the 5-S quality control concept used by the Japanese. The concepts used from the Japanese are *seiri* (discard the unnecessary), *seiton* (arrange tools in the order of use), *seisoh* (keep the workplace clean), *seiketsu* (keep yourself clean), *shitsuke* (follow workshop disciplines)—to which Haier added the sixth S—safety. Work teams at the plant learn the 6 S's and use the open floor space (6-S squares) to explain or provide examples of the particular "S" on which they stand during team news exchange time.

The Chinese system of managing teams is dominated by the leader. The American system used in teams is a two-way system in which leaders and members exchange ideas, suggestions, and recommendations. Blending the Chinese style with the American style is difficult, but possible. Haier has brought its style, but is willing to modify it to fit the Camden, South Carolina, employees' needs, which illustrates an effective approach to team building and effectiveness.

Source: Adapted from Jonathan Sprague, "China's Manufacturing Beachhead," *Fortune*, October 28, 2002, pp. I192A–I192J, and Ralph E. Wilson, E-Commerce in China, *Web Connect Today*, April 15, 2001, p. 8.

Europe, Central and South America, and North America. In Asia hybrid teams were studied. The hybrid team cultures consisted of an emergent and simplified set of rules and actions; work capability expectations; and member perceptions within a team to develop, share, and enact after mutual interactions. The study found homogeneous and highly heterogeneous teams outperformed moderately heterogeneous teams. Heterogeneity was determined on the basis of perceived difference among team members on nationality and team background. For example, a team that included members from Thailand (3), Australia (2), the United States (3), Malaysia (1), Hong Kong (1), and Indonesia (1) was rated as high heterogeneity. Another team with members from Thailand (5), Britain (1), and the United States (1) was rated as low heterogeneity. The national country makeup and perceptions of team members appeared to be significant factors in the team performance determined by these researchers.

The highly heterogeneous teams found ways to interact, communicate, and create a common identity. The moderately heterogeneous teams showed ongoing communication problems, conflict, and low levels of team identity. The researchers concluded, "Diversity—at least, national heterogeneity—is not an inherent characteristic of effective teams."[42]

Research about group teams suggests that the effectiveness of the unit depends on its stage of development, the training and skill possessed by members, and the manager's skill to manage diversity. A manager who doesn't possess the understanding and skill to integrate the abilities, skills, and experience of a heterogeneous group or team is likely to have difficulty optimizing the unit's performance.[43]

GLOBAL AND TEAM OUTCOMES: PERFORMANCE AND SATISFACTION

The purpose of group and team membership is to achieve performance. A number of social psychologists have conducted research to improve the understanding of group and team performance. Some factors proposed to improve group and team performance are (1) perceived freedom to participate, (2) perceived goal attainment, and (3) status consensus.

Perceived Freedom to Participate

A group member's perception of freedom to participate influences his need satisfaction and performance. Work group members who perceive themselves as active participants report that they are more satisfied, whereas those who perceive their freedom to participate as insignificant are typically the least-satisfied members in a work group.

The freedom-to-participate phenomenon is related to the entire spectrum of economic and sociopsychological needs. For example, individuals' perceived ability to participate may lead them to believe that they are valued members of the group. This assumption can lead to the satisfaction of social, esteem, and self-actualization needs, which in turn leads to high levels of performance.

Perceived Goal Attainment

Perceiving progress toward the attainment of a desired goal is an important factor in the performance of group members. Members of groups and teams who have clearly progressed toward results indicate higher levels of satisfaction than members of groups who have not progressed adequately. Goal attainment is important to better job performance.

Status Consensus

Status consensus is defined as agreement about the relative status of all group members. Suppose an Egyptian employee (host-country national) has a high rank or worth because he has an exceptional education but is not experienced to perform a group role. In this case, a lack of status consensus, or **status incongruence,** would exist. A recent college graduate might face status incongruence if she is placed in a position to lead a group of experienced technicians. This lack

EXHIBIT 8.9
Checklist for Learning about Groups

Area of Concern	Questions to Answer
Activities	Who does what job in the unit?
Interactions	Who initiates contact? How frequently? On what issues?
Norms	What are the task and the behavioral norms? How clear are the norms to the members?
Leaders	Who are the informal leaders?
Status	What is the status order?
Cohesiveness	How cohesive is the group? On what issues is its cohesiveness greatest?
Group politics	How much political maneuvering goes on?
Performance	How does the group's performance compare to that of other units? Has its performance fluctuated? When?

of consensus between education and experience for the position would create an uncomfortable work atmosphere. According to formal organizational procedures, the leader has the authority and the responsibility to direct the group. However, the experienced workers likely would not trust the untested opinions and ideas of the new, inexperienced leader. The result might be covertly slowing down performance or even sabotaging the young leader's directives. A lack of status consensus within a group can cause decreased performance and less satisfaction.

Managers must work with groups and acquire an understanding about how they function and perform. Managers who understand groups are better able to turn inevitable group characteristics into positive forces to accomplish desirable performance objectives. Without a solid understanding of group structure, processes, development, and consequences, the manager is placed at an uncomfortable disadvantage. Exhibit 8.9 presents guidelines that managers can use to learn more about their groups or teams.

Key Terms

Cohesiveness, *245*
Command group, *230*
Cross-functional team, *233*
Formal group, *230*
Friendship group, *232*
Group development, *237*
Group politics, *249*
Groupthink, *247*
Informal group, *232*
Interest group, *232*
Intergroup conflict, *251*
Received role, *240*
Role, *240*
Role ambiguity, *241*
Role conflict, *241*
Role overload, *241*
Self-managed team, *235*
Social loafing, *249*
Status, *243*
Status consensus, *256*
Status incongruence, *256*
Task group, *230*
Team, *228*
Virtual team, *234*
Work group, *228*

Review, Critical Thinking, and Discussion Questions

1. How does an individual member of a group or team identify and follow the norms established by the unit?
2. What are the advantages and disadvantages of a virtual team?
3. Managing a diverse, multicultural team could be very challenging. What skills would a manager most likely have to utilize to manage such a team?
4. Would groupthink be more likely to develop in a culturally homogeneous or heterogeneous team? Why?
5. What should be measured to determine if a group or team is effective?
6. Is it possible for effective groups to exist and develop in an individualistic-oriented national culture? Explain.
7. What type of leader (characteristics) emerges from within the group? Describe an informal leader's characteristics.
8. Explain the forming stage of group and team development.
9. What are the distinct features of a team?
10. What type of national culture dimensions should a manager be knowledgeable about to effectively oversee a group or team?

Endnotes

1. Jon R. Katzenback, "The Discipline of Teams," *Harvard Business Review,* March–April 1993, p. 112.
2. Marie Reed and Richard Hammelsley, *Communicating Successfully in Groups: A Practical Guide for the Workplace* (Philadelphia: Routledge, 2000).
3. J.R. Evans and W.M. Lindsay, *Management and the Control of Quality* (Cincinnati: South-Western, 2001).
4. T.B. Kenne, "Boundary Busting Teamwork," *Industry Week,* March 21, 1994, pp. 72–78.
5. Jerald Greenberg and Robert A. Baron, *Behavior in Organizations* (Upper Saddle River, NJ: Prentice Hall, 2003), p. 298.
6. Anthony M. Townsend, Samuel M. DeMarie, and Anthony R. Hendrickson, "Virtual Teams, Technology and the Workplace of the Future," *Academy of Management Executive,* August 1988, pp. 17–29.
7. K. Kiser, "Working on World Time, *Training,* March 1999, pp. 29–30.
8. K. Fisher, *Leading Self-Directed Teams* (New York: McGraw-Hill, 1993).
9. T. Petzinger, Jr., "How Lynn Mercer Manages a Factory That Manages Itself," *Wall Street Journal,* March 7, 1997, p. B1.
10. Howard Risher, "Eyes on the Prize," *Government Executive,* September 1997, pp. 25–29.
11. Vanessa Urch Driskett and Steven B. Wolff, "Building the Emotional Intelligence of Groups," *Harvard Business Review,* March 2001, pp. 80–91.
12. Barbara Pate Glace, "Teamwork's Top Ten Lead to Quality," *Journal for Quality & Participation,* January–February 1997, pp. 12–16.
13. Michael M. Byerlein, ed., *Work Teams: Past, Present, and Future* (Boston: Kluwer, 2000).
14. Christine Avery and Diane Zabel, *The Flexible Workplace: A Sourcebook of Information and Research* (Westport, CT: Quorum, 2001).
15. D. Levi, *Group Dynamics for Teams* (Thousand Oaks, CA: Sage, 2001).

16. Erika Rasmusson, "Brief Case: Wild Ideals at Work," *Sales and Marketing Management,* July 1999, pp. 22–23.
17. Philip M. Podsakoff, Michael Ahearne, and Scott B. MacKenzie, "Organizational Citizenship Behavior and the Quantity and Quality of Work Group Performance," *Journal of Applied Psychology,* April 1997, pp. 262–70.
18. P. Hinds and S. Kiesler, *Distributed Work* (Cambridge, MA: MIT Press, 2001).
19. George Homans, *The Human Group* (New York: Harcourt Brace, 1950).
20. Robert L. Kahn, D.M. Wolfe, Robert P. Quinn, J.D. Snock, and R.A. Rosenthal, *Organizational Stress: Studies in Role Conflict and Role Ambiguity,* (New York: John Wiley, 1964).
21. Holly B. Thompson and Jon M. Werner, "The Impact of Role Conflict/Facilitation on Core and Discretionary Behaviors: Testing a Mediated Model," *Journal of Management,* August 1997, pp. 583–601.
22. Ruth C. King and Vikram Sethi, "The Moderating Effect of Organizational Commitment on Burnout in Information Systems Professionals," *European Journal of Information Systems,* June 1997, pp. 86–96.
23. Jill Hecht, "Fourteen Heads—and Budgets Are Better Than One," *Inside Technology Training,* March 1998, p. 37.
24. Janice R.W. Joplin and Catherine S. Davis, "Challenges of Leading a Diverse Workforce," *Academy of Management Executive,* August 1997, pp. 32–47.
25. This definition is based on Stanley E. Seashore, *Group Cohesiveness in the Industrial Work Group* (Ann Arbor: University of Michigan, Institute for Social Research, 1954).
26. Marvin E. Shaw, *Group Dynamics: The Psychology of Small Group Behavior* (New York: McGraw-Hill, 1981).
27. J. Lipman-Blumen and H.J. Leavitt, *Hot Groups: Seeding Them, Feeding Them, and Using Them to Ignite Your Organization* (New York: Oxford University Press, 1999).
28. Fred Luthans and Alexander D. Stajkovic, "Reinforce for Performance: A Need to Go Beyond Pay and Even Rewards," *Academy of Management Executive,* May 1999, pp. 49–57.
29. Irving L. Janis, *Victims of Groupthink: A Psychological Study of Foreign Policy Decisions and Fiascos* (Boston: Houghton Mifflin, 1972), and Irving L. Janis and Leon Mann, *Decision Making: A Psychological Analysis of Conflict, Choice, and Commitment* (New York: Macmillan, 1977).
30. Clarence W. Bon Bergen, Jr., and Raymond J. Kirk, "Groupthink: When Too Many Heads Spoil the Decision," *Management Review,* March 1978, pp. 44–49.
31. Kenwyn K. Smith and David N. Barg, *Paradoxes of Group Life* (San Francisco: Jossey-Bass, 1987).
32. D.A. Kravitz and B. Martin, "Ningleman Rediscovered," *Journal of Personality and Social Psychology* 50 (1986), pp. 936–41.
33. P.C. Earley, "East Meets Mideast: Further Explorations of Collectivistic and Individualistic Work Groups," *Academy of Management Journal* 36 (1993), pp. 319–48.
34. R. Nordstrom, P. Lorenzi, and R.V. Hall, "A Review of Public Posting of Feedback in Work Settings," *Journal of Organizational Behavior Management* 11 (1990), pp. 101–23.
35. N.L. Kerr, "Motivation Losses in Small Groups," *Journal of Personality and Social Psychology* 45 (1983), pp. 919–28.

36. Louis R. Pondy, Órganization Conflict: Concepts and Models," *Administrative Science Quarterly,* September 1967, pp. 296–320.

37. Martin W. Rempel and Ronald J. Fisher, "Perceived Threat, Cohesion, and Group Problem Solving in Intergroup Conflict," *International Journal of Conflict Management,* July 1997, pp. 216–34.

38. Suzy Wethaufer, "Common Sense and Conflict," *Harvard Business Review,* January–February 2000, pp. 114–24.

39. Levi, *op. cit.*

40. Chantell E. Nichols, H.W. Lane, and M.B. Brechu, "Taking Self-Managed Teams to Mexico," *Academy of Management Executive* 13 (1999), p. 15.

41. P.C. Earley and Elain Mosakowski, "Creating Hybrid Team Cultures: An Empirical Test of Transnational Team Functioning," *Academy of Management Journal* 43 (2000), pp. 26–49.

42. Betty Jane Punnett and Jason Clemens, "Cross-National Diversity: Implications for International Expansion Decisions," *Journal of World Business* 34 (1999), pp. 128–38.

43. Joseph J. DiStefano and Martha L. Maznevski, "Creative Value with Diverse Teams in Global Management," *Organizational Dynamics,* Summer 2000, pp. 45–63.

Part 2/Reading 1

The Hidden Challenge of Cross-Border Negotiations

James K. Sebenius

Cultural differences can influence business negotiations in significant and unexpected ways, as many a hapless deal maker has learned. In some cases, it's a matter of ignorance or blatant disrespect, as with the American salesman who presented a potential Saudi Arabian client with a multimillion-dollar proposal in a pigskin binder, considered vile in many Muslim cultures. He was unceremoniously tossed out and his company blacklisted from working with Saudi businesses. But the differences can be much more subtle, arising from deep-seated cultural tendencies that influence how people interact—everything from how people view the role of the individual versus the group to their attitudes, say, about the importance of time or relationships. In response to these challenges, a great body of literature has emerged to help executives navigate differences not only in protocol and deportment but in deeper cultural tendencies as well.

But my research shows that there's another, equally treacherous, aspect to cross-border negotiation that's been largely overlooked in the literature: the ways that people from different regions come to agreement, or the *processes* involved in negotiations. Decision making and governance processes, which determine either a "yes" or a "no," can differ widely from culture to culture, not just in terms of legal technicalities but also in terms of behaviors and core beliefs. In my experience observing and participating in scores of international negotiations, I've seen numerous promising deals fail because people ignored or underestimated the powerful differences in processes across cultures. In these pages, I will examine how systematic differences in governance and decision making can disrupt cross-border negotiations, and I will offer advice on how to anticipate and overcome possible barriers on the road to yes.

Source: *Harvard Business Review,* March 2002, pp. 76–85.

MAP THE PLAYERS AND THE PROCESS

In any negotiation, you are always interacting with individuals, but your real purpose is to influence a larger organization—representing a diverse set of interests—to produce a meaningful yes. In an international deal, just as at home, you need to know exactly who's involved in that larger decision process and what roles they play. But in unfamiliar territory, the answers might surprise you. Indeed, applying "home" views of corporate governance and decision making to international deals may seriously hinder the negotiation process. I find it's useful to break down the decision-making process into several constituent parts: Who are the players? Who decides what? What are the informal influences that can make or break a deal? Let's look at each of these factors, which can vary dramatically when you cross national borders.

Who Are The Players?

If you're accustomed to deal making in the United States, you know that extra players beyond those representing the two companies may influence the deal: the SEC, the Federal Trade Commission, and the Justice Department, among others. In his book *Masters of the Universe,* Daniel J. Kadlec writes that when Travelers and Citicorp were contemplating a merger, the heads of both companies together visited Federal Reserve Chairman Alan Greenspan to get a reading on the Fed's likely attitude.

Abroad, you'll of course find extra players as well, but they will be different and often less obvious. For those executives experienced in North American shareholder-based corporate governance, it may come as a surprise to discover that in Germany, labor has virtually equal representation on many supervisory boards of directors. It will probably be less surprising, though no less discomfiting, to discover that local party officials play an integral part in Chinese negotiating teams in the People's Republic, even when the Chinese company is nominally "private." In the European Union, various Brussels commissions may get involved in business negotiations. If an acquisition target has foreign subsidiaries, the skein of negotiating partners may grow even more tangled. All these constituencies bring their own interests to the table, as well as varying abilities to block or foster negotiations. Even GE, one of the most experienced acquirers, suffered a humiliating defeat in its attempted merger with Honeywell, in part because GE's management underestimated the nature and seriousness of European concerns about competitiveness and the potential for these concerns—and GE's European competitors—to obstruct the deal.

Another example is drawn from the research of my colleagues William A. Sahlman and Burton C. Hurlock: Near the time of the collapse of the Soviet Union, California-based venture capital firm Sierra Ventures was negotiating with the director of the Institute for Protein Research in Russia, hoping to get the rights to an apparently revolutionary biotechnology process. Marathon negotiations with the institute's management team—heroically bridging huge gaps between East and West, business and science, bureaucracy and venture capital—seemed as if they would finally culminate in an acceptable deal for both sides. Although the deal ultimately succeeded, nearing the finish line it suddenly became clear that several Moscow ministries, each with its own point of view and agenda, also had to approve the agreement. This posed a potentially fatal set of obstacles that could have been anticipated had the Sierra team made more than a perfunctory effort early on to learn about the real decision process.

Who Decides What?

Even if you know who's playing, a failure to understand each player's role—and who owns which decisions—can be very costly. For example, when Italian tire maker Pirelli sought to acquire its German rival, Continental Gummiwerke, Pirelli claimed control of a majority of Continental's shares and received tacit backing from Deutsche Bank and support from Gerhard Schröder, then Prime Minister of Lower Saxony, where Continental is based. In a U.S. transaction, merely owning enough equity often allows the acquirer to control the target. But not in this setting.

Unfortunately for Pirelli, German corporate governance provides a structure in which other key players can block the will of even a majority of shareholders. While the management board in most large German companies has day-to-day management responsibilities, it is only one of four sets of players—along with shareholders, a supervisory board, and labor—that can play a significant role in any major decision. What's more, under union codetermination, labor elects fully half of the members of the supervisory board, which in turn elects the management board. And the management board can prevent any single shareholder, no matter how large his or her holdings, from voting more than 5 percent of the total company shares. Thus, having failed to gain real buy-in from all the players, especially labor and key managers, Pirelli couldn't complete the transaction, even though it claimed effective control over Continental's shares and had powerful allies—a humiliating defeat that cost the Italian company nearly half a billion dollars.[1]

There are some impressive stories of executives deftly navigating these potential barriers—U.K.-based Vodafone's successful acquisition of Germany's Mannesmann is a notable recent example—and such cases might seem to herald major changes in German law and governance. But the circumstances and tactics in Vodafone's case were highly specific to the deal, and the general implications for Euro-governance seem limited. Deeply entrenched structures continue to blindside many a corporate suitor—and not just in Germany. In fact, versions of this cautionary tale could be repeated in locales as distinct as Switzerland and Japan, where boards of directors representing constituencies other than shareholders may exert powers unfamiliar to those accustomed to Anglo

[1]Razeen Sally, "A French Insurance Firm and 'Fortress Germany': The Case of AGF and AMB," and the associated "Appendix," Insead Cases 394-052-1 and 394-052-5, 1994.

Saxon-style governance, including voting caps and the power to block share registration or voting of outside equity holders.

Cultural assumptions can sometimes make it very difficult to recognize or acknowledge who has formal decision rights. For example, when Honda invested heavily in an extensive relationship with British automaker Rover, workers and managers at the two companies developed very positive working relationships for more than a decade. The partnership intensified after the government sold Rover to British Aerospace (BAe), but as Rover continued to lose money, BAe decided to discard the relationship, abruptly selling Rover to BMW through a secretive deal that caught Honda completely unawares. The Japanese automaker considered its connection with Rover a long-term one, much like a marriage, and it had shared advanced product and process technology with Rover well beyond its effective contractual ability to protect these assets. Honda's leaders were dumbfounded and outraged that BAe could sell—and to a competitor, no less. Yet while Honda's prized relationship was at the level of the *operating* company (Rover), the Japanese company had not taken seriously enough the fact that the decision rights over a Rover sale are vested at the *parent* (BAe) level. From a financial standpoint, the move made sense for BAe, and it was perfectly legal. Yet Honda's cultural blinders made the sale seem inconceivable, and its disproportionate investments in Rover in effect created a major economic opportunity for BAe. The bottom line: Understanding both formal decision rights and cultural assumptions in less familiar settings can be vital. (For more on how cultural assumptions can influence negotiating behavior, see Exhibit 1 "Cross-Cultural Etiquette and Behavior: The Basics.")

A final note on identifying decision rights: Even the experts may stumble over their assumptions. U.S. attorneys apparently told Bernard Arnault's French luxury conglomerate LVMH that companies traded on the New York Stock Exchange could not increase their share base by a significant amount without shareholder approval. With this

EXHIBIT 1 Cross-Cultural Etiquette and Behavior: The Basics

Lapses in etiquette can trip up negotiations on two levels: the visible manifestations of protocol and deportment, and the deeper cultural characteristics that influence how people interact in subtle yet powerful ways.

Protocol and Deportment

Books on regional protocol and deportment offer a stew of dos and don'ts that attempt to generalize about the specifics of surface behavior. To quote a handful of rules from Dean Allen Foster's *Bargaining Across Borders:* Never show the sole of your shoe to an Arab, for it is dirty and represents the bottom of the body. Look directly and intently into a French associate's eye when making an important point, but avoid direct eye contact in Southeast Asia until the relationship is firmly established. In Italy, don't touch the side of your nose; it is a sign of distrust. The lists go on and on and can certainly help you avoid mistakes. But the rules are so complex and detailed that it's difficult to keep them straight, and the likelihood of regional variation further complicates matters.

Nonetheless, negotiators would do well to consider a range of questions about these behaviors when preparing for international negotiations, either by consulting the literature or by engaging in conversations with people who have experienced the culture at hand. I've outlined the categories of surface behaviors most likely to affect the tenor of negotiations. While the list is not exhaustive and must be read in light of obvious caveats about regional, professional, and national variation, seeking answers to these questions will at least provide a degree of familiarity with the basic dos and don'ts in any given culture.

Sensitivity to these basics allows you to avoid giving offense, demonstrate respect, enhance camaraderie, and strengthen communications. But cultural codes of protocol and deportment are not likely to interfere dramatically in your negotiations, absent blatant disrespect.

(*continued*)

(concluded)

Deeper Cultural Characteristics

Somewhat more difficult to see are the underlying cultural tendencies affecting how people interact, such as the relative emphasis on the individual versus the group and on the deal versus the relationship. Indeed, some compare culture to an iceberg: The danger of collision is not so much with the part you see but with what's below.

The idea that such deeper cultural traits can profoundly affect negotiation is not new. In an influential 1960 *Harvard Business Review* article "The Silent Language in Overseas Business" (May–June), anthropologist Edward T. Hall, along with collaborator Mildred Reed Hall, developed four categories of underlying cultural variables that may drive surface behavior. Complementing Hall's work, academic Geert Hofstede conducted surveys, beginning in 1980, of more than 60,000 IBM employees in more than 40 countries to develop four dimensions of cultural differences.

In addition to the characteristics raised by Hall and Hofstede, there are other cultural issues to consider, such as a society's views on fairness and justice or how a culture accords status (by accomplishment, knowledge, social position, age, and so forth).

Dos and Don'ts

Greetings

How do people greet and address one another? What role do business cards play?

Degree of Formality

Will my counterparts expect me to dress and interact formally or informally?

Gift Giving

Do businesspeople exchange gifts? What gifts are appropriate? Are there taboos associated with gift giving?

Touching

What are the attitudes toward body contact?

Eye Contact

Is direct eye contact polite? Is it expected?

Deportment

How should I carry myself? Formally? Casually?

Emotions

Is it rude, embarrassing, or usual to display emotions?

Silence

Is silence awkward? Expected? Insulting? Respectful?

Eating

What are the proper manners for dining? Are certain foods taboo?

Body Language

Are certain gestures or forms of body language rude?

Punctuality

Should I be punctual and expect my counterparts to be as well? Or are schedules and agendas fluid?

understanding, LVMH acquired almost 35 percent of Gucci in a takeover bid.[2] However, it turns out that different stock rules apply to companies based outside the United States—Gucci, for instance, traded in New York but was chartered in the Netherlands and is headquartered in Florence. Gucci's defense team discovered this loophole and used it to shut down the deal. The company first issued 20 percent new shares to its employees in an ESOP-like transaction and then offered 42 percent additional new shares to a group controlled by François Pinault, Arnault's French rival. LVMH's massively diluted position in effect handed ultimate control to Pinault, leaving LVMH trapped as a relatively powerless minority shareholder in Gucci.

What Are the Informal Influences that Can Make or Break a Deal?

It's important to understand which people must sign the contract to finalize a deal, but that's often not enough. Many countries have webs of influence that are more powerful than the actual parties making the deal, even though those webs don't have the formal standing of, say, government agencies. In Japan, it may be the *keiretsu*—industrial groups that are linked by a web of business ties, lending, and cross-shareholdings. In Germany's financial sector, it might be the insurance giant Allianz. In Italy, it may be a set of powerful families. In Russia, it can be the Russian mafia and other protection rackets. Outsiders need to understand these webs and factor them into their negotiating approach. It's a lesson many companies have learned the hard way.

And influence on negotiations need not be driven by an informal, underlying power structure, as U.S. Stone Container Corporation learned. While negotiating the terms of a major forest project in Honduras, Stone Container's executives assumed that the Honduran president and his relevant ministries had the power to decide whether to allow the project and therefore dealt primarily with the president. But while the president did have the legal authority to make the deal and ultimately approved it, the company's proposal and negotiating strategy seemed to signal a possibly corrupt deal among elites. This inadvertently triggered the involvement of the Honduran Congress, labor unions, political parties, potential business competitors, indigenous people in the affected region, and domestic and international environmental groups. Had Stone taken into account the history of strained relationships between Honduras and the U.S. government and multinationals, as well as the fragile status of the presidency in this fledgling democracy, it could have developed a strategy that accommodated this informal web of potential influences. Instead, Stone's lack of foresight caused it to become enmeshed in an adversarial, multiparty process that ultimately failed. When interviewed for a Harvard Business School case, Stone executive Jerry Freeman likened the experience to being "caught in a drive-by shooting with no place to hide."

U.S. companies like Stone—and others from cultures with strong legal systems—frequently underestimate the power of informal influences because they assume that foreign legal systems will enforce formal contracts just as they are expected to at home. What they may ultimately learn is that dispute resolution can look very different in different cultures. In Japan, which has a relatively small legal system and few lawyers, companies rely on relationships and negotiation to sort through most commercial disputes. Present-day Russia has practically no functioning judiciary. Many countries' legal systems are corrupt or controlled by local political powers.

The fact is, there can be a great gulf between the laws on the books and how things really work, as one U.S. electrical goods manufacturer learned after it entered a joint venture with a Chinese company and hired a local manager to run the Chinese operation. As described in Charles Olivier's 1996 *WorldLink* article, "Investing in China: 12 Hard Lessons," the company tried to expand its product line, but the Chinese manager balked, insisting there was no demand for the additional products. The U.S. management team tried to resolve the dispute through

[2]Bryan Burroughs, "Gucci and Goliath," *Vanity Fair,* July 1999.

negotiations, and when the Chinese manager wouldn't budge, the team fired him—but he wouldn't leave. The local labor bureau refused to back the U.S. team, and when the U.S. executives tried to dissolve the venture, they discovered they couldn't recover their capital because Chinese law dictates that both sides need to approve a dissolution. A foreign law firm, hired at great expense, made no headway. It took some behind-the-scenes negotiation on the part of a local law firm to finally overcome the need for dual approval—an outcome that demanded local counsel well versed in the intricacies of Chinese culture.

In short, successful cross-border negotiators begin by discarding home-market presumptions and developing a clear map of the players who are likely to influence the formal and informal decision process. Only when you know exactly who these players are can you develop a strategy that targets their interests.

ADAPT YOUR APPROACH

Unfortunately, however, knowing who's involved in the process is only half the battle. While you negotiate with people, you are typically seeking to influence the outcome of an organizational *process*. That process can look different in different cultures, and different processes may call for radically different negotiation strategies and tactics. Even seasoned executives often fail to adapt their approaches to those different processes, with costly consequences. While it's difficult to generalize, such processes tend to take one of several forms: top down, consensus, and multistage coalition building.

Top Down

In some cases, you will deal with a "real boss," a top-down authority who won't delegate in any meaningful way and will ultimately make the decision unilaterally. When there is the local equivalent of a very much in charge Admiral Rickover, Harold Geneen, or Robert Moses, revealing key information or making premature concessions to those not genuinely in the decision loop can work to your disadvantage. The most effective negotiators avoid making deals with relatively powerless agents who function as important messengers or emissaries but not as powers in their own right. Instead, these negotiators find ways to interact directly with the boss—or, if that's not possible, to connect with people outside the process who have close ties to or influence over the boss.

In some cultures, even if the boss delegates authority, going directly to the top can sometimes be more effective. For example, when one Italian industrial products firm wished to acquire a large division of a French conglomerate, it first made friendly overtures to the target unit. But as it became clear that unit management wouldn't even consider discussions about a possible sale, the Italian chief went quietly to the top. He eventually closed the deal with the boss, who—consistent with that company's top-down culture and, in fact, much of French corporate governance—simply "crammed it down" on the division, softening the blow somewhat by offering any reluctant managers a chance to be absorbed into the French parent. This strategy must be used cautiously, however. It can easily backfire when subordinate players have opportunities to sabotage the deal or erode its effectiveness.

What's more, it can be risky to impute omnipotence even to apparently powerful bosses. U.S. executives almost reflexively ask, "Who is the real decision maker?" But the answer can be misleading, as Stone Container learned in its negotiations with the Honduran president. This is not a problem limited to less-developed countries. Even in negotiating with U.S. presidents, parties such as the Shah of Iran or South Vietnamese leaders have made deals or reached critical understandings, only to learn later that limits on presidential power would prevent the deal from transpiring as expected. And even in one-party, relatively authoritarian countries, deals at the top may not translate into action on the ground.

The case of Armand Hammer's protracted negotiations to form, and later manage, a joint venture between Hammer's Occidental Petroleum (Oxy) and the state-run China National Coal Development Corporation (CNCDC) reveals how even the highest-level backing can be insufficient. Hammer and China's then-paramount leader Deng Xiaoping, who met in person about the project, both expressed their serious commitment to making the venture work, despite signals during preliminary negotiations that the deal would not succeed. As Roderick MacLeod recounts in his book, *China, Inc.: How to Do Business with the Chinese,* Hammer saw the project as the crowning achievement of his career: the largest-scale foreign investment in China in history. Deng, for his part, was anxious to show the world that his market reforms were transforming China into an economy ripe for investment. The two ordered their subordinates to reach an agreement, and the Oxy–CNCDC project became a highly visible test case. Yet because of bureaucratic conflicts, clashing expectations and interpretations, and escalating antagonisms, the formal negotiations dragged on for years, and Oxy ultimately pulled out after more than a decade of frustration.

Consensus

If top-down authority is at one end of the decision-making spectrum, then consensus is at the other. The consensus process can have many variations and is especially common in Asia. It sometimes requires agreement among the members of the other side's negotiating team; at other times, it requires agreement from the broader enterprise and can include external stakeholders and governments.

When a consortium of U.S. companies submitted a proposal to assist in building a dam in the Three Gorges section of China's Yangtze River—a project debated by the Chinese for more than 70 years—they were blindsided by the consensus process. The consortium's negotiating team largely directed its efforts at a single agency, the Yangtze Valley Planning Office (YVPO). But in China, bureaucratic units like the YVPO are explicitly ranked, and no one unit has authority over another of the same rank; permission from above is required if there is disagreement. As a result, decisions are pushed up to the highest authority possible, overloading the top levels of bureaucracy. The only practical solution is consensus, which has become a cornerstone of the modern Chinese bureaucracy.

To move a process along, each affected unit must engage in a complex bargaining system to establish compatible goals and to protect interests. By failing to appreciate the involvement of these other units, the U.S. team didn't anticipate enemies or, even more important, help potential allies back its plan. (Hampered by U.S. government opposition to the project—driven by environmental and human rights concerns—the U.S. team also made some classic negotiation errors, such as failing to understand the other side's interests. For example, the team's proposal emphasized efficient machinery and a lean labor force, while maximum employment is one of China's top priorities, With a little more thought, the U.S. group might have placed greater stress on elements such as technology transfer, training, and foreign investment, rather than cost cutting and speed.)

The need for consensus among players on the other side will affect your negotiating strategy in other ways as well. First, since consensus cultures often focus on relationships rather than deals, the parties involved will often want to take substantial amounts of time to learn about you and forge a deeper relationship before talking about the deal. In consensus cultures, relationship building is critical not only to reaching an agreement but also to making it work. The lengthy timetable may be very frustrating to teams from decisive, top-down cultures; unfortunately, there's usually little they can do to speed up the process unless the other side is desperate for a deal—which generally means the consensus is already there—or the other side wants a deal and you're credibly engaged in parallel conversations with one of their serious rivals.

Second, since consensus processes often go hand-in-hand with near-inexhaustible demands for information, you should be prepared to provide it—in many different forms, in great detail, and repeatedly. Third, to the extent that you can pinpoint the source of delay—usually the doubts of specific people or units—you can and should design your approach to help your proponents on the other side convert the doubters, giving them the data they need and supplying them with arguments they can use internally to address specific concerns.

Fourth, you may need to shift your focus away from the bargaining table and instead interact extensively and informally with the other side as it tries to reach a position internally. With some bitterness, U.S. trade negotiators dealing with seemingly immovable Japanese counterparts have puzzled, "Before the Japanese have reached a consensus, they can't negotiate; after consensus is attained on the other side, there is nothing to negotiate." Your objective is to get your interests, point of view, and plans incorporated into *their* consensus process. If you wait to do this until you are at the bargaining table, you will have to pry open their now-fixed position, reached before the players officially sit down to negotiate. As John Graham and Yoshihiro Sano, authors of *Doing Business with the New Japan,* explain, "In Japan, what goes on at the negotiation table is really a ritual approval of what has already been decided through numerous individual conversations in restaurants, bathhouses, and offices. In Japan, the negotiating table is not a place for changing minds. Persuasive appeals are not appropriate or effectual." Often, breaking apart a previously settled mind-set requires near-collusion between you and their bargaining team, in which you make such a public fuss that their team returns home with a powerful argument to reopen the process.

And finally, you'll need to adjust your own expectations—and your organization's—of how long the deal will take. Failure to do so can put you into a bargaining vise, with your home management team pressuring you for quick results and the relaxed other side exploiting your own side's impatience. Caught in the middle, you may feel as though your choices are limited: You can walk away (and undermine your effectiveness and waste resources), or you can make major concessions (and dilute the value of the deal). In general, if you think your side cannot handle a lengthy negotiation, you may be better off avoiding the negotiation altogether.

As frustrating as the need for consensus may be to those from fast-moving cultures, there can be offsetting advantages. A slow and painstaking negotiation process may lead to a decision that has more staying power. What's more, actual implementation may occur more quickly than with a top-down agreement. People may also be more attached to the deal after investing so much in it. In one case, a U.S. firm negotiated for two years with a major Japanese company to create a large-scale joint venture under Japanese control. During this excruciatingly detailed process, the negotiations were halted several times due to what the Japanese team described as a breakdown in its consensus process. Each time, however, the Japanese company resumed negotiations with a stronger consensus on the central role of the deal to its long-term global strategy.

When a European firm unexpectedly made a tender offer for the entire U.S. business, the Japanese company had to decide whether to drop out of the process or seek to acquire the whole firm. After years of negotiations and mentally integrating the U.S. operations into its long-term strategy during its exhaustive consensus process, the Japanese company had essentially fallen in love with its target. Rather than face the internal organizational costs of "losing," it was willing to pay an extraordinarily high price for the U.S. firm—far more than it would have paid had it not been part of the frustratingly long consensus process.

In short, you should not be blindsided by the need for consensus. It may require more time, relationship building, and information than expected. Dealing with a consensus process effectively requires facilitating it while doing what you can—with real external deadlines and competitors—to speed it up, but also recognizing what you can't do and setting realistic expectations.

Coalition Building

Decision processes don't always come in pure forms such as top down or consensus. Sometimes, they're less defined and don't require the agreement

EXHIBIT 2 **How Negotiation-Specific Expectations Shape the Process**

In addition to the general cultural differences that influence negotiations, different cultures will influence expectations as to what the specific process and outcome will look like. The expectations revolve around four key areas:

Underlying View of the Process

People may view the negotiation process as cooperative (win-win) or competitive (win-lose). Some people will seek mutual advantage; others won't. Making assumptions about which view the other side will take can be misleading and even dangerous.

Approach to Building Agreement

U.S. negotiators often seek agreement on specifics first, building up toward an overall deal. Their Chinese counterparts often focus first on what seems to many Americans to be a very general historical and national frame for discussion. Then, as many French negotiators do, they seek agreement on general principles, later working through the details. This tendency also manifests itself in thought processes: Many Chinese tend to reason about the whole while Westerners often proceed by breaking the whole into parts and reasoning incrementally.

Form of Agreement

What level of detail is required? In many parts of East Asia, negotiators are content with a fairly broad agreement that focuses on general principles rather than detailed rules. By contrast, North American and European executives often insist on a detailed contract in which as many contingencies as possible are foreseen.

Implementation of Agreement

Is adherence to an agreement expected or contingent? U.S. negotiators generally expect to stick with the letter of the contract, treating renegotiation as a very unusual, even aberrant, event. In many other cultures, an agreement is merely a starting point in what is expected to be an evolving relationship; renegotiation may occur as warranted under the assumption that all contingencies cannot possibly be foreseen. The precise terms are expected to unfold as the process does. Moreover, while a U.S. negotiator can rely on its court system to serve as a fairly reliable enforcer of contracts, there is little such expectation in many parts of the world.

of every player but rather the support of a sufficient subset of players—a "winning coalition" that can effectively pressure, sidestep, or override dissenters. At other times, a "blocking coalition" that has interests no one can ultimately overrule can bring a proposal to a halt. Pirelli's failure to win over Continental Gummiwerke's all-important management board and labor force in its failed takeover foray into Germany left a blocking entity in control. Stone Container in its negotiations with the Honduran president, and Armand Hammer in his attempts at an agreement with Deng Xiaoping both fell victim to ad-hoc blocking coalitions. Navigating such coalitions requires an understanding of the likely interests and options of the players who will be needed as allies in a winning coalition or who may seek to form a blocking entity.

Governance processes often drive these considerations, so taking a close look at the key players and how they work together can help you anticipate opportunities and obstacles as well as appropriately sequence your approach. For example, one foreign would-be acquirer of a German company first approached the supervisory board and obtained agreement in principle to go forward. Then, to the surprise of the board, the acquirer suddenly put the deal on hold. The acquirer had delayed the negotiations in order to approach the German company's management board, lay out the terms it had proposed, and offer it total veto power over the transaction. In reality, the management board already had the ability to obstruct the deal, but the move felt like a concession because the board was not accustomed to being incorporated into the process in this way. Finally, after spending a great deal of time working out the strategy with the management board, the acquirer went back to the shareholders on the supervisory board to conclude what became a very successful transaction.

In closing, it's worth noting that cultural allegiances are often not as simple as they appear. While national culture can tell you a lot about the person sitting across the table from you, every individual represents a number of cultures, each of which can affect negotiation style. Beyond her French citizenship, an ABB executive may well be from Alsace, have a Danish parent, feel staunchly European, have studied electrical engineering, and earned an MBA from the University of Chicago. Gender, ethnicity, and profession all play a role. But along with assessing the person across the table is figuring out the intricacies of the larger organization behind her. And to do that, you need to diligently map the governance and decision-making processes, which can take devilishly unexpected forms across borders. Then, you must design your strategy and tactics so that you're reaching the right people, with the right arguments, in a way that allows you maximum impact on the process to yield a sustainable deal.

Part 2/Reading 2

The Multicultural Organization

Taylor Cox, Jr.

As we begin the 1990s, a combination of workforce demographic trends and increasing globalization of business has placed the management of cultural differences on the agenda of most corporate leaders. Organizations' workforces will be increasingly heterogeneous on dimensions such as gender, race, ethnicity, and nationality. Potential benefits of this diversity include better decision making, higher creativity and innovation, greater success in marketing to foreign and ethnic minority communities, and a better distribution of economic opportunity. Conversely, cultural differences can also increase costs through higher turnover rates, interpersonal conflict, and communication breakdowns.

Source: *Academy of Management Executive,* 5, no. 2 (1991), pp. 34–47.

To capitalize on the benefits and minimize the costs of worker diversity, organizations of the '90s must be quite different from the typical organization of the past. Specifically, consultants have advised organizations to become "multicultural."[1] The term refers to the degree to which an organization values cultural diversity and is willing to utilize and encourage it.[2]

Leaders are being charged to create the multicultural organization, but what does such an organization look like, and what are the specific ways in which it differs from the traditional organization? Further, what tools and techniques are available to assist organizations in making the transition from the old to the new?

This article addresses these questions. I have used an adaptation of the societal-integration model developed by Milton Gordon, as well as available information on the early experience of American organizations with managing diversity initiatives, to construct a model of the multicultural organization.

CONCEPTUAL FRAMEWORK

In his classic work on assimilation in the United States, Milton Gordon argued that there are seven dimensions along which the integration of persons from different ethnic backgrounds into a host society should be analyzed.[3] I use "integration" to mean the coming together and mixing of people from different cultural identity groups in one organization. A cultural identity group is a group of people who (on average) share certain values and norms distinct from those of other groups. Although the boundaries of these groups may be defined along many dimensions, I am primarily concerned with gender, race, ethnicity, and national origin. Gordon's seven dimensions are:

1. Form of acculturation.
2. Degree of structural assimilation.
3. Degree of intergroup marriage.
4. Degree of prejudice.
5. Degree of discrimination.
6. Degree of identification with the dominant group of the host society.
7. Degree of intergroup conflict (especially over the balance of power).

Although Gordon's interest was in societal-level integration, I believe his model can be easily and usefully adapted for analysis of cultural integration for organizations. Therefore, an adaptation of his seven-point framework is used here as a basis for describing organizational models for integrating culturally divergent groups. Exhibit 1 shows my proposed six-dimensional adaptation of the Gordon framework along with definitions of each term.

Acculturation is the method by which cultural differences between the dominant (host) culture and any minority culture groups are resolved or treated. There are several alternatives, the most prominent being: (1) a unilateral process by which minority culture members adopt the norms and values of the dominant group in the organization (assimilation); (2) a process by which both minority and majority culture members adopt some norms of the other group (pluralism); and (3) a situation where there is little adaptation on either side (cultural separatism).[4] Pluralism also means that minority culture members are encouraged to enact behaviors from their alternative culture as well as from the majority culture. They are therefore able to retain a sense of identity with their minority-culture group. Acculturation is concerned with the cultural (norms of behavior) aspect of integration of diverse groups, as opposed to simply their physical presence in the same location.

Structural integration refers to the presence of persons from different cultural groups in a single

EXHIBIT 1 A Conceptual Framework for Analysis of Organizational Capability for Effective Integration of Culturally Diverse Personnel

Dimension	Definition
1. Acculturation	Modes by which two groups adapt to each other and resolve cultural differences
2. Structural Integration	Cultural profiles of organization members including hiring, job-placement, and job status profiles
3. Informal Integration	Inclusion of minority-culture members in informal networks and activities outside of normal working hours
4. Cultural Bias	Prejudice and discrimination
5. Organizational Identification	Feelings of belonging, loyalty, and commitment to the organization
6. Intergroup Conflict	Friction, tension, and power struggles between cultural groups

organization. Workforce profile data has typically been monitored under traditional equal opportunity and affirmative action guidelines. However, to get a proper understanding of structural integration it is important to look beyond organization-wide profile data, and examine cultural mix by function, level, and individual work group. This is because, it is commonplace in American companies for gaps of 15 to 30 percentage points to exist between the proportion of minority members in the overall labor force of a firm, and their proportion at middle and higher levels of management.[5]

Even within levels of an organization, individual work groups may still be highly segregated. For example, a senior human resource manager for a Fortune 500 firm who is often cited as a leader in managing diversity efforts, recently told me that there are still many "white-male bastions" in his company. As an assistant vice president with responsibility for equal opportunity, he indicated that breaking down this kind of segregation was a focal point of his current job.

The informal integration dimension recognizes that important work-related contacts are often made outside of normal working hours and in various social activities and organizations. This item looks at levels of inclusion of minority-culture members in lunch and dinner meetings, golf and other athletic outings, and social clubs frequented by organization leaders. It also addresses mentoring and other informal developmental relationships in organizations.

Cultural bias has two components. Prejudice refers to negative attitudes toward an organization member based on his/her culture group identity, and discrimination refers to observable adverse behavior for the same reason. Discrimination, in turn, may be either personal or institutional. The latter refers to ways that organizational culture and management practices may inadvertently disadvantage members of minority groups. An example is the adverse effect that emphasizing aggressiveness and self-promotion has on many Asians. Many managers that I have talked to are sensitive to the fact that prejudice is a cognitive phenomenon and therefore much more difficult than discrimination for organization managers to change. Nevertheless, most acknowledge the importance of reducing prejudice for long-range, sustained change.

Prejudice may occur among minority-culture members as well as among dominant-culture members. Putting the debate over whether rates of prejudice differ for different groups aside, it must be emphasized that the practical impact of prejudice by majority-culture members is far greater than that of minority-culture members because of their far greater decision-making power (except under extraordinary conditions, such as those of South Africa).

Organizational identification refers to the extent to which a person personally identifies with, and tends to define himself or herself as a member in the employing organization. Levels of organizational identification have historically been lower in the United States than in other countries (notably Japan). Indications are that recent changes in organizational design (downsizing and de-layering) have reduced organizational identification even further. Although levels of organizational identification may be low in general in the U.S. workforce, we are concerned here with comparative levels of identification for members of different cultural identity groups.

Finally, intergroup conflict refers to levels of culture-group-based tension and interpersonal friction. Research on demographic heterogeneity among group members suggests that communication and cohesiveness may decline as members of groups become dissimilar.[6] Also, in the specific context of integrating minority-group members into organizations, concerns have been raised about backlash from white males who may feel threatened by these developments. It is therefore important to examine levels of inter-group conflict in diverse workgroups.

TYPES OF ORGANIZATIONS

This six-factor framework will now be employed to characterize organizations in terms of stages of development on cultural diversity.[7] Three organization types will be discussed: the monolithic organization, the plural organization, and the multicultural organization. The application of the six-factor conceptual framework to describe the three organization types appears in Exhibit 2.

The Monolithic Organization

The most important single fact about the monolithic organization is that the amount of structural integration is minimal. The organization is highly homogeneous. In the United States, this commonly represents an organization characterized by substantial white male majorities in the overall employee population with few women and minority men in management jobs. In addition, these organizations feature extremely high levels of occupational segregation with women and racioethnic minority men (racially and/or culturally different from the majority) concentrated in low-status jobs such as secretary and maintenance. Thus, the distribution of persons from minority-cultural backgrounds is highly skewed on all three components of function, level, and work group.

To a large extent, the specifications on the frameworks' other five dimensions follow from the structural exclusion of people from different cultural backgrounds. Women, racioethnic minority men, and foreign nationals who do enter the organization must adopt the existing organizational norms, framed by the white male majority, as a matter of organizational survival.

Ethnocentrism and other prejudices cause little, if any, adoption of minority-culture norms by majority group members. Thus, a unilateral acculturation process prevails. The exclusionary practices of the dominant culture also apply to informal activities. The severe limitations on career opportunities for minority-culture members creates alienation, and thus the extent to which they identify with the organization can be expected to be low compared to the more fully enfranchised majority group.

One positive note is that intergroup conflict based on culture-group identity is minimized by the relative homogeneity of the workforce. Finally, because this organization type places little importance on the integration of cultural minority group members, discrimination, as well as prejudice, are prevalent.

EXHIBIT 2 Organizational Types

Dimension of integration	Monolithic	Plural	Multicultural
Form of Acculturation	Assimilation	Assimilation	Pluralism
Degree of Structural Integration	Minimal	Partial	Full
Integration into Informal Organization	Virtually none	Limited	Full
Degree of Cultural Bias	Both prejudice and discrimination against minority-culture groups is prevalent	Progress on both prejudice & discrimination but both continue to exist especially institutional discrimination	Both prejudice and discrimination are eliminated
Levels of Organizational Identification*	Large majority-minority gap	Medium to large majority-minority gap	No majority-minority gap
Degree of Intergroup Conflict	Low	High	Low

*Defined as difference between organizational identification levels between minorities and majorities.

While the white-male dominated organization is clearly the prototypical one for the monolithic organization, at least some of its characteristics are likely to occur in organizations where another identity group is dominant. Examples include minority-owned businesses, predominantly black and predominantly Hispanic colleges, and foreign companies operating in the United States.

Aside from the rather obvious downside implications of the monolithic model in terms of underutilization of human resources and social equality, the monolithic organization is not a realistic option for most large employers in the 1990s. To a significant degree, large U.S. organizations made a transition away from this model during the '60s and '70s. This transition was spurred by a number of societal forces, most notably the civil-rights and feminists movements, and the beginnings of changes in workforce demographics, especially in the incidence of career-oriented women. Many organizations responded to these forces by creating the plural organization.

The Plural Organization

The plural organization differs from the monolithic organization in several important respects. In general, it has a more heterogeneous membership than the monolithic organization and takes steps to be more inclusive of persons from cultural backgrounds that differ from the dominant group. These steps include hiring and promotion policies that sometimes give preference to persons from minority-culture groups, manager training on equal opportunity issues (such as civil rights law, sexual harassment, and reducing prejudice), and audits of compensation systems to ensure against discrimination against minority group members. As a result, the plural organization achieves a much higher level of structural integration than the monolithic organization.

The problem of skewed integration across functions, levels, and work groups, typical in the monolithic organization, is also present in the plural organization. For example, in many large U.S. organizations racioethnic minorities now make up 20 percent or more of the total workforce. Examples include General Motors, Chrysler, Stroh Brewery, Phillip Morris, Coca-Cola, and Anheuser-Busch. However, the representations of non-whites in management in these same companies averages less than 12 percent.[8] A similar picture exists in work groups. For example, while more than 20 percent of the clerical and office staffs at General Motors are minorities, they represent only about 12 percent of technicians and 13 percent of sales workers. Thus, the plural organization features partial structural integration.

Because of the greater structural integration and the efforts (cited previously) which brought it about, the plural organization is also characterized by some integration of minority-group members into the informal network, substantial reductions in discrimination, and some moderation of prejudicial attitudes. The improvement in employment opportunities should also create greater identification with the organization among minority-group members.

The plural organization represents a marked improvement over the monolithic organization in effective management of employees of different racioethnic, gender, and nationality backgrounds. The plural organization form has been prevalent in the United States. Since the late 1960s, and in my judgment, represents the typical large firm as we enter the 1990s. These organizations emphasize an affirmative action approach to managing diversity. During the 1980s increased evidence of resentment toward this approach among white males began to surface. They argue that such policies, in effect, discriminate against white males and therefore perpetuate the practice of using racioethnicity, nationality, or gender as a basis for making personnel decisions. In addition, they believe that it is not fair that contemporary whites be disadvantaged to compensate for management errors made in the past. This backlash effect, coupled with the increased number of minorities in the organization, often creates greater intergroup conflict in the plural organization than was present in the monolithic organization.

While the plural organization achieves a measure of structural integration, it continues the assimilation approach to acculturation which is characteristic of the monolithic organization. The failure to address cultural aspects of integration is a major shortcoming of the plural organization form, and is a major point distinguishing it from the multicultural organization.

The Multicultural Organization

In discussing cultural integration aspects of mergers and acquisitions, Sales and Mirvis argued that an organization which simply contains many different cultural groups is a plural organization, but considered to be multicultural only if the organization values this diversity.[9] The same labels and definitional distinction is applied here. The meaning of the distinction between containing diversity and valuing it follows from an understanding of the shortcomings of the plural organization as outlined previously. The multicultural organization has overcome these shortcomings. Referring again to Exhibit 2, we see that the multicultural organization is characterized by:

1. Pluralism.
2. Full structural integration.
3. Full integration of the informal networks.
4. An absence of prejudice and discrimination.
5. No gap in organizational identification based on cultural identity group.
6. Low levels of intergroup conflict.

I submit that while few, if any, organizations have achieved these features, it should be the model for organizations in the 1990s and beyond.

Creating the Multicultural Organization

As I have discussed issues of managing diversity with senior managers from various industries during the past year, I have observed that their philosophical viewpoints cover all three of the organizational models of Exhibit 2. The few who are holding on to the monolithic model often cite geographic or size factors as isolating their organizations from the pressures of change.

Some even maintain that because American white males will continue to be the single largest gender/race identity group in the U.S. workforce for many years, the monolithic organization is still viable today. I think this view is misguided. By understanding the generic implications of managing diversity (that is, skill at managing work groups which include members who are culturally distinct from the organization's dominant group), it becomes clear that virtually all organizations need to improve capabilities to manage diverse workforces.

Further, focusing too much attention on external pressures as impetus for change, misses the fact that gross underutilization of human resources and failure to capitalize on the opportunities of workforce diversity, represent unaffordable economic costs.

Fortunately, the monolithic defenders, at least among middle and senior managers, seem to represent a minority view. Based on my observations, the majority of managers today are in plural organizations, and many are already convinced that the multicultural model is the way of the future. What these managers want to know is how to transform the plural organization into the multicultural organization. Although progress on such transformations is at an early stage, information on the tools that have been successfully used by pioneering American organizations to make this transformation is beginning to accumulate.

Exhibit 3 provides a list of tools that organizations have used to promote organization change toward a multicultural organization. The exhibit is organized to illustrate my analysis of which tools are most helpful for each of the six dimensions specified in Exhibit 1.

Creating Pluralism

Exhibit 3 identifies seven specific tools for changing organizational acculturation from a unilateral process to a reciprocal one in which both minority-culture and majority-culture members are influential in creating the behavioral norms, values, and policies of the organization. Examples of each tool are given on the following page.

EXHIBIT 3 Creating the Multicultural Organization: Tools for Organization Change

Model Dimension	Tools
I. Pluralism *Objective/s:* – create a two-way socialization process – ensure influence of minority culture perspectives on core organization norms and values	1. Managing/valuing diversity (MVD) training 2. New member orientation programs 3. Language training 4. Diversity in key committees 5. Explicit treatment of diversity in mission statements 6. Advisory groups to senior management 7. Create flexibility in norm systems
II. Full Structural Integration *Objective/s* – no correlation between culture-group identity and job status	1. Education programs 2. Affirmative action programs 3. Targeted career development programs 4. Changes in manager performance appraisal and reward systems 5. HR policy and benefit changes
III. Integration in Informal Networks *Objective/s* – eliminate barriers to entry and participation	1. Mentoring programs 2. Company sponsored social events
IV. Cultural Bias *Objective/s* – eliminate discrimination – eliminate prejudice	1. Equal opportunity seminars 2. Focus groups 3. Bias reduction training 4. Research 5. Task forces
V. Organizational Identification – no correlation between identity group and levels of organization identification	1. All items from the other five dimensions apply here
VI. Intergroup Conflict *Objective/s* – minimize interpersonal conflict based on group-identity – minimize backlash by dominant-group members	1. Survey feedback 2. Conflict management training 3. MVD training 4. Focus groups

Training and orientation programs. The most widely used tool among leading organizations is managing or valuing cultural diversity training. Two types of training are most popular: awareness and skill-building. The former introduces the topic of managing diversity and generally includes information on workforce demographics, the meaning of diversity, and exercises to get participants thinking about relevant issues and raising their own self-awareness. The skill-building training provides more specific information on cultural norms of different groups and how they may affect work behavior. Often, these two types of training are combined. Such training promotes reciprocal learning and acceptance between groups by improving understanding of the cultural mix in the organization.

Among the many companies who have made extensive use of such training are McDonnell Douglas, Hewlett-Packard, and Ortho Pharmaceuticals. McDonnell Douglas has a program ("Woman-Wise and Business Savvy") focusing on gender differences in work-related behaviors. It uses same-gender group meetings and mixed-gender role-plays. At its manufacturing plant in San Diego, Hewlett-Packard conducted training on cultural differences between American-Anglos and Mexican, Indochinese, and Filipinos. Much of the content focused on cultural differences in communication styles. In one of the most thorough training efforts to date, Ortho Pharmaceuticals started its three-day training with small groups (10 to 12) of senior managers and eventually trained managers at every level of the company.

Specific data on the effectiveness of these training efforts is hard to collect, but a study of 75 Canadian consultants found that people exposed to even the most rudimentary form of training on cultural diversity are significantly more likely to recognize the impact of cultural diversity on work behavior and to identify the potential advantages of cultural heterogeneity in organizations.[10]

In addition, anecdotal evidence from managers of many companies indicates that valuing and managing diversity training represents a crucial first step for organization change efforts.

New member orientation programs are basic in the hiring processes of many organizations. Some companies are developing special orientations as part of its managing diversity initiatives. Procter and Gamble's "On Boarding" program, which features special components for women and minority hires and their managers is one example.

Language training is important for companies hiring American Asians, Hispanics, and foreign nationals. To promote pluralism, it is helpful to offer second language training to Anglos as well as the minority-culture employees, and take other steps to communicate that languages other than English are valued. Leaders in this area include Esprit De Corp, Economy Color Card, and Pace Foods. For many years, the women's clothier Esprit De Corp has offered courses in Italian and Japanese. At Economy Color Card, work rules are printed in both Spanish and English. Pace Foods, where 35 percent of employees are Hispanic, goes a step farther by printing company policies and also conducting staff meetings in Spanish and English. Motorola is a leader in the more traditional training for English as a second language where classes are conducted at company expense and on company time.

Insuring minority-group input and acceptance. The most direct and effective way to promote influence of minority-culture norms on organizational decision making is to achieve cultural diversity at all organization levels. However, an important supplemental method is through ensuring diversity on key committees. An example is the insistence of *USA Today* President Nancy Woodhull on having gender, racioethnic, educational, and geographic diversity represented in all daily news meetings. She attributes much of the company's success to this action.

Another technique is explicitly mentioning the importance of diversity to the organization in statements of mission and strategy. By doing this, organizations foster the mind-set that increased diversity is an opportunity and not a problem. Examples of organizations that have done this are the University of Michigan and the Careers Division of the National Academy of Management. The latter group has fostered research addressing the impact of diversity on organizations by explicitly citing this as part of its interest.

Another way to increase the influence of minority-group members on organizational culture and policy is by providing specially composed minority advisory groups direct access to the most senior executives of the company. Organizations which have done this include Avon, Equitable Life Assurance, Intel, and U.S. West. At Equitable, committees of women, blacks, and Hispanics (called "Business Resource Groups") meet with the CEO to discuss important group issues and make recommendations on how the organizational environment might be improved. CEO John Carver often assigns a senior manager to be accountable for following up on the recommendations. U.S. West has a 33 member "Pluralism Council" which advises senior management on plans for improving the company's response to increased workforce diversity.

Finally, a more complex, but I believe potentially powerful, tool for promoting change toward pluralism is the development of flexible, highly tolerant climates that encourage diverse approaches to problems among all employees. Such an environment is useful to workers regardless of group identity, but is especially beneficial to people from nontraditional cultural backgrounds because their approaches to problems are more likely to be different from past norms. A company often cited for such a work environment is Hewlett-Packard. Among the operating norms of the company which should promote pluralism are: (1) encouragement of informality and unstructured work; (2) flexible work schedules and loose supervision; (3) setting objectives in broad terms with lots of individual employee discretion over how they are achieved; (4) a policy that researchers should spend at least 10 percent of company time exploring personal ideas. I would suggest that item four be extended to all management and professional employees.

Creating Full Structural Integration

Education efforts. The objective of creating an organization where there is no correlation between one's culture-identity group and one's job status implies that minority-group members are well represented at all levels, in all functions, and in all work groups. Achievement of this goal requires that skill and education levels be evenly distributed. Education statistics indicate that the most serious problems occur with blacks and Hispanics.[11]

A number of organizations have become more actively involved in various kinds of education programs. The Aetna Life Insurance Company is a leader. It has initiated a number of programs including jobs in exchange for customized education taught by community agencies and private schools, and its own in-house basic education programs. The company has created an Institute for Corporate Education with a full-time director. Other companies participating in various new education initiatives include PrimAmerica, Quaker Oats, Chase Manhattan Bank, Eastman Kodak, and Digital Equipment. In Minnesota, a project headed by Cray Research and General Mills allows businesses to create schools of its own design. I believe that business community involvement in joint efforts with educational institutions and community leaders to promote equal achievement in education is critical to the future competitiveness of U.S. business. Business leaders should insist that economic support be tied to substantive programs which are jointly planned and evaluated by corporate representatives and educators.

Affirmative action. In my opinion, the mainstay of efforts to create full structural integration in the foreseeable future, will continue to be affirmative action programs. While most large organizations have some kind of program already, the efforts of Xerox and Pepsico are among the standouts.

The Xerox effort, called "The Balanced Workforce Strategy," is noteworthy for several reasons including: an especially fast timetable for moving minorities up; tracking representation by function and operating unit as well as by level; and national networks for minority-group members (supported by the company) to provide various types of career support. Recently published data indicating that Xerox is well ahead of both national and industry averages in moving minorities into management and professional jobs, suggests that these efforts have paid off (*Wall Street Journal,* November 5, 1989).

Two features of Pepsico's efforts which are somewhat unusual are the use of a "Black Managers Association" as a supplemental source of nominees for promotion to management jobs, and the practice of hiring qualified minorities directly into managerial and professional jobs.

Career development. A number of companies including Mobil Oil, IBM, and McDonald's have also initiated special career development efforts for minority personnel. IBM's long-standing "Executive Resource System" is designed to identify and develop minority talent for senior management positions. McDonald's "Black Career Development Program" provides career enhancement advice, and fast-track career paths for minorities. Company officials have stated that the program potentially cuts a 15 year career path to regional manager by 50 percent.

Revamping reward systems. An absolutely essential tool for creating structural integration is to ensure that the organization's performance appraisal and reward systems reinforce the importance of effective diversity management. Companies that have taken steps in this direction include the Federal National Mortgage Association (Fannie Mae), Baxter Health Care, Amtrak, Exxon, Coca-Cola, and Merck. Fannie Mae, Baxter, Coca-Cola, and Merck all tie compensation to manager performance on diversity management efforts. At Amtrak, manager promotion and compensation are tied to performance on affirmative action objectives, and at Exxon, evaluations of division managers must include a review of career development plans for at least ten women and minority men employees.

For this tool to be effective, it needs to go beyond simply including effective management of diversity among the evaluation and reward criteria. Attention must also be given to the amount of weight given to this criterion compared to other dimensions of job performance. How performance is measured is also important. For example, in addition to work-group profile statistics, subordinate evaluations of managers might be useful. When coded by cultural group, differences in perceptions based on group identity can be noted and used in forming performance ratings on this dimension.

Benefits and work schedules. Structural integration of women, Hispanics, and blacks is facilitated by changes in human resource policies and benefit plans that make it easier for employees to balance work and family role demands. Many companies have made such changes in areas like child care, work schedules, and parental leave. North Carolina National Bank, Arthur Andersen, Levi Strauss, and IBM are examples of companies that have gone farther than most. NCNB's "select time" project allows even officers and professionals in the company to work part-time for several years and still be considered for advancement. Arthur Anderson has taken a similar step by allowing part-time accountants to stay "on-track" for partnership promotions. Levi Strauss has one of the most comprehensive work–family programs in the country covering everything from paternity leave to part-time work with preservation of benefits. These companies are leaders in this area because attention is paid to the impact on advancement opportunities and fringe-benefits when employees take advantage of scheduling flexibility and longer leaves of absence. This kind of accommodation will make it easier to hire and retain both men and women in the '90s as parents struggle to balance work and home time demands. It is especially important for women, Hispanics, and blacks because cultural traditions put great emphasis on family responsibilities. Organization change in this area will promote full structural integration by keeping more racioethnic minorities and white women in the pipeline.

Creating Integration in Informal Networks

Mentoring and social events. One tool for including minorities in the informal networks of organizations is company-initiated mentoring programs that target minorities. A recent research project in which a colleague and I surveyed 800 MBAs indicated that racioethnic minorities report significantly less access to mentors than whites. If company-specific research shows a similar pattern, this data can be used to justify and bolster support among majority-group employees for targeted mentoring programs. Examples of companies which have established such targeted mentoring programs are Chemical Bank and General Foods.

A second technique for facilitating informal network integration is company-sponsored social events. In planning such events, multiculturalism is fostered by selecting both activities and locations with a sensitivity to the diversity of the workforce.

Support groups. In many companies, minority groups have formed their own professional associations and organizations to promote information exchange and social support. There is little question that these groups have provided emotional and career support for members who traditionally have not been welcomed in the majority's informal groups. A somewhat controversial issue is whether these groups hinder the objective of informal-network integration. Many believe that they harm integration by fostering a "we-versus-they" mentality and reducing incentives for minorities to seek inclusion in informal activities of majority-group members. Others deny these effects. I am not aware of any hard evidence on this point. There is a dilemma here in that integration in the informal networks is at best a long-term process and there is widespread skepticism among minorities as to its eventual achievement. Even if abolishing the minority-group associations would eventually promote full integration, the absence of a support network of any kind in the interim could be a devastating loss to minority-group members. Therefore, my conclusion is that these groups are more helpful than harmful to the overall multiculturalism effort.

Creating a bias-free organization. Equal opportunity seminars, focus groups, bias-reduction training, research, and task forces are methods that organizations have found useful in reducing culture-group bias and discrimination. Unlike prejudice, discrimination is a behavior and therefore more amenable to direct control or influence by the organization. At the same time, the underlying cause of discrimination is prejudice. Ideally, efforts should have at least indirect effects on the thought processes and attitudes of organization members. All of the tools listed, with the possible exception of task forces, should reduce prejudice as well as discrimination.

Most plural organizations have used equal opportunity seminars for many years. These include sexual harassment workshops, training on civil rights legislation, and workshops on sexism and racism.

Focus groups. More recently, organizations like Digital Equipment have used "focus groups" as an in-house, on-going mechanism to explicitly examine attitudes, beliefs, and feelings about culture-group differences and their effects on behavior at work. At Digital, the center piece of its "valuing differences" effort is the use of small groups (called Core Groups) to discuss four major objectives: (1) stripping away stereotypes; (2) examining underlying assumptions about outgroups; (3) building significant relationships with people one regards as different; (4) raising levels of personal empowerment. Digital's experience suggests that a breakthrough for many organizations will be achieved by the simple mechanism of bringing discussion about group differences out in the open. Progress is made as people become more comfortable directly dealing with the issues.

Bias-reduction training. Another technique for reducing bias is through training specifically designed to create attitude change. An example is Northern Telecom's 16-hour program designed to help employees identify and begin to modify negative attitudes toward people from different cultural backgrounds. Eastman Kodak's training conference for its recruiters is designed to eliminate racism and sexism from the hiring process. This type of training often features exercises that expose stereotypes of various groups which are prevalent but rarely made explicit and may be subconscious. Many academics and consultants have also developed bias-reduction training. An example is the "Race Relations Competence Workshop," a program developed by Clay Alderfer and Robert Tucker of Yale University. They have found that participants completing the workshop have more positive attitudes toward Blacks and inter-race relations.

Leveraging internal research. A very powerful tool for reducing discrimination and (to a smaller extent) prejudice, is to conduct and act on internal research on employment experience by cultural group. Time Inc. conducts an annual evaluation of men and women in the same jobs to ensure comparable pay and equal treatment. A second example comes from a large utility company which discovered that minority managers were consistently under-represented in lists submitted by line managers for bonus recommendations. As a result of the research, the company put pressure on the managers to increase the inclusion of minority managers. When that failed, the vice president of resources announced that he would no longer approve the recommendations unless minorities were adequately represented. The keys to the organization change were, first obtaining the data identifying the problem and then acting on it. My experience suggests that this type of research-based approach is underutilized by organizations.

Task forces. A final tool for creating bias-free organizations is to form task forces that monitor organizational policy and practices for evidence of unfairness. An example of what I consider to be a well-designed committee is the affirmative action committee used by Phillip Morris which is composed of senior managers and minority employees. This composition combines the power of senior executives with the insight into needed changes that the minority representatives can provide. Of course, minority culture-group members who are also senior managers are ideal but, unfortunately, such individuals are rare in most organizations.

Minimizing Intergroup Conflict

Experts on conflict management have noted that a certain amount of interpersonal conflict is inevitable and perhaps even healthy in organizations.[12] However, conflict becomes destructive when it is excessive, not well managed, or rooted in struggles for power rather than the differentiation of ideas. We are concerned here with these more destructive forms of conflict which may be present with diverse workforces due to language barriers, cultural clash, or resentment by majority-group members of what they may perceive as preferential, and unwarranted treatment of minority-group members.

Survey feedback. Probably the most effective tool for avoiding intergroup conflict (especially the backlash form that often accompanies new initiatives targeting minority groups of the organization) is the use of survey feedback. I will give three examples. As one of the most aggressive affirmative action companies of the past decade, Xerox has found that being very open with all employees about the specific features of the initiative as well the reasons for it, was helpful in diffusing backlash by whites. This strategy is exemplified by the high profile which Chairman David Kearns has taken on the company's diversity efforts.

A second example is Procter and Gamble's use of data on the average time needed for new hires of various culture groups to become fully integrated into the organization. They found that "join-up" time varied by race and gender with white males becoming acclimated most quickly, and black females taking the longest of any group. This research led to the development of their "onboarding program" referred to earlier.

A final example is Corning Glass Works' strategy of fighting white-male resistance to change with data showing that the promotion rate of their group was indeed much higher than that of other groups. This strategy has also been used by U.S. West which recently reported on a 1987 study showing that promotion rates for white men were 7 times higher than white women and 16 times higher than nonwhite women.

The beauty of this tool is that it provides the double benefit of a knowledge base for planning change, and leverage to win employee commitment to implement the needed changes.

Conflict-resolution training. A second tool for minimizing intergroup conflict is management training in conflict resolution techniques. Conflict management experts can assist managers in learning and developing skill in applying alternative conflict management techniques such as mediation and superordinate goals. This is a general management skill which is made more crucial by the greater diversity of workforces in the '90s.

Finally, the managing and valuing diversity training and focus group tools discussed previously are also applicable here. AT&T is among the organizations which have explicitly identified stress and conflict reduction as central objectives of its training and focus group efforts.

CONCLUSION

Increased diversity presents challenges to business leaders who must maximize the opportunities that it presents while minimizing its costs. To accomplish this, organizations must be transformed from monolithic or plural organizations to a multicultural model. The multicultural organization is characterized by pluralism, full integration of minority-culture members both formally and informally, an absence of prejudice and discrimination, and low levels of intergroup conflict; all of which should reduce alienation and build organizational identity among minority group members. The organization that achieves these conditions will create an environment in which all members can contribute to their maximum potential, and in which the "value in diversity" can be fully realized.

NOTES

1. See, for example, Lennie Copeland, "Valuing Workplace Diversity," *Personnel Administrator,* November 1988; Badi Foster et al., "Workforce Diversity and Business," *Training And Development Journal,* April 1988, 38–42; and R. Roosevelt Thomas, "From Affirmative Action to Affirming Diversity," *Harvard Business Review,* Vol. 2, 1990, 107–17.
2. This definition has been suggested by Afsavch Nahavandi and Ali Malekzadeh, "Acculturation in Mergers and Acquisitions," *Academy of Management Review,* Vol. 13, 83.
3. In his book, *Assimilation in American Life* (New York; Oxford University Press, 1964), Gordon uses the term assimilation rather than integration. However, because the term assimilation has been defined in so many different ways, and has come to have very unfavorable connotations in recent years for many minorities, I will employ the term integration here.
4. These definitions are loosely based on J. W. Berry, "Acculturation: A Comparative Analysis of Alternative Forms," in R. J. Samuda and S. L. Woods, *Perspectives in Immigrant and Minority Education,* 1983, 66–77.
5. This conclusion is based on data from nearly 100 large organizations as cited in "Best Places for Blacks to Work," *Black Enterprise,* February 1986 and February 1989, and in Zeitz and Dusky, *Best Companies for Women,* 1988.
6. Examples of this research include: Harry Triandis, "Some Determinants of Interpersonal Communication," *Human Relations,* Vol. 13, 1960, 279–87 and J. R. Lincoln and J. Miller, "Work and Friendship Ties in Organizations," *Administrative Science Quarterly,* Vol. 24, 1979, 181–99.
7. The concept of stages of development toward the multicultural organization has been suggested in an unpublished paper titled "Toward the Multicultural Organization" written by Dan Reigle and Jarrow Merenivitch of the Procter and Gamble Company. I credit them with helping me to recognize the evolutionary nature of organizational responses to workforce diversity.
8. See note 5.
9. A. L. Sales and P. H. Mirvis. "When Cultures Collide: Issues of Acquisitions," in J. R. Kimberly and R. E. Quinn, *Managing Organizational Transition,* 1984, 107–33.
10. For details on this study see Nancy J. Adler, *International Dimensions of Organizational Behavior* (Kent Publishing Co., 1986), 77–83.
11. For example, see the book by William Julius Wilson which reviews data on educational achievement by Blacks and Hispanics in Chicago: *The Truly Disadvantaged: Inner City, the Underclass and Public Policy* (University of Chicago Press, 1987). Among the facts cited is that less than half of all Blacks and Hispanics in inner city schools graduate within four years of high school enrollment and only four in ten of those who do graduate read at the eleventh grade level or above.
12. For example, see Gregory Northcraft and Margaret Neale, *Organization Behavior: Conflict in Organizations* (The Dryden Press, 1990), 221.

Part 2/Reading 3

Building an Effective Global Business Team

Vijay Govindarajan and Anil K. Gupta

Every global company's competitive advantage depends on its ability to coordinate critical resources and information that are spread across different geographical locations. Today there are myriad organizational mechanisms that global corporations can use to integrate dispersed operations. But the most effective tool is the global business team: a cross-border team of individuals of different nationalities, working in different cultures, businesses, and functions, who come together to coordinate some aspect of the multinational operation on a global basis.

It is virtually impossible for a multinational corporation to exploit economies of global scale and scope, maximize the transfer of knowledge or cultivate a global mind-set without understanding and mastering the management of global business teams. That, however, is easier said than done. In our study of 70 such teams, we discovered that only 18 percent considered their performance "highly successful" and the remaining 82 percent fell short of their intended goals. In fact, fully one-third of the teams in our sample rated their performance as largely unsuccessful.[1] How can companies reverse the weak performance of faltering global business teams? First, they must understand the obstacles to success that global business teams confront. Then they can take concrete steps to avoid those pitfalls and build effective and efficient teams.

WHY GLOBAL BUSINESS TEAMS FAIL

Domestic teams and global teams are plagued by many of the same problems—misalignment of individual team members' goals, a dearth of the necessary knowledge and skills, and lack of clarity regarding team objectives, to name a few. But global business teams face additional challenges resulting from differences in geography, language, and culture. Teams can fail when they are unable to cultivate trust among their members or when they cannot break down often-formidable communication barriers. The results of our survey of 58 senior executives from five U.S. and four European multinational organizations confirm that important, unique challenges confront global business teams—challenges that tend to exacerbate the more common problems all teams face. (See Exhibit 1.)

The Inability To Cultivate Trust Among Team Members

Trust is critical to the success of global business teams in that it encourages cooperation and minimizes unproductive conflict.[2] Each member of a global business team brings a unique cognitive lens to the group. If harnessed effectively, the resulting diversity can yield significant synergies and produce a collective wisdom superior to that of any individual. Without mutual trust, however, team members may shy away from revealing their true beliefs; or if they do express their viewpoints, they may not be "heard." In one way or another, the absence of trust is likely to turn a team's diversity into a liability rather than an asset.

Global business teams are particularly prone to problems of trust. Among the many factors that determine how much trust people feel, three important ones are individual characteristics, quality of communication and the broader institutional context. More specifically, research shows that, on average, people trust one another more when they share similarities, communicate frequently and operate in a common cultural context that imposes tough sanctions for behaving in an untrustworthy manner.[3] Global business teams, by their very

Source: *MIT Sloan Management Review,* Summer 2001, pp. 63–71.

EXHIBIT 1 The Challenge of Managing Global Business Teams

We asked 58 senior executives to rank the importance of the following tasks as indicators of the effectiveness of global business teams and to rank how difficult it is to accomplish each task.

Importance of task*	Task	Ease or Difficulty of Accomplishing Task†
6.52	Cultivating trust among team members	6.06
6.35	Overcoming communication barriers	5.56
6.04	Aligning goals of individual team members	5.44
5.62	Ensuring that the team possesses necessary knowledge and skills	4.66
6.05	Obtaining clarity regarding team objectives	4.61

*Ranking is based on a 1–7 scale, where 1 = "not at all important" and 7 = "very important."
†Ranking is based on a 1–7 scale, where 1 = "very easy" and 7 = "very difficult."

nature, suffer from severe limitations on all three dimensions. Not surprisingly, when global business teams fail, it is often because the team process did not emphasize cultivating trust.

Hindrances to Communication

Communication barriers resulting from differences in geography, language and culture also can sabotage global business teams.

Geographical Barriers

With members living in different countries, separated by time zones and conflicting schedules, arranging team meetings can pose logistical challenges. Undoubtedly, technology (e-mail, teleconferencing, and videoconferencing) can enable members to work together despite geographical distance; but technology should be viewed as a complement to, not as a substitute for, team meetings. Face-to-face meetings foster familiarity and trust—not easily established through virtual meetings. When members cannot see one another's body language and directly experience one another's reactions, the emotional dimension critical to a team's success suffers. Moreover, certain types of deliberations demand face-to-face meetings. Brainstorming, for instance, requires unstructured free-form interaction over an extended period that is not suited to a virtual meeting.

Language Barriers

The inability to understand what another person is saying is always a potential barrier to communication in cross-cultural settings. If language barriers are not adequately addressed, the likelihood of creating an atmosphere conducive to candid sharing of different viewpoints—and hence conducive to achieving creative solutions—is greatly diminished.

One extreme example would be a team whose members all speak different languages and have poor facility in a common language. Such a team would undoubtedly require interpreters, who, regardless of their skill, may not capture the full richness of the communication. Even in the case of global teams whose members speak the same language, differences in semantics, accents, tone, pitch, and dialects can be impediments. For example, whereas the term *table a motion* means to postpone discussion in the United States, in the United Kingdom it means to discuss the issue right away.

Cultural Barriers

Members of global business teams typically come from diverse cultures and, as a result, may bring different values, norms, assumptions, and patterns of behavior to the group.

Consider, for example, differences between "individualistic" and "collectivistic" cultural norms for decision making.[4] The need for consensus deemed critical in collectivistic cultures is a relatively low priority in individualistic cultures. What if some team members come from highly individualistic cultures (such as the United States and Britain) and others from highly collectivistic cultures (such as Japan and Venezuela)? Unless the differences in assumptions and beliefs inherent in that diversity are explicitly addressed, the cohesiveness of the group is likely to suffer and impede effectiveness.

DEFINING THE TEAM CHARTER

In order to overcome the unique challenges confronting global business teams and create a high-performing, effective unit, executives must carefully craft the team's charter, composition and process. All three areas demand equal attention (see Exhibit 2). A clear charter without the appropriate mix of team members leads to failure. Similarly, when a team's composition is sound but its process is not, effectiveness suffers. In short, the three work as a system to determine overall team effectiveness.

Given the communication problems and trust issues that plague global business teams, structuring the team charter is particularly critical to success. Three primary questions need attention: Is the charter defined correctly? Is it framed correctly? And is it clearly understood?

Is the Charter Defined Correctly?

One of the first concerns for any global business team must be to explicitly discuss the team's agenda and ensure that it is defined clearly and correctly. Many teams doom themselves from the start because they skip that step or do not fully resolve the issues involved.

In 1995, a certain European manufacturer of industrial components set up a global-customer-account team to coordinate the company's marketing, sales, and service offerings to one of its largest customers. At the team's first meeting, members identified three possible objectives: to help the customer move toward coordinated global sourcing at a faster pace, to offer the customer global volume discounts (and thus, lower prices), and to offer a more attractive bundle of products and services based on a better, more comprehensive understanding of the customer's global needs than its individual buying locations might have. After considerable discussion, the team decided against the first two alternatives and embraced the third. The third alternative was seen as the most appropriate because it accomplished several key corporate objectives simultaneously: It eliminated internal price competition across plants, thus boosting gross margins; it made the company's product and service offerings more comprehensive; and it dramatically enhanced the company's ability to respond appropriately to a customer's moves toward coordinated global sourcing.

Is the Charter Framed Correctly?

Ensuring that the charter is framed correctly is a more subtle challenge. By framing, we mean the way an idea is expressed or a problem is formulated. Issues can be framed in multiple ways, and different framing of the same problem can produce different outcomes.[5]

Because global teams have members from different subsidiaries that typically compete with one

EXHIBIT 2
A Framework for High-Performing Global Business Teams

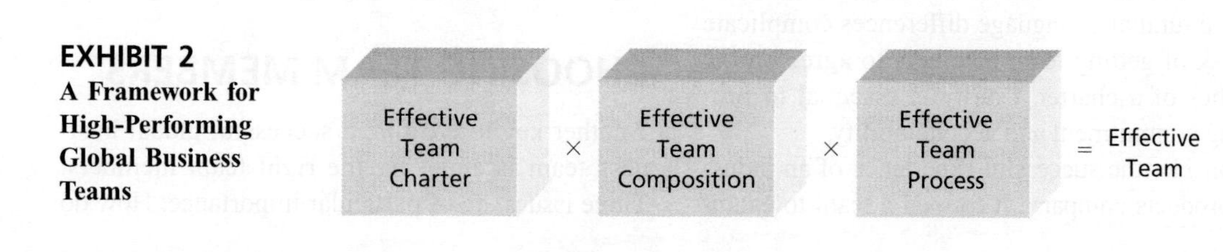

another for scarce corporate resources, they tend to have a high degree of internal conflict—in addition to a low level of trust. As a result, it is generally best to frame the team's charter in terms of the company's position vis-à-vis the external marketplace instead of emphasizing internal dynamics.

For example, in the mid-1990s, senior executives of a consumer-products company assembled a global manufacturing team to rationalize the company's production network. Given the objective, there were at least two ways of framing the team's charter. Consider this option: "The team's charter is to cut costs by reducing the number of factories in our worldwide network from 15 to 9 and by downsizing the work force." Compare it with the following: "We want to be the clear industry leader in terms of creating customer and shareholder value. This goal requires that we be world-class in manufacturing, better than our best-in-class competitor in terms of cost, quality, and service. Given these targets, the team's charter is to propose the optimal network of factories for our business." The second option is by far the preferable charter. Its broad, external focus encourages benchmarking, fosters creativity, and provides a compelling rationale for making the tough decisions inherent in any manufacturing rationalization and work-force reduction.

Is the Charter Clearly Understood?

When teams have frequent face-to-face meetings, they are able to iron out ambiguities in the team charter. If they meet less often, the charter has to be crystal clear so that tasks can be delegated effectively. Given the communication problems inherent in global business teams, it is imperative that members understand the specifics of the charter: in particular, the scope of the project, the expected deliverables, and the timeline. Understandably, cultural and language differences complicate the task of getting team members to agree on the specifics of a charter. Clarity is essential to promoting commitment and accountability.

Consider the successful experience of an industrial-products company. It formed a team to examine the organizational design of its global businesses. Several meetings were arranged between the internal sponsor and the team members to ensure that the team charter was clearly understood. The scope of the project included: an analysis of the current organizational design across the company's five growth-platform businesses (part of the diagnostic challenge was to determine whether a single organizational design made sense across all five); external benchmarking of world-class global organizations, with attention to the latest research on the best approaches; and recommendations, with development of the business case, for an organizational design that would optimize global growth potential across the five businesses including ways to capture potential synergies in areas such as research and development, information technology, human resources, and the supply chain).

The project also was intended to be a personal learning experience that could help the team members become experts on organizational design and understand the many facets of globalization within the company's businesses. Furthermore, the team members were explicitly told *not* to work on nongrowth business units or subsidiaries or to reformulate the global strategies of the five businesses.

Two deliverables were expected from the team: a set of recommendations on the optimal worldwide organizational design for the five major growth-platform businesses and a presentation of the team's key findings, including a process or a methodology for tackling potential global-organizational issues.

The specificity of the objectives, project scope, and deliverables, along with the time spent at the start of the project getting the team members to internalize and accept the charter, helped the team stay on course and make progress.

CHOOSING TEAM MEMBERS

Another key to creating a successful global business team is choosing the right team members. Three issues are of particular importance: How do you balance diversity within the team? How big—or small—should the team be? And who should occupy positions of leadership?

The Question of Diversity

There are at least three reasons why global business teams have high levels of diversity. First, members come from diverse cultural and national backgrounds. Second, team members generally represent subsidiaries whose agendas may not be congruent. Third, because team members often represent different functional units, their priorities and perspectives may differ. Is the high level of diversity a necessary evil that must be curbed or a source of strength that should be cultivated? The answer depends on whether the type of diversity is cognitive or behavioral.

Cognitive diversity refers to differences in the substantive content of how members perceive the team's challenges and opportunities, options to be evaluated, and optimal course of action. Diversity of nationality can account for substantive differences on issues such as whether the free Internet-service model pioneered in the United Kingdom can be transferred to other countries. Diversity in subsidiaries' histories and charters can account for substantive differences on issues such as whether Singapore, Hong Kong, or Tokyo is the optimal location for a company's Asian headquarters. Diversity in functional backgrounds can account for substantive differences on issues such as the relative importance of "market pull" and "technology push" in a company's new-product-development efforts. Because no single team member ever can have a monopoly on wisdom, cognitive diversity is almost always a source of strength. Divergent perspectives foster creativity and a more comprehensive search for and assessment of options. But the team must be able to integrate the perspectives and come to a single solution.

Behavioral diversity, by contrast, refers to differences in language as well as culture-driven norms of behavior. Consider, for example, a cross-border business team in a Franco-American company. The norm in most U.S. teams is that the most senior member presents the team's perspective, but in a French team, the most junior member typically does so. Unless the members of the Franco-American team are sensitized to such differences, misunderstandings easily can emerge and block or distort communication. Behavioral diversity is best regarded as a necessary evil: something that no global business team can avoid but the effects of which the team must attempt to minimize through language training and cultural sensitization.

The Ideal Team Size

The optimal size of a global business team is one that can ensure the required knowledge and skill base with the smallest number of people.

Deciding on team size is never easy. On one hand, representing every required knowledge and skill calls for a large team. On the other hand, very large teams become cumbersome and dysfunctional, making it difficult to foster broad participation, bring out diverse viewpoints or get the unity needed for meaningful action.[6] An effective solution is to establish a core team and supplement it as needed. Membership in the core team would be limited to a relatively manageable number—say, 10 people or fewer. Then, if the core team requires input from others, those individuals could be brought in on an ad hoc basis. Thus, the extended team could include all relevant stakeholders both within the organization and outside. If for some reason, the core team itself has to be large, then it is best to break it into subteams, each assigned to tackle specific aspects of the overall team's objectives.

The Selection of Team Leadership

Structuring the leadership of a global business team involves critical decisions about three roles: the team leader, the external coach, and the internal sponsor.

Choosing an Effective Team Leader

Despite an increasing emphasis on team self-management, the leader plays a pivotal role in cross-border teams. Effective leaders must manage the organizational, linguistic, cultural, and physical distances that separate members, create severe

EXHIBIT 3 When Do Global Business Teams Need a Coach?

An external coach is nedded when the process-management task is complex.

For example, when:

- A global business team (GBT) consists only of part-time and ad hoc members.
- A GBT consists of members from different organizational levels.
- Members' cultural backgrounds are significantly diverse.
- Team members are GBT novices.
- Team members' initial perspectives are strongly held and in conflict.
- Radical change is required.
- A GBT is formed for a single project.

...and when very high levels of process-management skills are needed

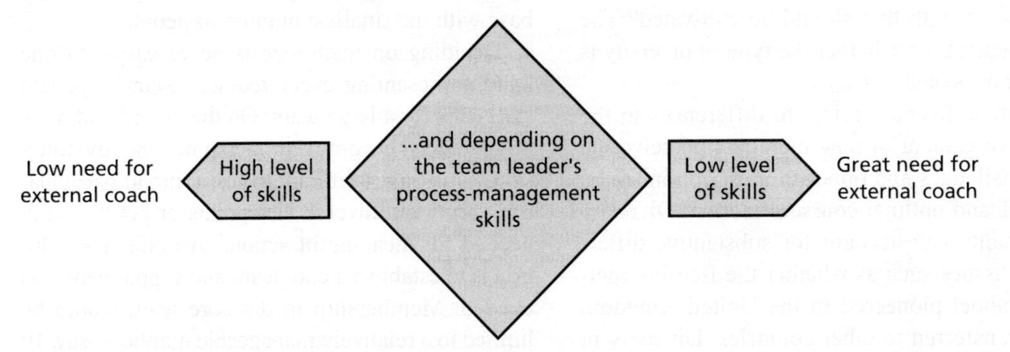

communication barriers, impede the development of trust, and contribute to the misalignment of members' goals. They are likely to be those with the biggest stake in the outcome of the project. Other important qualities: credibility resulting from a proven track record; conflict-resolution and integration skills; and expertise in process management, including diagnosing problems, assessing situations, and generating and evaluating options.

Determining the Need for an External Coach

An external coach serves as an ad hoc member of the team and is an expert in process rather than content. The more complex and challenging the process to be managed, the greater the need for and the value added by an external coach. A global business team will find using an external coach beneficial under certain conditions. (See Exhibit 3.) The need for such a coach is likely to be particularly high when the process-management task is complex and the process-management skills of the best available team leader are inadequate. Consider a global financial-services firm that set up a cross-border task force to rationalize the number of its offices spread across three continents. The appointed leader, a team member with a major stake in the project's outcome, turned out to be rigid, inflexible, and overbearing. Alternative views were stifled. The team was able to make progress only when an external coach was brought in.

Selecting a GBT Sponsor

The sponsor of a GBT is typically a senior-level executive in the company who has a strong interest in the success of the team. The sponsor who performs the role well indirectly encourages open and candid conversations among team members drawn from different countries and cultures. Among the responsibilities of the sponsor are to: clarify and interpret the charter; clarify performance expectations and deliverables; provide ongoing guidelines, input, and support; facilitate access to resources; manage political roadblocks on behalf of the team; be an intellectual sounding board on content; review team progress; and hold the team accountable.

MANAGING TEAM PROCESS

Having a clearly and correctly defined charter and an optimally constituted membership is merely the foundation of an effective global business team. Without skillfully managing process, the team is more than likely to fail in accomplishing its objectives. The primary goals of an effective team process are to facilitate open and rich communication among the team members and to cultivate a culture of trust.

Overcoming Communication Barriers

Several process mechanisms can be used to overcome the communication barriers that plague global business teams.

Language and Culture

In order to overcome the barriers to communication created by the linguistic and cultural divides separating members of the typical global business team, companies need to invest in language education and cross-cultural training. Language training reduces the need for third-party mediators such as translators and thus fosters more direct, spontaneous, and free-form communication. The ABB Group provides a good example of how even a bit of progress on linguistic skills can go a long way toward reducing communication barriers. Goran Lindahl, ABB's former CEO, was explicit in referring to his company's official language as "poor English" to drive home the point that no one should be embarrassed to express an idea because of a lack of perfection in English.

Investments in cross-cultural skills also help global business team members. A better understanding of team members' different cultures can improve richness of communication: People pick up the signals in verbal and nonverbal communications more comprehensively and accurately. Investment in cross-cultural skills also can improve team members' ability to understand and respect diversity and turn it into a competitive advantage.

Agreeing on Norms of Behavior

Establishing ground rules that reflect desired norms of behavior can serve as a powerful self-policing mechanism to overcome communication barriers, enrich the content of team discussions, and keep the team operating as an integrated whole.

A global-customer-account-management team created by a European industrial-packaging company illustrates how agreeing on certain ground rules can facilitate a team's smooth functioning. The team established two ground rules: First, whenever a member of the account team had any meeting with the customer, that member would send a briefing to every other member of the team; second, the customer's primary contact would be with one or more of the members of the global account team, with no other employee authorized to discuss or decide policy or strategy issues with the customer. The ground rules proved especially useful when the customer tested the relationship. Occasionally, the customer would contact employees other than those on the account team, but the employees would always refer them to someone on the team. When the customer would contact different members on the account team about issues such as prices and delivery times, the ground rules ensured that the customer always got the same answer from every member.

Adopting Data-Driven Decisions

In the absence of facts, people often resort to opinions. As everyone knows, discussions based largely on opinion can degenerate into personal attacks. By contrast, if opinions are accompanied by factual data, conflicting ideas can be evaluated more objectively. Fact-based discussions encourage team members to be more forthcoming in sharing their viewpoints, even if their views are at odds with the prevailing wisdom.[7]

For instance, a certain global consumer-products company formed a cross-border team to recommend ways to improve the profitability of one of its global businesses. The team, with the help of a consulting firm, assembled a detailed base of facts, including fundamental shifts in the industry, competitors' moves, and the company's current positioning. The concrete data helped elevate the team's level of discourse. Instead of denying problems, shifting the blame to uncontrollable external factors, or focusing on individual personalities, the team was able to brainstorm and come to terms with the critical vulnerabilities in the company's competitive positioning. A clear agreement emerged that the vulnerabilities required immediate, decisive, and visible action.

Developing Alternatives to Enrich the Debate

Surfacing alternatives is often useful in ensuring the expression of diverse views within a global business team. Two well-recognized formal mechanisms—*dialectical inquiry* and *devil's advocate*—are aimed at uncovering alternatives.[8] In a dialectical inquiry, for every potential solution, the team is instructed to develop a full-fledged counterapproach based on different assumptions; then a debate ensues on the merits of the plan and the counterplan. In the devil's-advocate approach the team critiques a potential solution (but doesn't necessarily develop a full-blown counter-approach). Both methods can benefit the process and the outcome of team discussions by giving creative license to members to express different views.[9]

The team established by the industrial-products company described earlier explicitly sought multiple alternatives to draw out its members' intellectual diversity. For each of the company's five major global businesses, the team collectively generated three distinct organizational forms and assigned subteams to develop the best arguments for each form. The resulting recommendations reflected the comprehensive discussions that followed each subteam's presentation of its approach to solving the problem.

Rotating Meeting Locations

Rotating the location of team meetings to different parts of the world is yet another mechanism to enrich the cognitive base of the team and also legitimize the expression of divergent viewpoints. VeriFone, a market leader in the automation and delivery of secure payment and payment-related transactions, uses that approach to keep its top management team informed about the global environment. The team, consisting of the CEO and his direct reports, meets for five days every six weeks at different locations around the globe.[10]

Cultivating a Culture of Trust

Just as process mechanisms can help global companies break down barriers to communication, so too can they help organizations cultivate trust among team members.

Scheduling Face-to-Face Meetings

Face-to-face interaction is the richest form of communication. It can help develop the solid social foundation and mutual trust that distance technologies can build on later. It is critical that the first few meetings of a global business team occur face to face.

In our interviews, the CEO of a global consumer-products company underscored the importance of early face-to-face meetings in cultivating trust: "There is an enormous premium on good, clean, nonbureaucratic communication, and that depends enormously on a high level of trust. That's why at the start of the team process, you have to be together personally. You can't start them with memos or telephone calls or things like that. You've got to get the group together to know each other and get a level of comfort and trust with one another. After that you can resort to the phone calls and video conferences."

Rotating and Diffusing Team Leadership

By rotating and diffusing team leadership across countries, managers in several subsidiaries gain an appreciation for cross-border coordination and learn to iron out conflicts en route to achieving their objectives. Moreover, diffusion of team leadership creates mutual interdependencies across countries because a country manager typically will lead one global business team while acting as a contributing member in another. Mutual dependence does not eliminate all conflicts, but it minimizes politicking and the more destructive types of conflicts.

To quote John Pepper, chairman of Procter & Gamble: "We felt that if each subsidiary manager also led a team, they would come to understand the value and challenge of working on a regional basis. We set up a brand team on Lenor, another on Pampers, another on Pantene, and so on. We assigned different country managers to lead these. Really wanting to get everybody into the fire, so to speak, in experiencing it. What made the teams work was the mutual interdependency that grew."[11]

Linking Rewards to Team Performance

Linking rewards to team performance encourages members to resolve conflicts and reach effective solutions. Consider two scenarios. In the first, a subsidiary manager's incentive bonus is based solely on country-level performance, even though part of the manager's time is devoted to being a member of a global team. In the second scenario, the manager's bonus also is linked to attaining the team's goals. The motivation for the manager in the second scenario to behave in a distrustful manner is low because that would compromise his bonus. Such considerations lie at the heart of Procter & Gamble's policy to give explicit weight to both country and team performance in computing annual incentive payments to its country managers.[12]

Building Social Capital

At any given time, a global enterprise typically will have many teams working on different cross-border coordination issues. It therefore makes sense for the company to undertake corporatewide initiatives to create interpersonal familiarity and trust among key managers of different subsidiaries. Initiatives to build social capital could take many forms. For example, Unilever uses several approaches to building social networks among managers who hail from different countries—including merging together managers from different subsidiaries in executive-development programs and horizontally rotating managers across locations.

GLOBAL BUSINESS TEAMS CAN SUCCEED

Global business teams are abiquitous throughout multinational corporations. But managing them effectively and steering them toward their intended goals is not easy. Barriers to communication and to cultivating trust routinely sabotage the most well-intentioned team. By making the right choices for the team's charter, composition, and process, global teams can overcome the problems and efficiently achieve their ends.

A solid framework for designing high performing global business teams is essential. (See Exhibit 4.) When a team consists of members with distinct knowledge and skills, drawn from different subsidiaries in different countries, the potential for cognitive diversity is high. That can be a source of real competitive strength. But intellectual diversity almost always will bring with it some degree of interpersonal incompatibility and communication difficulty. Process mechanisms that recognize and anticipate such pitfalls—and integrate the best of individuals' ideas and contributions—are needed to help the team reconcile diverse perspectives and arrive at better, more creative and novel solutions.

ADDITIONAL RESOURCES

Readers interested in learning more about teams in general and global business teams in particular should note: D. Ancona and D. Caldwell's 1992 article, "Demography and Design: Predictors of New Product Team Performance," in *Organization Science;* K. Bantel and S. Jackson's 1989 "Top Management and Innovations in Banking" in *Strategic Management Journal;* J.R. Hackman and associates' 1990 book *Groups That Work and Groups That Don't,* from Jossey-Bass; D. Hambrick,

EXHIBIT 4
Effective Process for Global Business Teams

Configuration of the Global Business Team

	Low Cognitive Integration	High Cognitive Integration
High Cognitive Diversity	A fragmented team, unable to converge on a decision	An effective global business team
Low Cognitive Diversity	A team that cannot add value	A team with high-speed decision making but also high risk of poor-quality decisions

Management of Team Process

T. Cho and M.-J. Chen's "The Influence of Top Management Team Heterogeneity on Firms' Competitive Moves" from a 1996 *Administrative Science Quarterly;* L.H. Pelled, "Demographic Diversity, Conflict and Work Group Outcomes: An Intervening Process Theory," in a 1996 *Organization Science;* S. Finkelstein and D. Hambrick's 1996 Jossey-Bass book, *Strategic Leadership,* J.R. Katzenbach and D.K. Smith's 1993 article in *Harvard Business Review,* "The Discipline of Teams"; and P.C. Earley and E. Mosakowski's "Creating Hybrid Team Cultures: An Empirical Test of Transnational Team Functioning," published last year in *Academy of Management Journal.*

REFERENCES

1. To date, no empirical study has presented data on the effectiveness of global business teams. A broad treatment of the international dimensions of organizational behavior, however, suggests that, although cross-cultural teams are necessary, the challenge of managing diversity often renders them ineffective. See Nancy Adler, *International Dimensions of Organizational Behavior* (Boston: Kent Publishing, 1986), 99–118.
2. D.J. McAllister, "Affect- and Cognition-Based Trust as the Foundations for Interpersonal Cooperation in Organizations," *Academy of Management Journal* 38 (1995): 24–59.
3. R.M. Kramer and T.R. Tyler, eds., *Trust in Organizations: Frontiers of Theory and Research* (Thousand Oaks, California: Sage Publications, 1996).
4. G. Hofstede, "Motivation, Leadership and Organization: Do American Theories Apply Abroad?" *Organizational Dynamics* 9 (Summer 1980): 42–63. According to Hofstede, cultures can differ across four dimensions: *power distance,* the extent to which power is centralized; *individualism/collectivism,* the extent to which people view themselves as individuals as opposed to belonging to a larger entity; *uncertainty avoidance,* the difficulty people have in coping with uncertainty and ambiguity; and *masculinity/feminism,* the extent to which people value materialism as opposed to concern for others.

5. A. Tversky and D. Kahneman, "The Framing of Decisions and the Psychology of Choice," *Science* 211 (January 1981): 453–458.
6. K.G. Smith, K.A. Smith, J.D. Olian, D.P. O'Bannon, and J.A. Scully, "Top Management Team Demography and Process: The Role of Social Integration and Communication," *Administrative Science Quarterly* 17 (1994): 36–68.
7. K.M. Eisenhardt, J.L. Kahwajy, and L.J. Bourgeois, "How Management Teams Can Have a Good Fight," *Harvard Business Review* 17 (July–August 1997): 77–85.
8. Ibid.
9. M.N. Chaniu and H.J. Shapiro, "Dialectical and Devils' Advocate Problem Solving," *Asia Pacific Journal of Management* (May 1984): 159–168.
10. D.B. Stoppard, A. Donnellon, and R.I. Nolan, "Verifone," HBS case no. 9-398-030 (Boston: Harvard Business School Publishing Corp., 1993).
11. John Pepper, chairman of the board, Procter & Gamble: remarks to an MBA class at the Tuck School, Dartmouth College, May 1995.
12. Ibid.

Part 2/Case I

Joint Venture #1: The Corning-Vitro Divorce

Monterrey, Mexico—Seldom do either marriages or business alliances develop without crises. Still, when Corning and the giant Mexican glass manufacturer Vitro made a cross-border alliance two and a half years ago, it seemed a blessed union.

"Vitro and Corning share a customer-oriented philosophy and remarkably similar corporate cultures"—that was the enthusiastic toast offered at the time by Julio Escamez, a Vitro executive. Both companies had long histories of successful joint ventures, both were globally oriented, and both had founding families still at their centers.

In February, however, Corning handed back Vitro's $130 million dowry and called off the joint venture. "The cultures didn't match," said Francisco Chevez, an analyst with Smith Barney Shearson in New York. "It was a marriage made in hell."

The 25-month union was hurt by constant cultural clashes. Corning managers were sometimes left waiting for important decisions about marketing and sales because in the Mexican culture only top managers could make them and at Vitro those people were busy with other matters. Vitro's sales approach was less aggressive, the remnant of years in a closed economy, and this sometimes clashed with the pragmatic approach Corning had developed over decades of competition.

To varying degrees, such cultural issues have plagued many mergers and alliances with their roots in the North American Free Trade Agreement. "Mexico initially appears to be the United States except that people speak Spanish," said Harley Shaiken, a labor economist who often works in Mexico. "That's just not the case, which everyone finds out in the short term rather than the long term."

The trade pact may have created false expectations about how much like the United States Mexico has become. In discussing cultural differences, it's difficult not to slip into stereotypes about "mañana" Mexicans who move at a slower pace. But what the gap separating the two business cultures really amounts to is a different approach to work, reflected

Source: Anthony DePalma, "A Corning-Vitro Joint Venture Was a Case Study in Clashing Styles," *The New York Times,* June 26, 1994, p. F5.

in everything from scheduling to decision making to etiquette.

When Banc One of Columbus, Ohio, was contracted to assist Bancomer, one of Mexico's largest banks, in setting up a consumer credit card operation, it found that cultural differences made working difficult because simple things like scheduling meetings became ballets of clashing customs. The Americans were used to eating lunch at their desks, but in Mexico City, bankers go out, often for hours, for leisurely meals. The solution: full lunch in the company dining rooms.

There was also a problem with schedules because Mexicans, with their long lunches, typically have a much longer workday, starting at 9 and often lasting until 9 at night. So Bancomer executives wanted to hold 7:30 p.m. meetings, and even then were often late, but Banc One advisers wanted to be home by that time. The solution: meetings could be held into the evening, but a piggy bank was placed on the center of the table and anyone arriving late had to pay a few pesos per minute. In the Corning venture, the Mexicans sometimes saw the Americans as too direct, while Vitro managers, in their dogged pursuit of politeness, sometimes seemed to the Americans unwilling to acknowledge problems and faults. The Mexicans sometimes thought Corning moved too fast; the Americans felt Vitro was too slow.

But it wasn't just cultural differences that undid the alliance. Added complications came from a strong peso, increased overseas competition, and a rethinking of marketing strategies by both companies. But the cultural disparities hurt the companies' ability to react to a fast-changing market, and in the end led both sides to throw in the towel.

Corning and Vitro continue to market each other's products and are reluctant to rehash their squabbles. But the abrupt end of the alliance still has them trying to figure out exactly what went wrong.

"We've reflected on this a lot ourselves," said John W. Loose, chairman of the Corning Consumer Products Company, the successor to Corning-Vitro in the United States.

Corning is most often associated with oven-ready glassware but has diversified into fiber optics, environmental products, and laboratory services. Vitro, Mexico's largest industrial group, makes dozens of products, including beer bottles, automobile windshields, and, in a joint venture with Whirlpool, washing machines.

Although both are aggressive global concerns, their cultural differences are sometimes quite obvious. Take their headquarters. Corning's offices in upstate New York are in a modern glass-enclosed building, while Vitro's headquarters in Monterrey, often thought of as Mexico's Pittsburgh, are in a replica of a 16th-century convent, with artwork, arched ceilings, and antique reproductions.

Another difference quite obvious from the beginning was the manner of making decisions and the time it took to make them. Vitro and other Mexican businesses are much more hierarchical, with loyalty to fathers and patrons somehow carried over to the modern corporation. As a matter of either loyalty or tradition, decisions are often left either to a member of the controlling family or to top executives, while middle-level managers are often not asked their opinions.

"If we were looking at a distribution decision or a customer decision," said Mr. Loose, "we typically would have a group of people in a room, they would do an assessment, figure alternatives, and make a decision; and I as chief executive would never know about it. My experience on the Mexican side is that someone in the organization would have a solution in mind, but then the decision had to be kicked up a few levels."

Even the way they have responded to the failure of the venture shows how different the cultures sometimes are. Americans are normally willing to discuss what went wrong and learn from it, while Mexicans are often reluctant to criticize anyone, especially a partner, preferring simply to focus on the fact that the marketing arrangement between the companies continues in spite of the breakup. In interviews, Vitro executives expressed dismay that Mr. Loose had spoken so openly, "It is unfortunate that he made those comments," one Vitro executive said in private.

The president of Vitro, Eduardo Martens, denied that corporate cultures in Mexico and the

United States differ any more than the cultures of any two corporations. But in an interview last year, before his comments could be taken as being in any way critical of Corning, he said, "Business in Mexico is done on a consensus basis, very genteel and sometimes slow by U.S. standards."

Richard N. Sinkin, a corporate consultant said cultural differences generally are "the No. 1 problem for doing business in Mexico." Though that may be an exaggeration, it underscores the difficulty of transferring a culture across the border. His own experience, he said, bears that out. He is bilingual and often works in Mexico, but has found that it isn't always easy to get paid because the Mexican view of contracts differs markedly from the one commonly held in the United States.

In Mexico, the terms of a contract "are kind of ideal things that you strive to achieve," he said, "while in the U.S. they are law."

In general, corporate style is more formal in Mexico than in the United States. Titles are common, and nearly everyone is "licenciado," which loosely refers to having any professional training. Forgetting the honorific can be seen as a serious insult.

While executives in Mexico can expect the unquestioned loyalty of employees, outsiders are often viewed with mistrust. Horace E. Scherer, director general of Hobart Dayton Mexicana, the Mexican subsidiary of Hobart Corporation, said his salespeople must often make four trips to complete one transaction because of that lack of trust. To sell the company's scales and other equipment, a salesperson starts with a visit to the client's top official. If a sale is made, a representative of the company itself must deliver the goods because the customer won't accept delivery from DHL or some other service. If all the papers are in order on delivery, the company representative is told to come back on an appointed day to present an invoice, in person, and if the invoice is accepted an appointment is made to return to receive payment.

Joint Venture #2: The Volvo-Renault Marriage

The most successful alliances result from the union of two companies that share a common business vision and have complementary resources and skills. Take the case of Volvo of Sweden and Renault of France. "Volvo understood long ago that in order to compete in the worldwide automotive market, it had to recognize economies of scale that were just not possible when you are a very limited niche manufacturer," says Rick Dowden, president and CEO of Volvo North America. Volvo manufactures 400,000 cars a year in an industry where major competitors manufacture millions, so in order to remain competitive Volvo sought a partner.

In searching for its partner, Volvo had several criteria in mind: to ally itself with a company that understood its business, offered complementarity, and was not so large that it would swallow up Volvo and dominate the relationship. Having previously been involved in a successful project to jointly produce engines with Renault, Volvo felt comfortable with the company. The product lines and marketing strengths also were complementary, according to Dowden. Essentially, both Volvo and Renault are in the same business—the manufacture of cars, trucks, and buses. Renault is strong in small cars and diesel engine technology, and Volvo is strong in larger cars and gasoline technology. And, geographically, Volvo is strong in northern Europe and North America, whereas Renault is relatively weak in North America, but strong in southern Europe and Latin America.

Aside from strategic fit of the two companies, there was a great deal of chemistry between the top executives. Volvo Chairman Pehr Gyllenhammar and Renault's then-Chairman Raymond Levy were very close in their philosophy about what kind of products they wanted, how they wanted to market them, and how they wanted their companies

Source: Julie Cohen Mason, "The Marriage of Volvo and Renault," *Management Review*, May 1993, p. 12.

to be viewed in the marketplace, according to Dowden. "These were two people who knew and respected each other and had common goals and aspirations for their companies," he says. "If the people don't work together, I don't care how much the numbers seem to work, you won't get that (spirit) of cooperation."

In order to facilitate the alliance between Renault and Volvo, working groups were set up to examine the elements of the industrial system, such as product design and procurement, as well as the manufacture of components for cars, trucks, and buses, to determine if an alliance would benefit both Renault and Volvo in terms of competitiveness and long-term profitability. The groups came up with some projections that were appealing to both parties. In February 1990, the Volvo-Renault alliance was officially announced.

The alliance with Renault covers every aspect of Volvo's business and is viewed as a permanent arrangement. "There are no provisions in our agreement for dissolving this relationship. It is intended to be a marriage," says Dowden.

Furthermore, each company bought a significant percentage of each other's stock. "They created such an economic interdependence that people couldn't succeed in their own part of the business without assuring that the partner succeeded," Dowden adds. "This (alliance) is not just a couple of people from Renault and a couple of people from Volvo who have lunch once in a while. This is a company that has to produce on a bottom line of its own."

Bringing together two companies from not only different countries but also different corporate cultures potentially could cause some problems. In the Volvo-Renault alliance, however, there have been no major clashes. "Volvo is an increasingly decentralized company and Renault has remained a very centralized company. But by setting up these joint (work groups) to administer different parts of the industrial system, we have found a very good way to bridge (gaps) because it forces a certain amount of decentralization and compromise between them," Dowden explains.

And for now, Volvo doesn't expect to enter into any major alliances of the same size and scope as the one with Renault any time soon, even though the company will continue to pursue joint ventures.

Part 2/Case 2

Moto: Coming to America

Moto arrived in Chicago in the middle of winter, unprepared for the raw wind that swept off the lake. The first day he bought a new coat and fur-lined boots. He was cheered by a helpful salesgirl who smiled as she packed his lined raincoat into a box. Americans were nice, Moto decided. He was not worried about his assignment in America. The land had been purchased, and Moto's responsibility was to hire a contracting company and check on the pricing details. The job seemed straightforward.

Moto's firm, KKD, an auto parts supplier, had spent 1½ years researching American building contractors. Allmack had the best record in terms of timely delivery and liaisons with good architects and the best suppliers of raw materials. That night Moto called Mr. Crowell of Allmack, who confirmed the appointment for the next morning. His tone was amiable.

Source: Patricia Gercik, *On Track with the Japanese*, 1992. (New York: Kodansha International, 114 Fifth Ave., NY, NY 10011) (OR Kudanske America).

Moto arrived at the Allmack office at nine sharp. He had brought a set of *kokeshi* dolls for Crowell. The dolls, which his wife had spent a good part of a day picking out, were made from a special maple in the mountains near his family home in Niigata. He would explain that to Crowell later, when they knew each other. Crowell also came from a hilly, snowy place, which was called Vermont.

When the secretary ushered him in, Crowell stood immediately and rounded the desk with an outstretched hand. Squeezing Moto's hand, he roared, "How are you? Long trip from Tokyo. Please sit down, please."

Moto smiled. He reached in his jacket for his card. By the time he presented it, Crowell was back on the other side of the desk. "My card," Moto said seriously.

"Yes, yes," Crowell answered. He put Moto's card in his pocket without a glance.

Moto stared at the floor. This couldn't be happening, he thought. Everything was on that card: KKD, Moto, Michio, Project director KKD meant University of Tokyo and years of hard work to earn a high recommendation from Dr. Iwasa's laboratory. Crowell had simply put it away.

"Here." Crowell handed his card.

"Oh, John Crowell, Allmack, President," Moto read aloud, slowly trying to recover his equilibrium. "Allmack is famous in Japan."

"You know me," Crowell replied and grinned. "All those faxes. Pleased to meet you, Moto. I have a good feeling about this deal."

Moto smiled and laid Crowell's card on the table in front of him.

"KKD is pleased to do business with Allmack," Moto spoke slowly. He is proud of his English. Not only had he been a top English student in high school and university, but he had also studied English in a *juku* (an afterschool class) for five years. As soon as he received this assignment, he took an intensive six-week course taught by Ms. Black, an American, who also instructed him in American history and customs.

Crowell looked impatient. Moto tried to think of Ms. Black's etiquette lessons as he continued talking about KKD and Allmack's history. "We are the best in the business," Crowell interrupted. "Ask anyone. We build the biggest and best shopping malls in the country."

Moto hesitated. He knew Allmack's record—that's why he was in the room. Surely Crowell knew that. The box of *kokeshi* dolls pressed against his knees. Maybe he should give the gift now. No, he thought, Crowell was still talking about Allmack's achievements. Now Crowell had switched to his own achievements. Moto felt desperate.

"You'll have to come to my house," Crowell continued. "I live in a fantastic house. I had an architect from California build it. He builds for all the stars, and for me." Crowell chuckled. "Built it for my wife. She's the best wife, the very best. I call her my little sweetheart. Gave the wife the house on her birthday. Took her right up to the front door and carried her inside."

Moto shifted his weight. Perhaps if he were quiet, Crowell would change the subject. They could then pretend the conversation never happened. "Moto-san, what's your first name? Here, we like to be on a first-name basis."

"Michio," Moto whispered.

"Michio-san, you won't get a better price than from me. You can go down the block to Zimmer or Casey, but you got the best deal right here."

"I brought you a present," Moto said, handing him the box of *kokeshi* dolls.

"Thanks," Crowell answered. He looked genuinely pleased as he tore open the paper. Moto looked away while Crowell picked up a *kokeshi* doll in each hand. "They look like Russian dolls. Hey, thanks a lot, my daughter will love them."

Moto pretended that he hadn't heard. I'll help by ignoring him, Moto thought, deeply embarrassed.

Crowell pushed the *kokeshi* dolls aside and pressed a buzzer. "Send George in," he said.

The door opened and a tall, heavyset man with a dark crew cut stepped inside the room.

"George Kubushevsky, this is Moto-san. Michio . . ."

"How do you do?" Kubushevsky's handshake was firm.

Moto took out his card.

"Thanks," Kubushevsky said. "Never carry those." He laughed and hooked his thumbs in his belt buckle.

Moto nodded. He was curious. Kubushevsky must be a Jewish name—or was it Polish, or maybe even German? In Japan he'd read books about all three groups. He looked at Kubushevsky's bone structure. It was impossible to tell. He was too fat.

"George, make sure you show Michio everything. We want him to see all the suppliers, meet the right people, you understand?"

"Sure." George grinned and left the room.

Moto turned to Crowel. "Is he a real American?" Moto asked.

"A real American? What's that?"

Moto flushed. "Is he first generation?" Moto finished lamely. He remembered reading that Jews, Lebanese, and Armenians were often first generation.

"How do I know? He's just Kubushevsky."

During the next few weeks Moto saw a great deal of Kubushevsky. Each morning he was picked up at nine and taken to a round of suppliers. Kubushevsky gave him a rundown on each supplier before they met. He was amiable and polite, but never really intimate. Moto's response was also to be polite. Once he suggested that they go drinking after work, but Kubushevsky flatly refused, saying that he had to work early the next morning. Moto sighed, remembering briefly his favorite bar and his favorite hostess in Tokyo. Yuko-san must be nearly fifty now, he thought affectionately. She could make him laugh. He wished he were barhopping with his colleagues from his *ringi* group at KKD. Moto regretted that he had not brought more *kokeshi* dolls, since Kubushevsky had not seemed delighted with the present of KKD pen.

One morning they were driving to a cement outlet.

"George."

"Yes, Michio-san."

Moto paused. He still found it difficult to call Kubushevsky by his first name. "Do you think I could have some papers?"

"What kind of papers?" Kubushevsky's voice was friendly. Unlike Crowell, he kept an even tone. Moto liked that.

"I need papers on the past sales of these people."

"We're the best."

"I need records for the past five years on the cement place we are going to visit."

"I told you, Michio-san, I'm taking you to the best! What do you want?"

"I need some records."

"Trust me, I know what I'm doing."

Moto was silent. He didn't know what to say. What did trust have to do with anything? His *ringi* group in Tokyo needed documentation so they could discuss the issues and be involved in the decision. If the decision to go with one supplier or the other was correct, that should be reflected in the figures.

"Just look at what's going on now," George said. "Charts for the last five years. That's history."

Moto remained silent. George pressed his foot to the gas. The car passed one truck, and then another. Moto looked nervously at the climbing speedometer. Suddenly Kubushevsky whistled and released his foot. "All right, Michio-san, I'll get you the damned figures."

"Thanks," Moto said softly.

"After we see the cement people, let's go for a drink."

Moto looked uneasily at the soft red light bulb that lit the bar. He sipped his beer and ate a few peanuts. Kubushevsky was staring at a tall blonde at the other end of the bar. She seemed to notice him also. Her fingers moved across the rim of the glass.

"George," Moto said gently. "Where are you from, George."

"Here and there," Kubushevsky said idly, still eyeing the blonde.

Moto laughed. "Here and there."

Kubushevsky nodded. "Here and there," he repeated.

"You Americans," Moto said. "You must have a home."

"No home, Michio-san."

The blonde slid her drink down the bar and slipped into the next seat. Kubushevsky turned more toward her.

Moto felt desperate. Last week Crowell had also acted rudely. When Imai, KKD's vice president, was visiting from Japan, Crowell had dropped them both off at a golf course. What was the point?

He drained his beer. Immediately the familiar warmth of the alcohol made him buoyant. "George," he said intimately. "You need a wife. You need a wife like Crowell has."

Kubushevsky turned slowly on his seat. He stared hard at Moto. "You need a muzzle," he said quietly.

"You need a wife," Moto repeated. He had Kubushevsky's full attention now. He poured Kubushevsky another beer. "Drink," he commanded.

Kubushevsky drank. In fact they both drank. Then suddenly Kubushevsky's voice changed. He put his arm around Moto and purred in his ear. "Let me tell you a secret, Moto-san. Crowell's wife is a dog. Crowell is a dog. I'm going to leave Allmack, just as soon as possible. Want to join me, Michio-san?"

Moto's insides froze. Leave Crowell. What was Kubushevsky talking about? He was just getting to know him. They were a team. All those hours in the car together, all those hours staring at cornfields and concrete. What was Kubushevsky talking about? Did Crowell know? What was Kubushevsky insinuating about joining him? "You're drunk, George."

"I know."

"You're very drunk."

"I know."

Moto smiled. The blonde got restless and left the bar. Kubushevsky didn't seem to notice. For the rest of the night he talked about his first wife and his two children, whom he barely saw. He spoke of his job at Allmack and his hopes for a better job in California. They sat at a low table. Moto spoke of his children and distant wife. It felt good to talk. Almost as good as having Yuko next to him.

As they left the bar, Kubushevsky leaned heavily on him. They peed against a stone wall before getting in the car. All the way home Kubushevsky sang a song about a folk hero named Davy Crockett, who "killed himself a bear when he was only three." Moto sang a song from Niigata about the beauty of the snow on the rooftops in winter. Kubushevsky hummed along.

They worked as a team for the next four months. Kubushevsky provided whatever detailed documentation Moto asked for. They went drinking a lot. Sometimes they both felt a little sad, sometimes happy, but Moto mostly felt entirely comfortable. Kubushevsky introduced him to Porter, a large, good-natured man in the steel business who liked to hunt and cook gourmet food; to Andrews, a tiny man who danced the polka as if it were a waltz; and to many others.

Just before the closing, Kubushevsky took him to a bar and told him of a job offer in California. He had tears in his eyes and hugged Moto goodbye. Moto had long since accepted the fact that Kubushevsky would leave.

Two weeks later Moto looked around the conference room at Allmack. Ishii, KKD's president, and Imai had flown in from Tokyo for the signing of the contract for the shopping mall, the culmination of three years of research and months of negotiation. John Crowell stood by his lawyer, Sue Smith. Sue had been on her feet for five hours. Mike Apple, Moto's lawyer, slammed his fist on the table and pointed at the item in question. The lawyers argued a timing detail that Moto was sure had been worked out weeks before. Moto glanced nervously at Ishii and Imai. Ishii's eyes were closed. Imai stared at the table.

Moto shifted uneasily in his seat. Sue was smarter than Mike, he thought. Perhaps a female lawyer wouldn't have been so terrible. While it was not unusual to see females in professional positions in Japan, this was America. Tokyo might have understood. After all, this was America, he repeated to himself. Internationalization required some adjustment. A year ago he would have had total loss of face if confronted with this prolonged, argumentative closing. Today he did not care. He could not explain to Tokyo all he'd learned in that time, all the friends he'd made. When he tried to communicate about business in America, the home office sent him terse notes by fax.

Now the lawyers stood back. President Ishii opened his eyes. Crowell handed a pen to Ishii. They signed the document together. The lawyers smiled. Sue Smith looked satisfied. She should be pleased, Moto thought. Her extensive preparation for the case made him realize again that the Japanese stereotype of the "lazy" Americans was false. Sue's knowledge of the case was perfect in all details. I'll have to use her next time, Moto thought. She's the smart one. Yes, he thought, his friend Kubushevsky had taught him many things. Suddenly he felt Kubushevsky's large presence. Moto lowered his head in gratitude.

CASE QUESTIONS

1. What was Moto's purpose and agenda for the first meeting with Crowell? How does he try to implement his agenda?
2. What happened to introduce "noise" in the communication from Moto to Crowell, and then from Crowell to Moto?
3. What was the significance of the doll? What went wrong?
4. Why did Crowell's remarks about Allmack threaten a loss of *face* from Moto's perspective?
5. How did Moto feel about Kubushevsky's behavior early on? How did their relationship change?

Part 2/Case 3

José Ignacio López De Arriortúa

Iñaki, the nickname José Ignacio López preferred, was the long overdue savior which GM had been in search of. His success in reducing the cost and improving the quality of General Motors Europe's procurement practices was already the stuff of legend. And now he would bring these same charismatic and competitive skills to General Motors North America. But it was impossible to separate López *the purchasing czar* from López *the visionary,* López, the man, continued to be driven by his lifelong ambition to build his model factory, what he called *Plant X,* in the remote town of his birth, Amorebieta in the Basque country of Spain. The pursuit of Plant X, however, would drive López to make personal and professional ethical decisions which would contribute to his downfall.

 This case was prepared by Professors Michael H. Moffett and William E. Youngdahl for the purpose of classroom discussion only, and not to indicate either effective or ineffective management.

EUROPEAN SUCCESS

Known as the "Grand Inquisitor" in European automotive circles, López had taken over purchasing for GM Europe in 1987. López, after earning a doctorate in industrial engineering, had worked tirelessly for Firestone in Bilbao, Spain, from 1969 to 1980. In 1980 he moved to GM Europe's Spanish offices in Zaragoza, working in the relative obscurity of this backwater of GM's European operations until late 1986. At that time he moved to

EXHIBIT 1 Contributions to the Cost of Producing and Delivering an Automobile

Source: Citibank and *The Financial Times*, Wednesday March 4, 1998, p. 13.

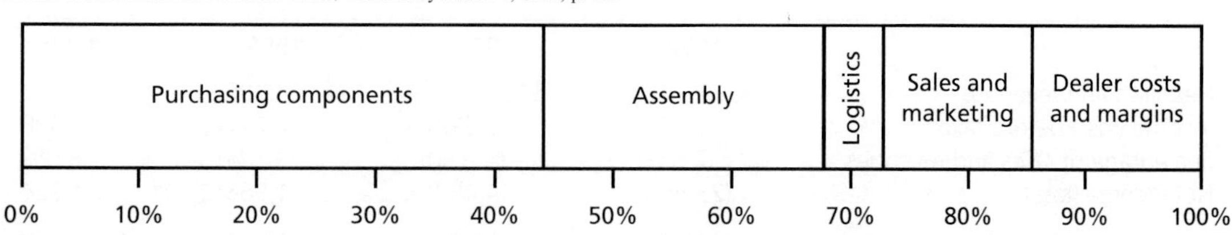

GM's flagship operations in Continental Europe, Adam Opel A.G. in Russelsheim, Germany. The new president of GM's European Operations, Jack Smith, quickly identified López's unique skills and he was promoted to head of purchasing for Europe in 1987.[1]

Jack Smith and Jose López helped lead the turnaround of GM's European operations in the 1980s. Auto industry analysts credited them with consolidating what had been a divided, expensive operation which depended nearly entirely on German suppliers into a highly profitable and diversified supplier-base business with well-managed marketing, distribution, and cost-control operations. The critical role purchasing played in the cost structure of the automobile could not be overemphasized. As illustrated in Exhibit 1, purchased components made up the single largest portion of the cost of manufacturing. If GM was to be cost competitive, purchasing would have to lead the way. In the process of cutting component costs, López had somehow been able to build increasing cooperation and teamwork among different GM-controlled units such as Opel and Vauxhall.

Following record losses of $4.5 billion in 1991, Roger Stempel was ousted as president of General Motors in the spring of 1992 and immediately replaced with Jack Smith. GM was in trouble.[2] As illustrated in Exhibit 2, GM was headed toward a record third year of losses, which although probably could not be prevented for fiscal 1992 had to be reversed as soon as possible.

It was hoped that Smith could achieve successes in GM North America similar to those that had forged his legacy at Opel in Europe. Smith moved quickly to assemble his team, including the appointment of Jose Ignacio López as vice president for worldwide purchasing in April 1992. In May, López moved to Detroit to assume his new duties.

López surrounded himself with his top assistants, his *Warriors,* who were known to follow his every word. He was openly emotional, a characteristic seen in few board rooms around the globe, and definitely a foreign concept in the halls of GM which was known more for the sterility and coldness of its founding genius Alfred P. Sloan, than the gushing effusiveness of a López who once hugged GM president Jack Smith and announced that "He is my brother and I love him!"

> López also had a flair for the grand gesture. During a dinner at Smith's house, he dramatically stripped his watch off his left wrist and strapped it to his right, proclaiming he would keep it there until General Motors made record profits in North America. Smith instantly followed suit; within days, the Warriors had also transferred their watches from left to right wrists.[3]

[1]Jack Smith had been the original negotiator in 1984 for GM in the GM-Toyota Motor Company joint venture in San Jose, California, the New United Motor Manufacturing Inc. (NUMMI) project. NUMMI's innovative use of Japanese production methods and inventory policies was considered revolutionary in American industry.

[2]It was rumored that at one point in 1991 GM came within 16 hours of not meeting payroll.

[3]*Fortune*, April 14, 1997, p. 92.

EXHIBIT 2 Selected Financial Results for General Motors, 1989–1992 (millions except for per share data)

Source: *GM Annual Reports,* Supplementary Information, Selected Financial Data (unaudited).

	1992	1991	1990	1989
Net sales and revenues	$132,242	$123,109	$124,705	$126,932
Income (loss) before taxes	(3,333)	(5,892)	(2,217)	6,398
Percentage of sales and revenues	(2.5%)	(4.8%)	(1.8%)	5.0%
Net income (loss)	(23,498)	(4,459)	(1,986)	4,224
Earnings per share (loss)	($38.28)	($7.97)	($4.09)	$6.33
Return on common equity (loss)	(169.3%)	(15.9%)	(6.1%)	12.0%

REVOLUTIONIZING PURCHASING

López wasted little time. Within days of occupying his new office, he declared that: (1) all contracts with GM suppliers were to be put up for bid; (2) GM would no longer favor its internal manufacturers (who were currently supplying 70 percent of the components used in GM vehicles); and (3) that 50 percent improvements in productivity were expected by 1995.

> A few weeks before López arrived in North America he issued a hand-written note to all the North American managers about our purchasing practices; we read, we laughed, then he showed up.[4]

López felt no particular loyalty to internal suppliers with GM's UAW wages approaching $50 per hour—quite the contrary. López was keenly aware that having 70 percent of automobile content supplied by internal GM operating units represented tremendous opportunities for cost savings. He felt that many tier-one suppliers such as TRW and AMP offered lower costs, excellent delivery, and design capabilities that could be integrated into GM's product development activites. The primary criterion driving the move to external suppliers, however, was cost reduction. Some of the managers of internal suppliers such as Delco believed that López was hollowing-out GM's core capabilities for the sake of short-term cost savings.

All GM purchasing agents were ordered to obtain a minimum of 10 bids for each supply contract, including one bid from outside the United States (excluding Canada). This was the first step in what he termed *PICOS,* the *Program for Improvement and Cost Optimization of Suppliers.*[5] What GM's North American suppliers were about to find out, however, was that López wished to change the rules on pricing, rules on contract term, rules on internal/external suppliers, rules on domestic and foreign suppliers, rules on intellectual property, in short—all the rules.

In contrast to the approach taken by GM in the early 1990s, Chrysler management decided that assistance should lead to long-term partnering with suppliers rather than short-term price concessions. Furthermore, Chrysler management believed that cost should not be the singular criterion when selecting suppliers. Rather, suppliers should be selected based on their abilities to contribute to the entire product development and manufacturing value chain. By involving suppliers up front in the design of products and processes, cost savings were shared evenly between Chrysler and its suppliers. This practice, known as *concurrent engineering,* involved suppliers as design partners, and provided quality and delivery benefits in addition

[4]Confidential interview with authors, February 1998.

[5]A later article in the *Wall Street Journal* defined *PICOS* as *Purchased Input Concept Optimization with Suppliers.*

to lower costs. Since suppliers would have to produce to Chrysler designs, their upfront involvement in the design process helped to ensure producibility, reduce engineering change orders and resultant cost, and shorten product development cycle time.

Thomas Stallkamp, vice president of Chrysler purchasing, described the difference between his partnering approach and the approach taken by Lopez:

> In general, the cooperative approach is the quickest route to better, lower-cost parts. When you start to see your suppliers as the experts, then they become valuable partners instead of a switchable commodity. You have to have some technique other than just bludgeoning to get some efficiency out of them.[6]

The state of the relationship between GM North America and its suppliers prior to López coming on-board was already in disarray. Of the Big Three automakers, GM was considered to be worst in cost competitiveness and quality assurance. One Midwestern supplier described the state of affairs.[7]

> We were already in the process of dropping GM as a customer. They were not the kind of company we wanted as a major part of our business. For example, they wouldn't pay. One Friday I finally instructed the general manager to stop shipment. I listened to the phone calls bounce back-and-forth all day long until they got to me. I talked to GM's CFO and explained to him we would ship when we got paid. He promised to cut a check immediately so I released the shipment. In the end, even with the CFO's promise, they were so inept they couldn't get a check to us until the next Thursday. We didn't need customers like that. López simply made it that much easier to drop them.

Pricing

López, at least in these early stages, focused on price, resulting in confrontational relationships with suppliers. This was in many ways in direct conflict with the principles of lean manufacturing supplier pricing strategies which emphasized the attitude and willingness of suppliers to work cooperatively with the manufacturer towards cost reduction, eventually accomplishing price competitiveness.

The basic premise of this method is that rather than having a model price set by the cost of components plus profits, component prices are set as a function of a target price for a new model; reverse cost-engineering, in principle. It is a strategy which is most easily applied in the creation and construction of entirely new models, but is difficult to apply in practice to existing chassis and existing product/price agreements. López, by focusing almost totally on price, positioned one supplier against another in terms of obtaining valuable contracts with GM, with a single objective criteria for selection.

A common criticism of this focus on price alone is that it cultivates no significant interaction between buyer and supplier, and in many cases, destroys any semblance of cooperation or joint-production. It is considered by many a short run strategy for cost reduction which often introduces a sequence of low price/low quality/low commitment/longer delivery times/little flexibility.

> Dr. López declared in his speech to supplier executives that both GM and its suppliers could prosper under his system. Teams from GM have held cost-cutting workshops and have achieved average productivity gains of 63 percent in certain areas of individual plants.[8]

Supplier Education/Development

The cost of meeting López's demands was often great, and in many cases, the suppliers could not meet his unrelenting demands. In early July 1992 López moved to the second stage of cost reduction action by sending his own crack engineering troops, his engineering cost efficiency warriors, into the suppliers' shops themselves to aid in the process.

[6] *Wall Street Journal,* May 14, 1993.

[7] Confidential interview with authors, February 1998.

[8] *Wall Street Journal,* August 26, 1992.

> "We had López into our plant," said Jack Withrow, the president of Lectron Corporation, a GM supplier in Rochester Hills, Michigan. "There's a lot of pressure on price—all our supply contracts are being rebid. He wants double-digit decreases, not the 2 or 3 percent GM had been asking for."[9]

Even in the event that GM's engineering teams could find additional cost savings in the suppliers' production and distribution processes, a number of firms found GM taking all of the cost savings itself. The Toyota Motor Company/NUMMI model typically distributed cost savings benefits on a 60/40 or 70/30 split between manufacturer and supplier.

Stories of López's methods, his use of coercion and intimidation to acquire the cost reductions he desired, followed him from Europe. Suppliers were frequently called into López's office. After reviewing the long and established relationship between the supplier and GM (many of GM's suppliers were privately held frms which were sometimes second-and third-generation suppliers to GM), López would purportedly make a dramatic production of tearing up the existing contract and instructing the supplier to resubmit the contract bid "with double-digit percentage reductions in price."[10] When challenged on the legality of such contract-busting practices, López would, according to story, note that GM represented a major portion of the firm's sales, and the firm would be long bankrupt by the time the supplier's grievance found its way to a court hearing.

> "He's delivering two messages at the same time," said James Womack, co-author of *The Machine That Changed the World,* a 1990 book on Toyota Motor Corp's. lean manufacturing system. In the long term, many suppliers could achieve big savings adopting his approach to manufacturing—which is similar to the Toyota manufacturing system, Mr. Womack said. "For the short term," Mr. Womack said, "the only way many of the big bloated suppliers can meet his targets is by selling to [Dr. López] at a loss.[11]

But Hanspeter Ryser, a spokesman for GM Europe and former colleague of López, said that Mr. López did not accept that his methods had been copied from Japan or were in any way coercive. His message to manufacturers was, look, you can do better, and we can help you get there. López was often successful in getting manufacturers on-board by offering lifetime contracts to those meeting his standards; a lifetime being that of a *particular model.*

Internal/External Suppliers

Early attention focused on the 70 percent of components in GM vehicles which come from in-house suppliers. The fear was that López would out-source the current in-house GM supplier operations. While maintaining the price focus of supply success, GM and López needed to maintain a larger supplier pool to promote competitive pricing and lowest cost bids. But outsourcing had become synonymous with low-cost non-union workers. This was not a popular move with the United Auto Workers (UAW), but López worked tirelessly to maintain their support. Steve Yokich, head of the UAW's GM Department, was quoted after meeting with López in August 1992:

> He said he admires union workers and they should work together to make operations competitive. But he said there is only one class of GM supplier, not internal and external. He's said to workers, "Let's work together."[12]

One particularly attractive part of his program, to some groups at least, was to allow firms to be suppliers to both North American and European operations, a relationship not previously allowed. In a meeting in late June 1992, López invited European parts suppliers to bid for contracts at

[9] *New York Times,* September 2, 1992.

[10] A typical renegotiated five-year contract would require the supplier to "give-back" sequentially 5 percent, 3 percent, 2 percent, 2 percent, and 1 percent of the sales value per year.

[11] *Wall Street Journal,* August 26, 1992.

[12] *New York Times,* September 2, 1992.

GM's North American operations. Once again, this was a move in defiance of traditional organized labor's stands, and was met with opposition by the UAW.

Intellectual Property

One alleged practice employed by López which could have repercussions for many years to come was his practice of taking proprietary manufacturing and engineering plans developed with suppliers as part of a growing co-production effort and putting these same plans out to competitive suppliers for bid. Many of those suppliers exploited responded by severing their GM relationship and telling GM to "take its tools."

Not only was the supplier's propriety research and development flowing directly to its competition, the supplier was forced to propose and, if lucky, accept returns on the investment which were inadequate to cover the R&D expenditure. As a result, there was a growing reluctance by even GM's long-term suppliers to work cooperatively toward future plans when they were not assured control over their own intellectual property.

A confrontational basis for buyer-supplier relationships typically fosters little long-term commitment on either party's part, and decreases the number of routine interactions requiring shared information and trust of more full partnership supplier programs. A spring 1993 automotive survey of 110 automotive suppliers conducted by ELM International found GM had reopened contracts more frequently than other auto manufacturers (10 times that of Ford for example).[13] When asked to rate their relationship with auto companies from 1 (dictatorship) to 10 (partnership) the approximate results were staggering: GM—3.8; Mazda—4.1; Ford—4.3; Saturn—5.0; Honda—5.2; Chrysler—5.5; Nissan—5.8; Toyota—6.0. Relationships and supplier trust were deteriorating. Still, it was estimated López had saved GM an estimated $4 billion in parts and manufacturing expenses, at least in the short term.

[13]*Business Week,* August 23, 1993, p. 26.

BURNING BRIDGES: GM TO VOLKSWAGEN

On Saturday, March 6, 1993, López, in a speech in Detroit to 246 major GM suppliers from around the world, reiterated his philosophy: "Please don't use any more excuses, like our prices are already low and our profits cannot be cut further. We must change our attitude from excuse generation to creativity in action." López emphasized that GM was still interested in building long-term supplier alliances, and reaffirmed his own personal commitment to GM and its leadership. In a rare show of emotion by a GM executive, López referred openly to "my hero, Jack Smith."

Three days later, Tuesday, March 9, a *New York Times* article cited rumors that López would be leaving GM to join Volkswagen of Germany. The rumors, although not all that uncommon for controversial corporate executives, raised concern immediately within GM due to the purported timing: López would be accepting the position immediately, joining VW the Tuesday of the following week when VW was scheduled to announce a corporate restructuring. On Wednesday, March 10, GM denied rumors that López was leaving.

On Thursday, March 11, an article in the *New York Times* titled "Cost-Cutter Is Leaving G.M. Post" carried the announcement by López himself that he was leaving GM. GM shares immediately lost $1.375 per share during the course of the day to close at $38.75. GM issued a statement after the close of trading which quoted Jack Smith as acknowledging López's departure but "the team and process remain intact."

On Friday, March 12, Jack Smith and several other senior executives from GM visited López at his home outside Detroit in continuing efforts to convince him to reconsider. On Saturday, March 13, Smith spoke with López again, finally convincing him to stay on in a new capacity. That night, Smith, while attending a black tie gala in Detroit, acknowledged that he still did not know what López would do.

On Sunday, March 14, GM confirmed López had changed his mind once again, and would be staying on in a more senior role, the details to be announced in a Monday press conference with Jack Smith. On Monday, March 15, a *New York Times* article announced that López had decided over the weekend to stay. At a press conference scheduled for 3 PM that day, the greater role López would be taking at GM would be outlined by Jack Smith.

In what has become known as *Black Monday,* the president of General Motors, John F. Smith, Jr., received a handwritten note from López 30 minutes prior to the press conference stating that he would not be staying on at GM after all. At the time the note was handed to Jack Smith, López was aboard a trans-Atlantic flight to Europe to join Volkswagen as chief of production optimization and purchasing. The melodrama in Detroit ended with the embarrassing acknowledgment in a live press conference by the senior corporate executive of arguably the world's largest company that he had been personally duped.

On Wednesday, March 17, 1993, the Chief of VW's Management Board, Ferdinand Piëch, named López chief of production optimization and purchasing, and simultaneously appointed him to VW's management board.

PLANT X

López had, however, never forgotten his roots and never realized his dream. Although new to the corporate offices of GM-North America in June 1992, he had promoted his personal vision of what he called *Plant X.* It was to be, in López's view, the world's leanest and most efficient automobile manufacturing facility, and he wished to build it in the city of his birth, Amorebieta in the Basque region of Spain. Unfortunately for López, GM was not interested.

López repeatedly submitted his proposal for the construction of Plant X to the GM planning committee during his brief Detroit stay. Despite repeated rejections, upon direct lobbying by López with Jack Smith himself, it was resubmitted once again only to be opposed outright by the Chairman of GM-Europe, Lou Hughes. The European automobile market was currently in a slump, and even in the event of a recovery, the location of Amorebieta, Spain, made little economic sense for GM. López would not, however, acknowledge that the idea was not to be. Even after a personal meeting with Jack Smith in which the president explained that it did not make sense for General Motors to build Plant X, López still refused to acknowledge the idea was dead and would not be heard by the consortium of operating units to which he continually marketed the idea. "I tell [the consortium], 'Let's wait, but let's at least have this hope.' "[14] On the same day that GM's board once again denied the Plant X proposal, they voted to promote López to group vice president and increase his compensation package. For López, the rejection was a major disappointment.

But Volkswagen would listen. Ferdinand Piëch needed to change Volkswagen from being Europe's *largest* automobile manufacturer to being a *profitable* manufacturer. VW was widely known as one of the most inefficient manufacturers in the world. Piëch needed López.

> Piëch knew exactly how to press López's hot buttons. He offered López the chance to be a savior: For instance, during two days of secret talks that took place in January 1993, Piëch took the GM cost cutter on a private tour of the company's massive auto works in Wolfsburg, Germany, just to show him how appallingly inefficient the whole operation was. He offered López power, promising to make him a member of Volkswagen's Vorstand—its management inner circle. He offered money: According to GM's lawsuit, López would get a hefty $1.6 million salary (López made less than $400,000 at GM). And Piëch offered López the hope that, at VW, Plant X might become a reality. When López brought up Plant X during their negotiations, Piëch promised to give it serious consideration.[15]

[14] *Fortune,* April 14, 1997, p. 93.

[15] *Ibid.*

THE GM-VW BATTLE

Beginning with Black Monday in March of 1993, until final legal settlement in January 1997, GM and VW took part in one of the ugliest and most intense corporate battles ever seen.

After a detailed inventory of materials, GM concluded there were four sets of materials taken by López which comprised the most damaging loss (1) a 3,350-page listing of the 60,000 parts, their suppliers, their cost, and their delivery schedules for GM-Europe; (2) a collection of materials detailing GM-Opel's future product lines; (3) a detailed manufacturing and cost study on the prospects for López's Plant X; (4) a portfolio of presentation materials used by López in cutting supplier costs.[16]

GM proceeded immediately in the spring of 1993 to file lawsuits preventing López and VW from poaching additional GM employees (in the end López took seven of his warriors with him). GM then filed a criminal complaint in Germany against López, citing industrial espionage. Spearheaded by GM-Europe's chief operating officer Lou Hughes, GM hired private detectives in Europe to pursue López and his select warriors, leaked information to the German press regarding all accusations, and continued a public relations assault on both López and VW. On June 22, 1993, German police discovered four boxes of internal GM documents in the apartment of two of López' warriors in Wiesbaden, Germany (including evidence that López himself directed a copy and shred operation of GM documents). VW, in its defense, then commissioned an independent evaluation by KPMG Peat Marwick which found, in a final report in late 1993, no evidence of wrongdoing on VW's part.

The battle continued for the next three years. Ferdinand Piëch, the CEO of Volkswagen and grandson of Ferdinand Porsche, became increasingly aggressive in his defense of his new friend López, and the verbal exchanges between GM and VW became increasingly nasty. Finally, on March 7, 1996, GM filed a racketeering suit against López and VW. Volkswagen's share price dropped markedly on the Frankfurt exchange. On November 29, 1996, VW announced that López had resigned. Days later, on December 13, 1996, German prosecutors indicted López on charges of industrial espionage.

Faced with mounting evidence and the potential triple damages which would accompany a successful racketeering conviction in the United States, VW settled with GM in January 1997. The final settlement called for VW to pay GM $100 million in damages, purchase over $1 billion in parts from GM over the next seven years, exchange letters of apology, and bar López from working for VW in any capacity through the year 2000.

[16]For a more detailed description of the three-year battle between GM and Volkswagen, see "Bloodfeud," *Fortune*, April 14, 1997, pp. 90–102.

VOLKSWAGEN: RESENDE, BRAZIL

In the end, Lopez saw his Plant X dream realized in the form of VW's new truck and bus plant in Resende, Brazil, in the state of Rio de Janeiro. Plant X was the realization of what GM would argue was a not-very-new idea, the *modular consortium.* VW maintained primary responsibility for vehicle design, selection of suppliers, and provision of the basic manufacturing facility. VW's suppliers performed the actual assembly in the Resende plant. That is, they replaced Volkswagen employees on the assembly line. The manufacturing floor, or *modular consortium,* was divided by yellow lines separating one supplier group from the next. Traditionally, these yellow lines were used by the manufacturer to separate production-line employees.

On November 1, 1996, Volkswagen initiated production of large passenger buses at the Resende plant. Of the $300 million invested in the plant, $50 million was put up by the suppliers themselves. In stark contrast to suppliers' recent dealings with VW, the capital commitment was part of a long-term production agreement ranging from

EXHIBIT 3 The Seven Tier 1 Suppliers at the Volkswagen Resende Factory

Source: "VW Plant at Resende Inaugurated," http://www.univ-evry.fr/labos/gerpisa/lettre/numeros/109/firmest.html.en.

Supplier	Module Responsibility
Tamet (Brazil)	Cabin—stamping and body shop
Eisemann (Germany)	Cabin—painting
VDO (Germany)	Cabin—trimming
MWM (Germany) and Cummins Engine (US)	Engine
Maxion (Brazil)	Chassis
Rockwell International (US)	Suspension and axles
Remon (a Brazilian joint venture of Maxion, Borlem, Bridgestone)	Wheels and tires

5 to 15 years in length with seven Tier 1 suppliers (see Exhibit 3). Total plant employment of 1,000 workers was divided into the 800 assembly workers, all employees of the suppliers, and 200 VW employees working in support roles including quality control, marketing, and engineering.

The Tier 1 suppliers assumed responsibility for assembly, production control, inventory management, and the procurement associated with all parts included in their production modules, or subassemblies. They would assume full responsibility for the selection and coordination of Tier 2 suppliers that supplied parts and components according to a just-in-time production schedule to the Tier 1 supplier assembly area of the modular consortium.

An example of a Tier 1 supplier in the Resende plant is VDO Kienzle, a German instrument maker:[17] VDO starts with the steel shell of a truck cab. About 200 VDO workers, working within their taped-off area, install everything from seats to instrument panels. They then attach the truck cab to the chassis to move down the conveyor line (supplied by VW) through other suppliers' work spaces. Improvements in the assembly process cut work hours during the pilot stage of operations by 12 percent according to Roberto Barretti, VW's operations manager at the Resende plant. Additionally, suppliers' infusion of their own capital equipment reduced VW's share of the capital burden. For example, VDO invested nearly $12 million in its own tools and fixtures to support assembly operations.

The economics of the co-production process was revolutionary when compared to traditional assembly line approaches originated by Henry Ford and further refined from an organizational standpoint by Alfred P. Sloan over 70 years ago. Cost savings went beyond reduced assembly hours and capital expenditures, extending to overhead expenses associated with planning and coordination. The transfer of product in process technology no longer depended on complicated boundary spanning activities managed by large procurement organizations. (Exhibit 4 illustrates the premise of the traditional supplier/producer assembly facility.) Rather, suppliers would transfer their knowledge and capabilities where they provided the greatest value—on VW's production floor. Furthermore, they were responsible for much of the internal coordination such as inventory control previously managed by legions of staff specialists who did not possess equivalent process and product knowledge. As a result of this shifting responsibility, the role of Volkswagen was no longer that of automobile assembler. VW's new role was that of conductor of this complex, yet at the same time simplified, orchestra of suppliers.

Suppliers were no longer simply parts sellers; they were now integral to the production of the co-designed and co-produced product (see Exhibit 5).

[17] *Business Week*, October 7, 1996.

EXHIBIT 4 The Supplier-Product Flow in the Traditional Assembly-Line Manufacturing Unit

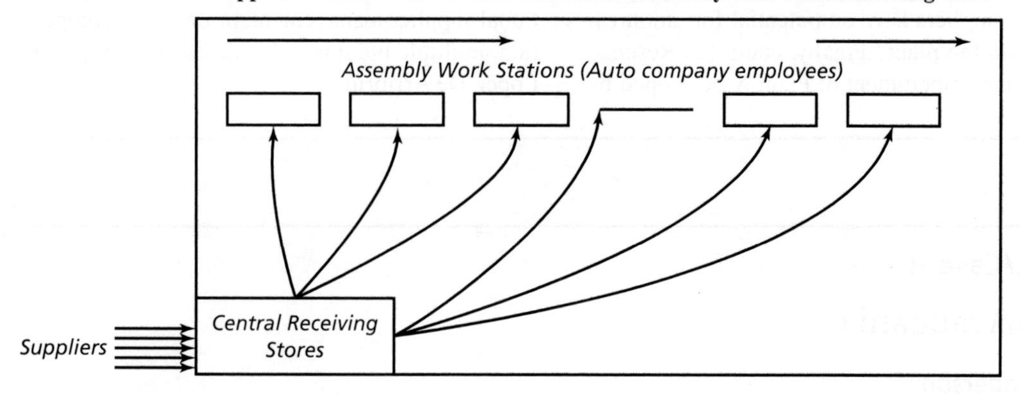

The automaker assumes responsiblity for inventory management, production control, and assembly. Suppliers deliver parts, components, subassemblies, and systems to Central Receiving. All capital equipment used in the assembly operations is owned and operated by the auto manufacturer.

They now shared responsibility for the elimination of defects, the prevention of delays, the quality of the final product. They were now subordinated stockholders as well as suppliers and workers; they were partners.

Forming partnerships with Tier 1 suppliers and allowing them to assume design and assembly responsibility was not a new approach. Virtually all automakers had done so. However, replacing line and staff positions with suppliers' employees was nothing short of revolutionary. The impacts of the changes on supplier relations, supply chain management, and the management of plant operations, had yet to be fully determined. Is it possible to become *too* dependent on Tier 1 suppliers? Should Tier 2 suppliers be integrated into the

EXHIBIT 5 The Supplier-Product Flow in the Volkswagen Resende Facility, Brazil

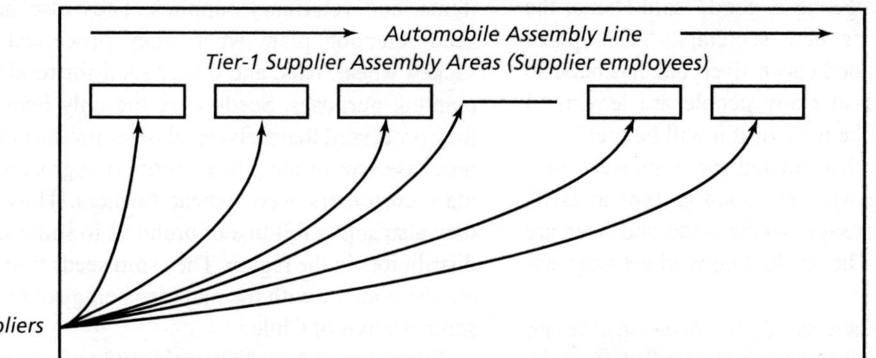

Suppliers assume responsibility for inventory management, production control, quality management, and assembly of their own parts components, subassemblies, and systems at Tier 1 supplier areas along the assembly line. Additionally, much of the capital equipment used in assembly operations is owned and maintained by the Tier 1 suppliers.

plant as a next step? What effect will the partnering with suppliers have on potential for unionization within the plant? Finally, could the Resende plant be the embodiment of Plant X developed by Lopez, the same man who advocated confrontational supplier management, price-based competition, multiple bidding—the ideals of José Ignacio López De Arriortúa?

Part 2/Case 4

AgroAraucania

Amy Anderson

TEMUCO, CHILE

The smell of the charcoal grill filled the office of this local Chilean farm supply company as the workforce prepared to finish the day's work. The light mist falling from the gray sky threatened the pending social event, but a feeling of anticipation was in the air. The employees buzzed around the office speculating about the meeting they had been invited to attend. "What do you think of all this?" asked Paula, a new employee.

"I have no idea," replied Rodrigo, one of the most senior employees. "We have never had a meeting like this before. This kind of thing usually happens when someone pays the *piso*."[1]

"I hope this meeting is good," said Diana, the general manager's new secretary. "This place could use some good cheer. Everyone has been so down lately and so many people are leaving. I wonder who will be next, or if it will be me!"

The company had invited the employees to a general meeting with an *asado* (a typical BBQ with beef and sausage, where wine and beer are usually served). The production workers were excluded, however, as management felt that they tended to drink too much and would not understand the purpose of the meeting. Management planned to use the opportunity to introduce a new initiative into the company, a Total Quality Management program, which they believed would help improve morale in the office.

THE COMPANY AGROARAUCANIA

Commerical AgroAraucania was a retail business selling a full line of over 2,500 different agricultural products, including fertilizers, herbicides, insecticides, fungicides, seeds, tractors, hardware items, and veterinary supplies. They also had a seed selection plant where they processed and sacked wheat, oats, and clover seed for resale for planting purposes. Seeds were the only item that they processed themselves; all other products were purchased for resale. The majority of AgroAraucania's customers were wheat farmers. However, they also sold a full line of products to some small distributors in the region. They sold seeds throughout the country with the majority being sold in the southern half of Chile.

Commercial AgroAraucania was an outgrowth of AgroAraucania Limited, a set of retail meat outlets. It began in 1977 in Temuco, founded initially to supply AgroAraucania Limited with the agricultural products it needed to operate grain and cattle

Source: This case was written by Amy Anderson of Wright State University. It is intended as a basis for class discussion rather than to illustrate either effective or ineffective handling of an administrative situation. Special thanks to Robert F. Scherer, Ph.D., Department of Management Chair at Wright State University, for his help and guidance in the development of this case.

farms. Eventually, it began to sell products to other farmers. Sales increased and the company grew to a US$3 million retail operation.

The company was started by four Chilean agribusinessmen. Each invested equal amounts of money, 10,000,000 Chilean pesos (approximately US$27,000). Elías Jiménez, one of the four owners, was actively involved in the daily operations of the company and served as the commercial manager. The other three owners lived and worked in Santiago, the country's capital, but all three had farms in the area and came to Temuco once a month for the company's board meeting.[2]

In 1984 they bought the property located at the edge of town near the airport. They purchased a seed selection machine and began buying local wheat crops to process and resell the seed. They now purchased not only local wheat crops, but also imported wheat, processing a total of 6,000 to 7,000 tons of seed annually.

In 1985, they opened a branch site, Mackenna, in a relatively poor section of Temuco. This office mainly made small sales to the Mapuche Indian community in the area. The manager of this office was himself a Mapuche and one of the two indigenous people employed by the firm. Many of the customers who came to this office purchased needed goods using credit slips distributed by the government agency, INDAP.[3]

At present, the company had branch offices in two other communities, Carahue and Victoria. Carahue was located 25 kilometers from Temuco in the heart of Mapuche territory. This area was fairly famous in Chile for having the highest rate of alcoholism in the country. The owner of the building AgroAraucania rented often stood in front of the store reciting poetry and talking of the glory days when Allende[4] was in power. The Victoria office was 35 kilometers to the north of Temuco, and many of the farmers in that area were of English descent. Branch offices dealt primarily with small farmers except for a few big customers who had personal relationships with the managers of these locations.

AgroAraucania's main office was located in downtown Temuco. Almost all of the competition was located on the same street. Management rented a building owned by three of the company's owners (the three that lived in Santiago). They had recently doubled the rent. Rents in this district were going up, and several banks had approached the owners offering to pay considerably more than Commercial AgroAraucania's rent for the use of the building. Management was thus considering moving its main office to the seed selection plant.

AGROARAUCANIA AND TOTAL QUALITY

Identifying the Problem

For the past year, management had been perplexed by the low morale and high turnover in the company. Although sales had increased, they felt something was not quite right in the organization. Eleven of the 42 employees had been with the company less than four months, and four others had been employed less than a year. In September 1992, they hired a psychologist to study the company and make some recommendations.[5] Using a questionnaire, she interviewed each employee, including management. During the interview with Roberto Gutenschuiger, general manager, the psychologist asked about AgroAraucania's future. He replied:

> We've been thinking about doing many things. We think the plant will make a good sight for a large farm and garden superstore. The market is moving outside of town; besides, the company rents the main office building and the owners could decide to sell it at any time. We are also thinking about putting in equipment at the plant to process frozen fruits and vegetables. Exports to American markets are really growing. We also want to try to capture as much of the forestry market as we can to make up for the loss in the traditional wheat farmer market. Seed sales are very important to us and we want to increase our market share nationally.

When asked what he felt was causing the company's problems, Gutenschuiger responded:

> Our salesforce has too much power. They are running their own mini-companies out there. We try to give them flexibility and autonomy but all they do is complain and take advantage of their freedom. We needed someone to manage and control their activities, so we created the general sales manager position. We need someone who will hold the sales force to quotas.

Each employee was asked what they would like to see changed in the organization. Over 80 percent responded that they would like more information about changes in the organization and greater participation in decision making.

One month later, the psychologist returned to AgroAraucania to submit a report. Here are excerpts from her presentation:

> AgroAraucania has experienced rapid growth over the past 10 years. Because of this growth, many new positions have been created to support the needs of the organization. But these job duties and responsibilities were not clearly organized. Jobs were created without definition. People in these new positions don't have clearly defined job descriptions. The older employees also do not understand the new responsibility structure. As a result, there is a great deal of misunderstanding within the organization.
>
> AgroAraucania lacks structure and has poor communications. Nearly all communications are verbal and very sporadic. In general, the management style is very patriarchal and centralized, with almost all decisions made by Elías Jiménez (one of the four owners). There is a general lack of focus on any long-term goals and objectives; almost all of the day-to-day activities are focused on meeting immediate needs and dealing with crises.
>
> The internal environment is uncooperative. Employees with seniority are protective of their positions and they do not always help the new people. The new people perceive an unfriendly environment where everyone looks out for themselves and no one cooperates with anyone. Now, no one is willing to work together because they don't know how long others will be around. Relationships are very important to Chileans. We do not want to get emotionally attached to fellow employees if they are not going to stay with the organization.
>
> Employees feel they do not have any say in decision making and feel very unsure about their performance. There is no feedback system, formal or informal. The employees also expressed a desire to become involved in the decision-making process and they want to be informed about decisions.
>
> The high turnover at AgroAraucania is caused by these problems. Many of these problems can be resolved by introducing more structure into the organization. I submit the following recommendations:
>
> 1. Develop a company mission.
> 2. Create an organization chart.
> 3. Write job descriptions.
> 4. Implement an evaluation program.
> 5. Develop an incentive program.

After she left the office, Roberto and Elías were not convinced that her suggestions were the answer to their problems. "We have always operated on an informal basis," Elías said. "The company is too small to worry about all that formality. We have to be able to react and change with the market. We don't want to pin ourselves down to anything."

"I think you're right," said Roberto, "I'm not sure this is the solution. We always tell the people they can come to us with their problems. We do have an open door policy. And besides, we have an incentive program. Look at the trips we give to the salespeople every year."

Each year the company provided an incentive program to motivate the salespeople. For the past two years, they had offered vacation trips to neighboring South American countries. The program was based on the level of operating profits earned during the year at each location. "We think that trips are a good idea because it is good for people to travel to see other parts of the world," said Roberto Gutenschuiger. "It is good for their development as people." In 1992, the salespeople at the main office earned trips to the capital cities of Argentina, Brazil, and Uruguay. In general, the salespeople were not happy with the premium. One salesman commented, "I'm really not interested in this trip. It will end up costing me more money to spend one week in Argentina with my wife than it would to spend three weeks in Chile with my whole family."

Roberto and Elías continued to discuss the turnover situation and the psychologist's report. They decided to put the matter on hold. "Let's think about this for a while," said Elías.

THE SOLUTION

Several months went by and no action was taken to change the situation. The turnover rate continued to be a problem; two more people left the company. In January 1993, Juan Fernandez, the company controller, returned from his summer vacation.[6] He had spent part of it in Santiago where he visited several colleagues. "Everyone's talking about Total Quality Management (TQM) in Santiago," he told Roberto on his first day back. "All the gringo companies use it.[7] I think it's the way of the future and could help us with all our problems. I brought back this book, *Using the Deming Method in Practice,* by Mary Walton (translated into Spanish).[8] I think it makes a lot of sense."

He gave the book to Elías to read. A week later, Elías came back and said, "I really like this book. Though I don't understand the whole thing and the call for single suppliers really doesn't make sense for us, the North Americans and the Japanese use it and they are good enough examples for me. Let's do something with it. Isn't this the same thing as Quality Circles?" he asked.

After Roberto read the book, he, Elías, and Juan got together to talk about it. Elías explained his enthusiasm for the idea to the group. Roberto spoke up and said, "I don't think we are ready for statistics here. We *just* started using computers last year. That stuff is complicated. Our employees will never understand it. I think we need a profit-sharing program. That is very popular in the United States and they say it really works."

"According to my friend in Santiago, there are stages to implementation. He says that the organization culture is the hardest to change and that we need to work on the attitudes of the employees and the work environment first," said Juan. "You know how our people think. They won't take the initiative to change anything and besides, everyone is out to protect their own space. This working-together concept will be difficult for them. Moreover, they are accustomed to the top-down style of management."

"What else did your friend tell you?" asked Roberto.

"He said commitment to the idea and formulation of a mission statement is the first step," explained Juan. "He also told me that training, and lots of it, is very important."

"We do plenty of training," said Roberto. "It seems to me that we need to organize ourselves first. Maybe we should reconsider what the psychologist said a few months back," he said. "Her recommendations seem to fit in with all this."

After much discussion, they all agreed that, at the conceptual level, TQM was a philosophy in which they all believed. They also agreed that the company would have to address the psychologist's recommendations to achieve a TQM environment. In addition, they decided to start using *Comisiones* or problem-solving groups to encourage participation in the decision-making process. They felt that this plan would start them down the road toward an effective TQM environment.

Roberto thought about the situation for the next several weeks. He formulated and wrote the company mission and determined the company's top five priorities. He also thought about how the employees could help by participating in the problem-solving groups. He wanted to give them a problem that would interest them and that they could solve themselves. He decided the first group problem would be the uniform problem.[9] The company had so much turnover that none of the women had uniforms. These women were concerned because they were told, when hired, that the company would provide uniforms. Olivia, the only woman with enough seniority to have a uniform, had stopped wearing hers.

EXHIBIT 1
Training and Development Program 1993

In 1993, AgroAraucania employees took the following courses:

Name	Course
Juan Fernandez	Fluency in English
Diana, Olivia, Lana and Julia	Basics of WordPerfect
Diana, Olivia, Lana and David	Basics of QuatroPro
All salespeople	Selling Skills II
Olivia	Managing a Warehouse
Lana	Labor and Legal Procedures
Julia and Olivia	Customer Service

AgroAraucania takes full advantage of the government tax incentive program. They spend the maximum allowable tax credit on training each year.

THE ASADO (THE BARBECUE)

Everyone gathered in the graveled patio area behind the main building with a glass of wine in one hand and a shish kebab in the other. Elías busied himself making sure everyone had wine. The mist had stopped but the sky was still cloudy.

Roberto cleared his throat to signal the beginning of his speech. He thanked everyone for coming and encouraged them to continue eating and drinking. He explained that the company was concerned about the negative atmosphere in the office and that this negativity was due to the company's disorganization as a result of growth. He explained that they needed to address their growing pains. "We feel the best way to do this is with your help," he said. He asked for each employee's participation in the process, then read the company mission and the top five priorities.

> Company Mission: Commercial AgroAraucania
>
> Our mission is to develop ourselves with the productive sectors of the Ninth Region, forming a company that benefits the economy of the region while providing the best products and services to the forestry and agricultural sectors, stable and rewarding jobs to our collaborators[10] and reasonable profits that permit the company's continued growth.
>
> The needs of our clients are our principal concern. We should seek excellence in everything we do to provide them with the best products and services.
>
> The people that work in the company are its principal and most valuable capital. The development and progress of each one of them will translate into further development of the company, the region, and the country. We wish to work in an environment of mutual respect and cooperation, working in teams to solve problems. To accomplish the mission, we solicit the participation of everyone to develop and grow the company.

He went on to read the priorities.

1. Establish a company structure that complements the mission and that will permit us to have good communication and cooperation among all employees of the company.
2. Improve our information systems and decision-making processes.
3. Analyze and choose the best business activities.
4. Increase our client base and improve the coverage of the market area.
5. Investigate new markets or new business opportunities.

Next, he presented the organization chart awkwardly, explaining with hand gestures the tasks and responsibilities of the people in each box. Then he gave each employee a copy of the mission, the priorities, and the organization chart. Blank-looking faces started back at Roberto. They did not fully grasp the meaning of these documents.

Next, Roberto explained that management wanted each employee to get involved in the decision-making process by participating in problem-solving groups. "The first problem we need to solve is the uniform problem," he stated. "Do we have any volunteers?" The employees all stood there looking at each other. No hands went up. Privately, Roberto had already asked Juan Fernandez to volunteer. Pedro Larrain, the outspoken branch manager from Carahue, volunteered first. Jose Soto stuck his hand up, too.

Someone commented, "We have all men in this group, yet the uniforms are for the women. We need some women on this committee." After a little coaxing, three women volunteered.

Someone else yelled, "Why should only the women have uniforms? What about the men?"

Roberto explained that the idea was to talk about the problem, examine all the alternatives, and come up with a recommendation. "We should talk about uniforms in general: men, women, management, nonmanagement, etc. The idea is for you who know the problem to find the best solution."

After the meeting was adjourned, the women left in a mass exodus and the men stayed behind to finish off the rest of the good Chilean wine.

The following day at the office, employees huddled together in small cliques to discuss what Roberto had said the night before. "I really don't believe any of it means anything," said Olivia. "They (management) are big at saying things, but they never follow through."

"Well, I think they are giving us a real opportunity here," said Diana, Roberto's secretary. "Not many companies would allow their employees to give input like this. Half of it is up to us to give them the input they need. I agree with what they say; we have the information to help them. Don't we all want to participate in what happens around here?"

THE EMPOWERED GROUP

In mid-February the first meeting was to be held immediately after work.[11] Everyone finally showed up at 8:00 pm.[12] The meeting started out with everyone talking at once. They started talking about everything except the uniforms. Juan, the company's plant in the group, tried to focus the group and suggested that they assign roles: president, secretary, and others. They all looked at him as the logical choice for president. "Let's make Diana the secretary, that's her job anyway," said Pedro.

"No, that's not the idea, everyone is on equal footing here—worker and management alike," explained Juan. About that time Elías, not officially part of the group, stepped out of his office and joined the group.

They continued to throw out ideas about the benefits of uniforms. Suddenly, Elías started talking about the *asistente social* that worked at the company several years back.

"Don[13] Elías, do you remember the *Bien Estar* fund that she tried to implement?" asked Olivia.

The meeting transformed into a discussion of ideas and suggestions that had nothing to do with the uniform problem. However, everyone was excited they had the opportunity to be heard and felt good about the meeting. They assigned responsibilities for researching uniform options and agreed to meet again four days later.

The next day, Elías met with Roberto and told him about the meeting. "It was a good meeting. We talked about all kinds of things. They (the employees) have good ideas to improve things around here. I think we need to hire an *asistente social* and start a *Bien Estar* fund," explained Elías. "The last time we had an *asistente social* at the company was one of the best periods we've had as far as people being happy."

"What about the uniforms?" asked Roberto.

"We didn't get into that very much," Elías explained. "They are going to meet again soon to talk about it."

They talked more about Elías's suggestion for an *asistente social*. They agreed to start the *Bien Estar* fund, but waited until they had some money built up in the fund to tell the employees. They contacted Juan Pere, an *asistente social* currently working part-time at another company, and contracted him to start visiting AgroAraucania's employees at their homes.

The Uniform *Comision* met several more times throughout the month of January and talked about alternatives. After several meetings they decided that they didn't necessarily have to stick with the

EXHIBIT 2 AgroAraucania Organization Chart

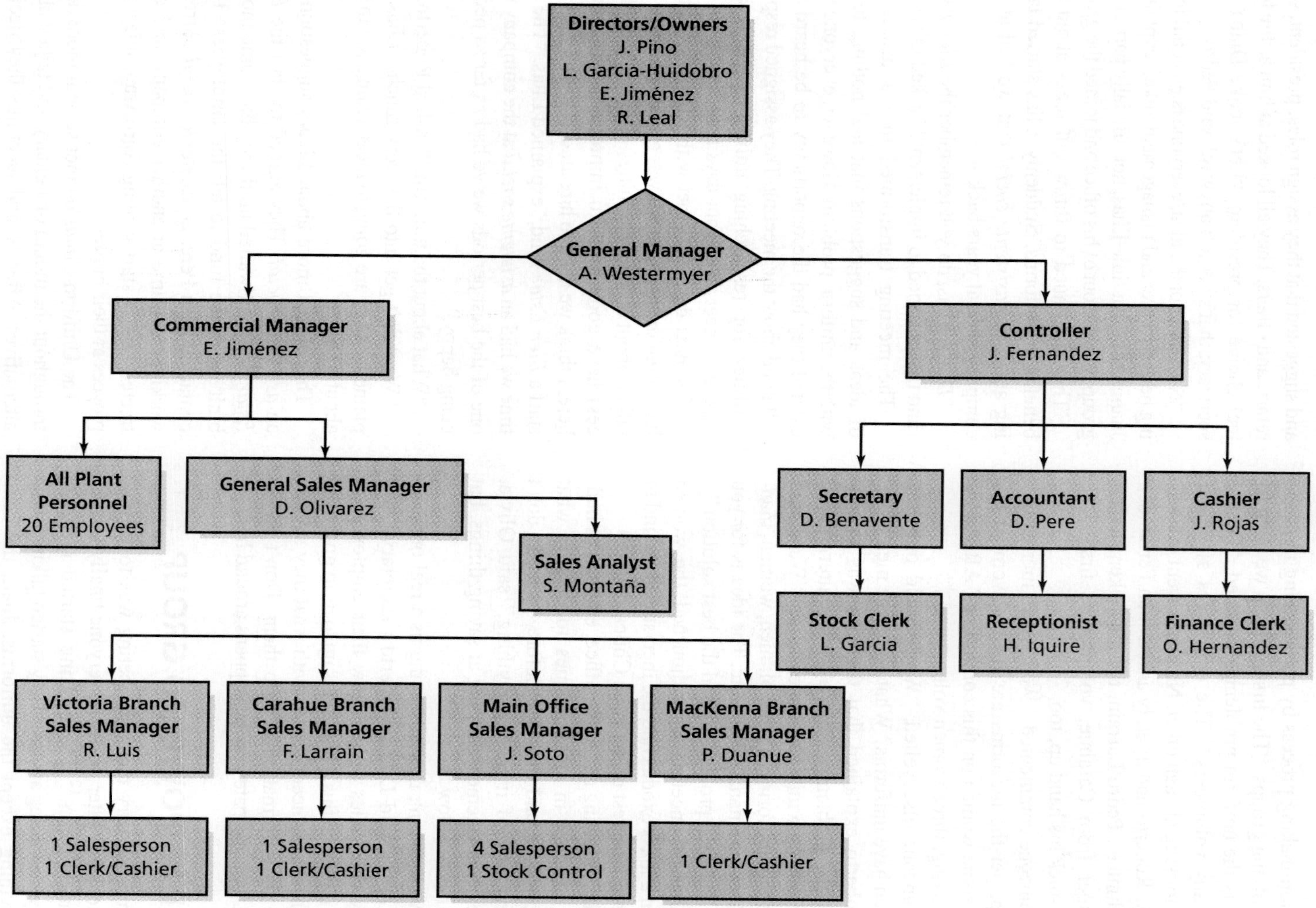

Directors/Owners
J. Pino
L. Garcia-Huidobro
E. Jiménez
R. Leal

General Manager
A. Westermyer

Commercial Manager
E. Jiménez

All Plant Personnel
20 Employees

General Sales Manager
D. Olivarez

Sales Analyst
S. Montaña

Victoria Branch Sales Manager
R. Luis

1 Salesperson
1 Clerk/Cashier

Carahue Branch Sales Manager
F. Larrain

1 Salesperson
1 Clerk/Cashier

Main Office Sales Manager
J. Soto

4 Salesperson
1 Stock Control

MacKenna Branch Sales Manager
P. Duanue

1 Clerk/Cashier

Controller
J. Fernandez

Secretary
D. Benavente

Stock Clerk
L. Garcia

Accountant
D. Pere

Receptionist
H. Iquire

Cashier
J. Rojas

Finance Clerk
O. Hernandez

EXHIBIT 3 Asistente Social (Social Worker)

Some companies in Chile contract social workers to work with their employees as a form of in-house social assistance program. They work with each employee, visiting their homes and determining their individual needs. They complete a worksheet (see example in Exhibit 4) and work with management to improve the standard of living of each worker.

They focus on the worker's living conditions, health issues of the entire family, and any other personal problems the worker might have, such as alcoholism or parental difficulties. They try to help the worker obtain available benefits from the company and government social programs to resolve these problems. One of the main functions today is to facilitate the purchase of a home. Typically these persons have degrees in social work.

The idea of these private social workers grew out of the socialist regime and carries over into today's organizations. During the Pinochet years, these professionals were considered leftist and were not very popular in companies. In recent years, however, the profession is regaining respectability, filling in part of the human resource gap that exists in most companies.

traditional uniform for women only. They decided to break the employees into groups (men, women, management, production) and ask their opinions. After all, this was a "democratic" process.

The women of the company got together to talk about options. In the winter, the office was very cold as there was no central heating.[14] "Personally, I would prefer to wear jeans and a sweater to work," said Julia. "It's freezing in the office in the winter season." They all agreed that would be nice.

"They will never accept that," said Diana. "Women are expected to wear skirts to work. You know what *machistas* Chilean men can be!"[15]

"I think that we should just wear whatever we want to work," said Lana. "I've been wearing a uniform almost all my life, since my school days. Frankly, I'm getting tired of it."

After much discussion, the women decided to go with the traditional uniform. They felt it would be what management was looking for from them. They wanted Roberto and Elías to be pleased with the group so they could continue to participate in the problem-solving process.

The following week, the problem-solving group met to discuss their findings. Diana told the group about the women's desire to wear pants, but that they had decided to go with something more traditional. The men in the group reported that the other males did not really care whether they had a uniform or not. Since all managers were men, they decided management should not have uniforms. In the end, the group agreed that the women should have uniforms and the men should continue to wear what they wanted.

The following week, the group presented their recommendation: uniforms for the women—one jacket, two blouses, and two skirts.

MANAGEMENT'S QUANDARY

Management, along with the psychologist, got together to talk about the results of the group and the progress on the TQM program. "I'm really surprised and frustrated by this group," said Roberto. "It's a real disappointment. They decided to go with the same old thing, and I know that's not what they really wanted. I heard that the women really preferred jeans and sweaters. I'm not opposed to that idea; after all, we do work with farmers in the agriculture business, and besides, it would be a lot cheaper for the company."

"I know," said Juan, "this was a real mistake. Our employees just don't have the capacity to participate in this kind of thing."

The psychologist explained that Chilean workers, in general, are not accustomed to giving their opinion. "Most have never been given an opportunity like this," she said. "The majority of workers at Agro-Araucania have worked most of their lives under a military dictatorship where speaking out was strictly out of the question. However, if you recall their reaction at the first meeting, there was a flood of ideas and suggestions. There were many unaddressed

EXHIBIT 4 Asistente Social Worksheet

EMPLOYEE WORKSHEET

R.U.T.	
Date:	

Employee Name:	
Birth Date:	Age:
Profession:	Marital Status:
Job Title:	Education:

FAMILY MEMBERS

NAME	RELATION	BIRTH DATE	RUT*	MARITAL STATUS	EDUCATION	ACTIVITIES	INSURANCE	SUBSIDY PROGRAMS	MONTHLY INCOME	OBSERVA-TIONS

HOUSING SITUATION

Owner	House	Condition
Renter	Apartment	Good
Multi-Family	Other	Fair
Parental Home		Poor

CHARACTERISTICS

Ceiling		Floor		Rooms		Other		
Plaster	Good	Cement	Good	Total #		Dining Room		Radio
Tin	Fair	Wood	Fair	# Bedrooms		Kitchen		TV
Straw	Poor	Dirt	Poor			Living Room		Other
						# Beds		

UTILITIES

Meters	Electricity	Water	Heating
Network	Connection at the home	Connection at the home	Electricity / Gas
Private	Other	Community Pump	Wood / Paraffin
Other		Other	Other

FUTURE PLANS

No Changes	Number of people living in the home:
Repairs	Number of children:
Additions	
Applied for subsidy?	
How much?	

HEALTH STATUS

Name	
Age	
Diagnosis	
Follow-up	

Nutrition Status	
Meat	
Fish	
Eggs	
Vegetables	
Beans	
Balance	
Variety	
Observations	
General Comments	

*R.U.T. = Chilean equivalent of social security number

EXHIBIT 5 **The *Bien Estar* (Well Being)**

This is a type of in-house insurance policy administered by the company. Typically, the company contributes a fixed amount of money per employee, and the employee either contributes a fixed amount or a percentage of his/her salary. It is an optional benefit that the employees manage. They elect a management committee and decide what benefits they would like to have. Often the fund covers medical expenses not covered under the company's other insurance policies. It may include special benefits for employees who have short-term cash flow problems or who face an extreme financial situation and need assistance. The fund is usually managed with the help of an *asistente social.*

issues that the employees were able to talk about. That doesn't mean that the workers aren't interested in the problem you gave them. I believe in that informal environment they were more open and were able to talk about their true feelings and perceived needs. You must keep in mind that half of your staff is relatively new to the organization. This is relevant because they are trying to please management. They really need more training on working in groups and possibly a facilitator to help the process.

"At this point, I think we need to work with the individual's performance and job before we work on group behavior. They don't have much feedback concerning their own performance so they don't yet feel confident enough to give you opinions on other issues. Considering the lack of individual feedback, I think we really should work on an individual performance/feedback system before we focus on group efforts."

They all agreed to think about it and meet the following week.

NOTES

1. It is a Chilean tradition for any new employee to *pagar el piso* (pay the floor) when they receive their first paycheck. The event is akin to a rite of passage in an organization. Typically, the person buys a cake and champagne and shares a little with all the employees. Managers usually do something more extravagant such as a luncheon or a BBQ. The employee makes a toast asking for the support and help of colleagues as he or she adjusts to the new position.
2. The evening before a board meeting, the directors/owners invited several people to dinner to discuss various issues concerning the business. Traditionally, they invited people involved in agriculture. Recently, they started to invite other members of the business community to talk about other issues, such as training, human resources, and marketing techniques. This was almost unheard of in small- or medium-sized Chilean businesses, particularly outside Santiago.
3. The government agency INDAP (Institute for the Development of Small Farmers) provided technical and financial assistance to small farmers. They advised these farmers on modern farming techniques and gave them a voucher to purchase necessary products.
4. Salvador Allende was Chile's president from 1970 until the military coup led by Augusto Pinochet toppled him in 1973. Allende was a socialist and aimed for a massive redistribution of income to benefit the poor.
5. Human Resource or Personnel Departments are usually not present in Chilean companies, particularly outside the capital city. Psychologists are commonly used by companies to assist in the human resource function, most commonly in selecting and hiring personnel. Chilean companies typically contract with a psychologist to evaluate potential employees and often rely heavily on these evaluations to make their final selections.
6. January and February are vacation months in Chile. During these two months, nearly the entire country shuts down and nothing much gets accomplished. Even if a person is not on holiday, the other parties needed to complete

any given task are likely to be absent, preventing work from getting done.

7. *Gringo* is the Spanish word for North American.
8. Mary Walton, *The Deming Method in Practice,* Spanish Edition (Barcelona: Grupo Editorial Norma S.A., 1992).
9. In Chile, many women have uniforms that they wear to work. These are usually provided by the employer, and they usually consist of a business suit (a jacket and two skirts) and two blouses. Most women prefer to use uniforms to save their own money and reduce the competition among women trying to outdress each other. Typically there is a calendar of combinations; everyone wears the same articles specified for any given day.
10. This writer has never heard a Chilean manager refer to employees as *collaborators*. The Deming book uses this term.
11. In most retail businesses, the work day starts at 9:00 AM and runs until 1:30 PM when they break for an hour and a half long lunch, the biggest meal of the day. They then open again at 3:00 PM and remain open until 7:00 PM.
12. Punctuality is not a strict rule. Most meetings start late. Employees are expected to participate without overtime pay.
13. *Don* is used before a man's name as a title of respect. All the employees use *Don* before Roberto and Elías. When speaking to a woman, *Señora or Señorita* is used. *Doña,* the feminine equivalent of *Don,* is not commonly used before a woman's name.
14. Central heating is very rare in Chile. Most homes and offices are heated with wood stoves and/or portable gas heaters. Relative to U.S. standards, buildings are cold and drafty. Small space heaters are often used under desks to keep feet warm.
15. *The Latin American Political Dictionary* defines *Machista* (adjective) *or Machismo* as: "A cultural trait that stresses male pride, virility and aggressiveness in social and political relations. The *machista* is an active man who displays strength, courage, self-confidence, daring, and sexual prowess. He is an extremely competitive man of action, proud of his manliness, ready to exploit weaknesses in any social relationship. In his self-image he combines the roles of Don Juan, the *conquistador,* the solitary hero, the risk-taking adventurer, and the revolutionary fighter. The origins of machismo have been traced to both Spanish and Latin American sources. It is related to Spanish pride, to personal honor and dignity, to the Indian-*mestizo* fatalistic view of life and to emotional self-expression encouraged in Latin culture. Some writers project that as social, economic, and political systems become more modern and as the movement for women's rights becomes more widespread, the influence of *machismo* will decline."

Part 2/ Exercise 1: Bribery in International Business

Purpose

To discuss issues related to ethical behavior in international business dealings.

Group Size

Any number of groups of four to six members.

Time Required

One class period.

Preparation Required

Students read mini-cases and decide what action should be taken in each one.

Cases

1. You are driving to a nearby country from your job as a manager of a foreign subsidiary. In your car are a number of rather expensive gifts for family and friends in the country you are visiting. When you cross the border, the customs official tells you the duty will be equivalent to $200. Then he smiles, however, hands back your passport and quietly suggests you put a smaller sum, say $20, in the passport and hand it back to him.

   What do you do?

2. You have been hired as an independent consultant on a United States development grant. Part of your job involves working with the Ministry of Health in a developing country. Your assignment is to help standardize some procedures to test for various diseases in the population. After two weeks on the job, a higher-level manager complains to you that money donated by the World Health Organization to the ministry for purchasing vaccines has actually been used to buy expensive computers for top-ranking officials.

   What do you do?

3. You have been trying for several months to privatize what was formerly a state-owned business. The company has been doing well and will likely do better in private hands. Unfortunately, the paperwork is slow and it may take many more months to finish. An official who can help suggests that if you pay expenses for him and his family to visit the parent company in the United States (plus a two-week vacation at Disney World and in New York City), the paperwork can be completed within one week.

   What do you do?

4. One of your top managers in a Middle Eastern country has been kidnapped by a terrorist group that has demanded a ransom of $2 million, plus food assistance for refugees in a specified camp. If the ransom is not paid, they threaten to kill him.

   What do you do?

5. On a business trip to a developing country, you see a nice leather briefcase (which you badly need) for a reasonable price in the local currency (the equivalent of $200 on the standard exchange rate). In this country, however, it is difficult for the locals to get U.S. dollars or other hard currency. The shop clerk offers you the briefcase for $100 if you pay in U.S. dollars.

   What do you do?

6. You are the manager of a foreign subsidiary and have brought your car with you from the United States. Because it is a foreign-purchased car, you must go through a complicated web of lines and bureaucracy (and you yourself must do it—no one can do it for you), which takes anywhere from 20 to

40 hours during business hours. One official tells you, however, that he can "help" if you "loan" him $100 and buy him some good U.S. bourbon.
What do you do?

7. Your company has been trying to get foreign contracts in this developing country for several months. Yesterday, the brother-in-law of the finance minister offered to work as a consultant to help you secure contracts. He charges one and one-half times more than anyone else in a similar situation.
What do you do?
8. You have been working as the director of the foreign subsidiary for several months. This week, you learned several valued employees have part-time businesses that they run while on the job. One of them exchanges foreign currency for employees and visitors. Another rents a few cars to visitors. And so on. You are told this has been acceptable behavior for years.
What do you do?
9. As manager of a foreign subsidiary, you recently discovered your chief of operations has authorized a very convoluted accounting system, most likely to hide many costs that go to his pocket. Right now, you have no real proof, but rumors are circulating to that effect as well. This chief, however, has close ties to officials in the government who can make or break your company in this country.
What do you do?
10. You have been hired to do some management training in a developing country. The costs of the program are almost entirely covered by a U.S. government agency. The people responsible for setting up one of the programs in a large company tell you they want the program to be held in a resort hotel (which is not much more expensive than any other) in a beautiful part of the country. Further, because they are so busy with all the changes in their country, they cannot come to a five-day program, which is what has been funded. Could you please make it a little longer each day and shorten it to three days? You would get paid the same.
What do you do?
11. You have been hired by an investment firm funded by U.S. dollars. Your job is to fund companies in several former communist countries. If you do not meet your quota for each of three months, you will lose your job, or at least have your salary severely cut back. One of the countries is still run by communists, though they have changed the name of their political party. They want you to fund three companies that would still be tightly controlled by the state. You know they would hire their relatives to run those companies. Yet, if you don't fund them, no other opportunities will exist for you in this country.
What do you do?
12. Your new job is to secure contracts with foreign governments in several developing countries. One of your colleagues takes you aside one day to

give you "tips" on how to make sure you get the contracts you are after. He tells you what each nationality likes to hear, to soothe their egos or other psychological needs. For example, people in one country like to be told they will have a better image with the U.S. government if they contract with your company (of course, this is not true). If you tell them these things, he says, they will most definitely give you the contracts. If not, someone in another company will tell them similar things and they will get the contracts.

What do you do?

Part 2/ Exercise 2: Babel Interpersonal Communication

Goals

1. To examine language barriers, which contribute to breakdowns in communication.
2. To demonstrate the anxieties and frustrations that may be felt when communicating under difficult circumstances.
3. To illustrate the impact of nonverbal communication when verbal communication is ineffective and/or restricted.

Group Size

An unlimited number of equal-sized groups of four, six, or eight members each.

Time Required

Approximately 1 class period.

Physical Setting

A room large enough for the groups to meet comfortably.

Materials

1. A pencil and paper for each participant.
2. A blindfold for each group member.

Process

I. The facilitator divides the large group into subgroups.

II. When the groups have assembled, the facilitator announces that each group is to create a language of its own. This language must be significantly different from English and must include the following:

1. A greeting.
2. A description of some object, person, or event.
3. An evaluative statement about an object or a person.
4. A farewell.

Group members must be able to "speak" their group's language at the end of this step. (45 minutes)

Source: "Babel Interpersonal Communication," by Philip M. Ericson from *A Handbook of Structured Experiences for Human Relations Training,* Vol. V, pp. 16–17.

III. Within each language group, members number themselves sequentially, i.e., 1,2,3,4, etc. The facilitator announces the location of a new group to be composed of all participants numbered 1. He likewise forms new groups of participants numbered 2,3,4, and so on.

IV. The facilitator directs members to pair off in the new groups. Each member must teach his new language to his partner without using English or any other recognized language. (20 minutes)

V. The facilitator distributes a blindfold to each group. A blindfolded volunteer from each group teaches his language to the group. A second volunteer repeats this task. (20 minutes)

VI. The facilitator distributes blindfolds to all remaining participants. Participants are told to stand in their second groups, and all chairs are moved aside. Participants blindfold themselves and are instructed to find their original groups without the use of any conventional language or people's names.

VII. When the original groups have been re-formed, the facilitator instructs them to discuss the activity and to answer the following questions:

1. What did this experience illustrate about communication?
2. How did you feel during the experience?
3. What did you learn about yourself from it?

VIII. The facilitator leads a general discussion on the problems faced by people who do not understand a language and on the difficulties that blind people may have in communicating.

Variations

I. The requirements for the new vocabulary can be changed to make the task more difficult or less difficult.

II. All participants can be blindfolded for step V.

III. Real language can be used. The phrases can be preset.

Part 2/ Internet Exercise 1: Cross-Cultural Negotiation 101: Some Tips

Purpose

To research and learn how to negotiate price reductions from international vendors.

Group Size

To be performed individually.

Time Required

Approximately one hour.

Other

Internet connection and search engine needed.

Exercise

Due to the sluggish global economy and slashed travel budgets in many global organizations, the commercial aircraft manufacturing company you work for has experienced a 10 percent decrease in sales over the past six months. As the new vice president of purchasing, you have been asked to negotiate a 10 percent discount from each of the international vendors that supply your firm with raw materials. Assume the vendors are located in Mexico, Singapore, and Nigeria. If successful, your company will achieve its year-end profit goals. Knowing how important it is to understand the dynamics of cross-cultural negotiations (e.g., the other side's personality, the different types of negotiation tactics, etc.), you turn to the Internet to find some helpful websites to learn more about how to succeed in negotiating a reduction in vendor prices. Go to and review the following two U.S.-oriented websites that discuss general negotiation tips. After that, use a search engine to locate three more websites that provide tips on how to negotiate with Mexicans, Singaporeans, and Nigerians.

1. www.negotiatingedge.com (click on "links")
2. www.batna.com (click on "difficult negotiations")

Part Three

Managing Human Resources

Chapter Nine

Global Human Resource Management

Learning Objectives

After completing Chapter 9, you should be able to:

- Describe how strategy and global human resource management practices are related.
- Define the different types of emerging assignments for global managers.
- Identify the reasons many organizations are increasingly turning to short-term and traveling global assignments.
- Discuss the challenges associated with recruiting, selecting, training, compensating, and appraising expatriate managers and employees.
- Understand how increases in global competition and cross-border interfirm agreements are shaping the nature of global human resource deployment in the early part of the 21st century.

Paragon-Mart's Deployment of Global Assignees

The Paragon-Mart Corporation, a U.S.-based retail firm, has enjoyed tremendous growth and success in the U.S. market over the past few decades. The company's executive management team has developed an aggressive global business strategy that entails opening at least 100 new stores in China and Japan within the next five years. The vice president of human resources, Maria Johnson, is creating a human resource action plan to ensure that this new global strategy will be accomplished.

Johnson's first step is to define the number and types of global assignments necessary to accomplish the global strategy. She determined that it would involve approximately 50 global assignees: Some would have to have previous international start-up experience and similar problem-solving skills; others would need to be able to transfer the company's global vision and implement coordination and control systems that would interface effectively with the headquarters' office and stores in other countries; and, some assignees would focus on building trust-based, long-term relationships with key stakeholders in the two countries. In reviewing Paragon-Mart's global staffing philosophy, it seems that the company has always relied on assignees from the United States. Johnson and other Paragon-Mart executives assumed that parent-country nationals could help transfer the company's vision and technology, but failed to see how they could help build stakeholder relationships and develop locally responsive business plans. So, Johnson decided that the company would also utilize key host-country nationals to ensure that these latter objectives were met.

Johnson's job was not finished because she had several additional critical human resource issues for which she would have to develop action plans, including:

- How will these individuals be recruited? Which selection criteria should be used?
- Should Johnson rely on their previous job performance in the United States or consider their cross-cultural skills?
- What kind of cross-cultural and language training programs will be offered?
- How much should these individuals be compensated?
- How should their performance be appraised?
- What kind of a repatriation plan should be developed to decrease turnover after the assignment?

INTRODUCTION TO GLOBAL HUMAN RESOURCE MANAGEMENT

The integration of the world's economies and the globalization of business continue unabated at the beginning of the 21st century. Evidence of globalization can be inferred from several different macroeconomic indicators. First, international trade is growing at a more rapid rate than world output. Over the past 50 years, trade flows have increased 17-fold while real output has expanded by only a factor of 6.[1]

Second, foreign direct investment (FDI) flows, the volume of cross-border investment, have set record levels in recent years. For example, global flows of FDI increased by 18 percent in 2000 for a record US$1.3 trillion. The world's 63,000 transnational corporations, along with their 800,000 foreign affiliates, consider FDI as the main force in global economic integration.[2]

Third, the number of cross-border interfirm agreements, another indicator of globalization, has risen dramatically during the past two decades. Defined as joint ventures, licensing, subcontracting, franchising, marketing, manufacturing, research and development, and exploration, cross-border interfirm agreements reached record levels in recent years.[3]

Finally, social, economic, and political developments throughout the world have contributed to dramatic changes in the way global business is conducted. Such changes include the development of regional trade agreements such as the North American Free Trade Agreement (NAFTA), the emergence of a more economically powerful European Union (EU), the continued opening of China to trade and foreign investment, and the growth in influence of such supranational entities as the General Agreement on Tariffs and Trade (GATT) and the World Trade Organization (WTO).

The trend toward greater economic integration has led to a dramatic increase in the amount of competition for U.S. businesses both abroad and in the domestic market. In the early 1960s, U.S. firms produced more than 40 percent of the world's output. By 1996, the U.S. share of world output slipped to 20.8 percent.[4] Domestically, U.S. businesses are facing more foreign competition than in the past. This trend continued throughout the 1990s and does not show signs of slowing in the 21st century.

How will firms such as Paragon-Mart in the opening vignette survive in such a competitive, global environment? Effectively managing the human factor can help make the difference. Global managers need to strengthen their firms' presence, involvement, and relative positions in domestic and global markets by utilizing their human resources in a manner that helps them establish and sustain competitive advantage. One method to achieve these goals is to align the firm's global management policies so as to support its overall business strategy.

STRATEGY AND GLOBAL HRM FIT

To compete and thrive in the competitive global marketplace of the early 21st century, global managers and their organizations must increasingly improve at managing three (sometimes conflicting) activities:[5]

1. Be more responsive to the different host-country markets (i.e., act locally).
2. Be more integrated globally (i.e., think globally).
3. Facilitate more learning and knowledge transfer (i.e., learn continuously).

To achieve this complicated balancing act, global managers and decision makers must identify, develop, and utilize its employees in a manner that fits with and supports its overall global or transnational strategy. As traditional sources of competitive advantage (e.g. technology, location, and financial capital) become more accessible to competitors, organizations are increasingly turning to rare and harder to imitate resources such as human capital.

Human Capital

Developed by Nobel Laureate Theodore W. Schultz of the United States in 1961, *human capital* refers to the skills and knowledge possessed by employees and the labor costs relative to return on investment (i.e., future productivity) for developing employee skills and knowledge.[6] Human capital is critical to the long-term success of organizations. Schultz referred to the potential impact that human capital can exert over productivity when he wrote: "The quality of human effort can be greatly improved and its productivity enhanced."[7]

Resource-Based View of the Firm

Related to the concept of human capital is a theory that came into prominence in the 1990s and continues to influence strategic management thought in the early part of the 21st century and is referred to as the **resource-based view of the firm.** This theory argues that sustainable competitive advantage can be achieved when the organization's resources, whether they be physical, organizational, or human are valuable, rare, hard to imitate, and without substitutes.[8] Considering the critical role that human resources play in many global organizations, human resource departments and top management alike spend considerable time and financial resources on achieving the right fit between their global business strategies and the internal development and deployment of their employees.[9] The best strategies in the world will not be successful without the right individuals in the right positions to implement and refine the plans.

Considering that human resources are seen as an important means to achieving and sustaining competitive advantage, what can global managers do to facilitate this process? Managers need to pay special attention when making decisions that influence such key areas as global assignment management, recruitment, selection, training, adjustment, performance, repatriation, and labor issues. Exhibit 9.1 includes a comprehensive list of the different areas that make up global HRM.

EXHIBIT 9.1
Global HRM Model

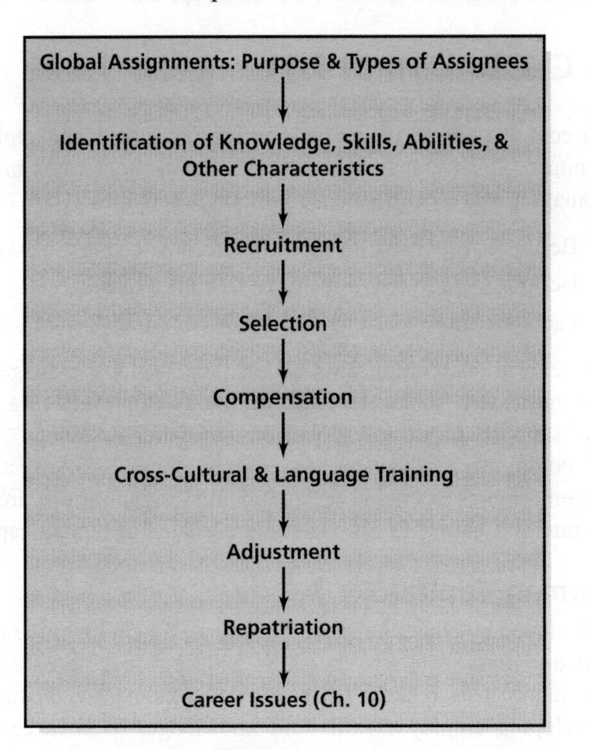

GLOBAL ASSIGNMENTS

As mentioned earlier, transnational organizations must develop and utilize their global managers in a manner that helps them establish and sustain competitive advantage. This idea was captured in a quote by Black and colleagues:[10]

> If multinational firms are to prosper now and in the future, they must develop people who can successfully function in global context-formulating and implementing strategies, inventing and utilizing technologies, and creating and coordinating information. International assignments are the single most powerful means for developing future global leaders.

In contrast to the wide-scale reductions in the use of U.S. long-term global assignees by large multinational firms in the 1970s and 1980s, the number of Americans deployed by U.S. firms remained fairly constant during the latter part of the 1990s. For example, over half of the non-U.S. and U.S. companies completing an annual survey on global relocation trends indicated an increase in the use of overseas-based long-term global assignees over the previous year. The steady use of U.S. expatriates in the 1990s can be attributed to an increase in the utilization rates of global assignees by smaller firms as those firms become more globally active. Similar trends were reported in a large-scale study of 270 European-based multinational organizations that employ approximately 65,000 expatriates. The largest increases in expatriate deployment occurred in Western, Central, and Eastern Europe, and Southeast Asia and China.[11]

In the early part of the 21st century, however, the number of expatriates deployed internationally appears to have decreased. A study found that just 26 percent of U.S. firms reported an increase in the use of expatriates over the previous year; while 39 percent reported no change in expatriate deployment. The study concluded that this temporary lull in expatriation is due to sluggish economies in many parts of the world and to a general feeling of international uncertainty and risk on the part of many companies.[12]

In addition to the continued use of expatriates, global organizations are expected to transfer more non-parent-country managers (i.e., inpatriates) to the home market or headquarters location. Driven by a global skills shortage and the need to expose host-country managers to headquarters' organizational culture and global strategies, inpatriate transfers are likely to increase.[13] Related to this trend is the increased use of third-country nationals who are being placed in many intraregional assignments. For example, a French executive for General Motors (a U.S.-headquartered company) might be placed in charge of European Union operations and transferred to regional headquarters in Zurich, Switzerland.

Given the continued pressure on global firms from international competitors abroad and in domestic markets, companies are likely to continue to develop their managers and future leaders through global assignments. Thus, the utilization of host- and parent-country global assignees is likely to continue in the first few decades of the 21st century.

Global Focus What Do Managers Do on Global Assignments? Some Examples

PROBLEM SOLVING

Assignees may be sent to an overseas subsidiary, customer, vender or other key stakeholder to assist in the resolution of a problem. For example, a Dutch petroleum engineer from Shell Oil may be sent on a six-month assignment from Rotterdam to assist in an oil exploration project in Venezuela.

COORDINATION AND CONTROL

Global assignees are used to help ensure that the organization's global vision and strategies are understood and followed. For example, a computer software development firm in India may assign a high-level manager to one of its sales centers in Thailand to make sure that pricing, promotion, and service policies are being implemented consistently.

STAKEHOLDER RELATIONSHIP BUILDING

Global assignees serve as ambassadors and lobbyists to gain support for organizational initiatives from key stakeholders. For example, an entrepreneur from Kenya, who wants to market his e-business services to the Chinese government, travels several times throughout the year to visit key officials in Beijing to build trust and to identify a need for his services.

TECHNOLOGY, INNOVATION, AND INFORMATION TRANSFER

Global managers aid in the process of transferring key technologies and information from one location to another. For example, Westinghouse Nuclear Fuel in the United States has established close working relationships with licensees, fuel vendors, and nuclear plant operators worldwide, through participation in joint fuel and core design, training, and licensing activities. Westinghouse Nuclear Fuel has shared nuclear fuel and plant operating technology with over 30 companies, providing fuel users and associates with design methodologies, engineering computer programs, manuals, and documentation, as well as training in the use of computer programs and other services.

Global assignments can serve a variety of purposes. The accompanying Global Focus identifies and describes how global assignees are expected to engage in one or more of the following activities: problem-solving, coordination and control, stakeholder relationship building, and technology transfer.

Types of Global Assignees

Generally, there are three sources of employees for global assignments. For key managerial and technical positions, all three sets of employees are frequently used by global organizations. The most commonly used source depends, however, on the international staffing philosophy of the company's top management.[14] The following section highlights the advantages and disadvantages of using parent-, host-, and third-country nationals in global assignments.[15]

Parent-country nationals (PCNs) are citizens of the country in which the organization is headquartered and are usually referred to as expatriates. For example, a Chilean manager representing her family's overseas business venture (e.g., a wine vineyard) in California would be considered an expatriate or parent-country national.

Organizations that rely heavily on PCNs for key overseas positions are following an ethnocentric staffing approach. This staffing strategy tends to be utilized when overseas ventures have little autonomy, strategic decisions are made at headquarters in the parent country, and most of the key positions at the foreign venture are occupied by parent-country nationals. Firms use this approach in early stages of internationalization and when a firm is establishing a new business or product overseas and prior experience is critical. Firms employing this approach will attempt to achieve control over foreign operations by utilizing expatriates and technical staff to transfer its reporting and operational systems. Although its advantages are clear, this approach is not without its problems.

One of the disadvantages of the ethnocentric staffing approach is that it can undermine productivity and encourage turnover due to limited promotion opportunities for host-country nationals. Japanese companies that used a high proportion of Japanese expatriates in international operations experienced higher levels of turnover and complaints by host-country nationals.[16] Additionally, host-country nationals can become upset after comparing compensation packages with those of the parent-country nationals. These sentiments can undermine working relationships and the exchange of valuable information.

Host-country nationals (HCNs) are employees from the host locations in which an international organization is operating. Sometimes referred to as local nationals, these individuals often bring a tremendous amount of knowledge regarding customer needs, business practices, language, and how best to manage and motivate HCN employees. The sales representative in France who meets the Chilean parent-country national would be considered an HCN.

Organizations that rely mostly on HCNs to staff their overseas business operations are following a polycentric staffing approach. This tends to occur when a multinational company considers each of its overseas ventures as a unique national entity that possesses autonomy in decision making. These overseas ventures tend to be managed by host-country nationals who rarely receive promotions to headquarters in the parent country. That is, a firm believing in this approach will decentralize on a country-by-country basis; coordination between overseas ventures will be minimal, and the individual locations will be responsible for developing their own personnel policies and guidelines.

As for advantages, first, the polycentric staffing approach employs more HCNs (thus, removing many of the problems associated with the use of expatriates: language barriers, premature return, and costly business mistakes). Second, the use of host-country nationals can placate local government officials concerned with local employment policies. Third, the employment of host-country nationals is less costly than that of expatriates and provides for continuity in managerial succession.

Disadvantages of the polycentric approach include language barriers and cultural differences between the host and headquarters' personnel, and conflicting national loyalties on the part of the host-country staff. Each of these potential problems can widen the gap between the international venture and the staff at the headquarters location. Another problem related to this approach is the limited career mobility for the host-country national staff.

Third-country nationals (TCNs) are employees from a country other than where the parent organization's headquarters or overseas operations are located. A Nigerian from Lagos who was working for a Chilean organization in France would be considered a TCN.

Organizations that use this type of assignee along with PCNs and HCNs are following a geocentric staffing approach. These firms will attempt to send the right person to the right job anywhere in the world without concern for borders, national culture, or geographic distance. Advantages of this staffing approach include the ability of organizations to develop a highly skilled set of global managers. It also helps ensure that the firm's global vision and strategy are accepted in the different operations around the globe. Disadvantages of geocentric staffing include resistance from host-country governments in terms of visa restrictions in an effort to preserve jobs for their own citizens. Also, this approach to staffing can be quite expensive when considering the relocation, training, and extra compensation costs typically associated with a high number of international transfers each year.

IDENTIFICATION OF KNOWLEDGE, SKILLS, ABILITIES, AND OTHER CHARACTERISTICS

Knowledge, skills, abilities, and other characteristics (KSAOs) are the qualifications needed to perform a global assignment effectively. Research indicates that the criteria for selecting an expatriate in the United States is often based on one's professional/technical ability and domestic track record, while European firms tend to place additional emphasis on cross-cultural and language skills.[17] The U.S. model, often used under intense time pressures to get someone into the global assignment as quickly as possible, is risky because it often does not consider other key aspects of success. Although many lists of critical success factors for expatriates are available, the accompanying Global Focus summarizes some key dimensions that influence global assignees' cross-cultural adjustment.

In addition to these characteristics, the global assignee's spouse and/or family needs to possess the interest and cross-cultural adaptability to succeed overseas as well. As Chapter 10 will discuss, support of the family is a critical factor in the global assignee's adjustment and performance in the overseas assignment.

RECRUITING POTENTIAL GLOBAL ASSIGNEES

Recruiting refers to organizational activities that influence the number and types of applicants who apply for a job and whether the applicants accept jobs that are offered. From a global manager's perspective, recruiting is especially

Global Focus Dimensions of Cross-Cultural Adjustment

Self-orientation refers to global assignees' ability to adapt to the new culture and use healthy stress-reduction techniques. Global assignees with high levels of self-orientation learn how to replace activities that bring pleasure in the home culture with similar, yet different activities in the host culture. For example, a manager who plays cricket in his home country might try to learn how to play baseball or softball during the expatriate assignment.

Others-orientation refers to global assignees' ability to relate to and interact effectively with host-country nationals. Global managers with high levels of others-orientation value making relationships and communicating with host-country nationals. For example, a global manager can signal her interest in host-country nationals by dedicating time and effort to learning and using the host-country language. The effort alone shows respect and can often enhance relationship building between the global and host-country managers.

Perceptual orientation refers to global assignees' ability to understand and learn why host-country nationals behave in such "different" ways. Well-adjusted global managers tend to be more open-minded and less judgmental in their worldview, and have a high tolerance for ambiguity. These individuals act more like cultural anthropologists who are interested in learning about cultural differences as opposed to the more ethnocentric manager who is constantly frustrated by comparison between the host and home country cultures.

Cultural toughness refers to the amount of differences between home- and host-country cultures (the larger the difference, the more difficult the adjustment process). A global manager who takes a long-term assignment in a country with a very unique culture (and language) may find that the adjustment period takes longer and that he or she needs more assistance in understanding the new culture from fellow expatriates or a bicultural host-country manager.

Sources: Mark Mendenhall and Gary Oddou, "Acculturation Profiles of Expatriate Managers: Implications for Cross-Cultural Training Programs," *Columbia Journal of World Business* 21 (1986), pp. 73–79, and Mark Mendenhall and Gary Oddou, "The Dimensions of Expatriate Acculturation: A Review," *Academy of Management Review* 10 (1985), pp. 39–47.

important because many employees may not be willing to accept multiyear global assignments, despite the perceived importance of developing a global perspective and international skills. According to a recent survey of companies with more than 33,000 expatriates, finding qualified candidates to accept global assignments was the most important concern of senior managers of human resource and/or international relocation.[18] Managers' reluctance to transfer internationally can create problems for growing international firms as they attempt to become more globally competitive. In many instances, organizations are forced to send their second- or third-choice candidates. For example, one U.S. study asked respondents how frequently they were forced to shift from first- to second-choice candidates due to refusals. Results indicated that up to 74 percent of companies with high refusals rates (between 10 and 25 percent) used less-qualified home-country nationals to fill international positions.[19] This may help explain why the majority of U.S. firms are not very satisfied with the performance (and thus, the return on investment) from their expatriates.[20]

Although there are many potential determinants of one's willingness to accept or reject an overseas assignment, career and family-related issues play a prominent role in the decision of whether to relocate internationally.[21] These issues will be covered in detail in Chapter 10.

Government Restrictions

Government restrictions can influence recruitment practices in a given country. Most countries begrudgingly issue work visas to nonlocal employees and managers who are transferred there by their companies. These companies often must show evidence that the incoming global assignee possesses skills and knowledge not readily found in the host-country population. One exception to this is Singapore, whose government believes that the continued recruitment of foreign skilled workers is critical to the long-term economic health of the country even in the face of growing unemployment locally.[22]

In addition, many governments around the globe try to control the illegal flow of immigration by placing strict restrictions and penalties on companies that conduct unauthorized recruitment and employment of foreign-born individuals. In the United States, the Immigration Reform and Control Act (IRCA) of 1986 has made companies and organizations the chief enforcers of stopping illegal immigration.

Regional Trade Agreements

Related to this issue of immigration is the growing popularity of regional trade agreements and their potential impact on the flow of employees and workers across borders. The most integrated region in the world, the European Union, provides for the free movement of labor between member countries. However, little labor movement actually occurs because the regulations are difficult to put into practice because of their complexity.[23] European Union leaders have placed illegal immigration and the flow of workers on the top of their agenda as talks continue with 12 applicant states from Eastern and Southern Europe.[24]

E-Recruiting

E-recruiting is growingly rapidly throughout the world. Companies can post an ad or ask for online applications on their own website. For example, Nestlé's (Switzerland) website (www.nestle.com) has a section for individuals who want to join the company and describes the characteristics it wants in its people (e.g., respect other cultures, embrace diversity, and never discriminate on any basis).

For companies that want a more proactive search, the cost on many Internet-based job search websites is reasonable. For example, the "post a job express" option at Monster.com (http://www.monster.com) in which a job is posted for 60 days in a single geographic location costs about US$300. This e-recruiting option provides almost immediate access to thousands of prospective applicants. The largest job-placement websites have reported huge increases in the number of resumes that were posted in 2001. For example, Monster.com listed 8.3 million

EXHIBIT 9.2
Some Job Search Websites for Global Recruiters

www.Monster.com—Search by location, job title, and keyword; a leading online career services provider in the United States.
www.StepStone.com—Search by job, location, and company; a leading online career services provider in Western Europe.
www.HotJobs.com—Search by career field, location, and company.
www.CareerBuilder.com—Search by location, job title, keyword, and salary.
www.Dice.com—Leading technology job board with permanent and contract jobs.
www.FlipDog.com—Search thousands of employment opportunities gathered directly from organizations' websites.
www.Jobs.com—Search for jobs, post a resume, and review career resources.
www.Jobsonline.com—Search job postings, find samples of resumes and cover letters, seek career advice and use a salary calculator.
www.NationJob.com—Job listings will be identified and sent to personal e-mail addresses.

resumes, while CareerBuilder.com indicated that it listed 2.0 million. In Western Europe, StepStone.com reported over 3 million users per month in 2002. Overall, the e-recruiting market was expected to grow rapidly from just $500 million in 2000 to $4.6 billion in 2004.[25]

To help fill job vacancies, recruiters can use any number of Internet-based job searching websites that are popular among job seekers. Exhibit 9.2 provides examples of such websites.

In addition to job search websites, recruitment continues to be conducted by more traditional means such as placing media advertisements in local newspapers and on the radio, contracting with employment agencies and executive search firms, and cultivating internship and permanent placement programs with colleges and universities.

Realistic Job Previews

A **realistic job preview** provides prospective employees or global assignees with realistic information about a job without distortion or exaggeration. In contrast, traditional job previews present the job in a very positive light, as attractive, interesting, and stimulating. From a realistic perspective, most jobs have both positive and negative features.[26]

When realistic job previews are given to job candidates, some will self-select out of the selection process and seek employment elsewhere. For those who remain interested in the job and are hired, research indicates that these individuals will experience higher levels of job satisfaction and job survival while experiencing lower intention to leave the job.[27]

When interviewing candidates for global assignments, realistic job previews are especially important given the fact that the risks to family and career are substantially higher for those individuals who work for an extended time overseas. These issues will be covered in Chapter 10.

SELECTING THE BEST CANDIDATE

Within the United States, Western Europe, and Japan the face-to-face interview is the most commonly used device for selecting global assignees.[28] Though often criticized for their lack of accuracy and consistency, face-to-face interviews can be good predictors of international job performance if they are structured. Typically, structured interviews possess the following characteristics:[29]

1. The questions are based on a job analysis (a systematic analysis of the job's tasks, duties, and responsibilities).
2. The same questions are asked of each candidate.
3. Consistent scoring is applied to each of the candidate's responses (e.g., 1 for "very poor" . . . 5 for "very good").
4. Detailed notes are taken.

Structured interview questions attempt to assess a candidate's behavior, either in past jobs or in future hypothetical work situations. For example, a candidate who is applying for an export manager position might be asked: "Tell me about a time in a previous job when you had to resolve a problem with an overseas-based client who did not speak your language."

The types of questions interviewers can ask candidates differ dramatically by country. For example, in the United States where equal employment opportunity laws are enforced, questions about a candidate's family, marital status, and nationality are prohibited. In comparison, in many parts of Latin America, such questions are more common.

In addition to interviewing candidates, some global companies use standardized tests to assess the candidate's (and his or her family's) potential to succeed overseas, including cross-cultural adaptability, interest in living overseas, language ability, and conflict-resolution skills. One of the issues with these instruments is that individuals in certain countries (e.g., Norway) perceive them as intrusive. Also, such tests may not be valid in predicting job performance for all types of global assignments. A wide variety of tests are available, including the Global Assignment Preparedness Survey (G-A-P-S™), which assesses candidates on six criteria: cultural flexibility, willingness to communicate, ability to develop social relationships, perceptual abilities, conflict-resolution style, and leadership style.[30]

Another standardized test for global assignees is the Cross-Cultural Adaptability Inventory (CCAI™). This self-assessment, self-scoring test can help individuals and groups identify their abilities to adapt to new situations, interact with people different from oneself, tolerate ambiguity, and maintain a sense of self in new and unique surroundings.

In addition to testing cross-cultural preparedness, standardized tests that measure certain personality factors should be used when assessing qualifications for global assignments. For example, expatriates who have contact with host-country nationals and who possess the personality trait of openness (i.e., enjoy trying new and different things, etc.) will tend to experience higher levels of cross-cultural adjustment. Also, expatriates who are conscientious (i.e., persistent and always get the job done) tend to receive higher performance ratings from supervisors. In addition to openness and conscientiousness, the personality trait of self-monitoring also helps predict expatriate behavior overseas. It was reported that expatriates who are more aware of how they behave and appear to others tend to achieve higher assignment-specific performance.[31]

Despite the existence of such standardized tests and evaluations, many global organizations do not use them extensively because they can be perceived as overly intrusive. However, many global organizations do make them available to candidates (and their families) to help them self-select in or out of the potential assignment.

COMPENSATING GLOBAL ASSIGNEES

To build competitive advantage, a global organization needs to develop and employ compensation policies capable of attracting, retaining, and motivating global assignees. In general, compensation policies should be consistent with the company's overall strategy and business needs. Also, when designing international compensation systems, companies try to achieve perceived fairness and equity, cost reduction and administration, ability to attract qualified candidates, and flexibility to modify when necessary.[32]

Types of Compensation Approaches

Although many approaches are available,[33] one of the most popular international compensation approaches for U.S., European, and Japanese firms is known as the **balance-sheet approach.** The objective here is to ensure that the expatriate maintains a similar standard of living as in the home country and to ensure employee mobility by providing some financial incentives to accept the global assignment. The major components include assistance with home- and host-country income taxes, host-country housing, goods and services (e.g., food, clothing, medical care), and a reserve for contributions to savings, benefits, pensions, and so on.

Key advantages to the balance-sheet approach are that it maintains equity between expatriates from the same home country and for the same expatriate on different assignments. Also, this approach is fairly logical, is easy to explain to prospective global assignees, and tends to motivate individuals to accept assignments. The disadvantages to this approach include the higher cost (compared to using the going rate of some host-country markets), complexity of administration, disparities between expatriates and host-country national managers, and reentry problems back into the home country.

Another common international compensation approach is the **going or local market rate approach** in which global assignees' compensation is linked directly to local compensation conditions. Base pay is established by host-country wage surveys and norms. For low-paying countries, this amount might be supplemented by additional compensation from the home-country office.

Though not as popular as the balance-sheet approach, one research study of European expatriation policies reported that 18 percent of responding firms used the local market rate when sending their expatriates from Europe to the United States and within Europe itself.[34] This reflects the idea that management salaries in several industrialized countries are converging and do not have huge discrepancies in compensation.

Advantages to this approach include the achievement of equity between global assignees and host-country nationals, equity between different nationalities of global assignees, and lower administration costs. Unfortunately, this approach also has some drawbacks, including variation between assignments for the same global assignees and potential reentry problems when the assignee returns to the home country.

Allowances in Expatriate Pay Packages

Long-term global assignees are often provided with a variety of extras to provide incentives for relocation and to make sure they are able to maintain their home-country standard of living. According to Milkovich and Newman, there are three broad categories of allowances:[35]

1. Financial: company-paid children's education allowance, home leave allowance, mobility premium, and assignment completion bonuses.
2. Social adjustment: rest and relaxation leave, language and cross-cultural training, club memberships, and assistance with locating a new home.
3. Family support: child care providers, assistance locating spousal employment, and assistance locating schools for children.

Does One Size Fit All?

Global assignments are extremely variable in terms of their purpose, length, and destination. For example, a global assignee from Ericsson in Norway may be asked to relocate to India for three months to assist in the development of a new customer service center. In terms of compensation, perhaps a onetime lump-sum payment equaling 10 to 20 percent of their base pay in Norway would be sufficient to ensure the individual accepts the position and feels equitably rewarded. It would not make sense to incur the administrative or financial costs of placing this individual on a balance-sheet compensation approach for such a short-term assignment, whereas, if the assignee were going to be in India for three years, a balance-sheet or local market rate approach would be applicable and appropriate.

In addition, companies are increasingly utilizing global assignees that are diverse in terms of their levels within their organizations, ages, gender, country of origin, and so on. For example, some companies, in response to the inherent difficulty of persuading middle managers (who are often married with school-age children) to accept global assignments, turn to younger, single employees and/or more senior "empty nesters" (i.e., no school-age children at home) to accept these positions. Also, research indicates that the percentage of female expatriates deployed by U.S. firms has increased in recent years to approximately 16 percent of total expatriates.[36] Similarly, there is evidence that organizations are providing host- and third-country nationals with more opportunities to accept global and intraregional assignments. Also, these individuals are often brought to the home-country operation for training and cross-fertilization purposes (this process is referred to as inpatriation).[37]

National culture can also influence the design and implementation of international compensation strategies. For example, U.S. and Canadian compensation policies tend to encourage individualism and high performance. In contrast, many continental European programs often focus on social responsibility. In Japan, seniority and company service are major determinants of compensation programs.[38]

In sum, international compensation approaches need to be standardized when possible to achieve consistency and cost efficiencies, but they also need to be flexible to accommodate the unique issues that arise as companies attempt to use strategic compensation approaches to support their business strategies and objectives.

CROSS-CULTURAL AND LANGUAGE TRAINING

Providing global managers with cross-cultural training leads to increased understanding and awareness about the target culture, which encourages greater attitude and behavior flexibility; ultimately resulting in faster adjustment and higher levels of performance.[39] A review of 29 research studies assessed the efficacy of cross-cultural training on three global assignment outcomes: cross-cultural skill development (self, relationship, and perceptual), adjustment, and performance. The review found strong support that cross-cultural training programs influence all three outcomes with 11 of the 15 studies finding a direct link between training and performance.[40]

Considering that training helps in global assignee adjustment and performance, it would be logical to assume that all companies would offer this to their employees. Unfortunately, this is not the case. According to a survey of 150 senior human resource and/or managers of international relocation programs from companies with a combined total of 33,340 expatriates, only 69 percent of respondent companies offer cross-cultural training for at least one day.[41] Since many of these companies do not make this training mandatory, only 67 percent of expatriates actually participate.

Reasons more global organizations aren't offering and mandating training programs include lack of top management support for such programs and the lack of time between when the assignment is made and the date of departure. Other reasons include lack of trainers, lack of awareness of training needs, and lack of long-range planning.[42]

Types of Training

Cross-cultural training programs vary considerably, by content, intensity, and number of days for delivery, but overall they each attempt to increase the participant's understanding and awareness of the target culture and the knowledge, skills, and abilities needed to succeed while working in that culture. Training typically occurs before departure, but some organizations supplement this with follow-up postarrival training within the host country. According to Ronen, training methods and techniques can be categorized in the following ways:[43]

1. Informational training—lectures, reading material, and videotapes to provide basic information about a destination country's history, economy, political institutions, languages, and religions.
2. Experiential seminars—simulations and role-plays designed to develop cross-cultural negotiation skills and to decrease ethnocentrism.
3. Sensitivity training—communication workshops to build understanding of self-awareness, communication style, empathy, listening skills, and nonjudgmental behavior.
4. Field experiences—meetings with ex-global assignees and microcultures within the home country to lead to understanding of customs, values, beliefs, and nonverbal behaviors of the destination culture.
5. Language skills—classes, CDs, PC and Web-based learning, and tutoring used to develop proficiency in interpersonal, and survival communication skills.

Exhibit 9.3 lists some organizations that provide these and other types of cross-cultural training programs.

The intensity or rigor of each of these approaches differs.[44] Generally, informational training is considered low in rigor from both the trainer and trainee perspective; the effort and energy required for this approach is modest. In contrast, the remaining four types of training are considered to be much more rigorous and demanding. Rigorous cross-cultural training programs are recommended for those individuals undertaking multiyear global assignments in culturally distinct host countries where frequent interaction is required with host-country nationals. For example, a global assignee from a Hong Kong financial services firm who will be based in Frankfurt, Germany, for three years would benefit from intense cross-cultural and language training.

In addition to these formal training approaches, premove visits to find adequate housing, practical in-country assistance (e.g., information about medical institutions, grocery stores, safety tips, etc.), and job-specific skills training may be offered by the global assignee's organization.

Which Approach to Use?

Tung reasoned that global assignees whose job will include a high degree of interaction with host-country nationals (e.g., subsidiary employees, customers, etc.) in a culture that is very dissimilar to the assignee's home culture, will need the most rigorous training available.[45] Others have argued that global assignee training in the 21st century should consist of in-country, real-time training; global mind-set training; and CD-ROM/Internet based training.[46]

EXHIBIT 9.3 Cross-Cultural Training and Consulting Companies

The following are companies that provide cross-cultural training, consulting, and other services for global assignees. For more information, please visit http://www.shrmglobal.org/function/xculture.asp.

Cendant Intercultural (http://www.cendantintercultural.com/)

Cendant Intercultural is an international training and consulting firm, specializing in international human resources support services. The firm's primary service areas are global workforce development and international assignment support services, such as cross-cultural training, destination services, assessment and selection, and repatriation workshops. Cendant Intercultural has trainers, associates, and destination services representatives in over 100 countries worldwide.

Berlitz International, Inc. (http://www.berlitz.com)

Berlitz, provider of international language training services, offers customized language instructions, cross-cultural training, translation and interpretation services through 400 offices worldwide, including more than 70 in the United States and Canada. Private, semiprivate, and group programs are available, and the total immersion program delivers conversational proficiency in as little as 2–6 weeks. Certain Berlitz courses are recommended for college credit by the American Council on Education.

Farnham Castle (http://www.farnhamcastle.com)

For 50 years the castle has been the home of the world-renowned Farnham Castle International Briefing and Conference Centre, providing intercultural training to employees of the world's leading companies as well as U.K. and overseas governments. In addition, specific programs are available in intercultural management, country and business briefings, repatriation, and intensive language training.

ITAP International (http://www.itapintl.com)

Based in Princeton, New Jersey, ITAP International provides cross-cultural consulting, training, and coaching to global organizations throughout the world. ITAP helps companies understand the business impact of cultural assumptions as well as focuses organizations and individuals to look at problems through the cultural diversity lens. In addition, ITAP helps individuals focus on their cultural preferences and leverage these in business interactions; global teams improve performance; and companies with global workforces improve cultural effectiveness.

Prudential Relocation Intercultural Services (303/546-1011)

For more than 30 years, Prudential Relocation Intercultural Services has provided custom-tailored training, consulting, assessment, and research in support of international human resource managers, expatriate employees and families, international business travelers, and workforce diversity. Services include cross-cultural and language training, diversity skills, foreign business practices, negotiations training, international human resource management skills development for host-country nationals, technology transfer training, repatriation programs, and international relocation management and overseas settling-in assistance. Programs have been conducted in 95 countries at training facilities in New York, Colorado, Texas, London, and Tokyo, as well as at client locations worldwide.

Sietar International (http://www.sietar.org)

Sietar International is an international professional organization for managers, consultants, and educators who are involved in facilitating contact, exchange, and integration for students, trainees, migrants, and professional personnel operating in a host culture different from their own. Members include educators at primary, secondary, and third level whose subject areas include languages, geography, civics, international relations, or conflict resolution; administrators and faculty of study abroad and foreign student programs; Third World development administrators and trainers; international business and language trainers, intercultural exchange facilitators. Sietar publishes *Communique International Journal of Intercultural Relations.*

More comprehensive models have been developed and include such factors as the assignee's motivation to apply learned behaviors on the job overseas, length of assignment, nature and type of job. For example, a traveling global assignee that is based out of Madrid, Spain, whose sales territory includes parts of France, Portugal, and Germany, makes short one-day visits to each of his customers. He would be expected to have a fundamental grasp of each of the languages and a strong understanding of how to relate to each of his customers. In sum, the global assignee and his or her company need to identify the types of cross-cultural training that are most appropriate for the type, length, nature, and objectives of the global assignment in question.

ADJUSTMENT IN THE HOST COUNTRY

When a parent-country national from Japan is sent on a three-year global assignment to Spain, the Japanese individual will need to adjust to working in a new and unfamiliar job, to interacting with host-country nationals, and to fitting in and functioning in the unfamiliar host culture. It is generally believed that individuals who make these adjustments more rapidly are at a distinct advantage and will tend to reach their performance levels sooner than those who struggle through a long adjustment process. In contrast, those global assignees who cannot adjust often return prematurely to the parent country or remain in the global assignment as an underperformer.

Culture Shock

When global assignees relocate or travel extensively to a different country, often they will be bombarded with unfamiliar signs, words, nonverbal gestures, laws, social customs, driving rules, and other cultural artifacts that do not make sense to them. For example, the OK sign (with thumb and forefinger in a circle) is a harmless gesture in the United States, but has severe connotations when used in Brazil. Though many host-country nationals forgive such mistakes when done by a newly arrived foreign national, the cumulative effect of being exposed to unfamiliar cues results in what is known as **culture shock.** Though the intensity may vary, many individuals who are transplanted into a new culture will typically go through the following stages of adjustment:[47]

1. Honeymoon stage. This can last from a few days to six months and is characterized by a great deal of excitement about being in a new place, eating new types of food, meeting new and interesting host-country nationals, and so on.
2. Hostile attitude stage. The honeymoon stage starts to slip as problems start to occur with school, health care, shopping, transportation, telephone systems, and so on. In essence, the host country is blamed for everything. This is a crisis stage that needs to be overcome for a successful sojourn; if not, underperformance in the assignment or premature return to the parent country is likely.

3. Acceptance stage. As the global assignee resolves successfully the crises that occur in the last stage, then he or she will begin to accept and enjoy the host country and its people for they are not better or worse than the home-country culture, just different and interesting in its own right. The assignee accepts the food, habits, customs, and language(s) of the hosts.

Types of Adjustment

Global assignees face a variety of adjustment challenges. Researchers have identified three major categories of adjustment: work/job, interacting with host-country nationals, and general nonwork environment.[48] Adjustment to work is thought to be the least stressful due to the fact that the assignee has experience with the company and in many cases has a good idea of the task performance requirements. More difficult is the adjustment to interacting with host-country nationals. This is more challenging due to possible differences in social, political, educational, economic, religious, and language influences. Learning how to fit into the general nonwork environment can also be quite challenging and often includes adjustment to food, transportation, medical services, entertainment, schooling, and more.

Poor Adjustment and Its Consequences

Global assignee failure is typically defined as the premature return of an expatriate (i.e., before the assignment is completed). Although there are many possible reasons, insufficient adjustment to the host culture is a major contributor to both premature return and/or reduced performance while on assignment. Many of the reasons for such failure are family-related (which will be discussed in Chapter 10), but global assignee maladjustment is a critical issue. Although no reliable large-scale empirical research projects have been conducted to pinpoint the true extent of expatriate failure rates in the past 20 years, there is some indication that failure rates among U.S. expatriates is slightly higher than that of European and Japanese expatriates.[49]

When failure does occur, there are a variety of costs to the global assignee, the parent-country organization, and the host-country operation. The assignee, once seen as a "fast tracker" and future star, may find his or her image tarnished within the organization. This can lead to decreased motivation, performance, and even turnover during or after the global assignment. The parent-country organization will bear the direct costs of relocating the individual and his or her family back to the parent country, conducting another candidate search, and relocating a new assignee and his or her family to the country of assignment. The host-country operations will have to repair the damage often done by the failed global assignee, rebuilding confidence and trust with government officials, customers, vendors, and the venture's host-country employees.

What Influences the Adjustment Process?

Before departing to the new culture, a rigorous cross-cultural training program can assist the global assignee to develop realistic expectations of the new culture. Also, selecting candidates who have a track record of having worked successfully in the culture of the assignment is critical. If none exist within the organization, then external recruitment may be a viable alternative, or an internal candidate with regional or any successful previous overseas work experience might prove acceptable. Previous expatriates who had successful overseas assignments are great sources of information for the soon-to-be-sent global assignees. They can provide tips and information on how to stay connected with the parent-country office, adjust to the new culture, manage the postassignment career, and so on.

After arriving in the host culture, several factors can assist in the adjustment process, including seeking to clarify one's job or role, developing an understanding for the host-country nationals, and helping one's family to adjust.[50] In addition, research indicates that global assignees who perceive that their companies are supporting them in the adjustment process (e.g., giving assignees some time off at the start of the assignment for themselves and their families to get settled) tend to adjust more successfully.[51] Global assignees' personalities can also aid or hinder the adjustment process. For example, one research study found that expatriates who had contact with host-country nationals and possessed the personality trait of openness (i.e., enjoy trying new things, working with new concepts and ideas, etc.) were better able to adjust to the new culture. Based on this and similar research findings, selection programs should identify candidates who possess the personality trait of openness to help ensure a successful adjustment to the host culture.

REPATRIATION

For many global assignees who are about to finish their international assignments and return home, the repatriation process will be filled with relief, anxiety, and a great deal of expected and unexpected change. Returning to the home country, especially for first-time global assignees, is a difficult process. Evans and associates summed up many of the reasons why this is such a difficult process:[52]

- Repatriates have to rebuild their professional networks and simultaneously work to get their careers back on track.
- Many repatriates lose the autonomy, freedom, and social status they had only weeks or months earlier in the global assignment (they go from being "big fish/little pond" to "little fish/big pond").
- Repatriates are often placed into meaningless "holding pattern" jobs when they first arrive at the home office until a suitable position opens up.
- Many repatriates relinquish the financial extras they received while on the global assignment, leading many to experience a type of financial shock.
- Family problems such as spouse reemployment and children's social integration often lead to family problems (see Chapter 10).

A study that analyzed some of the influences on the maladjustment of British repatriates found that length of time overseas, unrealistic expectations of job opportunities in the home country, downward job mobility, reduced work status, and negative perceptions of organizational support were all linked to repatriation adjustment problems.[53]

These issues often culminate in a type of reverse culture shock for the repatriate and his or her family. The returning assignee often expects the process of "coming home" to go much more smoothly than it usually does. Many things have changed in the home country during the assignee's absence such as housing costs, neighborhoods, the economy, job market, and so on. Also, key players and politics at headquarters may have changed, adding to the repatriate's sense of disorientation.

Repatriate Turnover

The combined effect of these issues can influence the repatriate's intention to quit and leave the organization. Although estimates vary widely, research has consistently reported that the repatriation turnover rate within two years of returning from the global assignment is between 10 and 25 percent.[54] This issue of turnover is especially worrisome when one considers the investment the organization made in the global assignee's selection, training, compensation, relocation, and repatriation. Global companies cannot afford to lose these internationally trained human resources.

Ways to Improve the Repatriation Process

The repatriation adjustment process can be improved during the pre- and post-return periods. Prereturn adjustment can be improved by a variety of means: (1) continuously exchanging information between the global assignee and his or her superiors and mentors in the home country, (2) assigning an organizational sponsor or mentor who is likely to remain in the home-country location for the duration of the expatriate's assignment, and (3) allowing occasional home leave visits to let the global assignee stay in touch with colleagues, superiors, friends, and so on. At Honeywell, employees and their families complete a repatriation program within six months of returning to the home country. The one-day program consists of counselor-facilitated discussion of potential readjustment issues and ways to apply the international skills in the home-office environment, as well as meeting with a former repatriated family.[55]

After the global assignee returns to the home country, several additional steps can be taken by the organization to ensure a smoother transition. First, organizations can provide repatriates with jobs that take advantage of the assignee's new international skills and allow for employee discretion. For example, repatriates at Deloitte & Touche are often placed in positions that allow them to have contact with clients from the country in which they lived.[56] Although not necessary in all cases, promotions for repatriates who did outstanding work overseas would send a clear message to potential candidates for future assignments that international work is clearly rewarded within the firm. Organizational variables such as a transition period of one to three months in which some financial incentives are kept by the repatriate until his or her spouse finds gainful employment or a new house is purchased, can ease the financial shock of the assignee. Job search assistance for the spouse would also help with important nonwork factors that can have an impact on the repatriate's productivity during the transition period (see Chapter 10). In general, repatriates whose companies provided supportive practices and policies were less inclined to leave their companies.[57]

The bottom line when it comes to many repatriation programs is to help the repatriate become quickly reintegrated into the home office (and help the family get situated) so that he or she can make a meaningful and strong contribution to the organization. To that end, a well-developed repatriation program can increase the return on investment of expatriate assignments, decrease repatriate turnover, and send a positive signal to future candidates that returning global assignees are important to the organization.

LABOR RELATIONS AND THE GLOBAL CORPORATION

Global corporations encounter a variety of labor relations issues that are different from purely domestic operations. There are many differences in the structure of unions and the influence they have over an organization's operations worldwide. In addition, labor laws will be unique to every nation with which an organization wishes to do business. In Mexico, for example, management places much less emphasis on the details of written contracts, instead relying on informal agreements to achieve desired work goals. In Germany, employee codetermination is a legally guaranteed right. German law gives employees three different degrees of participation, depending on the issue in question. German worker councils participate in HRM decisions such as dismissals, work procedures, design of the workplace, working hours, training programs, and safety regulations.[58]

Government regulation is another area where the global firm will encounter vastly different systems around the world. For example, in Singapore, the National Wages Council sets guidelines for annual wage adjustments, while legislation regulates working conditions throughout the country.[59]

CONCLUSION

This chapter covered a variety of topics and issues that global and transnational managers need to be aware of as they attempt to utilize their human resources in effective and competitive ways. As world economies become more tightly linked and the need for international skills and perspectives increase, global organizations will continue to develop their human capital by deploying their parent-, host-, third-country managers and employees on a variety of global assignments. To accomplish this, e-recruiting on career services websites such as Monster.com and StepStone.com as well as using cross-cultural adjustment skills testing for global candidates and their spouses will be used in greater amounts. Expatriates (and spouses and families) should continue to receive cross-cultural and language training before and during the early stages of assignments.

Compensation packages will tend to be more standardized across global assignees and not be as generous as a couple of decades ago. Many companies are sending the signal that overseas experience is an expected part of career progression with the organization and not a huge personal sacrifice requiring large foreign service premium payments and other incentives. Global organizations will continue to prepare their assignees for the cross-cultural adjustment of going to the host country and then retuning home upon completion of the assignment. Several of these issues have a substantial impact on the global manager's career and on his/her spouse and family. Because of the unique nature of these additional issues, the next chapter is dedicated to discussing these issues in greater detail.

Key Terms

Balance-sheet approach, *341*
Culture shock, *346*
E-recruiting, *338*
Global assignments, *333*
Going or local market rate approach, *341*
Host-country nationals, *335*
Parent-country nationals, *334*
Realistic job preview, *339*
Resource-based view of the firm, *332*
Third-country nationals, *336*

Review, Critical Thinking, and Discussion Questions

1. What is the difference between a parent-, host-, and third-country national? Explain.
2. Compare and contrast an ethnocentric staffing policy with a polycentric staffing policy.
3. What is a realistic job preview? Why is it important to help a candidate for a global assignment develop realistic expectations of the job?
4. Structured interviews tend to be more valid and reliable than unstructured interviews. Describe the characteristics of a structured interview.
5. Identify and describe three typical allowances found in many expatriate compensation packages.
6. Assume you are being sent on a three-year global assignment in which you will be expected to interact with host-country nationals and speak the host-country language. Which cross-cultural training methods/techniques would you need to prepare you for this assignment?
7. Identify and describe the three stages of culture shock.
8. What problems can undermine the effectiveness of performance appraisals?
9. Why do some repatriates leave the organization after returning from their global assignment?
10. Would you consider taking a two-year global assignment? Under what conditions would this opportunity be more enticing? Less enticing?

Endnotes

1. Charles Hill, *Global Business,* 2nd ed. (New York: Irwin-McGraw Hill, 2001).
2. UN Conference on Trade and Development, *World Investment Report* (New York and Geneva: United Nations, 2001).
3. Nancy J. Adler, *International Dimensions of Organizational Behavior,* 4th ed. (Cincinnati: South-Western, 2002), p. 4.
4. UN Conference on Trade and Development, *World Investment Report* (New York and Geneva: United Nations, 1997).
5. Paul Evans, Vladimir Pucik, and Jean-Louis Barsoux, *The Global Challenge: Frameworks for International Human Resource Management* (New York: McGraw-Hill/Irwin, 2002).
6. E.G. Flamholtz and J. Lacey, "The Implications of the Economic Theory of Human Capital for Personnel Management," *Personnel Review* 10 (1981), pp. 30-41; G.S. Becker, *Human Capital: At Theoretical and Empirical Analysis, With Special Reference to Education,* 2nd ed. (New York: National Bureau of Economic Research: University Press, 1975); and Theodore W. Schultz, "Investment in Human Capital," *The American Economic Review* 1 (1961), pp. 1–17.
7. T.W. Schultz, *Investment in Human Capital: The Role of Education and of Research* (New York: Free Press, 1971), p. 25.
8. Jay Barney, *"Firm Resources and Sustained Competitive Advantage," Journal of Management* 17 (1991), pp. 99–120.
9. Patrick M. Wright, Benjamin B. Dunford, and Scott A. Snell, "Human Resources and the Resource Based View of the Firm," *Journal of Management,* 27 (2001), pp. 701–21, and Randall S. Schuler and N. Rogovsky, "Understanding Compensation Practice Variations Across Firms: The Impact of National Culture," *Journal of International Business Studies* 29 (1998), pp. 159–77.
10. J. Stewart Black, Hal B. Gregersen, Mark E. Mendenhall, and Linda K. Stroh, *Globalizing People Through International Assignments* (Reading, MA: Addison-Wesley, 1999).
11. Windham International, New York, NY, National Foreign Trade Council, New York, NY, and Institute for International Human Resources, Alexandria, VA, *Global Relocation Trends 1999 Survey Report* (Society for Human Resource Management, 1999), and Windham International and National Foreign Trade Council, *Global Relocation Trends 1998 Survey Report* (Publisher: Windham Intnl., June 1998).
12. GMAC Global Relocation Services, Warren, NJ, National Foreign Trade Council, New York, NY, and SHRM Global Forum, Alexandria, VA, *Global Relocation Trends 2001 Survey Report* (Publisher: GMAC G.R.S., 2002).
13. Michael Harvey and Milorad M. Novicevic, "The Influences of Inpatriation Practices on the Strategic Orientation of a Global Organization," *International Journal of Management,* 2000, pp. 362–71, and Michael G. Harvey, Michael F. Price, Cheri Speier, Milorad M. Novicevic, "The Role of Inpatriates in a Globalization Strategy and Challenges Associated with the Inpatriation Process HR," *Human Resource Planning,* 1999, pp. 38–50.
14. H.V. Perlmutter, "The Tortuous Evolution of the Multinational Corporation," *Columbia Journal of World Business* 4 (1969), pp. 9–18.
15. For a review, see Peter J. Dowling, Denice E. Welch, and Randall S. Schuler, *International Human Resource Management: Managing People in a Multinational Context,* 3rd ed. (Cincinnati: South-Western, 1999).

16. Rochelle Kopp, "International Human Resource Policies and Practices in Japanese, European, and United States Multinationals," *Human Resource Management* 33 (1994), pp. 581–99.
17. Evans et al., *Global Challenge;* V. Suutari and Chris Brewster, "International Assignments across European Borders: No Problems?" in *International HRM: Contemporary Issues in Europe,* eds. C. Brewster and H. Harris (London: Routledge, 1999); and J. Stewart Black, Hal B. Gregersen, and Mark E. Mendenhall, *Global Assignments: Successfully Expatriating and Repatriating International Managers* (San Francisco: Jossey Bass, 1992).
18. GMAC Global Relocation Services, *Global Relocation Trends*.
19. Michael G. Harvey, "The Impact of Dual-Career Families on International Relocations," *Human Resource Management Review* 5 (1995), pp. 223–44.
20. J. Stewart Black and Hal B. Gregersen, "The Right Way to Manage Expats," *Harvard Business Review,* March–April 1999, pp. 52–63.
21. J. Ball, "DaimlerChrysler's Transfer Woes: Workers Resist Moves Abroad—And Here," *Wall Street Journal,* August 24, 1999, p. B1; J. Hauser, "Managing Expatriates' Careers," *HR Focus* 76 (1999), pp. 11–12; Michael G. Harvey, "Addressing the Dual-Career Expatriate Dilemma," *Human Resource Planning* 19 (1996), pp. 18–39; and Jeanne M. Brett and Linda K. Stroh, "Willingness to Relocate Internationally," *Human Resource Management* 34 (1995), pp. 405–24.
22. Shu Shin Luh, "Singapore Recruits Foreigners Despite Qualms at Home," *Wall Street Journal,* October 9, 2001, p. B1.
23. Francois Vandamme, "Labour Mobility Within the European Union: Findings, Stakes and Prospects," *International Labour Review* 139 (2000), pp. 437–55.
24. "Europe: Huddled Masses, Please Stay Away: The European Union and Immigration," *The Economist,* June 15, 2002, pp. 49–50, and Dick Leonard, "Eye on the EU: Enlargement Talks Focus on Immigration Worries," *Europe* 408 (July/August 2001), p. 3.
25. Elisabeth Goodridge, "Online Recruiters Feel the Pinch," Informationweek.com, May 14, 2001, pp. 1–2.
26. Yoav Ganzach, Asya Pazy, Yehudit Ohayun, and Esther Brainin, "Social Exchange and Organizational Commitment: Decision-Making Training for Job Choice as an Alternative to the Realistic Job Preview," *Personnel Psychology* 55 (2002) pp. 613–28.
27. John P. Wanous, "Tell It Like It Is at Realistic Job Preview," *Personnel* 52 (July–August 1975), pp. 50–60.
28. Black, Gregersen, Mendenhall, and Stroh, *Globalizing People,* and Evans et al., *Global Challenge*.
29. Herbert G. Heneman III and Timothy A. Judge, *Staffing Organizations,* 4th ed. (New York: McGraw-Hill/Irwin, 2003).
30. Black, Gregersen, Mendenhall, and Stroh, *Globalizing People*.
31. Paula M Caligiuri, "Selecting Expatriates for Personality Characteristics: A Moderating Effect of Personality on the Relationship between Host National Contact and Cross-Cultural Adjustment," *Management International Review* 40 (First Quarter, 2000), pp. 61–80; Paula M Caligiuri, "The Big Five Personality Characteristics as Predictors of Expatriate's Desire to Terminate the Assignment and Supervisor-Rated Performance," *Personnel Psychology* 53 (Spring 2000), pp. 67–88; and Paula M Caligiuri

and David V Day, "Effects of Self-Monitoring on Technical, Contextual, and Assignment-Specific Performance," *Group & Organization Management* 25 (June 2000), pp. 154–74.

32. Carla Joinson, "Save Thousands per Expatriate," *HRMagazine* 47 (July 2002), pp. 73–77; Calvin Reynolds, "Global Compensation and Benefits in Transition," *Compensation & Benefits Review* 32 (2000), pp. 28–38; and Geoffrey W. Latta, "Expatriate Policy and Practice: A Ten-Year Comparison of Trends," *Compensation and Benefits Review* 31 (July/August 1999), pp. 35–39.
33. For a review, see Dowling et al., *International Human Resource Management,* and Calvin Reynolds, "Expatriate Compensation in Historical Perspective," *Journal of World Business* 32 (Summer 1997), pp. 118–32.
34. PricewaterhouseCoopers, *International Assignments European Policy and Practices* (Toronto: PricewaterhouseCoopers, 1999/2000).
35. George T. Milkovich and Jerry Newman, *Compensation,* 7th ed. (New York: McGraw-Hill/Irwin, 2001).
36. GMAC Global Relocation Services, *Global Relocation Trends.*
37. Harvey and Novicevic, "Influences of Inpatriation Practices," and Roger Herod, "Expatriate Assignments to the United States," *Benefits & Compensation International* 28 (June 1999), pp. 23–28.
38. Reynolds, "Global Compensation and Benefits in Transition."
39. S. Ronen, "Training the International Assignee," in Goldstein, I. (Ed.), *Training and Career Development,* ed. I. Goldstein (San Francisco: Jossey-Bass, 1990), and P. Christopher Earley, "Intercultural Training for Managers: A Comparison of Documentary and Interpersonal Methods," *Academy of Management Journal* 30 (1987), pp. 685–98.
40. J. Stewart Black and Mark E. Mendenhall, "Cross-Cultural Training Effectiveness: A Review and Theoretical Framework for Future Research," *Academy of Management Review* 15 (1990), pp. 113–36.
41. GMAC Global Relocation Services, *Global Relocation Trends.*
42. Evans et al., *Global Challenge.*
43. Ronen, "Training the International Assignee."
44. Black and Mendenhall, "Cross-Cultural Training Effectiveness," pp. 113–37.
45. Rosalie L. Tung, "Selection and Training of Personnel for Overseas Assignments," *Columbia Journal of World Business* 16 (1981), pp. 68–78.
46. Mark E. Mendenhall and Gunter K. Stahl, "Expatriate Training and Development: Where Do We Go From Here," *Human Resource Management* 39 (2000), pp. 251–65.
47. Kalervo Oberg, "Cultural Shock: Adjustment to New Cultural Environments," *Practical Anthropology* 7 (1960), pp. 177–82.
48. J. Stewart Black, Mark E. Mendenhall, and Gary Oddou, "Toward a Comprehensive Model of International Adjustment: An Integration of Multiple Theoretical Perspectives," *Academy of Management Review* 16 (1991), pp. 291–317.
49. Ann K. Harzing, "The Persistent Myth of High Expatriate Failure Rates," *The International Journal of Human Resource Management* 6 (1995), pp. 457–74.
50. Black, Gregersen, Mendenhall, and Stroh, *Globalizing People,* and Black, Mendenhall, and Oddou, "Toward a Comprehensive Model of International Adjustment."

51. Maria L. Kraimer, Sandy J. Wayne, and Renata A. Jaworski, "Sources of Support and Expatriate Performance: The Mediating Role of Expatriate Adjustment," *Personnel Psychology* 54 (Spring 2001), pp. 71–99.
52. Evans et al., *Global Challenge*.
53. Nick Forster and M. Johnsen, "Expatriate Management in UK Companies New to the International Scene," *International Journal of Human Resource Management* 7 (1996), pp. 178–206.
54. GMAC Global Relocation Services, *Global Relocation Trends;* Linda Stroh, "Predicting Turnover among Repatriates: Can Organizations Affect Retention Rates?" *The International Journal of Human Resource Management* 6 (1995), pp. 443–56; and Earl Naumann, "A Conceptual Model of Expatriate Turnover," *Journal of International Business Studies* 23 (1992), pp. 449–531.
55. Leslie G. Klaff, "The Right Way to Bring Expats Home," *Workforce* 81 (July 2002), pp. 40–44.
56. Ibid.
57. Mila Lazarova and Paula Caligiuri, "Retaining Repatriates: The Role of Organizational Support Practices," *Journal of World Business* 36 (2001), pp. 389–401.
58. Peter Conrad and Rudiger Pieper, "Human Resource Management in the Federal Republic of Germany," in *Human Resource Management: An International Comparison,* ed. Rudiger Pieper (Berlin: Walter de Gruyter, 1990), pp. 109–39.
59. Dahlia Hackman and Brian Kleiner, "The Nature of Effective Management in Singapore," *Leadership and Organizational Development Journal* 11 (1990), pp. 28–32.

Chapter Ten

Career and Family Considerations

Learning Objectives

After completing Chapter 10, you should be able to:

- Describe why global assignments can be so important to a manager's career.
- Understand the risks and benefits associated with accepting global assignments.
- Identify the different types of new alternative global assignments.
- Learn how family issues such as dual-career couples can affect the success of organizational global recruiting efforts.
- Discuss the different types of assistance programs that organizations can provide for spouses of global assignees.

Eduardo Diaz: Virtual Expatriate

Eduardo Diaz, an Argentinean, has worked for a multinational company headquartered in Buenos Aires for more than seven years. Perceived as a fast-track manager destined for executive-level status, Diaz has performed well in a variety of domestic assignments. However, his supervisor has just asked him to accept a three-year expatriate assignment in a high-potential overseas subsidiary in Egypt. Although Diaz recognizes the importance of developing language, cultural, and global business skills, he has several concerns regarding this long-term assignment: It could make him "out of sight, out of mind" with regard to promotions and the shifting political landscape at headquarters; his spouse may not be willing to put her career on hold for three years; and his children are about to enter high school and are vehemently opposed to leaving their peer groups. Diaz solved this potential dilemma by offering to become a **virtual expatriate,** meaning he would commute back and forth between the Egyptian subsidiary and headquarters. Even though he would be away from home for several days each month, Diaz and his family would not have to sell their house and relocate overseas. This way, he would be able to protect his career interests at the home office while not disrupting his spouse's career or children's social development by relocating internationally.

Source: The "virtual expatriate" is a relatively new type of global assignee that has been referred to by a variety of authors, including Julia Flynn, "Multinationals Help Expatriate Couples Deal with the Strains of Living Abroad," *Wall Street Journal,* August 8, 2000; Stephanie Armour, "Commute a Chore? Try USA to London—Quick Trips Can Make More Sense than Relocating for Short-term Jobs," *USA Today,* November 9, 2000; and A. McErlain, *International Assignments: European Policy and Practices* (PricewaterhouseCoopers, 1999/2000).

As can be seen in the opening vignette, Eduardo Diaz had to consider career, spouse, and family issues before making a decision about whether to take a global assignment. In the end, he opted for a traveling, or virtual expatriate, assignment. He believes this is the best alternative for him and his family. This chapter will delve more deeply into these career and family-related issues that global managers need to be aware of as they attempt to deploy talented individuals throughout the world. The end of the chapter will cover emerging trends that are affecting potential international assignees and their organizations.

INTRODUCTION

As mentioned in the previous chapter, the demand for qualified, world-class global managers is outstripping the current supply.[1] This shortage is leading many transnational companies to encourage managers and future leaders to develop international skills and to become more globally oriented. For example, future global managers are encouraged to develop the following capabilities: (1) understand the worldwide business environment from a global perspective, (2) work effectively with people from many cultures simultaneously, and, (3) interact with foreign colleagues as equals.[2]

Global assignments are an effective way to develop these international skills and capabilities. Traditionally, these assignments have formed a key part of most global managers' careers. International management researchers have reinforced the importance associated with working overseas: "An international assignment is the single most powerful experience in shaping the perspective and capabilities of effective global leaders."[3]

The importance of developing a global perspective and capabilities has contributed to the perception that overseas assignments play a critical role in one's career success.[4] Top leadership of global and transnational corporations is increasingly emphasizing international experience as a requirement to stay on the corporate fast track.[5]

But from a career perspective, managers are concerned with the longer-term implications of being disconnected and removed from the home office for an extended period. In a survey of U.S. and non-U.S. companies with a combined overseas-based population of 33,000 expatriates, it was found that only 36 percent of respondents believe that international assignments lead to faster promotions within the global organization.[6] Contributing to such concerns is the perception that overseas assignments are often a "haphazard, ill-planned affair" that too frequently lead to job displacement upon repatriation.[7] Research also suggests that the annual turnover rate for expatriate managers is approximately 20 percent or about twice the domestic managerial turnover rate.[8]

In addition to career concerns, many potential global assignees are reluctant to undertake global assignments for a variety of family-related reasons. Research has consistently found that the failure of the spouse and/or family to adjust to the overseas environment is a major factor in the lack of adjustment and premature return of the expatriate.[9] The direct costs for such a "failure" can reach as high as $150,000 per expatriate.[10] Indirect costs such as lost or damaged business in the host country and a blow to the confidence of what was once a fast-track employee, though not as easily quantifiable, are thought to be quite high as well.[11] Considering the costs associated with premature return and the fact that the manager's spouse and family play an important role in the expatriate's success overseas, companies would be well-advised to include spouses and family members in the selection process.

CAREER ISSUES

When a candidate is considering whether or not to accept a global assignment, a variety of questions can be asked: How well does this assignment fit with long-term career goals? What are the career, family, financial, and personal risks and benefits associated with this global assignment? What kind of personal development and challenges will result? These and other issues related to one's career will be discussed in the following section.

Perceived Career Fit

When asked to take a global assignment, many candidates will consider how such an assignment will impact their overall career with the transnational organization. Although there has not been a great deal of research on how global assignments affect career development, some evidence shows the better the perceived fit between one's particular overseas assignment and long-term career plans, the more likely the expatriate will have a positive attitude toward a variety of job and organizational factors.[12]

Research in this area has been fairly convincing that **career fit** is an important issue in global assignment planning. For example, one study found a positive relationship toward career advancement due to the result of an international assignment.[13] Other researchers have studied the extent to which expatriates perceive a direct connection between their current international assignment and overall career path by asking expatriates questions such as this: "This expatriate assignment fits in logically to my career path." It was reported that this "fit" variable was positively related to expatriate performance, relations with host-country nationals, international skill acquisition, job satisfaction, and intent to remain overseas.[14]

Extending this line of research, Stroh studied the effect of career development planning on repatriate turnover.[15] She reported that companies that worked with expatriate candidates to create a career development plan experienced lower turnover rates among repatriates. In sum, these findings suggest that fit between the global assignment and manager's career plans plays an important role in influencing managers' willingness to assume an overseas assignment. Companies that carefully plan global assignments and how global assignees will fit in upon returning from the overseas sojourn are much more likely to retain repatriates with valuable international experience and to recruit top candidates who are willing to accept the assignments.

Risks Associated with Accepting Global Assignments

When candidates are offered a global assignment opportunity, they not only consider the potential fit with their careers, but also some of the risks associated with such assignments. The following are some of the risks (during and after the assignment) that candidates should consider when evaluating whether to accept a global assignment. Exhibit 10.1 summarizes several of these risks.

During the Global Assignment

1. *Risk of failure*. Though the premature return (or "failure" rate) of U.S. expatriates is estimated to be between 5 and 10 percent, or only slightly higher than that of European and Japanese expatriates,[16] most managers with an excellent domestic track record should not automatically accept a global assignment without considering the softer skills necessary for success. As discussed in the previous chapter, managerial and technical skills are not enough to ensure success in most global assignments. Cross-cultural skills and personality traits such as openness, adaptability, empathy, and language skills are very important as well.
2. *Risk of being "out of the loop" regarding office politics*. Although e-mail, telephone calls, videoconferencing, and occasional visits can help global assignees keep abreast of important political developments at the home office, nothing replaces being there. That being said, potential candidates need to accept the fact that they may be out of touch on several developments and

EXHIBIT 10.1
Summary of Career Risks Associated with Global Assignments

During the Assignment	After Repatriating from Assignment
1. Risk of failure or premature return	1. Risk of not having a job upon return
2. Risk of being out of the loop regarding office politics	2. Risk of not using skills/knowledge in next job
3. Risk of losing touch with mentor(s)	3. Risk of lost social standing, autonomy, and financial extras

should expect some surprises from time to time, including announcements of leadership changes, layoffs, and so on. Many expatriates complain about feeling "out of sight, out of mind" when on assignment.[17]

3. *Risk of losing touch with a mentor(s).* It is not uncommon for a global assignee to lose a home office mentor during the actual assignment due to the mentor's departure from the home office, whether because of layoffs, transfer, or voluntary separation.

After Repatriating from the Global Assignment:

1. *Risk of not having a job upon repatriation.* Most U.S. organizations provide no postassignment guarantees of employment. For example, one research study found that only 29 percent of companies provide guarantees of home-country employment, not necessarily promotions or at the same preassignment level.[18] In a related survey of 270 organizations based in Europe that employ more than 65,000 expatriates, it was reported that approximately 47 percent of firms offer postassignment employment.[19] Many of these European organizations, when faced with redundancy (i.e., the repatriate's skills overlap with those of someone already in the home office), are increasingly laying off the repatriate. Taken together, the research indicates that a meaningful job may not be available for many repatriates.
2. *Risk of not using skills or knowledge in the next job.* Many organizations, while not ready to utilize their returning expatriates, place them into short-term temporary holding jobs until a suitable position can be found. Other repatriates receive a position similar to what they had before the assignment and are unable to apply the global skills they acquired in the international assignment. Either way, this leads to a feeling of frustration on the part of returning expatriates, which contributes to the estimated 10 to 25 percent turnover rate within the first two years of repatriation.[20]
3. *Risk of lost social standing, autonomy, and financial extras.* As mentioned in the previous chapter, many global assignees enjoy the perquisites of an international assignment, including exposure to high-level government and business leaders, a great deal of job autonomy and decision-making latitude, and the financial extras of relocation bonus, foreign service premiums, paid private education for children, and so on. Unfortunately, repatriates often go through shock upon returning to their home country and discovering that they are just like everyone else again and no longer have the social standing, autonomy, or earnings they had only months earlier while on assignment. Added to this last point is the fact that their spouses, often employed before the assignment, will need time to enter the workforce again (resumes need to be prepared, skills updated, networks established, etc.).

Why Take a Global Assignment?

Although there are risks associated with taking global assignments, many individuals are very enthusiastic and are willing to jump at the opportunity. Many reasons exist for this positive attitude, including the personal development that comes with living and working internationally, the benefit of meeting company expectations, and the ability to take a less risky alternative global assignment.

Personal Development and Challenge

Despite the potential risks associated with going on a global assignment, there are several very solid career-related reasons for doing so. Full-time MBA students from seven graduate schools in the United States, Canada, and Europe were queried about their reasons for accepting or rejecting an international assignment. An overwhelming amount (84 percent) of the respondents indicated an interest in an international assignment at some time during their careers. In addition, the three most frequently cited reasons for accepting an international assignment were:

- Cross-cultural experience and personal growth (52.2 percent).
- Job and type of work (40.2 percent).
- Money and compensation package (27.7 percent).

The cross-cultural experience and personal growth factors included the MBAs' desires to broaden their horizons and to expand their knowledge of other ways of life through traveling, living among people from other cultures, and becoming proficient in other languages. MBAs perceived that an overseas job would be inherently more interesting and difficult to master. Such a job would offer more responsibility and autonomy when compared to a domestic position in the MBA's home country. Also, the potential to receive a higher salary and benefits package was attractive to just over a quarter of the respondents.[21]

Similar findings were reported in a study of German expatriate managers on assignment to 59 countries. Although such international assignments may not help the individuals' careers in their own companies, many felt that global assignments were a great opportunity for personal and professional development and career advancement in the job market in general, outside of their companies.[22]

Company Expectations

In addition to personal and professional reasons, many potential assignees see the "writing on the wall" from their organizations that future career progression within the company hinges partially on their ability to acquire critical global skills and an international perspective. Many reasons exist to explain why global organizations need to develop such international business and management skills in their human resources: the proliferation of regional trade agreements (e.g., ASEAN, NAFTA, and the EU), the untapped profit potential of emerging markets (China, India, and Brazil), and the geo-political risks affecting business ventures in several parts of the world. This type of leadership development is best achieved through participating in one or more global assignments. John Pepper, former CEO of Procter & Gamble, reinforced this idea when he stated that international assignments played a critical role in shaping him as an effective leader and helped him to refine four key global leadership competencies: dealing with uncertainty, knowing customers, balancing tensions, and appreciating diversity.[23]

Global Focus Optimas® Award for Excellence in HRM

Each year, *Workforce* (formerly *Personnel Journal*) congratulates several corporations for their efforts in HRM by honoring them with an Optimas® award. The Optimas is *Workforce*'s "Oscar for an outstanding performance" in some aspect of HRM. Past winners of this award include the United Nations, Royal Dutch/Shell, and Colgate-Palmolive Corporation.

The 2002 award winner for excellence in the Global Outlook category was Deloitte Touche Tohmatsu (DTT). DTT, a leading global professional services organization, delivers world-class assurance and advisory, tax, and consulting services through its national practices. The firm employs 95,000 individuals and operates from 700 offices in 140 countries. One of its more pressing concerns has to do with the development of its international human resources. DTT is constantly dealing with the issue of identifying enough internationally mobile talent to accomplish its global business goals and objectives.

To solve this problem, DTT utilizes a global development program (GDP), which is designed to advance fast-track professionals through the use of international assignments. The GDP aims at strengthening the global firm's worldwide service capabilities through development of future leaders—teams of people who understand the challenges of international business, have knowledge in specialized fields and markets, and have strong awareness of the world's economic environment.

Soon after its launch in 1998, participation in the GDP was less than expected. In response, DTT upgraded several policy elements, focused on recruiting more candidates, and developed a comprehensive communications program to increase awareness of the program. To assist potential candidates in determining their suitability for global assignments, DTT created and made available a host of self-assessment tools.

The hard work paid off. The enhanced communications project increased participation in the GDP by approximately 35 percent from 1998 to 2000. Equally outstanding was the fact that individuals from 50 countries participated during that time period. Now, the GDP is responsible for half of all international assignees within the entire worldwide company and has become DTT's key international assignment program.

Sources: David Read, "Deloitte Touche Tohmatsu Wins Human Resources Award," www.deloitte.com, June 25, 2002, and "Workforce Optimas Awards 2002," *Workforce,* March 2002, pp. 26–31.

As a global maker of shaving and other consumer products, Gillette manages a successful global assignee program that includes 450 expatriate managers worldwide.[24] Facing a potential global skills shortage 20 years ago, the company took a proactive approach and began to identify and send its best and brightest on assignments throughout the world. Specifically, it chose individuals who were recently hired, were adaptable, had good social skills, were fluent in English, were internationally mobile, and were enthusiastic and aggressive. These trainees were given the broad goals of learning everything they could about their particular functional area and to work effectively within the Gillette organization.[25]

The accompanying Global Focus shows how one award-winning company, Deloitte Touche Tohmatsu, uses international assignments to build global managerial skills and experience.

Less Risky "Alternative" International Assignments

To broaden the appeal of international assignments to more fast-track managers, global organizations are increasingly turning to creative alternatives.[26] Fueled by what many consider to be a growing resistance to accept lengthy overseas assignments, two major trends appear to be surfacing as international human resource managers attempt to fill global openings and to provide opportunities to domestic managers to develop critical international work skills and capabilities. These trends include shorter-term overseas assignments and home-country-based traveling global assignments.

Short-term international assignments require global managers to relocate to the overseas location (with or without one's spouse and family) for less than one year.[27] Though not really expatriates in the traditional sense, these individuals are quickly immersed into the operations and culture of the host country. Typically, the purpose of these assignments is to solve a well-identified problem and/or to expose the assignee to international business and cross-cultural issues. An example of this would be if Singapore Airlines assigned 10 of its best and brightest managers to key commercial markets throughout the world to learn more about international business practices, customer relations, and the different aviation laws and guidelines. After six months, these individuals would either be transferred to a different host-country operation or brought back to the home-country office in Singapore.

In contrast, **traveling global assignments** expose assignees to several aspects of international business without having to relocate overseas. Traveling global assignments require frequent international travel to one or more host countries, but do not include relocation of self or family to an overseas location.[28] Often, the purpose of these types of global assignments is for problem solving and career enhancement. The accompanying Global Focus discusses this emerging trend in global assignments. The jobs may include both domestic and international responsibilities, but they are usually based out of the headquarters or some other home-country location. For example, a marketing manager for Olivetti Group of Italy, whose core businesses are telecommunications and Internet businesses, may have responsibility for the Italian, Swiss, and German markets. She will likely be based out of Ivrea, Italy (headquarters for Olivetti), and travel extensively to Zurich, Frankfurt, and other key markets for the company.

Several advantages are associated with short-term and traveling global assignments. First, headquarters has more control over who assesses and resolves the problems affecting the international venture. Second, the risk of premature return tends to be lower. Traveling assignees don't actually relocate, and most individuals can ride out a short assignment, even in some difficult parts of the world. Third, there may be much less disruption to the assignee's spouse and/or children if they remain in the home country while the assignee is away. Fourth, there is little risk of being derailed from the fast track at company headquarters because the assignee will not be out of sight for very long. Also, short-term global assignments typically include two or three home leave

Global Focus Rapid-Response Expatriates: The Generation of Global Managers

Expatriate managers have become an integral part of the global marketplace. Historically, organizations have needed qualified managers willing to travel overseas regardless of the cost. And the costs of traditional expatriate managers have been well documented, easily running two to three times more than a domestic peer. Now, however, organizations are increasingly cost-conscious when they assess the usefulness of international assignees. As a result, a new generation of expatriate manager is emerging. Today, record numbers of short-term assignment expatriates are stationed around the globe. Organizations are also employing "just-in-time" expatriates, managers with specialized skills who are hired for assignments of limited duration.

A number of potential advantages are associated with the new-generation expatriate. First, organizations find that short-term assignments are more attractive to a significant number of managers who otherwise would opt out of an international assignment. Second, when structured properly, these assignments create much less stress and strain on the expatriate's family, frequently requiring no relocation. Third, the organization may identify and arrange for the transfer of a short-term expatriate much more quickly than for the traditional expatriate. Toward this end, the Internet has become an invaluable tool. By posting global assignments on the Web, organizations can quickly identify qualified candidates from a much larger pool than parent-country managers alone. In today's business environment, rapid response can be the difference between winners and losers bidding for lucrative overseas contracts. And last, but certainly not least, short-term assignments prove to be substantially less costly overall to the organization than more traditional assignments. The savings stem from a number of factors including lower foreign service premiums, reduced relocation costs, and perhaps, most importantly, dramatically lower turnover and failure rates.

A new generation of expatriate is clearly on the business horizon. Experts warn, however, that not all overseas projects can be handled effectively by short-termers. More traditional long-term expatriates will still be needed in the foreseeable future, but the new perspective on global management is clearly changing the nature of expatriate recruitment, selection, and deployment.

Sources: GMAC Global Relocation Services, Warren, NJ, National Foreign Trade Council, NY, NY, SHRM Global Forum, Alexandria, VA, *Global Relocation Trends 2001 Survey Report*, (GMAC G.R.S., February 2002), pp. 1–77; Robert Konopaske, "Willingness to Assume a Global Assignment," excerpts from unpublished doctoral dissertation, (Spring 2001); Michelle Neely Martinez, "Hiring Just-In-Time Global Managers," *Institute for International Human Resources: International Update*, (June 1999), pp. 1–3; and Charlene Marmer Solomon, "Short-Term Assignments and Other Solutions," *Workforce* (*Global Workforce Supplement*), (March 1999), pp. 38–40.

allowances during which the assignee can meet with key mentors and decision makers at the home office. Last, these approaches help the assignee to gain at least some knowledge of international business and its cultural nuances, albeit not a deep exposure.

Disadvantages revolve around the short-term nature of these assignments. Typically, many traveling and short-term global assignees end up cocooning themselves and fail to immerse in the culture or language of the host country.[29] Host-country managers often give visiting "dignitaries" from headquarters the ambassador treatment in which they provide drivers, are ever-present during meetings with key host-country stakeholders (e.g., customers, vendors, government officials, etc.), escort them to cultural and social events, and essentially troubleshoot for and protect the global assignees. Although usually well-intentioned, this sheltering by the host-country managerial staff needs to be minimized (after an initial orientation period) so that the global assignee can learn firsthand about the culture, economic conditions, business-related social customs, language, and other critical components of doing business internationally. The global assignee must take a proactive role to extract key lessons from the assignment that can be applied later in subsequent international business decisions.

In sum, potential candidates have to sort through a plethora of issues when it comes to assessing the potential impact of a global assignment on one's career. On one hand, the top leadership of many leading organizations (such as Colgate-Palmolive) promotes and encourages its employees and managers to take global assignments to develop scarce and badly needed global skills and perspective. On the other hand, many potential candidates view such assignments as high risk in that being out of sight while overseas can derail an individual's career in the company. Interestingly, many individuals appear to take this in stride and feel that gaining international business experience is not only inherently challenging and possibly lucrative, but also will make them much more marketable to other companies that need globally competent managers and executives.

Another key variable in the global assignment area has to do with spouses and families, which influence every step of the global assignment process.

SPOUSE AND FAMILY ISSUES

As companies attempt to globalize their human resources, an often-overlooked variable in the process is the spouse and family. Spouses, children, and more and more elderly parents exert a considerable amount of influence on potential and actual global assignees at different points in the global assignment cycle. An important family issue to consider is when both the global assignee and his or her spouse have careers, commonly referred to as dual-career couples.

Recruitment

Dual-Career Couples

In the United States and Europe, many couples are classified as **dual-career couples**—both partners in a marriage earn incomes and have a career orientation and commitment to their work.[30] The phenomenon of dual-career families has grown in importance during the past three decades. For example, data from the U.S. Department of Labor indicate the labor force participation rate among married women increased from 35 percent in the 1960s to more than 60 percent in the 1990s. In absolute terms, there were 53.7 million dual-income families in the United States in 1998. In addition, 20 to 25 percent of the wives in dual-career couples earn more than their husbands, giving women more input into family financial and career decisions.[31] There is evidence to support similar trends in several countries in Europe.[32]

Dual-career families are also prevalent among global assignee couples. For example, a recent survey indicates that approximately 70 percent of expatriates are married, most of these spouses (87 percent) accompany the manager on the overseas assignment, and nearly half (43 percent) of the spouses were employed before the overseas assignment.[33] Once overseas, many spouses are not able to pursue their careers due to work permit restrictions and lack of suitable career opportunities. Many governments throughout the world try to protect jobs for their own citizens. As a result, many potential global assignees may not be willing to accept an assignment because of the negative consequences such a geographic move would have on their spouse's career.[34]

Elderly Parents and Children at Home

In addition to spousal resistance to relocate, other family variables include children's opinion of the relocation opportunity and whether elderly parents require care from the potential assignee and spouse.[35] Worldwide, the population of individuals aged 65 and older is growing by an unprecedented 800,000 people a month. Italy replaced Sweden as the world's oldest country in 2000, with 18 percent of Italians having reached their 65th birthday.[36] To learn more about this issue, Exhibit 10.2 contains some questions and answers regarding global aging.

In the United States, the growth rate of the elderly population (persons 65 years and older) over the past several decades has greatly exceeded the growth rate of the population as a whole. Population projections indicate that the number of persons 65 years and older will more than double early this century to 80 million.[37] This will result in 1 in 5 Americans being elderly by the year 2030.

An inevitable by-product of this growth in the elderly population is the increased pressure placed on their children and younger relatives to provide personal and financial care. Though many individuals remain healthier for longer periods, longer lives mean higher rates of chronic illness, long-term disability, and, in many cases, dependency.[38] Consequently, working employees (male and female) will be faced with the difficult task of balancing work and parent care demands.

These elder care issues can also affect employees' attitudes with regard to global assignments. Employees and spouses who live near elderly relatives may find it difficult to either bring them on an overseas relocation or to leave them while on the overseas assignment. This latter case is especially true if the employee and/or spouse is the primary care provider. Landau and Associates[39] reported that the existence of elderly relatives is negatively related to employee willingness to relocate for career enhancement.

EXHIBIT 10.2 Questions about Global Aging

Source: Adapted from Kevin Kinsella and Victoria A. Velkoff, "An Aging World: 2001," *International Population Reports* (Washington, DC: National Institute on Aging and U.S. Department of Commerce, November 2001).

1. True or false: In the year 2000, children under the age of 15 still outnumbered elderly people (aged 65 and over) in almost all nations of the world.
   Answer: True. Although the world's population is aging, children still outnumber the elderly in most nations.
2. The world's elderly population is increasing by approximately how many people each month?
   a. 50,000 *b.* 300,000 *c.* 500,000 *d.* 800,000
   Answer: d. The estimated change in the total size of the world's elderly population between 1999 and 2000 was 9.5 million, or 795,000 per month.
3. Which of the world's developing regions has the highest aggregate percent elderly?
   a. Africa *b.* Latin America *c.* The Caribbean *d.* Asia (excluding Japan)
   Answer: c. The Caribbean, where 7.2 % of all people are 65 or older.
4. China has the world's largest total population (more than 1.2 billion people). Which country has the world's largest elderly (65+) population?
   a. Japan *b.* Germany *c.* China *d.* Nigeria
   Answer: c. China also has the largest number of elderly, 88 million in 2000.
5. True or false: More than half of the world's elderly today live in the industrialized nations of Europe, North America, and Japan.
   Answer: False; 59% of elderly live in developing countries.
6. Of the following countries, which had the highest percentage of elderly people in 2000?
   a. Sweden *b.* Turkey *c.* Italy *d.* France
   Answer: c. Italy, with 18.1% of its population aged 65 or older.
7. True or false: Current demographic projections suggest that 35% of all people in the United States will be at least 65 years of age by the year 2050.
   Answer: False. Although the United States will age rapidly when the baby boom generation reaches 65, 20% of the population will be elderly by year 2050.
8. More than one-third of the world's oldest old (people aged 80 years or older) live in which three countries?
   a. Germany, United States, and United Kingdom
   b. India, China, and United States
   c. Japan, China, and Russia
   d. Russia, India, and Brazil
   Answer: b. India has approximately 6.2 million people aged 80 and over, China has 11.5 million, and the United States has 9.2 million. Added together, these three nations account for 38% of the world's oldest old.

A related issue is children at home. Research suggests that employees who have children at home are less likely to relocate; specifically, the number of children at home was negatively related to employee willingness to move internationally for career advancement.[40] In another study, of the 77 percent respondents who were married, couples without children tended to be more open to moving internationally than those with children.[41]

Organizational Response

Organizations can increase the likelihood of being able to recruit and select their best candidates for global assignments by providing organizational support to the spouse and/or offering the candidate alternative global assignments. Motorola offers a **spouse assistance program** to deal with the dual-career issue. The company provides spouses of global assignees with a maximum reimbursement of $7,500 per year (for a total of three years) for expenses related to maintaining or improving career-related skills. Reimbursement is made for such things as: (1) fees to join professional associations, (2) tuition, books, and fees for educational courses, and (3) costs associated with obtaining a work permit and using an employment agency. Spouses who take advantage of this program often decrease the sense of loneliness and meaninglessness that can affect unemployed spouses in a foreign country and receive the added benefit of having up-to-date skills upon reentering the home-country workforce after the assignment is complete.[42]

Another option is not to relocate the spouse and/or family, but rather offer the candidate a home-based traveling or overseas-based short-term global assignment. These flexible arrangements may fit only certain types of global assignments and cannot be used in every instance. If a short-term assignment (one year or less without relocating permanently) is made available, then a generous home-leave policy is important for the assignee to maintain his or her family and business relationships.

Selection and Adjustment

In addition to influencing whether an assignee accepts a global assignment, the ability of a spouse to adjust to living in the host country should be considered in the overall selection process. In comparison with the global assignee who has a well-defined role and purpose working in a similar office environment everyday, the spouse often has a more difficult time adjusting because he or she has to reestablish some sense of routine, find meaningful activities to engage in, and develop a support structure within the host country. All of this takes time, especially when language barriers must be overcome.

Spouse adjustment can have a strong influence (both positive and negative) on global assignee adjustment. One study evaluated 220 U.S. global assignees and their spouses and found that the adjustment of the spouse was highly related to the adjustment of the global manager.[43] Another study, in attempting to identify the major reasons U.S. expatriates return prematurely from their assignments, found that the spouse's inability to adjust was the number-one cause of such failure.[44]

Organizational Response

Unfortunately, many companies do not include spouses in the interview process when selecting global assignees. Black and colleagues, in summarizing the results of several research studies, reported that just 52 percent of U.S. firms, 41 percent of European companies, 18 percent of Scandinavian organizations, and 12 percent of Japanese firms interview spouses.[45] Overall, these low rates can be explained by organizations not wanting to be perceived as interfering with employees' personal lives, especially in the United States, Europe, and Scandinavia. In Japan, however, another explanation is likely. Given the strong commitment that many Japanese employees have to their companies and the nature of husband-spouse relationships, many decision makers do not expect Japanese spouses to exert much influence over the global assignee, before or during the assignment.

Companies can take other steps to involve spouses in a noninvasive manner. First, spouses of candidates can be introduced to spouses of repatriated assignees. This will give the potentially relocating spouse a realistic preview of what lies ahead and may help decrease the anticipatory stress involved in the upcoming move. Second, organizations can provide both the candidate and spouse with the opportunity to visit the host country before the actual move. Also used as a home-hunting trip, this visit can help the assignee and spouse develop a realistic preview of how living in that country will be. Last, the company can provide the assignee and spouse with a home-use-only personality assessment to gauge their level of cross-cultural and relocation readiness. Results are for the assignee and spouse only and should be used by them in making the final decision whether to accept the assignment.

Cross-Cultural Training

As mentioned in the previous chapter, cross-cultural training has been shown to increase one's adjustment to a new culture.[46] Such training, which includes area briefings, language training, and role-playing, can be offered before departure and after arrival in the host culture. Unfortunately, many companies do not provide cross-cultural training for the spouse and family. A study indicated that just 21 percent of U.S. companies provide cross-cultural training for the spouse.[47] In contrast, 62 percent of European firms provide cultural awareness training for spouses of global assignees.

Organizational Response

Organizations can help prepare spouses for the major cultural adjustment of a global relocation. In addition to providing information about the host culture, organizations should also provide language training both before departure and for the initial postarrival period. At the very least, the spouse should learn key survival phrases that can help make the day-to-day living safer and more enjoyable. Also, in-country settling-in assistance can be extremely beneficial to a spouse who will suddenly find himself or herself at home while the assignee is working long hours in the early stage of the assignment. Such support would include assistance with finding a pediatrician and good hospital, obtaining a driver's license, finding reasonably priced grocery stores, and so on. In addition, the settling-in process can be improved by helping the spouse develop a supportive network of host-country individuals and other spouses of global assignees. A list of volunteer opportunities can be provided and introductions

EXHIBIT 10.3 Percentage of Companies Providing Assistance for Spouses of Midmanager Global Assignees

Source: Adapted from Michael G. Harvey, "The Impact of Dual-Career Families on International Relocation," *Human Resource Management Review* 5, no. 3, (1995), pp. 223–44.

Assistance	Before Assignment	During Assignment	After Assignment
1. Training programs	72%	35%	60%
2. Job search assistance upon international relocation	30	35	27
3. Employment opportunity with transferring company	12	8	5
4. Extended adjustment time during international relocation	22	57	18
5. Educational opportunity support	47	45	12
6. Introduction/recommendation to other companies in host country	27	46	n/a
7. Income replacement for designated time period	n/a	12	n/a
8. Assistance with government requirements and/or restrictions	27	45	12

made so that the spouse can get involved with interesting and meaningful activities.

In addition to considering spouses in the recruitment, selection, adjustment, and training aspects of global assignments, special support should also be afforded during the repatriation stage. Because close to half of all spouses who accompany global assignees worked before the relocation,[48] many of these individuals will be reentering the workforce upon returning to the home country. Organizations can play a critical role at this stage of the process by providing job search assistance, networking leads, and paying for courses or other career-related training to update the spouse's skills. Exhibit 10.3 provides a partial list of assistance that global organizations are offering spouses of global assignees prior, during, and after global assignments.

Emerging Trends

Two major issues that increasingly affect global assignments include the move toward increasing (though still relatively underutilized) the use of female expatriates and the potential negative impacts of travel-related stress. Transnational managers need to be aware of these issues in order to enhance the productivity of their global assignees.

Female Expatriates

The proportion of women among U.S. expatriates has inched upward over the past several years. Current estimates are that 16 percent of U.S. expatriates are female.[49] Though conclusive estimates are not available, it is believed that the percentage of female expatriates in other parts of the world, such as Europe, is also quite low. This relatively low percentage of females is attributed to a variety of organizational and family-oriented issues. One study found that international career opportunities are often given almost exclusively to senior male candidates as a result of gender disparity in organizations as well as the role that females have in family responsibilities.[50] From a family role perspective, females tend to bear a great deal of responsibility (especially when both spouses are employed), but there are many excellent female candidates who can effectively balance these responsibilities or do not have children and/or a spouse). Organizations that take a proactive approach to identifying qualified female managers who are interested in international assignments are more likely to achieve competitive advantage in the global business environment.

Another issue contributing to the low percentage of female expatriates is the perception that these individuals will not be treated with the same amount of respect overseas as compared to their male counterparts, especially when conducting business in male-dominated cultures such as Japan, South Korea, or Saudi Arabia.[51] An expert in the area of female expatriation has argued that women succeed as global managers because their international hosts see them as representatives of their companies who can help them achieve their international business goals, not as women from their own host culture.[52] The global assignee who can offer the best price, highest-quality service, or other key attribute to the international customer will be seen in a positive light and will command respect, regardless of the assignee's gender.

A related issue has to do with the way in which female candidates and their supervisors interact. The results of an extensive survey of potential female expatriates found that the female candidates and their supervisors typically do not openly discuss the issues surrounding the decision of whom to send on the global assignment. The findings suggest that women can increase their chances of being chosen for international assignments by communicating openly their international career goals and their ability to overcome perceived obstacles in their path.[53]

Travel-Related Stress

Many would agree that a new era of globalization and business-related travel began on September 11, 2001. In the wake of the terrorist attacks, people from many countries are, and will likely remain, more reluctant to travel. Despite these risks, many managers recognize the significance of face-to-face business interactions to close deals, solve problems, negotiate contracts, and develop mutual trust and respect. Some suggest that distance can be overcome by using "groupware," e-mails, and/or videoconferencing.[54] Though there is certainly a place for these high-tech approaches, face-to-face meetings and personal interactions have unique, irreplaceable value, especially for those cultures that rely heavily on interpersonal contact for developing trust in relationships.

As managers and executives continue to travel internationally to conduct business, they are at higher risk of experiencing travel stress. **Travel stress** is defined as the perceptual, emotional, behavioral, and physical reactions to a misfit between an individual's needs and responsibilities and an organization's demands and expectations at three distinct travel phases—pre-, during, and post-trip.[55]

Pretrip stressors include such issues as planning the actual trip (plane tickets, rental cars, hotels, whom to meet, when, where, what time, etc.), clearing out one's inbox (physical and e-mail) before departure, finding someone to troubleshoot at the home office in case problems arise while traveling on business, packing, getting appropriate vaccinations, making arrangements for children or elderly parents, and assisting one's partner or spouse with key chores, and other home-related issues.

During-trip stressors include dealing with problems that arise from the home office and/or at home while away, health concerns, multiple airport security processes, delays/cancellations of flights, jet lag, in-country language and cultural differences, reactions to different foods and eating schedules, and other unexpected issues.

Posttrip stressors include coming back to a full inbox (physical and e-mail), multiple briefings on work-related issues that came up while overseas, and catching up on family and other personal activities that were missed or delayed (chores, family time, doctors' appointments, etc.). Exhibit 10.4 contains a list of organizational and individual interventions that can help prevent or diminish many of the effects brought on by travel stress.

EXHIBIT 10.4
Organizational and Individual Travel Stress Interventions

Source: Richard S. DeFrank, Robert Konopaske, and John M. Ivancevich, "Executive Travel Stress: The Perils of the Road Warrior," *Academy of Management Executive,* 2000, pp. 58–71.

Organizational Interventions	Individual Interventions
Work scheduling	Jet-lag reduction program
Family plans (spouse and children)	Eating plan
Travel arrangements	Exercise
Hotel accommodations	Sleep adjustment
Jet-lag seminars	Music
Travel stretching exercises	Massage
Communication links	Relaxation techniques (e.g., meditation)
Web-based contact	Web-based contact
Immunizations	Biofeedback
Safety and crime prevention workshops	Nutritional supplements
Antiterrorist training	Discussions with experienced travelers
Food and water precautions	Effective packing
General travel training programs	Improvement of destination knowledge
Procedures for obtaining medical help	Medications
"Concierge" programs	

CONCLUSION

This chapter covered several personal, career, and family-oriented factors that need to be considered by global managers as they attempt to recruit, select, and deploy their human resources around the globe. Creating flexible assignments that meet the personal and career needs of global assignees will help make these opportunities more attractive. Also, providing support services for spouses, children, and possibly elderly family members in the host country (or in the home country if the family does not relocate with the manager) will decrease the stress of the global assignee, allowing him or her to be more productive in the job. Women candidates for global assignments should be considered based on their qualifications and stated interest levels, and not for their gender and perceived lack of interest. Given that many of the new entrants into the labor force in many countries will be female, global organizations that utilize this group to the fullest will be in a better position to compete in the world marketplace during the 21st century.

Key Terms

Alternative global assignments, *364*
Career fit, *359*
Dual-career couples, *366*
Global assignee failure, *360*
Repatriate turnover, *361*
Short-term international assignments, *364*
Spouse assistance programs, *369*
Travel stress, *373*
Traveling global assignments, *364*
Virtual expatriate, *357*

Review, Critical Thinking, and Discussion Questions

1. There is a shortage of qualified employees for global assignments. Explain why.
2. What are some major direct and indirect costs associated with expatriate failure or premature return from an overseas assignment?
3. Assume you were just offered an opportunity by your company to take a three-year global assignment to Singapore. What factors would you need to know before you make your decision?
4. Why don't more organizations provide job guarantees to returning global assignees? Explain.
5. Why is cross-cultural work experience and personal growth more important to many expatriate candidates than a compensation package?
6. Compare a traveling global assignment (in which you don't relocate overseas, but rather travel to several countries each year) with a long-term expatriate assignment (in one country). What are the advantages and disadvantages of both approaches in terms of global skill development?
7. Assume you want to recruit a colleague for a global assignment, but he declines the opportunity because his spouse doesn't want to disrupt a good career. What company-sponsored assistance programs could be provided to convince this couple to take the global assignment?

8. Would you relocate on a three-year overseas assignment if you had small children at home? How about elderly parents to care for? What if the assignment was for just six months?
9. Considering how important spouses' attitudes are in the overall selection and adjustment process, why don't more companies interview spouses during the selection process?
10. What is travel stress? Describe some steps that individuals and organizations can take to decrease the potential harm associated with it.

Endnotes

1. J.A. Quelch and H. Bloom, "Ten Steps to a Global Human Resource Strategy," *strategy+business* (McLean, VA: Booz Allen Hamilton, First Quarter 1999), pp. 1–6.
2. Nancy J. Adler and S. Bartholomew, "Managing Globally Competent People," *Academy of Management Executive* 6 (1992), pp. 52–65.
3. J. Stewart Black, Hal B. Gregersen, Mark E. Mendenhall, and Linda K. Stroh, *Globalizing People Through International Assignments* (Reading, MA: Addison-Wesley, 1999).
4. Rosalie L. Tung, "American Expatriates Abroad: From Neophytes to Cosmopolitans," *Journal of World Business* 33 (1998), pp. 125–44.
5. Quelch and Bloom, "Ten Steps," and Gary Oddou and Mark E. Mendenhall, "Expatriate Performance Appraisal: Problems and Solutions," in *Readings and Cases in International Human Resource Management* (Boston: PWS-Kent, 1991), pp. 364–74.
6. GMAC Global Relocation Services, Warren, NJ, National Foreign Trade Council (NFTC), NY, NY, and SHRM Global Forum, Alexandria, VA, *Global Relocation Trends 2001 Survey Report* (GMAC G.R.S., 2002).
7. Daniel C. Feldman and David C. Thomas, "Career Issues Facing Expatriates," *Journal of International Business Studies* 23 (1992), pp. 449–531, and Mark E. Mendenhall, E. Dunbar, and Gary Oddou, "Expatriate Selection, Training, and Career-Planning: A Review and Critique," *Human Resource Management* 26 (1987), pp. 331–45.
8. Nancy J. Adler, *International Dimensions of Organizational Behavior,* 4th ed. (Cincinnati: South-Western, 2002), and Earl Naumann, "A Conceptual Model of Expatriate Turnover," *Journal of International Business Studies* 23 (1992), pp. 449–531.
9. GMAC, *Global Relocation Trends*; J. Stewart Black and Greg Stephens, "The Influence of the Spouse on American Expatriate Adjustment and Intent to Stay in Pacific Rim Overseas Assignments," *Journal of Management* 15 (1981), pp. 529–44; and Rosalie Tung, "Selection and Training of Personnel for Overseas Assignments," *Columbia Journal of World Business* 16 (1981), pp. 68–78.
10. Black and Stephens, "Influence of the Spouse."
11. Anne-Wil Harzing, "The Persistent Myth of High Expatriate Failure Rates," *The International Journal of Human Resource Management* 6 (1995), pp. 457–74.
12. Feldman and Thomas, "Career Issues Facing Expatriates."
13. Naumann, "Conceptual Model of Expatriate Turnover."
14. Feldman and Thomas, "Career Issues Facing Expatriates."
15. Linda Stroh, "Predicting Turnover Among Repatriates: Can Organizations Affect Retention Rates?" *The International Journal of Human Resource Management* 6, no. 2 (1995), pp. 443–56.

16. Paul Evans, Vladimir Pucik, and Jean-Louis Barsoux, *The Global Challenge: Frameworks for International Human Resource Management* (New York: McGraw-Hill/Irwin, 2002), Harzing, "Persistent Myth of High Expatriate Failure Rates;" and Tung, "American Expatriates Abroad."
17. Anne-Wil Harzing, *Environment, Strategy, Structure, Control Mechanisms, and Human Resource Management in Multinational Companies* (Maastricht: University of Limburg, 1996).
18. GMAC, *Global Relocation Trends.*
19. A. McErlain, *International Assignments: European Policy and Practices* (PricewaterhouseCoopers: 1999/2000).
20. Stroh, "Predicting Turnover Among Repatriates;" Naumann, "Conceptual Model of Expatriate Turnover;" J. Stewart Black and Hal B. Gregersen, "When Yankee Comes Home: Factors Related to Expatriate and Spouse Repatriation Adjustment," *Journal of International Business Studies* 22 (1991), pp. 671–94.
21. Nancy J. Adler, "Do MBAs Want International Careers?" *International Journal of Intercultural Relations* 10 (1986), pp. 277–300.
22. Gunter K. Stahl, Edwin L. Miller, and Rosalie L. Tung, "Toward the Boundaryless Career: A Closer Look at the Expatriate Career Concept and the Perceived Implications of an International Assignment," *Journal of World Business* 37 (2002), pp. 216–27.
23. Christopher B. Bingham, Teppo Felin, and J. Stewart Black, "An Interview with John Pepper: What It Takes to Be a Global Leader," *Human Resource Management* 39 (Summer/Fall 2000), pp. 287–92.
24. Joann S. Lublin, "How to Know Whether Another Overseas Stint Will Help Your Career," *Wall Street Journal,* July 3, 2001, p. B1.
25. Jennifer J. Laabs, "How Gillette Grooms Global Talent," *Personnel Journal* 72 (August 1993), pp. 64–69.
26. Caroline M. Fisher, "Increase in Female Expatriates Raises Dual-Career Concerns: International," *Benefits & Compensation International* 32 (July/August 2002), pp. 73–81, and Julia Flynn, "Multinationals Help Expatriate Couples Deal With the Strains of Living Abroad," *Wall Street Journal,* August 8, 2000, p. A19.
27. Rachel Emma Silverman, "Career Journal: The Jungle," *Wall Street Journal,* January 16, 2001, p. B12, and Siobhan Cummins, "Short-Term Assignments: Combining Employer and Employee Interests," *Benefits & Compensation International* 30 (October 2000), pp. 8–12.
28. Flynn, "Multinationals Help Expatriate Couples," and Charlene M. Solomon, "Short-Term Assignments and Other Solutions," *Workforce* 4 (1999), pp. 38–40.
29. Gary Oddou, Mark E. Mendenhall, and J. Bonner Ritchie, "Leveraging Travel as a Tool for Global Leadership Development," *Human Resource Management* 39 (Summer/Fall 2000), pp. 159–72.
30. Michael G. Harvey, "The Impact of Dual-Career Families on International Relocation," *Human Resource Management Review* 5 (1995), pp. 223–44.
31. Anne E. Winkler, "Earnings of Husbands and Wives in Dual-Earner Families," *Monthly Labor Review*, April 1998.
32. Irene Hardill and David T. Graham, "The New Economy, Labour, Work, and Welfare: A Regional Perspective," Regional Studies Association, Gdansk Meeting, September 15–18, 2001.

33. GMAC, *Global Relocation Trends.*
34. Michael G. Harvey and M.R. Buckley, "The Process for Developing an International Program for Dual-Career Couples," *Human Resource Management Review* 8 (1998), pp. 99–123; Charles A. Handler, Irving M. Lane, and Michael Maher, "Career Planning and Expatriate Couples," *Human Resource Management Journal* 7 (1997), pp. 67–79; and Calvin Reynolds and Rita Bennett, "The Career Couple Challenge," *Personnel Journal* 70 (1991), pp. 46–48.
35. Robert Konopaske, "Determinants and Moderating Influences of U.S. and Foreign National Managers' Willingness to Assume a Global Assignment and Spouses' Willingness to Relocate Globally," Dissertation, University of Houston, 2001.
36. Kevin Kinsella and Victoria A. Velkoff, "An Aging World: 2001," *International Population Reports,* November 2001.
37. "Profiles of General Demographic Characteristics," *2000 Census of Population and Housing—United States* (Washington, DC: U.S. Census Bureau, May 2001).
38. L. Pulliam, "Time to Talk," *Los Angeles Times,* September 12, 1999, p. C1.
39. J.C. Landau, B. Shamir, and M.B. Arthur, "Predictions of Willingness to Relocate for Managerial and Professional Employees," *Journal of Organizational Behavior* 13 (1992), pp. 667–80.
40. Jeanne M. Brett, Linda K. Stroh, and A.H. Reilly, "Job Transfer," in *International Review of Industrial and Organizational Psychology,* eds. C.L. Cooper and I.T. Robinson (New York: John Wiley & Sons, 1992), pp. 323–62.
41. Jeanne M. Brett, Linda K. Stroh, and A.H. Reilly, *Impact of Societal Shifts and Corporate Changes on Employee Relocation* (Washington, DC: Employee Relocation Council, July 1990).
42. M.T. Pellico and Linda K. Stroh, "Spousal Assistance Programs: An Integral Component of the International Assignment," in *New Approaches to Employee Management,* (Greenwich, CT: JAI, 1997), pp. 227–43.
43. Black and Stephens, "Influence of the Spouse."
44. Tung, "American Expatriates Abroad."
45. J. Stewart Black, Hal B. Gregersen, Mark E. Mendenhall, and Linda K. Stroh, *Globalizing People Through International Assignments* (Reading, MA: Addison-Wesley, 1999).
46. J. Stewart Black and Mark E. Mendenhall, "Cross-Cultural Training Effectiveness: A Review and Theoretical Framework for Future Research," *Academy of Management Review* 15 (1990), pp. 113–36.
47. GMAC, *Global Relocation Trends.*
48. Ibid-, and Black et al., *Globalizing People.*
49. GMAC, *Global Relocation Trends.*
50. Margaret Linehan and James S. Walsh, "Key Issues in the Senior Female International Career Move: A Qualitative Study in a European Context," *British Journal of Management* 12 (March 2001), pp. 85–95.
51. Hilary Harris, "Think International Manager, Think Male: Why Are Women Not Selected for International Management Assignments?" *Thunderbird International Business Review,* 44 (March/April 2002), pp. 175–203; Kathryn Tyler, "Don't Fence Her In," *HRMagazine* 46 (March 2001), pp. 69–77; Geert Hofstede, *Culture's*

Consequences: International Differences in Work-Related Values (Beverly Hills, CA: Sage Publications, 1980).

52. Adler, "Do MBAs Want International Careers?"
53. Linda K Stroh, Arup Varma, and Stacey J. Valy-Durbin, "Why Are Women Left at Home: Are They Unwilling to Go on International Assignments?" *Journal of World Business* 35 (Fall 2000), pp. 241–55.
54. Thomas E. Weber, "After Terror Attacks, Companies Rethink Role of Face-to-Face," *Wall Street Journal,* September 24, 2001, p. B1.
55. Richard S. DeFrank, Robert Konopaske, and John M. Ivancevich, "Executive Travel Stress: The Perils of the Road Warrior," *Academy of Management Executive* 14 (2000), pp. 58–71.

Part 3/Reading 1

Adapting to a Boundaryless World: A Developmental Expatriate Model

Juan I. Sanchez
Paul E. Spector
Cary L. Cooper

Adjusting to an international assignment can provoke feelings of helplessness in an unprepared executive, who may have difficulty sorting out appropriate from inappropriate behavior. In fact, learning to manage in and cope with a foreign environment involves such a profound personal transformation that it has an analog in the process of human development throughout the life span. Expatriate executives are removed from the comfortable environment of their parental culture and placed in a less familiar culture. Indeed, a management style that works at home may fail to produce the desired response abroad, or it may be even counterproductive.[1] The sudden loss of control in one's environment that results from cultural shock abruptly disrupts one's equilibrium.[2] This uneven relationship between the executive and an environment that is perceived to exceed the executive's coping resources perfectly fits the definition of stress, which threatens well-being.[3] A recent comparison of expatriate executives with a similar group that did not relocate revealed an alarming increase in the stress-sensitive hormone prolactin, reduced mental health, and an increase in cigarette and alcohol consumption in the expatriate group during the first year abroad.[4]

Rivers of ink have been dedicated to the need to develop globally minded leaders. A better understanding of the stages involved in a successful adjustment to a foreign environment should help in the development of a global mind-set. A profound personal transformation, involving the formation of a multicultural identity, is necessary to buffer the stress provoked by an international assignment.

Coping with stress can be seen as a process involving two steps—primary and secondary—in the evaluation of such adverse environmental conditions as having too much work and uncertain job responsibilities.[5] Adverse environmental conditions function as work stressors when an individual recognizes them as stressful through the mental process known as primary evaluation. Secondary evaluation involves the selection of a coping response to deal with the stressor. The same two steps can be distinguished in coping with stress during an international assignment. First, coping requires an understanding of the new environmental conditions or stressors that demand adaptive responses from the executive.[6] Second, leverage of the new stressors demands a revision of one's old repertoire of coping responses, which may no longer be effective in the new setting.[7] Our goals in this article parallel these two steps and are to shed light on the nature of the primary stressors faced by the expatriate executive, and formulate recommendations regarding strategies that facilitate the adjustment of expatriate executives. Our recommendations are divided into two categories—those directed at expatriate executives and those directed at their employers. To provide a framework or roadmap, our review draws a parallel with the process of human development, proceeding along the developmental stages experienced by expatriate executives as they struggle to adapt to their new world. This progression is summarized in Exhibit 1, which presents each stage, its primary stressors, and the recommended coping strategies for both executives and their employers.

Source: *Academy of Management Executive*, May 2000, pp. 96–106.

EXHIBIT 1 Stressors and Coping Responses in the Developmental Stages of Expatriate Executives

Stage	Primary Stressors	Executive Coping Response	Employer Coping Response
Expatriate selection	Cross-cultural unreadiness.	Engage in self-evaluation.	Encourage expatriate's self and family evaluation. Perform an assessment of potential and interests.
Assignment acceptance	Unrealistic evaluation of stressors to come. Hurried time frame.	Think of assignment as a growth opportunity rather than an instrument to vertical promotion.	Do not make hard-to-keep promises. Clarify expectations.
Pre- and post-arrival training	Ignorance of cultural differences.	Do not make unwarranted assumptions of cultural competence and cultural rules.	Provide pre-, during, and post-assignment training. Encourage support-seeking behavior.
Arrival	Cultural shock. Stressor reevaluation. Feelings of lack of fit and differential treatment.	Do not construe identification with the host and parent cultures as mutually exclusive. Seek social support.	Provide post-arrival training. Facilitate integration in expatriate network.
Novice	Cultural blunders or inadequacy of coping responses. Ambiguity owing to inability to decipher meaning of situations.	Observe and study functional value of coping responses among locals. Do not simply replicate responses that worked at home.	Provide follow-up training. Seek advice from locals and expatriate network.
Transitional	Rejection of host or parent culture.	Form and maintain attachments with both cultures.	Promote culturally sensitive policies at host country. Provide Internet access to family and friends at home. Maintain constant communication and periodic visits to parent organization.
Mastery	Frustration with inability to perform boundary spanning role. Bothered by living with a cultural paradox.	Internalize and enjoy identification with both cultures and walking between two cultures.	Reinforce rather than punish dual identification by defining common goals.
Repatriation	Disappointment with unfulfilled expectations. Sense of isolation. Loss of autonomy.	Realistically reevaluate assignment as a personal and professional growth opportunity.	Arrange prerepatriation briefings and interviews. Schedule post-repatriation support meetings.

EXPATRIATE SELECTION STAGE

Technical skills, family situation, relational skills, and motivational state all play a crucial role in effective cross-cultural adjustment.[8] However, 90 percent of all companies base their international selections on technical expertise while ignoring the other areas.[9] Technically qualified candidates are not always capable of easily adjusting to critical cultural differences, such as those involving social status and group dependence.[10]

Openness to the profound personal transformation that awaits the expatriate executive is perhaps the most fundamental sign of expatriate readiness. It is not surprising that courage and risk taking are among the core characteristics of successful expatriates who, knowing themselves, are willing to revisit their most deeply held assumptions.[11] Authoritarianism, rigidity, and ethnocentrism are personality aspects that impede adaptation to a foreign culture.[12] Because these are deeply ingrained personality traits that are not easily malleable, selection rather than training should be the strategy used to ensure that candidates possess these characteristics from the first day on the job. Although traditional personality inventories have not proven very effective at predicting expatriate success, available measures specifically designed to evaluate expatriate potential appear promising.[13]

A frequently reported explanation for expatriate failure has been poor adjustment of spouses.[14] Despite the key role of family-related variables in successful expatriate management, assessing the family situation without violating privacy rights is a real challenge. A practical and potentially useful strategy involves providing a realistic preview of the assignment, then instigating a self-evaluation of readiness among family members. By reflecting on the results of this evaluation, the executives can appraise their family situation and can voluntarily withdraw if the prospect is not altogether favorable.

ASSIGNMENT ACCEPTANCE STAGE

The excessive emphasis on technical skills also seems to dominate the decision-making process that the expatriate executive and family go through before the offer is accepted. Typically, the candidate selected has technical expertise and experience related to the assignment. Therefore, the candidate does not envision being incapable of performing an assignment abroad that he or she has already done at home. Why are some managers and employers prone to overlook the cross-cultural demands of the assignment? The answer lies in the psychological perspective of work stress, which is driven by subjective appraisals of the executive's environment.[15] The objective reality of the situation does not directly provoke a stressful experience, but the subjective appraisal of the situation does. The subjective appraisal of stressors is, in essence, a judgment of person-environment fit.[16] Therefore, when an offer to take an international assignment is extended, candidates are probably unable to anticipate stressors they have not experienced before, unless they have had a prior international assignment. Ignorant of the alien environment to which they are about to be transplanted, executives might also overestimate the effectiveness of coping responses that work at home but may not work abroad. For instance, being outgoing, as it is normally understood in the U.S., may be perceived as being rude in other cultures, thereby provoking rather than preventing social isolation.

Consider the case of an executive with a demonstrated competence in launching start-ups who was selected to head the Asian operations of a U.S. corporation. When considering the transfer to Asia, the executive dismissed the possibility of feeling socially isolated because he considered himself and his family outgoing and friendly, and thought they would have no problems making friends and adjusting. Six months after his arrival in Japan, the executive expressed frustration at his inability to communicate effectively with others and at his feelings of social isolation.

When weighing the pros and cons of an international assignment, the stressors to be encountered are thought to be alleviated by the prospect of career advancement once the executive returns home. Promises of immediate promotion upon return are often the main driver of an executive's decision to accept relocation.

The executive may use these promises to convince a spouse who hesitates to give up local friends, family, and perhaps a good job. However, once the executive starts the international assignment, the management representatives who were involved in selecting the executive may very well move on to other posts or other corporations. Witnessing these departures from afar, the expatriate may feel that the expectations that motivated the transfer are vanishing too. In the absence of a future payoff, the new stressors will be reappraised and may appear more unbearable than when the prospect of a red-carpet return was alive.

The offer to take an international assignment frequently comes from out of the blue. For instance, an executive previously uninterested in living abroad was motivated by a hefty relocation bonus to accept an unexpectedly sudden but nevertheless career-enhancing assignment.[17] This kind of hurried decision may lead to an unrealistic appraisal of both the stressors awaiting abroad and one's cross-cultural skills.

How should executives and their employers cope with such unanticipated circumstances? One of the answers appears to lie in the clarification of expectancies beforehand. Executives who take on international assignments hoping that an immediate promotion will materialize upon return are oblivious to the pace of change in today's business environment, where vertical career paths are no longer the norm. Instead, executives should consider international transfers as an additional growth opportunity in their career development plans.

Rather than delivering hard-to-keep, long-term promises of promotion, employers should clarify expectations and highlight the developmental growth that will result from having completed the international assignment. For example, a U.S. executive who decided to take an assignment in Japan because it fit into his general career plan was not guaranteed a specific promotion upon repatriation. Instead, he was made aware of what his general opportunities would be if he met his goals in Japan.[18]

PRE- AND POSTARRIVAL TRAINING STAGE

Intercultural training can partly remedy cross-cultural insensitivity, but intercultural competence involves more than a series of country statistics and cultural gimmicks learned in a short, predeparture training session. Making executives aware that they will face different business and social customs is not sufficient, because awareness does not necessarily bring competence in the host culture.[19]

The classic burnout symptoms of emotional exhaustion and a sense of reduced accomplishment of an American expatriate six months after he was put in charge of operations in Taiwan illustrate this point.[20] Because he was unable to obtain collaboration from local executives, he followed the recommendations of his California team. The implementation of such recommendations, however, worsened the situation he had been called to improve. Even though this executive was made aware of such cultural differences as Asians being more deferential and less straightforward in their business dealings than Americans, he had neither the interest nor the patience to participate in extended discussions of family and nonbusiness matters with his new business acquaintances. He decided to cut his losses and gladly accepted his CEO's invitation to repatriate him.

Many corporations are becoming aware of the need to provide continued hands-on training rather than just predeparture awareness training. An executive's predeparture evaluation of the stressors experienced abroad may be unrealistic. Without some on-site experience in the culture, executives may overestimate their future ability to cope. In contrast to predeparture training, postarrival training gives expatriates a chance to evaluate their stressors after they have encountered them. A good example of this kind of on-site training is provided by the British trade giant Jardin Matheson.[21] The training format is project-based, with participants spending much of their time in their respective business areas. At regular intervals, they are brought together to discuss their experiences under the guidance of facilitators. Cultural differences are addressed when they surface in the context of working together, rather than as part of theoretical discussions regarding why Asians and Westerners behave differently.

Experiential training formats also provide an opportunity to react to cultural stressors and receive feedback about the adequacy of one's coping responses. One of these formats is the cultural assimilator, which employs descriptions of critical incidents involving stressful situations together with possible ways of coping with them.[22] With the help of a facilitator, participants discuss the consequences of their individual responses. The exchange helps reduce feelings of stress, because it reinforces the perception that they hold a reservoir of potentially effective coping responses. Foreigners trained using a Greek assimilator, for instance, felt significantly better adjusted to Greece than untrained individuals.[23]

From the employer's point of view, training is an opportunity to provide the social support that the expatriate executive needs.[24] Social support, however, can either reduce or alleviate the effects of stressors. Predeparture training sessions, for instance, can significantly reduce stressors by providing basic information about housing, schools, foods, and transportation that may help the executives get by in the first few weeks of their assignments. Predeparture training, however, is not likely to buffer or alleviate the cultural stressors to be faced by the expatriate executive, because cultural differences are best understood in postarrival training sessions once they have been experienced. Although identifying the potential sources of social support is a difficult task for executives who are still unfamiliar with their host environment, training can provide the encouragement and motivation to seek the social network and activities that will make the new stressors more bearable.

ARRIVAL STAGE

Understandably, the prospect of an international assignment provokes quite a bit of excitement. However, the executive's arrival in an unfamiliar environment may soon bring almost as much frustration. Many of these frustrating times can be explained by feelings of inadequacy. In fact, the executive's sense of control, which plays a significant role in healthy adjustment, may be dramatically affected by the transfer.[25] Stressors like an excessive workload, which was not perceived as such because of the individual's sense of environmental control, suddenly turn worse because of what appears to be an uncontrollable new environment.

Feeling different, especially feeling that one is subject to differential treatment because of membership in a particular culture, can induce stress above and beyond that resulting from typical stressors such as conflict and ambiguity over perceived responsibilities.[26] If the expatriate executives attribute differential treatment to their membership in a different culture or group, their rejection of the host culture is likely to intensify. Thinking of the environment as beyond one's control induces a sense of helplessness.[27] For example, a U.S. expatriate executive in a Central American nation felt that his written requests for equipment maintenance were ignored because he was a foreigner. Later in his assignment, he learned that such written requests were routinely ignored, and that the way to get the work done was to drop by the maintenance shop or ask a maintenance employee for help at the beginning of the workday.

Social identity theory provides a vehicle to better understand and cope with feelings of cultural rejection. Individuals are likely to experience internal conflict when concurrent identification with two or more social entities is perceived as unacceptable. For instance, a U.S. expatriate in Mexico

EXHIBIT 2
Successful Evolution of Parent- and Host-Culture Identification

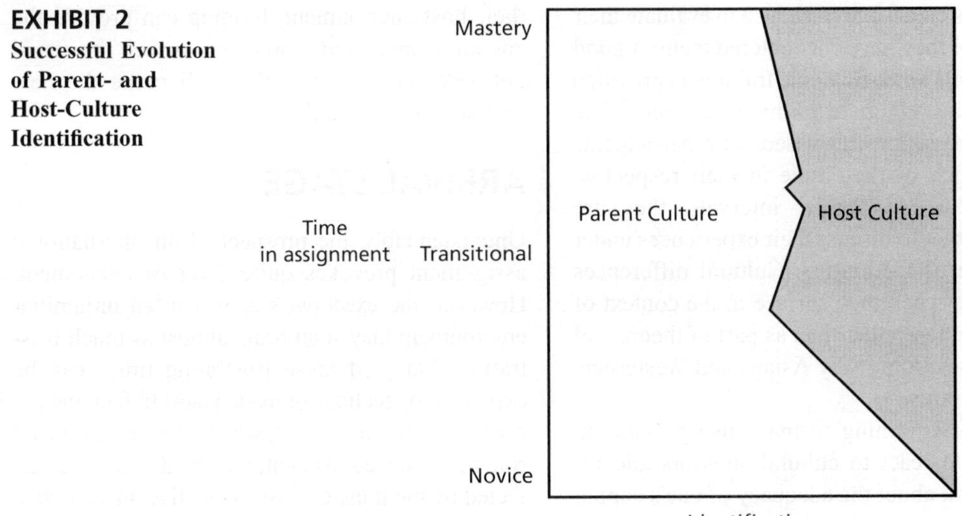

may feel that being an American and identifying with the Mexican culture are opposite poles of the same continuum and are therefore mutually exclusive. Feelings of frustration early in the international assignment may strengthen identification with the U.S. culture to the detriment of the host culture. When the executive construes his or her identification with the two cultures in this us versus them manner, devastating psychological consequences may follow.

Expatriate executives who reject the host culture are destined to experience continuous frustration and negative feelings as they are forced to conduct business according to local usage. Exhibit 2 depicts the tortuous evolution of the internal struggle between executives' identification with the host versus the parent culture. The two identifications compete for the same space. Whereas identification with the parent culture dominates in the early phases of the assignment, identification with the host culture will dominate later on. A successful adjustment implies a final identification midway between the host and parent cultures.

Understanding that identification with both cultures is possible is the safest way to prevent acculturative stress.[28] The different degrees of identification with the host and the parent culture can be summarized in four quadrants (Exhibit 3). The upper-right quadrant represents dual identification, which is indeed possible and least stressful. A U.S. executive on assignment in Japan indicated that his high allegiance to both the parent and the Japanese operation led him to try to bring their interests together rather than choose one over the other whenever he perceived discrepancies in their expectations and goals.[29] Reacculturation, as represented by the lower-right quadrant, is significantly more stressful because one's parent culture is neglected rather than incorporated into the expatriate's new identity.

A better understanding of the host's ways should not necessarily be accompanied by a rejection of the parent culture. Executives run the risk of drifting in either direction by identifying too much with one of the cultures while rejecting the other. Rather than absorbing oneself in an internal battle for self-definition, the executive should learn to view identification with the host as compatible with identification with the parent culture.

EXHIBIT 3
A Model of Expatriate Cultural Identification and Stress

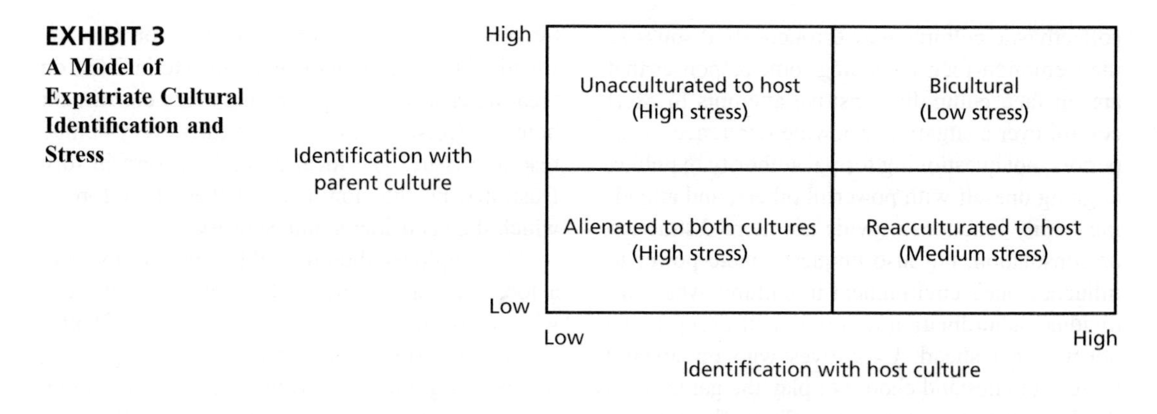

NOVICE STAGE

At the beginning of their international assignments, expatriates may make the mistake of ignoring culturally critical aspects. Why is it so difficult to make sense of and cope with the new stressors? Executives who feel stressed are likely to search their repertoire of coping responses for adequate ways to confront situations.[30] However, the choice of coping response would be determined by the effectiveness of responses used to cope with similar stressors in the past. Notions of response effectiveness are influenced by prior personal experience and culturally bound notions of response adequacy and likelihood of success. In other words, the choices of coping responses have been shaped throughout the executives' personal and cultural experience. The problem is that such responses are no longer valid in a different culture characterized by different norms and values. Thus, the experience and knowledge of social norms that the expatriate executive used to select adequate coping responses at home have lost much of their informative value.

Expatriates need to become aware of the consequences that their old repertoire of coping responses has in the host culture. Ambiguity will be overwhelming at first. Uncertainty about what is demanded will be aggravated by one's inability to decipher the meaning of a situation. Blunders can be unwittingly committed by executives who misread culturally different situations.[31] An American expatriate in Beijing dared to challenge his Chinese colleague's idea by saying, "That's a very good point, but I don't agree with you." Although this observation was respectfully made in the eyes of the American, it offended the Chinese executive, thereby straining the business deal.[32] Another U.S. executive inadvertently offended his senior Mexican managers by asking for the junior manager's opinion in their presence.

Expatriate managers should pay attention to the functional value of the coping mechanisms employed by local executives, who make useful role models. Responses that imitate local uses can be successful, but expatriates should be sensitive to the true function of such responses, which can be rather subtle. Expatriate managers should think a bit like anthropologists trying to make sense of human behavior in a different cultural context.[33]

Coping styles have been classified as problem-solving (taking direct action to solve a problem) versus emotion-focused (taking action to make oneself feel better about a situation one cannot control).[34] Emotion-focused coping might be more characteristic of collectivistic societies, such as Asians or Hispanics, than of individualistic societies, like the United States or Australia, because members of collectivistic cultures are encouraged to subordinate their personal goals to those of stable groups. However, expatriate executives in collectivistic cultures may erroneously dismiss as mere emotion-focused coping some responses that are, in fact, culturally sensitive attempts to exert control over a situation. Showing deference to superiors, not questioning formal authority in public, aligning oneself with powerful others, and attending family functions provide not mere distraction or consolation, but also unquestionable power to influence one's environment in cultures where individual subordination to a powerful group is the norm to get ahead. Executives who understand these subtleties and choose to play the game stand the best chances of coping effectively with an unfamiliar situation.

An American executive who understood the importance of family and friendship in the Middle East made a point of reminding his business contacts there of his friendship by taking their picture together at every occasion and then mailing copies to them. This action may seem a bit manipulative to some, but we can attest to the sincerity of the American expatriate, who had already internalized some of the values and customs of his Middle Eastern partners.

More straightforward coping styles involving direct attempts to control situations of the kind expected in individualistic countries like the United States may be even counterproductive. A study of managerial stress in 24 countries revealed that exercising direct control over one's environment is associated with mental and physical well-being in the United States, but not in many other countries.[35] Thus, expatriates who insist on employing the kind of direct control responses that have made them successful at home may only add to their stress level abroad.

Expatriates from individualistic societies should be reminded that the lengthy social interactions observed in collectivistic cultures are not a waste of time, but a necessary conduit to doing business. Executives from collectivistic cultures transplanted to an individualistic one may make the opposite mistake. For example, a southern European executive assigned to a financial institution in a U.S. territory was used to having decisions backed by social consensus, which are the norm in the world of European labor relations. He insisted on creating task forces representing every constituent before a decision was made on nearly every human resource issue. The local executives were in turn frustrated by the slow pace of these task forces, which they considered unnecessary.

The employer should facilitate integration into a local or regional network of other expatriates, who can be an extremely valuable source of tangible and informational support in the beginning of the assignment regarding schools, shopping, obtaining a driver's license, and the like. Whereas physically distant friends and family provide simply emotional support and consolation, other expatriates provide the kind of tangible support that directly reduces stressors.

TRANSITIONAL STAGE

Executives' continued frustration may lead to identity crises when they choose to reject the parent culture by fully embracing the host culture, or vice versa.

The ability to form and maintain attachments plays a significant role in executive health in general.[36] For example, keeping in touch with the expatriate community overseas allows executives to maintain their links with the parent culture. These links can be reinforced by Internet access to family, friends, and media from the parent culture. The employer's investment in such electronic communications should provide a significant return in the form of emotional support. Even though this support cannot reduce the stressors faced abroad, it should help alleviate the strain felt by the executive.[37]

Going native by becoming too identified with the host culture may elicit a negative reaction at headquarters, because the executive's allegiance may be questioned.[38] This reversed identification phenomenon may have the same kind of negative impact on the executive's well-being that the rejection of the host culture does, because a significant part of the self is being rejected.

Expatriate executives' conflicting feelings about identification with one culture to the exclusion of the other exacerbate the normally high levels of role conflict characteristic of executive positions. Successful expatriate executives cope with these conflicting roles through constant communications. Lags in communications provoke the kind of unhealthy us versus them attribution mentioned earlier. An American expatriate in Holland negotiated for a trip to the United States every four months so he could bring the points of view of the Dutch operations to headquarters and also take headquarters' perceptions back to Holland. Physical separation and cultural differences made it difficult for the groups to understand each other's actions, and the tone of communications invariably deteriorated after three to four months.[39] The executive's trips back and forth kept negative feelings from getting too far out of hand. In essence, expatriates are forced to cope with conflicting demands imposed by their dual identification with the host and parent organizations by functioning as boundary spanners that walk the line separating the two cultures. The need to maintain this delicate equilibrium among multiple stakeholders calls for skills similar to those possessed by political diplomats.[40] The parent organization should not create additional role conflict for the expatriate with policies that are insensitive to cultural differences.

MASTERY STAGE

By the end of their assignments, successful expatriates have already developed the knowledge of cultural norms that allow them to understand their environment more fully. Over time, expats have also crafted a repertoire of coping responses adapted to their new stressors. Seasoned expatriates are capable of choosing among potential responses with a minimum of uncertainty because they have seen their choices succeed in the past. However, the developmental stages discussed here do not always follow a linear sequence, and making sense of a foreign culture will remain puzzling at times.[41] This ambiguity should not bother effective expatriates, who have already learned to cope with feelings of divided loyalty. They understand that feelings of identification with the host and the parent culture are not mutually exclusive. Instead of being frustrated, they enjoy their boundary-spanning roles of bicultural interpreters who walk between two or more cultures.

Accepting the profound personal transformation that comes with an international assignment is not easy. Fearing identity loss and unable to cope with a myriad of new stressors, nearly 40 percent of American expatriates return early.[42]

However, those who successfully complete their assignments become different people because they have experienced radically different events. Armed with the dual experience of having lived and worked both abroad and at home, expatriates are capable of seeing one culture through the eyes of the other. The ability to understand the cultural paradox that surrounds them and, most importantly, the fact that living with such a paradox does not bother them, represents the pinnacle of expatriate executive transformation. Not surprisingly, the healthiest expatriates are those who possess a strong sense of coherence and control.[43] These individuals have learned to live with and enjoy membership in more than one culture—the essence of being a global executive. A U.S. executive working in Holland described how he had learned over the course of his assignment that being conspicuous was often frowned on in that country. He learned to be more reserved in what he said and to wear more formal clothes even when grocery shopping, so that he would not stand out as much. He and other expatriates explained that these changes did not interfere with their identification with the United States, which they still genuinely felt.[44]

REPATRIATION STAGE: THE MOST STRESSFUL PART OF THE ASSIGNMENT?

Executives' repatriation can turn into the most stressful time of the entire international assignment. A survey of repatriated executives found that

33 percent were still holding temporary assignments three months after repatriation, more than 75 percent felt than their permanent post upon repatriation was a demotion from their international assignment, and 61 percent felt that they did not have opportunities to put their experience abroad to work. Perhaps the most dramatic finding was that 25 percent of the executives had quit their jobs within three months of repatriation.[45]

An expatriate banking executive working in Mexico returned to the United States to find an organization whose top management had radically changed and seemed unwilling to fulfill his previous bosses' promises of upward promotion. After lingering in support roles for about a year, the executive landed a job as vice president of international banking in another financial institution. Similarly, a Mexican executive was disappointed to learn that his employer planned to repatriate him to a relatively low-level management job back home. The executive had been known to share with his co-workers in the United States what he thought were his high chances of securing the general manager position in Mexico's operations. Dissatisfied with the repatriation offer, the executive quit his job and started an import-export partnership with one of the business acquaintances he had made during his assignment in the United States.

Repatriation brings new stressors to executives. Feeling that others do not share their multicultural identification can create a sense of isolation. An expatriate who spent two years implementing a training program around the world characterized his repatriation as a much more traumatic event than going abroad. He complained about feelings of not belonging and about not having anyone to confide in.[46] Repatriated executives may also find themselves making an effort not to stand out by hiding the new interests and behaviors they acquired abroad. An expatriate who headed the Dutch operations of a U.S. firm admitted that he was afraid that others might label his new manners as snobbish.

How can expatriate executives cope with these feelings of lack of fit? In a way, the repatriated executives had already coped with the feeling of not fitting in when abroad. The essence of being bicultural is being proficient in both cultures, and that includes dealing with members of one culture who, unlike the repatriated executive, are unfamiliar with the other. In short, learning to live with and not be bothered by these multiple cultural identities continues to be necessary even when executives return home.

Another dramatic change confronted by repatriated executives is the frequent loss of autonomy, augmented by possibly unrealistic expectations about being promoted upon return. The kind of bold management style that was accepted and even praised abroad may be unwelcome at headquarters. Insisting on this kind of bold style might provoke turf battles with executives from other functional areas. Employers can smooth this difficult transition by providing a sensible repatriation program that takes into account executives' interests and newly developed talents. In this sense, reentry training is at least as important as predeparture training. Setting expectations about reentry well before it takes place is a fundamental component of this kind of training, which should begin when the expatriate is first selected and continue throughout the assignment prior to the return.[47] Prerepatriation briefings and interviews with parent organization representatives to inform executives of available opportunities should help clarify how such opportunities fit into executives' postrepatriation career plans. After reentry, follow-up meetings are critical because they provide information regarding how executives are adjusting, whether they need additional support to cope with new stressors, and whether their coping strategies should be revised. When suitable openings are not immediately available at the parent organization, Swedish employers place expatriate executives in a multi-employers pool. Executives from this pool are loaned out to other employers who need them as a short-term solution.[48]

There are limitations to the recommendations presented here. First, the available research from which we drew is based primarily on the experiences of U.S. expatriates working abroad.

Although many of our conclusions should apply to expatriates regardless of nationality, the unique aspects of every culture should not be ignored. Similarly, about 90 percent of all expatriate managers may be male, and the recommendations presented here are therefore based on primarily male samples.[49] However, contrary to stereotypical assumptions, the case of a female executive who received equal treatment during her assignment in Japan illustrates that female expatriates need not necessarily experience more frustration than their male counterparts, even if female executives are not common in the host country.[50]

A SURVIVAL GUIDE FOR EXPATRIATE EXECUTIVES AND THEIR EMPLOYERS

Employers need to actively support the adjustment process of their expatriate executives. Cross-cultural competence-oriented training should be provided before, during, and after the assignment. In addition, the parent firm should be sensitive to the delicate balance between the interest of the parent and the host firm that executives need to maintain, listening and working with them to define and achieve common goals.

Expatriation uproots executives from a familiar environment, thereby breaking the balance between the individual and his or her ability to cope with the environment. Feelings of internal conflict are likely to be aggravated by executives' inability to decipher the meaning of culturally different situations. Even though the strain associated with such negative feelings can be partly prevented by competence-oriented intercultural training, individual predisposition and courage to cross cultural boundaries of both a physical and a psychological nature are necessary for healthy expatriate adjustment. Perhaps the most challenging of all transformations is the ability to develop a dual identification.

Otherwise, the conflicting roles experienced by expatriate executives may be exacerbated by a divided sense of social identity that views identification with the host and the parent culture as mutually exclusive. In essence, an international assignment is not only a physical adventure in a more or less remote land, but also a psychological adventure that requires the willingness to revise deeply held beliefs concerning one's own identity.

ENDNOTES

1. Selmer, J. 1999. Effects of coping strategies on sociocultural and psychological adjustment of Western expatriate managers in the PRC. *Journal of World Business,* 34(1): 41–51.
2. Cummings, T. G., & Cooper, C. L. 1998. A cybernetic theory of work stress. In C. L. Cooper (Ed.), *Theories of organizational stress:* 101–121. Oxford, U.K.: Oxford University Press.
3. Lazarus, R. S., & Folkman, S. 1984. *Stress, appraisal, and coping.* New York: Springer, 19.
4. Anderzen, I., & Arnetz, B. B. 1997. Psychological reactions during the first year of a foreign assignment: Results of a controlled longitudinal study. *Work & Stress,* 11(4): 304–318.
5. Lazarus, R. S. 1966. *Psychological stress and the coping process.* New York: McGraw-Hill.
6. Beehr, T. A., & Newman, J. E. 1978. Job stress, employee health, and organizational effectiveness: A facet analysis, model and literature review. *Personnel Psychology,* 31: 665–699.
7. Shupe, E. I., & McGrath, J. E. 1998. Stress and the sojourner. In Cooper (ED.), op. cit., 86–100.
8. Teagarden, M. B., & Gordon, G. D. 1995. Corporate selection strategies and expatriate manager success. In J. Selmer (Ed.), *Expatriate management. New ideas for international business*: 17–36. Westport CT: Quorum.
9. Earley, P. C. 1987. Intercultural training for managers: A comparison. *Academy of Management Journal,* 30(4): 685–698.
10. Spreitzer, G. M., McCall, Jr., M. W., & Mahoney, J. D. 1997. Early identification of international executive potential. *Journal of Applied Psychology,* 82(1): 6–29.

11. Ibid.
12. Locke, S. A., & Feinsod, F. 1982. Psychological preparation for young adults traveling abroad. *Adolescence,* 17: 815–819.
13. Spreitzer, et al., op. cit.
14. Teagarden & Gordon, op. cit.
15. Lazarus, op. cit.
16. Edwards, J. R., & Cooper, C. L. 1990. The person-environment fit approach to stress: Recurring problems and some suggested solutions. *Journal of Organizational Behavior,* 11: 293–307.
17. Schell, M. S., & Solomon, C. M. 1997. *Capitalizing on the global workforce*. Chicago: Irwin.
18. Black, J. S., Gregersen, H. B., Mendenhall, M. E., & Stroh, L. K. 1999. *Globalizing people through international assignments*. Reading MA: Addison Wesley.
19. Black, J. S., & Gregersen, H. B. 1999. The right way to manage expats. *Harvard Business Review,* March–April: 52–62.
20. Schell & Solomon, op. cit.
21. Williams, G., & Bent, R. 1996. Developing expatriate managers for Southeast Asia. In D. Landis & R. S. Bhagat (Eds.), *Handbook of intercultural training,* 2nd ed.: 383–399, Thousand Oaks CA: Sage.
22. Brislin, R., Cusgner, K., Cherrie, C., & Yong, M. 1986. *Intercultural interactions: A practical guide*. Beverly Hills CA: Sage.
23. Fiedler, F., Mitchell, T., & Triandis, H. 1971. The culture assimilator: An approach to cross-cultural training. *Journal of Applied Psychology,* 55: 95–102.
24. Fontaine, G. 1996. Social support and the challenges of international assignments. In D. Landis & R. S. Bhagat (Eds.), op. cit.: 264–281.
25. Spector, P. E. 1998. A control theory of the job stress process. In Cooper (Ed.), op. cit. 153–169.
26. Sanchez, J. I., & Brock, P. 1996. Outcomes of perceived discrimination among Hispanic employees: Is diversity management a luxury or a necessity? *Academy of Management Journal,* 39: 704–719.
27. Spector, P. E., 1982. Behavior in organizations as a function of employee locus of control, *Psychological Bulletin,* 91: 482–497.
28. Sanchez, J. I., & Fernandez, D. M. 1993. Acculturative stress among Hispanics: A bidimensional model of ethnic identity. *Journal of Applied Social Psychology,* 23: 654–668.
29. Black, J. S., Gregersen, H. B., Mendenhall, M. E., & Stroh, L. K. op. cit.
30. Shupe & McGrath, op. cit.
31. Ricks, D. A. 1993. *Blunders in international business*. Cambridge MA: Blackwell.
32. Schell & Solomon, op. cit., 7.
33. Osland, J. S., & Bird, A. 2000. Beyond sophisticated stereotyping: Cultural sensemaking in context. *The Academy of Management Executive,* 14(1): 65–77.
34. Bhagat, R. S., O'Driscoll, M. P., Babakus, E., Frey, L., Chokkar, J., Ninokumar, H., Pate, L. E., Ryder, P. A., Fernandez, M. J. G., Ford, D. L., & Mahanyele, M. 1994. Organizational stress and coping in seven national contexts: A cross-cultural investigation. In G. P. Keita and J. J. Hurrell, Jr. (Eds.) *Job stress in a changing workforce:* 93–105. Washington, DC: American Psychological Association.
35. Spector, P. E., Cooper, C. L., Sanchez, J. I., et al. 1999. A twenty-four nation study of work locus of control, well-being, and individualism: How generalizable are western work findings? Manuscript submitted for publication.
36. Quick, J. C., Nelson, D. L. & Quick, J. D. 1990. *Stress and challenge at the top. The paradox of the successful executive.* Chichester U.K.: John Wiley.
37. Viswesvaran, C., Sanchez, J. I., & Fisher, J. 1999. The role of social support in the

process of work stress: A meta-analysis. *Journal of Vocational Behavior:* 54: 314–334.

38. Adler, N. J. 1997. *International dimensions of organizational behavior*. Cincinnati, OH: South-Western.
39. Osland, op. cit. 118.
40. Saner, R., Yiu, L., & Sondergaard, M. 2000. Business diplomacy management: A core competency for global companies. *The Academy of Management Executive,* 14(1): 80–92.
41. Osland & Bird, op. cit.
42. Keally, D. J. 1996. The challenge of international personnel selection. In Landis & Bhagan Eds.), op. cit., 81–105.
43. Anderzen & Arnet, op. cit.
44. Osland, J. S. 1995. *The adventure of working abroad*. San Francisco: Jossey-Bass.
45. Black & Gregersen, op. cit., 60.
46. Osland, op. cit., 171.
47. Martin, J. N., & Harrell, T. 1996. Reentry training for intercultural sojourners. In D. Landis & R. S. Bhagat (Eds.), op. cit.: 307–323.
48. *Sunday Telegraph*. Home truths await the returning executive. November 21, 1999.
49. Solomon, C. M. 1994. Success abroad depends on more than job skills. *Personnel Journal,* April: 51–60.
50. Black, et. al., op. cit.

Part 3/Reading 2

Don't Fence Her In

Kathryn Tyler

FOCUS ON GLOBAL HR MANAGEMENT

Myths and misperceptions about what happens to women sent abroad—from the belief that they are crime targets to the assumption that some cultures won't accept them in business—prompt managers to overlook women when filling international assignments, according to expatriates and experts.

Women are only 14 percent of the expatriates working for U.S. companies, but they make up nearly 50 percent of the middle management pool from which employers choose most candidates for international assignments. So says the study, "Why Are Women Left at Home: Are They Unwilling to Go on International Assignments?" published last year by the International Personnel Association (IPA), a business group whose members include 60 of the top 100 businesses in the Fortune 500.

Source: *HR Magazine,* March 2001, pp. 69–77.

Even though women rejected foreign assignments no more often than men did, supervisors believed women weren't interested or wouldn't work out and were reluctant to recruit them, the IPA found.

"Most often employees, whether male or female, find out about assignments from their immediate supervisor," says Linda K. Stroh, co-author of the IPA study and professor of human resources and industrial relations at Loyola University in Chicago. "If the supervisor thinks women are less willing [to go on international assignments], there lies the dilemma. It relates so much to the stereotypes we're beginning to chip away at domestically."

IPA "put to rest many of the myths in regards to female expatriates: That women don't want international assignments; that the male spouse is the bigger breadwinner; that women were less inclined to disrupt their families," says Raj Tatta, partner with PricewaterhouseCoopers in Florham Park, N.J. "Good people with the most honorable intentions made the wrong assumptions."

The business group's study got backup from a separate survey by the women's advocacy group Catalyst, based in New York. Catalyst's "Passport to Opportunity," published last year, found that supervisors believe women are not as internationally mobile as men—even though 80 percent of the women expatriates surveyed had never rejected a new assignment, compared to 71 percent of the men.

Catalyst also found that while management assumed that men would be interested in expatriate assignments, women had to ask management to be considered for an international job.

Companies that ignore women when making international assignments are putting their business at risk, Tatta says. "This is the tightest labor market the world has ever seen. If you do not draw upon your women for your international assignments, you are hurting yourself." Sending women on international assignments "is no longer a matter of good corporate citizenship . . . it's a matter of the corporation's survival."

SAFETY CONCERNS

If women are willing to go on international assignments, why do supervisors and managers keep sending men while women stay home?

Expatriates and experts note that employers express two major—but usually unfounded—worries. Employers fear that women posted abroad could become crime victims and they believe that some societies' cultural prejudices against working women could hamper female expatriates' effectiveness on the job.

Patti Bellinger, an American expatriate in London and vice president of global diversity and inclusion for BP Amoco, labels the crime concern a myth. "There are basic rules of the game when traveling that men and women have to follow," she says.

Katie Koehler, vice president of HR for the Caribbean and Latin American region for Marriott International Inc., agrees. She accepted an assignment in Mexico City, which she says is considered one of the most dangerous cities in the world. "In Mexico . . . it doesn't matter if you're a man or a woman. If it's a dangerous city, it's dangerous for whomever."

Expatriates add that in some cases, women working abroad may be safer than men because women are less likely to underestimate risks. "Women take more precautions. Men don't feel as at risk," says Bellinger.

PREJUDICES AGAINST WORKING WOMEN

Managers also may say that women might have difficulty being accepted in business because of prejudices against working women in the host countries.

Cultural prejudice against businesswomen can be subtle or pronounced. In some countries, Stroh says, workers may refuse to acknowledge women during meetings, question women's decisions, or make derogatory comments about a woman's role in society. In some cultures, women may be forced to alter their attire and change their habits, such as going out in public only with their husbands because the local culture prohibits women from being seen with other men.

While such strictures can affect women, they do not necessarily prevent women from succeeding as expatriates, Stroh notes. "Even in the more harsh cultures, once they recognized the woman could do the job, once her competence had been demonstrated, it became less of a problem," she says.

That was Koehler's experience in Mexico. "In dealing with the men who run the unions, there was a noticeable shock that I was . . . to be treated as an equal," she says. "At one breakfast meeting, immediately after graciously welcoming me, one union leader told a dirty, sexist joke in Spanish. I knew it was a test—one, whether I understood it, and two, how I would react." She merely smiled politely to indicate that she understood the joke but didn't think it was funny. After that incident, she notes, "He didn't mess with me. There's a lot of 'sweetie' stuff. You just have to work around it."

Jill Walsleben, director of HR development for Watson Wyatt Worldwide, an international HR consulting firm based in Washington, D.C., spent two years working for Citibank in Zurich, Switzerland, where she found that attitudes varied depending on her co-workers' positions.

"Among my leadership team, the female thing was not a problem," she says. But she noticed a different attitude among other employees. "I did feel there was this underlying feeling of 'Why are you pushing for this change? You should be home with your kids. You dragged your poor husband here?' "

Bellinger says that in male-dominated cultures like Saudi Arabia "it's impossible to be as effective [as a man], but there aren't many examples like that. We have women in other Middle Eastern countries who are doing well." Generally, she says, employees in the host country tend to assume that if a company spends the money to send a woman on an international assignment, the woman must be highly competent.

Bellinger adds that an expatriate faces more prejudice as an American or as a corporate executive than as a female.

"The stereotypes weren't gender-specific. They were about an American coming from corporate [offices]," says Lori Roland, who recently returned from a stint in London working as a program director for the Gillette Co. of Boston. "It's important for an expatriate in a new culture to be open and not presume they know the business."

WHAT ABOUT THE SPOUSE?

"People assume that . . . the husband's job is more important," Roland says. "That is the biggest fallacy that a company can fall into. You can miss some really good opportunities to develop talent by making that assumption."

The spouses of married female expatriates are likelier to work than are the spouses of married male expatriates, according to Catalyst. When the group surveyed married expatriates, it found that 91 percent of married female expatriates are in dual-career marriages, while only 50 percent of married male expatriates are in dual-career marriages.

Host-country immigration laws, language barriers, and work limitations often make it extremely difficult, if not impossible, for trailing spouses, male or female, to find suitable employment.

That's what led Walsleben to terminate her assignment in Zurich. Walsleben, who moved there in 1995 with her husband and their two young children, says she found there was no day care available because most Swiss women quit working when they have children. Her husband, who had hoped to find work, tended the children. "My husband was the only dad in the parking lot at the international school, the only man in the village grocery store," she says.

The family came home when her husband, who had been a project manager for an aerospace company in the United States, couldn't find work in Zurich. "He said, 'I'm too young to be retired. I'm going home and I hope you come, hon.' I was left with torn emotions between doing what my husband needed and what I had committed to the business to do."

Female expatriates also may have a tough time dealing with their spouses' adjustment to a move abroad because male "trailing spouses" often find that corporate support and social arrangements assume that the spouse will be female.

"There isn't a lot of community for my husband to be a part of," Bellinger says, adding that most events for spouses are geared toward women. She notes that her company's internal publication for trailing spouses is called *Woman*.

DON'T MAKE ASSUMPTIONS

In advising employers on how to expand the number of women in expatriate assignments, Koehler and Roland say employers should not make assumptions about anyone's interest or willingness to go, but should keep asking.

"HR departments need to be creative in recruiting more women," says Koehler. "Sometimes all it takes is for the company to plant the seed. There may be a lot of women out there who would want to do it and be good at it, but they don't consider it themselves." Despite living abroad as a child, Koehler says she never considered an international assignment until an executive at Marriott presented her with the idea.

Roland urges supervisors to "ask and ask again," even if a woman turns them down the first time. She notes that she rejected an international assignment before saying yes to a post in England. "Don't assume because someone has turned an assignment down once, they are not willing and interested," she says. "Sometimes timing is just not right, especially when they have a dual-income situation."

Roland's case also shows that employers shouldn't assume that a woman's personal life will make her turn down an assignment. Roland was nine months pregnant with her first child when she accepted the assignment in England. Her employer agreed to send her and her family overseas after she completed her maternity leave.

"From a personal point of view it was a busy time, but it was the logical next transition in my career," she says.

DRAWING WOMEN TO EXPATRIATE JOBS

Experts and expatriates say companies can increase the number of women in expatriate positions if they try these tactics:

- Create a system for identifying employees willing to take these assignments. Employers need to set up organized selection systems that "develop pools of potential candidates so that when there's a position that becomes available, it isn't a matter of random selection," Stroh says. At Gillette, managers use the annual performance review as a time to ask employees about possible moves. "Having [the employee's interest] in writing and in the database puts it into the formal process and hopefully gets rid of those assumptions before they even ask the employee," says Roland. If your corporate culture leans more toward expecting employees to volunteer their interest in assignments, make that expectation clear, Bellinger says. Use successful female expatriates to recruit others. "Let these people do recruiting, have seminars and talk about the pros and cons and how to make it successful," advises Koehler. Tatta adds: "One successful assignment breeds more assignment requests."
- Be flexible about timing. The Catalyst study recommends giving employees a reasonable deadline for deciding whether to accept an assignment and being flexible about the starting date. For example, Roland's employer held her assignment for three months while she was on maternity leave. Bellinger's company delayed her departure until children finished the school year in the United States.
- Provide employment assistance for the trailing spouse. The Catalyst study showed that 60 percent of trailing spouses would like career assistance from the expatriate's employer, but only 17 percent receive it. If local immigration laws prevent the spouse from working, offer alternatives, such as volunteer opportunities or tuition allowances for local universities.
- Address social needs. Expatriates cite isolation as one of the most difficult obstacles to assimilation in the host country. The Catalyst study showed that only 52 percent of women felt included in the informal expatriate network or in socializing with local nationals, while 68 percent of men felt included in such networks and local socializing. Catalyst also found that 73 percent of trailing spouses would like the employer to provide a formal spouse network but only 11 percent had one. "It's incredibly lonely," says Koehler of her experiences as a single female expatriate. "I wanted to meet other people, but all of the [expatriate social] events were during the day. There was nothing for working women or trailing spouses." Bellinger says she would have liked some opportunities for her children to meet other expatriate children because her family moved to England at the start of summer and had to wait until school began in the fall to meet other playmates.

- Provide mentors. Expatriates benefit when they can discuss problems, both on and off the job, with someone who knows their host country. The Catalyst study showed that 72 percent of women expatriates would like a formal host-country mentor, but only 30 percent had one.
- Plan for the employee's return. "Companies need to think about repatriation," advises Walsleben, who says she left her company 18 months after returning from abroad because she felt it did not plan adequately for her return. The only job available to her that took advantage of her new experience was in New York, but she lived in Virginia. The commute helped fuel her decision to leave.

IMPROVING THE INTERNATIONAL EXPERIENCE

How can employers improve all expatriates' experiences and make the idea of an international assignment more attractive to women? Female expatriates and Catalyst, a New York-based women's advocacy group, recommend that employers do the following:

- Provide information packs on the host country with emergency telephone numbers and information on contacting basic services, such as schools, utilities, and doctors.
- Expand and improve education about the host country's culture before and during the assignment.
- Offer flexible, cafeteria-style benefits so that expatriates can tailor the benefits to their individual situations. For example, most companies offer a free plane ticket to the home city every year, but some expatriates would rather use that ticket to visit family living elsewhere in the United States or for family from the United States to visit them. Still others would prefer the cash to use for private school tuition in the host country.
- Offer concierge-type services to help expatriates set up their households. For example, these services could arrange for someone to wait at the employee's home for the telephone to be installed.
- Provide opportunities for employees and their families to build social networks. Make sure there are events in the evenings or on weekends and that events aren't oriented toward one gender. Some husbands of female expatriates complain that the employer-organized social events seem to be geared toward women, on the assumption that trailing spouses are female.
- Use gender-neutral terms when referring to the trailing spouse.
- Provide a checklist, organized by date, of what the employee should consider doing when leaving the home country, when arriving in the host country, and when leaving the host country.

Part 3/Reading 3

Global Fatalities: When International Executives Derail

Morgan W. McCall, Jr.
George P. Hollenbeck

Developing global executives is an expensive proposition, especially when expatriate assignments are involved. But the investment can produce a significant return—provided that the corporation uses the knowledge and expertise gained from the experience effectively. When things go wrong, the investment is lost, and usually, so too is a person who was judged to be quite talented. Can these

Source: *Ivey Business Journal,* May–June 2002, pp. 74–78.

loses be prevented? Maybe, but the answer to that question depends on what causes such derailments. If the complexity and ambiguity of international work makes selection errors unavoidable, then the derailment of executives is just another cost of doing business. However, if derailments occur because of something that can be corrected or prevented, then a significant payoff is possible.

To shed some light on the dynamics underlying the derailment of global executives, we interviewed 101 individuals who were successful in their international postings. With an average of nine years experience abroad, they were in a unique position to observe other global executives come and go. The 121 tales they told are the basis for the conclusions we have developed about the underlying causes of international executive failures.

Three factors contribute to the failure of international executives:

The individual
The cultural context
Organizational mistakes

1. THE INDIVIDUAL

Executives contributed to their failure in two ways. Some personal attributes and types of behaviours just don't play in international settings. However, more often, it wasn't simply a personal flaw that prevented an individual from succeeding. Rather, it was the complex interaction of a person's strengths or weaknesses with a change in the situation. We will consider both causes.

Fatal Flaws

The successful executives we interviewed described over 300 flaws in the behaviour and management skills of the executives they had observed. A few of these flaws were factors regardless of the situation or context.

Foremost among them was a failure to adapt to change. What needed to be adapted to varied considerably—bosses, business strategy, leadership philosophy, changes in markets and technology. For many of those ill-fated executives, their inability or unwillingness to change was rooted in a career spent in a silo, or in a single function, which gave them a narrow perspective and made them unable to see the big picture. Unwilling to appreciate another point of view, some executives either refused to accept change or would not put energy into their effort to change.

Another flaw or set of flaws in the "clearly lethal" category resulted in bungled relationships with key people—customers, partners, senior management, or peers. The bungling was especially toxic when it occured in conjunction with a decline in performance or some significant mistake. In a global environment, quality relationships are crucial in certain countries and business situations (such as sensitive negotiations, joint ventures, and cross-cultural alliances). Although a lack of people skills is annoying in any environment, the consequences are particularly severe in an international setting.

Other flaws led some executives to hesitate when action was needed, to default on promises made to senior management, and, when things subsequently went wrong, not to ask for (or accept) outside help. Powerful and successful executives in trouble may try to deal with matters on their own, viewing offers of assistance or advice as interference from the outside. This can be a fatal mistake, made all the more likely whenever, as an expatriate, the executive has lost contact with the rest of the company.

Complex Interaction

But just having flaws is too simplistic an explanation for the derailments that were described to us. As we have all observed, there are people who have glaring flaws who don't derail, while some with overpowering strengths actually do. Still other with no apparent flaws early in their careers seem to develop them later on. And for still others, there is no apparent cause for the flameout. Moreover, the international executives in this derailed group were unusually talented to begin with. They were often described as having multiple strengths, rarely found together, such as brilliant and interpersonally skilled, technically skilled and shrewd about people, or people-and results-oriented. How could such gifted and successful people derail?

The paradoxes can be resolved if derailment is considered as a dynamic process rather than the inevitable result of some personality flaw. Indeed, if one assumes that there are no unqualified strengths and few universally fatal flaws, the data begin to make sense. We identified four patterns that describe the dynamics of many of the derailment scenarios.

1. Early strengths that led to success became weaknesses later on. Most often, this took the form of exceptional technical, functional, or market expertise that resulted in early successes and promotions, but later on blinded the executive to the bigger picture or the need for different skills essential to a higher-level job.
2. Long-standing flaws that became salient when something changed in an executive's situation. Some leaders, for example, had always been abrasive and arrogant, but because they got great business results, they were never damaged by their flaws. Their sins were forgiven in light of their bottom-line performance. When the results weren't as good as expected or when the situation changed so that relationships (and not single-handed bravado) were critical to meeting the bottom line, the flaws "suddenly" emerged and the executive derailed.
3. An executive's constant success. Some executives began to believe that they were as good as they seemed and, like the Greek tragic heroes, their hubris led to their demise.
4. Some executives appeared to be just unlucky, ending up in the wrong place at the wrong time or running afoul of the wrong person. What happened, at least on the surface, was not the person's fault. But while ill fortune appeared to cause these derailments, other factors usually contributed to the fall. It was frequently suggested that the same events might not have derailed someone else—that there was something about the way the executive handled the situation, or about bridges burned in the past, that contributed to the outcome. In short, one of the other dynamics—not bad luck—may have been the real culprit.

While some flaws were uniformly problematic (e.g., failing to adapt to changed situations or an "appalling lack of people skills"), and others emerged when an executive's immediate situation changed, the vast majority of international derailments were anchored in the cultural context itself.

2. THE CULTURAL CONTEXT

It was rarely sufficient to say that an executive's traits or flaws "caused" him or her to derail—most of these executives were extraordinarily talented individuals—unless one could place that trait or action in a larger context. For global executives, that context was almost always cultural.

Working abroad increases stress through its isolation, family pressures, and the broader job responsibilities it often entails. International executives may find themselves dealing with political issues, government corruption, bribery, and a variety of contextual issues without the help that would be available in the home country. Contributing to the stress, but demanding in their own right, are the difficulties of understanding and being understood in one or more foreign languages, and the often subtle differences in values, norms, beliefs, religions, economic systems, and group and community identities.

The natural reluctance of people in organizations to be candid with each other can be magnified by cultural norms, as well as by the inability of outsiders to read the subtle cues. One executive, quite successful in a series of functional assignments, was promoted to a general manager's job outside of his own country. He did well initially, probably because of his functional expertise, but when things started to go wrong, he did not realize it. When he realized it, he didn't have the ability or business knowledge to diagnose the problem and figure out what was wrong. One can't help but wonder if he could have drawn on the expertise of others had this happened in his home country.

Different economic, religious, government, and social systems in some countries have direct effects on how business is carried out. Here, complexity again takes several forms, including the potentially lethal—or at least convoluted—web of relationships and the presence of different business models and practices. As we interviewed executives, we saw how the web of relationships can grow more and more complex: from subordinates from a different culture who don't speak the executive's first language, to subordinates from multiple cultures speaking multiple languages in one region, to subordinates from multiple cultures speaking multiple languages and physically dispersed around the globe. To thicken the mix, add a boss from a different country who speaks a different language or multiple bosses from different countries in a matrix structure, and so on, through suppliers, customers, partners, shareholders, peers, consultants, and others. As if that weren't complicated enough, different countries may have different business models, different definitions of ethical behaviour, and different business approaches and systems.

All these complexities and others too numerous to recount, create a fertile context for derailment. The more relationships an executive has to cultivate, and the more varied they are, the greater the chances that some of them will go wrong. The greater the differences in how business operates in the countries involved, the greater the likelihood that an executive will make erroneous assumptions or commit errors without even knowing that anything is amiss. The more diverse and culturally different the countries, the greater the likelihood that seemingly extraneous factors—or what would be extraneous factors in the home country—will affect business results, the outcomes of deals and negotiations, and other activities for which the executive is accountable. In other words, not only are the executive's actions more likely to be ineffective or even counterproductive, but more circumstances will be beyond the executive's control and more likely to affect outcomes, regardless of the executive's actions. And for all the reasons we pointed out above, the executive may not get timely feedback or pick up the clues that anything is wrong in time to do anything about it.

Although cultural and business differences create a complex and sometimes treacherous context for executive action, international assignments also come with particular seductions that can lure executives onto the path to derailment. Being on their own, often far from direct supervision and with tremendous authority over local operations, global executives can come to believe that they are all-powerful, even above the law. Feeding self-aggrandizement were the perks of foreign duty, which might include servants, cars and drivers, luxurious homes, impressive expense accounts, invitations to galas and state affairs, and other special treatment that, over time, some executives began to view as entitlements.

Even if an executive completes an expatriate assignment successfully, he or she still faces a final risk that may cause derailment—repatriation. Though it is tempting to view coming home as an easy transition, it turns out to be anything but. Executives may return to find that they have lost their business networks and their friends, that their home country is not the same as it was when they left, and—perhaps the unkindest cut of all—that no one cares. Their living conditions may actually be worse, with no servants, drivers, luxurious homes, access to exciting events, or relationships with top business and government leaders. They may come back to less important jobs and reduced responsibility, they may find themselves outside the mainstream, and they may feel that their organization does not take advantage of or appreciate what they have learned. In such circumstances, the skids are greased for derailment.

3. ORGANIZATIONAL MISTAKES

Neither individual attributes and behaviour, nor the cultural context, were sufficient to explain all of the derailments. The organizations for which the derailed executives worked made numerous mistakes that contributed to, or in some cases directly caused, their derailment. The fall of one executive provides an example: "The company contributed [to the derailment] when they led him to believe they would back him up no matter what. But they didn't. They backed him when things went right, but they deserted him when things went wrong." Absence of honest feedback was pervasive, as were mixed messages or unclear expectations from "back home." Companies picked people who were obviously wrong for the assignment, promoted people too fast (they were "untested"), or kept them out too long. Frequently, expatriate executives did not have access to the kinds of technical or other support that domestic executives could call upon.

The complexity of the global context increases the odds that the organization will make various mistakes that contribute to derailments, most of which are avoidable: giving little or no feedback, little monitoring, tolerating existing flaws, and lack of support. Because organizations can influence these and similar factors, we fault them for being lazy, or worse, negligent. Although we don't absolve executives from being responsible for their actions, the organizations' lapses increase the probability that flaws and inappropriate or ineffective behaviour will go unnoticed and uncorrected until it is too late.

Some cases of global derailment resulted from poor selection decisions, usually made for technical or political reasons without considering the potential consequences. Organizations chose people who obviously would not fit in the environment, failed to prepare them properly for the challenges ahead, and/or failed to communicate their expectations or changes in expectations. In still other cases, organizations made decisions that directly affected the executive's operation without considering the situation "on the ground." At times, an organization made strategy or design changes without consulting, or even informing, the local executive.

Derailment risk is high for foreign nationals coming to headquarters and for other executives returning home. Organizations seem to botch their part in both events consistently, contributing to an already difficult situation for the executive.

Finally, we were told of derailments in which an executive's career was exploited for short-term gain. In these circumstances, the organization, purposely or not, knew that the situation was not viable—the executive was assigned an impossible job, or one that would almost certainly create an aftermath so intolerable that the executive could not survive.

PREVENTING DERAILMENTS

A single intervention or a smattering of human resource programs for international executives will not prevent events as complex as those leading to global derailments. Like global executive development itself, preventing derailment requires an integrated approach that connects strategic intent with the systems and practices that affect the selection, development and movement of global executives.

To begin with, solutions must address all three culprits in derailment: the executives' strengths and weaknesses, the global context in which the executives are placed, and the organizational practices that surround the whole process. All three depend on the fundamental strategic issues facing a global business. Only the strategy can determine how many and what kinds of global executive jobs are required, and how many and what kinds of executives are needed to fill them. Only the strategy can determine how many truly global executives are needed (if any), how many foreign nationals are necessary, how the international jobs will be structured and positioned, the extent and nature of alliances, how business will be done internationally, and so on.

There are important differences in the development of local nationals, host-country nationals, and third-country nationals, and for this reason lock-step or undifferentiated development programs are likely to be ineffective for many in the international pool.

Further, global executive jobs, whatever the home country of the executive, are fraught with dangers, not the least of which is the increased probability of derailment associated with poorly designed and poorly managed assignments. Much can be done to improve the ways these jobs are structured, the processes by which performance is monitored, and the feedback processes associated with them.

To emphasize the strategic and structural aspects of developing international executive talent is not to say that individual development should be ignored. There is no question that many of the essential skills needed in global careers can be learned, and that very few individuals are so naturally gifted that they need no further development. While there are limits to what an organization can do to make someone grow, there is a lot they can do to help people who want to grow. These include providing opportunities, early in a career, to work with people from other countries and to be part of activities that cross borders, to work under competent bosses with international experience and perspective, and to live and work as an expatriate. These kinds of experiences, combined with effective assessment and feedback, seem to be essential ingredients in developing global talent.

This article was adapted with permission of the Harvard Business School Press. Source: Developing Global Executives: The Lessons of International Experience, by Morgan W. McCall, Jr., and George P. Hollenbeck. Copyright 2002 by Harvard Business School Publishing Corporation.

Part 3/Reading 4

The Right Way to Bring Expats Home

Leslie Gross Klaff

You make a significant investment when you send an employee overseas, but many workers leave companies when they return home. Here's how to keep your repatriates, and make sure your investment doesn't go to waste.

Employers often dole out as much as $1 million for each employee they send on an overseas assignment. So when an employee returns home and jumps ship, it's a huge investment loss.

Almost a third of repatriates end up quitting within two years of returning from abroad, research shows. Why do they leave? Often there's no career path in place for them, they're not using skills they gained overseas, or they've grown accustomed to more autonomy abroad and don't feel challenged.

Source: *Workforce*, July 2002, pp. 40–44.

But there are steps that employers can take to retain repatriates. Consultants say the key is having a full-circle repatriation program, one that supports employees and their families before they leave, during their stay, and—perhaps most important—after they return.

THE HIGH COST OF NOT HAVING A PROCESS

"Sometimes the repatriation process is an afterthought for many companies," says Laura Herring, CEO of The Impact Group, a relocation consulting firm in Minneapolis. "The number one reason for having a repatriation program is to protect your $1 million investment."

An increasing number of companies today do have repatriation programs, but many still can't retain people because the organization doesn't guarantee jobs when the assignment ends, says John Wada, business development consultant at Runzheimer International, a relocation firm in Rochester, Wisconsin. Two-thirds of companies offer no job guarantee, according to the *Global Relocation Trends 2001 Survey Report,* a study on relocation data trends sponsored by GMAC Global Relocation Services, National Foreign Trade Council, and SHRM Global Forum. And many repatriation programs don't counsel employees when they come home—when repats are at the highest risk of quitting.

That reentry counseling is not only the most critical aspect of keeping the employee, it's also the cheapest, says Margery Marshall, president of Prudential Financial's Relocation Services in Irvine, California. "And that's what companies are ignoring the most."

An effective repatriation program costs between $3,500 and $10,000 per family, Herring says. To retain a repatriate, smart companies plan a program that spells out career goals, prepares the family for cultural differences and adjustments, keeps the person connected to the home office, and allows the employee to use the international skills when he returns.

RETURN PLANNING BEGINS BEFORE THEY LEAVE

A strong repatriation program begins well before an employee moves to a foreign post. Unfortunately, Wada says, HR professionals tend to get bogged down in the logistics of the assignment when they should be focusing on setting career expectations. They should define assignment goals and specify how they fit into the employee's long-term career plan.

The *Global Relocation Trends* report, which surveyed 150 human resource professionals, shows that more than a third of companies are unsure of how international assignments affect expats' careers. At the New York-based accounting firm Deloitte & Touche, managers discuss which job each of the company's 200 expats will take after returning—before the person goes abroad, says John McNamara, national director of international assurance. That is when they sign a written commitment letter, which includes a "return ticket," a job guarantee at the end of the assignment.

"If they come back and you don't take advantage of what they've learned . . . they can easily get disillusioned," McNamara says.

Karen Schwindt, a Deloitte & Touche repatriate who returned from Melbourne, Australia, in April 2000, speaks from experience when she says, "If you have a vision of what you want to bring back, you can build those skills while you're there."

It's not easy to place every repat in a job that uses international experience, so don't define goals too narrowly, Wada says. If the expat is going to London, for example, the goal might be learning how best to interact with the British and how to negotiate with a diverse group of people.

LEVERAGING OVERSEAS EXPERIENCE

Employees will view working abroad as valuable if a company's high-level executives have international experience, Wada adds. At FedEx, many former repats fill leadership positions, including FedEx Express President and CEO David Bronczek and International Executive Vice President Michael Ducker.

"As we become more and more global, it shows that experience overseas is leveraged back home," says Tom Mullady, manager of international compensation planning and administration at FedEx. The global mail and transportation company understands the need for expats to be secure about their employment future.

Before an assignment begins, employers should counsel employees and their families on what to expect culturally and logistically in their new host country. Research shows that the most common reason assignments fail is that the family is unhappy. Honeywell, a global technology and manufacturing company based in Morristown, New Jersey, offers employees and their families a two-day cultural orientation on the region where they will be living, says Sharon Byrnes, manager of international compensation. As early as one year before the employee leaves, the company conducts an assessment to identify certain skills the employee might need to be successful, such as learning a foreign language. The assessment assists the company in identifying successful expatriate candidates, and helps the potential expat decide whether to accept the assignment.

STAYING CONNECTED

While the employee is overseas, one of the factors critical to retention is keeping the person in the loop with her company and co-workers at home. One effective way of accomplishing this is for the employer to assign the employee as mentor, ideally a former repat, says Tara Brabazon, director of intercultural services at GMAC Global Relocation Services in Warren, New Jersey. These sponsors keep expatriates abreast of job openings and organizational changes at home so they can more easily feel comfortable and fit in when they return.

At the medical technology company Medtronic, based in Minneapolis, mentors are usually at the vice-presidential level, says Martha Hippe, manager of global assignments. The mentor helps to set career goals and to place the repat in a job when she comes home. The two stay in close communication through phone calls, e-mail, and visits.

Employers also can keep in touch with expats by giving them access to the company's intranet and monthly newsletters. Many companies require mentors to make at least one face-to-face visit with the expat each year. In an effort to ensure that relationships in the home office are nurtured, FedEx encourages its expats to "have one foot in each country" while they're abroad, Mullady says. In order to stay connected and ease the transition, discussions about returning home should begin six to eight months before an assignment ends, Wada says. "Most companies wait until the last minute."

For Schwindt, keeping on top of her next career move was especially important, because she had decided while she was away that upon her return home, she'd move from the audit department to mergers and acquisitions. Her mentor put her in touch with other employees in the new department.

"I never felt really forgotten," she says.

THE HOMECOMING CHALLENGE

Most employers don't realize that coming home from an overseas assignment is often harder than leaving. Repats face a myriad of changes, often referred to as "reverse culture shock." When they return, there's a tendency to expect that life will be just the way it was when they left, but it rarely is. There are professional changes that may require adapting to a different corporate culture, and personal adjustments. A spouse who didn't work abroad, for example, has to learn how to reenter the workforce, and the children are now older and have different needs, Herring says. The family's friends may have moved, and they may find that co-workers and others get tired of hearing stories about life abroad. At the office, they often are placed in temporary jobs and feel as though they're being put on hold.

"Repatriation is many, many times more difficult than relocation," Brabazon says. "To fix the situation, [repats] look to change something. It's often the job."

Many managers perceive the repat as difficult. They don't understand how hard a homecoming can be, she says. Gaye Reynolds-Gooch, a consultant for Window on the World, a relocation consulting firm headquartered in Minneapolis, says it's vital to offer employees and their families counseling. Counselors should help repats step back and consider how they might want to live their lives differently. Some, for example, might have changed their priorities and want more work-life balance, she says. It could take a repat nine months to a year to settle into a job and learn how to leverage his international experience.

At Honeywell, employees and their families go through a repatriation program within six months of returning home. Counselors discuss issues such as the challenges of adjusting, and also help employees understand how to apply what they've learned abroad. The one-day program includes a roundtable discussion with members of another former repat family.

Employers also must make sure that repats are able to use their international experience. Researchers at American University found that expatriates are eager to use the skills they developed overseas, but that only 39 percent actually ever do, according to a paper by David Martin, a professor of management and human resource management at American University's Kogod School of Business.

At Deloitte & Touche, managers try to place repats in positions that allow them to conduct business with clients from the country where they lived. Sometimes they are placed in offices in big cities that are more involved in international business so that the employee can associate with other people who have worked abroad. Former repats also can participate in an orientation program for future expats.

Reynolds-Gooch also suggests sponsoring brown-bag lunches for discussions about life overseas, and encouraging repats to join international associations tied to the country where they lived, such as a local Australian, French, or Chinese-American community association.

"You don't want to lose your best and brightest talent. And if a repat leaves the company, it could discourage other employees from wanting to go abroad and hurt the success of the program."

10 TIPS ON MANAGING A SUCCESSFUL REPATRIATION PROGRAM

- Make sure you're sending the right people abroad. Carefully assess who will be successful. Don't just look at their technical skills; consider the employee and his family's ability to adapt to a new culture.
- Clearly define the expat's career goals before the overseas assignment begins and make sure the goals reflect your company's overall objectives. If the purpose of overseas assignments, for example, is to give your company global reach, then view the trip as a stepping-stone toward that goal. Have a strong sense of where the assignment will lead next for the employee.
- Discuss the challenges of repatriation before the employee leaves. Let the expatriate know that coming home can be difficult, and stress the importance of staying connected to the home office.
- Create a mentor program. Assign mentors before employees go abroad so they're involved from the start. The mentor should continue to help throughout the stay and for six months after employees return home. If possible, mentors should be previous expats who worked in the same region as the employees they are mentoring.
- Encourage expats to make regular visits to the home office through a home-leave policy. They can reconnect with colleagues and new employees, and help prevent feeling "out of sight, out of mind." Help expats stay in the loop by including them in companywide e-mails and newsletters. Managers at home can serve as advocates by looking for job openings and mentioning their names in discussions.
- Understand and educate management on the challenges of repatriation. Recognize that when returning home, repats can experience reverse culture shock. Look for symptoms, which include boredom, withdrawal, feelings of frustration, and distancing from co-workers. Help repats by letting them know they're not alone and their feelings are normal.
- Find positions and activities that use repats' new skills. Allow them to act as mentors, put them on assignments in which they can interact with overseas colleagues, and encourage them to continue to learn a foreign language or join a community organization related to the country where they lived.
- Provide support to the entire family. Help the repats spouse find a new job, and offer counseling

to the parents and children on readjusting to life after living abroad.

- Encourage repats to approach repatriation similarly to relocating overseas. Many people are well prepared for their move abroad and expect that life will be different. Repats should have a similar mind-set when they return home. They should approach it as another new adventure. Make sure that repats set realistic goals, are aware of changes in their home offices, and reflect on personal changes and new priorities.
- Once repats have returned home, offer a counseling program. Review their international experience and discuss the challenges of repatriation both personally and professionally. Discuss with the repats how their business has changed and how to capitalize on their global experience.

AT AT&T, REPATS GET A SAFETY NET

The telecommunications giant AT&T has crafted a repatriation program that aims to help overseas employees feel as connected to home as possible.

Unlike many companies, the company runs the program in-house rather than contracting the service to an outside firm. The arrangement makes expatriates feel more connected, because they're dealing with people they already know, says Barbara Maria, an international human resources district manager at AT&T.

The three-part program starts with what the company calls a "safety net." Employees and their families are matched up with a psychologist trained in repatriation issues. The mental-health professional meets with the family before they go overseas to discuss the challenges of life abroad. They talk about what it will be like for the spouse not to have a job, and for the children to adapt to a new life. The family is also given an assessment that measures how well they'll adapt to a new culture. The employees and their families call the psychologist throughout the assignment when concerns crop up. "It gives them a comfort level," Maria says. "It's someone to lean on when a problem arises. It softens the shock."

Having such a formal program in place can make all the difference in retaining repatriates. At companies that have formal repatriation programs, 5 percent of repatriates resign within a year of returning from abroad, compared with 22 percent at companies without such programs, according to a recent paper written by David C. Martin, a professor of management and human resource management at the Kogod School of Business at American University.

AT&T also offers a mentor program that helps expats stay connected to colleagues and news in their home office. The company makes sure that expats periodically return home for meetings and to hang around the office and be seen. About six months before the end of the overseas assignment, expats go through a "journeying home" program. The psychologist and a representative from human resources visit the expat family and prepare them to come home. They focus on updating the expat's resume, planning the next career move, and getting in contact with at-home supervisors. They also plan the logistics of the move back home, everything from transferring household goods to arranging for housing and schools.

About one month after the employees return home, AT&T invites repatriates and their families to a " welcome home" seminar. Families participate in counseling sessions on dealing with the stress of repatriation, and, if needed, retirement planning. Spouses are offered job counseling. The psychologist checks in with the family a few months later for a follow-up visit.

AT&T has another tool to prevent turnover among repatriates. It gives a bonus to repats who stay with the company for six months after returning home. In the past, bonuses were given on a monthly basis, and it was more likely that employees would "take the bonus, their knowledge, and expertise and just leave," Maria says. "There's nothing there holding them. It's an incentive to stay."

Part 3/Case 1

Whom to Hire?

Richard M. Hodgetts
Fred Luthans

OBJECTIVES

- To explore participants' cultural biases and expectations.
- To examine cultural differences.
- To consider the impact culture has on hiring decisions.

INSTRUCTIONS

Step 1 (10–15 Minutes)

Read the background information and descriptions of each of the applicants. Consider the job and the cultures within which the individual to be hired will be operating. Rank the candidates from 1 to 5, with 1 being your first choice, and enter your rankings on the ranking sheet in the column marked "My Ranking." Briefly, list the reasons for each of your rankings.

Do not discuss your rankings with your classmates until told to do so.

Step 2 (30–40 Minutes)

Working with three to four of your classmates, discuss the applicants, and rank them in the order of group preference. Do not vote.

Rank the candidates from 1 to 5, with 1 being the group's first choice, and enter your group rankings on the ranking sheet in the column marked "Group Ranking." Briefly list the reasons for each of the group's rankings.

If your group represents more than one culture, explore the ways in which each person's cultural background may have influenced his or her individual decisions.

Step 3 (Open-ended)

Report your rankings to the class, and discuss the areas of difference that emerged within your group while you were trying to reach consensus.

QUESTIONS FOR DISCUSSION

1. Was your group able to explore openly any culturally based biases that came up—for example, feelings about homosexuality, religion, personality traits, politics?
2. Did you make any comments or observations that you feel would have been fully acceptable in your own culture but were not accepted by the group? Explain.
3. If the answer to number 2 was yes, how did the reaction of the group make you feel about your membership in it? How did you handle the situation?
4. What implications do you believe these cultural differences would have in business dealings?

BACKGROUND

You are a member of the management committee of a multinational company that does business in 23 countries. While your company's headquarters are in Holland, your offices are scattered fairly evenly throughout the four hemispheres. Primary markets have been in Europe and North America; the strongest emerging market is the Pacific Rim. Company executives would like to develop what they see as a powerful potential market in the Middle East. Sales in all areas except the Pacific Rim have shown slow growth over the past two years.

Source: Richard M. Hodgetts and Fred Luthans, *International Management: Culture, Strategy, and Behavior* (Burr Ridge, IL: McGraw-Hill/Irwin), pp. 574–576.

At present, your company is seeking to restructure and revitalize its worldwide marketing efforts. To accomplish this, you have determined that you need to hire a key marketing person to introduce fresh ideas and a new perspective. There is no one currently in your company who is qualified to do this, and so you have decided to look outside. The job title is "vice-president for international marketing"; it carries with it a salary well into six figures (US$), plus elaborate benefits, an unlimited expense account, a car, and the use of the corporate jet. The person you hire will be based at the company's headquarters and will travel frequently.

A lengthy search has turned up five people with good potential. It is now up to you to decide whom to hire. Although all the applicants have expressed a sincere interest in the position, it is possible that they may change their minds once the job is offered. Therefore, you must rank them in order of preference so that if your first choice declines the position, you can go on to the second, and so on.

APPLICANTS

PARK L., AGE 41, MARRIED WITH THREE CHILDREN

Park L. is currently senior vice president for marketing at a major Korean high-technology firm. You have been told by the head of your Seoul office that his reputation as an expert in international marketing is outstanding. The market share of his company's products has consistently increased since he joined the company just over 15 years ago. His company's market share is now well ahead of that of competing producers in the Pacific Rim.

Mr. Park started with his present company immediately after his graduation from the University of Seoul and has worked his way up through the ranks. He does not have a graduate degree. You sense that Mr. Park has a keen understanding of organizational politics and knows how to play them. He recognizes that because the company he works for now is family controlled, it is unlikely that he will ever move much higher than his present situation. Mr. Park has told you that he is interested in the growth potential offered at your company.

In addition to his native tongue, Mr. Park is able to carry on a reasonably fluent conversation in English and has a minimal working knowledge of German and French. His wife, who appears quiet and quite traditional, and his children speak only Korean.

KIRAN K., AGE 50, WIDOW WITH ONE ADULT CHILD

Kiran K. is a Sikh woman living in Malaysia. She began her teaching career while finishing her DBA (doctorate in business administration) at the Harvard Business School and published her first book on international marketing 10 months after graduation. Her doctoral dissertation was based on the international marketing of pharmaceuticals, but she has also done research and published on other areas of international marketing.

Two months after the publication of her book, Kiran went to work in the international marketing department of a Fortune 500 company, where she stayed for the next 10 years. She returned to teaching when Maura University offered her a full professorship with tenure, and she has been there since that time. Her academic position has allowed her to pursue a number of research interests and to write authoritative books and papers in her field. At present, she is well published and internationally recognized as an expert on international marketing. In addition, she has an active consulting practice throughout Southeast Asia.

You have learned through your office in Kuala Lumpur that Kiran's only child, a 23-year-old son, is severely mentally and physically disabled. You sense that part of her interest in the job with your company is to have the income to guarantee his care should anything happen to her. Her son would go with her to Holland, should she be given the job, where he will need to be enrolled in special support programs.

In addition to fluency in Malay, English, and Hindi, Kiran speaks and writes German and Spanish and is able to converse in Japanese and Mandarin.

PETER V., AGE 44, SINGLE

Peter is a white South African. He had worked in a key position in the international marketing division of an American Fortune 100 company until the company pulled out of his country eight months ago. While the company wanted to keep him on, offering to move him from Johannesburg to its New York headquarters, Peter decided that it was time to look elsewhere. He had begun to feel somewhat dead-ended in his position and apparently sees the position at your company as an opportunity to try out new territory. Like your other candidates for the position, Peter has a long list of accomplishments and is widely recognized as outstanding in his field. People in your company who have had contacts with him say that Peter is creative, hardworking, and loyal. In addition, you have been told that Peter is a top-flight manager of people who is able to push his employees to the highest levels of performance. And, you are told, he is very organized.

Peter has a PhD in computer science from a leading South African university and an MBA from Purdue's Krannert School of Business.

Peter had been a vehement opponent of apartheid and is still very much a social activist. His high political visibility within South Africa had made his life there difficult, and even now, with the end of apartheid, he would like to get out. His constant male companion, P. K. Kahn, would be coming with him to Holland, and Peter would like your personnel office to help P. K. find an appropriate position.

Peter speaks and reads English, Dutch, Afrikaans, and Swahili and can converse in German.

TEX P., AGE 36, DIVORCED WITH ONE CHILD

Tex is currently job hunting. His former job as head of marketing for a single-product high-technology firm—highly specialized work stations for sophisticated artificial intelligence applications—ended when the company was bought out by Texas Instruments. Tex had been with his previous company virtually from the time the company was started six years earlier. Having to leave his job was an irony to Tex as it was largely due to the success of his efforts that the company was bought out. You sense that he is a little bitter, and he tells you that jobs offered to him by TI were beneath him and not worthy of consideration.

Tex has both his undergraduate and MBA degrees from Stanford University. In addition, he was a Rhodes Scholar and won a Fulbright scholarship, which be used to support himself while he undertook a two-year research project on the marketing of high-technology equipment to Third World countries.

You have learned through your New York office that Tex has a reputation for being aggressive and hard driving. Apparently he is a workaholic who has been known to work 18 to 20 hours a day, seven days a week. He seems to have little time for his personal life.

In addition to his native English, Tex has a minimal command of French—which he admits he hasn't used since his college days.

ZVI C., AGE 40, MARRIED WITH FIVE CHILDREN

Zvi began his career after receiving his MBA from the Sloan School of Management at the Massachusetts Institute of Technology (MIT). His first job was as marketing manager for a German company doing business in Israel.

Zvi's phenomenal success with this company led to his being hired away by an international office equipment company in England. Again, he proved to be outstanding, boosting the company's market share beyond all expectations within two years. After five years, Zvi was offered a chance to go back to Israel, this time to oversee and coordinate all the international marketing programs for an industrial park of 14 companies run as an adjunct to Israel's leading scientific research institution. It has been his responsibility to interface the research component with product development and sales as well as to manage the vast marketing department. Again, he has shown himself to be a master.

You have learned through your Haifa office that Zvi is highly respected and has extensive contacts in the scientific and high-tech worlds. He is exceptionally creative in his approach to marketing, often trying bold strategies that most of his peers would dismiss as too risky. Zvi, however has made them work and work well.

Zvi is a religious man who must leave work by noon on Friday. He will not work Saturdays nor any of his religion's major and minor holidays—about 18 a year. He will, however, work on Sundays.

In addition to his native language, Dutch (Zvi and his family moved to Israel from Holland when Zvi was six), he speaks and writes fluent Hebrew, English, German, and Arabic.

Ranking Sheet

Rank candidates from one to five with one as your first choice.				
Applicant	**Rank**	**Group Reasons**	**Ranking**	**Reasons**
Park L.				
Kiran K.				
Peter V.				
Tex P.				
Zvi C.				

Part 3/Case 2

Steve Parker and the SA-Tech Venture (A)

On September 2, 1996, SA-Tech, a joint venture between Standard Industries (Standard) of the United States and Good Fortune Enterprises (Good Fortune) of China, began operating in Huadong, a small town about 100 miles from Shanghai. The joint venture was created to manufacture various automotive heating ventilation and air conditioning (HVAC) parts. On September 13,1996, Good Fortune's president stopped venture operations and would not allow the joint-venture general manager into the plant. The general manager had been hired in China by Standard specifically for the joint venture. Good Fortune's president wrote a letter to Standard HVAC's Asia

 This case was prepared by Professor Andrew Inkpen for the purpose of classroom discussion only, and not to indicate either effective or ineffective management.

Pacific director and demanded that the general manager be replaced. After various meetings and communications between the partners, it was decided that a new general manager would be appointed and that the general manager would come from Standard. Steve Parker, a Standard manager who was in China working as Asia Pacific purchasing manager for Standard HVAC, was asked if he would be interim general manager in SA-Tech. It was now up to Parker to decide whether he should accept the position and if so, what he would do to get the joint venture back on track.

STEVE PARKER'S AUTOMOTIVE CAREER

Steve Parker, 32 years old, began his automotive career with Ford Motor Company in Michigan. While attending Michigan State University, he had summer jobs at a Ford plant. After graduation with a degree in MIS in 1988, Parker worked as a manufacturing foreman in two different Ford plants for six years. In his last position at Ford, he had about 30 unionized-workers reporting to him and about $12 million of budget responsibility. In 1993 Parker left Ford and joined Standard, a large automotive supplier and a tier one supplier to various automotive firms. Standard manufactured many different types of automotive components, including HVAC parts, seat systems, steering systems, and metal pressings. Parker became a buyer at Standard with responsibility for purchasing about $75 million of components for the Standard HVAC division.

Parker viewed his manufacturing and buying experience as critical to his career because:

> I was comfortable in a factory and had worked with base level workers. The buying job gave me experience in negotiating. I negotiated several long-term contracts and developed a good understanding of competitive sourcing and the value that materials and negotiating play in the business.

In 1995 Parker attended a presentation by Standard's head of business development and ventures. The presentation showed how Standard's HVAC business would go from $600 million in sales to $700 million over the next five years as a result of foreign joint ventures. Even though Parker had never traveled outside the United States, the presentation triggered his interest. After the presentation, Parker told his boss, the director of purchasing, that he would be interested in any international opportunities that might come up, especially in the area of venture negotiations. Two days later Parker's boss told him that if he was interested, there was a new purchasing position in China that had to be filled immediately. The manager selected for the position would be required to spend 50 percent of the next six months in China. The assignment was to look for suppliers in the Asia Pacific region who could support four joint ventures that were being negotiated by the HVAC division: two in China, one in Taiwan, and one in Japan. At the time, Parker was not married so moving at short notice was possible. Also, Parker's buying responsibilities had been secured with three to five year contracts, with annual cost reductions locked in, so he could easily leave his current position. Parker agreed to take the China job and within a week was in Beijing.

THE CHINESE AUTOMOBILE INDUSTRY

Standard Industries was interested in the Chinese automobile market because of the significant expected growth. Sales in 1996 were expected to increase by 20 percent to about 380,000 units, although capacity over the next few years was expected to grow to greater than 700,000 units. More than 95 percent of Chinese production was by joint ventures between Chinese firms and the major international automobile producers. In 1996 new joint-venture investments were under way by General Motors, Daimler-Benz, Citroën, Honda, and other firms. In response to concerns about overcapacity, the Chinese government announced that it would not license any more automobile manufacturing joint ventures and revised its projections for future car demand in 2000 from 1.2 million units to 850,000. Adding to the competition was rampant smuggling of vehicles from Japan and South Korea, which was estimated to have reached 100,000 units.

Most of the foreign automobile firms in China were struggling. For example, in 1993 Peugeot began investing in its joint venture plant in Guangzhou to increase production to 150,000 units. In 1996 the Peugeot plant produced fewer than 3,000 units, down from 6,600 in 1995. Citroën would produced only 13,000 vehicles in 1996, even though its joint-venture agreement permitted production of up to 300,000 units. Nevertheless, Citroën was expanding steadily. With the possible exception of Peugeot none of the automakers appeared willing to withdraw from China, and Japanese firms, latecomers to China, were scrambling to gain a foothold.

Shanghai VW, the joint venture between Volkswagen and Shanghai Automotive Industry Corp., was unique in two respects: It was the only profitable foreign joint venture and the only one to have achieved commercially viable levels of production. Shanghai VW was formed in 1984 as the first foreign automotive venture in China. By 1996 Shanghai VW was producing more than 200,000 vehicles and had built strong supply and distribution channels. Nevertheless, until recently, Shanghai VW had minimal serious competition and, consequently, invested little in product development. The Santana model produced by Shanghai VW was more than a decade old. In addition Volkswagen's second joint venture with First Auto Works in Changchun, formed in 1988 to produce the Jetta model, was in serious difficulty. Sales in 1996 were 25,000 units, half the target output and far less than the plant's 150,000-unit capacity. The joint venture lost an estimated $100 million in 1996.

The Chinese car market was heavily protected, with import tariffs of close to 100 percent and quotas on the number of cars imported. Foreign producers were prohibited from consolidating sales organizations of imports and joint ventures. Joint-venture producers were required to have 40 percent local content in the first year of production and 60 percent and 80 percent in the second and third years. The local content rules meant that firms like General Motors actively encouraged their suppliers to invest in China. In the event that China entered the WTO tariffs, local content rules and other protective measures would have to be dismantled.

Despite the problems with overcapacity and profits, most industry observers expected the China automobile market to grow significantly. Discretionary incomes were rising, especially in the major cities, and with the arrival of General Motors and other OEMs, many automotive suppliers, including Standard, believed that the China market was too important to ignore. In fact, the strategic issue for most of the major auto producers and suppliers was not whether to enter the market or how to compete with Chinese companies but rather securing or consolidating profitable market share.

PARKER ARRIVES IN CHINA

Parker went to China in May 1995 as the purchasing representative to the Standard HVAC division joint-venture negotiating team, which was headed up by Joe Ryan, a manager from the Standard's business development and ventures group. Two joint-venture partners in China had been identified and negotiations were underway. Because material costs for the HVAC division were always over 50 percent of total costs, it was critical to assess the supplier base during the negotiation phase. Also, because tariffs at that time were often as high as 100 percent, domestic sourcing in China was essential if the ventures were to be profitable.

Parker's job was to meet with potential suppliers and assess their suitability for the proposed ventures. During the venture negotiations, Joe Ryan was the only real contact with the Chinese partners and was largely on his own in terms of assessing partner competencies and designing the joint-venture organization. For finance and legal issues, Ryan had to work closely with Standard's corporate legal and treasury departments. Because

Ryan's personal compensation was in part dependent on successfully forming joint ventures, he was anxious to conclude the negotiations.

Almost as soon as he arrived in China, Parker began a four-week trip through northeast China, an area full of crumbling state-owned manufacturing plants often referred to as China's rust belt. For about a year, Parker traveled between China and the United States, with four weeks in China and one week in the United States. During this period he visited about 200 firms all over China as a preliminary investigation of their potential to become suppliers to Standard's joint ventures. Besides his work with the HVAC division, Parker helped support China purchasing for several other Standard divisions.

In April 1996, Parker became an expatriate based in China and was appointed Asia Pacific purchasing manager for the Standard HVAC division. In a matrix structure he reported to both Mark Hunt, Asia Pacific director of Standard HVAC and the Standard HVAC purchasing director based in Detroit. Besides Hunt and Parker, five other American expatriates in the HVAC division were also in China. These managers were responsible for finance, sales, engineering, venture development, and marketing. Parker was based in Shanghai because most of the potential automotive suppliers were in the Shanghai region. The other Standard expatriates were based in Beijing.

Standard HVAC signed one joint-venture agreement in June 1996 and the SA-Tech agreement in August 1996. After the two joint-venture agreements were signed, Parker's job shifted to support for venture purchasing. He had two main tasks: train the Chinese purchasing managers in competitive sourcing and bring the ventures' purchasing departments up to QS9000 levels.

SA-TECH

The SA-Tech joint venture was negotiated over the period June 1995 to late August 1996. The Chinese partner, Good Fortune Enterprises, was a large diversified Chinese company that contributed its automotive HVAC division to SA-Tech. The HVAC division, which had more than 700 employees, represented about one-third of Good Fortune's total business. The other main business was tools such as pliers and screwdrivers. Good Fortune was also trying to launch a joint venture to build small cars. Good Fortune was a Chinese Township Enterprise company that was, as far as Standard and Parker knew, family controlled. At times Good Fortune deferred to higher authorities but throughout the life of the venture, Parker and other Standard managers never truly understood who owned and controlled the partner. The venture equity split was 60 percent for Standard and 40 percent for Good Fortune. The board included three members from Standard and two from Good Fortune. The chairman of the board was from Good Fortune but this position did not have any veto rights.

Good Fortune was interested in forming the joint venture for two main reasons. One, without new technology it was only a matter of time before the company would be unable to compete against other HVAC firms that had access to Western technology. Two, in return for contributing its HVAC business to the joint venture, Good Fortune would receive a significant cash payment. The cash would come from Standard. In a worst-case scenario, if SA-Tech failed, Good Fortune had managed to divest 60 percent of its HVAC division assets. The valuation of the assets was based on projected profits from SA-Tech. Standard agreed to pay Good Fortune $20 million in two installments of $10 million; one at the start of the joint venture and another 18 months later. The first payment would be due one month after the official start of the joint venture.

Standard's contribution would be in two areas, technology for new products and cash. There were four different technology agreements for four different products. These agreements included a lump-sum payment to Standard from the joint venture plus a royalty on units sold. When the joint venture was formed there was no guaranteed new business associated with the new technology.

Because the joint venture was not a greenfield business, joint venture startup was quite straightforward since the workforce, plant, customers, and suppliers were already in place. The most important early issue to resolve was the selection of a joint-venture management team. A Chinese manager named Yin Chung Li[1] from Dalian was hired by Joe Ryan to be SA-Tech's general manager. Mark Hunt, Standard HVAC's Asia Pacific director, believed that the best approach to joint-venture management was to appoint local Chinese managers to represent Standard and then support them with the functional area expatriates based in China (like Steve Parker). Yin started work in July 1996 and was not involved in the joint-venture negotiation. One of Yin's first actions was to hire 20 new employees including three managers to fill management positions for engineering, including manufacturing operations, quality, and sales. Standard hired a Chinese manager to be SA-Tech's chief financial officer. All of the new managers spoke English.

Good Fortune appointed the venture's HR manager, purchasing manager, and deputy general manager. The deputy general manager was Li Chu Kang, the son of Li Hong Tan, the founder and president of Good Fortune. Prior to the joint venture formation, Li Chu Kang ran Good Fortune's HVAC division. None of the managers in Good Fortune or those appointed by Good Fortune to SA-Tech had a university education.

SA-Tech began operating on September 2, 1996, with a $1 million cash contribution for working capital from Standard. Ten days later, Good Fortune's president, Li Hong Tan, stopped SA-Tech from operating and would not allow Yin and his 20 hires into the plant. They were allowed only in the SA-Tech office. In reality, the business kept operating as if it was 100 percent owned by Good Fortune and not a joint venture. At this point, the first $10 million payment had not yet been made to Good Fortune—it was due in a few weeks.

[1]This case follows the Chinese custom of placing the surname first.

Li Hong Tan wrote a letter to Standard's Mark Hunt (Hunt was an SA-Tech board member) with 14 demands. The 14 demands were viewed by Standard as both serious, such as the request for a new general manager for SA-Tech, and frivolous, such as the general manager must have a less expensive car and the CFO must not get a car. Most issues were viewed as "face" issues by Standard. In a meeting with Mark Hunt, Yin accused the Good Fortune managers of cheating and he was unhappy about the $20 million asset agreement, even though this agreement was in place before he was hired. Yin argued that at $20 million, Standard was significantly overpaying for its 60 percent investment in Good Fortune's HVAC business.

A meeting was held on Monday, September 23, at Standard's Beijing office. Participating were Li Hong Tan, his son Li Chu Kang, Mark Hunt, and Standard's HVAC assistant director of Asian operations. It was conceded by both sides that Yin Chung Li was unsuitable as joint-venture general manager and would have to be replaced. Mark Hunt had never trusted Yin (he had been hired by Joe Ryan without any consultation with Hunt) and now that Good Fortune was unhappy with Yin, Hunt was willing to side with the partner. The Chinese side demanded that an American from Standard be appointed as general manager. It was their belief that Standard was not committed because they did not bring any expatriates to the venture. They also believed that an American manager would help them sell to other Chinese automotive OEMs.

A second meeting involving the same people was held on the following Wednesday. Steve Parker was called to a meeting on Friday afternoon with Mark Hunt. Hunt explained the situation to Parker:

> We would like you to be the interim general manager in SA-Tech. I am committed to doing the venture so you need to go in and establish a plan and a timeline for getting the business back on track. Originally I was not in favor of putting expatriates in our ventures because of the cost.

> However, I now think that we need to have our own people on the ground and be willing to pay for it. We really need to start over and do our due diligence to understand what it is going to take to bring this plant to world-class level. We also need to make sure that we get this venture back on track with a process that is consistent with the way Standard runs new businesses.

Other than being told to "fix the problems and rescue the joint venture," Parker was given no specific instructions as to what should be done, mainly because, within Standard, there was very little understanding of the situation. By this time, Joe Ryan, the venture development manager, had returned to the United States. His replacement was unfamiliar with the history of the joint venture. In fact, nobody in Standard knew much about the venture's operations because Ryan had worked on the project by himself and had coordinated more closely with his U.S.-based boss than the HVAC Asia Pacific director. If he accepted the position, Parker would be seconded to SA-Tech and paid by the joint venture. He would report directly to the joint-venture board. He would also report informally to Mark Hunt who, in reality, was Parker's boss and responsible for decisions that would impact his career.

Part 3/ Exercise 1: Global Labor Relations IQ

Purpose

To understand labor-management relations differences that could result in problems.

Group Size

Complete report individually. Then form into four-to-six-person groups.

Time Required

Approximately one hour.

Exercise

Parent companies have experienced difficulties adjusting to host-nation labor practices. Examples of blunders being made by American, Japanese, French, British, and Swedish firms have continued to make news for decades. For example, a Japanese company doing business in Indonesia hired primarily Bataks, members of an ethnic group with characteristics similar to the Japanese. Other Indonesians, however, resented this hiring practice, viewed it as discriminatory, and forced the company to change its policy.

As an assignment, collect three examples of blunders or problems encountered when addressing labor practices in a host country and prepare a one-page report on each for discussion with class colleagues.

Blunders are reported in news reports, books, articles, and white-paper reports. Meet with your class group, compare notes, and examine blunders. Develop a group-produced list of the labor practice blunders to share with the rest of the class.

Source: Robert Konopaske and John M. Ivancevich, © 2004.

Part 3/ Exercise 2: The Family Unit

Purpose
To illustrate that within different cultures and subcultures the family unit exerts various degrees of influence.

Group Size
Create in terms of age, nation of birth, and gender, diverse groups of five to eight.

Time Required
Approximately 45 minutes.

Exercise
Families play various roles in the decisions a person makes with regard to occupation, career plans, education, and self-improvement. Each group of students is diverse in terms of personal life experiences, background, and family cohesiveness.

Be prepared to identify the "influence" your family has had on your life to date in terms of:

- Where you go to school
- Career plans
- Work ethic
- Family responsibility
- Ethical behavior
- Motivation
- Displays of affection
- Celebrations/holiday gatherings

Describe your family patterns and how they influence your behavior. Share some of your thoughts, concerns, and positive and negative experiences about family in the national cultural context and subcultural context from the perspective of the national culture in which you spent most of your development years (birth to 16 years old).

Source: Robert Konopaske and John M. Ivancevich, © 2004.

Part 3/ Internet Exercise 1: Cross-Cultural Training on the Web

Purpose
To learn how to conduct basic Internet-based research on cross-cultural issues.

Group Size
To be performed individually.

Time Required
Approximately 45 minutes.

Other
Internet connection and search engine needed.

Source: Robert Konopaske and John M. Ivancevich, © 2004.

Exercise

As the director of a midsized U.S. firm, you have just been asked to provide cross-cultural information to five of your company's employees who are about to leave on a two-part global assignment: one year in Lima, Peru, followed by another year in Tokyo, Japan. Use the website below to prepare a brief report for these employees that compares and contrasts these two locations on such dimensions as (1) overview of economy, (2) type of political system, (3) languages spoken, (4) religions practiced, (5) safety and security precautions, and (6) other tips that "new" expatriates should know before arriving.

1. www.expatexchange.com (click on "countries," then Peru).
2. www.outpostexpat.nl (click on "Latin America," then Peru).
3. www.odci.gov/cia/publications/factbook (click on "country listings," then Peru).

Note: repeat steps above substituting "Japan" for "Peru."

Part 3/ Internet Exercise 2: Expatriate Sources on the Web

Purpose

To become familiar with a website that has information for current and future expatriates.

Group Size

To be performed individually.

Time Required

Approximately 45 minutes.

Other

Internet connection and search engine needed.

Exercise

Using the Internet, visit www.expatexchange.com and become familiar with its information and hyperlinks. Then, research and prepare a three-to-four-sentence response for each of the following scenarios:

Scenario 1—Assume your organization is about to send you to Thailand for a three-year expatriate assignment. Knowing that your spouse would like to do some volunteer work while in Thailand, you decide to do some research on this issue. Using the website above, please identify three leads for your spouse that could lead to volunteer opportunities in the host country.

Scenario 2—Assume you are about to be assigned to Sao Paolo, Brazil, and would like to "chat" with former expatriates who have lived there to gather information about the quantity and quality of international schools for your children. How could you go about doing that using this website? Please describe.

Source: Robert Konopaske and John M. Ivancevich, © 2004.

Scenario 3—Assume that you have just been promoted to global marketing manager for a large consumer products company. This new role will require you to visit customers in several countries each year. Please identify five countries that have "travel advisories" for U.S. citizens. Please summarize why these countries have travel advisories.

Part 3/ Internet Exercise 3: Global Netiquette: Effectively Communicating via E-mail

Purpose
To research and understand best practices regarding the sending of international e-mail.

Group Size
To be performed individually.

Time Required
Approximately 45 minutes.

Other
Internet connection and search engine needed.

Exercise
How many times have you wished, right after pressing the "send" button of your e-mail program, that you could take back and soften the message you just launched into global cyberspace? What kind of emotion was behind your e-mail? Maybe none, but will the international recipient perceive it that way? Also, which language should you communicate in? If you speak only English, is it OK to use this when communicating with important global customers, vendors, or government officials?

Several articles and websites can be found on the Internet to help improve effectiveness with international e-mail communication.

Using your favorite search engine (e.g., www.northernlight.com or www.google.com), search for and identify 10 sources that provide tips and advice on how to use e-mail (both domestic and international) in an effective manner. Summarize the best practices and be prepared to present/write a brief overview. Be sure to include which tips are particularly important to help you improve your own e-mail use.

Source: Robert Konopaske and John M. Ivancevich, © 2004

Glossary

A

affirmative action Company actions that are meant to overcome the effects of past or present discriminatory practices, policies, or other barriers to equal employment opportunity.

B

balance sheet approach Type of compensation plan for expatriates in which pay is adjusted so that the financial responsibilities the expatriate had before the assignment are kept at the same level while on assignment.

bargaining zone model A model of negotiation in which there is a starting, target, and resistance point. The target point is a realistic goal or expectation in which both parties attempt to achieve.

bribery A subset of corruption and fraud, the paying of money or providing a benefit to someone in business or government to obtain an inappropriate market, workplace, or individual economic advantage.

C

career fit Refers to the perceived match between an employee's particular global assignment and his or her long-term career plans.

code of ethics A statement of behavioral ideals or prohibitions that are common to the organization.

cohesiveness The extent that group members are attracted to each other and to the group values and accept group goals.

collectivism The opposite of individualism. People view themselves as a working and connected member of a team, family, organization, or clan.

command group A group of subordinates who report to a manager as specified in a formal organization chart.

communication process model A widely used model that describes the general process of communication from a communicator to a receiver.

Confucianism Founded in the fifth century B.C. by Confucius, this is a comprehensive ethical code that establishes guidelines for relationships with others; central elements include loyalty, and high ethical and moral conduct.

contingency or flexible approach States that there is no one best way to manage in every situation. Manager must find ways to manage to fit different situations.

corporate codes of conduct A formal document that provides guidelines on expected conduct from employees.

corruption Dishonest behavior that a firm will not tolerate.

cross-cultural communication Occurs when two managers from different national cultures exchange meanings with one another.

cross-cultural communication model General framework of communication that includes the communicator, encoding/sending, message, medium, decoding/receiving, and noise.

cross-cultural negotiation The process by which two or more parties from distinct national cultures decide what each will give and take in a given exchange.

cross-functional teams Individuals from about the same hierarchical level, but from different areas of expertise, who join together to accomplish a task.

culture shock The stressful, accumulated effect of being exposed to unfamiliar cues and behaviors in another culture. The three stages of culture shock include: honeymoon, hostile attitude, and acceptance.

D

decoding The mental procedure that the receiver of a message gives to decipher a message.

distributive negotiation Win-lose or zero-sum approach to negotiation in which resources are limited. This approach is characterized by negotiators who decide who gets what portion of the resources.

diversity Refers to a vast array of physical and cultural differences that constitute the spectrum of human differences, including age, ethnicity, gender, physical attributes, race, and sexual/affectional orientation. These core elements of diversity have a lifelong impact on behavior and attitudes.

diversity management A voluntary organizational program designed to create greater inclusion of all individuals into informal social networks and formal company programs.

dual-career couples Refers to marriages or partnerships in which both partners earn incomes and have a career orientation and commitment to their work.

E

enacted role How the received role is expressed or redefined by the individual assuming the role.

encoding The conversion of an idea into an understandable message by a communicator.

equal employment opportunity laws The U.S. government's attempt to ensure that all individuals have an equal opportunity for employment, regardless of race, sex, color, religion, age, disability, or national origin.

e-recruiting Refers to any activity related to recruiting individuals via the Internet.

esteem needs Needs comprised of both the awareness of one's importance to others (self-esteem) and the actual esteem of others.

ethics Ethics is the study and evaluation of human conduct in the light of moral principles.

ethnocentrism The belief that one's native country, culture, language, customs, mores, and way of conducting an operation is superior to any other nation.

Executive Order 11246 Issued by U.S. President Lyndon B. Johnson in 1965, this prohibits employment discrimination on the basis of race, color, religion, sex, or national origin by federal contractors, subcontractors, and federally assisted construction contracts; it required these organizations to create an affirmative action program.

expectancies Probabilities calculated by a person's thought processes.

expectancy theory of motivation Views motivation as a process governing choices. Thus, an individual who has a particular goal must practice a certain behavior to achieve it. He or she weighs the likelihood that various behaviors will achieve the desired goal, and if a certain behavior seems to be more successful than another, that behavior likely will be the one the goal-seeker selects.

F

Foreign Corrupt Practices Act A United States Law (1977) which prohibits a U.S. company from making payments to foreign government officials to influence those officials to make decisions beneficial to the company.

formal group A group sanctioned by management to accomplish the goals of the organization.

fraud The practice of deception a person uses to gain something or an advantage.

friendship group People drawn together by common characteristics such as age, ethnic background, political sentiment, or family structure.

G

glass ceiling A barrier to advancement to higher-level jobs and positions within an organization that adversely affects women and minorities. The barrier may be due to lack of access to training programs, development experiences, or mentoring relationships.

global assignee failure Refers to those incidences in which an expatriate returns prematurely from his or her overseas assignment.

global assignments A position requiring a manager or employee to travel to or live in one or more countries outside of the country in which headquarters is located.

global organizational behavior Used in this book is an extension of the traditional OB definition cited. By adding the notion of studying "human behavior in organizations in any world setting" a global orientation of organizational behavior is introduced.

goal The object of an action.

goal setting theory An approach to motivation proposing that goals and intentions are cognitive and serve as regulators of human behavior.

going or local market rate Type of compensation plan for expatriates in which the expatriate's pay is based on the compensation received by host country or local nationals.

group development The progression from a collection of people brought together for a common purpose to a well-functioning unit whose individual members cooperate to pursue a common goal.

groupthink Characterized by high conformity and cohesiveness, groupthink exists when a group believes that it is invincible, rationalizes away criticisms, believes that everyone should comply with a group norm, and is characterized by unanimity among its members.

H

Herzberg's two-factor theory View that job satisfaction results from the presence of intrinsic motivators and that job dissatisfaction stems from not having extrinsic factors.

hierarchy of needs Based on two important assumptions: (1) Each person's needs depend on what he already has. Only needs not yet satisfied can influence behavior. A satisfied need cannot influence behavior. (2) Needs are arranged in a hierarchy of importance. Once one need is satisfied, another emerges and demands satisfaction.

high-context communication Refers to how information is used in a culture. Individuals from low-context communication cultures exchange information that is embedded in the context of relationships. Examples of high-context communication cultures include Korean, Vietnamese, Japanese, Chinese, Middle Eastern, and Latin American.

host-country nationals Employees from the host location in which a global or transnational organization is operating.

human rights Basic standards of treatment for all people, regardless of nationality, gender, race, economic status, or religion.

I

individualism Exists when people look at themselves primarily as individuals and secondarily as members of teams or groups.

informal groups Natural groupings of people in the workplace.

instrumentality Whether or not high performance is associated with desired outcomes is determined by examining what is called *instrumentality* in the expectancy theory. Instrumentalities are correlations or indicators of association, which range from −1.00 to +1.00.

integrative negotiation Win-win or positive-sum approach to negotiation in which both (all) parties gain without a corresponding loss from the other party(ies).

interest group Members share a common interest in some particular job-related event or possible outcome join together to achieve some objective.

intergroup conflict When one party perceives that another party has frustrated, or is about to frustrate, the accomplishment of a goal.

ISO 9000 and ISO 14000 A series of standards for quality control and environmental management systems.

L

lowballing Type of general negotiation tact in which ridiculously low offers and/or concessions are used to lower the other group's expectations.

low-context communication Refers to how information is used in a culture. Individuals from low-context communication cultures require an exchange of detailed information such as contracts, business plans, etc., in order for business transactions to be conducted. Examples of low-context cultures include: Scandinavian, German, Swiss, and North American.

M

maintenance or hygiene factors Herzberg's theory is that they are necessary to maintain a minimum level of need satisfaction. He also noted that these have often been perceived by managers as factors that can motivate subordinates, but that they are, in fact, more potent as dissatisfiers when they are absent.

masculinity Masculine-dominated cultures emphasize assertiveness, proaction, and acquisition of wealth as opposed to concern for people growth and development.

McClelland's Learned Needs Theory McClelland proposed a theory of motivation that is associated with learning concepts. He believed that the need for achievement, the need for affiliation, and the need for power are acquired from national culture.

monochronic time cultures Refers to the use of time in a culture. Individuals from monochronic cultures tend to do things in a linear fashion, one activity at a time.

monolithic organization Refers to organizations that are in the early stages of developing a diversity management orientation. Women and ethnic minority men tend to be segregated into low-status jobs, reflecting a low degree of integration and inclusiveness into the organizational structure.

motivation Refers to an individual's selection of behaviors and what lies behind making choices.

motivators Cause high levels of motivation and job satisfaction when present. However, absence of these factors does not prove highly dissatisfying.

Meaning of Work (MOW) International Research Team A group of global researchers that created, designed, and conducted a series of studies. The MOW survey collects data on such factors as work centrality, work life, relationships to work, and employer responsibilities.

multicultural organization Refers to organizations that not only contain different cultural groups but also value the diversity that these groups bring to the table. Full integration is achieved in terms of including minorities into informal networks. Discrimination is minimized in employment decisions and the diversity is used to gain competitive advantage in the marketplace.

multinational organization An organization that has operations in more than one country, sales revenue generated globally, and a diverse mix of managers, employees, and owners.

N

national culture Like organizational culture, provides the basic assumptions used to guide behavior.

nationalism The devotion and honor bestowed on the goals, vision, customs and ritual of one's nation.

O

organizational behavior The study of human behavior, attitudes, and performance within organizational settings; drawing on theory, methods, and principles from such disciplines as psychology, sociology, and cultural anthropology to learn about individual, groups, structure, and process.

organizational culture The system of values, beliefs, and norms in an organization. It can encourage or discourage overall effectiveness, depending on the nature of the values, beliefs, and norms.

organizational socialization The process by which organizations indoctrinate and encourage new employees on the firm's cultural norms and expectations.

P

parent-country nationals Employees from the country in which the headquarters is located. Also known as expatriates.

physiological needs The basic needs of the human body, such as food, water, and sex.

plural organization Refers to organizations that have a heterogeneous group of employees and that take steps to be more inclusive of persons who are different from the majority group. Steps can include giving preference to minority-culture groups in hiring and promotion decisions, as well as training all managers and supervisors on equal employment opportunity issues.

political risk A government action or motivated event that could negatively affect the economic gains, market share, value, ownership, and opportunities of a firm.

politics The behavior of a group that is specifically self-serving. The group acts to enhance its own position, regardless of the costs of the action.

polychronic time cultures Refers to the use of time in a culture. Individuals from polychronic cultures tend to do many things at the same time.

power distance Power distance is a measure of the extent to which those who have less power in society accept that power is distributed unequally among members of the society.

proxemics Refers to the study of how people use and structure space in work and personal relationships.

R

realistic job preview Provides accurate information about the attractive and unattractive aspects of a global assignment, working conditions, location, to ensure that potential employees develop appropriate expectations.

relativist The view that language influences perception and behavior.

repatriate turnover Occurs when a returning expatriate leaves voluntarily from his or her organization for personal or career-related reasons.

resource-based view of the firm Theory of strategic management that argues that sustainable competitive advantage can be achieved when the organization's resources—physical, organizational, or human—are valuable, rare, hard to imitate, and without substitutes.

role A set of shared expectations regarding a member's attitude and task behavior within the group.

role ambiguity Results when the role occupant is not sure how to fulfill role requirements.

role conflict The incompatibility between the role's requirements and the individual's own beliefs or expectations.

role overload A condition where a task's demands overwhelm the role occupant's ability to perform the task.

S

safety needs Protection from physical harm, ill health, economic disaster, and the unexpected.

self-actualization needs Maslow defines these needs as the "desire to become more and more what one is, to become everything one is capable of becoming."

self-managed team Groups of members that have the autonomy to lead and manage themselves and determine how the team will perform its tasks.

shared values Values represent the core values and beliefs shared by employees about what is important.

short-term global assignee Short-term global assignments require managers to relocate to an overseas location for a period of less than one year. The assignee's partner and family may or may not accompany him or her on this assignment.

Social Accountability 8000 (SA 8000) A code of conduct for companies seeking to make the workplace more humane.

social loafing The tendency of some individuals to exert less effort and attention when performing tasks while working as a part of a group or a team.

social needs Needs related to the social nature of people and to their need for companionship.

spouse assistance programs Programs developed and sponsored by the expatriate's organization to assist spouses who accompany expatriates on their international assignment. This can include funding for education or job search activities, in-country living orientations, language training, etc.

stakeholder management devices (SMDs) Mechanisms through which organizations respond to stakeholder concerns.

status The rank, respect, or social position that an individual has in a group.

status consensus Agreement about the relative status of all group members.

status incongruence A lack of status consensus.

stereotypes Type of categorization that organizes previous experiences and guides future behavior.

subculture Within a nation's culture, a number of subcultures will likely exist. The subculture is a set of values, beliefs, and norms shared by individuals in the group making up the culture.

T

task group A team or group assembled by management to complete a specific task.

team A group of people interacting and working closely together with a shared commitment to accomplish goals.

terrorism The use or threat of the use of violence for political purposes.

Thematic Apperception Test (TAT) Reflects a person's values, interests, and motives.

third country nationals Employees from a country other than where the parent organization's headquarters or overseas operations are located.

time orientation The extent to which people focus on the past, present, or future. A short-term perspective of time generates pressure to accomplish short-term performance results.

transnational firm A company that operates across national boundaries and attempts to learn and work within the customs, laws, politics, and history of each country in which it operates.

travel stress The perceptual, emotional, behavioral, and physical responses made by an individual to the various problems faced during one or more travel phases.

traveling global assignments Traveling global assignments require the manager to make frequent international trips to one or more host countries, but do not include relocation of self or family to an overseas location. Also known as virtual expatriate or a commuter.

U

uncertainty avoidance This measures the extent to which a culture programs its members to feel either comfortable or uncomfortable in unstructured situations.

unethical conduct Conduct that does not conform to approved standards of social or professional behavior.

universalist View that all languages share common elements and therefore result in common thought processes and perceptions.

V

valences The values an individual attaches to work outcomes, such as a merit pay increase, a promotion, a transfer to a new group, more job responsibility, or having a longer workday. If one desires an outcome, it has a positive valence.

values Vary from culture to culture and are defined as the concepts people believe in and the standards they live by, which are different in various countries.

virtual expatriate A person who is considered an expatriate is linked electronically to assignments across geographical boundaries.

virtual teams Group of individuals who operate across space and time and who communicate mainly through electronic technologies.

W

work group A collection of interacting employees (managerial or nonmanagerial) who share certain norms and are striving toward member need satisfaction through the attainment of group goals.

Index

Note: Page numbers followed by "n" indicate material in footnotes, sourcenotes, or endnotes.

J

K

T

U

V

W

X

Y

Z